Ex Libris

Howard R. Gilbert

The Feast of St Pius V

5 May 1962

THE CARDINAL SPELLMAN STORY

FRANCIS CARDINAL SPELLMAN

THE
CARDINAL SPELLMAN STORY

✠

ROBERT I. GANNON, S.J.

✠

ILLUSTRATED WITH PHOTOGRAPHS

DOUBLEDAY & COMPANY, INC.
GARDEN CITY, NEW YORK
1962

The author has given the rights
to this book to Fordham University.

Acknowledgments

Grateful acknowledgment is made to the following for permission to reprint selections included in this book:

Quotation from *Cardinal Mindszenty Speaks* reprinted by permission of Longmans, Green & Company, Inc. These quotations originally appeared in *Weissbuch Von Kardinal Mindszenty* by József Cardinal Mindszenty and are reprinted by permission of the publisher, Thomas-Verlag, Zürich.

Quotations from "The Catholic-Protestant Feud" by Rev. Alson J. Smith published in the November 1947 issue of the *American Mercury*. Reprinted by permission.

Personal letter of Madame Chiang Kai-shek to Cardinal Spellman, reprinted through the courtesy of the Chinese News Service.

Quotations from letters of President Franklin D. Roosevelt to Cardinal Spellman reprinted by permission of the Franklin D. Roosevelt Library, Hyde Park, New York.

Quotations from Mrs. Eleanor Roosevelt's columns in the New York *World-Telegram*, copyright 1949 by United Feature Syndicate, Inc. Reprinted by permission.

Quotations from *F.D.R. His Personal Letters*, edited by Elliott Roosevelt. Copyright 1950, by Elliott Roosevelt. Reprinted by permission of Duell, Sloan & Pearce, Inc. and George G. Harrap & Company Limited.

Quotation from Methodist Bishop G. Bromley Oxnam in an article by a staff writer of *The Christian Science Monitor* and reprinted in a Boston news dispatch of June 21, 1949. Reprinted by permission of *The Christian Science Monitor*.

Quotation on pages 9 and 10 summarized in a 1946 Close-up from *Life* Magazine. Reprinted by permission.

Quotations from *Popes and Cardinals in Modern Rome* by Lincoln MacVeigh. Reprinted by permission of The Dial Press.

Quotations from AP Newsfeatures, reprinted by permission.

Quotation from the April 29, 1939, issue of the *New York Journal-American*, reprinted by permission.

Quotations from *Sermons, Addresses and Pastoral Letters* by William Cardinal O'Connell. Reprinted by permission of Benziger Brothers, Inc.

Quotation from *The New York Times* of November 5, 1936, reprinted by permission.

Quotation from the April 25, 1939, issue of *The Boston Herald*, reprinted by permission.

Quotations from *The Memoirs of Cordell Hull* and *Wartime Mission in Spain* by Carlton J. H. Hayes. Reprinted by permission of The Macmillan Company.

Quotation from *Memoirs* by Franz Von Papen, translated by Brian Connell. Reprinted by permission of E. P. Dutton & Co., Inc. and Andre Deutsch Ltd.

From "Archbishop Spellman Visits Baghdad" by Rev. Clement J. Armitage in *Jesuit Missions*, September 1943. Reprinted by permission.

Quotations from *Calculated Risk* by Mark W. Clark. Reprinted by permission of Harper & Brothers.

Quotation from the August 6, 1949, issue of *The Catholic News*, reprinted by permission of the publisher.

Quotations from *No Greater Love* by Francis J. Spellman, reprinted by permission of Charles Scribner's Sons. Quotations from *Action This Day* by Francis J. Spellman, reprinted by permission of Charles Scribner's Sons and Sheed & Ward Limited.

Quotation from *My Three Years with Eisenhower* by Harry C. Butcher, © 1945, 1946 by The Curtis Publishing Company. Reprinted by permission of James Brown Associates, Inc.

Foreword

Writing the biography of a living Prince of the Church is not an enviable task but neither is it a pointless one. Even though the account can never be considered definitive because it lacks the completeness and perspective that come only with the passage of time, it can be much more true to life than a scholarly analysis which depends entirely on documents. Fifty years from now the great men and women mentioned in these pages, and especially the harvests they reaped in their lives, can be more accurately appraised but it is still something to have seen them in the flesh.

The author has had the advantage of knowing his subject for a quarter of a century and of being with him often at times of relaxation and worry and strain when he was very much himself. More important still it has been his privilege to spend long hours with His Eminence discussing his extraordinary story with its many lights and shadows. This does not mean that anyone could hold Cardinal Spellman responsible for all the color, overtones, and judgments of men and events that may be found in the text. But when it comes to setting down what he actually said and did and thought in the course of seventy-two years, the authority for its accuracy can be found in his own testimony direct or indirect.

This testimony is direct when taken from his signed letters, private and official, his published books, sermons and addresses and his private diaries which he kept with surprising candor from 1925 to 1943. Where the information stems from the personal observations of the author and private conversations or from the reminiscences of the Cardinal's family, friends, associates, subordinates, and critics, the testimony is indirect, deriving its authority from the fact that His Eminence has always been able to comment on its accuracy before it was used.

Many sources of material like the diaries will never be available again and contemporaries are already beginning to disappear so that future historians will be dependent on the Archives of the Archdiocese of New York, including ninety-six large bound volumes full of clippings, speeches, invitations, and pictures; on the Archives of the Archdiocese of Boston, the Archives of the Military Ordinariate, the President's Personal File in the Roosevelt Library, the newspaper files of the world, magazine articles without end and a stream of books, chiefly memoirs touching on war and international affairs or on Church history and the lives of modern Popes. Most of the material identified in the notes is to be found in such public sources as these. Where no reference is given to a quote or a statement of fact not publicly known, it is because the source was private and can never again be rechecked.

Grateful acknowledgment is made of all the generous assistance offered by the heads of various bureaus and services of the New York Archdiocese beginning with the Right Reverend Monsignor Terence J. Cooke, Chancellor; also by the Right Reverend Monsignor Joseph F. Marbach, Chancellor of the Military Ordinariate. To these we add many distinguished and discerning readers of the manuscript like His Eminence J. Francis Cardinal McIntyre of Los Angeles and the late John Cardinal O'Hara of Philadelphia, the Most Reverend James H. Griffiths, Auxiliary Bishop of New York, the late Honorable Frank C. Walker, Postmaster General in President Roosevelt's cabinet, and Cardinal Spellman's personal counsel, Lawrence X. Cusack. Their opinions were not unanimous, but their comments and criticisms were invaluable.

Finally, due credit is very gladly given to a devoted research assistant, Dr. George J. Gill, assistant professor of history in the School of Education, Fordham University. His critical eye and scholarly habits were just what the author needed most.

Contents

I'll Call Him Francis

EARLY March is still winter in Massachusetts, but on Tuesday, March 5, 1946, the noon sun was as warm as spring. Looking down on the little town of Whitman from a plane circling at a thousand feet, the passengers could see workers strolling out of the shoe factories for lunch, children just released from morning classes, and shoppers along South Avenue and Washington Street. Most of them were looking up. They were not used to having planes circle the little town, especially big commercial planes. One they recognized as a Douglas Skymaster. The other was a brand-new model. It might be one of those Constellations that the papers had been featuring—that would seat forty or fifty people. The mention of "Constellations" reminded them that their fellow townsman Frank Spellman, now Francis Cardinal Spellman, had chartered two planes for his trip to the Great Consistory, and one of them was a Constellation, *The Star of Rome*. They had followed every dispatch in the Boston papers from the day when His Eminence took off from LaGuardia. They had pored over all the pictures taken in Ireland and France and Italy, and only last night had read that he was setting out from Lisbon to New York by way of Gander. That must be *The Star of Rome*. Many of them smiled and waved their hands.

Inside the planes there were a dozen personally conducted tours in progress at the crowded windows, where various members of the Spellman family were pointing out the sights to the Cardinal's friends. Over there was the Dyer Grammar School, and Whitman High, and the old house on Beulah Street. There was South Avenue where Pa had the store for forty-six years, and the Holy Ghost Church where Frank was baptized and made his First Communion. There was the road to Abington where his younger sister Helene lived with her husband; and this was the attractive new place where Marian Pegnam, his older sister, kept house for Pa, who was still expressing himself with vigor after eighty-eight years of rugged individualism. At that very moment, the old man was waving from the front lawn and talking to his practical nurse.

"It's nothing to get excited about," he told her. "We have to take things as they come. The boy has done all right after all; a whole lot better than I ever thought he would. Seems to have taken the advice I gave him when he was growing up. I used to tell him, 'Always go with people who are smarter than you are—and in your case it won't be difficult to find them.' I must say he picked some pretty smart people."

Pa was happy in his own way—happy and very proud. But his way had a lot of the Yankee about it and an irreducible minimum of Irish effusion. His father, Patrick, had come direct from Clonmel, Tipperary, but had not settled in South Boston, where his son and four daughters would have grown up impervious to the influence of Plymouth Rock. Instead he had pushed on twenty miles southeast—quite a distance in those days with a horse and cart—to a little town called Abington. This was a center even then for shoes, and Patrick was a bootmaker who had his trade from the Old Country and was proud of it. So he settled down, as events were to prove for life, and soon after married one of the very few Catholics in town, Honora Hayes, young and pretty and fresh from Limerick. That part of the sprawling community which they selected for their home changed its name in 1875 to South Abington, and eleven years later to Whitman.

The newcomer was industrious and before long formed a partnership with the proprietor of a general store, but kept on working in a loft upstairs making shoes for rich Bostonians. Integrity and thrift did the rest. He soon owned a modest white frame house on Glen Street, a quiet place still surrounded with elms, and there in 1858 William Spellman was born. There was no Irish neighborhood, no Irish consciousness, and the scattered Catholic neighbors who, rain or shine, walked three or four miles to their beloved Sunday Mass, were too few to arouse any bigotry even in a self-satisfied town that had no particular use for outsiders. They were loyal to their pastor and to their plain white parish church but otherwise, as years passed and the Civil War came and went, they melted imperceptibly into "the rocks and rills and templed hills" around them. So it was that in appearance, speech, mannerisms, and habits of thought William grew up a complete, if not quite proper, Yankee.

While attending the local public schools he helped his father when classes were out, and once he had finished the grammar grades, settled down full time at the Jones & Reed shoe factory on Washington Street. He could have paid his board at home, but his father said no. Patrick knew his son well enough to trust his Yankee thrift. Like the neighbors around him, William was quietly putting one dollar on top of another until at the early age of twenty-two, he opened a grocery store of his own in rented quarters on South Avenue. About a year later he had sold enough sugar and spice to buy the entire block. The down payment was only $100, but he always said it was the best business deal he ever made, and on that spot he kept his store for nearly half a century. It was not the beginning of a spectacular success story. It remained for all those years "William Spellman's cash grocery, full of assorted canned goods, warranted as represented, for sale at lowest possible prices for cash." But it brought him a success that meant happiness.

It brought him a blessed marriage, a comfortable home, and a united family that remained a source of enormous pride throughout his almost fivescore years of life.

All this was New England, but one Irish trait asserted itself. He was in no hurry to marry, and remained until he was thirty the most eligible Catholic bachelor in Whitman. The store was to blame for keeping his thoughts so long on other things, but in the end it was the store that found him a wife. One afternoon in the spring of 1886, a girl in her early twenties came in to buy, let us say, a pound of dried prunes. In no time at all, the undemonstrative William found out that her name was Ellen Conway. She was the daughter of John Conway, a farm hand, who had come over from Whitechurch, Cork, and settled in Plympton, down Plymouth way, where Ellen was born. It was a nice enough place, but the nearest church was thirty miles distant in Sandwich, so spurred on by Ellen Kehoe, his wife from Kildavin in County Carlow, John had been glad to get a job driving an ox team for a Whitman tack factory. The big inducement in the move was the fact that the family now had only five miles to walk to Sunday Mass.

By mid-summer Ellen and William were keeping company in an 1886 sort of way and a note is still extant on fancy paper with a rosebud at the top, written in a very careful hand and dated July 8:

Friend Will:

I suppose you will be somewhat surprised on receiving this note, but as it will be impossible for me to leave the shop on Saturday, I thought I would let you know by writing for a change. I am very thankful for the invitation, & only wish I could go.

Yours
NELLIE

Two years later they were married over in Abington and rented a small house on Temple Street in Whitman where their first child was born, May 4, 1889. It was a boy and when Nellie Spellman took him in her arms she said in her quiet way, "I'll call him Francis." A few days later in the little mission Church of the Holy Ghost, Father George J. Patterson christened him Francis Joseph—not for anyone in the family circle, still less for the Austrian Emperor, but just for two great saints in heaven, the Little Man of Assisi and the Spouse of Mary. Two more children, Martin and Marian, followed in rapid succession, and then Helene and John.

For the next eighteen years, Francis Joseph, who was Frank by the time he could walk, lived the life typical of a lucky American boy at the turn of the century—small town, good schools, active parish, brothers and sisters, a store to tend, papers to sell, delivery wagon to drive, horses in the stable, with a pony for his little sister, enough prosperity to provide a comfortable home and the prospect of college—all brought to a happy focus by a good, hard-working father and a devoted mother. Small wonder that his love for

Whitman has been lifelong and deeply personal. Returning on his sixtieth birthday for a greeting at the Town Hall, he read the following lines:

WHITMAN—MY MOTHER-TOWN

In joyous soul I come back to thee,
Bearing upon my brow
The frost of mounting years;
Wearing above my heart
A garland of living memories
Binding me with constant love for thee.

Three score years ago today
My mother first beheld my infant face,
Giving light from her eyes for my light
And the love in her heart for my heart.
Through the years she has accompanied me,
My lodestar, lighting my way to God.

Whitman, my mother-town!
Dear to my soul are the scenes of thy keeping.
Beneath thy sod my kinsfolk sleep,
      their eyes turned starward,
And I dream the dreams of long ago,
I, a priest of God, son of this soil of America.
Whitman, my mother-town!

After eight years in the house to which he had brought his bride, William Spellman saw an opportunity to buy one of the finest places in town. It was just across the way, at 96 Beulah Street. A large white frame building, of Georgian design and practically new, it stood on five acres of land covered with fruit trees and shrubs. Best of all, there was a glorious stable attached, with a carriage house and hayloft and feed bins and chutes—a perfect clubhouse for the short-pants brigade, and destined to be the main youth center of the neighborhood. Years later in Rorschach, where he was summering with Cardinal Pacelli, Frank wrote to his mother:

There is much about this part of German Switzerland bordering the Lake of Constance that reminds me of my childhood and boyhood days in Whitman. There are many farms hereabouts and as I walk over the roads with the Cardinal I see the boys helping their fathers and their grandfathers in much the same way as I did. I remember very well being with Grandpa Spellman in his garden. I remember haying. I remember taking care of the horses. I remember raking up the leaves to use as bedding for the horses and then for the pigs. I remember how I learned to be economical, shaking out the straw or the meadow hay used as bedding as I see the boys here doing.

Then the stores here are like the stores of thirty years ago in Whitman. I could walk right into them and start waiting on the customers. Some of them still have big kerosene lamps like Pa had in his oldest store and which, after he got electric light, he still kept to heat his office while he posted the order books in the ledger during the winter mornings.

The people here get water from pumps also and that reminds me of Grandma Conway's when sometimes we would have to prime it with hot water to thaw it out and start it working.

Then there was the pump at Grandma Spellman's where I used to go for water with a can because factory pond water was not good to drink and we did not then have water from Silver Lake.

I hope these children are as happy as I was, but I am afraid not.

Pa's "oldest store" gave way in 1897 to a new store, which proved to be his last. There was a grand opening "from six to half-past nine o'clock. Music by Mosaic Orchestra. Refreshments." Frank was only eight at the time, but before many years had passed he regarded himself as one of the most valued employees in the establishment—an appraisal that was not completely endorsed by his employer. Pa was never too busy to keep one eye on his eldest son. It worried him that Frank could take the sale of groceries so lightly. The boy had entirely too much fun in the front of the store, where he could joke with the customers and wave at the passers-by. Moreover, he tended to specialize too much in his salesmanship. He would always suggest rice or some other substitute for potatoes because the dirt got in his fingernails, and he tried to impress his father with his ability to sell slow-moving items like catsup. One day the elder Spellman said to him:

"Is that the only thing in the store? Try selling tea for a change. There's a bigger profit. And another thing . . . don't say 'Is that all?' Ask 'Isn't there something else?'"

The fact was Frank's heart was not entirely in groceries. He had other interests, photography for example. He had an old box camera and his own darkroom, where he could spend rainy afternoons with kindred spirits developing his prints. But athletics was even more absorbing. There were boxing gloves upstairs in the stable and hockey on the frozen streams, and when the spring came round again, good old American baseball. Two items on the subject appear in the files of the Whitman *Times*. One is the box score of a game between Whitman High School and Oliver Ames High School of North Easton. "Spellman played first base, batted seventh, got one of five Whitman hits and made no errors." The account goes on to say that "Spellman for the visitors did the best work. Spellman's hand was injured in the last inning"—doubtless accounting for the fact that Whitman lost rather handsomely, 15–6. The second item concerns his executive ability. In 1906 he was manager of the team, which at that time involved not only recruitment in a school where most of the students were girls, but finance of a very high order. The greater part of their liquid assets came from whist parties. It is gratifying therefore to read that "Frank Spellman recently resigned his position as manager of the baseball team at the High School, but the pupils would not have it. They unanimously asked him to resume the position and he finally consented."

Meanwhile schoolwork was not entirely neglected. Like most of the boys in town, he was content to let the girls lead the class. After all, they had nothing more important to do. A clue to his rank and average is revealed in a letter to his mother dated August 1930. He was in Paris with Monsignor Borgongini-Duca and met Mr. and Mrs. Benjamin S. Atwood, old-time neighbors from Whitman. He wrote:

> Mr. Atwood said you were the smartest girl in your class at school and when you did problems on the board all the other children marvelled. Now I can understand why you were so dissatisfied with Martin and Marian when they bothered you by bringing home their report cards. I at least spared you the worry of ever looking at my card and the energy of signing it. I always signed it so well that the teachers thought what a nice writer my mother was.

As it happened, it was this same Mr. Atwood who was instrumental in starting him off on his literary career in 1904. Once more we refer to the files of the Whitman *Times*:

> B. S. Atwood, who has always taken a deep interest in the public schools, a few weeks ago offered a reward to the pupils in the ninth grade for the best essay on the Battle of Gettysburg. Hon. William M. Olin [Secretary of State for the Commonwealth] was selected as judge, and the essays from the school were submitted to him. Frank Spellman, son of Mr. and Mrs. William Spellman of Beulah St., was yesterday awarded the prize.

The prize was only ten dollars, but the satisfaction of winning strengthened an already competitive spirit and helped to shape the formative years of his life. The next opportunity came in fourth year high. The class formed the ambitious project of a trip to Washington, with funds raised by a series of benefits that absorbed the attention of the whole town. The Whitman Women's Club posted a prize for the student who would write the best account of this thrilling adventure.

The entire class, with three unhappy exceptions, left Whitman on the twenty-second of March 1907, "after receiving a splendid ovation"—which was repeated at Brockton. Frank's first impression of New York was that of a passenger on the old Fall River Line:

> Most of us got up about four o'clock and we enjoyed ourselves very much especially as we neared New York, passing Blackwell's Island, going

under Brooklyn Bridge and then around Battery Park and docking in full view of the Statue of Liberty and the three great cities of New York, Brooklyn and Jersey City.

No one seems to have pointed out St. Patrick's Cathedral, which could be seen in 1907 from the East River.

Washington fascinated him. He noted that "the carriages we met were not very good-looking and the horses showed no signs of overfeeding," but the government buildings "more than counterbalanced the bad appearances of other things." They saw the President, Theodore Roosevelt, at the Dutch Reformed Church, and did not miss a building or a patriotic shrine. On the other small-town boys and girls, all the wonders made separate and surface impressions. For Frank, the visit to the Smithsonian Institution gave the whole trip perspective:

> When one has gazed upon the greatest works of his fellow man, beautiful works of art and feats of engineering, he gets an exalted opinion of human achievements. Then when he looks at the plumage of birds and the handsome colorings blended by God, he sees how much greater is the humblest creation of God's hand than the best that man's intellect can produce.

Shortly after their return, the Whitman *Times* noted that a "committee of the Whitman Women's Club has awarded to Frank Spellman the prize for the best essay on a trip to Washington. He will read the essay before the Club this afternoon."

More exciting than even the trip to Washington, however, was the graduation from high school, with its music, "Pomp and Circumstance," its procession, its speeches, its diplomas, the swelling hearts and misty eyes of fathers and mothers. Out of a total of twenty-two graduates, eight decided to go to college, a larger number than usual for Whitman High School, and Frank was one of the lucky ones, because his mother had quietly made up her mind that he would be. It had to be a Catholic college, of course, and the choice narrowed finally to Notre Dame in South Bend, Indiana, and Fordham in New York. The Middle Western institution had offered him a partial scholarship, a fact that carried weight in the family councils. But Katherine E. Conway, his mother's cousin, was a dressmaker in New York, and Pa's sister, Mrs. Mary A. Hayes, lived in Brooklyn; and besides, what advantage would it be to a small-town boy to spend the four most impressionable years of his life in another small town? Four years in New York would be an education in itself! So the partial scholarship was sacrificed and Fordham was selected, even though it meant private lessons in Greek from Father Augustine F. Hickey, the brilliant new curate who had just returned from his studies in Rome.

CHAPTER TWO

Fordham—Class of 1911

FORDHAM in the fall of 1907 was in its early morning as a university. Founded in 1841 by the first Archbishop of New York, the zealous, indomitable, and somewhat difficult John Hughes, it had remained a traditional Jesuit college, St. John's College, until the rectorship of the Reverend John J. Collins, S.J. Two months after his appointment the new rector announced at the 1904 Commencement that Schools of Law and Medicine would be opened in the fall as parts of what would henceforth be known as Fordham University. The name of the College Department remained St. John's for many years. When young Spellman arrived therefore to register for the class of 1911, there were signs of future greatness everywhere though the College was still of modest proportions with only one hundred and five students in all. The teaching was handled by ten priests and two scholastics who were able to know intimately every boy committed to their care. In such a school the rector was still able to interview all the new students and decide on their fitness for the one course offered—an A.B. with Latin and Greek. So it was that Frank Spellman and his mother's cousin, John J. Conway, principal of a New York public school, were ushered into the office of the Reverend Daniel J. Quinn, S.J., who inspected his diploma, asked a few questions about the second aorist of an irregular verb and handed him over to the prefect of studies, a dignitary to be known later by a conforming generation as a dean.

The classes were small, but the extracurricular activities were unusually vigorous and Frank set out to sample every one of them. In his favorite sport, baseball, the competition was a little too keen for a boy from Whitman. Filling the position he coveted was a certain Jack Coffey destined after graduation for the Big Leagues and later still for the Graduate Managership of Athletics at his alma mater. Jack wrote long afterwards, "There was just one big reason why he did not make the Fordham team—Jack Coffey." In Jack's memory, Frank was "a little fellow with a springy step—didn't like to let his heels touch the ground. A good fielder but not much power at the bat." So philosophically and providentially Frank turned to tennis, a game that was destined to enter into the shaping of events in his later life.

Ample time remained for intellectual and social activities as well. The Fordham University Dramatic Association, known from 1885 to 1904 as the St. John's Dramatic Society, and since 1920 as the Mimes and Mummers, stood high on the list. In his sophomore year young Spellman played the Dauphin in "King John"—with what success we can only speculate, but as a junior he stepped into the varsity play on short notice, and with very satisfactory results. A clipping in the college scrapbook reads:

The Fordham University Dramatic Association gave an elaborate scenic production of Shakespeare's "Macbeth" in the Auditorium on Tuesday evening. Vincent H. Isaacs '11 did some remarkable work as Macbeth and James M. Dunn '14 as Lady Macbeth won a good share of the applause. Banquo was played by Francis J. Spellman '11. As in former plays he proved himself an able actor.

Accompanying the article was his picture in costume, with a make-up that would sufficiently explain Macbeth's loss of poise at the banquet.

Oratory was a kindred interest. As a member of the debating society, he gained much valuable experience and at least one future friend, a young debater named Louis F. Kelleher, who visited Fordham as a member of the Boston College team. Neither could have dreamed that some day they would both be members of the American hierarchy. One year, as a matter of principle, he tried out for the oratorical contest. There were two conditions laid down by the faculty moderator: speeches had to be original and memorized. Seven boys entered the preliminaries for six places in the contest, and young Spellman was the only one not chosen. He had written out the speech and had it letter perfect, but another contestant who had not fulfilled the essential requirements was preferred before him. He never forgot the incident. He never forgot anything which he thought was unfair.

In the literary field he was more successful. The early promise of high school days developed at college, and the pages of the Fordham *Monthly* mark his progress from freshman to senior. One article that reveals not only the improvement of his style but the trend of his thought is a review, in his capacity as exchange editor, of the Vassar *Miscellany*. It was thus summarized many years later by a national magazine:

One month the *Miscellany* carried a short story by Margaret Culkin '12 (now Margaret Culkin Banning, the well known novelist) about a servant girl who refused to wear sensible shoes and who fell to ruin eventually because of an uncontrolled craving for lace jabots and long white gloves. This little story moved Frank Spellman to preach the first sermon of his entire career.

"That the story is founded on fact we do not deny," he wrote. "But we must confess that we are tremendously amazed to see such 'facts' brought out in the pages of a young ladies' college publication. Moreover, the sad story is narrated in language which is shockingly plain, language which could scarcely be expected from an undergraduate of the fair sex. Preaching is a new and unwelcome role to us. We could not, however, in conscience let such an article pass by unnoticed, and we trust that no ill-feeling will result from our remarks."[1]

Two years before, as a sophomore, he had entered a national contest open to all Catholic college students, with an essay which is full of characteristic touches. The title prescribed was "Why Should I Take a Part in Organized Total Abstinence Work?" and Frank proceeded to answer the question systematically:

When I have seen, even in my limited experience, the dreadful consequences of strong drink manifested in so many horrible ways, I am stirred by Christian charity to do all in my power to lessen the ravages of this crying evil. These examples also warn me to avoid drinking myself, and one of the surest methods of doing so is taking an active and earnest part in the organized crusade against drink. The prime motive of my interest in this work, namely that of Christian charity may be considered under three heads; the love of God, the love of my fellowman, and the love of myself.

The first two motives were handled traditionally:

The third motive, namely the love of myself, though seemingly selfish, is nevertheless a strong one. In common with all men, I am seeking how I can be most happy. Some attain what they think is ideal pleasure by humoring the senses, pampering the body and yielding to its every whim. Others, on the contrary, as for example, the members of the Trappist Congregation of Religious, derive their pleasure and happiness in looking beyond the few short years of mortal life, and subjecting their body to every possible denial, eating the plainest food, wearing the coarsest garments, and rarely conversing with even the others of their own household, and all this in atonement for sin. My pleasure at present is the gratification of my ambition to amount to something worthwhile, both for my own sake and the sake of my parents who are educating me. Now would the pleasure seeker in the first case willingly allow any suffering or mortification to alloy his happiness? Would the humble Trappist allow any worldly pleasure to distract him from his chosen life of prayer and retirement? No, they would not. Should I therefore allow anything to interfere with or thwart my ambition? With God's help, no. And drinking could perhaps be one obstacle that might impede my way. That temptation overcome, I will be reasonably sure of success.

It would be misleading to give the impression from such quotations that there was too much of the future seminarian in our Fordham student. He was one of the most fastidious dressers in the class and cut quite a figure at social events in tails and a top hat. During his junior year we find him listed as a member of the reception committee for the Prom, which was held in the new Hotel Astor on January 31, 1910. His dance order which happens still to be extant, lists a partner for every one of the twenty dances and for the four extras besides, though the names, written in pencil, are after more than half a century understandably indecipherable.

That June, at Commencement time he was called to the stage to receive the Hughes Medal for Religion, a prize open to the competition of the whole college and much sought after. Returning to Whitman for the summer, he arrived a little after bedtime, but felt that the good news of his success could not wait till morning. So he went up to his parents' room, ostensibly to say good night, but really to hear them express their pride and gratitude in words that he could cherish always. Pa met him at the door, looked at the medal for a moment and said, "Did you put out the light downstairs?"

The next morning, Frank and his brother Martin went to the Hyde Park office of the old Bay Street Railway Line and asked to be hired as conductors. Before being appointed to such important posts, they submitted to a special examination which was considered quite difficult. They had to learn the names of the streets from Grove Street, Boston, to East Walpole, make out report slips, and when the cars came to a turnout on the single-track system, throw the blocks in time to get the right of way and avoid disaster. In forty-eight hours Frank had come back and passed what was called by the astonished boss the best exam ever taken in the car barns.[2] So all summer long he rang up fares, called out the names of streets, and threw the blocks with the greatest skill imaginable. But success as a conductor and the lure of a private income could never go to his head with Pa around. Once when he squandered an extra dollar to get home an hour faster by train, his father warned him, "Don't do that again until your time is worth a dollar an hour—and I don't think it ever will be."

Thus he was in every way a normal, happy, healthy American boy of twenty, but deep in his heart there were undercurrents already set in their courses. The following letter to a man who worked for his father and who was evidently inclined to take his religious duties somewhat lightly, is indicative of the development that was taking place.

My Dear Jim:—

I was very sorry to learn you were sick and meant to write you as soon as I heard the news. I was so very busy with my school work, however, that it was a week before I had an opportunity and by that time mother wrote me that you were much better. I trust by this time you are as well as ever and are already back to work. I hope so, not only for your own sake, though of course that is the chief reason, but also for the horses and pigs, for Pa isn't exactly "struck on" feeding and caring for them. I'd be willing to bet that there were more pans of corn went down the scuttle during your absence, than there were buckets of food in the trough.

Let us get down to the present and the real reason I am writing to you. When I heard that next Sunday was Trinity Sunday, the thought at once occurred to me that perhaps you might have forgotten to make your Easter duty. At once it seemed that it was a ridiculous thought, because I knew you wouldn't be so foolish as to neglect a thing so important as that, especially as you are fulfilling so nobly all the other demands of our Holy Mother Church and I at once banished the thought.

But it came back again later on, as I thought there was at least a possibility, that on account of your illness, you might not have been present the Sunday it was announced. So in order to make sure, I determined to send you a few lines, so that in case you hadn't as yet received Holy Communion during the present Easter Season, you could do so on next Sunday.

Now Jim in case you have not already gone to Confession please go in the name of God, next Saturday night and go to Communion on Sunday. Make a good Confession and be assured you will be well rewarded. Now is the time. Make up your mind this minute that you will go. Don't think what people will say. What do you care what they say? Let others be brave and stay away from their duty, because they want to be "one of the boys"—in other words, one of the fools. Little do they realize the danger of "being brave" but there is such a thing as being too brave. Now, for God's sake, Jim don't neglect this both for your own sake and your mother's. You needn't say a word about this letter for I'll not mention it, but just show them next Sunday that you are a man and a Catholic.

It might reasonably be thought that when he sent this somewhat pastoral exhortation he must have already been aware of his priestly vocation, but such was not the case. Like any typical American boy with a good Catholic background, he was still thinking of it merely as one of many possibilities. At home the religious tone had reflected principally the influence of his mother. She was no more Irish than his father but had much more Irish warmth in her devotions. The Church was, in fact, the great interest of her life, and as soon as the Church of the Holy Ghost was opened as a mission of the parish of Abington, she became one of the pillars of the new congregation. When Archbishop John J. Williams in 1898 appointed Father James F. Hamilton as the first pastor of the new Whitman parish, the Spellman home began a tradition of entertaining the clergy that has grown with the years. At the age of ten, Frank was trained as an altar boy by Father John J. Cronin, the young curate, and until he went away to college he always served the seven o'clock Mass. While Pa was known locally as a "Cape Cod Catholic"—one, that is, who practices his faith with a minimum of external devotion and sentiment—he too had a hand in Frank's religious development. In a letter from his son, written at Malta in 1943, we read:

The Church was thronged to its capacity, and I was reminded of Mission Masses long ago in Whitman where we would all get up in time to walk to Church for five o'clock Mass and instruction and then walk back home again for breakfast, so that you and everybody else in town could be working at seven o'clock.[3]

On the same trip, during his visit to the Near East, the son wrote again:

How well do I remember you in my very youngest days, teaching me Bible History, and the book you bought me with the engravings by Gustave Doré so that I could more easily remember what you had told me. Many of the episodes illustrated in that book took place in Babylon; and to Babylon I went and was well repaid.[4]

After the excitement of high school graduation, he had mentioned the possibility of a priestly vocation to his mother, who immediately sought advice from a neighboring pastor. The incident has been described by the Right Reverend Monsignor Walter H. Gill, pastor for many years of St. Patrick's in Brockton:

About the year 1906, a very pleasing Catholic woman, almost in fear and trembling in the presence of a priest, came to me and said, if I could spare the time, she would like to talk to me about one of her boys. The boy had just told her that he thought he wanted to be a priest.

"Send him over," I said. "But first tell me who you are."

She said, "I am Mrs. William Spellman of Whitman and my boy's name is Frank."

In due course the young man came to me and I was pleased with his appearance and address. Not too great in stature, he wore a light summer suit. His manner and conversation marked him immediately as the product of a Catholic home. Polite, diffident, eager to listen and obey. Aside from this he was a typical American boy, swayed perhaps more by likes and dislikes than by cold reason. He was a lover of sports, especially baseball, and at times thought more of a ball and bat than of his marks in school. I can look back now to that day. It was summer. There was a summer house at the back of the yard space between the Rectory and the Church. There was where we had our first interview.

I did not keep him long the first time. I have often wondered if he was not glad to be released from the intimate questions I threw at him. That evening when I had time to compare my impressions I decided there was sufficient foundation on which to build and with God's grace he might weather the storms and sunshine of college and seminary life and come back to us a priest.[5]

As a student in Fordham, Frank Spellman continued to be an active, intelligent young Catholic with a layman's interest in his Church. He was regular in his reception of the sacraments and active in the "Parthenian"— the oldest and most distinguished of the student sodalities. As a sophomore, he read an essay on "Devotion to Mary in Modern Times" as part of a literary academy for the Feast of the Purification, and in his junior year we find him listed as "sacristan." But even his gold medal for religion would not in itself prove a thing. As far as a vocation was concerned, he was content to keep an open mind and stay in the state of grace until the senior retreat came around. This opportunity, he quietly determined, was not to be wasted.

Following the Spiritual Exercises of St. Ignatius, he weighed every word of the Foundation with its inexorable logic, and like any generous youth of blameless life, he came prepared to the "Meditation on the Kingdom." There he saw Our Blessed Lord as the perfect Captain of men's souls, calling for a new crusade to win back the world to His Eternal Father, and bowing down with his head in his hands, he whispered, "Lord, I shall follow You wherever You go!" He talked things over with his favorite scholastic, Mr. Edward P. Tivnan, S.J., who told him that he had the required aptitude and if he made application, would, no doubt, receive the call from his Bishop.

The day of Commencement came at last, June 14, 1911. Mr. Francis V. S. Oliver of the class of 1860 addressed the graduates, Vincent Isaacs was valedictorian, and degrees were distributed by His Excellency—soon to be His Eminence—Archbishop John Murphy Farley, a fellow alumnus of the class of '67. Among the proud and happy parents who crowded the auditorium were the Spellmans from Massachusetts, his mother in a warm glow, his father satisfied. After the ceremonies they all sat together on a bench, looking out on the tidy lawns of the campus shaded by towering elms, talking quietly over the events of the great day. It was then that he told them for the first time that he definitely wanted to be a priest. His father said he had better be sure. He said he was as sure as young men ever are. Where would he go to study? Brighton? No, he would rather go away some place far from home, so that if he failed it would be easier for the family. Father Hickey, when he was tutoring him in Greek, used to talk about the North American College in Rome. That might be just the place. Very well then, they would see him through. His father hoped he was doing the right thing. His mother's heart was singing.

Monsignor Gill again takes up the narrative:

> Naturally I did not see too much of him, except a visit now and then, during the vacation time. In June of 1911 he returned home with his sheepskin and his first degree, that of Bachelor of Arts.
>
> As yet from our beloved Plymouth County none had gone to study in

Rome. I had always had that idea in mind. Boys were going from other sections of the Diocese and why not from ours. To be sure, besides the question of expense, Rome seemed the other side of the world and most boys would prefer home training, during which they would not be so long separated from their people.

The Spellman home was the first likely place where I could find a member who could go to Rome. The thought of breaking up a family circle, urging one to leave for a period of five years, was indeed a serious one, and so with some trepidation I went over to see the Spellmans with my proposal. In a moment I found all my fears were groundless. The parents were glad to make the sacrifice and the young man was delighted to go.[6]

This was not as easy to arrange as the candidate used to suggest in later life when he explained with a smile, "In those days you did not have to be bright to go to the North American College. The only qualification was financial." The fact was he had the other qualifications too; so a distant relative, Father Michael J. Owens, spoke to Bishop Anderson, the Auxiliary of Boston, and he in turn obtained the consent of His Excellency, Archbishop William Henry O'Connell.

On September 26 two identical postcards depicting the Cunard R.M.S. *Franconia* were mailed from the ship. On Pa's he wrote, "*I will do my best for you*"; on his mother's, "*This is my last card and properly sent to my Mother. Thank you for my life and my hopes. May they both end happily.*"

CHAPTER THREE

The North American College

THE North American College in 1911 had been located on the narrow Via dell' Umiltà for all of its fifty-two years. There had been a time of uncertainty in 1884 when the highest Italian Court had decided that as title was held by the Sacred Congregation of Propaganda, the building came under the anticlerical statutes of the day regarding religious corporations and was forfeit to the secularist government. At the time, however, there was still a certain prestige attached to the name "American," so that the Cardinal Archbishop of New York, John Cardinal McCloskey, and his Coadjutor Archbishop, Michael Augustine Corrigan, could appeal to President Chester A. Arthur with some hope of success. They sent him a joint letter on March 3, 1884, requesting that he "ask the King of Italy for stay of proceedings, if it be not possible furthermore to exempt the institution as virtually American property from the operation of the law."[1] Three weeks later, our ambassador, William W. Astor, cabled to Secretary of State Frederick T. Frelinghuysen that the college had been exempted.

This was not the first time that New York had been identified with the Via dell' Umiltà, nor was it to be the last. It was the great John Hughes, Cardinal McCloskey's predecessor and patron, who had suggested to Pope Pius IX that the Catholic Church in the United States, having come of age, could profit by having a college of its own in Rome. He had in mind rather a collegiate residence, like many others in the city, whose seminarians went for their lectures to one of the old-established universities there, like the Gregorian or the Propaganda. The most venerable institution of the kind still existing was the Capranica, which had been founded before the Reformation for poor clerics from any part of the world. The stormy days of the sixteenth and seventeenth centuries, however, saw the rise of the national colleges which followed the pattern established in the German College by St. Ignatius Loyola.

In 1854 Archbishop Hughes had come to Rome with two hundred other prelates for the proclamation of the dogma of the Immaculate Conception. Europe was just recovering from the violence of 1848 and Pius IX had not long since returned from his exile at Gaeta, but hope was in the air and a spirit of progress was in the field of education. Four new colleges had been recently opened: the Lombard Seminary that very year; the French Seminary the year before; Beda College, for converted Anglican ministers, in 1852; and the Belgian College within the decade.

It was appropriate, then, that when the Archbishop of New York and his friend the venerable Archbishop of Baltimore, the Most Reverend Francis Patrick Kenrick, had audience with His Holiness, they should bring up the matter of a North American college. Pio Nono was sympathetic, and dispatched a letter to the First Provincial Council of New York proposing that they take the steps necessary for organization. The Pope himself bought the old Visitation Convent of the Umiltà for $42,000, and Archbishop Hughes raised $50,000 more to pay for its restoration and remodeling. Finally the great day came—the Feast of the Immaculate Conception, Patronal Feast of the United States of America, December 8, 1859—and the college opened its doors to receive what has become over the years an uninterrupted stream of future professors, chancellors, vicars general, bishops, archbishops, and cardinals.

Such was the future home of young Frank Spellman, who now arrived late in the fall of 1911 to begin five years that would profoundly influence his whole life. He had landed in Liverpool after the thrills of his first ocean voyage, and hand in hand with Thomas Cook & Son had made his way through Liverpool, London, Paris, Cologne, the Rhine, Heidelberg, Lucerne, Milan, Venice, and Florence to Rome. The fares were $46.00; the hotels, $27.75.

Arriving in Humility Street, he was promptly assigned to a cell that would have satisfied any Carmelite's thirst for mortification. There was a bed, a desk, and a chair, but no fireplace, no central heating, and no sunlight. It was a far cry from the comfortable home on Beulah Street, but the natural tourist in him came to the rescue. It was all so different. So Roman! He put on his new uniform: a black cassock with pale blue piping and buttons and a maroon sash, adjusted his round little Roman hat, and grinned.

His first interview with the head of the college was noncommittal enough, though Mr. Spellman may have sensed the fact that their future relations could be less than ideal. This present rector, the seventh in line of succession, was Bishop, afterward Titular Archbishop, Thomas Francis Kennedy. A priest of the Archdiocese of Philadelphia, he had been generally recognized until a few months before as a likely successor to the aging Ordinary of his diocese, Archbishop Patrick John Ryan. Then the Holy Ghost had done one of those unexpected things. The Auxiliary Bishop of Philadelphia, the Most Reverend Edmond Francis Prendergast, was appointed to the see although not resident in Rome, so that Bishop Kennedy was in the process of making a difficult adjustment when the first-year men of 1911 arrived in Humility Street. Added to this was the fact that young Spellman did not seem sufficiently impressed in conversation with personages of importance. All through his life he was to be incurably natural in dealing with everyone, and in almost every other case it won him friends. According to the Boston *Globe*, "Mr. Spellman was personally one of the most popular young men in the town and was foremost in social and athletic circles."[2] But now Massachusetts was far away, and for the first time he had a superior who thought he needed to be put in his place and kept there. The rector was not alone in this. His opinion was shared by the vice-rector, Monsignor Charles A. O'Hern of Chicago, who was destined to succeed Bishop Kennedy in office. As a result, the young seminarian never became in his five years an officer of the house, a sacristan, a beadle, or a prefect; could never aspire to the joy of an early ordination; could never win the right to exchange his "bags"—as the uniform was called—for the simple black cassock of a priest and go out on the streets without a companion. When, on a rare occasion, he did enjoy the latter experience, it was a privilege contrived by himself and grudgingly conceded.

By way of compensation he made deep and lasting friendships among his fellow students. Only one had he ever seen before—Louis F. Kelleher, formerly of the Boston College debating team. Now, two years later, he was delighted to recognize him as a first-year theologian, one year ahead in the American College. His classmates included Gerald T. Bergan of Peoria, Francis O. McCarthy of Chicago, Edward Quinn of Cincinnati, Laurence B. Killian of Boston, and other kindred souls who were never to be divided over the years by jealousies or misunderstandings. One who knew them only in their maturity, when they could sit together all evening, singing and laughing like boys at the memory of their days in Rome, can still capture some of the spirit that made their early twenties the dearest part of their lives.

The routine of the college had not been designed to amuse the students as much as it did—at least in retrospect. From the rising bell at 5:30 A.M. (Rome can be very cold and dark at 5:30 A.M.) till "lights out" at 10:00 P.M. (when so many fascinating things remain to be done) bells were ringing all day. Recreation on school days consisted in a walk for one hour and a half as a member of a *camerata*, a group of eight or ten students supervised by an older seminarian acting as a prefect—in young Spellman's case, John Mogan, destined one day to be Chancellor in Nashville, Tennessee. The beadle was Francis Malone, who died as Chancellor of the Diocese of Toledo. As a band they visited all the churches, palaces, and ruins of Rome. Perhaps after four college years in the big city of New York this might have seemed at first to be sufficiently pale entertainment, but life lived in the state of grace can do strange things to the exuberance of youth and the most ordinary things become vastly entertaining.

In like manner, impressive events are more overwhelming in early life. What a thrill it was, for example, two months after his admission to the seminary, to have his own Archbishop, the Most Reverend William Henry O'Connell, an extraordinary figure who dominated his native New England

and any other place he happened to visit, come to Rome for the greatest honor in the gift of the Pope. The public consistory took place in the Sala Consistoriale, and not one American seminarian was missing.

While they waited for the procession to enter, Spellman and his friends chatted with Anton Lang, the recent Christus at Oberammergau, and discussed the great prelates about to be honored, among them the Archbishops of Paris, Westminster, and Vienna. Frank could not resist bragging moderately about the great little Archbishop of New York, John Cardinal Farley, who had given him his diploma only last June as one alumnus of Fordham University to another, but most of his bragging, which had the loyal support of Louis and Larry and other Bostonians, was for Cardinal O'Connell who, it seemed, had never been less self-effacing. He was superb. He always made the most of a situation and this was a situation. The other Americans, however, could feel that they belonged in the chorus too, because although they could not claim this Prince of the Church as an Ordinary, they could, as a previous rector of the North American College. Gaetano Cardinal Bisleti and Gennaro Cardinal Belmonte probably went unnoticed in the excitement, although the first was to figure prominently in young Spellman's early adventures and the second was to live on into his nineties and attend the Great Consistory of 1946. There is no reason to believe that Frank made up his mind then and there to be a Cardinal, but just as in high school and college where he had tried out for every team on the field and every medal that was offered without being crushed when he was overlooked, so in his subsequent career he always wanted to get to the top. His ambition was not to have wealth and wield power and push people around. It was just to win. Perhaps it merely reflected the motto of Whitman High: *Excelsior*.

In any case, the young seminarian planned his immediate future systematically, and the first assist came from Louis F. Kelleher. This sensitive, quiet, brilliant boy was always loyal to his friends, so from the height of his experience in first-year Theology, he took time out to teach Frank the facts of university life. At that time, the students of the American College marched over every day to the Propaganda for their university courses, or to be more precise, to "The Pontifical Atheneum of the Urban College *de Propaganda Fide*." Here Louis analyzed for the newcomer the various members of the faculty that graced the Propaganda of 1911. In his first year, while he reviewed the philosophy he had studied at Fordham, he would have Enrico Dante for logic; for ethics, Giovanni Corti, a diffident man who shunned ecclesiastical dignities and dignitaries; and for metaphysics, the great Pietro Ciriaci. For theology there was the famous Servite who had written several good books, Alexis Lepicier, O.S.M., and Domenico Tardini, who Louis said had a brilliant future. There were also several of the second magnitude and one or two of the third. But the man to keep an eye on and the teacher who was *facile princeps* among them all was the young

Don Francesco Borgongini-Duca. At twenty-seven he was not yet even a monsignor, and not to be a monsignor in Rome is to be very young or very overlooked indeed. But Louis said that he was the man, and Frank respected Louis's judgment.

After six months of this strange new life, young Spellman wrote the following letter to Monsignor Gill of Brockton, Massachusetts, who had been so anxious to have him study in Rome:

DEAR FATHER:

It is but a few days since I completed my six months as a student in the American College, and by this time I am fairly well settled in my new surroundings. So I thought it high time to write you and let you know how things are going for me and how I like my present life. . . . I have not regretted for one single fleeting instant the step I took, when, on the nineteenth of last September, I sailed away from home. Nor have I been at all homesick or discouraged.

The fellows here have been especially kind, and I have already a number of friends whom I like very much. The one whom I think I like the best is a Cambridge boy, a graduate of Boston College in the class of 1910 and a chap head and shoulders over any Boston man at present a student here. His name is Kelleher.

In my studies I am progressing as well as I expected. This year, however, does not amount to much as far as lessons are concerned as there is nothing that depends on it. It is a general review of philosophy and is useful in so far as it acquaints one with the methods in vogue here, and is also useful in accustoming oneself to taking Latin lectures. There is no degree to be competed for, as the Ph. D. is only given at the end of a two years' philosophical course.

But of course the degree is purely accidental and so I consider it. It would make one disgusted at times to hear a few of the fellows (and fortunately they are very few) talking about degrees. Sometimes I think they consider the degree and its concomitant imagined prestige, to be more than the priesthood. But as I have said above, thank God they are in the minority. I am working just as hard this year as I would were a degree at stake. I am, however, taking more time for the study of Italian than for Philosophy. My reason is that I have already had a good course in Philosophy and the Italian may be useful in my future life. There is no year like the first for studying it, for two reasons, that you have the next four years for conversational practice and study of the literature, and secondly because the study of Theology allows no such time for outside work as does this present year. I am going to try to make a good solid theological course.

And now for the purely material aspect of the life here. True it is that Rome is more renowned for beauty than for comfort, but I manage to get along very well. There is some griping going on here, the same as in every institution of its kind; but they get no encouragement nor sympathy from the majority who are determined to look on the bright side of things. I get enough to eat to keep me alive and as my health has been excellent I have no cause to complain. . . .

If convenient I should be grateful if you would sometime call on my people for they would be delighted to receive you. Thanking you for your many kindnesses to Martin and myself, I remain

Gratefully your friend,
Frank Spellman

Rome, April 21, 1912.

The first year passed pleasantly enough, and it was summer in the Alban Hills. The Villa Santa Caterina, which had belonged to the great Orsini family, was beautifully situated at Castel Gandolfo near Lake Albano. It had been purchased in 1899 by Cardinal O'Connell when he was rector of the North American College, and was everything the students could desire —at least in a seminary villa. There they lived and worked and played from early in July till the end of October. There they studied their modern languages and history, and wrote essays and sermons for the coming year. In addition, there were long trips over the fascinating hills and valleys that lie to the west and south of the Campagna, trips on which they could choose their own companions. In later years gray-haired bishops and monsignori recalled that on their journeys they met many Americans whose names were promptly forgotten by all except young Frank Spellman. He always kept their names and addresses, and got Christmas cards from the most unexpected people.

One incident of that first summer stands out in the memory of everyone concerned. Tramping along the countryside, McCarthy, Quinn, Killian, Finn, Kealey, Mullin, Halleran, Wagener, Mahoney, and Spellman came to a little town called Veroli, where they learned that the newly created Cardinal Bisleti had his villa. Spellman proposed that they call on him and do him the favor of taking his picture with a new Kodak that he always brought along with him on their "gitas." His Eminence was amused, and Frank was not one to waste an opportunity. He chatted away in his new-found Italian, which was still full of Massachusetts. He had his distinguished subject pose in front of every bush and balcony. He caught him smiling, severe, pensive, inspired; and then asked casually if he could call to deliver the finished pictures in the fall. "Perchè no?" The Cardinal would be charmed!

On their return, therefore, to the Via dell' Umiltà, Spellman informed his rector that he had an appointment with Cardinal Bisleti. That involved changing the blue buttons and piping for the black of a priest's cassock— and, of course, permission to go alone, just as if he were in favor and an officer of the house. Despite the fact that he wore his most innocent look

—an expression that was to become internationally famous in time—Bishop Kennedy did not credit him with complete ingenuousness. His call at the palazzo was a great success at the time and afterward in recreation, for he had brought with him not only the finished prints but the new Kodak as well. This time he got a photo of His Eminence sitting at his desk beside his mother's picture which made such a successful and touching print that another visit to the Cardinal's palazzo was necessary, and by this time his new patron was so well disposed that the young American was asked to drop in any time, even without the camera.

Meanwhile his second year at "del Nord" was beginning. After a review of scholastic philosophy, he was ready for his first year of theology under Don Borgongini-Duca. This extraordinary man was everything that Louis had said he was. Time after time, as the courses progressed, Frank's intimates would watch him as he waylaid the popular professor to walk up and down in the corridor in deep conversation, not realizing that Spellman who had begun by cultivating a promising man was falling under the spell of a great teacher.

The class repetitions followed an ancient pattern: the order of seniority among the colleges; the alphabetical order among the students. When the turn came for the North American College and they reached Q on the list, it was time for Louis Kelleher, now a second-year theologian, to display his coaching ability. Bergan had led the way. Killian had covered Harvard, his alma mater, with distinction. McCarthy and Quinn had followed suit, all of them reflecting glory on the Stars and Stripes. So Louis and Frank put their heads together. Spellman's repetition would be a Grand Act. The day came and the professor lectured without interruption. The next day he postponed the repetition, and the next day again. The two friends began to feel that they would be up all night every night until Easter, but their big moment finally came on the fourth day. The repetition covered three lectures instead of one, and was further complicated by the fact that as the young American rattled off the Latin, aided by a phenomenal memory that was to be an important asset all his life, Borgongini-Duca unexpectedly kept interrupting him with questions. A kind Divinity, however, was shaping the end of a future cardinal, and it just so happened that the answer to every question was the next sentence he had memorized. It was a triumph. Larry and Ed exchanged a glance that said, "What have we been nourishing in our bosoms all these months—another Suárez?" And when it was over, the delighted professor said very quietly, "*Bene dixisti.*" ("You have recited well"), the only time he expressed his approval of anybody in the class for four years. This may be taken as the real beginning of a great career.

The second year of theology opened auspiciously enough. Father Lepicier, who had been expected to continue with the dogma class, was suddenly called away to become prior general of his order, later still the Apostolic Visitor to England and Scotland and India, and finally a member of the

Sacred College of Cardinals. This was a great loss. He was a brilliant man, but his place was to be taken by none other than Don Borgongini-Duca, so all was well. It was the fall of 1913. Unsuspected by the wisest man alive, the world was beginning the last normal year that it would know for many decades to come. Pius X seemed very weary. He had been through the apostasy of France with its *lois laïques*, through the ravages of modernism, through the revolution in Portugal, and the carnage in Mexico. In another year his sufferings would be complete. But that winter, for young Spellman, life was still made up of little things, and he wrote every week to his mother in Whitman describing how the Holy Father had looked at the most recent audience and how he himself had done in his latest repetition.

Finally the year was over. He had worked hard and had really deserved the treat that was in store for him. Through July and August, instead of going as usual to the Villa Santa Caterina, he was to join his cousin, John Conway, who was assisting the director of a large party of McGrane tourists and was to visit several of the capitals of Europe. "When the war broke out," Frank recalled later, "I was in the city of Milan and the next day we were to leave Italy for Switzerland. But instead of the planned-for ride in the railway train, I was given a ride in an ambulance, and instead of Alpine scenery on the morrow, my eyes rested on the white ceiling of a little room in the Yolanda Hospital of Milan. My cousin had to leave me alone in the hospital and hurry away with his party to Luzerne where they barely managed to catch the last train that left Switzerland for nearly a month. In the meantime I had become very ill and remained in the hospital more than three months." When he felt that he was on the road to health, he wrote to his father on September 8, 1914:

My Dear Father:

I am starting a letter to you that I think will be very long, as I have a great deal to tell you. First of all, let me assure you in all frankness and sincerity that I am perfectly cured. There are absolutely no traces of any disease, I feel well and my appetite is splendid. Kelleher says that he never saw me looking better and that he cannot realize that I have been sick.

And now I will tell you all about my sickness. I wouldn't tell you if I thought it would worry you, but it is only justice that you should know. I didn't know what it was myself until I was practically cured and thought all the while it was pleurisy and bronchitis, but it was pneumonia. Now please don't let mama worry for it is all over now and we must all thank God that I came out of it so well. If you think mama will worry, perhaps you had better not tell her, but I think she will be brave as I would have to be brave in my anxiety if one of us were sick at home. And of course I hate to worry you, realizing all your troubles and sacrifices perhaps more keenly than does anyone else except mama. But I feel that I must tell you, that I would be dealing underhanded if I did not do so. So forgive me if I have given you a shock. Please continue to have confidence in me and with the help of God Who has preserved us all together for so long a time, I will yet make you proud of me.

My expenses here are not heavy and I have over a hundred dollars. The doctor is a dollar a day and the hospital charges are one dollar a day also and that includes meals and everything except medicines and I take no medicines now and have not taken any in two weeks. The meals are splendid. I have bread and butter and coffee at seven; oatmeal at ten and it tastes great, the first I have had since I left home except once at the Dahlgrens. At twelve I have rice in broth, half a chicken, bread, butter and milk. At three I have more milk and as much as I can drink at any time in the day. For supper I have a sort of a tapioca custard, something like mama makes without the white of egg frosting and then either another half chicken or some fried eggs. I don't see how they do it and the nursing, etc. for only a dollar a day.

I only had the pneumonia in my right lung and in only a small area of that lung. I will be able to leave here so the doctor says in about three weeks, fat and strong. But he advises me very strongly to go to some quiet place in the foothills of the Alps which are really mountains on one of the beautiful Italian lakes for the month of October and perhaps the first week in November, that is, until lectures begin again. Then he says all danger of any falling back in health would be averted and it is much better this way than to plunge directly back into the routine of college life. Then I will be able to resume school work in the "fullness of my forces" as the doctor says, literally translating the Italian expression.

I know the first thing that comes to your mind when I have anything the matter with my lungs for I remember your injunctions of old and how you always explained to me that the boys of both families were weak, so I took pains to ask him especially on the chances of consumption and besides I had Kelleher ask him. And the reply was all-assuring. There is no danger, but naturally he says the one lung will be weak for a little while and that is why he wants me to take the complete rest at one of the beautiful places on the Italian lakes.

Now about the money. I have enough, I think, to pay my expenses here and besides Kelleher has insisted on giving me some money which he says I shall not return, at least until after my ordination.

I hate to ask you for any money, but if you can spare any or whether you can spare any or not, I will never take a trip again during my course, and I will sail directly home from Naples to save every expense. Besides I think I can get along on five dollars a month instead of the ten you have been so generously allowing me. I think that forty or fifty dollars will be enough to pay my expenses during October if you can spare it and perhaps I can get the Rector to take that amount off of the bill for next year.

And now I must close asking you to please be happy. One of the reasons the disease was light was because I never smoked or drank and took good care of myself. With love to all I remain

Your loving son,

FRANK

It was a brave letter from a sick boy, who left the Yolanda Hospital early in October only to enter another in Rome, the Hospital of the Blue Nuns. In a letter to his sister Marian he describes the transfer:

Well, when I changed hospitals from Milan to Rome I thought there would be some sort of a change as regards people towards me. I didn't suppose that I would be quite as big a curiosity in the English hospital in Rome where all the students go as I was in an Italian hospital in Milan. But I was wrong again.

From the very first night that I arrived (and after I was abed beginning to wonder what would be the next thing on the program for me) the head Sister of my floor came in to see me and said, "Well tell your mother all about it now." I had met her several times before and Mother Agnes, a dear friend of mine in the same Order, had told me that I could tell her anything with perfect confidence. And I would probably have told her anyway as she certainly had a kind, motherly appearance. But I couldn't help remarking at the start, to myself of course and not aloud, that here I am a baby again. Nobody seems to want to let me grow up.

In Rome the case was diagnosed as kidney complication with pleurisy and in addition to what are now regarded as old-fashioned medicines, the doctors prescribed deep drafts of the famous Roman virtue—*pazienza*. Of the latter Frank needed as much as he could get. All through August and September, while the other seminarians were studying in the cool gardens of Santa Caterina or planning "gitas" to Frascati, or even Tivoli and Anagni, he had been without visitors, looking out the window at a warm patch of northern Italian sky. A great war was starting. Russia was mobilizing the day he went to bed, and a few days later Belgium was invaded by the Germans. It began to look like a big-scale operation, but fortunately the experts said the destruction was so great the fighting could not go on a hundred days, and he was very tired. Now it was the end of October, and back in Rome his friends could drop in every day with stories of a wonderful summer. Some had seen the coronation of Benedict XV, and there were exciting arguments about the Battle of the Marne and the defense of Ypres. Their companionship was a real lift, but progress was so slow. Classes had resumed and to the tedium was added anxiety about his studies. Would he lose his year? Would he be left behind when the other musketeers sailed for home after ordination? The nuns were good to him of course (he said, "They came near to spoiling me!") and, noticing that one of them was in need of shoes, he wrote to his mother and asked her to send a pair of Whitman's best. The size? "About as big as Sister Philomena wears." So his mother sent three pairs—one a size larger and one a size smaller than his beloved aunt's. He smiled when he opened the package. It was just like his mother.

October passed, and soon it was Thanksgiving Day, with letters from Whitman and echoes of a celebration over in the Via dell' Umiltà. The Boston men had agreed the year before that New England mincemeat cannot be reproduced east of the Cape and Italian turkeys simply do not feed on the right stuffing, but what would he not have given to be at the end of the table again with the old crowd and able to eat. On December 25 he was surprised and pleased to have a visit from the rector of the college, but soon found that the good Bishop had not come to wish him a Merry Christmas. He told him instead that the doctors held out no hope for his recovery, and since he was never going to get any better, it would be the prudent thing to return at once to the United States. Cardinal O'Connell, he was sure, would allow him to continue in the diocesan seminary in Brighton, where he might live to be ordained and even say a Mass or two before he died. Young Spellman was stunned. Where was the Divinity that was shaping his end? Finally, after a moment of silence, he said:

"The doctor told me that I could get better if I could stay in the hospital till the warm weather comes again."

Bishop Kennedy rose to go. "We shall not argue the point. You will either be back in the college by January the first or go home."

On the afternoon of December 31, a thin, pale, shaky seminarian was back at his desk on the Via dell' Umiltà.

January was a trying month, but it taught him a lesson in the value of friends. Ed Quinn, who was higher in seniority and an officer of the house, had a room where the sunlight streamed in for part of the day. So the sick man soon found himself transported, bag and baggage, to the better neighborhood of those who were "approved." Ed and Larry and the rest of the faithful *camerata* took care of him by turns, shopped for his Horlick's malted milk, and repeated for his benefit the lectures he had missed since the previous October.

About this time the student discussions on Italian neutrality were more and more linked with the approaching examinations for the licentiate in sacred theology. Conservative Catholic and diplomatic circles were for staying out of the war—partly because they felt some obligation to the Triple Alliance of 1882, partly because they foresaw that even if Italy could gorge herself with booty as an ally of England and France, disaster would eventually follow. But the Democrats, Freemasons, Republicans, and Reformed Socialists were bound to France and England by close ties—historic, philosophic, and antireligious. The Nationalists were eager to seize Trentino and the rest of "*Italia irredenta*." D'Annunzio and a certain Benito Mussolini were shouting for war, and most people in the street thought they saw a chance to get something for nothing. As the seminarians talked it over in unofficial sessions, it seemed inevitable that Italy would soon be in the conflict on the side of the Allies. It was not strange, then, that in no time at all a healthy rumor was going the rounds that the students of the North American College would soon be packed off to Salamanca in Spain, where the requirements for the licentiate were thought to be less exacting than in Rome. So, human nature being what it is, some of the worldly wise decided not to register for the examination when the time came in June, preferring to take a chance on Salamanca. Young Spellman sized it up differently. Sick as he was all through January and still behind the class after six months' illness and three months' absence from lectures, he concluded that if Salamanca did not materialize, he would be taking his licentiate in fourth year, and never would get a chance at the doctorate. So he registered.

For the examination four subjects were included: scripture, and moral, dogmatic and sacramental theology, from which three would be selected by lot. Each examiner at the conclusion of his own subject matter could drop three little balls, white or black, into the box on the table, varying them as he saw fit, for example, two whites and a black. To attain the degree two-thirds of the number of votes cast, six whites out of nine that is, were required. Scripture was first; his worst subject. He wrestled with the examiner, Dr. Colombo, on the authorship of the Psalms of David, skirted the two accounts in the Book of Genesis, and mistook the Colossians for the Thessalonians. Three black balls were rather ostentatiously dropped in the box. Bloodied but unbowed, he turned to Monsignor Domenico Tardini, who was duly impressed by his knowledge of the Sacraments, and with slightly more ostentation dropped three white balls into the box. The score was a tie and Borgongini was absent: the perspiring young American needed a perfect mark in moral. His examiner for the third and crucial subject was the Dominican, Paban-Segond, who made no attempt to conceal his approval, so the last three balls were also white. Frank had just squeezed by, but with the physical handicap he had overcome it was a triumph.

The next year, when he appeared as a candidate for the doctorate, he was a better prepared but equally fortunate young man. For the written examination, it was the custom at the Propaganda to fill an urn with one hundred slips of paper, each bearing the title of a thesis whose subject matter would form the basis of a four-hour paper. A candidate could reject the first two if he felt they were not his best subjects, but he had to accept the third. After a silent prayer, young Spellman looked at the first slip. It was a thesis in scripture, and he quickly discarded it. The second was drawn. It was scripture again. The sands were running out. Providence was looking the other way. If the third was the same as the first two, he had little hope of being a doctor of sacred theology. He closed his eyes. When he opened them again, he saw on the final slip a thesis in sacramental theology, his best subject. At the successful end of this ordeal, he passed on to the orals, and this time the margin of white balls was a comfortable one.

More important, however, and more deeply satisfying than his doctorate, was his ordination to the priesthood, which had taken place May 14, 1916. The whole year had been one of prayerful preparation under the guidance of the spiritual father of the college, Dr. Bernard J. Mahoney, later Bishop of Sioux Falls, South Dakota. He had received the subdiaconate the previous June in the chapel of the South American College, and while it was a step in the right direction, it had not been a completely happy occasion, because the same day Frank McCarthy, Larry Killian, and many other classmates were raised to the priesthood. They had all entered the seminary together, but Frank Spellman had failed to impress the rector and vice-rector sufficiently to be placed on the list for early ordination. It was not easy to be left behind, but he took it philosophically and prepared for the diaconate, which was conferred by Basilio Cardinal Pompili, Vicar General of His Holiness, Benedict XV, in the chapel of the South American College. These were the preludes, solemn, impressive, and important, but preludes. The great day was, as always, the day of priesthood, and although many days of pomp and glory lay ahead in the distant future, Father Spellman would always look back on May 14, 1916, as the high point of his career. He knew his theology and realized that the difference between a cardinal archbishop and a simple priest is infinitely less than the difference between a priest and a deacon. A priest can say Mass; and the Holy Father himself, Bishop of Rome, Patriarch of the West, Successor of the Prince of the Apostles, and Vicar of Christ on earth, can do nothing greater.

The scene was the Church of the Apollinare, which had been given to the Jesuits by Gregory XIII in 1575 as part of the German College. The ordaining prelate, the Most Reverend Giuseppe Ceppetelli, Patriarch of Constantinople, was seated on a faldstool before the main altar as the archdeacon spoke out in a clear voice: "Let those come forward who are to be raised to the order of priesthood." A group of young men in spotless albs advanced to the altar. They were of various nationalities, ten of them Americans. One of them was Frank Spellman. On his arm were folded the priestly vestments which he had not yet the right to wear.

There was no one from home in the old eighth-century church that morning, but when it was eight o'clock in Rome one light was burning in the second floor of the house on Beulah Street. Ellen Spellman was on her knees, saying her beads again, her one intention, repeated afterward a dozen times in her letters, that no matter what he became in after life, her boy would always be a holy priest.

As Frank knelt and bowed his head, the Archbishop crossed the stole upon his breast with the words, "Receive the yoke of the Lord, for His yoke is sweet and His burden light." In God's own time it would seem heavy enough, for trials and failures and misunderstandings lay in wait for him at home in Boston and, later still, in many strange and distant places he didn't dream of yet. But heavy or light, he would carry it through to the end because it was the yoke of the Lord. After the chasuble of charity had been placed on his shoulders and the oil of the catechumens spread upon his palms from thumb to fingertip in the sign of the cross, he placed his hands together and one of the Archbishop's attendants wrapped them about with a linen cloth—a little white strip which always remains the dearest treasure of any woman who has a son at the altar. It is to be carefully put away at home, and when the mother dies and her body is laid out for veneration, her hands are placed as her boy's were at his ordination and wrapped with the same little strip of white. Then Frank went forward to touch with his fingers the chalice and paten of gold with the Host upon it. "Receive," said the Archbishop, "the power to offer sacrifice to God and to celebrate Mass for the living and the dead."

The next morning at the Tomb of St. Peter, Father Spellman whispered for the first time: "*Introibo ad altare Dei*." As Nicholas Murray Butler used to say, the sense of apostolicity is overpowering in Rome, but nowhere more so than at the Tomb of Peter himself. So that when he came to the words of consecration, the young priest felt as if the hands of the Twelve had been laid upon his head the day before.

As he walked back through the streets with his friends to a simple breakfast, he heard more news of disaster in the Trentino and the Asiago plateau. Italy had been fighting for a year. The casualties had been disproportionately heavy and, except for initial success, fruitless. The conviction was widespread that walking out on the Triple Alliance had not paid off. A spirit of defeatism was in the air. The government was about to fall. It was a depressing picture for one as sympathetic as Father Spellman was, but nothing could dampen the spirits of a new priest on the day of his ordination. New priests are like lovers—single-minded. What is a mere world war when a man can look forward to Mass in the morning? Thus another two months sped by, his doctorate was safely achieved, and a few days after the last examination he set out with Father Quinn and Father Frank Cummings for Whitman by way of Lourdes and London. It was an exciting trip through wartime France, but for him the special feature was a visit in London with Vincent Isaacs, his brilliant friend of Fordham days, who was then a barrister in the Inner Temple, wig and all. Vincent subsequently fought for England and was killed in action. Twenty-two years later, with a long memory and a thoughtfulness that were characteristic, Father, by that time Bishop, Spellman paid a special call on Vincent's mother in Kingston, Jamaica. He had written to his father a few days before in a letter dated March 14, 1938:

> Then, unexpectedly, I am also to visit Kingston, Jamaica, and this will give me an opportunity not alone to see the island, but also the privilege of visiting someone whom I have never met, but whom I have desired to

meet and have admired for twenty-five years,—the mother of one of my classmates in Fordham who was one of the closest friends I had there, and one of the four of my Fordham classmates killed in the World War. His name was Vincent Isaacs. He was not only the smartest man in the Class or in the College at that time, but he was one of the best all round men that I have met in my lifetime. He was a great student, a fine speaker, an exceptional actor, and above all, he was a wonderful Catholic and remained one until the end. I met him for the last time, and the only time after graduation, in 1916. We met in London and had a few pleasant days together. He was a British subject and an officer in the British Army. He had finished his legal studies and was an English Barrister, and above all, he was still the same individual with the same splendid character and ideals that he had had at Fordham. You remember that he had visited with me in Whitman during short vacations and how much the family liked him.

CHAPTER FOUR

The Boston Chancery

As FAR as Whitman was concerned, the full realization of Father Frank's priesthood came only on July 23, 1916, when he celebrated his first Solemn Mass in the little Church of the Holy Ghost. The Whitman *Times* carried the following account:

> In the congregation were many from the surrounding towns, and personal friends and relatives of the young priest attended to do him honor. There was a delegation from his College in New York City. The Solemn High Mass was celebrated with Rev. Fr. Spellman as celebrant, Rev. Michael Owens of Lexington, as deacon, Rev. Augustine Hickey of Holy Cross Cathedral in Boston as sub-deacon, Rt. Rev. Msgr. George J. Patterson of St. Vincent's Church of South Boston, a former pastor of the local church, assistant priest; John Spellman, a brother, as master of ceremonies; Richard J. Quinlan of this town, a student at the Brighton Seminary, as thurifer; Michael Hayes of this town, of Boston College, incense bearer, William Burke and Joseph Whalen, acolytes, and 20 altar boys. The service was most impressive.
>
> The sermon was preached by Rev. James F. Hamilton, the senior priest of the parish, a warm personal friend of the young man. In the sanctuary were seated Rev. J. J. McGrath, the local curate, Rev. Alexander J. Hamilton, pastor of St. Margaret's Church of Brockton, and Rev. Edward Quinn, a classmate of Rev. Fr. Spellman in Rome, who returns soon to his home in Cincinnati, Ohio, where he is to receive the honors yesterday accorded his brilliant classmate.
>
> When called upon to speak by Father Hamilton, the newly ordained priest said in part:
>
> "I cannot tell you how happy I am, but I think you can imagine what five years away from home means. Of course I am not sorry that I went away, as I have been able to learn some things that I could not have learned at home. But the two most important things that I learned were not new things. They are things taught in every Catholic Church, in every Catholic home, in every Catholic school, throughout the United States, and they are love of God and love of country.
>
> "Seeing other countries makes us realize as does nothing else, the great-

ness of the United States and the greatness of the Catholic Church. A Catholic cannot but feel proud that he is a Catholic and an American that he is an American. In the last audience with the Pope he congratulated our country and praised America, and told us to work with every ounce of strength in our bodies for our Church and for our great and glorious country. He blessed our work with all the affection of a father and gave us each permission to give his own blessing to the congregations in our widely scattered homes."

The residence of the young priest's father was the scene of an exceptionally pleasant gathering yesterday afternoon, where many called to tender congratulations upon his success. Over 500 called to do him honor. Not only Whitman was represented, but Abington, Rockland, the Weymouths, Bridgewaters, Boston, New York, Washington, Marlboro, Milford. . . . One of the pleasing features of the reception was the presentation of a handsome watch, suitably engraved, the gift of a number of his Whitman friends. . . . Among the priests who assisted in the reception, aside from those present at the Church, were Rev. Walter H. Gill of Brockton, Rev. Laurence Killian of the Sacred Heart Church of East Cambridge and Rev. Louis F. Kelleher of St. Thomas's Church of Jamaica Plain.

The editor of the paper went on to presume that "he will rest for a short time at his home in this town and will then enter the ministry [sic!]. His exceptional advantages and recognized ability should meet with ready recognition at the hands of the Church authorities." There seems, however, to have been a minimum of excitement at Cardinal O'Connell's residence following the young priest's return from Rome. He was appointed first as chaplain at St. Clement's Home for old ladies on Brookline Street, Boston, and in due time received a routine assignment as second curate at the Church of All Saints in Roxbury. His first pastor, the Reverend Charles F. Regan, was an invalid and had Father John J. Duran as administrator, but a year later, Father Mark J. Sullivan was placed in charge of the parish and continued the pleasant tradition of friendliness with his curates that made 167 Center Street a real home for all of them. The new curate felt as if he had been placed in charge of the archdiocese when, in addition to his sick calls, parlor duty, and preaching every Sunday, he was made responsible for the Holy Name Society, the First Communion class, the Confirmation class, the Sunday school, and the baseball team, but he loved the people and was so content in his vocation that everything seemed easy, even sick calls on Christmas Day. A letter of thanks written on Christmas Eve forty-two years later gives us a glimpse of our second assistant in 1916:

My eldest brother who was an altar boy in Roxbury when you were a young curate was very sick and the city doctor had visited him and left a prescription to be filled at the drug store. My mother who had eight children did not have the money to have it filled.

I was walking along Marcella St. when I met you and you asked about Joseph. I told you about the Doctor, etc. and you took me down to Cyrus Davis Drug Store in Jackson Square and paid for the medicine and told the druggist to give me any more medicine needed. . . .

I pray for your success and enclose $20.00 which I know you will use in your wonderful work to help some deserving family.

An Ex-Marine from Marcella St.

In fact Father Spellman had settled down at All Saints as if his whole life was going to be spent as a parish priest, but the World War which he had seen face to face in Europe, was coming closer to Boston every day. President Wilson had urged the United States to maintain "neutrality of thought," but Walter Hines Page, our Ambassador to the Court of St. James's, was very subtly bringing him into line with the British point of view, aided and abetted by a marked lack of subtlety on the part of Germany. President Wilson was re-elected on the slogan that "he kept us out of war," and yet just one month after his second inauguration we were in it for better or worse. No matter what may have been the divisions in American public opinion up to that point—and the pro-German sentiment was much stronger than afterward seemed possible—the declaration of war was remarkably effective in achieving substantial unity. The word "propaganda" became part of the ordinary American vocabulary, and by the time the first contingent of Pershing's troops left for Europe on May 28, 1917, the whole country had caught fire.

All Saints, Roxbury, Massachusetts, was no exception. War was on everyone's mind from the pastor down. It was the first real war we had had since 1865—the first time there had been any general call for chaplains—and many an evening the curates talked it over after supper. By the following February, Father Spellman had made up his mind, so he wrote to his Ordinary, volunteering to be a chaplain in any branch of the service. The Cardinal designated the Navy.

Meanwhile he had been invited to make the address at the raising of the service flag honoring the boys of his old parish in Whitman. Five days before, Marshal Foch, one of the most devout Catholics in the Allied ranks, had been made commander-in-chief of all our armies, and Father Spellman chose to speak on the patriotism of American Catholics. He said in part:

Seventeen million, in round numbers, of the one hundred and ten million people in our United States are Roman Catholics, that is, about fifteen per cent. It is then with pardonable pride that we reflect on the statement of the Secretary of War, Mr. Newton Baker, made last September, that thirty-five per cent of the Army are Catholics, while we have it on the authority of the chaplains that Catholic boys form sixty per cent of the Navy.

He went on to point out the role played by Catholics in the War for Independence and concluded:

Now our Country has entered this war to win for other countries the blessings that we enjoy. From a material standpoint, we have nothing to gain, everything to lose, but we enter the struggle in the words of our chosen leader, Woodrow Wilson,—we enter the war unselfishly, self-sacrificingly, that universal right and justice may prevail. And we are proud to follow his leadership.

One more word and I am done,—a word to those most closely related to the young men whom we honor today. There is sadness as well as gladness in your heart and in my heart. It is almost certain that some of our loved ones will not come back to us, that our next meeting with them will be in our heavenly home, where suffering and sadness will be no more. But the sunlight of divine consolation pierces the mist of our human tears, and we realize that it makes absolutely no difference when we die, —old or young,—it is all the same,—the one thing that matters, and the only thing that matters, is how we die. And we have the word of the Catholic chaplains that our boys are living well and are dying well. "As a tree falls, so shall it lie, and as a man lives, so shall he die." "Greater love than this hath no man, that a man lay down his life for his friend," and greater patriotism hath no man than to give up his life for his country. Nor is there greater heroism, my friends, than the heroism of the father and mother who give up their son, flesh of their flesh, blood of their blood, dearer to them than their own life, who give up their loved one to their country.

And when, in the course of time, everything will be over for you and for me, when all within sound of my voice will have crossed the threshold of death,—will have passed before the judgment seat of Almighty God,— and when those of us who have served Him faithfully here upon earth will have begun to enjoy that happiness that will never end, we can look down upon the heavens to which we now look up, and we can see the stars on God's celestial service flag, not only one for every son who has served Him well, but one, also, for every mother and father, whose martyrdom of tears is just as meritorious as their loved one's sacrifice of blood.

His patriotism was at the burning point, and everything was progressing with dispatch. He was not as tall as the regulations demanded nor was his eyesight all that it might be, but he had won exemptions for both defects. Only the mental test remained. This, he was assured, was a mere formality for a graduate of the North American College, so he ordered his naval uniforms. They cost $140—real dollars, the parting gift of Father Lowney, an old friend, who had married his mother and father.

In charge of the mental test was a head chaplain of the Navy, who was reading a newspaper, with his feet on the desk, when the young priest entered the room. For two full minutes the great man never looked up. Unimpressed as usual by earthly majesty, Father Spellman opened the conversation.

"I came here to be examined." The tone may have been a trifle more firm than that prescribed for one who could not yet rank even a single-striper.

The captain looked up and glared. "You Catholic priests are all too arrogant for your own good. I suppose it is because you are so used to bull-dozing your congregations."

The young man, instead of retreating, answered quietly, "We don't have to bulldoze them. They know we have something to give them."

There was a pause before the chaplain remarked icily, "I see you have a lot of lessons to learn in the Navy. If I give you a text and an hour to prepare can you preach a sermon for me?"

Father Spellman shot back, "I could preach one now on the subject of arrogance."

That was the end of his mental test. He was rejected as "temperamentally unfit for the Navy." There was no appeal, since the captain was an intimate of Secretary of the Navy Josephus Daniels and said to be friendly with Woodrow Wilson himself.

Still determined, however, to serve his country, Father Spellman now turned to the Army, and this time went through the various tests successfully. With every day that passed, the situation in Europe became more critical. Through the summer months, 10,000 American troops were sailing in convoys every day—300,000 in the month of June. When August came it was time to leave for the training camp, so he went to Brighton with a group of other chaplains to get the farewell blessing of Cardinal O'Connell. His Eminence was not informal. He said:

> I have called you together in audience this afternoon to bid you a fond farewell, to bid you Godspeed on the mission that takes you away from the Archdiocese to serve God and country as chaplains in the Army. First of all, I wish to congratulate you upon the special call you have received, because, in volunteering to be a chaplain, you have done nothing less than answer the voice of Almighty God.
>
> Yours is an unusual opportunity. You have been brave and generous enough to take it. Now you must be prudent enough to make the most of it. You have been taken away from the restricted areas of a parish and have been given the larger fields of a missionary. You must enter into your new labors with the same spirit of prayer, the same thirst for the well-being of souls, and the same self-sacrificing devotion to duty that have characterized the work of missionaries since the time of the Apostles.

If you are to be true to your vocation, there will be no self-seeking in the fulfillment of your duty—nothing vainglorious. There will be only the supreme oblation of self, wholly, entirely, undividedly, upon the altar of sacrifice, sacrifice, first of all, for God and for God's children, and sacrifice also for our beloved country, the United States of America.

I strongly advise you to take notes of your experiences, for your observations will be invaluable in years to come. You are taking important parts, very important parts in the making of history, and you should write to me frequently, giving me your impressions, telling me of your duties and the results of your labors.

I wish to keep in constant communication with you, for I have a special interest in your work. I am ever anxious to hear of your progress, your successes; anxious also with the solicitude of a father to assist in your trials and crosses. I would that I were able to go with you personally, but my prayers, my thoughts and good wishes are with you always. My parting word that I give with my blessing is to prepare for your departure as did the Knights of Old. Let your first action after putting on the uniform of a soldier of your country, let your first action be a visit to the Blessed Sacrament. There with Christ let everything begin; there, too, with Him, let everything end. And so if in the course of the fulfillment of your duty, you lose your life for Christ, it will be only to gain immediately and eternally your new life with Christ Jesus in Heaven.

Having concluded his discourse, His Eminence descended suddenly to the conversational plane and turned to Father Spellman. "Did you understand what I said?" He did. "Then go in the next room and write it out while you remember it." The young man obeyed enthusiastically, and when he brought the text back, with just the right degree of balance and polish that such utterances always acquire before publication, the Cardinal almost revealed his satisfaction. To the consternation of the would-be chaplain, however, his Ordinary, without warning, changed the whole course of his life. As offhandedly as he might have moved him from the nine to the ten o'clock Mass, he took him out of the Army. "I have decided," he told him, "that you will not be a chaplain after all. You are appointed to the staff of the *Pilot*. The circulation has gone down, and you are to promote subscriptions." Of course, as St. Leo says, "Nothing is difficult to the humble and nothing hard unto the meek," but the young priest left the Cardinal's presence in a daze. His mother was brokenhearted. She had trained herself through hours of prayer to accept the sacrifices and dangers involved in war service. After all, it was a sublime vocation to keep up the morale of a fighting force and prepare heroic boys for Heaven, but to come back after five years in Rome a doctor of sacred theology and be assigned to selling papers was just too much. Besides, she had to live in a small town.

On August 17, the Boston *American* carried a few lines to the effect that

"Father Spellman has been appointed to the Cathedral of the Holy Cross and placed in charge of work on Catholic literature." That certainly presented the situation in its best light, and the following month His Eminence in a letter to the Catholic Press Association referred at least to the appointment, if not to the appointee. "Recently," he wrote, "one of the diocesan priests was assigned to the special duty of preaching in the churches of the Archdiocese on the necessity and value of the Catholic press." Not a name, just a number, but the young priest set to work as if this was the one apostolate he had been praying for. His appointment was a complete surprise to the editor of the *Pilot*, and though he was welcome enough, there was no room for him at the headquarters in the Blake Building on Washington Street, so most of his work was to be done at the cathedral rectory. That all was not smooth sailing from the start appears from a letter which he received from the Chancellor, the Right Reverend Monsignor J. P. E. O'Connell, a nephew of the Cardinal:

I trust it will not be wasted advice to suggest to you that it may be well, while you are yet in the beginning of your career, not to allow yourself to get any false conception of your importance, or the importance of your particular work, thus leading you to either the one extreme, temerity, or the other, timorousness. I make this statement because one of your recent letters to me savored of arrogance, a quality which ill befits a subordinate. I passed it over without comment at the time because I attributed the display to your callow inexperience. A change in the attitude which you have so far displayed to my personal knowledge will have wholesome effects for yourself in the future.

For the next four and a half years he visited a different church each Sunday, preaching at all the Masses, sometimes at ten or eleven. It was monotonous enough, Sunday after Sunday, thinking up fresh ways of saying "Buy the *Pilot*," but the obvious success of the campaign was encouraging, and it gave him the opportunity of knowing every church and every pastor in greater Boston. Nor was time heavy on his hands in the middle of the week. Father John Starr, who was appointed curate at Whitman in 1918, recalled that Father Spellman took no vacation through all these years, but devoted his summers to the study of journalism and Spanish. If his career was to be on the *Pilot*, he would be ready for any emergency. Some of the courses were followed during the winter as well, and to make sure that his days would be full, he translated from Italian two books of devotion that had recently come from the pen of his old professor and friend, Monsignor Borgongini-Duca. In 1920 his English rendering of *The Word of God* was published by The Macmillan Company. It was this little volume that brought the translator to the attention of the Apostolic Delegate who sent him the following note:

DEAR REV. FATHER:

It gives me great pleasure to learn that you have translated from the Italian into English a volume of short meditations on the Gospels for every Sunday of the year, written by Monsignor Francis Borgongini-Duca, professor of dogmatic theology at the Propaganda, Rome, and Secretary of the Tribunal of the Sacred Penitentiary.

Knowing the author personally and admiring his qualities of mind and heart, his sound learning, his rare powers of exposition as a teacher, his priestly zeal and earnestness, I feel confident that his book will be helpful to many souls in this country.

With best wishes, I am

Sincerely yours in Xt.,

✠ JOHN BONZANO
Archbishop of Melitene
Apostolic Delegate

Four years later, the second translation appeared, *In the Footsteps of the Master*.

There may have been something here of Father Spellman's infallible sense for public relations, but he could not have foreseen the circumstances that made these translations another link in the chain of destiny. As far as he knew, he would stay on the *Pilot*, do a little writing himself for the glory of God, perhaps eventually succeed to the post of editor, and ultimately be rewarded with one of the better parishes. So he kept on building up the circulation and helping out in the office, writing an occasional editorial, fashioning headlines, rewriting stories, and proofreading miles of galley sheets—sometimes far into the night. On one occasion, an address of His Eminence was prepared for the front page. Four or five times in the course of the article, the words "Divine Law" appeared as "Divine Lamp" and the Cardinal, being very much upset, addressed a few well-chosen words to his second assistant editor. When the storm had spent its force, Father Spellman, respectful but unimpressed as usual, told his Ordinary that by eleven o'clock at night, after twelve hours in the office, he had no way of telling the Divine Law from the Divine Lamp and could promise no improvement.

On May 24, 1922, there was a brief note in the *Pilot* saying that Father Spellman had been made a member of the Executive Curia of the Archdiocese. Father Starr and Mrs. Spellman talked it over in Whitman, and while she was inclined to be optimistic, he was inclined to await further clarification. This came on Father Spellman's next trip home. It seems that Monsignor Richard J. Haberlin, P.A., D.D., the chancellor at the time, had asked for him as an assistant chancellor, but His Eminence appointed him as an assistant in the chancery—a somewhat different and less impressive position.

The circumstances of his appointment were thus outlined years later by
Monsignor Haberlin himself:

> Father Spellman and the late Louis Kelleher, who was later to become
> the Auxiliary Bishop of Boston, were close friends, and I met Father Spell-
> man through an introduction by Father Kelleher who was one of my
> dearest friends throughout his life. Naturally, with these two friendships I
> saw Father Spellman quite frequently and became very fond of him. I
> was impressed by his earnestness, his untiring devotion to his work and
> his outstanding ability. When an opening, therefore, came in the Chan-
> cery, I did not hesitate to recommend Father Spellman for the assignment,
> fully confident that he would live up to whatever would be required.[1]

The Cardinal may not have regarded it as a promotion, but may have
thought that this independent young man, whatever his name was, would be
safer under the eye of a dependable chancellor than left to himself to mix
up lamps and laws on the editorial board. In any case he made the appointment, and Dr. Spellman, as he was now called, moved into a small office
in the chancery. He had not asked for the change, but as long as he was not
going to be an editor after all, he set about being the chancellor's best assistant in the chancery, and maybe some day assistant chancellor. Father
Starr is again the authority for the statement that his summers were now
devoted to courses in accounting, and that for the next few years he was
seldom seen on a train without a small copy of the new *Code of Canon Law*
which had been promulgated after he left the seminary.

For a while the routine of the chancery moved along smoothly enough—
an easy knowledge of Italian and a fair grasp of French and Spanish proved
useful in the handling of correspondence, while his familiarity with Europe,
especially with Rome, was frequently called upon. When in time a third
assistant became necessary, he was gratified to be consulted on the possibilities under consideration, and urged the appointment of Father Francis A.
Burke, who was selected on his recommendation. All in all, he began to feel
that he was making his mark, that the future showed signs of taking definite
shape. In any case, his tasks were more congenial than proofreading, so he
worked all the harder at his accounting and canon law. It was only after
months and by degrees that he began to feel, vaguely at first, that his natural
objectivity was not popular; that he was a no man at a yes man's desk.
The crisis came with the death of the first assistant, Father William E.
Conroy. Returning from the funeral, Father Spellman found the first desk
occupied by the third assistant, Father Burke, and was told that the Cardinal
wanted to see him.

The interview was brief; no reasons were given, but his demotion was to
be immediate and conspicuous. His Eminence was appointing him archivist
—replacing nobody in particular. His office would be in the basement of the
chancery, near the archives of course. If any time remained after his more

important duties were done, he could help out with a little proofreading at the *Pilot*, and eventually perhaps write a history of the diocese. By this time the average young man would have lost his sense of humor, but Father Spellman was able to keep smiling. Even Father Starr and Father Harry O'Connor were amazed at his apparent lack of feeling. Those in the cathedral rectory and chancery office, who were something less than interested in his career, looked for the ordinary signs of wounded vanity, and saw none. As far as anyone could tell, the archives had been from the beginning the goal of his life's ambition. As he sat there hour after hour, there was nothing to do but read, so he read with the same enthusiasm that he had developed selling papers, and just as in the earlier days he had become better acquainted with the personnel of the archdiocese than anyone at headquarters, so now he was in no time at all an authority on the history of Catholic Boston. But the active ministry appealed to him more than reading about others' activities and when he met his old friends from the North American College, he had to admit that life had become very dull.

CHAPTER FIVE

Monsignor Borgongini-Duca

B Y THE end of 1924 every mail brought notices from various travel
agencies that 1925 would be a Year of Jubilee in Rome—the first since Leo
XIII had proclaimed the celebration of 1900. Every folder that came in made
the young archivist homesick: the dome of St. Peter's, the Tre Fontane,
St. Paul's-Outside-the-Walls, the Piazza del Populo, and the Pincian Hill at
sunset. Why had he been so anxious to get back to Boston?

For the solemn opening of the Holy Year, Cardinal O'Connell sailed for
Europe, taking Monsignor Haberlin with him. In their absence the chancellor's brother died, and the former assistant in the chancery did for the Haberlin family what he would wish another to do for the Spellmans in like circumstances. On his return Monsignor Haberlin did not disguise his gratitude
and asked the young priest if he could do anything to show his appreciation.
Father Spellman promptly admitted that he could and suggested that there
might be a chance of his going on the second pilgrimage. This the chancellor
was able to arrange with the Cardinal by proposing that Bishop Joseph
Anderson, the Auxiliary of Boston, who was to be the leader, might appropriately have a secretary for the trip. The secretary, of course, could pay
his own expenses. Unfortunately, Bishop Anderson was not enthusiastic
about the arrangement. He considered Father Spellman a fifth wheel, and
informed all and sundry that he had not asked for any secretarial assistance
and did not want any. It was embarrassing all around. But while the prospect
of a trip in such circumstances left much to be desired, it did offer at least a
temporary escape from the archives. So Father Spellman decided to join
the pilgrimage, welcome or no welcome, knowing that he could get along
with anybody for thirty days.

The first night out, the unwanted secretary reported for duty and informed
the Bishop that His Eminence had written a beautiful hymn for the group,
which he was to teach to the pilgrims on the boat. Bishop Anderson, without changing expression, said, "I have written a hymn of my own for you to
teach." The first verse he tried went as follows:

> *Christ's Vicar calls to Rome all faithful souls*
> *Come then and sing this hymn to God above,*
> *As marching on to visit sacred shrines,*
> *Where we shall offer acts of faith and love.*

Perhaps the music would have saved it, but in this department Father Spellman, who could scarcely carry a tune, was not an unqualified success. The situation reminded him of an incident in the fifth grade of the Dyer School when the children had been practicing a chorus for Memorial Day and the teacher had been trying in vain to track down a particularly sour note. He remembered what a look of relief had come into her eyes as she said, "Now we shall try it without Frank Spellman." After one or two sessions of practice, the Bishop made the same decision. He would try it without Father Spellman. Instead of choir master, he would use him as a lecturer. Secretaries must be able to do something. So the pilgrims were assembled in the lounge, and on very short notice Bishop Anderson ordered his fifth wheel to give a full-fledged lecture on the Holy Year. Far from being nonplused, the young man began in a light vein that sounded a little bit like ecclesiastical spoofing. He was in favor of Holy Years. They were great institutions. His only suggestion was that they should come more often. If it were not for this Holy Year, he would be back in Boston reading archives instead of on a glorious trip to Rome. At that, the Bishop, in the front row, interrupted with, "Stop that nonsense; give us something solid." So, putting on solemnity without changing the twinkle in his eye, the speaker continued, "According to the Pentateuchal legislation contained in Leviticus, a Jubilee Year is a year that follows immediately seven successive sabbatical years." He went on to explain how Boniface VIII in 1300 had proclaimed the first Christian Jubilee, intending that it should be kept every hundred years; how later the period had been reduced to fifty years and then to twenty-five; how Leo XIII had celebrated in 1900; and what the nature of the ceremonies would be when they arrived in Rome.

As it happened, it was an incident on their arrival that began a new relationship between the Auxiliary Bishop and the archivist. As the train pulled into Rome's Stazione Centrale, it was observed with satisfaction that an official party had come to welcome the pilgrimage, a party led by a high official of the Secretariat of State for the Vatican, Monsignor Borgongini-Duca. As in the old ballads when the king suddenly points to the neglected younger son as the savior of his country, the distinguished monsignor surprised them all by revealing at once that he had come to honor, not the pilgrimage, but his old friend and pupil, Francesco. The Bishop was not offended. He was tremendously impressed.

In due time, the Boston pilgrims were received in audience by Pope Pius XI. They were, of course, just a small fraction of the 1,250,000 pilgrims who visited the Holy Father that year, but he addressed them as though they were the first and only group. When he finished, he turned to the surprised Bishop Anderson and said, "You may translate what I have said into English." The embarrassed prelate summed up a rather long address in the words, "The Holy Father is pleased to see you and gives you his blessing." There was a moment of electric silence, and the observant secretary, standing in the back row, heard the virile and forthright Pope grunt significantly. As the Bostonians filed out of the Throne Room, a group from Rochester, Buffalo, Syracuse, and Albany filed in, and someone, perhaps an angel in disguise, asked Father Spellman to wait in case they might need the help of an interpreter. The Pope spoke again. It was amazing how he could keep up his interest and enthusiasm day after day. This time he even varied the talk. It was practically new. Looking around through his heavy glasses, he spied the young cleric standing at his elbow and asked him if he could understand Italian. It was another of those critical moments. Everyone has a few of them scattered through his life, but too often they are allowed to slip by in a paralysis of indecision. Dr. Spellman never had a touch of paralysis. He was not infallible in his judgment. He was to make his share of mistakes in the years to come, but not as the result of hesitation. So he stepped forward without coaxing and delivered himself of a very fair oration, eloquent and at least as long as the Holy Father's. He summarized everything that had been said to the Boston group as well as the message to the New York pilgrims, and Father Laurence Killian always claimed that he concluded with a phrase or two from the Gettysburg Address. In any case, the Pope, who understood English, was delighted, kept repeating, "Bene! Bene!" and remembered the incident vividly at the proper time.

That time came toward the end of the pilgrims' visit to Rome. It seems that in the summer of 1920 a large and important group of Knights of Columbus had an audience with Benedict XV. In the course of his address the Holy Father asked them to help him in his plan to provide playgrounds for the children of Rome, and they promised to do their best. At the next Supreme Convention, which was held in San Francisco, sufficient money was voted to construct the desired playgrounds, together with a maintenance fund of about a million dollars. The project had been placed in charge of Edward L. Hearn of New Haven, Connecticut. He had been resident in Europe since the summer of 1919 when the Knights of Columbus war work had been liquidated after the expenditure of $45,000,000, and he retained the title of European Commissioner, although his interests now centered exclusively in the Holy City. When Father Spellman arrived on the scene, the Oratory of St. Peter, the first recreation center, had been opened, and three more playgrounds had been completed but were not yet in operation, one on Gelsomino Hill, one near San Lorenzo, and the third in the Valle Giulia. Pius XI had expressed his gratitude in his *Motu Proprio* of March 25, 1924, when he said that the Knights of Columbus had met "his solicitude for youth in the most efficacious manner" and the project was placed under the direction of Monsignor Borgongini-Duca in the Department of State. But unfortunately, through no fault of the overworked monsignor, the progress had not been what it might have been. The Americans and the Italians were not seeing eye to eye. The Italian ideal of boy work was to build chapels on all playgrounds. The Americans, while equally devout, were by nature and experience more realistic.

This somewhat delicate situation was not unknown to Father Spellman even before he left Boston. On the invitation of the Reverend Dr. Louis Kelleher he had attended the annual convention of the Knights of Columbus in Philadelphia, and, returning to Boston on the boat with Mr. Hearn, had discussed with him the co-ordination that was necessary in Rome. As a consequence, when Monsignor Borgongini-Duca, inspired by the physical presence of his old pupil, thought of him as a possible solution to the playground difficulty, all the interested parties were ready for discussion. Before taking any further steps, however, the monsignor called his prospect aside and asked him if he would like the appointment. As usually happened, he had already thought it over carefully and had come to a conclusion. There were sacrifices involved, Rome was a long way from Whitman, and family ties were unusually strong. The job, moreover, was not one of extraordinary dignity. He would be merely joining the small army of young career men who spend their lives in clerical posts, watching for an opportunity in the Vatican. He knew all that. But anything was better than reading archives in the cellar of the Boston chancery office. So he said yes, he would like it.

His faithful diary, beginning September 2, records from day to day the progress of a situation that would change the whole course of his life and the lives of many others.

Wednesday:
  Had lunch with Ed Hearn at Pincio restaurant. Very enjoyable time together. He has certainly had his troubles but he appreciates the fact that I have improved the situation and have talked frankly.

Thursday:
  Monsignor Borgongini asked me again if I would be willing to come to Rome to continue helping him and Mr. Hearn. Monsignor Tardini present.

Friday:
  Told Mr. Hearn of Monsignor Borgongini's desire to have me in Rome and of his intention to ask Mr. Hearn. I asked him to think it over for 24 hours. He said he could answer at once and was sure it would help the work, but he was concerned with my happiness and welfare. I told him my one sacrifice, but a tremendous one, would be my family, especially because my mother was not well. Monsignor Borgongini very enthusiastic. I told him that cost what it would, if I was needed I would come.

Saturday:
  Monsignor Borgongini, Mr. Hearn and I went to Ostia for the afternoon. An enjoyable outing for all. It is certain that they are much closer together than they were a week ago and both are delighted at the change. I

am of course pleased that I contributed to the rapprochement. Mr. Hearn is convinced like Monsignor Borgongini of the desirability of my presence here but insists that for my protection and the protection of the Knights this call must come *Motu Proprio* from the Holy Father. It will be decided tomorrow.

Sunday:

Said Mass at 5:45 in Monsignor Borgongini's private chapel. Then served his Mass. We went at 7:15 to St. Peter's for the Holy Father's Mass. The Church was filled with Boy Scouts. As I knelt before the *Sedia Gestatoria* and gazed upwards at the face of the Holy Father, I thought that later that day he would decide the question that was to make such a difference in my life.

That afternoon the Secretary of Extraordinary Affairs went to the Pope to have the appointment confirmed. Pius remembered the young American and the ability he had displayed in the translation of His Holiness' address. Two things impressed the Pope: that Father Spellman had wanted to think it over and that Mr. Hearn had wanted to do the same. So he not only confirmed the appointment but was evidently pleased to do so. Someone who was present was tactless enough to remark, "Suppose His Eminence of Boston does not care to have him come to Rome?"

Pius, the most direct of all the modern Popes, looked up sharply and answered, "*Sopra di lui siamo Noi*" ("Above him are we"). That settled that. But of course the ordinary courtesies were still to be observed and the following letter was dispatched to His Eminence of Boston by Cardinal Gasparri, the Secretary of State:

Your Eminence knows of the work which the Knights of Columbus have initiated here in Rome. In addition to St. Peter's Oratory which has been in operation for more than a year, the Knights have provided three large fields as recreation centers for children. These are not yet in operation but will be soon. For all these new enterprises which are growing more important every day, the Holy Father desires that everything be done in the best possible way, considering the wishes of the Knights of Columbus and Roman traditions as well as the special characteristics of the children, of the families and of the public of this dear city. . . .

Because of the nature of the work and the necessity of contacts and the clear exchange of ideas between the Knights and the Curia, the Holy Father is anxious to have a priest attached to the offices of both the Knights of Columbus and the Roman Curia who enjoys the fullest confidence of both parties.

With a view to this end the Holy Father is considering the Reverend Francis Spellman of the Archdiocese of Boston whom His Holiness has seen more than once on the occasion of the Boston Pilgrimage, whom he has deigned to use as his interpreter and whose piety and Roman spirit he has appreciated.

Wherefore His Holiness has ordered me to ask that this priest be sent to Rome to remain here for at least one year.

Dr. Spellman, however, without questioning the authority of the Supreme Pontiff, realized that if the Roman venture proved to be something less than a success, he might soon be returning to his own diocese. So in spite of Monsignor Borgongini's repeated remark, *"Ut quid perditio haec?"* ("Why this waste of time?"), he begged leave to return to Boston that he might pack and attend to various odds and ends of personal business. Before leaving Rome, he wrote in his diary for September 10:

> Holy Father received me in private audience. Wonderful! *"Caro Spellman, speriamo di rivederci presto."* ("Dear Spellman, we hope to see you again soon.") Gave me a medal and sent rosary to mother. Said goodbye to Monsignor Borgongini-Duca. Monsignor Tardini went with me to station and also Ed Hearn. Mr. Hearn sent his auto for me. It has certainly been a most eventful visit to Rome. I am now eager to get home to talk everything over. Took the De Luxe train from Rome direct to Paris. Quiet restful trip in compartment by myself.

Arriving in Boston, he went at once to visit his Ordinary in Brighton. Having learned the details of the proposal, the Cardinal asked him, "What would you like to do yourself?"

The youthful diplomat replied, "Whatever would please my Cardinal Archbishop."

"You have given the right answer," said His Eminence. "What will you do for money?"

On this point Father Spellman was properly disinterested and the Cardinal offered very generously to continue his salary of one thousand dollars a year as long as he remained in Rome. Then he gave him a paternal blessing and assured him that he would always be welcome in the Archdiocese of Boston.

This time all the Boston papers carried the announcement of his departure. The Boston *Post* pointed out that it was the first time that an American had been attached to the Secretariat of State—and it was. The *Herald* quoted Father Spellman as saying that "his special duty would be in connection with the projects which the Knights of Columbus have established in Rome," and the *Pilot* added that "Monsignor Borgongini-Duca had asked for him." His friends were delighted, and it was agreed in informal clerical circles that Providence had been kind to him. Down in Whitman the news was received with mixed emotions. His mother had recovered by now from the severe illness of his ordination year, but though she wanted as much as ever to see him do well, she felt as very fond mothers always do about long separations. He promised he would write to her every week, a promise he kept till his return to America in 1932.

The details of his departure from Boston as reported in the local press for November 2, 1925, convey a sense of triumph that under the circumstances must have been very heartening:

> One of the warmest farewells ever extended a traveller was given to the Rev. Francis J. Spellman, D.D., formerly of the staff of the Cathedral of the Holy Cross and editorial writer of the *Pilot*, when he sailed last night aboard the Cunard steamer *Scythia* en route for Rome where he will take up his new duties as a member of the Papal Department of State. He is the first American to be so honored.
>
> From shortly after two o'clock in the afternoon until the big liner slipped from her berth . . . hundreds of friends and associates grasped the hand of the priest and wished him "bon voyage" and success in his new field of endeavor. Bishop Anderson headed the large delegation of clergymen who were on the pier to say farewell. . . .
>
> One of the greatest demonstrations during the afternoon was the arrival in a body of a large group of friends from Father Spellman's home town of Whitman. Grand Knight John B. Brouillard of the Whitman Council . . . and Miss Loretta Quinlan, regent of the Massachusetts Catholic Women's Guild, headed this group.
>
> Grand Knight Brouillard presented Father Spellman with a purse of gold following a brief speech in which he wished him God-speed on his journey. Then the entire group recited a small speech in which they conveyed their wishes from the people of Whitman. This was followed by three cheers which rang throughout the pier.[1]

On his return to Rome, Dr. Spellman became first and foremost a playground director and remained such from 1925 until his consecration as a bishop in 1932. But he was a playground director responsible to the Secretary for Extraordinary Affairs in the Secretariat of State. In fact he was designated *Addetto alla Segreteria di Stato—la Sezione* (Attaché in the first section of the Secretariat of State). This was the nerve center of the Vatican with fascinating associations stretching back to the Middle Ages. Though the title Secretary of State was borne for the first time by St. Charles Borromeo in the middle of the sixteenth century, the great Hildebrand, later Gregory VII, performed the functions of the office for Leo IX and four of his successors, and before him each Pope's most trusted Cardinal had occupied the same position. In modern times, Consalvi, Antonelli, Rampolla, and most recently of all Merry del Val, had been part of the pageant of world history, but now Dr. Spellman, fresh from the basement of the Boston chancery, and walking wide-eyed through an ancient suite of offices hung with crimson damask, was to work with two of the greatest figures in the whole story of the Secretariat—Gasparri and Pacelli.

His first lesson was to read the official definition of duties and divisions in the department, as outlined in the Papal Constitution, *Sapienti Consilio* of June 29, 1908:

The department for the despatch of public affairs over which the Cardinal Secretary of State presides shall consist of the following three sections.

The first shall deal with extraordinary affairs which are to be submitted to the examination of the Congregation appointed for that purpose, and shall remit other business according to its nature to the respective Congregations.

The second shall carry on the routine work of regular administration and in addition to its other functions shall be competent to grant titles of honour both ecclesiastical and civil with the exception of those reserved to the master of the apostolic palace.

The third shall provide for the despatch of the apostolic briefs which the other congregations shall deliver to it for that purpose.

Over the first section shall preside the Secretary of the Congregation for extraordinary affairs, over the second his Delegate for ordinary affairs, over the third the Chancellor for apostolic briefs.

The Secretary of the Congregation for extraordinary affairs shall take precedence among the presidents of these sections, and after him the Delegate for ordinary affairs.[2]

In this eventful November of 1925, Dr. Spellman found Monsignor Spada, Chancellor for Apostolic Briefs, Monsignor Pizzardo, destined one day to be Cardinal Bishop of Albano and Prefect of the Congregation of Seminaries and Universities, the Delegate for Ordinary Affairs, and his old friend, Monsignor Borgongini-Duca, Secretary of the Congregation for Extraordinary Affairs. The Cardinal Secretary of State, to whom they were all responsible, was Pietro Cardinal Gasparri, now in his seventy-fourth year. His early life had been spent in the chair of canon law, first at the College of the Propaganda in Rome, and then until 1901 at the Institut Catholique of Paris. Returning to the Holy City, he had been appointed Secretary to the Congregation for Extraordinary Affairs, serving under Rampolla and Merry del Val, until his elevation to the College of Cardinals in 1907. It was Benedict XV who had appointed him Secretary of State, but Pius XI had continued him in office, an unusual tribute to unusual ability. His had been the tremendous task proposed by Pius X of codifying canon law, and the fruits of his labor had been promulgated throughout the world in the Apostolic Constitution of May 27, 1917. Although that in itself was achievement enough for any churchman, it had been the work of his leisure moments. For all through the First World War he had counseled and served the frail little Benedict in his struggle for peace, and after the armistice had handled all the problems that were created for the Church by the

Treaty of Versailles. In the conclave of 1922 he was commonly ranked as *papabilis*, and after the elevation of Pius XI was reappointed to his old post. He had seen the chaos of Italy's corrupt government in the postwar period and the rise of Benito Mussolini. He had seen the Bolsheviks seize power in Russia and had no delusions about the nature of communism. Here was a man worthy of Dr. Spellman's closest study and imitation.

Settling down in Rome again, even after an absence of nine years, was easy enough but a little lonely at first. After one or two false starts, he found a room at the Minerva, a quiet hotel close to Santa Maria Sopra Minerva, the titular church of New York's first two cardinals, John McCloskey and John Farley. There he lived for seven of the most formative years of his life, saying his Mass in the little private chapel of the hotel, which had been regularly used by Pius XI when he visited Rome as Archbishop of Milan. One of his friends of the fourth estate who knew him well during those early days records that "we ate lunch or dinner, irregularly but often, in the rather modest restaurant in Rome known as La Rosetta. He was as jovial with the manager as he was congenial with the waiters. He became a figure and land-mark of the place to such an extent that the enterprising proprietor hung his picture up in the garb of a simple priest, which was quite a distinction in Rome where simple priests are almost as plentiful as parishioners."[3]

The economic aspect of the picture was described by the new assistant in a letter to his mother:

Mr. Hearn was willing to give me $2400 a year. I told him I got $1800 a year and my board but for many reasons I was willing to work for half this amount viz., $900 a year and my board. He allows me two dollars a day for my board making my salary $135 a month. This isn't so bad. Be-sides he paid my expenses of $280 from Boston to Rome.

And again he wrote:

Thus I think I shall be well enough off and I am not anxious for many reasons to be too well off.

All in all, his first impressions were favorable, and he went on record as follows: "My opinion of Mr. Hearn is of the very best. He is my idea of a fine, intelligent, fearless, broadminded and square Catholic American gentle-man." Before long they were received together in an official audience at the Vatican, which drew attention to the importance of their task. The *Corriere d'Italia* carried the report that:

The Holy Father received in audience the pupils of the Pontifical Ora-tory of St. Peter, consisting of 750 boys and girls, ranging from the tender-est age to full adolescence, who on this day had completed the last of their Jubilee visits to the Vatican Basilica. . . . In the Consistory Cham-ber near the Throne was Mr. Hearn, Knight of the Grand Cross, Commissioner to Italy of the Knights of Columbus who founded the Oratory, making a gift of it to the Pope and assuming the cost of maintenance. With him was the Reverend Spellman of Boston, who has recently come here from America to assist in the work which the Knights of Columbus are carrying on in Rome, and who is also attached to the Office of Secretary of State.[4]

Meanwhile, Father Spellman was functioning successfully as the unofficial lubricator in the oratory. "You know," he wrote to his mother, "that Monsignor Borgongini and Mr. Hearn are both big men and smart men. They are both forceful, but they have opposite views on many things and neither one is very anxious to yield and each expects me to convince the other that his viewpoint is correct. That is only one of many things. But in the meantime everything is advancing smoothly and a few more months ought to see a great development."

The opening of the new playgrounds, however, was not the only development in progress. The young director found only enough routine duties to occupy his time during the afternoons, when the boys had their games and instructions. The mornings were free, and interesting things were always waiting to be done in the Vatican. "Everything goes smoothly and everyone is kind. I am with Monsignor Borgongini all the afternoon every afternoon. He is learning English very fast. It seems kind of funny for me to be serious so often and for such long times at a stretch but once in a while I get him to laugh a little. We are not a great deal alike you know in disposition." But this served only to add to their mutual admiration. "Yesterday was the big ceremony of the Consistory. I sat with Monsignor Borgongini in the diplomatic tribune and could see everything very well. It's the first time I ever got that close in a Consistory."

He was surprised as well as delighted by his reception in official circles. "I really had no idea I was in so strong over here. Monsignors Borgongini and Tardini are wonderful to me. That was true that Monsignor B. [Borgongini-Duca] wanted to ask Cardinal O'Connell to make me a Monsignor, but Monsignors Bernardini and Tardini advised him not to do so. Monsignor Tardini wanted to know this time if I thought the Cardinal would approve. I told him of course that it was unnecessary for me to be a Monsignor." *Father* Spellman was title enough for the time being, since it happened that he was the only American attached to the Secretariat and was known to enjoy the complete confidence of his superiors. Step by step, his horizon began to widen as his special assignments became more important than his official duties. Controversies on peace, labor, economics, and politics were taking place in the American press. There were the remnants of the great debate on the League of Nations and on the Immigration Act of 1924. There was the spectacle of tremendous industrial expansion, accompanied by constant strikes, especially in the coal fields, and a near-paralysis of the railroads, demoralized by wartime government control. There was the disgraceful campaign of 1928 which saw the dark forces of bigotry given free rein in American politics, and finally, the collapse of the stock market in October of 1929 which ushered in the worst depression of modern times. More and more, as the years went on, the young American priest was called on to evaluate such issues, as his judgment became more and more respected by his superiors. More and more he was regarded as the American door to the Secretariat by outsiders who had projects of their own. Businessmen came to him, like the unfortunate banker here described:

When Mr. X came to Rome the first time for the renewal of the loan and expected my assistance, I asked him innocently if he would give a better rate than any other bank. He answered, "Well I'll say I will, but I won't." He laughed and I laughed but we were both laughing at different things. He was laughing because he thought I was going to help him fool the people over here and I was laughing because he was such a big fool as to think so.

Then there were affairs of the noble heart—in debt.

On five distinct occasions during these past six years some member of the nobility or his representative has come to me with the request to try to arrange a marriage with some American lady.

The enclosed card concerns another such mission. The Master of the Household of Prince X came to see me the other day. He said the Prince would like to know me and that he and his brother, another Prince, and his brother's wife, a Princess, invited me to dinner any night next week.

I said I had dinner engagements for all next week and if the Prince wanted to know me, he could come to the Minerva and if he wanted to invite me to dinner, he could invite me himself, but that I never went to dinner unless I knew the people first.

So he told me the Prince was sixty years old. The Princess died a few years ago and now the Prince was very lonely and felt he needed a companion and I had been selected as the recipient of the high honor of choosing her. I told him that just at present I did not have any candidates on file, but that if I did have any applications I would surely bear his client in mind. However, he could understand himself that the Prince was not what could be termed a 100% Prince at the age of sixty.

The last agent I had before this had a number of opportunities listed, Dukes and Marquises and Counts, and he even was kind enough to offer me a percentage, but a percentage of what he did not say nor did I enquire.

Prominent Americans came to pay their respects to the Holy Father. Father Spellman was assigned to make the arrangements. Finally, there was the American Embassy and that large colony of English-speaking people who had succumbed to the eternal lure of Rome and were more or less permanent residents. For all of them he was a friend at court—tactful, thoughtful, and tireless. His position with the press became particularly important. For the first time, card indexing and mimeographing were brought into the historic premises. Speeches were translated ahead of time, and press releases were ready to be handed out to all the reporters. Father Spellman retained the modest title of playground director, but became in fact American assistant to the Secretary of the Congregation for Extraordinary Affairs.

Among the distinguished Americans who frequently wintered in Rome and kept a town house there, none was more distinguished than the Nicholas F. Bradys. Nicholas, the son of Anthony N. Brady, a pioneer in public utilities, had been brought up a Protestant, and only after his college days had he recaptured for himself with study and prayer the ancient Faith of his ancestors. His sense of spiritual values had something to do with his interest in Genevieve Garvan, whom he subsequently married. They both regarded themselves as mere stewards, dedicating their lives and everything they owned to the service of God, so that their associations were very close with the Vatican, where they were known for a princely generosity to every cause of religion. Their home when they were in the Eternal City was the charming Casa del Sole on the Janiculum Hill at 16 Via Aurelia Antica, where there were tea gardens and tennis courts for the younger visitors, terraces with views of St. Peter's in the distance, and silent alleys lined with cedars where a Prince of the Church could walk up and down saying his Office. There the best of two worlds met, with the ecclesiastical world represented at different times by such figures as Cardinal Bonzano, Cardinal Gasparri, and Cardinal Pacelli, who were particularly intimate friends.

On his first Thanksgiving Day in Rome, Father Spellman wrote to his mother:

> I saw Cardinal Bonzano yesterday and he was great to me. He said that Monsignor Borgongini had told him all about me, the sacrifice I made in leaving home, the good work that was expected of me here, etc. He gave me some fine advice and kept me at least a half-hour. He is going to arrange to have me preach some sermons here in Rome in the American Church which is his Titular Church.

Cardinal Bonzano had been for eleven years the Apostolic Delegate in Washington, where he had become one of the Bradys' dearest friends. It was through him that Father Spellman joined the interesting and important circle at the Casa del Sole. The occasion was described in a letter to Whitman:

> On the last day of the year when the Holy Father pontificated in Saint Peter's and solemnly proclaimed the new Feast of Jesus Christ, King, I

noticed Mrs. Brady in a row of seats behind where I was sitting. I had five seats for the Diplomatic Tribune, three of which were used by Father Walsh of Maryknoll, Father Crane and Father Martin. But I saw two fine seats in the front row vacant, where the Ambassador of Portugal was supposed to go. So I wrote a little note to Monsignor Borgongini and he and Monsignor Pizzardo did the rest. This worked out perfectly as Mrs. Brady was grateful and Cardinal Bonzano appreciated it too. . . . I also enclose the card on which Cardinal Bonzano wrote my address for the Bradys.

The acquaintance soon ripened into friendship. There was a private chapel in the Casa and the Bradys needed a private chaplain. The obvious choice was Father Spellman, who was soon regarded almost as a member of the family. "After Mass in the morning, I play tennis with Mr. Brady for an hour and then take a shower and get to work at 10:30 or 11. It does him good and I am certain that it does me worlds of good." The new chaplain seemed to know everybody in Rome and the answers to all the questions. His thoughtfulness, which was natural and was shown to the humblest people all his life, anticipated every occasion and smoothed out the difficulties before they arose. He played a fast set of tennis with the younger visitors as well, including Aunt Genevieve's nieces and nephews, somewhat to the surprise of his associates in the Vatican, and was, in short, so refreshingly and unaffectedly American that everyone liked to have him around, including Cardinal Bonzano, Cardinal Gasparri, and, a little later, Cardinal Pacelli.

From now on his letters home are full of the Bradys. "Yesterday was Monsignor Bernardini's feast day, the feast of St. Philip. Mrs. Brady gave a dinner in his honor. Cardinal Gasparri, Monsignor Borgongini, Monsignor Pizzardo, Monsignor Bernardini and I were the guests." In June, he wrote:

Yesterday Cardinal Gasparri, Monsignor Borgongini, Monsignor Pizzardo and Mr. Brady and I had a one hundred and fifty mile ride in the country. We brought our lunch and had it in the old Monastery of Subiaco which I had not visited since 1912 when I went there with my classmates on a walking trip. We all had a great time.

I suggested to Mr. Brady to give Cardinal Gasparri a new Chrysler Limousine 82 and he said, "Sure." Both Mr. Brady and the Cardinal are delighted.

On June 13, 1928, there is the following entry in the diary:

Mr. and Mrs. Brady sail *Majestic*. Received code message from Mr. Brady saying that John Ryan, intimate friend of Dwight Morrow, American Ambassador, urges Holy Father to accept Calles' oral promise not to interfere any more in religious matters. Have strongly urged acceptance on Monsignor Borgongini and Monsignor Pizzardo.

Meanwhile the hand of sorrow had been laid upon the intimate circle of friends at the Casa del Sole. The sudden illness and death of the great and gracious John Cardinal Bonzano is outlined in the staccato phrases of the Spellman diary for November 1927. The "Martin" and "John" referred to were Father Spellman's two brothers, who had by now become successful and experienced physicians in Boston. Martin had graduated from Georgetown Medical School in time to go overseas with a Medical Corps unit in World War I. John had finished at Harvard Medical School a few years later, and had specialized in cancer.

November 9: Cardinal Bonzano sick. X-rays very bad. Sent them by *Berengaria* to America. November 11: Operation advised for Cardinal. Sent long X-ray description message to Martin. November 12: Doctors will decide tomorrow on possibility and practicability of operation. November 13: Operation decided. So telegraphed America. November 14: Received answers. Opposed to operation. Martin says life shortened instead of lengthened; suffering increased instead of diminished. November 15: Went with Cardinal to inspect hospital. We even visited operating room. Telegraphed John to come. November 16: Cardinal fixes operation for end of week. Finally I tell him the alternatives. He considers them. He is marvelous. November 17: Operation decided on. Situation tense. November 19: Cardinal's operation. Professor Alessandri. November 24: John arrived. Cardinal getting worse. November 26: Cardinal died. Mr. and Mrs. Brady arrived. November 28: Said Mass Cardinal's House. November 30: Cardinal's funeral.

As soon as the Cardinal realized that his situation was serious, he asked his young friend to take anything in the house that he would like as a keepsake to remind him of their many happy hours together. The choice fell on a small, simply designed statue of the Little Flower, carved in wood by Mario Corbel. This has occupied ever since the place of honor in the Spellman house at Whitman.

The following summer, the young priest was himself near death. The story as outlined in his diary is important as a character study and also as an introduction to a friend who was destined to play a very important role in later events. Enrico Galeazzi was an engineer and architect who, being in charge of planning and constructing all the works done by the Knights of Columbus in Rome, formed an immediate friendship with the new director that was to prove lifelong. It was through his later association with the American priest in the Secretariat of State that he became acquainted with Cardinal Pacelli. His Eminence, who learned to esteem Galeazzi very highly, advanced him to the post of Architect of Vatican City. In 1946 he was ennobled with the title of count by Humbert of Savoy, Lieutenant General of the Realm.

The diary begins August 3, 1928:

August 3:

Had sore knee. Went to Victoria Hotel in Bern, Switzerland. In bed until Saturday, August 11th.

August 12:

Left Bern after twelve days—ten in hospital.

August 14:

Arrived Rome.

August 16:

My knee worse today. Decided to call a doctor. Mr. Galeazzi called Professor Giudice Andrea. He said knee was tubercular, but chest was clear.

August 17:

Called in another doctor at random—Professor Basili. He confirmed tuberculosis. Recommended seashore and putting knee in cast. Said I would get better but knee would always be stiff. Said chest was clear. Mr. Galeazzi got tuberculosis specialist—Professor Passini. He agreed diagnosis and also found right lung affected. Decided to stay in Rome and go to hospital.

August 18:

Went to Hospital Quisisana. Will try not to let anyone know I have tuberculosis. Had X-ray. Showed both lungs affected with new process. Have sweats and fever in the afternoon. Have confidence in doctor. He says process should be arrested in month, but that I will be very weak. Wrote to Monsignor Pizzardo cancelling trip.

August 22:

In bed. Knee improving. Started injections in vein of calcium chloride every other day.

August 23:

Started injections in pleura of gum oleo. The professor is not only the inventor of this, but only user. Hope at least they do no harm.

August 25:

X-rays show kneebone unaffected. Mr. Galeazzi is wonderful to me. How much better off I am now than in 1914. Now I am a priest, I am insured, I have no money worries or worries about being a burden on the family. They are now, thank God, all independent.

August 29:

I think I am getting better and slightly stronger. I am still lame but optimistic.

August 30:

Professor says I am improving, but will always be more or less delicate. I think I will be all right if I lead a more regular life which I intend to do.

September 2:

Feeling better. I think I shall get well. The fever has also diminished. I don't think anyone suspects the real trouble and I prefer that no one knows but Mr. Galeazzi. Of course, if I get better it won't make much difference and if I don't get better all will be known sooner or later.

September 6:

Fever continues. Knee no better.

September 9:

Mr. Galeazzi arranged for Professor Schibone to see me in Sangemini. I can never forget his goodness to me.

September 11:

Here alone in Sangemini.

September 12:

Sangemini: Professor Zanatelli is giving injections. Mother and Mrs. Brady and Monsignor Borgongini are getting nervous about me. I hope I will get better before they find out what is the matter.

September 13:

Routine at Sangemini: Mass—hypodermics—fountain—dinner—sleep —fountain—supper and sleep and not much progress.

Eventually he could write: "Returned to Rome cured. Thank God. Have written story to Martin and John."

At the end of the first exciting year of his new life, we find an entry in the diary: "October 19: Heard indirectly that I am to be made a Monsignor." A little later, "October 30: Monsignor Borgongini told me I was made a Monsignor on October the fourth." Such was in fact the date on the very official notice which might have been phrased by one of the Medici: "His Holiness Our Lord, Pope Pius XI, has benignly deigned to include among his Supernumerary Secret Chamberlains the Reverend Priest Francis Joseph Spellman." What the news meant to Whitman may be gathered from his mother's next letter:

Well dear boy we were certainly surprised yesterday when we received Monsignor Borgongini's cable telling us about your honors. We received the cable about five P.M. The Western Union telephoned it to Maurice Graney's store, and the news spread rapidly. Helene received it from Mr. Graney. Martin was lying down. He jumped up and said, "Isn't that wonderful!" Then Arthur and Marian came down and danced around. It was John's day on duty; we let him know and he was delighted also. Martin called up Father Starr and he was as pleased as we were. He came to me after Mass and shook hands, and said that ten minutes after Martin called he went out to hear Confessions. A man came to him and said, "Father Spellman has been made Monsignor." Father Starr said, "Yes, I know it, but how in the dickens do you know it?" He said, "A few of us were in Graney's and we doped it out that was what the code meant." . . . May Donovan called they read it in the Post and she said Catherine called her up and she was so excited.

Well dear Frank you know we are very happy and proud of you, and I know the best of all is that you are, thank God, a good Priest and my prayer is that God will give you the grace to always be good and be humble. If I thought for one minute the honors would make you conceited or change you from your simple way I would rather you would not be so honored.

When the time came for him to advance another step and be invested as a domestic prelate, the circumstances of the promotion brought echoes from the past. A letter from His Eminence of Boston had petitioned the Pope to honor Father Francis A. Burke, who will be remembered as having superseded Father Spellman in the chancery office. He wanted him made a domestic prelate in recognition of his valuable services. Monsignor Borgongini-Duca, who handled all such correspondence, was sure that the chancellor was entirely worthy, but suggested to His Eminence that it was perhaps incongruous that he should be so honored before his predecessor in the office, and invited him to request the same rank for his other subject, Monsignor Spellman. The Cardinal expressed surprise. He had been under the impression that Monsignor Spellman was already a domestic prelate. Thus was a delicate matter amicably settled.

Mr. Hearn, who was made a papal count at about this time, had anticipated that his new assistant would be somewhat less influential and prominent than he was proving to be, but two years passed before there was any serious friction. For September 23, 1927, there was an ominous entry in the Monsignor's diary: "Heard that Mr. Hearn does not wish me here any more." The trouble seems to have begun on August 17, when, according to the same diary, "the Pope asked me to find $45,000 for a work on Sarcophagi in five volumes, to take three years." What followed is outlined in a letter to Mrs. Spellman, dated November 5:

When I returned from my trip with Monsignor Borgongini, the Holy Father's idea was for the Knights of Columbus to give the $45,000. The Pope wished me to write directly to America. This I did not wish to do as I felt sure that my letter would be sent back to Mr. Hearn in Paris and he would disapprove and be displeased.

The upshot of the matter was that I wrote to Mr. Hearn telling him of the Holy Father's desire and telling him too that since the Knights of

Columbus had already done so much, I would understand his reluctance to ask, but that if he wished, I would ask as it would be very easy for them to say no to me.

Mr. Hearn didn't answer my letter, but as I learned afterwards sent it to Rome to Mr. Andreoli, his secretary, who has never been enthusiastic over my presence in the Eternal City. So after ten days I wrote the now famous letter to Mr. John J. Raskob, without saying anything to anybody about it, except to have Monsignor Borgongini ask the Holy Father if I could write to some one else and the Holy Father said, "Surely." I had a year's time to get the money, so I wasn't worrying and I waited the reply from Mr. Raskob before throwing any more bombs. In the meantime I had explained the matter in full to Monsignor Bernardini and he told me that if necessary, he could get the entire sum from Cardinal Dougherty. I have since written Monsignor Bernardini that he could now hold the Cardinal in reserve for some other emergency.

Now Mr. Raskob is a member of the famous Knights of Malta sponsored by Mr. Hearn and Mr. James J. Phelan of Boston. Some of my ideas about this matter were different from the ideas of Mr. Phelan and Mr. Hearn and on the fourth of January of the present year, I sent a long cablegram to Monsignor Pizzardo explaining that I thought some details should be held up until I could talk to him. I have never entered into the matter very deeply, have never discussed it with Mr. Hearn or Mr. Phelan but only with Monsignor Pizzardo, but Mr. Hearn is somehow under the impression that I have been a hindrance instead of a help. For example, the Knights of Malta wished to have the *exclusive* right to name other Knights of Malta in America. First of all, I did not think it convenient that they should have the exclusive right of nomination. Secondly, I didn't think they should have any right except unanimously to present the name of some person and then have the nomination approved here in Rome.

Meanwhile, time has been going on and nothing has been done for the hospital for children here which the Knights were supposed to help support. Now I have talked to Mr. Raskob. But Mr. Raskob did not know that Mr. Hearn was not enthusiastic about me and that Mr. Hearn has been convinced for some period of time that I would do much more efficient work in my chosen calling as a curate to Father Casey in Atlantic. So Mr. Raskob one fine day was busily engaged in finding work for a stenographer so he told her to make copies of my letter to him and these copies were sent merrily speeding over the ocean to give joy to Mr. Hearn. But the result was like the encounter of the U-Boat with the *Lusitania.* Mr. Hearn was not pleased. In fact he was decidedly irritated. He dispatched a strong protest through Mr. Andreoli to Monsignor Pizzardo.

In the meantime, I had thought it well to give a demonstration that the Knights of Malta hadn't the exclusive right to name other Knights of Malta or to confer the decorations on themselves, so Mr. Raskob was named Grand Cross and Mrs. Raskob "Dame" and when this news breaks on the eleventh of November, I imagine the irritation will increase. But I think the aggregate results will be good, as it may stir up a little action. The reason the eleventh of November is chosen is because Mr. and Mrs. Brady sail on the tenth and Mr. Brady might wonder why he wasn't named, but he will be made Grand Cross of St. Gregory some time in December and I have already written that Mrs. Brady and Mrs. Farrell will be named two of the three Dames of Malta in the whole United States.

Monsignor Pizzardo even wanted to make me a Knight of Malta like Cardinal Mundelein and Cardinal O'Connell, but I said, "No thanks." So he said, "Do you want to be made now or later?" And I answered, "Never."

And now to take up the narrative about Mr. Hearn. First I cabled Mr. Raskob to regard my letters in the future as confidential. Monsignor Pizzardo did not wish me to do this as he feared to offend Mr. Raskob. But I decided to do it.

However, I am laboring under no delusions that Mr. Hearn is not extremely irritated, but I hope for the sake of the Knights of Columbus and for Mr. Hearn's own sake that he restricts his attacks on me to a rebuke. Such an action I shall enjoy with great humility and docility. Monsignor Borgongini would not mind a bit of an argument and Monsignor Pizzardo says that if Mr. Hearn wants trouble when he returns from Paris, he will be accommodated.

The next letter home would indicate that Mr. Raskob's gift of $45,000 had created a stir in Rome.

Monsignor Pizzardo told me the Pope spoke again to him this morning about the $45,000 and me, and I suppose Monsignor Pizzardo takes occasion to speak well of me once in a while for the Holy Father said I was very necessary here and called me a *Monsignore Prezioso* which to go back to Sister Philomena's language would be a precious Monsignor. So today Monsignor Pizzardo was walking with Monsignor Cicognani and me, and he told Monsignor Cicognani the story of my writing to America and getting the $45,000 and that the Holy Father has rechristened me—Monsignor Precious.

The gift has certainly caused quite a sensation and just at present I am in very strong even if there were any efforts made by anyone to hurt me.

His mother replied: "My daily prayer is that your work is pleasing to God now and always, as the work and sacrifices of a good priest must be pleasing to His Most Sacred Heart." The next reference to the matter in the diary is for April 6, 1928: "Didn't see Mr. Raskob as Monsignor Pizzardo said Mr. Hearn was very bitter towards me and resented my knowing Mr. Raskob."

A few days later we read: "Mr. Hearn left for Paris. He has high blood pressure." The incident was not completely closed, however, until 1932, when the Monsignor wrote to his mother on March 11:

> Mr. Hearn's resignation has now become public and the Cardinal Secretary of State wrote him a nice letter accepting it. . . . Mr. Galeazzi is now in complete charge and things are going fine.

Meanwhile, events in Italy had become more absorbing than any personal misunderstandings, for arriving late in 1925, Monsignor Spellman was in time to see the first stirrings in the momentous settlement of the Roman Question. It was now fifty-five years since the fateful September 20 when Victor Emmanuel's troops breached the Porta Pia and overran Rome with pillage and sacrilege and bloodshed. Pius IX, outraged and brokenhearted, would have none of the settlement proposed by the invading Piedmontese, and in protest against their utter disregard for international law, let it be known that henceforth he would never again leave the Vatican until there was some return to reason and justice. Over the years, as generations died out and Pontiff succeeded Pontiff, opinions changed with regard to the details of the settlement, but two claims on the part of the Holy Father were regarded as immutable. First, he should be the ruler of a civil state, however small, whose sovereignty would be manifest so that the Pope's complete independence might be safeguarded, and secondly, a concordat should be signed that would recognize among other things the legality of a Church marriage.

While Pius IX lived, the wounds were too fresh to heal, and after his death the Freemasons attacked the funeral procession with the obvious intention of throwing his body in the Tiber. Under Leo XIII a mistrustful reserve was maintained on the part of the Vatican, which proved more effective in the end than violent opposition. On the side of the anticlericals, bitter laws were passed and scurrilous magazines like L'Asino, whose aim was to destroy the confidence of the people in the clergy, were subsidized by the government. Public officials of Rome thought up fantastic and childish insults. They erected a statue of Giordano Bruno on the Campo di Fiori and one of Garibaldi scowling at St. Peter's from the Janiculum. They encouraged soldiers and police to insult priests and nuns. They were proud of the fact that cardinals and bishops were not safe on the streets. The Pope on the other hand offered merely passive resistance. He refused to recognize that the seizure of Rome had changed anything. The widely acclaimed twentieth of September remained merely the Feast of St. Eustachius and Companions, Martyrs. The unilateral Law of Guarantees, with its assumption of authority over the Holy See, was never to be considered. There was to be a strict separation of the diplomatic corps accredited to the Pope and to the King, and no sovereigns or chiefs of state would be received at the Vatican if they had first visited the upstarts in the Quirinal. Symbolically, the great bronze doors of the apostolic palaces were closed, and the Holy Father ceased to appear above St. Peter's entrance to give his traditional blessing *urbi et orbi*—to the city and the world. Leo, moreover, continued the *Non Expedit* of Pius IX, forbidding Catholics to seek office or to vote in this unlawful and outrageous state.

Meanwhile, through the diplomatic genius of the Pope and the wide dissemination of his great encyclicals, the prestige of the Holy See was rising rapidly, and Italy began to realize that the papacy had not been done to death, but that the new state and her royal family were losing ground in world opinion because of their disreputable campaign. Little by little the atmosphere became less tense. Pius X lifted the ban on voting. Benedict XV allowed Catholic sovereigns to visit the Quirinal. Pius XI, immediately after his election, went to the balcony and gave his blessing *urbi et orbi*. It has been pointed out that in the crowd that day, applauding with the rest, was the Count of Turin, Vittorio Emanuele di Savoia-Aosta, grandson of Victor Emmanuel II, the king that Garibaldi made. From that day people began to predict that the Roman Question would soon be solved, regarding the Masonic lodges as the only insuperable difficulty in the way. Toward the end of 1925, Freemasonry, to consolidate the power of the Fascists, dissolved itself in Italy.

The following June, a Eucharistic Congress was held for the first time in the United States. His Eminence George Cardinal Mundelein of Chicago was host to the enormous throng of pilgrims from all over the world, and saw to it that everything was planned on the unprecedented scale which foreigners expected from the Middle West. His public relations were worthy of the occasion, and as nothing of much importance was happening elsewhere except for the general strike in England, the world press reported the congress at length. Detailed accounts penetrated the Palazzo Venezia and made a deep impression on an impressionable Duce. So it happened that Signor Francesco Pacelli, brother of the future Pope and legal counselor to Pius XI, had hardly returned from Chicago with the Cardinals of the Curia when he was visited by Professor Domenico Barone, legal counselor to the Italian government, who asked if informal conversations might be opened on the subject of the Roman Question. Pacelli went at once to the Secretary of State.

For the next two years every other project was secondary while the great work went on in secrecy with all the patience and skill expected of trained diplomats. The Holy Father was closeted for hours with Gasparri, and Gasparri was closeted for hours with Borgongini-Duca. In a letter to his mother, written the day before the Lateran Treaty was signed, we read:

> Monsignor Borgongini and I are together an hour or two a day but not as much as formerly. He thrilled me last night by telling me that some of my ideas were made use of in the Concordat. Of course this is only for

the family. For example, I was the one who explained that our church marriages are recognized by the Civil Law without our being obliged to go through a civil ceremony as has been obligatory hitherto in Italy.

Naturally I realize that this did not take much genius on my part but still if I had not explained it, they would not have known about it. So when he said, and I repeat it, because he says very few things like it—"some of your ideas are in the Concordat"—it meant a great deal.

The demands of the Pope were easily stated. He was fighting not for acreage but for principle. He wanted not power over others but complete independence. It was unthinkable that he should be another Canterbury. He wanted a concordat so that the religion of the people would be honored by the temporal rulers of the people. And finally there was a certain matter of restitution to be determined. The Piedmontese had plundered the Church. It was time they paid at least in part for what they took.

Thus when in November of 1928 the Pope and the King appointed official plenipotentiaries in the persons of Cardinal Gasparri and Benito Mussolini, three separate documents were prepared: the Lateran Pact, a monetary convention, and a concordat. Two months later the last drafts were complete, and on February 11, 1929, the Lateran Treaty was signed by the two official plenipotentiaries. After fifty-nine years of bitterness, there was to be at least a measure of understanding. Pius XI would henceforth be known as the Pontiff of Reconciliation and the papers were not slow to suggest that the one-time mountain climber had scaled his highest peak.

The day-by-day description of events which Monsignor Spellman sent to his mother breathes with the excitement which had gripped Rome as the time for the signing drew near. On February 8 he wrote:

> These are wonderful days! Wonderful days to be alive and still more wonderful to be alive and in Rome! And wonderful beyond imagination's power to conceive the possibility to be here in Rome and so closely associated with Monsignor Borgongini, Cardinal Gasparri and with the Holy Father in these historic moments!
>
> God be praised and be thanked for this great grace to His Church, to this nation and to the world!
>
> And God be praised and thanked from a personal standpoint that even though I had no part in it, I was a part of it in several ways.
>
> Everyone here is radiantly happy and well they might be. This Holy Father, Cardinal Gasparri and Monsignor Borgongini are assured of places in history and of course also Mussolini.
>
> The Holy Father asked Monsignor Borgongini today if I could get him a train and I thought he was joking. But he was serious. The Italian Government will give the engine and I am to find the car. First he wanted four cars. But I explained one car with three or four bedrooms and bath and dining room and sitting room and chapel would be sufficient for the

Holy Father and for his suite, the regular sleeping car for the necessary occasions would be quite sufficient. So I am now on the hunt for a nice car. But I have a year to find it.

The Holy Father told Monsignor Borgongini also to ask me about three automobiles, so I am getting Bob Graham who went to school with me in Fordham and who now makes the Graham Paige car to give them.

Monsignor Borgongini is going to ask Cardinal Gasparri to use my fountain pen when he signs with Mussolini. Nothing is sure yet about Monsignor Borgongini being nuncio but I think it most probable.

Cardinal O'Connell sent me a telegram today which said: "Communicate to Holy Father universal sentiment of joy and approbation here final settlement of Roman Question and peace with Italy and world. Congratulations to Cardinal Gasparri and Monsignor Borgongini. Am leading American pilgrimage leaving Boston April nineteenth.—O'Connell."

I answered: "Had already told Holy Father about pilgrimage and he was most pleased and consoled. Cardinal Gasparri and Monsignor Borgongini appreciate message of Your Eminence and will convey it to Holy Father tomorrow morning.—Spellman."

The ceremony in St. Peter's on Tuesday will be thrilling. I wish you could be present but perhaps the excitement would be too great.

Two days later he added subsequent details:

It is useless for me to tell you all about it now because the American papers will be full of it tomorrow. But as I write the papers do not know that Cardinal Gasparri and Monsignor Borgongini are leaving at ten o'clock in the Chrysler which Mr. Brady gave the Cardinal, to go by a round about way to the Lateran, and are to wait in the Roman Seminary near the Lateran until about half past eleven. There have been some threats from anarchists and anti-Catholics, but Monsignor Borgongini has not told the Cardinal about them.

I still think Monsignor Borgongini will be the nuncio and if so a Cardinal in two or three years at the age of forty-six or seven. Poor Cardinal Gasparri will be seventy-eight on May the fifth and he cannot last much longer, but I surely hope he lives a few more years even though tomorrow will be the crowning achievement of his life.

Monsignor Borgongini has become a world figure over-night and if Cardinal Gasparri lasts a couple of years, I do not see how it is possible for Monsignor Borgongini not to be next Secretary of State.

The Holy Father is delighted with everything and he is just fine to me. Monsignor Pizzardo, in the midst of all the excitement of these days, told me this morning that he had let the Holy Father know of the things I had done for him and that the Holy Father was most impressed and appreciative. When I think how good God has been to me the whole thing seems just like a dream, especially these last four years.

Then on February 15 he sent a personalized description of the great event itself.

> The day of the signing of the Treaty and Concordat came and I did not expect to attend. . . . Monsignor Pizzardo saw me and told me to come with him. And Cardinal Gasparri and Monsignor Borgongini went in the Chrysler and Monsignor Pizzardo, Mr. Pacelli and I went in the Cadillac. We arrived first and Monsignor Borgongini was thunderstruck when Monsignor Pizzardo told him I was there. I did not go in the room during the signature, but I was there in the Palace and saw the meeting of the two forces. And I was thrilled because I realized, if not to the full, at least I realized and visualized many of the effects of this agreement.

As events transpired after the signing of the treaty, only one of Monsignor Spellman's confident predictions with regard to his chief was fulfilled. On June 7, 1929, Monsignor Borgongini-Duca was appointed the first nuncio to Italy and was consecrated a titular archbishop later in the same month. But twenty-four years were to pass before his elevation to the College of Cardinals and he never served as Secretary of State. The Holy Father had made up his own mind as usual.

The various wheels within wheels that were involved in this promotion are outlined by the American Monsignor in a letter to his mother, written late in February 1929:

> What I am to tell you in this letter will seem hard to believe as it is hard for me to believe myself despite the experience of the events occurring as they did.
>
> You will recall that Monsignor Pizzardo told me the first night after my return from America that at the conclusion of the Conciliation between Italy and the Holy See in all probability Monsignor Borgongini would be the Ambassador from the Vatican to Italy. And that he wished me to ask Monsignor Borgongini to help him remain in Rome instead of being sent to Berlin as Ambassador when Monsignor Pacelli was made a Cardinal. Monsignor Pizzardo was desirous of being the successor of Monsignor Borgongini in the position which Monsignor Borgongini now occupies as Secretary to Extraordinary Ecclesiastical Affairs.
>
> Naturally I was most happy to do this and Monsignor Borgongini replied that he did not expect to be nuncio, would try to refuse it even if offered him, etc. But I insisted and said that any rate to keep it in his mind and he agreed.
>
> On last Saturday we returned from Naples and Monsignor Borgongini had an audience on Sunday morning with the Holy Father. The Holy Father told him then that he had decided to appoint him nuncio and overruled Monsignor Borgongini's objections. And so it was determined. And I was the first one he told. He thus becomes the head of the Diplo-

matic Corps of Italy, he heads the Papal Diplomatic Corps of the world and he is the youngest Ambassador.

Then Monsignor Borgongini asked for Monsignor Pizzardo and the Holy Father said yes. Then Monsignor Borgongini asked me if I would ask Monsignor Pizzardo to agree to have Monsignor Ottaviani as his successor and Monsignor Tardini as Monsignor Ottaviani's successor as Undersecretary of the Congregation of Extraordinary Ecclesiastical Affairs. And so I went to Monsignor Pizzardo and he agreed and I was most grateful.

So all seems adjusted. Cardinal Gasparri desired Monsignor Pizzardo to go to Berlin, but now that the Holy Father has approved the described arrangement, everything seems sure.

But I cannot help but think how strange it is that I, an American priest, should be consulted and requested by these men, my friends, in such high positions to help in such a matter. If it doesn't sound like a fairy tale, well I never heard a fairy tale. . . .

Monsignor Borgongini is very strong and firm and determined. Naturally it is a difficult position and many will be seeking favors and many will be disappointed and therefore cross. But he will ask the Pope—Who are my Superiors? Whom must I obey and whom may I disobey? I hope that he will be consecrated Bishop by the Holy Father. The consecration will probably take place in May.

CHAPTER SIX

Cardinal Pacelli

WHILE a concordat was being signed in Rome, Berlin was getting a concordat of its own, which Lutheran Prussia preferred to call a "*solemnis conventio.*" Thirteen years before its publication, Benedict XV, absorbed as ever in his effort to halt the suicide of Europe, had selected for service in Germany a young monsignor in the State Department whose very name suggested peace—Eugenio Pacelli, Secretary of the Congregation for Extraordinary Ecclesiastical Affairs and the "right arm" of Cardinal Gasparri. He appointed him nuncio at Munich and consecrated him with his own hands Titular Archbishop of Sardes. Soon after arriving in Germany, the Pope's new envoy had pleaded with the Kaiser in the imperial headquarters at Kreuznach to do his part in achieving peace and to put an end to the deportation of Belgian labor. But as William II still thought he had a chance to win the war, nothing came of the visit. The concordat with Bavaria, however, had been so completely successful, and the nuncio's relations with the German people between 1924 and 1929 so unusually cordial, that when the "solemn agreement" between Prussia and the Holy See was ratified on August 14, 1929, Pius XI was ready to show his appreciation. The fact that Hitler was to violate and then annihilate all agreements in four short years would not lessen the brilliance of the negotiation. The purple was obviously in order.

It was about this time that an eventful meeting took place which is referred to in the following letter written by the then Bishop Spellman to his brother John, March 6, 1939: "I begin with the memories of my first meeting with His Holiness, Pope Pius XII, when His Holiness was Papal Nuncio in Berlin. I went there with Cardinal Pizzardo and remained in the Nunciature as the guest of the future Pope for several days." As usual, his mother had been kept informed. In a letter dated September 8, 1929, he wrote:

Here in Berlin everything is wonderful. The Nuncio, Monsignor Pacelli, met us at the station in his automobile and brought us to his home where we shall be for four or five days. He is a wonderful man. He was Monsignor Borgongini's second predecessor. Cardinal Cerretti was his immediate predecessor and ordinarily Monsignor Pacelli would have been a Cardinal sooner although he is now only 52, but because of the war and complicated conditions in Germany he is not as yet a Cardinal.

However, seven out of ten people consider him as the most likely next Holy Father. But I hope there won't be any next Holy Father for a long time. Monsignor Pacelli is one of those men that you can really term charming.

Tomorrow the Nuncio will have President Hindenburg to luncheon and the following evening Chancellor Marx. I don't know German so I won't ask Mr. Hindenburg what he thought of the war!

Five days later he wrote again, this time from the Apostolic Nunciature in Prague:

Monsignor Pacelli and the members of his household came to the train to see us off. All the time I was with him in Berlin I kept thinking of the great possibilities he has of being the next Holy Father. Monsignor Pizzardo is his closest friend. He does not know Monsignor Borgongini very well and Monsignor Pizzardo told me that he asked about him and Monsignor Pizzardo answered, "He is the Holy See's first man."

Monsignor Pacelli gave me his photograph as Monsignor Micara did last year after our visit to Brussels.

Thanksgiving Day another milestone was recorded:

Yesterday Monsignor Pacelli arrived in Rome. Monsignor Pizzardo and I met him at the station. He goes back to Berlin tomorrow to notify President Hindenburg and then returns to Rome. After he returns it will be announced that he is the new Secretary of State.

Now Cardinal Gasparri is more reconciled and contented. And he and all my friends here are happy that it is Monsignor Pacelli who steps into the greatest position in the Church after the Pope—that of the Secretary of State.

When word reached the German Government of the popular nuncio's recall to Rome for his expected assignment, formal farewells were extended on December 10 at the Kroll Opera. Of his arrival in Rome, Bishop Spellman wrote: "I was one of three persons—Marquis Pacelli and Monsignor Pizzardo were the other two—to meet him in the railroad station when he was called back to Rome by Pope Pius XI to become the Cardinal Secretary of State." The following week, in the secret consistory of December 16, Archbishop Pacelli was created a Cardinal Priest. The red hat was conferred a few days later and in the last consistory he was given, as his titular church, Santi Giovanni e Paolo.

Cardinal Gasparri was now a tired old man with a lifetime of achievement behind him. He had served as Secretary of State for sixteen years. He had finished the Code of Canon Law and had signed the Lateran Treaty. Now he was occupied with the codification of laws for the Oriental Church and felt that the time had come to offer his resignation. So on February 7, 1930, Cardinal Pacelli received the following autographed letter from His Holiness:

> Now that We have agreed as We have today, not without sorrow, to satisfy the insistent wish of the Lord Cardinal Pietro Gasparri and accept his resignation as Secretary of State, We have decided before the Lord to call upon you with this Our letter to succeed him in this important and delicate office and to appoint you to this difficult and exacting post.[1]

"I think too," wrote Bishop Spellman ten years later, "of that day when Cardinal Gasparri relinquished the office of Secretary of State to Cardinal Pacelli. I accompanied Cardinal Gasparri to the reception given in his honor at the palace of the Italian Ambassador to the Holy See and I recall most vividly the meeting between the two great Cardinals on that occasion and Cardinal Pacelli's graciousness to Cardinal Gasparri." Graciousness was never an effort to Cardinal Pacelli, but least of all in the case of Cardinal Gasparri to whom he owed so much reverence and gratitude. The reception which brought together for the first time "the Blacks and the Whites"—the diplomatic corps accredited respectively to the Vatican and the Quirinal—emphasized the significance of the Cardinal's contribution to peace. As the guest of honor, he was the first to leave. Driving home with Monsignor Pizzardo and Monsignor Spellman, Gasparri murmured, "*Sic transit gloria mundi!*"

Pizzardo protested, "The glory of Your Eminence will never pass."

The old man did not reply, but as his custom was, blessed himself and started the Rosary.

Through the spring, the new Secretary had ample opportunity to evaluate the young American monsignor, and when the summer came, they went to Switzerland together. "The memories of the days and weeks in various years that I was permitted to be the sole companion of Cardinal Pacelli on the journeys which His Eminence was accustomed to make during vacation periods, periods that were supposed to be vacations, but which were in fact weeks of work and retreat, will remain engraven in my mind as long as life endures. His thoughtfulness and benevolence were supreme."

One spot that was dear to the Cardinal was Rorschach in the Canton of St. Gallen on Lake Constance. There, early in his career as nuncio to Germany, he used to spend a few weeks of peace at the Institute Stella Maris, conducted by the Sisters of the Holy Cross of Menzingen. It was a refuge in 1919 from the turmoil in Munich, when the Reds—or the Sparticists as they were called—threatened him with death at the door of his nunciature, and many times in the years that followed he had returned to this lovely lake resort for his vacation. So when the hot weather came to Rome after his first busy months in the Vatican, one spot had more appeal than any other. "Those weeks with His Eminence, those journeys, those experiences, unique and intimate as they invariably are when two persons are associated closely for extended periods, have always been memories most precious and most treasured." At the time they had their humorous aspects as well. The first trip was summed up in a postcard to Martin: "This is a view of the town of Rorschach, a little larger than Whitman. I am very happy here and am leading a very, very, very regular life." This was enlarged upon in a letter to his mother:

Well here I am lodged in a Young Ladies' Academy in a place called Rorschach on the Swiss shore of the Lake of Constance. The Austrian frontier is about fifteen miles away to the south at the end of the Lake and the German frontier is twenty-five miles to the north at Constance.

It is a funny place to pick out for a vacation, but a great place for a rest. As Mr. Galeazzi said when he wrote down my address, "Stella Maris, Rorschach—it's a far cry from the Ritz."

Of course it is a wonderful thing to be the travelling companion of the Cardinal Secretary of State and the person whom most people believe is to be the next Holy Father, but it does mean a regular life: up at 5:30 in the morning, celebrate Mass for the Sisters at 6:15, assist the Cardinal at his Mass at 7, breakfast at 8. Then study and read and say my Office until 11:45 when I go to the Chapel. Luncheon at 12, then a two hour ride or a walk or a visit to some convent and back here at Rorschach at 4 when I say the Rosary and give Benediction at 7 and at 7:30 there is supper. At 8:30 I am free for the night and I go to bed fairly early.

Instead of an ordinary bedroom I have a beautiful assembly hall to sleep in; something like sleeping in Grand Army Hall in Whitman. There are ten or twelve windows, a black board, chairs and tables, the teacher's desk and a bed and a wash stand. Everything is here except a piano. That is upstairs. Some girls who evidently did not acquit themselves brilliantly in music and have to practice in the summer are up there now playing "The Woodman Cutting Down A Tree."

There were distractions, of course. On a glorious trip through the Vorarl-berg Mountains to Merano and thence through the Dolomites to Innsbruck, Monsignor Spellman asked the Cardinal if he could go to the last perform-ance of the Passion Play at Oberammergau, as he had been in Munich twice without seeing it.

He could hardly say no because he had a companion (Monsignor Ludwig Kaas, the Head of the Center Party in Germany) and kindly gave me permission. I got to Oberammergau and found it was all booked up. But Anton Lang, the Christus of the performance, whom I knew; got me a seat and the American Express Company got me a room, so I was all set. Imagine my surprise when my seat was next to Henry Ford and Mrs. Ford and on the other side of me was Sir Percival Perry, the president of all Ford's European Companies. We talked at various times during the intermissions and I enjoyed meeting him immensely. I knew many Detroit people whom he knew and we talked about everything except religion and prohibition. He said if he ever got to Rome he would look me up. I was amazed and moved on my return from Oberammergau to see His Eminence standing alone on the dock in Rorschach awaiting the finish of my transit of Lake Constance.

But the main source of diversion was an interminable number of receptions at neighboring convents and monasteries.

We have visited a dozen convents and every time the Cardinal visits a convent there is a holiday. If we stay around here much longer, this will become the most ignorant country of the world. The way the holidays are distributed makes me wish I was a child again in Switzerland. And some days we go to Austria and Germany which are very near and give them a few holidays over there too. There is nothing narrow about the Cardinal when it comes to distributing holidays. All the nations are the same to His Eminence.

Here we are in another convent, Menzingen. It is the largest convent in my limited experience with convents. When we arrived all the town was out to meet us. It was one of those occasions on which, if Pa were Swiss, he would ride horseback and Pat Smith and Andy McCallum and Foster Rand (the entire police force of Whitman) would wear white cotton gloves. The local equivalents of the Grand Army and the Sons of Veterans and the Daughters of Rebecca and the Women's Club were waiting for us an hour before we arrived.

Another day we visited a Sacred Heart Convent and there were poems and songs and flowers presented and more poems and more flowers and then the Cardinal gave a holiday, but the holiday wasn't meant for me. . . . The World Series is going on in America.

There are no bananas in Italy. They do not grow there and since there is a lot of other fruit there, the importation of bananas is forbidden. And so one of the first days after being accepted as a student in this Academy, they had bananas, and I with memories, sweet memories, of the invariable custom of Pa to bring home a dozen bananas every Saturday night, took one. Now I have to eat one every meal or Mother Superior will think I am sick. Will you ever forget that bag of bananas?

I have thought of home so many times during this month, I suppose because I was leading such a quiet life. I remember all the different periods of my growing up, of my life at home, of my life at the store with

Pa, of my life at school. And it is surprising how many details I remember although I have not as good a memory as Martin. It is surprising with how much pleasure I live over the past, almost with as much pleasure as I lived those days then in actuality.

Yesterday was the Feast of St. Francis of Assisi. I received roses and pinks and we had chicken and pudding and flowers on the table and we stayed up half an hour and the children sang and played and spoke pieces, and I got my hair cut.

The Cardinal is in fine humor and delighted with everything. He is learning English very well. He is very kind and pleasant and confidential with me.

The Cardinal was a little nervous over a telegram he had received from Monsignor Pizzardo, but I was sure it was not anything alarming. However, we called Monsignor Pizzardo and found out it was only to sign the marriage dispensation for the King of Bulgaria and Princess Johanna of Italy. So then he felt better. However, he was in no hurry to get back because he said here we can breathe all we want to and back in Rome with the visits and the letters we shall be massacred.

Inevitably, however, the time came for the return trip.

Even though the tickets were in my name the Cardinal was at once recognized and in five minutes we were again surrounded by detectives after having ducked them for more than a month. It was the first time in over fifty years that a Cardinal Secretary of State had left Italy during his term of office. We had kept our arrival in Rome a secret and only Monsignor Pizzardo was at the train to meet us. The Cardinal was immensely pleased with everything and so was I. We shall probably take another trip together next year.

They did, and the letters describing the two visits are indistinguishable.

The world press became interested a few months later when it was announced that Guglielmo Marconi, the inventor of wireless telegraphy, was to present a fully equipped radio transmitting station to the Holy See. As events transpired the Holy See ended up by paying for the installation, but Marconi received public credit for a major benefaction. Vatican City already had its own railway station, post office, and cable facilities. Now, for the first time in history, the Pope could speak directly to his children all over the world. Formerly what he wrote could be read to them by others from the pulpit; now his voice would reach them in their sitting rooms.

The formal opening on February 12, 1931, had all the elements of drama and was awaited everywhere with more than ordinary interest. "Pius XI and members of his Court were received at the entrance by Marquis Guglielmo

Marconi who conducted the Pope through the various halls and then assisted him to a throne in the small transmitting room. The inventor personally superintended the pickup. It was he who introduced Pope Pius XI to the world. The speech lasted half an hour and in practically every country the broadcasting systems stood by and cancelled their usual programs to get the speech in full."[2]

The circumstances made it an unusually important statement and the text was worthy of the occasion. It rose to a universality that belonged not to the Bishop of Rome or to the Patriarch of the West, but to the Vicar of Christ on earth. He began with great solemnity:

> To all Creation: Having in God's mysterious designs become the successor of the Prince of the Apostles—of those Apostles whose doctrine and preaching were by Divine Command destined for all nations and for every creature—being the first Pope to make use of this truly wonderful Marconian invention, We, in the first place, turn to all things and to all men, and We say to them:
>
> Hear, O ye heavens, the things I speak. Let the earth give ear to the words of my mouth. Hear these things, all ye nations; give ear, all ye inhabitants of the world, both rich and poor together. Give ear, ye islands, and harken, ye people from afar.[3]

Then, after a prayer to God, he turned successively, with appropriate exhortations, to Catholics, to the hierarchy, to the religious, to missionaries, to all the faithful, to unbelievers and those outside the fold, to leaders of peoples, to subjects, to the rich, to the poor, to laborers and employers, to the afflicted, ending with the simple words: "It remains for Us to impart to the city and to the world and to all who dwell therein Our Apostolic Blessing. This We do in the Name of the Father and of the Son and of the Holy Ghost."

The Secretary of State suggested that Monsignor Spellman, who for some time had been translating all important documents into his own language, might for the occasion not only prepare the text for the English-speaking papers, but deliver a digest of the address in English after the Pope had finished. It was this suggestion which made Monsignor Spellman for the first time a national figure in his own country. He had met every American bishop who had come to Rome in the previous five years, and in five years practically every Ordinary from the United States makes an official visit "*ad limina.*" But now his name was briefly at least on every tongue. He received the Latin text at ten o'clock and went on the air at twelve. Transoceanic broadcasting was new to him and he expected a special signal to let him know when the general public was listening. As a consequence, an amusing dialogue was heard by millions of listeners between the Pope's translator and Monsignor Stephen J. Donahue, secretary of Cardinal Hayes, which began, "Hello Steve—Hello Frank," and was widely reported by the press. Referring to this and other circumstances of the broadcast, Monsignor Spellman wrote to Mr. Hernand Behn, president of the International Telephone and Telegraph Company:

My part in the affair was a distinctly minor one as there was nothing very difficult involved in reading the address from written pages. Some friends of mine wrote to me that I must have nerves like a fish because I was not excited. But there was really nothing to be excited about since I was all alone in a room with my manuscript before me and it was impossible not to do well.

Moreover I could not imagine that people were listening to me, and besides I did not know that anyone would recognize my voice. I told no one that I was to make the translation and transmission, not even the members of my own family, and since I had never broadcast before or heard anyone whom I knew broadcast, I was unaware that individual voices could be recognized. It was, therefore, a revelation when I began to be deluged with telegrams and letters from those of my friends who realized that it was I who was speaking.

And of course never in the world could I have imagined that people would listen in to my personal conversation with Monsignor Donahue. I asked Monsignor Donahue to remember me to the Cardinal and Bishop John J. Dunn, to Mr. George MacDonald and Mrs. Brady because I knew he sees them very frequently. But if I had had the remotest idea that people could have heard me, I would surely have included yourself, Mr. John D. Ryan and Mr. Cornelius F. Kelley and those with whom I had dined the evening that I sailed from New York.

What happened in Whitman that day was described by a writer on the Boston *Post:*

Thursday morning was just like any other morning in the Spellman household. Mrs. Spellman and her daughter, Mrs. Arthur Pegnam, were up bright and early preparing breakfast for the men folk. As Mr. Spellman took his place at the table, he reached for the morning paper. His eyes were immediately attracted to the large black type which read: "Wait Voice Of Pontiff." He read on until all at once his face brightened and he read aloud to the other members of the family that his son was chosen by His Holiness to translate his speech into English. For a moment silence fell over the family group. Each was thinking the same thing. Then all at once the telephone rang to break the silence. "New York is calling Mrs. Spellman," came a voice from the phone. It was Rt. Rev. Msgr. Stephen J. Donahue calling to advise her that her son was to speak over the radio that morning.

Breakfast was forgotten. The radio was given an extra onceover just to make sure that it was in perfect working order. Nothing should happen that would mar the reception of the voices from Rome. At exactly noon, Father Frank began his translation of the Pope's message. The eager group was seated around the radio, their heads bent in the direction of the loudspeaker to be sure they would not miss a word. "Here he is," said Mr. Spellman, not daring to speak above a whisper for fear something might be missed. Mrs. Spellman nodded. It was not in her power at that moment to speak. As if by magic the voice entered the room and through the entire program the family listened silently to their Father Frank.

The popular response was great. By the following morning Monsignor Spellman told the Associated Press that he had received more than 275 cable and radio messages from the United States alone, and a little later wrote to his mother, "For the last ten days I have averaged 70 letters a day." Bishop O'Leary of Springfield wrote:

But to the great majority who could not understand the Latin message, your interpretation and translation of it was a source of unspeakable satisfaction and pleasure. I had no idea that you were to be on the air—our local papers did not announce it—but no sooner had you begun than I said to myself, "This is Msgr. Spellman speaking," and I was delighted. I recognized your voice at once. It was just as familiar as if you were once again sitting in my study as you did last month. The transmission was flawless. Your voice was perfect. Your enunciation most distinct, your delivery full of unction and eloquence. What an honor to be selected to interpret the words of Our Holy Father urbi et orbi! I rejoice in your great privilege and distinction and beg to offer sincere congratulations on the perfect manner in which you rose to the occasion.

Harry Stanley, a real estate agent in Whitman, spoke for the home town:

Your talk over the radio was just great, and we of the old Town are mighty pleased. Whitman is surely on the Map. The papers are full of it as are also all the people.

I as a father can realize what the feelings of your Father and Mother must be. If it were me, Whitman wouldn't be big enough to hold me.

Meanwhile the Holy Father was finding Mussolini very difficult. Almost before the ink was dry on the Lateran Treaty, the Duce made a speech at Montecitorio which interpreted the agreement as a personal triumph for himself and gave deep offense to the Pope. It was clear that his attitude toward the Church was Napoleonic. In spite of a temporary reconciliation arranged by Father Tacchi-Venturi, S.J., which had brought him back to the sacraments and straightened out his invalid marriage, he remained at heart right up to his tragic end an antireligious Socialist, regarding the Church as something to be used by the omnipotent state for its own ends. As the editor of *Avanti*, he had fought Don Luigi Sturzo and his Popular Party.

Now as the *de facto* ruler of Italy, he crushed them. Brutal attacks by the Black Shirts began everywhere in the kingdom on Catholic Action groups. Their meeting places were sacked and their members beaten. By Easter 1929 it was clear that fascism was determined to capture all the youth of Italy and destroy the influence of the Church in education. The Duce had forgotten what opposition felt like. It would take a man like Pius XI to refresh his memory. The government could and did suppress the Pope's messages of protest, so the Holy Father determined to publish an encyclical for the whole world to read condemning the tyranny of Mussolini. It took form as the famous "*Non Abbiamo Bisogno*" ("We Have No Need") written in his own hand and printed in great secrecy in the Vatican printing shop. In it, the most aggressive and fearless of modern Popes stood toe to toe with the absolute master of fascist Italy and traded rhetorical blows. He defied him to prove that Catholic Action had overstepped the mark in politics. He championed the "sacred and inviolate rights of souls and of the Church," and excoriated the youth program of the fascists.

It was again the Secretary of State who suggested the name of his young American assistant when it was decided to have the text published outside of Italy. The suggestion was accepted promptly, and the Holy Father summoned Monsignor Spellman to his private library on June 29 for final instructions. He was to make the journey to Paris in the role of a diplomatic courier, taking the occasion to deliver some official letters to the apostolic nuncio and received a card to that effect signed by Monsignor Ottaviani. On his return he would be given a document signed by Monsignor Maglione with the assurance that he was carrying a packet to Cardinal Pacelli under the seal of the Apostolic Nunciature of Paris. He also carried a less official letter from John Evans, chief of bureau, Associated Press, Rome, to his associates in Paris: "You may have absolute confidence in the bearer. He is fully authorized to say whatever he says and to do whatever he does. Please offer him every facility of whatever nature that he wishes."

Leaving Rome by train, unnoticed, Monsignor Spellman had an uneventful trip to the Swiss border, spending most of his time on the translation of the encyclical. From Switzerland he could safely send the following telegram:

Associated
       Paris
Sharkey please have two fast capable stenographers at your office for highly important work midnight tonight Thursday

                                        EVANS

The courier had no intention, however, of confining his release to the Associated Press, so it went as well on July 4 to the United Press, International News, Havas Agency, Reuters, and the German and Polish press agencies.

As a measure of precaution, a dutiful son telephoned Whitman to forestall alarming rumors that might cause his mother unnecessary worry, and then with his task accomplished, took the express for Rome. On the train he wrote:

This is Monday and I am on my way back. I left Paris at 8 this morning and it is now 10. We are about three hours from the Swiss frontier so I will send you a little letter to be posted in France.

It was so lovely to hear your voice last night. I hope you could hear me as well as I could hear you. Well I'll say "So Long" now and read a little Office. I shall wire you as soon as I reach Rome or wherever I do reach. Love to Pa, Martin, Marian, Helene, John, you, Louise, Arthur, George, Helen and the babies.

A few days later, in a letter to Martin, he referred again to the eventful trip.

Things have quieted down a bit now as far as I am concerned. I did not know what to expect when I crossed the border into Italy but I was not molested. There were two or three attacks against me in the newspapers but naturally they did not bother me. If anything, they were an honor because I did what I was told and in the exact way I was told. I tried to keep my identity secret but it inevitably became known.

The first news of the coup to reach America came from a dispatch in *Il Lavoro Fascista*, revealing that Monsignor Spellman left Rome for Paris where he gave the encyclical to the press. This was done, according to the dispatch, because "they feared the violence of the encyclical would provoke, on the part of the Italian State, prompt and justified action with an order forbidding publication." Mussolini's anger glows through the following Associated Press dispatch, dated July 4:

A great deal of Fascist criticism was being leveled at the Pontiff's method of publishing the encyclical. The fact that the document was published abroad with no hint given here or at Vatican City until it had almost reached the newspapers was being construed as a reflection on the good faith of Fascism.

It was interpreted as meaning that Pope Pius believed Premier Mussolini might have prevented the transmission of the document which was said by officials tonight to be "absurd."

The next move, it was conceded, is up to the Government. The Vatican has demanded the reopening of the thousands of closed clubs. The Government's reply, it was understood tonight, will probably be based on the Pope's encyclical. Both Premier Mussolini and Foreign Minister Grandi take the view that the encyclical renders further conversations extremely difficult.

The belief prevailed that if the Pontiff should decide to withdraw the Papal Nuncio, he would leave a chargé d'affaires as the medium of further contacts. Neither side, it was believed, considered that there had been a complete rupture or nullification of all the work accomplished by the Lateran Treaty.

The final result was just what Pius XI had foreseen. Every step he had taken had been carefully planned. Mussolini could sequester the Catholic newspapers—all but the *Osservatore Romano* which was published inside Vatican City—and he did. He could go on the air and tell the world that the Pope was playing politics, but the Pope was wise enough in the ways of the press to know that an answering broadcast from the new Vatican radio would make only back-page copy. The little touch of the cloak-and-dagger was deliberate, and it worked. The personable young American priest fleeing from the tyrannical Fascists struck a responsive note, and the Pontiff's message made the front page of every American newspaper. World opinion turned still more against the Duce. Messages of encouragement and sympathy poured into the Vatican from every direction, but especially from the United States. This meant a great deal to the Palazzo Venezia, probably because every member of the Black Shirts had at least one cousin in New York. So that by September, conditions in Rome were taking an upward turn.

After a discussion on the definition of Clause 43, the clause which defines the scope of Catholic Action, a *modus vivendi* was arrived at, whereby the state would stop interfering with religion. The Pope had examined the program and activities of Catholic Action, and had proclaimed that whatever the organization had done was within its rights and within the Lateran Pact. Nevertheless, to make it easier for his adversary to save face, he agreed that Catholic Action would not interfere in politics. He did not, however, admit that it ever had. The only real concessions to the Italian Government were first, the transfer of athletic events from Catholic Action to the Fascist Physical Culture Division, and second, the agreement not to engage in any kind of trade-unionism.

Meanwhile the American Monsignor was anything but popular outside of the Vatican, but he rather enjoyed the excitement, and the scurrilous cartoons in which he figured appealed to his sense of humor.

One had me in an airplane scattering Encyclicals, tearing down from the heavens the motto, "Peace On Earth To Men Of Good Will," and putting up another slogan in its place—"Death On Earth To Men Of Good Will." The second had a *blind* man coming to me and asking help. And I say to him, "For you—read this!" and I hand him an encyclical. Then the funniest of all was a man running up to me while I was passing out encyclicals like handbills on the street and the man says to me, "Hurry up—come quick, there is a man dying!" And I answer, "Tell him to wait a few hours because I have a few hundred more encyclicals to distribute!"

He had feared that they might not let him back into fascist Italy, and some observers expected that he would see the inside of a jail. But the worst that happened was an occasional outburst of unpleasantness in the streets. A veteran correspondent at the Vatican gives the following account:

> He was watched by the Fascists and followed by a couple of them as he went about his daily schedule. He knew it, but ignored them for some time. Then one day he swung around on them and said:
> "Well, here I am. What do you want?"
> There was no answer.
> "I'll be back here again tomorrow," he challenged and stepped toward them. They backed up. "I am ready any time you want to start something. I can take care of myself. Now go."
> They did and were never put on his beat again.[4]

In 1932, at the request of the government of the Irish Free State, Dublin was graciously designated by the Pope as the site of the next International Eucharistic Congress, and His Eminence, Lorenzo Cardinal Lauri, was appointed to represent His Holiness as legate. The honor of accompanying him on this great occasion fell to the lot of three prelates—Monsignor Spellman, who was to be his secretary and translate all his speeches into English; Monsignor Domenico Tardini; and Monsignor Michael J. Curran, Rector of the Irish College. A letter to Whitman carried the great news:

> Cardinal Lauri is to be the Papal Legate and he is a friend of mine. He asked the Holy Father if I could be one of the prelates who will compose the mission and the Holy Father said, "Certainly—that is a good idea." And the other prelate will be Monsignor Tardini. This will be the first time for Monsignor Tardini to go outside of Italy. And he is delighted.
> It will be a nice thing as I am the first American ever to be a prelate official member of a Eucharistic Congress Mission. If I had gone to Chicago as Cardinal Bonzano desired and invited me to do, I would have gone as Private Secretary and not as a member of the mission and the same way if I had gone to Australia with Cardinal Cerretti.

A few weeks later he wrote:

> I am now preparing for the Eucharistic Congress. I am sure it will be a great experience. I am reading the history of Ireland and am studying its geography and memorizing its dioceses and Bishops so that I shall be as useful as possible to the Cardinal Legate.

Setting out from Rome together, the party reached Ireland on the afternoon of Monday, June 20. It was nearly three o'clock when the legate's chartered ship was seen from the Irish shore, and sturdy fishermen from the old village of Howth were among the first to welcome him. The royal salute of nineteen guns started as soon as the ship was sighted from Dún Laoghaire. Six Irish pilots flew above the boat, their planes in the form of a cross.

Only the year before Monsignor Spellman had paid a visit to Ireland, accompanied by the Reverend John F. Kelleher, then pastor of Sacred Heart Church in Haverhill, and his former adviser of seminary days, the Reverend Louis F. Kelleher, D.D., at this time a brilliant young professor at St. John's in Brighton. Together they had seen the sights from Blarney Castle to Dublin, but the high light for the young monsignor was the day he had wandered around the little village of Clonmel, Tipperary, the birthplace in 1831 of his Grandfather Spellman. Now he stood on the deck beside the legate—the first papal legate ever to visit Ireland in its 1400 years of Catholic history—and watched the pageantry through a mist of tears. Eight years later he said:

I remember very well entering the harbor of Dún Laoghaire with the hills all about the harbor literally black with people, more than a million souls. For me, it was a moment of great emotion as I beheld that spectacle and reflected that I was a member of that Papal Mission, escorted with boats and airplanes and accorded every honor, received by the President of the Irish Free State, by the Bishops and by other dignitaries and, above all, welcomed by the Irish people in the Irish manner as a representative of the Holy Father. With all these considerations crowding my mind, with the panorama of that glorious scene before me, you can, I am sure, my friends, imagine my emotions as my thoughts went backward through the vista of the years, and I recalled that from the selfsame harbor which I was entering triumphant, my ancestors had been driven by famine and by persecution, had been herded like cattle in sailing ships unworthy of the sea and brought to this land of the free, this home of liberty, this country of opportunity, my country, your country, our United States.

It was difficult to realize that in one hundred years I, their grandchild and great grandchild, since two of my great grandparents, as well as my four grandparents, natives all of them of Ireland, are now reposing in the little country churchyard in New England where they lived and struggled and died, to realize that I, through their sacrifices and patriotism and above all through their devotion to the Catholic faith, was privileged to enjoy their heritage and to return to their native land as an American with Irish blood in my veins to participate in the tribute the Irish people were paying, as no other people could, their tribute of love to the King of Kings in the Holy Eucharist and their tribute of devotion to the Vicar of Jesus Christ on earth, our Holy Father.[5]

Monsignor Tardini could grasp what he meant, but no foreigner could appreciate what the mere sight of Dublin does to a man with Irish blood in his veins. This garrison town, English since the days of Henry II and surrounded by the Pale, had always been the heart of every movement for national independence. Here Robert Emmet had been executed; here Daniel O'Connell and Charles Parnell had been imprisoned; here Sinn Fein had been founded; and here the glorious Easter Week rebellion of 1916 had triumphed after it was crushed. Following years of bloodshed, peace had come at last, and the people of Ireland were greeting it with a great manifestation of Faith. Their spiritual preparation began on June 5 with a retreat for women which closed on June 12 with a General Communion for women throughout the country. On the same day the men's retreat began, with General Communion on the nineteenth. So that on the twentieth they felt that they were ready to greet the Holy Father's legate.

The official welcome was extended by Archbishop Edward J. Byrne, D.D., of Dublin, and the newly elected president of the Executive Council, Eamon De Valera. The unofficial welcome was even more impressive. Thousands of men, women, and children—some 36,000 children alone—lined the way from Dún Laoghaire to the center of the city, cheering and waving little flags. The Lord Mayor, Alderman Alfred Byrne, greeted them at the Dublin boundary and accompanied them to St. Mary's Pro-Cathedral, where the ecclesiastical reception took place. On Wednesday Cardinal Lauri formally opened the congress by reading the papal bull in the pro-cathedral. The English version of the brief was read by Monsignor Spellman. That evening, exposition of the Blessed Sacrament began in all the Dublin parishes. The churches were filled for midnight Masses. Ceremony followed ceremony until the climax was reached with the Pontifical Mass on Sunday. A great altar was erected on the broad acres of Phoenix Park, which had once been sacred to the evolutions of the British Army. The celebrant was the Most Reverend Michael J. Curley, Archbishop of Baltimore, a native of Athlone, and the sermon came over the air waves from the Holy Father in Rome. At the Elevation an ancient little bell dating back to St. Patrick drew the attention of a faithless world to 1400 years of Irish fidelity, and in the silence that followed a voice was heard, the voice of John McCormack, the most popular Irishman of his generation, singing César Franck's "Panis Angelicus" to the largest audience he had ever faced. After Mass four processions were formed, and the people marched eight abreast by four different routes the five miles to O'Connell Bridge, which spans the Liffey in the heart of Dublin. Cardinal Lauri carried the Blessed Sacrament in a specially constructed car and then gave Benediction from an altar erected in the center of the bridge. When he got back to Rome, he told the Holy Father, "I had prepared myself to witness something extraordinary, but I am obliged to say, in all truth, that what has occurred is beyond anything I could have conceived as possible."[6]

The excitement and fatigue attendant on the ceremonies overtaxed the strength of one of America's most beloved Cardinals. The day after the congress closed, Patrick Cardinal Hayes, who had come from New York on pilgrimage for the occasion, suffered his first heart attack in the home of his host, Frederick A. Sterling, the American Minister. Monsignor Spellman paid him a special visit of solicitude and sympathy—without dreaming, of course, that the event had any connection with his own future. After a period of rest, His Eminence rallied and returned to the heavy round of duties in his archdiocese, but the experience in Dublin proved to be the beginning of the end. For the next six years until his death, he was watched very carefully by his physicians and devoted assistants, who shielded him as far as possible from every strain and from the anxiety of every unpleasant situation.

Among the many other visits of friendship, courtesy, policy, duty, charity, and respect that were paid in Dublin by the young American prelate, none was more interesting than the call upon His Eminence of Boston. Their relations in recent years had been increasingly cordial. The Cardinal had sent the Holy Father, the previous spring, a ten volume set of his *Sermons, Addresses and Pastoral Letters*, beautifully bound. The following letter refers to them:

DEAR SPELLMAN,

I have just returned from a good long rest at Nassau. Thanks for your kind letter. I think the little books will look very chic all in white robes, and it will be a great satisfaction to know that they will have even a modest place among so many great books by great men. After all, it is something to have written and spoken for nearly half a century, and never once written or spoken a sentence that was not perfectly orthodox. Not many, I think, can boast of that achievement. I find that the books are more and more being called for and widely used—even by Protestants. It is all God's work done for Him and His Church and He has certainly blessed it.

I am happy to say I am in perfect health and I trust you are also.

Affectionately,
W. CARD. O'CONNELL

A month later he was writing again, and found occasion to comment on the recent broadcast from the Vatican:

I am very grateful to you for your thoughtfulness and kindness in sending me the coins of the Vatican City. I appreciate it very much and was glad to receive these precious souvenirs.

I have recently received a letter from the Cardinal Secretary of State, His Eminence, Cardinal Pacelli, in which he conveys to me the thanks of His Holiness for the set of my works, and the congratulations of our Holy Father on the general character and importance of them. I was happy to receive such a fine endorsement of my humble efforts and I want to thank you for your kind offices in this matter. I am sure that the binding of the books must have been very beautiful and consequently very expensive, and I wish you to send me the bill in connection with it.

I was thrilled by the radio address of our Holy Father. Every word came over perfectly. I want to congratulate you on the excellence of your translation and explanation. I know you have heard from others how pleased everybody was with your contribution to this international broadcast.

I trust you are in good health. I felt that you were on hearing your voice on the radio. I would write personally if I were not so overwhelmed with work. I know you will understand.

Assuring you once more of my appreciation of your kindness in these various matters, I send you my blessing and every best wish.

Finally, there had been the Cardinal's unexpected suggestion to the Holy Father about sending Monsignor Spellman to Portland as bishop.

It seems that Archbishop Austin Dowling of St. Paul, the successor of the great John Ireland, had died November 29, 1930, and the following year the Bishop of Portland, Maine, the Most Reverend John Gregory Murray, had been advanced to the See of St. Paul. That left Portland vacant. A few months later on August 6, 1931, the elderly Bishop George Albert Guertin of Manchester, New Hampshire, died. Like Portland, his was one of the suffragan sees of the Boston metropolitan, and Cardinal O'Connell was expected to present candidates for both vacancies. He had been the Bishop of Portland himself for five years before he was called to Boston as coadjutor, with the right of succession to Archbishop Williams, and it is just possible that he was thinking of his own successor when he considered the name of Monsignor Spellman for the vacant see. But he was not exactly a simple man and the nomination gave rise to considerable speculation. The young Monsignor, on the other hand, while he was deeply grateful for the compliment that had been paid to him, saw a number of reasons for thinking that another appointment might be more appropriate and was grateful that the Holy Father had decided to keep him in Rome.

Four months before the Eucharistic Congress, the Auxiliary Bishop of Boston, the Most Reverend John B. Peterson, had briefed Monsignor Spellman on the local situation. They were old friends. Back in 1927, October 7, the Spellman diary had the following entry: "Monsignor Pizzardo told me that my friend Monsignor Peterson was Auxiliary Bishop of Boston"; and among his letters to his mother at the time was the following:

I shall cable you tomorrow morning that Monsignor Peterson is the new Auxiliary Bishop of Boston. He was the best choice of all mentioned. You know how I like him and admire him.

Monsignor Pizzardo was the one who told me. I had said that Monsignor Peterson would be the choice of 95% of the Boston priests, so he told me—"Your friend is chosen"—and I was happy.

For Cardinal O'Connell wished him for Portland. Therefore if good for Portland, also good for Boston Auxiliary. Then too Monsignor Peterson is fifty-four or fifty-five and therefore mature enough to be a Bishop and he is saintly, learned and kind. And also, I am, as you know, very friendly with him.

My cable to Monsignor Peterson will be: "You know how I feel."

As might have been expected, there were some in the archdiocese who believed that Monsignor Spellman had been consulted on the appointment. His Eminence was said to have taken cognizance of their opinion and to have suggested that perhaps the young man was swimming beyond his depth. This the young man referred to in his next letter home:

I want nothing and never asked for anything except an opportunity to serve. I have no fears. After all, after one's usefulness ceases in Rome as in other places, one must expect to be supplanted.

Of course it is a difficult place to be in, here in Rome, as there are so many elements and so many interests that are sometimes conflicting. But even if I should go home tomorrow, which by the way I have no intention of doing if I can help it, I would still be infinitely happy that I came, for each day is an intensely exhilarating experience and even the uncertainty makes it pleasant.

Perhaps it may be true that I could not again be quiet and happy as I was in All Saints when my activities and interests were somewhat more circumscribed than at present, but I intend to let the future take care of itself as the past has done and be just the same as I always was and remembering that every day I am getting closer to the end—to leave things to the Lord; to be fair and square with everyone, but at the same time to try and make everyone be fair and square with me and if not, not to play with him any more.

As the comment continued in Boston, he wrote again:

My friends are Monsignor Borgongini and Monsignor Pizzardo. I am loyal to them. I do everything I can for the Church and for the Holy Father with the proper motives. I have absolutely no ambitions to be anything else but a good priest. If I can cooperate with the grace God gives me to live and die as such, I shall be happy.

As events transpired, everyone was delighted with Bishop Peterson, including the Cardinal, and now five years later His Excellency was writing familiarly to his old friend in Rome:

Things here are in statu quo. H. E.'s absence is always a quieter. I saw Bishop Howard of Covington last week in New York. He had heard it said that you were talked of for Portland. I tried to trace the source of his information, but he was either coy or forgetful, for he did not remember. I judged from his recent associations that it came from either Washington through George Johnson, or from Cincinnati.

But, apart from conjecture, I would like to see you settled near home and on the nearer way to higher things. I would willingly yield my place to you if it would help. If my going to Manchester would open your way to come here as my successor, and you can do anything to help yourself in that way, do not consider me at all. I may have only a few years to live; you may have many. It is important for you to get a good start.

I say all this as if we were really being considered. Perhaps they do not even think of it at Rome. In fact all I have to base my statements on are the commendations of H. E. Perhaps they are not worth anything. But I wanted to make clearer to you my frame of mind and to insist that I would do anything to give you the right of way.

Actually they were giving it plenty of thought at Rome, as the following letters to Whitman reveal:

> March 17th
>
> There is nothing new about Portland or Manchester. Cardinal Pacelli would like to have me stay here. Monsignor Borgongini and Monsignor Pizzardo would like to have me go to Portland. Cardinal Gasparri, Monsignor Ottaviani and Monsignor Bernardini would like to see me succeed Bishop Peterson as Auxiliary. I am satisfied where I am because I know that I am as contented here as I can ever be anywhere. However, I am doing nothing and saying nothing.

> April 23rd
>
> I told you that notwithstanding all the talk about my going to Portland that I was not going. Neither am I going to Manchester. . . .
>
> As for myself, I am, of course, extremely happy here, even though there is much speculation about me and I do not suppose it will finish even when the new Bishops of Manchester and Portland are announced as they will be soon, since such a long time has now elapsed since the Sees became vacant.

The public announcements followed close upon the letter and the Most Reverend John B. Peterson, who had been since 1927 Auxiliary Bishop of Boston was transferred to Manchester where he served with much distinction until his death in 1944. On May 1, Monsignor Spellman wrote:

> This week Bishop Peterson is being transferred to Manchester. This will be a nice promotion for him as he will then have a diocese of his own and I imagine he will be more tranquil there. Certainly it is a splendid choice and the priests and people of the Diocese of Manchester may well feel pleased. Portland no doubt would have been larger and perhaps

better known, but I think probably Bishop Peterson is just as happy to go to Manchester.

And I presume Cardinal O'Connell will be happy too because he sees one of his priests so honored. It is true that no Boston man is going to Portland but after all, getting one-half of what one desires in this world is quite a lot and the Cardinal surely received one-half.

Speculation on a more interesting subject appeared in the following excerpt dated May 2:

Now I wonder whom the Cardinal will select for Bishop Peterson's successor. . . . You know generally there are three names submitted. The Cardinal was mighty good to have suggested me for Portland and even though it did not go through, it was not his fault and therefore I shall always be grateful to him. But then it is lovely over here, and I could not be happier.

His mother knew that he was not exaggerating. She wrote prophetically enough, "You are having your happy years now. May God bless you and keep you." His next letter described his birthday party—his forty-third. Mrs. Brady combined the celebration with Cardinal Gasparri's eightieth which fell on May 5 and gave a brilliant dinner. A few days later, he described another anniversary and his own reflections on current events at home:

Today is Pentecost Sunday, May 15th, the 16th anniversary of my first Mass. I said Mass very early today because after my Mass I went to the Vatican to Cardinal Pacelli's apartment where I assisted him at his Mass celebrated for Mrs. Brady who was present. Afterwards we all had breakfast together.

Then Mrs. Brady went to the Solemn Pontifical High Mass in St. Peter's and I went for a while to the Tomb of St. Peter where sixteen years ago I celebrated Mass for the first time.

I then worked a while on some of Cardinal Lauri's speeches for the Eucharistic Congress, had luncheon with Mr. Galeazzi and now in the afternoon I am back at the Minerva to write a few personal letters. This evening I go to Mrs. Brady's to dinner with Bishop Hoban of Rockford and Monsignor Bernardini.

I have just written a note to Bishop Peterson congratulating him on his nomination as Bishop of Manchester. I hope that he will be happy there. It must be a pleasant place. His nomination was published yesterday as well as the nomination of Father Joseph McCarthy of Hartford as Bishop of Portland. And I was talked of so much for Portland! Well I do not suppose that one can stop talk. But I do not feel jealous of Father McCarthy. I do not feel badly at all. It was nice even to have been considered. I wish him all the luck in the world. And I am so happy to know he speaks French fluently.

Of course, now, not too unnaturally comes up the question of a new Auxiliary Bishop of Boston. I imagine His Eminence will desire one because he has always had one. And then one is almost necessary. Of course I realize there will be much speculation. There always is in circumstances of this kind. I imagine that some will even mention me as a possibility. I do not know anything about it except I imagine it all depends on His Eminence. Of course His Eminence is very nice to me, but it would be too much to expect to have him include me among his candidates.

And now I am going to see His Eminence at the Eucharistic Congress in Dublin.

His mother answered, "I am so happy you are a good priest. All else is vanity."

It was on the return of the legate and his suite to Rome after the close of the Dublin congress that the Pope determined to offer Monsignor Spellman the vacant auxiliary bishopric of Boston, stating with his usual directness that he expected him ultimately to succeed Cardinal O'Connell in that distinguished archbishopric. And so it probably would have happened, had Pius XI outlived His Eminence of Boston. The details are described in a long letter home:

On Monday evening July 25th Cardinal Pacelli sent for me. I went into his big room and he at once came towards me and before saying a word he embraced me. Then he said, "I have something to communicate to you, something joyful and something sad, sad because it means you will leave me, joyful because it will be for the welfare of the Church and because it is clearly God's will,—the Holy Father has named you Auxiliary Bishop of Boston."

I said that I was sad and joyful too.

Then Monsignor Pizzardo came and we all three talked together. I asked Cardinal Pacelli to consecrate me in St. Peter's with Monsignor Pizzardo and Monsignor Borgongini as co-consecrators. He said, "All right," and then Monsignor Pizzardo interrupted to say he thought it should take place in Boston. I did not think so and do not think so. Monsignor Borgongini thinks that it should be in Rome. At any rate the matter is still undecided.

If it takes place in Rome, I imagine it will be during the first half of September. Just tell me who is coming and I shall make arrangements here. I should, of course, like to have you come and if Martin and John and Marian come, I imagine you will be taken care of sufficiently well. But no matter how well you are taken care of, there is bound to be considerable excitement and strain and naturally I would prefer to have you not come and live longer, than come and suffer even the slightest setback.

Of course I feel you all must be very happy and I am happy too. I realize that I have to leave Rome sooner or later and such a way of returning home could not be better. It will represent one of those complete changes of life that have come to me at intervals of every few years since I entered high school.

In answer to Cardinal Pacelli's request for permission to consecrate the Bishop-elect, Cardinal O'Connell sent the following answer: "Am very happy to give my consent for you to consecrate Monsignor Spellman. It will be a great honor to him and to the Diocese of Boston."

The pre-consecration retreat was made at the Casa del Sole where Archbishop Borgongini came three times each day to give the points for meditation. On the last day, the nuncio presented his old pupil, his beloved Francesco, with an episcopal ring containing a magnificent sapphire surrounded by diamonds with a fragment of the True Cross set in gold.

At first everyone in the family was coming and there were reservations on the *Saturnia* for nine, but his mother had had an unexpected sinking spell, so his father, Marian, and Helene stayed home in Whitman to keep her company. By way of substitution, most of the Vatican and half of Rome seemed to have accepted the invitation to share with him the happiness of his consecration.

In appropriate tribunes and benches arranged under the very particular direction of his old friend, Enrico Galeazzi, were seated many of the American colony, and for the first time since the seizure of Rome by the Piedmontese, representatives of the American Embassy headed by Alexander Kirk, the counselor. Opposite them sat the members of the diplomatic corps accredited to the Vatican; the Marquis Camillo Serafini, Governor of Vatican City; the Marquis Francesco Pacelli, brother of the Cardinal Secretary of State; heads of religious orders; bishops; archbishops; and His Eminence Lorenzo Cardinal Lauri, who occupied the principal place of honor. If any space was left in the enormous apse, which holds more than five thousand people, it was tightly packed by the ubiquitous seminarians, who are rather expected to infiltrate every gathering but the most secret consistories. Close to the altar sat a little group from Boston: Martin and John and their wives; Father Michael J. Owens; Father Edward J. Quinn, his old classmate from Cincinnati; Fire Commissioner Edward F. McLaughlin and a few close friends. It was a touch of home.

The altar—called the Altar of the Chair because the traditional cathedra of St. Peter is enclosed in a sumptuous baroque setting just above it—stands at the end of the apse facing the great Papal altar directly under the dome. It is there that the Holy Father usually venerates the relics of a new saint, and it is frequently the scene of public consistories, with the Papal throne erected on the predella. Neither is it an unheard of place for the consecration of bishops. Pius XI, for example, had consecrated on this spot the first six native bishops of China in October 1926, and on the same date the next year, the first native Japanese bishop. But never before had an American been consecrated there.

As he had promised, Cardinal Pacelli was the consecrator, with Archbishop Pizzardo and Archbishop Borgongini-Duca as co-consecrators. Monsignor Camillo Caccia-Dominioni and Monsignor Arborio-Mella di Sant'Elia assisted at the altar, while the Papal Master of Ceremonies, Monsignor Carlo Respighi, watched all details with a practiced eye. The Bishop-elect wore a rich but simple set of vestments, which have since become the treasured possession of the Fordham University Library. Fashioned of silver cloth without embroidery, their real value stemmed from the fact that fifteen years before, Cardinal Pacelli had worn them himself when, on March 13, 1917, he was consecrated Titular Archbishop of Sardes by Benedict XV. It was not lost on the young American that Benedict had in turn been consecrated by Pius X. Writing to his brother John in 1939, he said:

> To have been made a Bishop, and in St. Peter's, at the Altar of St. Peter's Chair, to have been consecrated by our Holy Father, the successor of St. Peter, who had himself been consecrated a Bishop by Pope Benedict XV, who had in turn been consecrated by Pope Pius X! What a heritage! What a succession! What a combination of circumstances!

After giving his episcopal blessing first to Martin and then to John, the Titular Bishop of Sila prepared to wait upon His Holiness in private audience. The redoubtable Pius XI, who always kept the enemies of the Church and some of her friends in awe of him, was this day a relaxed and affectionate father to the new Bishop, whom he called the Benjamin of the American hierarchy and his dearest friend. He told him that it was with a sense of personal loss that he had appointed him to Boston, but that he was satisfied as to the great things he would do there. When he asked about his new episcopal coat of arms and Bishop Spellman described a shield devised by Archbishop Borgongini-Duca with Columbus' ship, the *Santa Maria*, in full sail on an azure field, the Pope himself suggested the motto: *Sequere Deum*, a motto which was to remain even after the red hat had replaced the episcopal green and the ship had been sacrificed in the interests of heraldic purity. The words, "Follow God," were taken from St. Ambrose's *Book of the Prophet Abraham*, where they refer to Abraham's wandering from Haran to Palestine, thence to Egypt, and back to the terebinths of Mambre. Thus the Holy Father's suggestion was prophetic of the new Bishop's many voyages by sea, land, and air in the years to come.

The reception that followed in the Borgia Apartments established another precedent. It was the first time that the picturesque fifteenth-century Romans in Pinturicchio's gorgeous frescoes had looked down on a young American bishop, surrounded by a throng of cardinals, bishops, princes, and diplomats. At the end of the day, when the central figure of all this pageantry retired to his little room in the Hotel Minerva, he took out of his pocket a crumpled cablegram from Whitman and carefully spread it out on the desk. It read: GOD BLESS AND GUIDE OUR BOY. KEEP HIM KIND AND HUMBLE. THIS IS THE PRAYER OF FATHER AND MOTHER.

It had been a rather strenuous time for everyone concerned, especially for the Cardinal Secretary of State and his former assistant, so it was decided that before the new Auxiliary should report to his post, a short holiday was in order for both of them. It was to be their last real holiday together. His Eminence, it seems, had never been on an ocean liner, so accompanied by the Bishop and the Bishop's old friend of North American College days, Father Edward Quinn of Cincinnati, he sailed on the *Vulcania* as far as Gibraltar, where they changed for a boat to Cannes. From Cannes they made their way overland to Chamonix and next morning at Mass time presented themselves to the pastor of the village church. They were all dressed in simple black, with no color to indicate their various ranks, but the curé could not help noticing the majestic bearing of Pacelli even on vacation and called him "Excellency." With a twinkle in his eye, the Cardinal pointed to the new Bishop and said, "This is the only Excellency here." Whereupon the Papal Secretary of State was assigned to a side altar, to be served by a pious nun kneeling in the church. Before he began, she asked him if he would let the Bishop give her Holy Communion, as she could receive from a simple priest any day. No one enjoyed the little joke more than the future Pius XII.

On his return to Rome, there was just time for the Bishop to pack and say a few farewells. The boys and girls of the playgrounds, which had brought him to Rome in the first place and had opened the principal door to his future, gave him a heartwarming party with little speeches and songs and the presentation of two mitres, white and gold. Among the intimate friends who joined the children that day was Archbishop Borgongini-Duca, who did not try to disguise the satisfaction he felt at the confirmation of his own good judgment. The Holy Father received Bishop Spellman in a final audience which lasted two hours. He presented him with gold medals, a pectoral cross, and a ring before dismissing him with an affectionate message and apostolic benedictions for the Cardinal Archbishop and the faithful of Boston. It was well that he did so, in view of the reception that was awaiting the new Auxiliary at home.

On the last day, friends from all walks of life were down at the station to wave good-by as Bishop Spellman, accompanied by Father Edward Quinn and Monsignor Egidio Vagnozzi, who was to join the Apostolic Delegation at Washington, departed for Genoa. There on September 27 he boarded the *Rex*, Italy's first 50,000-ton steamer, which was sailing on her maiden voyage to New York.

CHAPTER SEVEN

Cardinal O'Connell

THE trip across the Atlantic was calm and uneventful except for a cablegram which arrived on the third day out. It was the official greeting to his new post and read: WELCOME TO BOSTON. CONFIRMATIONS BEGIN ON MONDAY. YOU ARE EXPECTED TO BE READY. CARDINAL O'CONNELL. Reading between the lines, the recipient felt that the tone was slightly ominous. Word had reached him about an unfortunate rumor circulated in Boston just before his consecration to the effect that he was to become coadjutor bishop with the right of succession, and he had seen the Cardinal's statement issued to the press on that occasion:

> There have been so many exaggerated press statements in relation to the recent appointment of Msgr. Spellman as Auxiliary to His Eminence, the Cardinal, that the office of secretary to Cardinal O'Connell wishes to make a plain statement about the facts of the matter.
>
> Some years ago Cardinal O'Connell was consulted regarding the charge of appointing someone who could assist in the Secretary of State's office in Rome in the work of translating English documents into Italian and vice versa. Whereupon Cardinal O'Connell sent Msgr. Spellman to act in that capacity. His task was merely to do the usual work given a cleric in the Secretary of State's office. . . . Msgr. Spellman showed the same assiduity in his work in Rome as he had in Boston. . . . As soon as possible after consecration Bishop Spellman will return to Boston to take up whatever work Cardinal O'Connell designates for him to do in regard to the confirming of the children of the archdiocese. . . .

The young prelate on the *Rex* began to realize that cold fogs settle at times on Boston Harbor; that he might in consequence feel less at home in Massachusetts than in the cordial and understanding atmosphere of Rome, where everyone had realized his relations with the Cardinal Secretary and even with His Holiness, the Pope. Much later he learned that the selectmen of Whitman had planned to go in a body to New York as a reception committee and greet their most distinguished townsman in behalf of his fellow citizens. Unfortunately, however, the Cardinal got wind of it and telephoned Father John Starr, the local pastor, that he felt the importance of the event was being exaggerated. So poor Father Starr had to call a meeting and explain to the enthusiastic group how possible it was that a prominent committee meeting the boat in New York might make the celebration in Whitman less impressive—"anticlimactic" was the word he used.

Nothing, however, could make the Bishop's arrival in the old home town an anticlimax, because it meant the reunion of a very united family after the most important event in its history. A mother who had written to him every week while he was away from her since the days when he was a freshman at Fordham saw him now for the first time a successor of the Apostles. When he officiated in the parish Church of the Holy Ghost, where he had served Mass as a little boy, and gave the triple blessing at the end she recognized the crowning of her life's work and was ready, like Simeon, to chant her "*Nunc dimittis.*" Nobody noticed the fact that, acting under orders, the pastor had to send away all the press photographers. The day was a complete success.

It was good to be home again, especially since home meant New England. No one could have a deeper and more spontaneous love for his own country than young Frank Spellman had passed on to his older self the Bishop, but for the rest of his life those golden years in the center of Christendom would color his thinking. His country was to be henceforth a part of the world. This can be read between the lines of an address he gave soon after the family reunion in Whitman:

> I wish to communicate to my friends some of the admiration, some of the sincere respect that I have for things European, and something of the sympathy which I feel for those Europeans who are struggling for a living and for peace in exactly the same manner as so many of my fellow countrymen.
>
> Being a 100 per cent American to my mind does not signify that one must believe that we Americans have or that we should have any monopoly of righteousness or intellectual prowess or of accomplishments in all departments of human activity. It does not mean, in my opinion, the despising or belittling of other nations or of the men or achievements of other nationalities. To my way of thinking, such an attitude is not American: it is decidedly un-American.
>
> True Americanism, like Christianity, is the engendering of the practice of brotherly love and of brotherly respect and of brotherly sympathy and of brotherly helpfulness. This love, respect, sympathy and helpfulness should be implanted and cultivated in the home and in the school. Gradually and inevitably, these virtues would infiltrate and extend throughout communities and embrace the whole world.
>
> Such improvement can be brought about by the injection of a little more of the spirit of Christianity, by the subtraction of selfishness, and by the addition of a little more common usage of that which is so uncommon

—common sense. The reapportionment of these elements in individuals and in peoples would make America, and Europe and the world, a happier, healthier, and holier place in which to live.[1]

Meanwhile the Confirmations were upon him. Sometimes he had two large parishes a day, with as many as 1800 children, to receive the sacrament. It seemed incredible that there could be so many young recruits for the Army of Christ in Boston. Thousands every week received the holy oils and the little blow on the cheek—177,141 in seven years. But this was the consoling part of the new life, which had to compensate for many personal embarrassments. Between the consecration of the new Auxiliary and his arrival in the States, for example, every vacant parish in the archdiocese had been filled. His assignment to the seminary as a residence underlined the Ordinary's coolness, and the fact that His Eminence had put his own suite at his disposal merely gilded the cage.

After five quiet months, Bishop Spellman wrote to his superior, March 20, 1933: "I respectfully request Your Eminence to appoint me Parish Priest of the Sacred Heart Parish in Roslindale." This had recently become vacant. On April 6, the Cardinal sent his secretary over to the seminary with a letter and instructions to wait for an answer.

YOUR EXCELLENCY:—

You are hereby appointed Removable Parish Priest of Sacred Heart Parish, Newton Center.

This appointment goes into effect immediately.

Please acknowledge receipt of this appointment without delay.

W. CARD. O'CONNELL
Abp. Boston

Over the years that have passed since then, this particular parish has been regarded as a prize. After Bishop Spellman's six happy years there, he was succeeded by Bishop Richard Cushing, and he in turn by Bishop Eric MacKenzie. But in 1933 it was considered distinctly less desirable than the Sacred Heart Parish in Roslindale. The church, dating from 1891, was ugly even for that period, and the school, built in 1922 by the zealous Father Timothy A. Curtin, was burdened with a heavy debt. The Pastor-Designate probably changed color and hesitated long enough to count ten. Then he sat down and wrote to His Eminence:

I have this moment received Your Eminence's letter appointing me removable Parish Priest of Sacred Heart Parish, Newton Center, requesting me to acknowledge receipt of this appointment without delay and the messenger is awaiting the acknowledgement.

I hereby gratefully acknowledge this appointment with the observation that I shall as always perform any duty to which I am assigned and cheerfully perform it. But frankness and fairness oblige me to state that I would prefer to remain where I am, if I have the alternative. I would be pleased to go to Roslindale but if Your Eminence has determined otherwise, I shall endure the humiliation of seeing some priest appointed to a better parish than the Auxiliary Bishop.

Kissing the Sacred Purple,

Your Eminence's servant in Christ,

✠ FRANCIS J. SPELLMAN

On closer acquaintance, the parish proved to be far more attractive than anyone at the chancery office had suspected. After all, the new appointee was coming under obedience, and that always has its compensations. As he told the congregation some time later:

> We priests are in a certain very definite way like unto soldiers. We must at all times be on duty or on call and obediently subject to the orders of our superiors, who destine us to the places and the duties which in their judgment before God they believe us best qualified to fill and to fulfill. . . . Ours is not the responsibility of judging these reasons. Ours is the responsibility of doing at all times our very best work in whatever places and in whatever position our superiors may designate for us.

The blessing that comes with obedience usually first manifests itself by revealing some hidden advantage in the new position. So in Newton Center it was not long before the Pastor found that he was blessed in his curates, blessed in his congregation, blessed in his teaching sisters and in his school. As for the rectory, the pastor's quarters were quite impressive. From a description in the Boston *Globe*, we gather that they were positively episcopal. "He sits in a comfortable armchair in the spacious library that is his office on the second floor of the rectory, at a wide dark maple desk in the alcove by a bay window, and talks with animation." With regard to the church, first impressions might be misleading. Those who had lived there for years seemed to have had a different perspective, for it is described in a commemorative booklet as "our beautiful church." "The structure," we read, "is novel in appearance. Departing from the classical type, the architects built mainly on American form and style. The exterior is of common brick with pink trimmings and a green tile roof. Rising eighty-eight feet above the ground are two immense towers. The Tuscan columns at the main entrance are of a highly polished granite. The loggia itself is fashioned in Italian Renaissance style with a touch of mosaic paving and tiling. The interior of the church resembles a simple Roman basilica. The life-size bas-relief of the Sacred Heart over the main altar is most imposing especially since it was recolored." Finally, the school, if one could forget the debt, was a joy and a consolation.

It was difficult, however, to forget first facts, and the parish debt stood in the way of every plan for expansion and improvement. So after his first

Sunday, Easter Sunday, had been spent in pleasant formalities, the new pastor took up the burning question the very next week. Six months later, the report made on his earliest efforts is so characteristic and revealing that we quote it at some length:

When I spoke before you the second Sunday of my presence here in the Parish, the Sunday after Easter, I told you clearly and frankly all about the situation in the Parish as I had been able to learn it. I explained the financial conditions and said that I intended to make no changes, and would follow through with the plans of Father Curtin. I said, further, that from time to time I would inform you if we were progressing and how we were progressing, and I made the assertion that I intended to have the smallest number of appeals for money that would be possible. I affirmed that I wanted no one to contribute anything at any time if such a person could not afford it. And I went so far as to state that I did not wish anyone to contribute anything, even if that person could afford to give, unless such a person wished to give freely and to contribute from spiritual motives.

It happened that on that particular Sunday, leaving the Church together, one parishioner said to another, "That is all very beautiful, but it won't work out as the Bishop thinks. We shall never get out of debt under that system, and he will be obliged to change his policy."

So far, what that parishioner observed has proved to be half true. So far, it is true that the system has not worked out as I anticipated, and we are having an extremely difficult and trying time. But the other observation of the well-meaning parishioner is not true. I shall not be obliged to change my policy. I shall not change it, first of all, because I am not convinced that just because it has not worked out well the first six months of my stay here, when times have been terribly bad, that it will not work out when times are better. And, secondly, I shall not change my policy because I cannot change it. It is too much a part of myself, and the principles upon which it is formulated are just principles. And, therefore, I reassert this morning that only on the rarest occasions will financial matters be mentioned from this pulpit, and then only by myself, and by me only in terms of explanation, and never in terms of rebuke. Because if explanations do not suffice to convince Catholic people and to persuade them to do their duty in this matter, then the responsibility is on their consciences and not at all on mine. . . .

The one bright feature of the whole situation is that the average attendance at Mass on a Sunday has increased from twenty to twenty-five per cent more than it was on the corresponding Sunday a year ago, and yet the contributions under my system of a simple announcement of a collection without any special appeal each time have been disastrously low. . . .

So you see, my dear friends, we are going in the wrong direction. Our debt remains the same as when I came here. It is, fortunately, no larger than it was. Our unpaid bills are different from the ones that were outstanding when I came, but they aggregate about the same amount,—insurance, heating repairs of a rather extensive nature, taxes, interest on mortgages, and the regular running expenses of the church, school, high school, rectory and convent require considerable money. . . .

And if I may be permitted, I would like to demonstrate that I have also done my share to help out the situation. As Pastor, I am entitled to a salary of fifty dollars a month and my board and lodging. The Parish is providing me with my board and lodging, but I am not drawing any salary, and, as a matter of fact, we were running on such a slim balance all summer that I could not have drawn any if I had wanted to. And I do not intend to accept this salary until the parish revenue justifies it. . . .

Now, we shall have the annual parish visitation beginning on Monday, October 9th. I ask you, please, to receive the priest who comes to see you. . . . If you cannot afford anything, I repeat with all the sincerity possible, do not have the slightest hesitation in saying so. That satisfies us and it satisfies the Lord. The Lord does not ask from anyone what He has not given. . . . But if you give, and whatever you give, please let it be given from a spiritual motive and given willingly. Otherwise it is useless for you, and certainly not desired by me.

Then, too, we shall have the usual parish reunion, which I anticipate attending and enjoying, as thus I hope I shall be able to meet personally a larger number of the parishioners than has yet been possible for me. . . .

So once more I say to the priests and people, I shall be most grateful for anything and everything that you can afford to do, that you have the time to do, and that you have the will to do, for the welfare of this our dearly beloved parish.

His worries for 1933, however, were not concerned exclusively with parish deficits. There was His Eminence. Between the Bishop's arrival home in September and the following June, the auxiliary saw his Ordinary only twice. The diary notes one occasion on April 20, 1934: "Met Cardinal for the first time in four months and sat beside him at table. Very genial." But it was one thing to be genial and another to be reconciled to the situation. Their next meeting was June 26: "Had stormy interview with the Cardinal. He looked fine and healthy contrary to wild rumors." Storms could rise over smaller issues, but in the present instance His Eminence was probably aware that there were many in Rome who would like to see the Bishop advanced from auxiliary to coadjutor with the right of succession. It was said that the Holy Father had decided on it. In any case, the possibility existed until the following September and created meanwhile a period of tension, in the midst of which Monsignor Tardini arrived in New York. Bishop Spellman met his old friend at quarantine together with Archbishop John T. McNicholas, Bishop John J. Dunn, and Bishop James Anthony Walsh, and accompanied him on a tour, which included Philadelphia, Washington, Cincinnati, Chicago, Detroit, Buffalo, and Scranton. When they arrived in Boston, the Bishop noted in his diary: "August 4th—Cardinal gave a dinner for Monsignor Tardini's feast day which I was supposed to give. It was scheduled for his home, but he gave it in the Seminary. He was in a bad humor. Upset at reports of his illness." With the passage of time, however, relations improved a little, and for the Cardinal's golden jubilee we read in the diary: "Arrived in Boston 8 A.M. Rather tired. Mass at 10 A.M. Cathedral jammed. I was the first speaker and did well. Cardinal said, 'Thank you, Bishop, that was beautiful,' and Bishop Cassidy wrote that he thought it was a masterpiece. That is satisfying the two extremes." The sermon began by pointing out that the life of His Eminence made imagination, oratory, and rhetoric superfluous. A mere outline of his accomplishments became eloquent without effort. "I have completely and carefully read the entire ten volumes of the *Sermons and Addresses* of His Eminence and to me the most noteworthy circumstance in the life of the Cardinal is that one which he himself tells us in most impressive, gripping language gives him the greatest happiness and consolation"—the fact that he owed everything to the Holy See. The Bishop then summed up the achievements of His Eminence in Boston and ended with an ordination prayer. No wonder the Cardinal said, "Thank you, Bishop, that was beautiful."

By then all thought of the coadjutorship had been laid aside, but for the next three years there was recurrent discussion reflected in the Bishop's diary about the possibility of being assigned to another diocese.

Received inquiry whether or not I would like to be transferred to another diocese.

Attended Board of Home Missions meeting. Became more convinced than ever that I wish to remain Auxiliary Bishop of Boston.

Had another letter from Rome saying that I should change.

Saw Delegate. He was very well disposed. Said I could be transferred to be Bishop of a diocese any time I desired it. I explained with emphasis that I wished to remain where I was.

In fact, he did not want to change even his parish. "Spent an hour with the Cardinal. He offered me St. Mary's, Waltham. I thanked him and told him I would prefer to remain where I was if he would permit me to do so. He commended me for my good sense." So it was that Newton Center remained his address until the next crisis in 1939.

When vacation time came around, it occurred to the busy Pastor that he had never been west of the Mississippi, and that a carefully planned tour could include a great many wonders that would have educational value on his return to the Sacred Heart School. As it turned out, he did not miss a thing. Characteristically, he climbed peaks, descended into caverns and mines, visited art galleries, oil refineries, smelters, universities, and churches. But the most important event proved to be a luncheon given to Bishop Cassidy of Fall River at Palm Springs by one of his most generous benefactors, Mrs. Mary Young Moore. She was a member of the Young family of California, which had distinguished itself for generations by its benefactions to the Church. Following the traditions of her fathers, she was in time to be created a Papal countess for her personal loyalty and assistance to the Holy Father, as well as to the Church in California and New York.

Oddly enough, the Bishop's career had run thus far in alternating periods of seven years, not too unlike the periods that brought fame to his namesake in Egypt. The years from 1911 to 1918, except for six months' illness, were carefree and happy; from 1918 to 1925, they were trying and uncertain; from 1925 to 1932, they were glorious—what his mother called the happiest days of his life; from 1932 to 1939, they were again trying and uncertain, but happier and more colorful than his days in the chancery.

According to the diary, many interests brought him frequently to New York and Washington. Fordham was one of them:

Went to Fordham Alumni Dinner and saw lots of old friends.

Presided at Fordham. First Commencement I have attended since I graduated in 1911. What a change and who then could have believed it possible that I should preside twenty-two years later. Everyone wonderful to me. Father Hogan, the President, especially kind.

Fordham Alumni Dinner. Well attended and most enjoyable. It was my first real public speech in New York. It was also to all intents my first speech at a banquet.

Letter from Father Hogan that I am to receive LL.D. from Fordham.

Fordham Commencement. It was quite a thrill to graduate again after twenty-four years. A number of my classmates present. Had dinner with faculty.

Another interest centered, appropriately enough, in St. Patrick's Cathedral.

Bishop Donahue's consecration in New York by Cardinal Hayes. It was a brilliant ceremony.

Big party of the laity at the Waldorf in Bishop Donahue's honor. It was wonderful. Everybody was there and his brother.

Mass at Mrs. Brady's. Cardinal Hayes pontificated at the Cathedral for the 19th Annual National Conference of Catholic Charities. Forty Bishops present. Cardinal says greatest ceremony in history of St. Patrick's. Luncheon at Waldorf. Great meeting at Metropolitan Opera House where Al Smith gave best speech.

Finally, there was always some little chore to do for friends in Rome who had confidence in his judgment. At times they were historic.

November 7, 1933:

Had letter from Mr. Galeazzi saying that Pope wished him to tell James Roosevelt to ask his father to request some guarantee for freedom of religion in Russia before recognition. Sent letter to Apostolic Delegate.

November 10, 1933:

The United States recognized Russia. Jack Kelly and Mr. Galeazzi whose names will never appear in history did much to get President Roosevelt to insist that American citizens at least should worship God as they wished in Russia.

Such matters, however, were only temporary distractions from the parochial duties which appealed to him more and more as time went on. They were so much more satisfying than diplomacy. As ever, he was absorbed in the problem at hand.

We are completely satisfied in the status of our school [he wrote in a report to the parish], and we know that, judged by every pedagogical standard, it ranks high. We know, too, that judgments made by standards other than pedagogical will also be favorable. It is of course true that the teaching of religion and, what is even more important, the teaching to live religiously, are considerations which are outside and beyond and above any category which will admit comparative analyses with secular schools. Likewise it is not fair to secular schools to consider the cost per pupil from a comparative standpoint, but I do not deem it to be unfair to mention these costs from a purely informative standpoint. Since the Sisters receive only enough for their board, clothing and lodging, plus small allotments for expenses in attending summer schools and providing higher education for younger Sisters and the support of the sick and aged Sisters, the annual cost of running our school is only fifteen thousand dollars, an average cost of $27.10 per pupil. The average cost per pupil in the Boston schools last year was $129, or four times as much as for our school. The average cost in the Newton High School was $152, the Junior High $122, and the first six grades $98. As we have an enrollment of over five hundred pupils, it would be useless for me to urge parents to send their children to the Parochial School because we cannot accommodate all who desire to attend. We have made admittances to the extent of our capacity, and we could not do justice to the pupils already in the school if we admitted others.

But we must observe that these children in the parish who do not attend the Parochial School are also obliged to learn their religion, and are obliged, too, to learn to live religiously. This obligation is threefold, on the child, on the parents, and on us. We guarantee to fulfill our duty in this regard if the children and the parents do their part. But we cannot do anything unless the parents send the children to us. The children, therefore, must attend Sunday School. . . . For pupils of high school age, there are special classes one night each week instead of Sunday morning. Last year it was one of my greatest consolations to know, from a comparison of the census books with the Sunday School roster, that nearly all the children and parents fulfilled this grave obligation, and I earnestly request you to bear in mind your responsibilities in this regard this year.

His own responsibilities were taken very seriously. The sister principal wrote of him twenty years later:

He was never satisfied with one statement or complaint about a pupil or group of pupils. He made it his business to hear both sides of the question. The amazing part of it all was that he did not count the sacrifice of his precious time to devote all his resourcefulness to the matter at hand. He was wholly concerned with being sure to decide on what was fair and just. . . .

I recall that when he came to Sacred Heart parish he admitted that he knew very little about the management of a school but since he had been assigned to this parish he would make it his business to find out all he could about school matters. He did. . . . He made very certain that his school had everything that was needed. He examined the requirements, syllabi etc. of public schools, brought representatives of the public school system to visit his school and thus made his own comparisons. He did not do this alone. He consulted the Superior and the Sister teachers of his school. In perfect harmony the Bishop and the Sisters talked over what was best for the school relative to changing courses, meeting the requirements of the College Board, etc.

He often told the children to make up their minds to be the very best in whatever they did. If they were playing ball, then to be the very best ball player, etc. I often thought that to try this was a reflection of his own way of doing things. . . .

Father, we were all aware that he was a truly great man, a great man in the Church, that he was then an international person. And yet we never stood in awe of him, we were never afraid when he came to our classroom, or to the convent. We all felt that if we had a problem we could approach him. Yes, he was "our father" as well as the children's.

He was never too busy to listen. He never referred to all he had to do.

Whenever a prelate, an author, or any distinguished visitor from our own or foreign countries came to visit him, he always found time to have the Sisters meet the visitor.[2]

This matter of distinguished visitors was not a rare occurrence. In a single year, the sisters met the Pope's private secretary, the Pontifical Master of Ceremonies, eight bishops, Archbishop McNicholas, Joseph Cardinal Mac-Rory, Archbishop of Armagh, and Archbishop Yu Pin of China, as well as prominent lay persons.

No pastor, of course, can enjoy the luxury of confining himself to spiritual and educational matters:

> In regard to finances, [he wrote] I think too that we can be satisfied with what has been accomplished in the last twelve months. All of last month's bills are paid; the parish property is in excellent condition; the school and church were kept warm last winter and, please God, will be kept warm and well lighted this winter. Many new books and other supplies for the school have been purchased, and finally, three thousand dollars have been paid off the principal of the mortgage, leaving forty thousand dollars as the balance now due. You already know that the annual cost of conducting this parish is thirty thousand dollars—the expenses connected with the church constituting about one-half of this amount and the school expenses constituting the other half.
>
> The seat money received during the year amounts to eleven thousand dollars, leaving a difference of nineteen thousand dollars which we must receive from special collections and social affairs in order not to go behind. About seventy-eight per cent of the parishioners are contributing to the support of the parish, but I am firmly convinced that ninety-eight per cent are doing their best, and I am further convinced that no parish in the Diocese is doing any better than we are in this regard. On an average Sunday there are approximately nineteen hundred adults who attend Mass in this church. If each person were able to contribute fifteen cents seat money, the receipts would average $285, and they actually average $250 which, considering the times, is I think remarkably good.

The improvement was encouraging, but at the rate of three thousand dollars a year it would be perhaps fifteen years before he could breathe freely, and in fifteen years he might be almost any place. Such were his sober reflections when one day he was talking to a loyal and generous parishioner who made a hobby of conducting annual horse shows around the fashionable outskirts of Boston. In the perfectly sincere but indefinite manner of one who says, "You must take dinner with us some time," Mr. Allan J. Wilson suggested that he would run a horse show one of these days for the benefit of Sacred Heart Parish. Within two weeks the author of *Action This Day* had his plans all laid. He found a beautiful estate in Dover called "Ard

Righ," whose owner, Mrs. Edward C. Donnelly, was only too happy to offer her green acres for such a worthy purpose. Other friends like Harry J. Blake, Joseph Sullivan, George Collins, and Hugh Nawn rallied round; entries poured in; the program grew to seventy-three pages; patrons multiplied; and of course the press coverage reflected the experience of the Pastor. "The Ard Righ Horse Show and Festival of 1935" was a tremendous success socially and financially. His Eminence the Cardinal in the beginning had not been too enthusiastic.

September 2nd:
    Saw Cardinal O'Connell at 10 A.M. He was angry at the horse show and forbade me to attend. It was his impression that Governor Curley was promoting it and making a tool of me for his own purposes.

September 6th: First Friday
    After Communion calls I went to see Cardinal again. We talked another hour and a half. After all was over I was permitted to attend the horse show.

The Cardinal still maintained that there was "too much ballyhoo," but that was a feature toward which the people of Newton Center felt no particular aversion, and they were as jubilant as their Pastor when he announced, "Not alone financially has this affair been successful. It has been helpful in divers other ways. Parishioners have been brought closer together. New friendships have been formed, and other friendships have been deepened by the associations and experiences of the weeks of preparation. Within the parish there has been a development and a fostering of the community spirit, the civic spirit, the family spirit, and the religious spirit. There has been progress in every direction." That year, principally because of the horse show, the debt was reduced by $13,000.

September 12th:
    Cardinal wrote me a letter congratulating me on the way in which I was paying off the debt.

Slightly tempering the consolation that the natural-born Pastor felt as he realized more and more his spiritual and temporal hopes for the parish was the ever recurrent displeasure of his Ordinary, who had never been in the custom of disguising his feelings toward anyone. During this year, for example, Boston College decided to bestow on the Auxiliary Bishop its choicest gift, the degree of Doctor of Laws. It would have been his first honorary degree—the first of many, but still the first. The Cardinal let it be known, however, that he saw no necessity for such an award, and the Jesuit rector with considerable embarrassment rearranged his plans for the commencement. As it turned out, the predicament of Boston College was the opportunity of Notre Dame in South Bend, Indiana. Father John F.

O'Hara, C.S.C., the charming and able president of the university, sent an invitation which was especially welcome at that particular time and was promptly accepted. It proved to be the beginning of a famous friendship, in the course of which Father O'Hara went to New York as auxiliary to the Military Vicar. On the death of the Most Reverend John A. Duffy in 1944, he succeeded to the See of Buffalo, and in 1951, upon the death of Dennis Cardinal Dougherty, became Archbishop of Philadelphia and eventually Cardinal.

At the Baccalaureate Mass in South Bend on June 2, 1935, the sermon was preached by the new Doctor of Laws:

> Unfortunately I am unable to tell you that youth is the only thing that is essential to success. Nor can I tell you that it is as easy to succeed today as it was in times that are past. I am unable to tell you this because I do not believe it. The combination of youth, ability, industry and integrity were an absolute guarantee to success in years gone by. But this recipe is not sufficient today. These four qualities are as important factors to success as they always were, but in addition to these endowments, which I believe you all possess, there are also required now more than ever before the supplementary qualities of courage and perseverance, which qualities I also confidently believe that you possess. . . .
>
> And for a closing thought of gratitude and of hope, I would adapt an expression of Abraham Lincoln in referring to the great and good mother whose knotted and toil-worn hands pointed out to him the way to goodness and to greatness, and from and in and through whose eyes he saw the light of mother-love, that light that we, my friends and brothers, have seen shine in mothers' eyes, a light that to us beams forth a three-fold radiance, and bears a three-fold significance, our mother's love, the love of Notre Dame, and the love of our Blessed Mother.
>
> And so paraphrasing the words of Lincoln we may say,—All that we are and all that we hope to be, we owe not alone to our mother,—but to our mothers. God grant that we may be worthy sons of all three mothers.

In ending on the note of mother love, the Bishop was speaking from the fullness of his heart. His own mother was dying. All through life they had shared every thought. Their letters, and hundreds of them were preserved for years at Whitman, were full of mutual understanding. Now they both knew the end was near.

It was a long time since Nellie Conway had sent "Friend Will" her formal regrets for the outing, and many things had changed for both of them. Over the years she had grown to be a large, handsome woman, a natural manager with a genius for cooking, and an unconscious disciplinarian who ruled the family with such tact and gentleness that even Pa hardly realized her influence. She had loved all her children and her in-laws and her grandchildren. All their losses and family worries were her troubles; all their joys and successes, her happiness. But no mother of a priest has to be told that her son is in a class apart. Frank could do no wrong because he was what she had always prayed he would be, a good priest. Now she was nearly seventy. Her health had been failing for years, so that she alone in the family had not been able to make one trip to Europe during her son's stay in Rome; she had not seen him ordained or consecrated. That was why these last few years since his return to Boston had been particularly dear to her. For his part, the Bishop had overlooked nothing that would add to her peace and comfort. It was principally for her sake that the family built the new brick house on the road to Abington, and August 13, 1933, was the big day when she took possession:

We moved mother tonight. John went with her in the ambulance. She took it very well. We were all with her except Martin who is ill. We wheeled her into the different rooms of the new house and she manifested a deep interest in everything. It was worth while building the house just to have the happiness of mother in it. She seems to look so comfortable in her new room and surroundings. Stayed all day in Whitman though I was not much help in getting settled.

For two years she lingered, suffering, but happy about the new house and the new babies, the happiness of the girls and Martin's success and John's success and all the wonderful things she heard about Newton Center. But toward the end of July 1935, the diary had the inevitable entries:

July 26th:
It is a long agony with mother becoming weaker all the time, but she is still able to receive Holy Communion when I say Mass in her room. I spend my day trying to adjust myself to her loss.

July 28th:
Mother died at 3:30 this morning. Said Mass in living room. After undertaker came I went to Boston to get ready for funeral and stopped to notify Father Owens. When I returned, mother was already in the casket. It was a hard moment for me. It is a day I have thought of for years, and I am better prepared than I expected to be.

July 30th:
Today is a beautiful day. All the funeral arrangements were perfect. I am able to do my part without permitting my emotions to get beyond my control.
Six Bishops were present, the Governor and Lieutenant Governor and the Mayor of Boston. The priests' choir sang beautifully. The time of the absolution was hushed and a bit tense, but at the same time triumphant with the joyful certain knowledge of a perfect and happy earthly life

transformed into a perfectly happy eternal one. The singing of the *Benedictus* at the grave was heavenly.

A graceful Celtic cross marks her grave in the quiet country churchyard of Abington. Nearby rest all the Conways and the Spellmans of a still older generation.

Newton Center was now a welcome distraction for the Bishop, and he threw himself more than ever into the details of church administration. During 1936 there was no horse show, and the debt could be reduced by only $6500. Under the circumstances, the amount was quite remarkable, for the year before the parish had been divided. On August 4, 1934, the following letter had come from the chancellor, Monsignor Francis L. Phelan:

> His Eminence, the Cardinal, has directed me to bring to the attention of Your Excellency that he is contemplating the establishment of a new parish in the Waban district of Newton, St. Philip Neri parish.
>
> His Eminence says that he notes in studying the map of the district that St. Philip Neri church is on the border of Sacred Heart parish and wishes to inquire if Your Excellency, in view of the proximity of St. Philip Neri church to Sacred Heart parish, could cede something in the neighborhood to round out the parish.

This matter of dividing parishes is a perennial source of difficulty in the history of the Church's expansion. It is always clear to the Ordinary that the public good demands another parish, but the old pastor and the members of his flock are often hard to convince. Sometimes it means that a large church heretofore comfortably filled will henceforth be partially empty, and sometimes that a part of the generous congregation which has just finished paying for one church will have to start paying for another. The Cardinal's decision about Sacred Heart parish took the form of a request and gave the Bishop a chance to make the enforcement embarrassing. Instead, he wrote an answer which may well serve as a model for pastors who sometimes find themselves faced with Hobson's choice:

> I hasten to say that I most willingly accede to the request of Your Eminence that the part of the Sacred Heart Parish, Newton Center, designated by Father Donovan be taken to form a portion of the new parish.
>
> Your Eminence will, I am sure, permit me to observe that Father Donovan's suggested line from Commonwealth Avenue to Beacon Street is an air line, and this type of boundary is often times unsatisfactory. For this reason I would suggest that the new boundary be extended even deeper into the Sacred Heart Parish territory in order to include all the land between Commonwealth Avenue and Beacon Street within Ward 5. . . . It is true, of course, that this portion which I suggest is more extensive than the portion included in Father Donovan's recommendations,

but I think it is more desirable as a boundary line from every point of view, except that of personal interest.

It is of course true that we in the Sacred Heart Parish have had a rather difficult time making both ends meet. I feel confident, however, that we can still continue to get along and maintain our High School and pay our bills. For many months the parish was operating at a continued loss but we have now all our bills paid and the mortgage has been reduced a trifle so that our interest charges are a little less. This gain on the situation convinces me that we shall continue to function satisfactorily, and I am sure the families in the territory comprising the new parish will constitute a desirable part of the new Waban parish.

The only unpleasant feature connected with the separation of this territory from the Sacred Heart Parish would come from parents of the children in our parochial school, but I think that this difficulty will be eliminated by permitting all the children at present in the school from that territory to remain here and finish their courses without any charge being made for their tuition.

I realize that the parish priest of the new parish will not have it easy, and it would be my pleasure—with Your Eminence's approval—to take one-half of the bank balance credited to the Sacred Heart Parish on the day the Parish is divided and give it to the new pastor. Of course, our bank balance is not very large, only a few hundred dollars, but this portion of this sum will at least be a gesture of moral support to him and to his parishioners in his and their new undertaking.

CHAPTER EIGHT

Inisfada

LATE in the summer of 1936 the Duchess Brady arrived in New York from Rome with news which she confided only to a trusted few as "her secret." Eugenio Cardinal Pacelli was coming in October to spend his vacation at Inisfada, her Long Island estate. Though caretakers and gardeners had kept it a show place, the duchess had found it depressing after Mr. Brady's death, and seldom, if ever, entertained there. Now it was to know one more brilliant season, perhaps the most brilliant of its history, before she made it over to a religious order for a country day school; a season that would be reminiscent of the gold and purple days of the Casa del Sole. The Cardinal was to be her house guest, and she would entertain him graciously for three full weeks without any intrusion by the world of affairs.

It was September 30 before the press had an inkling of the impending visit, and when the story broke, it came with as much surprise to the hierarchy as to the government. Only one prelate was fully prepared: Bishop Spellman. A brief entry in the diary for Thursday, August 6, indicates that he was probably the first in the country to receive the news: "Had telephone call from Mrs. Brady in Paris about proposed visit to America." He added no further comment at the time, but he was deeply troubled. It seemed like an awkward moment for such a trip, and he could not reconcile himself to the idea of the Cardinal Secretary of State living in seclusion on Long Island.

It happened to be a presidential year of peculiar importance. Franklin D. Roosevelt was just finishing his first term, and, as some thought, gloriously, but he was not yet entrenched, and those who saw in the liberalism of the New Deal a threat to private property were in a crusading mood. The President, whose strategy was to rule through combined minorities, was satisfied by now that three of them were already sympathetic to his ideals, so that logically enough his next step was to be an appeal to the imaginary Catholic vote. Already feelers had gone out from the White House on the subject of American representation at the Vatican, and the moment seemed propitious for some sort of understanding. To the President's acute annoyance, however, his most violent adversary at this juncture was a Catholic priest from the Archdiocese of Detroit, the Reverend Charles E. Coughlin.

Father Coughlin, a Canadian by birth and formerly a priest of the Community of St. Basil, was pastor of the Shrine of the Little Flower in Royal Oak, Michigan. A man of unusual eloquence and deep conviction, he had been for ten years, but especially since 1931 when a single broadcast brought a response of 350,000 letters, the most controversial radio personality in the United States. To supplement his broadcasts and furnish a mouthpiece for his "National Union for Social Justice," he began publication of a magazine called *Social Justice* in March 1936. By June he was knee-deep in the presidential campaign, denouncing both major candidates but devoting most of his attention to the President. In July, at Cleveland, he said "Franklin Double-Crossing Roosevelt" was "a liar," and later in the same month apologized.[1] As the campaign grew in warmth, however, he referred to him as "anti-God" and "a scab President," daring him on more than one occasion to repudiate his alleged communist support.[2] It was not easy to estimate the number of Father Coughlin's admirers, but it was large and it included his Ordinary, the Most Reverend Michael James Gallagher, D.D., the respected Archbishop of Detroit.

The situation had, of course, been talked about in Rome, and the *Osservatore Romano* considered his lese majesty "improper,"[3] but Archbishop Gallagher could still say to the Associated Press, "The Vatican never intervened in the Coughlin matter."[4] It is not surprising, then, that when Bishop Spellman hung up the receiver after his conversation with the Duchess Brady, he did not completely share her radiance. Experience told him that in the circumstances a vacation on Long Island for the Papal Secretary of State posed certain problems and he was not too sure of the answers. Only one thing seemed clear to him. The plans of the duchess were not realistic.

A month later there is an entry in the diary.

Monday, September 7th:
    Labor Day. Luncheon with Mrs. Brady and Kurt Roderburg. We spent the whole afternoon talking. I did not contradict her, but I shall have to oppose some of her plans. . . .

Devoted as he was to the Bradys and conscious of his debt to them, his seven years in the Vatican told him that the Cardinal Secretary of State on his first visit to this country could not remain in seclusion. So he wrote four long letters of explanation to Rome, and on September 16 received a telegram from Mr. Galeazzi saying that his suggestions would be followed.

On September 30 the news was released at the Vatican that His Eminence would sail the next day from Naples on the *Conte di Savoia*. The Associated Press quoted the Cardinal as saying, "I am going to America simply on a vacation. I have a great longing to see the United States. There is no political aspect to my trip whatever." Various dispatches appeared, however, in all the American papers purporting to give the real reason for the visit. A few mentioned Mexico, more said that he was interested in curbing communism, most agreed that he sought to have the United States establish diplomatic relations with Vatican City, and all brought in Father Coughlin and his repeated denunciations of "an upstart dictator" in the White House. Only four days previously, a letter signed by Archbishop Mc-Nicholas of Cincinnati had rebuked the radio priest for saying that he advocated the use of bullets "when any upstart dictator in the White House succeeds in making a one party Government and when the ballot is useless."[5] Father Coughlin made no comment on the letter at the time, but referred to it as follows on May 5, 1954:

It is true that careless if not smearing reporters from Cincinnati attributed certain words and sentences to me which were not founded on fact, for I said in the Cincinnati speech that "it was possible for America to so deteriorate socially and politically that what happened elsewhere could happen here, namely, hotheads would have recourse to bullets when the efficacy of ballots failed." . . .

I recognize that I was at least a small thorn in the side of the Roosevelt Administration and a small obstacle in Roosevelt's determination to engage us in war on the side of Great Britain and Russia against Germany, as if the Russian Government wore the halo and the German Government the cloven hoofs. Small as I was, it was necessary to silence my voice even though I must be smeared as an anti-Semite, as a pro-Nazi and as a bad priest, when really all I was, outside of trying to be a Christian and an American, was an anti-Bolshevik, anti-Nazi and an anti-warmonger. . . .

I am still proud of the opposition I displayed to the New Deal's foreign policy, particularly in its all-aid-for Russia. . . . After twenty years, this Rooseveltian policy seems to have been at one time supporting both British imperialism and Soviet Marxism, together with American Republicanism—a peculiar policy of triangular circle-ism at which we can now laugh through our tears twenty years later.[6]

Meanwhile, the apostolic delegate, the four cardinals, and many other members of the hierarchy were deliberating about the details of the unexpected honor being paid to the United States, while the Pastor of Newton Center was spending wakeful nights trying to anticipate all the complications. He decided against the plan of taking His Eminence off the liner by tug before the boarding cutter arrived, pointing out that Queen Victoria of Spain had recently taken the same short cut, with unpleasant consequences in the press. Then while the ship was still twenty hours out, he phoned to the Cardinal to prepare him for the informality of his first interview.

No preparation was necessary. The distinguished visitor put the reporters at their ease and charmed them with his affability and wit, without, at the same time, saying a single thing. The more experienced thought they could

see a twinkle in his eye as he read from a carefully prepared statement the
words:

> Despite the private character of my visit I know well that I am expected
> to make my little contribution to the representatives of the Press as a sort
> of "journalistic tax of entry" into the United States. Accordingly, I am
> happy to be able to say that the Holy Father in the midst of the heavy
> burdens of his apostolic office, with youthful energy and untiring devo-
> tion, ever labors by every means in his power to extend to all peoples and
> all nations in their present difficulties the incomparable aid and encour-
> agement found only in the teachings of Christ.

Thus began one of the most eventful months in the young Bishop's life:
crowded, thrilling, often anxious and troubled, but a glorious month. Writing to his brother John three years later, after the election of Cardinal
Pacelli to the papacy, only the sunshine remained in memory. All the shadows were gone.

> I have not done much for the Church, nothing in fact in comparison
> to the blessings and graces that I have received. But I do take some little
> satisfaction in knowing that I had some part in helping to bring to pass
> the visit of His Holiness to our country and through our country; and I
> am sure that this visit will continue to mean much, as it does already
> mean much, both to the Church and to our country. The newspapers of
> America are recalling and retelling the details of those eventful days. All
> newspapers and all commentators are unanimous in their jubilation be-
> cause Pope Pius XII came to us, lived among us, saw much of us, and
> visited so many of us.
> I think the statement of His Excellency, the Apostolic Delegate to the
> United States, sounds the keynote in the great symphony we are hearing.
> For His Excellency wrote,—"We might say that Pope Pius XI was in
> some way inspired when he allowed his beloved Secretary of State to visit
> this country in the fall of 1936."
> The whole month of Cardinal Pacelli's visit was just one succession of
> glorious triumphs. They were certainly full days. It is still a marvel to me
> how His Eminence was able to visit so many places and to do so very
> many things. I remember that I was torn between the emotions of anxiety
> not to overtax the strength of His Eminence and the desire to have His
> Eminence do all that was physically possible for the most people and
> as much good for the Church as was possible. For His Holiness never
> thinks of himself when the welfare of religion is concerned. No sacrifice of
> strength or of time is too great to make if souls are to be helped!

After four days of comparative quiet at Inisfada, a visit to Boston was
decided upon. The Bishop's diary describing the next few days is succinct
and complete.

Tuesday, October 13th:

Left Inisfada at 9. Over Triboro Bridge. Stopped at New Haven at Knights of Columbus headquarters. Cardinal and I in Mrs. Brady's car. Went to Mercy Academy of St. Joseph's College where Mrs. Brady's sister is Superior.

At Newton Center: Bishop Cassidy, Bishop Peterson, Bishop Rice and Bishop McCarthy. Had supper at Rectory.

Wednesday, October 14th:

Cardinal said Mass in our church and used chalice Holy Father gave me which I gave the parish in memory of my mother. Went to Seminary. Cardinal Pacelli met Cardinal O'Connell and both spoke to priests of the diocese in the library. Afterwards both spoke in Seminary Chapel to the students. Luncheon at Cardinal's house with Monsignor Haberlin, Father Minihan. Everything went well and Mr. Galeazzi made great hit with Cardinal O'Connell. Went to Home for Italian Children and the Jeanne d'Arc Academy. Went to Whitman for supper with friends. Some priests and friends met Cardinal after supper.

Thursday, October 15th:

Cardinal said Mass again in Newton Center. Received Italian Consul. Went to school for entertainment. Then to Boston College where I gave $125 to Father Gallagher to buy incunabula, an illuminated Bible, which the Cardinal wrote in and presented to the school. Went to Sacred Heart school in Newton. Took Yankee Clipper for New York. Cardinal had nice simple meal on the train. He, Enrico and I got off at 125th Street. They went to Inisfada and I to Commodore Hotel.

Friday, October 16th:

Drove to Manhasset for luncheon. Talked with Bishop Lamb about visit to Philadelphia. Cardinal thinks now he will make plane trip to coast.

Saturday, October 17th:

Atmosphere a good deal clearer today. Cardinal wrote speech for Philadelphia Seminary and received Father Murphy, Provincial of Jesuits. Bishop Molloy told of Thomas N. Perkins' inviting the Cardinal to a luncheon of bankers. The Duchess was in favor of the Cardinal's accepting. I was against. Dinner for twenty-five at Mrs. John D. Ryan's. Had planned to go home on midnight train, but Cardinal asked me to stay.

Sunday, October 18th:

Stayed at Inisfada all day and wrote letters. Went to Boston at midnight.

Tuesday, October 20th:

Met Cardinal Dougherty in Philadelphia and drove with him to Wernersville where we had luncheon and then with two Cardinals in one car and Mr. Galeazzi and Hugh Lamb in another, and Father Provincial and I in a third, went to Philadelphia. Saw Liberty Bell. Very long dinner at Cardinal Dougherty's home. Cardinal decided at my suggestion to stop at Baltimore and so telephoned Apostolic Delegate.

Wednesday, October 21st:
   Visited Rosemont College, Mercy Hospital and a big girls' high school in Philadelphia. Cardinal gave fine talk at Seminary at Overbrook. Then dinner with Suffragan Bishops in Seminary. Left at 3:30 for Baltimore. Archbishop Curley and Delegate met us in Baltimore and we visited Cathedral and Seminary. Then we drove to Washington.
   Cardinal Pacelli was told he was supposed to speak at Press Club Lunch and he was upset. I was not invited to the luncheon and Cardinal Pacelli insisted that I be invited.

Thursday, October 22nd:
   Cardinal gave speech at Catholic University, visited Congressional Library, and NCWC headquarters. Cardinal memorized speech during Press Club luncheon. He did well and speech was quoted all over America, while not a word was said about University speech. Went to Mount Vernon. I rode in auto with Cardinal Pacelli both coming and going and the Delegate rode with Mr. Galeazzi and Monsignor Vagnozzi. Visited Georgetown and Cardinal spoke and received degree. Stopped at Convent of Sacred Heart. Left at 6 P.M. for New York.

Friday, October 23rd:
   Back at Inisfada and found out that Mr. Lilly's offer of a private free plane had been withdrawn and that a plane had been chartered from United Airlines. Duchess has arranged for everything, but I am the only one in favor of extension of trip to coast.

Saturday, October 24th:
   Joe Kennedy arranged for President to invite Cardinal to lunch with him at Hyde Park on November 5th and so told me, but I said to have Cardinal invited directly and through neither of us.

   The rest of that day belonged to the duchess and ended with a reception that would have been notable in Rome. Long Island had never seen anything remotely like it, even when the Prince of Wales visited Clarence Mackay. As the guests arrived at dusk, the winding driveways were lined with hundreds of tallow lights like those used for solemn illumination at the Vatican. Inside, the house was filled with flowers, dozens of long-stemmed roses banked in every corner, lighted candles everywhere, Pietro Yon playing softly on the famous organ. The guests themselves were part of the picture with cardinals and bishops in their brilliant cinctures and silk *ferraiuoli* lending a striking accent to the customary feathers and furs and jewels around them. In the great hall, before a blazing fire, the duchess and her guest of honor were receiving. She knew that it was to be the last reception in the history of the lavish home which Nicholas Brady had built for her twenty years before. Already she was planning to sell the furniture and give the estate to the Jesuits. But there was no overtone of sadness on coming to the end. The end was too beautiful.

The following description of the historic tour of America by air is taken from one of the Bishop's letters to his brother John:

There was a stop in Cleveland and another in South Bend where His Eminence received an honorary degree from the University of Notre Dame, before we arrived in Chicago. Here the plane was met by Cardinal Mundelein and the Bishops of the Province with a large delegation of religious and civic personalities. Later His Eminence motored out with Cardinal Mundelein to inspect the beautiful Seminary of Our Lady of the Lake.

When we left New York the length and duration of the trip had not been determined. St. Paul was considered the ultimate in distance, and three or four days the utmost in time. But when I told His Eminence that if he would fly to the coast he would never regret it, and that I felt it would help religion in the West, His Eminence answered at once,—"If it will help religion, I shall go!" It was ten o'clock at night in St. Paul when I telephoned to Archbishop Mitty that His Eminence would be in San Francisco the next night. Then I telephoned to Archbishop Cantwell in Los Angeles that His Eminence would be there the following night; and to Archbishop Glennon of St. Louis I gave word that His Eminence would be his guest the night thereafter. I then informed Archbishop Mc-Nicholas that in four days His Eminence would be in Cincinnati and that on the fifth day, we would be flying back to New York. God was good to us with the weather, and all proceeded as per schedule for those glorious epochal days and nights. Nothing like that trip was ever made before. Nothing like it was ever even considered possible. His Eminence was the first Cardinal who ever travelled in an airplane in North America.

In addition to the religious considerations which motivated the trip and were paramount, His Eminence saw the greatest natural wonders in the United States. It was thrilling to be able to ask the pilot, "How is the visibility at Grand Canyon?" and to have the answer in a few minutes, "It is clear." "Good, let us make a little detour of a few hundred miles and fly above it and circle over it." And we did the same at Niagara Falls! His Eminence also saw the greatest engineering achievements in our country, the buildings of New York, the bridges of New York and San Francisco, one of which His Eminence blessed, Boulder Dam and other notable things. But as I said above, religious considerations were paramount. It was in order to know Catholic America that His Eminence came to us; and see it, know it and learn about it, His Eminence did. Cathedrals, seminaries, universities, churches, schools, hospitals and other institutions were visited. His Eminence is a quiet, but keen, accurate, all-perceiving observer. His Eminence's powers of observation are equal to his other more widely known powers, such as a phenomenal memory and a gift of languages which Pope Pius aptly described as "Pentecostal."

I have said that the one word or phrase that completely describes His Eminence is "Christ-like." I think of Christ's compassion for the lowly, His love of little children, and His care for things that the world regards as unimportant. The Cardinal's attentions are frequently centered in similar interests. I have seen the joy and contentment of His Eminence as benignly and unhurriedly he visited many assemblies of children and young people in schools and colleges. I have observed "Christ-like" manners with old people, poor people and sick people. I have known his poverty of spirit and his humility in grand environments. Yes, His Eminence is "Christ-like."

The readiness with which His Eminence acceded to Monsignor Quinn's petition to bless the corner stone of the parochial school that was to be built in his parish surprised some who knew of His Eminence's compact schedule. But to me, it was not surprising; and the laying of the corner stone of this Catholic school in a small parish, surrounded by children in the presence of the parents and parishioners who were making real sacrifices to provide that school and to support it, was one of the most typically Christ-like episodes in the Cardinal's American experiences.

By the time His Eminence had blessed Monsignor Edward Quinn's new school in Cincinnati the famous trip was nearly over. The diary for Saturday, October 31, records that "Cardinal celebrated Mass in Seminary Chapel and spoke to Seminarians and afterwards to people from balcony of Seminary. Left at eleven for New York. Beautiful weather over Niagara Falls. Arrived 4:30. Duchess met us at airport. It was a grand week."

The next day was a busy Sunday, beginning with Pontifical Mass at St. Ignatius Loyola, in which the representatives of many religious orders took part. A reception followed at the Carroll Club, a home endowed by Duchess Brady for business girls, and after luncheon the whole party proceeded to Fordham University. There His Eminence, surrounded by bishops, monsignori, the presidents of ten universities and colleges in the metropolitan area, consular representatives, and officers of the Army and Navy, received five hundred members of the faculty on the Terrace of the Presidents. Rising from a throne chair, he went in procession across the Edwards Parade, where five thousand people cheered him and some broke through the lines of the R.O.T.C. to kiss the hem of his silken cape. The honorary degree of doctor of laws was conferred upon him in the gymnasium before three thousand invited guests. Radio carried his address across the nation, and the four major newsreel companies recorded the entire ceremony. His statement on education was impressive because of its clarity and authority:

> The white-robed shepherd who dwells on the Vatican hill, wherein repose the relics of the first sovereign Pontiff, St. Peter, a hill that has been made fruitful through the blood of a great multitude of martyrs, as he yearns to protect his lambs and his sheep against the oncoming wolves, realizes as you know from his many pronouncements that there is a great need today of an education of the heart and of the will as well as of the mind and of the intellect, an education which develops the whole man, morally as well as intellectually, spiritually as well as scientifically, an education that rests upon the rock of truth and not upon the sand of mere materialism, a truly Christian education illumined by the light of Faith.

Afterward, in the Tower Room of the Graduate School, with Bishop Spellman at his side, he spoke to hundreds of guests as they were presented to him by the president of the university.

Meanwhile the excitement of the campaign was increasing. Father Coughlin was denouncing Roosevelt in an adjoining diocese when Bishop Spellman hurried home to Boston to cast his vote. In the diary for Tuesday, November 3, he noted, "Roosevelt elected by biggest electoral majority in a century. . . . Took midnight back to New York." The President had in fact swept the nation. He had carried forty-six states—all but Vermont and Maine—with a popular plurality of 11,000,000. Father Coughlin commented on November 5: "President Roosevelt can be a dictator if he wants to. The minority is purely theoretical. We now have a one party system. The National Union for Social Justice has taken a thoroughgoing good knockout."[7] In a radio speech on November 8, he announced his withdrawal from radio activity and the suspension of the National Union, which he said had been discredited by the election. He denied, however, that the withdrawal had been directed by his Ordinary.[8]

It had not been considered appropriate for the Papal Secretary of State to call on a campaigning candidate for the presidency, but now the way was clear for an unofficial visit, and November 5 was selected by the President. Typed on the stationery of the White House and dated October 28 is a "Memorandum for Kannee: Mr. McIntyre, before leaving the other night, told me to make an appointment at Hyde Park for Bishop Spellman on November fifth,—he said it was very confidential.—RB."[9] The venerable but still very charming Mrs. Sara Delano Roosevelt was the hostess for the occasion, and the guest list, which had been carefully made up in Washington—with a few surprising omissions—included only the following: Cardinal Pacelli, Bishop Spellman, Bishop Stephen J. Donahue representing Cardinal Hayes, Mr. Galeazzi, Joseph P. Kennedy, who was about to go to St. James's as ambassador, and Mrs. Kennedy, with Frank C. Walker, destined one day to be the only Catholic member of the Cabinet, and Mrs. Walker.

Two years later Bishop Spellman jotted down his memories of the day for his brother John:

> There is one American recollection that is etched in my memory as actually having taken place which, before the Presidency of Franklin Delano Roosevelt, would have been considered fantastic. And that was the morning visit and luncheon of His Eminence Cardinal Pacelli, the Secretary of State of His Holiness, Pope Pius XI, with the President of the United States and his family. I can see in my mind's eye as clearly as if it were yesterday, His Eminence and President Roosevelt talking alone near the fire place at the far end of the great living room in the President's home at Hyde Park . . . President Roosevelt had been returned to office by the largest plurality of votes that any President of the United States has ever received. That had been the greatest day in the President's life, greater than the first election day because it meant the approval of his policies and actions.
>
> This was a great day for America and a great day for Catholic America. I was so proud of the Cardinal on that day, and Mrs. Roosevelt, the President's mother, was proud too. I sat at her left at luncheon and she said to me, "What a joy to have His Eminence as our guest. He may be Pope some day."

Like most non-Catholic hostesses who wish to make a visiting prelate feel at home, Mrs. Roosevelt summoned all her Catholic servants to come upstairs and be blessed by His Eminence. But being more than an ordinary hostess, as they knelt, she knelt with them.

When the guests emerged, Hyde Park was full of determined reporters, who saw in this delightful luncheon the purpose and climax of the Cardinal's visit to America. They were sure he had discussed communism with the President, had agreed to silence Father Coughlin, and had arranged the preliminaries for the appointment of an envoy from Washington to Vatican City. All they needed was a quote. The interview, featured by all the Eastern papers, was thus described by the New York *Times*:

> Following their conversation, Cardinal Pacelli, smiling and friendly, greeted newspaper correspondents with warm affability, but attempts to hold a conference with him on current affairs were stopped before a single question could be completed. The Most Reverend Francis J. Spellman, Auxiliary Bishop of Boston, and one of the Cardinal's escort, declared that the Cardinal had given no interviews and should give none now.
>
> Bishop Spellman firmly declined an offer on the part of the correspondents to observe an agreement to ask questions only with the stipulation that if the Cardinal did not care to answer them all present would con-

sider the questions as not having been put. Accordingly, proposed questions concerning the activities of the Rev. Charles E. Coughlin and similar topics of public interest were barred, since Cardinal Pacelli would act only on the advice of Bishop Spellman. . . .

When he finally boarded his private car he asked to meet individually each of his interviewers, and then, speaking perfect English, although with a marked continental accent, he began what promised to be a fruitful talk. "I was very anxious to meet the President of the United States," Cardinal Pacelli said. "I am very happy to have had the opportunity of seeing him and congratulating him."

Here Bishop Spellman interrupted the Cardinal to explain that the latter must not be interviewed, but the visitor continued: "I enjoyed my visit very much. It was a great opportunity to meet the President and his truly American family and to have luncheon with them."

At this point occurred the debate over an interview, when one of the correspondents started to ask a question but was stopped in mid-sentence by Bishop Spellman. Cardinal Pacelli appeared momentarily bewildered by the rapid flow of conversation, but acquiesced to Bishop Spellman's desires and only added that he had enjoyed his visit to the United States and his opportunity to observe in a month's tour schools and institutions in various parts of the country.

On his return to Inisfada, the Cardinal sent the following telegram to Mr. Roosevelt: I AM GRATEFUL, MR. PRESIDENT, FOR THE CORDIAL WELCOME WHICH YOU EXTENDED TO ME. I AM HAPPY TO HAVE HAD THE HONOR AND THE PLEASURE OF MEETING YOU. THE MEMORY OF YOUR COURTESY AND FRIENDLINESS AND KINDNESS WILL LONG REMAIN WITH ME. I PRAY THAT GOD WILL BLESS YOU WITH THE BEST OF HEALTH AND THE UNITED STATES WITH PROSPERITY AND HAPPINESS.

The great thirty days had now come to an end, and His Eminence sailed on November 7. Riding to the pier with Cardinal Hayes and the Rector of St. Patrick's Cathedral, Monsignor Michael J. Lavelle, he greeted and blessed two thousand or more Italian-Americans come to wish him Godspeed. In his formal release given to the press, he described his travels in the United States, remarking that he had visited twelve of the sixteen ecclesiastical provinces and had had the privilege of meeting and conversing with bishops from fifteen of them; seventy-nine bishops in all. The New York *Times* reported for November 14 that "Cardinal Pacelli arrived in Rome this evening and was immediately received by Pope Pius to whom he made a detailed report on his journey to America. The concrete results of the trip, however, are not yet known and probably will not be announced until examined by competent Vatican Congregations."

Of the concrete results that were never announced, at least three concerned the Bishop. One can be inferred from the fact that his diary is practically a blank from November 5 to November 18 and records a week in bed from November 22 to November 29, followed by recuperation in Florida with Joseph P. Kennedy. And small wonder! It had been a month to remember; a month of many stresses and strains; the straining of some old friendships and the stressing of others. Another effect was the return of a future Pope to Rome more than ever convinced that in Bishop Spellman he had a disciple whose sound judgment and unwavering loyalty he would never have to question. He had seen him years before in the offices of the Vatican; he had seen him on vacation in the Alps, now he had seen him at home. He had sat down at dinner with Pa and the rest of the family in Whitman; he had seen the pastor in his church and surrounded by his children in the parish school; he had seen him in press conferences and an endless series of receptions, handling situations and people of every kind, nervous and unsmiling sometimes, but always firm and tactful. The fact that Cardinal Pacelli made no secret of the confidence that he had in Bishop Spellman led President Roosevelt to consult more and more on national and international affairs with the young Auxiliary of Boston. This was the third concrete effect of the famous trip that was never announced.

The situation was not without a background stretching over three years.

There is a note in the diary for Saturday, March 4, 1933: "All banks closed in Massachusetts. Heard it over the radio. Also heard President Roosevelt's inaugural address. It was very strong." A week later: "President Roosevelt's actions are meeting with popular approval and people have great confidence in him."

Washington buzzed with activity. In addition to national problems, the new President was busy paying off his election debts and one of the first was to Mayor James Curley for keeping Massachusetts in line. The mayor wanted the appointment as Ambassador to the Quirinal, but on March 16 phoned to the Bishop to say that the Italian Government had demurred. The diary for March 19 notes:

Mayor Curley told me that James Roosevelt told him in the name of his father the President that the President could not appoint him Ambassador to Italy because Cardinal O'Connell said that the Vatican did not wish a Catholic Ambassador. I denied that such could be the reason.

In two days the Bishop's opinion was confirmed.

The Holy See replied that neither officially nor unofficially, neither directly nor indirectly, neither through Cardinal O'Connell or any other person, did it express any opinion about Mayor Curley or anybody else as an Ambassador from the United States of America to Italy and Monsignor Marella gave Mayor Curley a letter to that effect which he showed to President Roosevelt, thereby contradicting him flatly.

This was probably the occasion that first brought Bishop Spellman into the great line of vision, and the entry on Saturday, April 22, reads: "Had talk with Jack Kelly. He said that President Roosevelt and Postmaster General Farley had heard that I was displeased because Mr. Curley did not get Rome."

Early the next year, a suggestion came to the Bishop from Mr. Galeazzi that he might explore the accuracy of some rumors that had reached Italy about a diplomatic exchange between Washington and Vatican City. By November 15, 1935, he could write in his diary:

> Wrote letter to Cardinal Pacelli that Joe Kennedy had conversation with President Roosevelt and the President had practically determined to recognize the Vatican. This conversation was held at my suggestion and request.

It was not surprising, then, that the President had thought of him when a perennial Mexican crisis had arisen in the spring of 1935. For July 10 there is a note in the diary:

> Judge Manton told me of conversation with President in which the President said that if I would secure authorization from the Holy See, he would arrange for me to be received by President Cardenas. This is obviously a shift in positions and I went to see Delegate. He was disturbed, had been trying to contact me all day by phone to Boston. I explained that Manton had told me that he had an invitation from Cardenas to go there and that I had asked for it in writing. Had conference with Father Burke over matter.

This diplomatic mission, however, was concluded the next day. "Had luncheon with Judge Manton and informed him that Archbishop Cicognani did not desire our services. Manton thinks the Church is missing a good opportunity."

The Bishop then was well and favorably known to the President before his first interview at Hyde Park. This occurred September 28, 1936, after Roosevelt had learned from very confidential sources of Cardinal Pacelli's proposed visit to the United States. This information must have reached him before the first announcement was made in Rome on September 30. The Bishop's diary for September 28 reads as follows:

> Took 6:20 A.M. train to Poughkeepsie. Phoned Phil Mylod. He came down to station for me and his partner, Joe Duggan, drove me to Hyde Park. The interview with the President lasted one hour and twenty-five minutes. Saw Franklin Jr. and the President's mother. Everything was most pleasant and interesting. We talked of election—Mexico—Daniels—Father Coughlin—Joe Kennedy—Archbishop McNicholas' statement—and the visit of Cardinal Pacelli.

It is fair to assume that the subjects were not mentioned in the order of their importance.

With the now famous meeting of the President and the Papal Secretary of State the pattern was fixed, and henceforth the principal channel of communication between the White House and the Vatican was to be the Pastor of Newton Center.

On November 20, two weeks after the Hyde Park visit, the diary records: "Had luncheon two hours in my room with Judge Burns and Tom Corcoran. I enjoyed the meeting and learned much. They told me that President Roosevelt wanted me to represent the Church in Washington. It was, of course, impractical and impossible." Ten days later, the Bishop was in Palm Beach at the Kennedy home. "Dinner with Miss LeHand, Mrs. James Roosevelt, Arthur Krock, Joe Kennedy and Eddie Moore." On December 1, they all listened to President Roosevelt speaking from Buenos Aires. With enthusiasm they signed a telegram of congratulation. The next day: "Played tennis for the first time in years with Betsey Roosevelt and Arthur Krock." Returning to Boston, he had a long visit on Christmas Eve from Miss LeHand.

This was the real beginning of an interesting relationship which increased in importance with the approach of war. On Roosevelt's side, it can be assumed that it was probably just one more of many friendships. The Bishop on his part was impressed by the good that could be accomplished through this distinguished contact and being already experienced in the ways of rulers was willing to be apparently won over. What came as a surprise after the ultimate disillusionment was the discovery that he really had been. His letters and diaries are full of evidence that he went through the successful processing that was experienced by so many of this gifted President's associates, and was for several years sincerely devoted to Roosevelt.

CHAPTER NINE

Interlude

THE year 1937 was as nearly an interlude as any Bishop Spellman was to know for the rest of his life. The same was true of the President. The country as a whole was settling down quietly for a second-term experiment with the no longer New Deal. It had already forgotten the shock of the United States' recognition of Soviet Russia and was largely unconcerned with its consequences. The Navy was being strengthened, but without too much emphasis, and certain foreign powers were marked out for "quarantine" in an academic sort of way. The Spanish Civil War raged on with ferocity—France and England ranged solidly with Soviet Russia on the side of the Reds, the desperate Nationalists forced to accept from Italy and Germany the help denied by the rest of Western Europe. But aside from the announcement of official neutrality and an embargo on the shipment of arms, the people of the United States felt safely out of the argument.

The Boston Archdiocese shared the atmosphere of interlude, and even before the end of 1936, the Peace of Pacelli had settled on the harbor. The diary records Cardinal O'Connell's first visit to his Auxiliary Bishop on Friday, November 27: "Still sick but much better. Cardinal O'Connell came to see me and spent an hour and a quarter with me. We are getting on fine and have identical ideas concerning many persons and things." For the following March 18, we read: "Harry O'Connor came to tell me that he had been called by the Cardinal and that I am to bless the oils in the Cathedral on Holy Thursday. It will be my first Pontifical mass except the funerals of my mother and of Father Hamilton. Also the first time in twenty-one years that Cardinal O'Connell has not performed the ceremony himself." By the following September, the Bishop had been made a diocesan consultor and on the twentieth he attended his first meeting. The diary notes that "the Cardinal was in poor humor," but not, apparently, with his Auxiliary.

Similarly, at Inisfada the Peace was spreading. On Christmas Eve, the Bishop had "a nice letter" from Mrs. Brady and on February 5, "a long talk" with her. On February 18, "Mrs. Brady told me she is to be married March 6 by Archbishop Murray in New York." This was the Archbishop John Gregory Murray of St. Paul who had married Genevieve Garvan to Nicholas F. Brady many years before when he was a young priest in the Hartford

Diocese. The bride and groom were deeply in love and remained so until the death of Mr. Brady in 1930. Now after seven years, the duchess, in spite of all her charity and public service, was a very lonely widow. She had met William Babbington Macaulay in Rome where he was serving as Minister to the Vatican from the Irish Free State and their marriage had been expected by their intimates for about six months. The ceremony, however, which took place at seven in the morning in the lower church of St. Ignatius Loyola was as quiet as possible. Few as the witnesses were, Bishop Spellman was one of them and when Mr. and Mrs. Macaulay sailed at noon on the *Conte di Savoia*, he was at the pier to see them off. On their return in the fall, he called on them with Monsignor Ottaviani and Monsignor Principi, old friends of Roman days, and noted: "Dinner and a pleasant evening. It was nice to see her again. She looks well."

Something over a year later, a cablegram arrived in Newton Center: GENEVIEVE DIED AT NOON. GALEAZZI. A routine visit to the dentist had resulted in complications, and death had followed suddenly in a matter of days. She was buried beside Mr. Brady in the Jesuit novitiate which they had built at Wernersville, Pennsylvania. For Bishop Spellman it was the end of a significant chapter, and his feelings are reflected in a note which he wrote to his nieces, Mary and Kathleen, who were away at the time in college:

I am glad, Mary, that there is to be a Mass celebrated at Manhattanville for Mrs. Brady. She was a marvelous woman and in several respects one of the most wonderful persons I have ever met. For over ten years I was associated with her very closely and in some ways no one was closer to her during several of those years than I was. Of course she may have made some mistakes but they were fewer than most of us make. Fundamentally she had a wonderful heart and a good brain, and she believed, I am thoroughly convinced, that everything she did was right. Certainly everything that she did was done with the right motive. She tried to be guided by supernatural considerations, and I know that even in her social activities she had religious motives. She was a daily communicant, and whenever possible she passed an hour each day in adoration before the Blessed Sacrament.

I have known of the devotion of wives to husbands, but I never saw and never knew any woman more devoted to her husband than was Mrs. Brady.

I shall always cherish her memory and remember her in my prayers. Knowing her influenced my life in many ways, and made it more interesting than it otherwise would have been, and while there was occasionally some element of unpleasantness, due to my fault and disposition, the ninety-nine per cent predominating experience of knowing her was one of happiness.

In conclusion I wish to say that I reverence her memory, and that it was one of my life's most wonderful blessings to have known both Mr. and Mrs. Brady. I know that as long as I live I shall not again meet their equals, for I have lived long enough and known people enough, to know that in some respects their equals do not exist.

Interlude or no interlude, however, the accumulated strain of the past year had taken its toll. On June 22, the Bishop wrote in his diary: "Doctor Nolan said I was frightfully run down, had low blood pressure, etc., and prescribed a three weeks' cure at Saratoga which I shall try to take." He succeeded in doing so, with fair results, but in September he was back where he had started, and on Sunday, October 3, he gave the parish a fright.

Started to say 8:30 o'clock Mass this morning. Read announcements at 7 o'clock and 8:30 o'clock Mass and as Father Winn was finishing his sermon I lost consciousness. I did not fall. Father Reynolds was seated beside me, but did not notice my plight until Mr. Boylan stood up in the church, pointed at me and said, "The Bishop!" Some policeman thought he had a revolver in his hand. I was carried to the sacristy and revived immediately.

I went to bed and Father Whalen finished the Mass. The incident caused some concern, but I was able personally to telephone the *Post* and it was kept from publication in the newspapers.

Two days later the entry reads:

I am feeling better and the doctors have concluded that my fainting spell was the result of a combination of various factors such as fatigue due to insufficient sleep, secondary anemia as a result of erysipelas, and of not having allowed sufficient time to recuperate from my illness of two weeks ago.

Left on the midnight for New York.

It was another two months, however, before he gave in to his family and the doctors, who had advised a South American cruise. Leaving Boston early in January and returning early in April, he visited Peru, Bolivia, Ecuador, Chile, Argentina, Uruguay, Brazil, Puerto Rico, Jamaica, Venezuela, Colombia, and Panama. He traveled as Father Spellman, a Boston pastor, and, insatiable tourist that he was, took innumerable pictures, went everywhere and recorded all his impressions for his favorite public in Whitman. "I always take one or two rides in streetcars anyway," he wrote, "but I am taking three or four in the Brazilian cities. It is a nice way to study the map of a city and also a convenient way to observe people and things."

Not very much escaped him. The scenery, the architecture, the economics, the politics, the social, and especially the religious conditions of the various countries were described in some detail. In doing so, he was consciously setting down a picture of South America in 1938, but unconsciously, even in his lighter observations, he was giving a picture of himself. There is an echo of affairs of state in his study of dead fish:

Shortly after leaving Salaverry, we passed the Guano Islands, where the warm current from the equatorial waters strikes the cold current from the Antarctic regions. The fish in the cold water are killed by the warm water, and the warm water fish are killed by the cold water, which shows what happens if one doesn't stay where one belongs. Good old Newton Center!

But on March 1 his thoughts were far from South America:

Today would be mother's birthday were she alive, and naturally I am thinking of her more today than I always do every day. I thought among other things of her letters to me at least once a week during the sixteen years I was away from home previous to 1932 when she was no longer able to write and I returned home. Absence from home would have been much harder and far, far less interesting did I not have her letters, and did I not have the opportunity of writing to her once or twice a week during those same years. I still have all those letters, over a thousand of her letters to me, and more than a thousand from me to mother. I have never reread them, but I keep them because I feel that I shall do so some day as Helene has done.

His mother would always remain one of the two great enthusiasms of his life. The other was, of course, the future Pius XII and he too seemed very close at times:

All through Chile and Argentina I have heard so much from so many people about Cardinal Pacelli. Naturally no one imagines that I know him, and it makes me so happy to hear him spoken of not alone with admiration, reverence and respect, but with enthusiasm and gratitude and almost with a feeling of ownership—that Cardinal Pacelli is their very own! And His Eminence really does belong to them as he belongs to every people he has ever visited. His Eminence is truly international and supernational, and above all His Eminence is supernatural in his life and his works, and that is the real secret of his greatness, the real reason for the veneration and affection all have for him, and none more so than we of the Sacred Heart Parish, Newton Center, where the memory of his visit is preserved not alone on the bronze tablet beside the altar, but in the minds and hearts of all those who saw him.

The religious situation interested him most of all. The casual tourist on a Caribbean cruise is given to sweeping statements about the entire continent, although as a rule what is true of Venezuela is seldom true of Argentina. But even experienced travelers can see a few difficulties which the Latin American states have in common. As the Bishop noted:

One of the fundamental troubles with religion here is its close association with the Government and the privileges accorded the Government in selecting Bishops. The Holy See makes the appointments, it is true, but the Government presents three candidates and it is possible all three may be unqualified individuals, and yet the Holy See may not have precise reasons for rejecting all three of them and so one of these is selected.

The government subsidy is another source of difficulty. Writing from Buenos Aires to Galeazzi, he summed up his impressions on the subject:

I am pleased with the religious situation here. The Sunday Masses are well attended by evidently devout people. The churches are clean and well cared for. And the priests are on a higher cultural plane than the priests of some other countries. The Americans here with whom I have talked, and there have been fifteen or twenty well informed ones, think that the greatest burden the Church has is the Government subsidy. They point out that it is relatively insignificant but yet every time it appears in the national budget, all the socialists and the anti-clericals use it as a reason to launch most bitter and untrue attacks on the Church. It is also an excuse to lukewarm Catholics not to contribute to the support of the Church. And it was really pathetic to see the infinitesimal offerings made by persons of apparent means. The Americans substantiate their opinion by pointing to Uruguay where things Catholic improved after the Government subsidy was terminated. I was glad to note that the priests are zealous, and the Salesians as usual are doing remarkable work.

The poverty of the people is not an unmixed evil nor does it account for all the neglect which he noted in various places. After deploring the fact that although the soil of Peru is rich, the minerals plentiful, and the people industrious and good-natured, the economic condition of the Indian is still a problem, he goes on to say:

I was happy, however, kneeling in the Church of Pisac because there is no question but that poverty and suffering can bring us close to God. The church was crowded to the doors. The priest gave a good sermon, the people listened attentively and with devotion. The men remained standing on one side of the church and the women sat on the ground. After the sermon all knelt on the stone-studded ground on bare knees until after the last blessing without shifting position. The mayors of the towns with maces in hand knelt near the altar.

The poverty was not so edifying in oil-rich Venezuela:

The churches are poor in this country of Venezuela and the priests are poorer. In Venezuela and in some other countries, there is a sad situation. The people do not assist the priests. There are few rectories and the priests have to board where they can. Naturally, their standard of living and culture is not very high, and then the people blame the priests when they themselves do not support them. And the worst symptom of the whole sad situation seems to me to be that fathers and mothers do not wish their boys to study for the Priesthood. While I have been edified and made very happy by many of the things I saw and heard in South America concerning the Catholic Church, I am afraid that my prevailing sentiments have been those of distress and depression. People tell me that things all over the continent are better than they were, but still they are not very good. Even in Curaçao, under Dutch Dominicans, there are broken panes of glass in the church and this situation cannot be attributed to poverty alone.

Brazil made a better impression:

Naturally, I go to many churches in every city and I generally can visit four or five on a Sunday morning. The churches that I have seen in Brazil are for the most part clean and well kept. Rio and São Paulo seem to be in situations similar to several large European cities where there is a concentration of churches in the central part and no timely provision was made or possibly could not be made to build churches in the newer residential sections. While the churches in Rio were well filled, it is absolutely impossible to accommodate the congregations that should attend Mass if Rio de Janeiro and São Paulo are as Catholic as they are reputed to be. I attended four Masses yesterday, and while there were boxes in which offerings might be placed, there was no collection taken up at any Mass. I am on the lookout for ideas that could improve things in Newton Center, but up to the present I can say that there are no radical changes that I contemplate making when I return.

In Puerto Rico he found the work of the Redemptorists particularly consoling:

There are two Redemptorist priests, Father Tansey and Father Wall, who accompanied us around Puerto Rico. Father Tansey and all his family used to go to All Saints Parish and he told me how he remembered my first sermon there in Roxbury, Massachusetts. Mr. Brady, Stella's father, frequently told me about it, and I still have it written out and memorized, as naturally I worked hard on it. Father Tansey is one of the several outstanding American priests I have met on the trip and meeting him and them has done me lots of good. We met the Bishop of San Juan, Bishop Byrne, and he had words of praise and gratitude for another outstanding American priest,—our own Father Richard Cushing. Conditions of the Church in Puerto Rico are not very good, but I think with priests like Father Tansey and Father Wall working here they must inevitably improve. Every day for the past three years these priests have visited the leper colony, insane asylum and the prison, and I was deeply edified to hear from them the simple eloquent story of their work and see with my own eyes the results of their work.

However, less than ten per cent of the people go to Mass and only one per cent of those who go are men. Think also of the difficulty of supporting the Church in Puerto Rico. There are priests there who receive only thirty cents a month from the people of their parish. And since these are not considered foreign missions, the priests receive no help from the Propagation of the Faith Society. However, the American Province of the Redemptorists is doing superhuman and supernatural work both in Brazil and Puerto Rico. And I am consoled by the generosity of Americans who in thirty-five years have contributed two million and a half dollars to build churches and schools in Puerto Rico. And each year the Provincial of the American Province pays a fifty-eight thousand dollar deficit to balance the budget for the support of the Puerto Rican Redemptorists.

A visit to Colombia, and the trip was over. His final comment was understandably inaccurate. "We steamed away from Cartagena last evening and as we left her harbor I breathed a prayerful farewell to South America, a farewell forever." That was something which he could never say with certainty of any place in the world.

CHAPTER TEN

Archbishop of New York

ON HIS return, the Bishop was amused to find that he had figured in one of New York's springtime rumors concerning the Diocese of Brooklyn. The rapid expansion of Long Island, following the development of subways and parkways and superhighways, had caused a considerable shift in the Catholic population. Cardinal Hayes used to say with gentle exaggeration that half his diocese had moved to Queens, and even suggested at one time that he would be willing to surrender Staten Island to Brooklyn in exchange for his wandering flock. But Bishop Molloy, being understandably attached to Queens and underestimating Grymes Hill, the highest point on the Atlantic Coast between Florida and Maine, showed little enthusiasm for the proposed arrangement. The incident, however, seemed to have prepared the way for the rumor of 1938 that the counties of Nassau and Suffolk would become a new diocese and that the choice of the new bishop lay between Bishop Kiley, then Ordinary of Trenton, and Bishop Spellman.

This flurry of speculation, however, was only a prelude to the momentous events of the following autumn. On September 4, New York was shocked to learn that Cardinal Hayes was dead. He had been spending a period of rest at St. Joseph's Villa in Monticello and had retired the evening before in excellent spirits. When he failed to appear the next morning at the usual hour for Mass, his secretary, Monsignor John J. Casey, entered his bedroom and found him resting peacefully against a pile of pillows neatly arranged, a crucifix in his hand. His health had been delicate ever since the first heart attack at the Dublin Eucharistic Congress in 1932, but he had taken part in liturgical functions at the cathedral, had presided at commencements and meetings of the clergy, had consecrated churches, and had dedicated many diocesan buildings. In 1935 he had even gone to Cleveland as Papal Legate at the Eucharistic Congress. But on all these occasions he was closely watched by his devoted circle for overexertion, and the sterner responsibilities and worries of administration were shared by his auxiliary bishop, the Most Reverend Stephen J. Donahue; his chancellor, Monsignor J. Francis McIntyre; his vicar general, the venerable rector of St. Patrick's Cathedral, Monsignor Michael J. Lavelle; and his secretary, Monsignor John J. Casey.

When news of the Cardinal's death reached Madison Avenue, the consultors were summoned at once to elect an administrator for the archdiocese. Though Monsignor Lavelle had twice taken part in previous elections, this time he was not present for the balloting. It was decided that up till now he had attended consultations not as a consultor, but only as vicar general, and that according to canon law, his tenure of office had ceased with the death of his Ordinary. So while the venerable administrator of the cathedral waited for word in an adjoining room, the consultors elected Bishop Stephen J. Donahue administrator of the archdiocese and forwarded his name to Rome for confirmation. This was given at once, and for the next eight months all the traditions established in the preceding decade were carefully preserved.

The attendance at the solemn obsequies of His Eminence at St. Patrick's Cathedral, which lasted four hours, gave testimony of the deep love that his children felt for the Cardinal of Charities and the veneration in which he was held by the entire American hierarchy. Twelve archbishops and fifty-five bishops, preceding three cardinals and the officers of the Mass, moved slowly up the aisle to the places prepared for them in the sanctuary. The rest of the clergy and the laity, as they watched the procession and identified the best-known figures, wondered inevitably which of them would be the successor of Cardinal Hayes, and before many days had passed the American press had taken up the speculation. It was thought at first that Cardinal Mundelein, who had grown up in the same neighborhood, had gone to the same college, had received his red hat in the same consistory, and who was in consequence the presiding prelate at the funeral, would on the occasion of his approaching visit to the Vatican practically nominate his old friend's successor. The choice was supposed to be limited to three. The first in dignity was Archbishop Edward Mooney of Detroit, the best-known in Rome was Bishop Spellman, and the hope of the New York consultors was Bishop Stephen J. Donahue. The local clergy were not critical of outside talent, while it remained outside, but they always had a small-town feeling with regard to "foreigners." Monsignor Lavelle, who served successively under five archbishops, once remarked that Archbishop Corrigan's principal difficulty was the fact that he was a foreigner. He came from Newark, New Jersey.

The Auxiliary Bishop of Boston was of two minds. He was willing to go to New York, but had no desire to go where he knew that he was not wanted. He had hoped to stay in Boston and eventually perhaps succeed his Ordinary, as superiors in Rome had intimated, but he realized that nothing insures longevity in a churchman like the presence of a successor. All this uncertainty with regard to his own attitude is reflected in the diary:

September 4:
    With all the opposition I believe my appointment is impossible.

September 14:

Had a talk with Cardinal O'Connell about the New York situation. Everything was most pleasant.

September 28:

Clayton Sheehan sent me clipping from New York *World-Telegram* saying I was mentioned for the Archbishopric of New York. That's as close as I'll get to it.

The debate in the press continued. By November, the dispatches from Rome were giving the margin of preference to Bishop Spellman. Over the Christmas holidays there was a change and by the middle of January, Bishop Donahue and Archbishop Mooney were still considered possible, but Bishop Walsh of Newark and Archbishop Rummel of New Orleans had been added, while a late starter, Archbishop McNicholas of Cincinnati was away out in front. Bishop Spellman had been dropped by the authorities in the copy rooms with the naïve explanation that "he was too valuable where he was." People smiled, but actually the Roman correspondents were not too far off the track. There were solid grounds for thinking that Pope Pius XI had always regarded Bishop Spellman as the logical successor of Cardinal O'Connell, and that on the other hand he had been deeply impressed by the zeal and scholastic accomplishments of the Dominican prelate of Cincinnati. It has even been said on good authority that the papers designating Archbishop McNicholas for New York had reached the Holy Father's desk.[1] It was at that point that Providence stepped in once more.

The previous October, the New York papers had carried the news that His Holiness would celebrate the tenth anniversary of the Lateran Pact with a solemn consistory on February 11 and mark the occasion by creating not only new cardinals but several archbishops as well. At the consistory of 1937, His Holiness had predicted that he would never preside at another, but his health had apparently improved, and everyone confidently expected him to be on hand at the date he had selected. For February 10, however, there is a note in the Bishop's diary: "Pope Pius XI died. Saw the news early in Miami paper and celebrated Mass for him." This was news indeed, far more significant than the death of Cardinal Hayes, and the next day the entry reads: "Guess there is a lot of speculation about new Pope and new Archbishop of New York. . . ."

The Bishop's superior, Cardinal O'Connell, was at Nassau in the Bahamas when the Pontiff died, and boarded the *Brittanic* at Hamilton on February 10. Sailing on the *Saturnia* from New York, February 15, His Eminence completed the six-thousand-mile journey on March 1 and entered the conclave in the late afternoon—the last of the sixty-two cardinals to arrive. Bishop Spellman had been assured that his presence was not necessary in Boston, and remained quietly where he was in Florida.

The international situation was deteriorating rapidly. It was obvious that the inexorable approach of World War II had contributed to the death of Pius XI. Everything in his nature and religious training loathed the appeasement of evil, and now his warnings were recalled as reports reached Rome of Hitler's progress. Within this very month the last of Czechoslovakia, and Memel on the Baltic, would be absorbed while Western Europe looked on petrified with fear. Armageddon was at hand, and the new Pope would be caught in the clash inevitably. He could not be an ordinary man. There were many who still maintained that no Secretary of State could be elected, backing up their opinions with statistics and historical references, but the conviction was spreading throughout the Catholic world that the providential choice would be Pacelli.

The diary for Thursday, March 2, shows only one line: "Cardinal Pacelli elected Pope Pius XII." The next day the Bishop wrote: "A few phone calls got through to me at Everglades Hotel. . . . I am so glad to be away from the pressure of visits, reporters, phone calls, etc., at this time." On Saturday: "Received first telegram from Pope Pius XII. Received wire from Apostolic Delegate asking for new Pope's coat of arms." On Sunday he noted: "The White House has been trying to locate me for two days."

Meanwhile he remained in the background, reading all the accounts, spending a couple of hours on the beach every day, taking long walks by himself. He was reliving the seven golden years in the Vatican. "Visualizing and enjoying the events described in eight or ten papers a day," he found time to write to his brother John:

> Of course I could write for hours and days of my memories of the Holy Father and of my thoughts. I am glad to be alone at this present time with these memories and thoughts. For even though I have believed for years that it was in the designs of God's Providence that Cardinal Pacelli would one day become our Holy Father, and it is easy and natural for me to visualize him as such, it is still absolutely impossible for me to comprehend how and why I have had the honor of knowing His Holiness personally and of enjoying so many and such extraordinary manifestations of his friendship.

After a week of seclusion, it was time to go home and face the interviews: "I am going North feeling well and strong and tranquil. I suppose I am back on the list again although I have seen no one and talked to no one. I have no desires and no hopes, but I have thoughts." By the fifteenth of March the thoughts were beginning to produce a little strain. "I am feeling well but the magnitude of all the happenings produces such a conflict that I am overcome with joy, apprehension and I don't know how many other things."

The suspense lasted for nearly a month. On March 16 an important letter arrived, which described the situation as of March 9. That had been only one week after the election of the Holy Father, and it revealed that already

New York was the subject of much earnest conversation among the highest officials of the Church. The same day the Bishop "received personally signed blessing in beautiful telegram of Pope Pius XII. Answered telegram supplicating." The supplication was that he be left out of consideration for the post. On top of this there was a phone message from Joseph P. Kennedy, our ambassador in London. He had been representing President Roosevelt at the Pope's coronation and could describe for the Bishop various crosscurrents in the Tiber. No wonder the diary records for March 20: "My pulse is running fast and I am unhappy." Ten days later it seemed to be all over. He would not succeed Cardinal Hayes after all. "Am feeling relieved to know what the serious reasons were that prevented my appointment to New York. The reasons are good ones and there is another good one—I don't want to go myself. Am informed there are three Cardinals against my going to New York. That is one reason why I should think I might go."

Cardinal O'Connell was, of course, fully aware of the situation and may have regarded the opposition to his Auxiliary with mixed emotions. He was in an excellent mood. His visit to Rome had been a complete success. At the coronation his seniority had placed him at the head of more than fifty cardinal priests, only six cardinal bishops preceding him. On his return to Boston he had been expansive in his description of the new Holy Father. He described him as "truly a beautiful character, a man of great intelligence and wide experience. He is humble and he is clever. He possesses great force and great restraint. He truly may be said to be a living saint. That is something of great importance in these troublesome times. I look forward to a remarkable Pontificate—something like that of Leo XIII."[2] When Bishop Spellman called to pay his respects, the Cardinal told him what he could about the conclave and then added characteristically, "The Holy Father asked for you and asked me if you were co-operating with me." He thought his Auxiliary would be pleased to learn that his Ordinary had given a favorable report on him, and was probably surprised when Bishop Spellman answered with his usual directness, "I do not understand such a query and consider it superfluous."

The good parishioners in Newton Center shared the joy of their pastor in the coronation of Pius XII. The next Sunday the following letter was read at all the Masses:

We of the Sacred Heart parish rejoice with 350,000,000 of our fellow Catholics and with other untold millions of men of good will of other faiths that such a saintly, talented, scholarly and courageous Shepherd has been chosen to direct and guide the flock of Christ. But also we rejoice in a special way because, for two days, we have had our Holy Father in our very midst as our guest. The recollection of this unique honor and distinction wells in our hearts today and forever will remain a hallowed memory. . . .

The days that followed were taken up with parish duties. Newton Center seemed very peripheral. There is only one line in the diary for April 4: "An eloquent silence in Rome and Washington."

This silence was suddenly broken, however, on April 12. "I heard at 10:45 this morning by an air mail special that the Holy Father intends to appoint me Archbishop of New York. I shall go to Washington tonight." The letter to which he referred had come from the Apostolic Delegate in Washington, and read as follows:

> I have the honor to inform Your Excellency that the Holy Father has in mind to name you Archbishop of New York; and I desire with this letter to offer you my heartfelt congratulations and felicitations on the high honor which His Holiness is about to confer on you. Before the appointment is made, however, an expression is desired of your willingness to accept it; and I would be pleased if you would make known your consent by telegram. If Your Excellency will wire me: "Letter of April eleventh received and suggestion approved," I shall understand it to indicate your acceptance.
>
> This communication is sent under the strictest secrecy and must remain entirely confidential until the information it contains is published in Rome. Your Excellency will be notified in due time of the date of publication.
>
> Once again permit me to offer Your Excellency sincere congratulations, and to assure you of my prayers in the position of high responsibility to which you will so soon be raised.
>
> With sentiments of esteem, and with all good wishes, I remain
>
> Sincerely yours in Christ,
>
> ✠ A. G. CICOGNANI

If his pulse had been running fast before, the Bishop was in a turmoil now. He was convinced that his selection for New York was a mistake. His spiritual formation had not been that of a Trappist. He loved being a parish priest and a bishop, but hoped that if he became an archbishop, he would be the Archbishop of Boston. Boston was his native land. He knew its history and its problems. He had visited every parish from Haverhill to Plymouth and could call every pastor by name. New York was a strange country. His student days at Fordham had given him a certain sense of familiarity with the city. He had made a few enduring friendships among the clergy and laity, and many of his Roman associates lived there, but he realized only too well that he was a foreigner. Then, too, as the huge metropolis was the capital of the New World, there would be great responsibilities added to the ordinary administration of the diocese, and he had good reason to believe that the financial situation was rather challenging. But the principal difficulty was this: that he would be regarded in a special sense as the personal appointee of the Pope, and he dreaded the thought, as he put it, "of letting him down."

All this was racing through his mind as he drove to the airport, determined to talk with the Delegate in Washington and then send a telegram in code to the Holy Father. He had already composed the message. It was to have read: "Father, if it be possible, let this chalice pass from me." He paced up and down the field for hours and was about to enter the plane when the flight was canceled due to weather conditions. Let the diary finish the story: "Since I could not go to Washington I decided that it was the Will of God to accept and so wired."

Twelve days were to pass before the announcement would come from Rome, but the secret was well kept by Archbishop Cicognani, and the Bishop merely wrote: "What thoughts I have and share them with no one!" On the seventeenth he arrived at the Apostolic Delegation in Washington and, after Mass in the new chapel, had a cordial talk with the Delegate, who was puzzled about the long delay in Rome over the expected announcement. Returning to Boston, he made the following entry for Sunday, April 23:

> These days of waiting between the appointment and the announcement are strangely feeling ones. I cannot realize that it is actually so that I am to be Archbishop of New York. I cannot foresee what the reaction will be.
>
> John and Helene invited all the family and some guests to their home in Brookline. I would have liked just the family at this particular time, but since I couldn't give a good reason decided to let John have his friends.
>
> At nine o'clock got a phone call from Delegate that publication would be tomorrow morning, the 24th at 10 o'clock. I feel that a bombshell is going to explode. The Delegate said I might tell the family. They all came to Newton Center and remained until after midnight. It was quite an emotional strain on us all.

There was just time between nine o'clock and midnight to dispatch a brief note to the President, dated April 23, and still preserved in the archives at Hyde Park: "I wish you to be the first one to know that the Holy Father has appointed me Archbishop of New York." The next day was feverish.

> The news broke at seven o'clock. I said Mass in the Convent at 6:30 and told the nuns after Mass. The news had come over the radio from Rome. Reporters and telegrams and people swarmed all over the place. I wrote a letter to the Holy Father, to President Roosevelt and I went to see Cardinal O'Connell. It was quite an interview. He was very nice. Of course he knew the past and also the immediate past, and I knew the past and also the immediate past. I gave out a statement which was well received. I asked the Cardinal to appoint Louis Kelleher as my successor in Newton

Center and he said he would. Then I asked him to let Sister Philomena and four others attend the installation and he said he would. He gave out a statement to the newspapermen speaking better of me than I have ever heard him speak of anyone in my life. It was quite a contrast with the statement which he issued when I was made a Bishop six years ago.

This one was more like the citation for an honorary degree, and was given to the press by Monsignor Minihan before the reporters were admitted to a joint interview. It read:

I feel very happy over the nomination of Bishop Spellman to the See of New York. I am glad to take this occasion to say that Bishop Spellman in the various positions which he has held has proved himself a faithful servant and a devoted priest and bishop.

It seems that Providence has directed him along the path which now leads to this very important post, the See of New York.

I chose him, among others, to go to the American College in Rome for his ecclesiastical training. He was an excellent student and while there made the acquaintance of those who afterwards took a hand in shaping his career. He came back as a priest and worked as a curate in Roxbury and there did very faithful service as a young priest.

At the request of Cardinal Gasparri, who was then Secretary of State to His Holiness Pope Pius XI, I loaned him to the Roman Curia. His immediate superior was Cardinal Pacelli, who in due time repaid the loan by sending him back to me as my Auxiliary Bishop. In that position he has given me the fullest co-operation and has proved his worth by laborious and efficient work both as Auxiliary Bishop and as a parish priest.

It has always been my opinion that when one was promoted to any office in the Church by those who have been his direct superiors he may well consider his promotion in the light of following God's will. Self-seeking in ecclesiastical affairs is sure to bring anything but happiness whereas accepting even the most difficult office by the direction of one's immediate superior without ambition or self-seeking is the surest road to success.

Bishop Spellman has been prepared for the burden which is now to land upon his shoulders by a wide experience both at home and abroad. I am sure he has learned here something of diocesan administration, for this archdiocese is well known to be one of the best-organized dioceses anywhere, and his experience in the Roman Curia is one of worldwide interest, so that both from a large worldwide point of view and in the line of diocesan administration he has had abundant experience to fit him for the task which is laid upon him by those who by every right and title have known him best. The Archdiocese of New York is one of the great Sees of the world.

It is the most natural thing in the world for the Sovereign Pontiff to want in this and similar Sees prelates upon whom he can absolutely rely for their firmness in the Faith, the courage of their position, and their loyalty to the center of Christian unity. Archbishop Spellman has the confidence of the Holy Father, and that in itself is the highest test of his fitness to be Archbishop of the great Archdiocese of New York. He has ability, courage and tactfulness, and I feel that I can say with certainty that in due time the priests and the good people of New York will come gladly to the aid of their Archbishop in the glorious work which faces the Church in this country of maintaining the highest standards of Christian Faith, of Catholic action, and of true patriotism. We are all rejoicing at his nomination and we all, Cardinal, priests and people, will pray God to give him the necessary health and strength to carry on the great work which faces him as the new Archbishop of New York.

As one reporter described the scene:

Standing beside the Cardinal in a little reception room of the Cardinal's home, Bishop Spellman at the urgent prodding of his superior, spoke haltingly, his voice choked with emotion, of his awe at the responsibility conferred upon him and his need of the prayers of the people of Boston.

"I am very happy that the Holy Father has thought me worthy of the high position, and I shall do my best to justify his confidence in me," he said. "I have been very happy in Boston and I ask the prayers of all that God may give me the strength to carry on this assignment."

"He is quite moved and has been having a trying time," the Cardinal explained.

"His Eminence has, through the years, been most fatherly, helpful and sympathetic," Archbishop Spellman added.

Later, after his return to his house in Newton, Archbishop-elect Spellman issued the following statement:

I realize the magnitude of the task to which His Holiness Pope Pius XII has assigned me. I know that I have not the preeminent qualities of Cardinal Hayes, but I know, too, that I shall have the help of those whom Cardinal Hayes has guided, and they will, I am sure, help to guide me. I am heartened to realize that I shall have the strong, practical and able cooperation of my companion of seminary days and my friend down through the years, Bishop Donahue. I shall rely greatly on the enlightened counsel of the venerable and beloved Vicar General, Monsignor Lavelle. I am confident that I shall have the loyal assistance of the experienced diocesan officials and the zealous clergy and religious.

I know that the ever faithful and devoted Catholic laity will cooperate with me in doing God's work for God's greater honor and glory. I shall dedicate myself in every way possible to the welfare of children, the hope of the future. I shall welcome the participation of all in the doing of good things for God, for country, for the poor, the sick, the suffering and the underprivileged.

For my part, I shall give my all and do my best. I shall pray and work —pray, because everything depends on God; work, as if everything depended on me. My completely absorbing interests will be the salvation of souls—including all, and the welfare of my fellow-man—excluding none.[3]

The American press could not have been more friendly and every paper in Boston and New York carried flattering editorials. There were personal sketches, anecdotes, and varying versions of his exploits in Rome. His boyhood friends were interviewed with all the inaccuracies and exaggerations customary on such occasions. Old files of the Fordham *Monthly* were sought for the first time on the shelves of the New York Public Library and his earliest efforts at verse were reproduced. The result was that everyone in the archdiocese knew all about the new shepherd even before he arrived. Bishop Donahue's statement was prompt and gracious:

As Administrator of the Archdiocese of New York and in the name of the priests, religious and laity of the Archdiocese, I desire to express our happiness that the Holy Father has given to New York an Archbishop in the person of His Excellency, the Most Reverend Francis J. Spellman, D.D., of Boston, to succeed His Eminence, the late lamented Cardinal Hayes. We pledge to Archbishop-elect Spellman our loyalty and obedience and pray for his health, strength, and every blessing to carry on the great burden that has been placed upon his shoulders.

It would be unrealistic, however, to imply that joy was universal. As in every change of government, some plans had to be altered—plans that in some cases affected careers. Then, as always, there were able men who had failed to consider the needs of the future. They had even made mistakes. One who believed his own irreparable went up to Newton Center at once and offered his resignation. The Archbishop-elect asked him, "Would you like to remain in office?"

"After what happened," the Monsignor answered, "I did not think it would be possible."

"Retaliation," said the Archbishop, "is a luxury I have never been able to afford."

The incident was the beginning of a long and very close friendship, as well as the keynote of the new administration. The fitness of every man in the archdiocese for the position he was holding was to be taken for granted until he proved himself unfit.

The rest of the month was given to clearing the debt, tying up loose ends, preparing addresses to be given in New York, and, of course, presiding at official and unofficial farewells. On May 14, the anniversary of his ordination, the Archbishop-elect confirmed the class at his own beloved school.

The next Sunday was his last in a parish which he was to love with a special predilection all his life. As Auxiliary Bishop, he might well have delegated his pastoral duties to the first assistant and no one would have criticized him for it, but being a pastor happened to be the joy of his life and with the nature God had given him, he was never satisfied to be nominally anything. At Newton Center he was the pastor. That meant to him that he should make the rounds of classes in the school and give out the honor cards; that he should be at the door of the church on Sunday for a word with Mary and Jim; that he should take his turn with preaching, confessions and sick calls; that he should keep up with his reading, enjoy his friends and sleep soundly at night. All this he was about to sacrifice for the heavy responsibilities and loneliness of honor and authority. It was a satisfaction, however, to realize that he had achieved most of the goals which he had set for himself. The church and the schools were models. The debt was paid. He had arrived in 1933 with a black bag and no money. Now he was leaving with the same black bag and still no money. The parishioners had, according to custom, subscribed to a purse for the departing Bishop, but he had used it to wipe out the parish debt and to extend the parking lot and playground across the street. His farewell address took the form of a letter to his still undesignated successor, which was to be read to his parishioners:

My dear Father:

I wish to offer you my heartfelt congratulations and to assure you of my good wishes and prayers in your work as pastor of the Sacred Heart Parish of Newton Center. I can wish you nothing better than to have the same happiness and receive the same consolations that I have had.

You will have the assistance of three zealous priests who are exact in the performances of their parochial duties, who prepare their sermons for the Sunday Masses and all other occasions, who visit each home in the parish once a year, and who visit the sick and those in difficulties regularly and frequently.

You will have here in the parish a Community of Sisters of St. Joseph who are conscientious observers of the rules of life for Religious, who are competent teachers, and who serve Almighty God in selfless service to God's children.

You will find a St. Vincent de Paul Society with its treasury depleted, but with its treasury of good works filled to overflowing.

You will find the parish with many activities functioning in conformity to the directions of the Sovereign Pontiffs concerning Catholic Action. You will learn that annually there are missions for the men, women and children of the parish and for the goodly number of our parishioners who speak Italian. Each year these spiritual exercises have been conducted by priests of different religious orders and congregations, and it has been a most gratifying experience for me to see that nearly all of the parishioners avail themselves of these opportunities to learn more about their holy religion and to follow more closely its teachings.

The great majority of the parishioners of the Sacred Heart parish are practical Catholics, loyal to their Faith, cooperative in the support of the works of religion, both parochial and diocesan.

They are also mission-minded and realize the sacrifices that priests and Sisters are making on the home and foreign missions to spread the gospel of Christ, and willingly and generously do they support them.

They are devoted to the Holy Father, and with a genuine and personal affection because of the visit of His Holiness to this parish.

You will find here an excellent grammar school, a high school, and a school of Christian Doctrine. It is an outstanding school of happy, healthy and successful children, and there are practically no failures. We take pride in the fact that students graduated from our schools who enter college have invariably received higher averages than they received in our school. Since, unfortunately, we have not the means to provide for the instruction of all the children who apply for admission to our school, we have a school of Christian Doctrine, where the children of the public schools assemble twice a week in the classrooms of their respective grades. Here they are taught religious living and religious subjects by the Sisters.

In regard to the material condition of the parish, I am pleased to report that all the buildings are in excellent condition. There is no debt on the parish and there is nothing in the treasury. You will find that most of the parishioners intelligently appreciate that it costs a great deal of money to maintain the parish property and the parish organization; that there are four priests and eighteen Sisters constantly at their service; that there are ten other persons employed in the school, the church and the rectory. You will also find that they are Catholic-minded and Catholic-hearted enough to contribute in proportion to their means to the considerable and constant expense of maintenance.

As I take leave of the parishioners today, I ask them to remember me in prayer as I shall remember them and you. I hope, and sincerely do I believe, they will be as cooperative with you as they have been with me.

And so, I bless you my dear parishioners, and I say and pray—God be with you.

Although the Archbishop-elect of New York was no longer a member of the Boston family, His Eminence invited him to speak at the last conference of diocesan clergy to be held before his departure. The pastors listened with deep interest as he described the lessons he had learned from the example of the Cardinal. He mentioned especially his devotion to the Holy See, to the Missions, and to little children; his charity towards all his priests, even the unfortunate. He spoke with feeling, and His Eminence was obviously touched.

The date of the installation was set by Bishop Donahue for May 23, so Sunday evening, May 21, the Archbishop-elect went down by train to Manresa, a Jesuit retreat center on Keyser Island near South Norwalk, Connecticut. There he remained in seclusion until the next morning at eleven-thirty, when Bishop Donahue arrived to escort him to New York. In the early afternoon, they crossed together the state line that marks the boundary of the archdiocese and proceeded through twenty miles of cheering and flag-waving children to the archiepiscopal residence on Madison Avenue. On the way, their car was joined by twenty-four others, filled with lay and ecclesiastical dignitaries, and, of course, the indispensable gentlemen of the press.

A Boston reporter found it hard to believe that there were so many schools so close together with such a mass child population. As he described it for the home paper:

> The sky was threatening when the automobile procession began. Half-way down the Bronx there were claps of thunder, and heavy downpours, but the children could not be driven or herded indoors. They stood along the curbs with uniforms wet and bedraggled and flags flapping in soggy whips.
>
> In Harlem a Catholic School turned out and the Bishop stopped the cavalcade to be received by the children and Nuns. In the preponderantly Jewish section of New York about 150 Jews had gathered and an elderly gentleman in the center held a banner aloft with the inscription: "Great Respect For Bishop Spellman."
>
> At a distinctly Irish settlement, a little further along, St. Catherine's School at 155th Street and Amsterdam Avenue, there were about 2,000 children and a band, costumed in blue caps, blue jackets and white trousers. The band struck up a lively tune and it was almost impossible to keep the children in check.[4]

Madison Avenue was black with cheering crowds as he turned for a moment with a little smile, gave them a blessing, and vanished into the old stone house on the corner of Fiftieth Street. It was 5:15 P.M. As he entered the foyer with its high ceiling and dark massive stairway, and walked with quick, short steps into a double parlor, mid-Victorian to the last touch, he was on familiar ground even if the role was unfamiliar. The ordeal that most people dread on such occasions is the traditional conference with the press, but after all his years in Rome and Boston, the Archbishop could take it in stride. He was asked for an interview.

He answered, "That is already prepared," and handed out a statement.

"Can you amplify this a bit further?" he was asked.

He smiled. "You gentlemen are all trained observers," he said. "Who could amplify your observations?"

Turning to Bishop Donahue, he inquired about the diocesan consultors and learned that they were waiting upstairs. So he bowed and smiled for some more pictures, and then one more before he went to the Board Room on the second floor, where he took his place at the head of the historic consultors' table and officially accepted the resignation of Bishop Donahue as administrator of the archdiocese. The formal statement given out at the time emphasized his sense of responsibility:

> I know that all realize that it will take some time for me to become personally acquainted with 1,695 priests, and to learn as much as I would like about the 685 churches and chapels of the Archdiocese. I am obliged to concern myself, as much as is humanly possible, with the welfare and progress of 354 schools, nine colleges and one university. With God's help and with the help of all, I must sustain with all my heart and soul, the pulsing, living monument to Cardinal Hayes, the great work of the Catholic Charities.
>
> On the day of my appointment I stated that I would pray and work. I now beg all to pray and work with me, and with reverence I appropriate the words of Saint Paul which he uttered on entering the largest city of the world of his day, as today I enter the largest city of the New World: "I give thanks to my God through Jesus Christ for you all because your faith is spoken of in the whole world." (Romans 1:8)

These well-chosen words, written out in the cool hours of anticipation, were not as colorful as the unforeseen events that followed his arrival. As soon as the new Archbishop took his place at the head of the table, he was presented with two copies of his own last will and testament, which he was requested to sign forthwith, leaving everything to his successor. The clear implication was that he might not live until morning. Then, to emphasize this wholesome realization, the consultors accompanied him on a visit of ceremony to his predecessor's tomb beneath the chancel floor in St. Patrick's Cathedral where he could hardly avoid noticing a similar space which had already been reserved for him. After a nervous dinner, the Apostolic Delegate, Archbishop Amleto Cicognani arrived and came to his room for a confidential priming session. There were, he said, four grave matters that required his immediate attention. One was financial, involving an archdiocese in Peru; one legal, and financial, involving a college in China; one concerned a religious congregation; and one a prelate living in retirement. Other difficulties could wait until he had caught his breath.

Some hours later, it was a weary Archbishop who said the last good night and closed the door of his study. The room was a mass of flowers. The desk was piled high with telegrams of welcome and spiritual bouquets from innumerable convents. Propped against a huge basket of red roses was a letter which had not come with them. It was probably from some benefactor offering to commemorate the happy occasion by the erection of a new home for foundlings! He opened it and read:

Most Reverend and Dear Archbishop:

This institution was founded in 1850 by eighteen merchants and citizens of the City, who were called together by Bishop John Hughes for the purpose of organizing a savings bank. Throughout its history, it has looked with favor upon Church and institutional loans, and has always had a substantial sum of money outstanding in the shape of mortgage loans on Catholic Churches and institutions. At the present time, such mortgages in the New York Archdiocese aggregate in the vicinity of $28,-000,000.

The Chairman of the Board and I would be delighted to call upon you at your convenience for the purpose of presenting our respects and of acquainting you personally with our policy towards applications for Church and institutional loans. I am wondering whether you would be kind enough to see us for this purpose, and, if so, whether you would name a time at which we might call on you.

Long and tiring as the day had been, he found himself smoldering, and could not sleep until he had planned the first steps in the refinancing of the archdiocese.

The next morning, a friendly crowd of perhaps 50,000 people braved a threatening sky to watch an unending procession of clerics who made their way from Madison to Fifth Avenue along Fiftieth Street and through the main portal of the cathedral. In addition to the seminarians, brothers, and priests, secular and religious, there were ninety-eight monsignori, including Monsignors Cushing, Minihan, Phelan, and Haberlin who represented Cardinal O'Connell, three abbots, forty-eight bishops, and seven archbishops with fifty papal knights attending them. The Apostolic Delegate presided as the enthroning prelate. Boston was well represented by one hundred and fifty priests, and Newton Center by six nuns from the parochial school. Sitting beside them was one of the Archbishop's special guests, John Burke, for many years the shy and devoted sexton of the Sacred Heart Church.

The most picturesque figure in St. Patrick's that day, however, was the Vicar General, Monsignor Michael J. Lavelle, now in his eighty-fourth and last year, who was already past his golden jubilee as administrator of the cathedral. With a halo of white hair and a slightly startled expression, he went through the reading of the papal bulls just as he had for Cardinal Hayes and Cardinal Farley before him. He read boldly, with a husky voice, his intonation and accent unmistakably local, until he came to the words, "Wherefore since the Metropolitan Church of New York has been bereft of its pastor by the death of its Archbishop of most cherished memory, Patrick Cardinal Hayes—" Here his voice faltered, then broke, and it was nearly half a minute before he could resume. There were three bulls read, which with the change of a name might have been addressed to Augustine at Hippo or Anselm at Canterbury. The first was:

Pius the Bishop, the Servant of the Servants of God, to His Venerable Brother Francis Spellman, heretofore the Titular Bishop of Sila, chosen the Archbishop of New York, greeting and apostolic benediction:

We, therefore, by the fulness of Our apostolic authority, do relieve you of the charge of the Cathedral Church of Sila, the title of which you have thus far borne, and do transfer you to the aforesaid Church of New York, constituting you its Archbishop and Pastor, and committing fully to you its charge, its government and its administration, both in spiritual matters and in temporal, with all the rights and privileges, all the duties and obligations inherent in that pastoral office.

The second was:

Pius . . . to Our beloved children, the clergy and laity of the City and Archdiocese of New York, greeting and apostolic benediction:

By these Our letters We inform you of this selection and We command you in the Lord that you receive this same Francis, who has been chosen as your Archbishop, with all respect and honor, as your father and as the shepherd of your souls; that you obey his wise commands and precepts; and, that you show to him the reverence which is his due, in such wise that he may rejoice to have found in you devoted children and you in him a genial loving father.

The third was:

Pius . . . to His Venerable Brothers, the Bishops Suffragan to the Metropolitan Church of New York, greeting and apostolic benediction:

We advise you, Brethren, of this selection, and command you in the Lord that you offer this same Francis, who has been chosen your Metropolitan, that obedience and show to him that reverence which the Sacred Canons require, in such manner that among you the grace of God may ever effect the greater benefit of souls.

The address of the new Archbishop which was carried by radio to millions of listeners was appropriate and eloquent:

As a child I was brought here by my father and mother. . . . As a youthful student in this city often did I come here to pray and never did I come without feeling renewed in the life of the spirit. On the altar in the Lady Chapel of this Cathedral on July 16, 1916, I offered my first Mass in America. Today I have walked the long aisle and approached the altar, not as a young man come to commune awhile with God and then depart fortified with new found grace to meet the problems of youth and of scholastic tasks, but I have come in my mature years to stay, to stay with the keys of this building of God and all that it typifies and signifies entrusted to my care—here to remain until God calls me to render an account of my stewardship.

The Archbishop praised the work of his predecessor, the Cardinal of Charity, and recalled the visit of the then Cardinal Pacelli to New York which "ratified between the Holy Father and all of us a deep and a solemn pact of mutual understanding and of friendship." He asked the clergy, religious, and laity to continue faithfully in the work of salvation as they had under Cardinal Hayes and concluded with a solemn pledge:

> What return shall I make for all that I have received?
> To my people, my care and solicitude.
> To my priests, justice and charity.
> To the Bishops, my brotherly affection.
> To the Apostolic Delegate who has installed me, my loyal devotion.
> To Our Holy Father, Pope Pius XII, gloriously reigning, who has appointed me, the love of a son, and the undying fidelity of a Catholic Bishop.
> And to God, for this grace to me unworthy, I bow my head and direct my prayer that His grace in me may not be in vain. The burden is heavy. Without God, my capacity is nothing.

The Solemn Pontifical Mass which followed was celebrated by Bishop Stephen J. Donahue, who had as deacons the rector of the seminary and the president of Fordham University.

Sometime in the course of the crowded and distracting day he paused long enough to write the following letter to his father who, at eighty-one years of age, had proudly witnessed the great events from a place of honor in the front pew:

> MY DEAR FATHER,
> I want to write my first letter after my installation and the ceremonies incident to it are finished to you to tell you of my love and veneration and of the appreciation and debt of gratitude I owe to mother and you and to my brothers and sisters, Martin, Marian, Helene and John and to say that I hope and pray that as we have all been so united here on earth and so happy that we shall one day be even more united and supernaturally happy in our heavenly home. This is the first letter that I sign myself
>
> ✠ FRANCIS J. SPELLMAN
> *Archbishop of New York*

When the time came for the formal reception given by the laity at the Commodore Hotel under the joint chairmanship of former Governor Alfred E. Smith and Lady Armstrong, seven thousand people filled the main ballroom, three other ballrooms, and ten public meeting rooms. But in the midst of the flash bulbs and excitement, the silent voice of the Archbishop's mother gave the occasion a touch of simple piety that was more impressive than all the compliments and applause. Lady Armstrong, founder and president of the Ladies of Charity, suggested in her speech of welcome that perhaps Ellen Conway Spellman had shown him as a boy "the way to the great distinction which he bears tonight," and would rejoice in his elevation.

"I had no intention of bringing such a personal note into the address I have prepared this evening," said the Archbishop, "but I would like to have it for the record that my mother never imagined that I would be any more than the priest I was ordained to be." He then took from his pocket a letter he had received from his sister Helene after his appointment as Archbishop and read the following excerpt:

> So many people say it is too bad that mother could not have lived for this day, but I cannot feel that way. She had never one ambitious thought and so often would say that all she asked of God was that you would be a good priest, and, of course, I feel too that she is so much happier now and can certainly help you so much more. Last night I found the scrap of paper on which she wrote the cablegram she was to send when she heard you had been made a Bishop. She had had the first shock and the handwriting was not as it once was. She wrote, "God bless and guide our boy. Keep him kind and humble. This is the prayer of father and mother."

Having cherished the cablegram since 1932, he knew the words by heart, and often in the years to come, with all their merited honors and honest praise as well as their inevitable invitation to worldly vanity and spiritual pride, that message would come back to him with the impact of the "*Memento homo quia pulvis es*" and the burning flax of a papal coronation.

Though the years that lay ahead would bring a variety of experiences—national and international; civil, religious and military; parochial, social, financial and educational—none would be a source of deeper satisfaction to the new Archbishop than the part he was to play in the growth of the American hierarchy. He could not have dreamed in 1939 that twenty years would see so many of his brother priests consecrated before the high altar of St. Patrick's. The late Cardinal Archbishop of Philadelphia, His Eminence John Cardinal O'Hara, C.S.C., whom he consecrated in 1940 at Sacred Heart Church, Notre Dame, was an exception, but twenty-four other bishops have been anointed in his cathedral, nearly all after the imposition of his own hands. The first was his chancellor, Monsignor J. Francis A. McIntyre, who became Auxiliary Bishop of New York in 1941, coadjutor archbishop without right of succession in 1946, Archbishop of Los Angeles in 1948, and Cardinal in 1953. The Very Reverend William Tibertius McCarty, a Redemptorist Provincial, was consecrated in 1943 with the title of Military Delegate and two years later was elevated to the See of Rapid City. The year 1945 saw a record of four consecrations in St. Patrick's in which the late Monsignor Joseph Patrick Donahue, a veteran administrator and vicar general, was made auxiliary bishop; Monsignor William A. Scully, the assistant executive director of Catholic Charities, became coadjutor with the right of succession to the Bishop of Albany; Major General William R. Arnold, former Chief of Chaplains, United States Army, took the place of Bishop McCarty as Delegate of the Military Ordinariate, and the Very Reverend Apollinaris V. Baumgartner, Capuchin superior and pastor of St. John Baptist Church, New York, was made Vicar Apostolic of Guam. At the time of Bishop Baumgartner's consecration, Archbishop Spellman was in Japan. On a visit to Rome with his Ordinary, the late Monsignor Thomas J. McDonnell, who had been since 1936 national director of the Society for the Propagation of the Faith, learned to his surprise that he had been selected for the episcopal dignity. He was consecrated in 1947 and in 1951 appointed coadjutor with the right of succession to the Bishop of Wheeling. Until 1948, Baltimore and Washington had had the same Ordinary, Archbishop Michael J. Curley. On his death, Monsignor Patrick A. O'Boyle, the executive director of New York Catholic Charities, was selected as Archbishop of Washington and consecrated by His Eminence in St. Patrick's. That same year, Monsignor Joseph F. Flannelly, the administrator of the cathedral, was made Auxiliary Bishop of New York. The "police action" in Korea brought problems akin to the Second World War and in 1950, Monsignor James H. Griffiths, the chancellor of the Military Ordinariate, was named Titular Bishop of Gaza and auxiliary to the Military Vicar. Subsequently he became Auxiliary Bishop of New York and Representative of the Holy See to the United Nations. About the same time, Monsignor Christopher J. Weldon, a former Navy chaplain and executive director of Catholic Charities, was elevated to the See of Springfield, Massachusetts. The next year, Monsignor Fulton J. Sheen, a professor in Catholic University, was selected by His Eminence as the successor of Bishop McDonnell in the Society for the Propagation of the Faith and consecrated in the Cardinal's Titular Church of Saints John and Paul in Rome. Ogdensburg had been left vacant through the election of its bishop, the Most Reverend Bryan J. McEntegart, D.D., consecrated in 1943, as rector of Catholic University, and in 1954, the Most Reverend Walter P. Kellenberg, D.D., chancellor and director of the building activities of the archdiocese, was named to succeed him. Bishop Kellenberg had been consecrated the previous year with Monsignor Edward V. Dargin, the vicar general, both as Auxiliary Bishops of New York. In 1957 on the death of the beloved Archbishop Thomas E. Molloy, D.D., of Brooklyn, his diocese was divided, the Counties of Nassau and Suffolk forming the new Diocese of Rockville Centre. Bishop McEntegart was then appointed to Brooklyn and Bishop Kellenberg to Rockville Centre. Both were formally installed by His Eminence. In 1955 it was the turn of Monsignor Joseph M. Pernicone, whose designation as auxiliary bishop was greeted with much enthusiasm by the large and influential group of Italian extraction in New York. Next in an illustrious line was Monsignor Philip J. Furlong, who took the place of Bishop Griffiths in the Military Ordinariate and in 1957, after many years of distinguished service as rector of the seminary, Monsignor John M.

Fearns, S.T.D., was consecrated as Auxiliary Bishop of New York. That same year the Most Reverend Charles Arthur Brown, M.M., became Titular Bishop of Vallis and Auxiliary Bishop of Santa Cruz in Bolivia, and the Most Reverend Vincent I. Kennally, S.J., Titular Bishop of Sassura and Vicar Apostolic of the Caroline and Marshall Islands. Again in 1959 there were three consecrations: Monsignor John J. Maguire, S.T.L., vicar general of the archdiocese, was made Auxiliary Bishop of New York; the Very Reverend John W. Comber, superior general of Maryknoll, the Titular Bishop of Foratiana, and the Very Reverend Thomas R. Manning, O.F.M., the Bishop of Corico in Bolivia.

This lengthy enumeration may have suggested to some great Homer's "Catalogue of the Ships," but it illustrates an important trait in the Cardinal Archbishop of New York—his zeal for the preservation of the highest standards in the American hierarchy. Added to this zeal is a deep and personal consideration to a fellow bishop that shows itself at every step of the consecration. A few days before, for example, His Eminence gets out what is left of the rings and chains and pectoral crosses that have been accumulating at the cathedral for more than a century and offers the bishop-elect his choice. One selects something that belonged to Cardinal Hayes who ordained him. One wants a souvenir of Cardinal Farley who baptized him, while another takes an emerald just because it reminds him of his mother.

This interest, however, extends beyond choosing the ablest candidates and making their great day memorable, to acts of justice and charity toward those already in the episcopal ranks. There was the strange and deeply moving case of the Most Reverend Bonaventure F. Broderick, D.D., Titular Bishop of Juliopolis, outlined in the following report sent by the Archbishop of New York to the Apostolic Delegate, November 27, 1939:

Your Excellency:

It will give Your Excellency great happiness to hear, as it gives me great consolation to recount that I have been able to bring to a satisfactory conclusion one of the problems which Your Excellency brought to my attention the night before my installation ceremonies as Archbishop. Your Excellency will remember that you told me that there was a Bishop living in the Diocese who was not living as a Bishop but instead was conducting a business establishment for the sale of automobile accessories and gasoline. Your Excellency told me that it would be a great blessing if this unfortunate individual could be reconciled with the Church, for many years have elapsed since he abandoned our Holy Religion. I made mental note of Your Excellency's story and resolved at the earliest opportunity to do what I could in this matter.

I had occasion to visit Millbrook, which is a town about eighty miles from New York City, on a matter concerning the acceptance of a gift of an estate to the Church for charitable purposes. After I had met the kind donor and inspected the property and expressed my gratitude for his gift, I excused myself from the company of priests and lay people and told the parish priest that I wanted him to take me in his own automobile to visit a convent. I actually went to the convent, but this visitation was only a pretext, as I did not care to have anyone know that my real mission was to meet the Bishop. When I was alone with the Pastor, I told him that I wished him to take me to the home of Bishop Broderick. After arriving at the place indicated to me as the Bishop's residence, I asked the parish priest to drive on a distance, and I walked back to the house and to the door of the residence which was some considerable distance from the road. The district is not very thickly settled and there were no houses in the vicinity so my going there would be unnoticed, but I did not wish the car to be parked in front of his house, in case some passing autoist might recognize it and speculate.

On my way to the house I asked the priest about the Bishop. He said that he was known as Dr. Broderick. He was respected in the community, even though it was known that he was a Bishop of the Catholic Church. Naturally, however, his presence there was, to say the least, a cause of wonderment to Catholics and non-Catholics alike.

I knocked on the door and it was opened by a man of about seventy years of age, dressed plainly in rough clothes and I took it for granted that it was the Bishop. I said, "Good afternoon, Dr. Broderick. I am Archbishop Spellman and I heard that you were here and I thought I would come to see you and ask you if there was anything I could do to help you." Immediately and spontaneously came his answer. "I have been waiting for thirty years for someone to say those words to me." I entered the house and sat down and told him that if he would like to tell me his story, that I would be pleased to hear it, as I knew nothing about him or the cause of his difficulties. I knew only that he was a Catholic Bishop, and I wanted to help him if I could.

He told me an interesting and moving story which I have since substantiated and have found out to be the truth. He told me that he was a priest of the Diocese of Hartford, that he had studied in Rome, received his degree, returned to America, and had been appointed professor in a Seminary. Subsequently he was a pastor of an Italian parish, and had been selected by Monsignor Sbarretti, his former professor, and at that time auditor of the Apostolic Delegation in Washington, to go with him to Havana and help him in adjusting matters concerning the relations of the United States government and the Church in Cuba. He was made an auxiliary bishop of Havana and did excellent work there. He succeeded in obtaining a conspicuous sum of money from the United States government in settlement of Church claims, and he showed me documents attesting the esteem of the highest American authorities because of his work in Cuba. He told me that Archbishop Chapelle of New Orleans became Apostolic Delegate to Cuba, and as time went on, the Archbishop became unfriendly to him. The Archbishop went to Rome and complained about Bishop Broderick. Bishop Broderick, on his own volition, went to Rome, and explained his position to the evident satisfaction of His Holiness Pius X and Cardinal Merry del Val because on the date of December 20, 1904, with document #9184 of the Secretary of State, Bishop Broderick was appointed delegate of the Holy Father to come to the United States to ("organizzare e promuovere in ciascuna diocesi della sua patria l'obolo dell' amor filiale") organize and promote in each diocese of the United States the Peter's Pence collection.

Bishop Broderick then returned to America to carry out this mission entrusted to him. When he arrived in New York he received a telegram to report to Cardinal Gibbons in Baltimore. Cardinal Gibbons treated Bishop Broderick in a somewhat abrupt manner and told him that the mission entrusted to him by the Holy See had been revoked. The Bishop was left without funds in the United States and without any work to do, and he wrote to His Holiness, Pius X and informed His Holiness of his plight. The Holy Father deigned to answer Bishop Broderick in a letter written March 29, 1905, entirely in his own handwriting. Bishop Broderick showed this letter to me, and permitted me to make a photostatic copy of it which I am sending to Your Excellency, and of which I have sent a copy to the Holy See by Father McCormick. Pius X explained to Bishop Broderick that he had been obliged to withdraw the authority granted to him to promote the Peter's Pence collection because of the protests that were received from many Bishops in the United States stating that this appointment of Bishop Broderick for this purpose would be interpreted as a reflection on their own capabilities and an implied reproof to the Bishops. The Holy Father then went on to say that it was not an easy thing for him ("di poter provedere *subito* l'Eccellenza Vostra di una sede vescovile o di una coadiuteria") to provide a diocese *immediately* for Bishop Broderick. The Holy Father referred to Bishop Broderick's plight as a ("piccola tribulazione") small trial, indicating that at least up to that time there had been no grave charges against the Bishop. Bishop Broderick showed me many letters and he also showed me a copy of a letter which he wrote to the Holy Father saying that his situation without a place to go or to work as a Bishop would be a scandal in America. The Holy Father interpreted this observation of Bishop Broderick as a threat to cause a scandal since the Holy Father exhorted him not to create a scandal by saying, ("non Le nascondo poi la grave amarezza che ha portato al mio cuore la minaccia fatta nella Sua lettera di evitare un grave scandolo.") "I do not hide from you the heavy sorrow that you have brought to my heart by your threat, in your letter, to cause a grave scandal." Bishop Broderick says he made no threat to cause a scandal. He only wanted to stress the fact that the lack of a definite assignment was in itself a scandal.

I then asked him if he would be willing to return to his duties as a priest. He told me that gladly would he do so, and the only reason that he was eking out his existence by conducting a little business was because the One Hundred ($100) Dollars pension which the Holy See had graciously granted to him thirty years ago and still continued was not enough for him to live on.

I made inquiries of several of the Bishop's contemporaries including Cardinal O'Connell and Cardinal Dougherty and also from Archbishop Murray who is from the Diocese of Hartford, and all agreed that the Bishop had not been guilty of anything wrong. There have been stories about the Bishop, but that was inevitable. Bishops, priests and people naturally concluded that there must have been something very serious that would have brought a Bishop to such a sorry plight. It would seem that since Pius X referred to his antecedent situation as a "small trial," and since the delicate nature of a task such as Bishop Broderick had entrusted to him by the Holy See was one that could of its very nature have provoked some annoyance or irritation, and since there is nothing definite of a grave nature in the files of the Apostolic Delegation concerning Bishop Broderick, and the Bishops who knew him and know him are desirous that he return to duty, and since the Bishop himself appeared to me to be very well disposed and very anxious to return to the work of the ministry and give the last few years of his life to the service of God, for all these reasons, I appointed him chaplain of the Frances Schervier Hospital, 227th Street and Independence Avenue, Riverdale, New York, where he will have an opportunity to celebrate Mass and care for the sick and comfort them and administer the Sacraments to them. This appointment will go into effect on December 1. The Bishop desired to be a parish priest, but when I indicated to him that this would be rather difficult, at least in the beginning, he readily consented to take up this post which I offered to him.

Rejoicing with Your Excellency at the happy solution of this case which I know will have Your Excellency's approval, and with sentiments of esteem and devotion, I am

Your Excellency's devoted servant in Christ,
✠ Francis J. Spellman
Archbishop of New York

A few days after the visit to Millbrook, Bishop Broderick wrote the following letter on stationery engraved with an episcopal coat of arms which had not seen the light for thirty years:

September 15, 1939

Most Reverend and Dear Archbishop:

Since it seems now that it may be ten days, or more, before I shall have given sufficient consideration to all the thoughts that have come into my mind in connection with your recent much appreciated visit, and shall have prepared all the materials that I shall then wish to submit to you, to justify my asking you for an interview at which to give you definite answers to the kindly suggestions you made in my favor, I have decided not to delay longer writing you this letter for the special purpose of expressing my admiration and gratitude for the Heaven-inspired, gracious and kindly visit. Even if no further benefit were to result to me from it, I would still always regard it as the most remarkable experience of my life. Never was there brought to my attention in any way an action more Christ-like or more noble. Every detail and incident of it, every word and look we exchanged shall always remain impressed on my memory as long as I live. You have done much to restore my badly shaken confidence in human nature. Fortunately I have never permitted bitterness to lodge in my soul. Divine grace has never allowed my faith in God to be weakened. Through all the years of my misery, my constant and fervent prayer has been: "God is Good." I like to believe that it was in answer to that prayer that He inspired you to visit me, and speak to me in the way you did last Tuesday.

Again thanking you for your great goodness to me, and praying God to bless you always, I have the honor to be

Very sincerely and gratefully yours in Christ,

✠ BONAVENTURE F. BRODERICK

Tit. Bishop of Juliopolis

Arrangements were completed and early in December the new chaplain of the Frances Schervier Hospital was writing to his Archbishop:

I arrived at this little heaven last Saturday afternoon, was enchanted with it from the very start, and am each day, becoming more strongly confirmed in my first impressions. The Sisters here are certainly doing God's work in an exemplary fashion.

My health is improving notably, I am getting accustomed to the routine of my duties rapidly, and I am very happy. I thank Your Excellency and am praying God to bless Your Excellency for all your kindness to me.

Very gratefully yours in Christ,

✠ B. F. BRODERICK

By the following February, the ceremony of conferring the pallium was to take place in St. Patrick's and the Archbishop decided that it was time for Bishop Broderick to appear in the procession wearing the robes of his rank. Thereafter, for the few years that were left to him, the Titular Bishop of Juliopolis was a familiar figure in the cathedral and at religious functions throughout the archdiocese, winning hearts everywhere with his simplicity, humility and gracious, courtly manner. When he died at the end of 1943, his body lay in state before the high altar of the cathedral where his best friend, the Archbishop, sang the Pontifical Mass. When his last will and testament was opened, it was found to be as brief and simple as the good Bishop's sorrows had been long and complicated:

First: I give and bequeath to the Most Reverend Francis J. Spellman, D.D., the Archbishop of New York, or to his successor in that office, my pectoral cross, pectoral cross chains, espicopal rings and crozier.

Second: All the rest, residue and remainder of my estate, of whatever kind or nature the same may be, whether real or personal or wheresoever situate, I give, devise and bequeath to the Sisters of the Poor of St. Francis. . . .

CHAPTER ELEVEN

Myron C. Taylor

WHEN the Lateran Treaty was signed in 1929, Italians, and especially Romans, were most interested in the fact that it cleared away so many awkward anomalies of social and political life. For foreigners the primary interest was in the unquestioned recognition of a very old sovereign state. To most governments this meant the sending of at least a chargé d'affaires, since the traditional function of diplomats had not been absorbed as yet by presidents and prime ministers. In the dark days between the seizure of Rome by the Piedmontese and the new peace, many nations had kept representatives at the Vatican, some as symbols of loyalty, some merely to take advantage of the "listening post of Europe." In recent years the number had increased, and when Pius XI received the congratulations of the diplomats accredited to the Holy See, March 9, 1929, there were more than seventy gathered around the Throne, representing thirty-five countries. Now that the world could call the Pope a temporal sovereign without offense to the Quirinal, official greetings poured in from every direction and the number of states represented rose to forty-two. England was there, and Japan and many other non-Catholic and non-Christian nations, but the United States was not.

To the American Catholic it seemed that his government was avoiding the normal course of action at the dictation of bigotry. Only the year before, Governor Alfred E. Smith had been defeated for the presidency in one of the most disgraceful campaigns in our history. All the wildest slanders of the Reformation had been drawn out of the pit; all the lowest instincts of backwoods sectarianism that had not been called upon since the days of the American Protective Association suddenly came into action. It was so violent, so indecent, that good Americans of every religious opinion were shocked, but after all, the solid South had been smashed and the Republican Party had profited by the outburst so that no one seriously expected the new administration to show any diplomatic courtesies to Vatican City.

With the election of Franklin D. Roosevelt, however, the picture changed. He was the President of the Minorities and realized that if they were all in his corner, the majority could be treated with detachment. He was an aristocrat and had a feeling for the fitness of things not always found in grass

roots, a sense of historical values that put the ancient Church of his ancestors into perspective. He was, for example, very proud that his father's first
cousin, Archbishop James Roosevelt Bayley, had been the third president of
Fordham and that he was himself related to the Venerable Mother Seton.
Finally, he was by temperament bold, imaginative, and consciously dramatic. For all these reasons it seemed possible that he would want to do
what the other civilized nations of the world were doing and appoint a
representative to the Vatican.

For this there was a long and honorable precedent. From 1797 till 1847,
consuls and consuls general had represented us in the Papal States. In 1847
Congress had raised the consulate to a legation and appointed a chargé
d'affaires. In 1853 Lewis Cass, Jr., of New York, who held the post, asked
President Franklin Pierce to accept a nuncio in Washington. Unfortunately,
the country just then was entering the throes of a hate wave called Know-
Nothingism, and some of our earlier families joined together in the persecution of later arrivals. At the moment, Irish Catholics predominated in the
immigration groups, so that the Catholic Church was soon the center of the
storm. Under pressure, therefore, the President had to refuse the nuncio and
could save face only by raising our chargé d'affaires to the rank of a minister.

This arrangement lasted until 1866, when Rufus King, who had been
appointed three years before, notified Secretary of State William H. Seward
that the Pope would probably seek refuge in the United States and asked
that a naval vessel be made available in case the necessity arose. Seward
approved, and the *Swatara* and the *Frolic* were sent for the purpose of
bringing the Pope to America. This prospect, however, was deeply offensive
to the Protestant public and probably gave rise to the popular tradition,
revived in 1928, that the Catholics were building a tunnel to Rome so that
the Pope could more easily invade the United States and take over the
government. At this juncture there was a regrettable incident in a Scottish
Protestant church within the walls of the Eternal City and the congregation
was quite properly ordered out to the suburbs. The story, however, was
garbled in the American press to make it appear that Americans were being
insulted, and it furnished the occasion for Congress to refuse a vote for
more funds to support the legation in Rome. Soon after the Pope was left
to the tender mercy of the Piedmontese, Rome was occupied, and the sending of a representative from the United States to the Vatican became a
subject of merely academic discussion. Such the situation might have remained indefinitely except for the personalities of Pius XII, President
Roosevelt, and the intermediary who was so highly esteemed by both of
them.

Bishop Spellman was discussing the question with his friends as early as
1932 when he returned to Boston, but it was two years later that the first
hint came from Mr. Galeazzi that it was time to study the preliminaries.
The Bishop began by suggesting to Joseph P. Kennedy that he mention

the possibility of a representative to the President and was delighted to learn from the account of the meeting that Roosevelt was sympathetic. It was, however, the visit of Cardinal Pacelli to Hyde Park that forged the most important link in the chain of events leading up to the final decision. No one ever stated officially that when the President and the Papal Secretary of State drew their chairs up to the fireplace at the far end of the great living room, well out of earshot of the other guests, they discussed the sending of a representative of the United States to the Vatican; but it would be difficult to deny that whether *propter hoc* or merely *post hoc*, things began to happen. Barriers dropped. The two men could talk freely, and each was aware that the other was satisfied to have Bishop Spellman as his channel of communication.

After the Christmas of 1936, a photograph of the photogenic Roosevelt arrived in Newton Center, autographed expansively, and the next month there was an invitation for an overnight stay at the White House. For Tuesday, February 16, 1937, there is an entry in the diary:

> Arrived in Washington at 1:15 in the midst of a snowstorm. James Roosevelt at train to meet me and bring me to White House where I was assigned to the Yellow Bedroom.
>
> We worked in his office on speech that he is to deliver Saturday night over national hook-up urging Massachusetts to ratify child labor amendment. Had tea with President and he was wonderful. He made the cocktails before dinner. For dinner he had as guests Colonel and Mrs. Watson, Commissioner and Mrs. Allen, James and Betsey Roosevelt, Miss LeHand. We saw movies after supper. It was quite an experience.

And the next day:

> Said Mass in the Monroe Room of the White House. It was the first time Mass was ever said in the White House. Miss LeHand, Miss Tully, Miss Eben and Miss Hackmeister present. Breakfast afterwards with them. The coffee cups were as large as bowls.
>
> Said good-bye to the President in bed. He said he had intended to get up for Mass.

The following summer, the White House was phoning the Bishop about a faculty change proposed for Catholic University. A well-known New Dealer was not seeing eye to eye with the Rector Magnificus and had been notified that his contract would not be renewed. The President wondered if something could not be done about it. Something was done. Later the same month (August 30, 1937) "Tom Corcoran came to visit me. We talked of Vatican recognition by the U.S.A. and the speech to be given by James Roosevelt showing how many of Roosevelt's reforms are like the Papal Encyclicals."

Two weeks later another delicate situation arose. Soon after the opening of the Seventy-fifth Congress, the President had startled the country with his Judiciary Reorganization Bill, which proposed to increase the United States Supreme Court by six new appointments. The number gave the impression that these representatives of the New Deal would neutralize the effect of the six conservative Justices who were over seventy and could not be made to conform or to resign. The bill was overwhelmingly defeated, and the proposed "court packing," as it was called, cost the President many admirers. But on June 2, Justice Willis Van Devanter resigned and a loyal and dependable progressive, Senator Hugo Black of Alabama, took his place. He was confirmed on August 12. Within a month, the Bishop's diary records: "Storm broke over documented copyrighted story showing Justice Black of the Supreme Court was a member of the Ku-Klux Klan." The Administration realized that unless the crisis were handled correctly, three minorities might be alienated at once, and turned to Bishop Spellman for an answer:

Friday, September 17th:
Told Jim Roosevelt that I thought Judge Black's only answer was to admit he joined the Klan, that he resigned, did not believe in it and repudiated it.

The advice was accepted and the storm blew over, but the incident opened at once into another.

Saturday, September 18th:
Eddie Brandon phoned me to New York that James Roosevelt wanted to see me. Took 1:00 P.M. train to Boston and went to Eddie's house in Cohasset where James and I discussed the possibility and the mode of having the U.S.A. recognize the Vatican and establish diplomatic relations. We talked for two hours and Ed Brandon who was present thought I did well and made progress.

While the President was thus relying more and more on his old friend in Newton Center, he was not averse to having an ally in the Middle West:

Tuesday, September 21st:
Phone call from Jim Roosevelt at White House inquiring about advisability of President's calling on Cardinal Mundelein. I saw nothing against it.

This was the great George Cardinal Mundelein, a prelate from the Brooklyn Diocese, who had been Archbishop of Chicago since 1915, and a Cardinal since 1924. He was a strong, energetic, and outspoken character with very pronounced and liberal views on social reform. He had supported the New Deal enthusiastically since 1932 and in 1936, when the administration was being fought on the subject of relief and a large part of the Catholic press was beginning to murmur "creeping socialism," he welcomed an invitation

from Notre Dame to preside at a convocation honoring the newly established Commonwealth of the Philippine Islands and took the occasion to
eulogize Roosevelt and his program. "Advised by reporters that the Notre
Dame speech practically renominated the President," Cardinal Mundelein
replied, 'I always go all the way for a friend.' "[1] So when Bishop Spellman
"saw nothing against it," the White House called the Cardinal and the
Cardinal wired the Bishop to have lunch with him in New York. Shortly
after, when Roosevelt went to Chicago, ostensibly to open a new bridge,
the Cardinal entertained him in his home at lunch.

The following January, on the ninth, "James Roosevelt telephoned, inviting me to Washington to stay at the White House." The Bishop arrived on
the twelfth:

> Went to Washington at 11:30, but Jim Roosevelt had been delayed in
> Boston by illness of his daughter so I went to the Mayflower instead of
> the White House where I had been invited. Called on Delegate in the
> evening.

The next day:

> Jim Roosevelt came for me and we went to his home for supper with
> Marguerite LeHand and himself. He liked the memorandum I prepared
> and I think I am making progress in persuading the President that it
> would be a good thing all around. The President looks tired. Went to
> Diplomatic Reception and Concert. Jim drove me to the station at mid-
> night and I took sleeper to New York.

Thereafter Bishop Spellman was in South America for some time and
on his return was seriously ill in Chicago through part of July and all of
August. The doctors could not agree on the diagnosis, the treatment was
in consequence ineffective, and on August 2 his brother Martin was sent for.
The crisis was reached on August 7:

> Got another 10 cc. of serum. I was very sick tonight. Thought I was
> going to die. Martin took dictation about what I wished done and how I
> wished my debts paid. I made a general Confession. Martin does not
> think I am to die. My nurse, Miss Butler, says I will go one way or the
> other soon in answer to my hope that it will be thus.
>
> Martin decided that we had been nice to people long enough and
> asked for a consultation. Dr. McNeeley was called. Dr. McNeeley was
> just one of the finest persons I have ever met. He confirmed the diagnosis
> I made on the very first day.

As result of this agreement, the crisis passed and His Excellency returned to
a world of rumors.

With the death of Cardinal Hayes early in September 1938, Washington
followed with some interest the speculation on his successor. It could be

very helpful if the right man were appointed. On October 12 the diary records:

Had momentous meeting with Tom Corcoran. Dinner together. I sent a cablegram at his request. Since I awoke at four o'clock I phoned Europe and had a very good connection and satisfactory conversation.

Two days later, he wrote to his father:

This evening [October 14th], I spent in the White House with the President. After I entered, the head usher showed me upstairs at once, and Miss LeHand came out of the oval room and brought me right in to the President. He greeted me with outstretched hands and his warm smile, and said, "How is my favorite Bishop? It's awfully nice of you to come, and I am so glad to see you."

I met Mr. William C. Bullitt, our Ambassador to France, for the first time. He is a very likeable individual. Grace Tully and Ray Cahill were the others there for dinner. The President and the Ambassador are Episco-palians. The other four at dinner were Catholics. It was Friday and we all had mushroom soup and lobster. The President and I were the only ones who ate whole lobsters. The President, Mr. Bullitt and I did most of the talking in the order named.

Mr. Bullitt was formerly Ambassador to Russia, and in fact, was our first Ambassador after President Roosevelt recognized the Soviet Govern-ment. So the most interesting topic of the dinner and evening was Russia. The President recounted his experiences with Mr. Litvinoff who was the Russian Plenipotentiary appointed to negotiate terms for the recognition of the Soviets. Mr. Bullitt said that after three days' conversations with President Roosevelt, Mr. Litvinoff said to him: "I can't understand the President; he hasn't talked about anything but religious freedom to me, and I want to discuss important things like trade relations, etc. What is the idea?"[2]

And the President continued and explained to Mr. Litvinoff, "You have a perfect right to be an Atheist if you want to be, but you ought to permit the same measure of liberty to others." And then the President turned to me—I was on his immediate right at the table—and gave me a repeti-tion of a dramatic moment in the conversation just before Mr. Litvinoff consented to allow American Catholics to have a Priest in Russia—"Mr. Litvinoff, you were born in Poland of Jewish parents. Your father and mother were believers and practiced the Jewish religion. They hoped you might be a Rabbi. They believed in God! Now Mr. Litvinoff—you are going to die and before you die you will think of your father and mother and the religion that they taught you. Mr. Litvinoff (and the President pointed his finger at me) before you die, you will believe in God!"

I don't know whether the President's prediction will come true or not, but at any rate, Mr. Litvinoff made some concessions. . . .

Mr. Bullitt, the Ambassador, spoke so very well of Father Braun, the priest from New Bedford who is the only [Roman] Catholic priest in Moscow, that I was deeply moved and edified. He said that he and the British Ambassador who was also an Episcopalian would collect flowers and decorate the chapel and sit in the front pews for services on Easter and Christmas. He is trying to have another priest sent now to help Father Braun.

But I cannot write everything that was said and happened. It was just one more perfectly thrilling experience, and it lasted until ten o'clock when the President had to broadcast on the "Mobilization for Human Needs," and I had to return to the hotel and pack and catch the midnight train to New Orleans to participate in the Eucharistic Congress.

At this Eucharistic Congress, Cardinal Mundelein was the legate representing His Holiness. When it was over, he set out for Rome to make the report customary on such occasions, and at the invitation of the President broke the journey by an overnight visit to the White House. A long, pleasant evening together gave the two friends an opportunity to discuss the question both had already considered and the meeting was regarded by both as a step in the negotiations. On his arrival in Naples, the Cardinal was pleasantly surprised to find that Roosevelt had directed Ambassador Phillips to meet the boat officially and escort His Eminence to Rome in a special train, underlining for the Italian public how highly the Archbishop of Chicago was regarded by the State Department. Unfortunately, the Nazi press, which had shrewdly guessed the subject of conversation during the evening at the White House, nourished a consuming grudge against His Eminence. No editor could forgive an American of German descent who had so bitterly denounced Hitler as "a paperhanger and a poor one at that." So the story was spread on the front page of every newspaper in the Fatherland that Mundelein had pledged himself to deliver the Catholic vote to Roosevelt in exchange for the establishment of diplomatic relations. As a result of the ensuing atmosphere, the project had to be postponed. Three months later Pope Pius XI was dead, and within a year George Cardinal Mundelein followed him.

The election of Cardinal Pacelli to the Throne as Pope Pius XII brought the question once more to the front. The President, who was returning from Navy maneuvers, cabled at once the following message from the cruiser *Houston*:

It is with true happiness that I learned of your selection as Supreme Pontiff. Recalling with pleasure our meeting on the occasion of your recent visit to the United States, I wish to take this occasion to send you a personal message of felicitation and good wishes.[3]

This was immediately followed by the appointment of Joseph P. Kennedy, our ambassador in England, to act as his special representative at the coronation. It was another first, the first papal coronation at which the United States Government had been officially represented.

Even Catholic opinion in the United States was not unanimous on the value of an American ambassador at the Vatican. Some felt that it was a deliberate slight not to have one when the rest of the world was represented, but others said, "Why stir up more clouds of bigotry for a gesture? What practical benefit will the Holy Father or the Church ever derive from it?" Some who held this view were very eminent indeed. The Bishop's diary for March 17, 1939, reads:

> Joe Kennedy phoned me from London expressing his joy at all that has taken place and the honors he has received from the Holy Father. He said Cardinal O'Connell is against recognition of the Vatican by the U.S.A.

The subsequent appointment of Bishop Spellman as Archbishop of New York made progress in the negotiations inevitable. To greet him on his installation in St. Patrick's, there was a letter in the President's own hand inviting him to Hyde Park:

My Dear Bishop Spellman—

Because I write only four or five longhand letters a year it takes me literally weeks to get around to one—but when [it] does get written it is truly an historic event in the family!

Do I have to tell you that very rarely have I been made so happy as when the announcement of your elevation to the Archbishopric came? It was what I had so hoped for, yes, and prayed for—and now best of all you will be near me in New York when I retire from Washington.

I am deeply regretful that I cannot come to the installation—but my heart and my thoughts will be with you. A little later in the summer you must come to us at Hyde Park and incidentally start the good habit of staying with us when you come to see your flocks in Dutchess County.

My congratulations—and my affectionate regards,

Faithfully yours,
Franklin D. Roosevelt

The answer read: "I shall of course be honored and delighted to go to you any time that you are free to receive me."[4]

As it happened, the President was free to receive him on several occasions, and before long the State Department was brought in on the discussion. Cordell Hull sets down in his memoirs the development of their thinking:

> Meanwhile the President had been talking over with us a project to establish some kind of relations with the Vatican. In early July, [1939] . . . Welles and I had discussed the advantages that might be gained through

such relations. We felt that the Vatican had many sources of information, particularly with regard to what was occurring in Germany, Italy and Spain which we did not possess. At my suggestion, Welles wrote a personal letter to Ambassador Phillips in Rome, asking his opinion. Phillips replied on July 19, recommending diplomatic relations and suggesting that a Protestant be named as the American representative. Welles sent this letter to the President.

In conversations with the President I cautioned that we could not send a regular ambassador to the Vatican and would have to limit ourselves to a personal representative from himself to the Pope. I favored Phillips' suggestion that this representative should be a Protestant. Great Britain had followed the procedure of naming a Protestant as her Minister to the Vatican, with a Catholic as first secretary of the Legation. I also said that, if he took this step, he should simultaneously enlist the similar cooperation of the American leaders of other churches.[5]

At the height of the conversations described by Secretary Hull, Enrico Cardinal Gasparri, the nephew of Pietro Cardinal Gasparri, arrived in this country for a visit with his uncle's former assistant. The Archbishop met His Eminence at the boat, steered him through a group of reporters, and then entertained him for a few days in New York and Whitman before his departure for Canada. A dispatch came from the *Times*' bureau in Rome the day after he landed with the information that "Cardinal Gasparri . . . has a mission of preparing the juridical status for the possible opening of diplomatic relations between the State Department and the Holy See, it was learned from good sources at the Vatican today. That is to say, Cardinal Gasparri bears no personal or specific message from Pope Pius, nor is he authorized to negotiate for the establishment of the relations; he is to work out a legal framework within which such a relationship could be placed if established." Once more, "good sources at the Vatican" had led the *Times* astray. The Cardinal had no such mission to perform, but the incident illustrates the general expectation of the public.

Meanwhile Roosevelt began to add new motives for the move which he had definitely in mind. On October 2, he sent the following memo to Secretary of State Hull:

This is a wholly original thought with me and I have discussed it with no one else.

We have, I think, all of us the thought that at the termination of the European War, whether it comes soon or next Summer or three or five years from now, there will be a very large number of refugees— refugees of various Christian faiths, as well as Jewish—refugees coming not from one country but from many countries, including even England and France and Italy. . . .

Mr. and Mrs. William Spellman, as they listen to their son, Monsignor Spellman, broadcasting a translation of Pius XI's radio message to the world, the first by a Pope, February 12, 1931.

The Spellman family. *Sitting*: John, Mrs. Spellman, Mr. Spellman, Martin. *Standing*: Marian, Frank, Helene.

The house in Whitman, Massachusetts, where Frank Spellman spent
his boyhood.

The Spellman grocery store in Whitman.

Frank Spellman and his roommate,
Edward J. Peters, in the room they
shared at Fordham.

Frank Spellman with some of his
fellow-seminarians in Rome. The
future Cardinal is second from left
in the first row.

Monsignor Spellman with Cardinal
Pacelli in Switzerland.

Monsignor Spellman and
Monsignor Pizzardo in the Vatican
with Archbishop Borgongini-Duca,
on the day of his consecration.

Bishop Spellman in St. Peter's Rome, just after his consecration, September
8, 1932. *Left to right:* Msgr. Alfredo Ottaviani, Under-Secretary of State;
Bishop Francis J. Spellman; Lorenzo Cardinal Lauri; Eugenio Cardinal Pacelli;
Archbishop Francesco Borgongini-Duca; Giuseppe Cardinal Pizzardo; Bishop
John M. Gannon, Bishop of Erie.

At Mount Vernon.

At Fordham. Father Gannon is on Cardinal Pacelli's left.

In Boston with Cardinal O'Connell, Archbishop of Boston and Monsignor Richard J. Haberlin, Vicar General of the Archdiocese.

Archbishop Spellman leading the
procession into St. Patrick's
Cathedral on the occasion of his
installation as Archbishop of
New York, May 23, 1939. Alfred E.
Smith, in the uniform of papal
chamberlain, is immediately behind
Monsignor J. Francis A. McIntyre,
Chancellor of the Archdiocese.

Archbishop Spellman receiving the
Pallium from Dennis Cardinal
Dougherty, Archbishop of
Philadelphia, March 12, 1940.

Archbishop Spellman, Cardinal-designate, leaving for Rome February 11, 1946, to receive his cardinal's red hat.

Archbishop Spellman in Rome as Bishop Kelleher, a close friend from Boston, reads the official notification of his elevation to the Cardinalate on February 18, 1946.

Francis Cardinal Spellman kneels before Pope Pius XII in the Basilica of St. Peter's as the Pontiff bestows upon him the red hat during the public Consistory of his elevation to the Cardinalate, February 23, 1946.

Later that day, Monsignor Toraldo di Francisca, papal chamberlain, presents to Cardinal Spellman for Pius XII the Pope's own cardinal's hat given to him by Pius XI when he was created a cardinal.

Archbishop Spellman, Cardinal-designate, offers Mass in world-famous Notre Dame Cathedral for America's soldiers who gave their lives in World War II.

Cardinal Spellman officiating at the consecration of the Most Reverend Joseph M. Pernicone, at St. Patrick's Cathedral.

The Cardinal ordaining a group of Paulists at the Church of St. Paul the Apostle, New York City.

Cardinal Spellman at prayer in St. Patrick's Cathedral.

Archbishop Spellman in Jerusalem after
celebrating a pontifical Mass in the
Church of the Holy Sepulchre on Easter
Sunday, 1943.

The Cardinal leading a group of
American pilgrims into St. Peter's in
Rome during the Holy Year of 1950.

The Cardinal at the head of a procession
during the 35th Eucharistic Congress in
Barcelona, Spain, May 1952.

It is my personal belief that there will be, in all probability, more Christian refugees than Jewish refugees.

A problem is, therefore, raised as to whether, because a very large number of them will be Catholics, the Vatican itself may not desire to take an active interest in helping the Catholic refugees to find homes in wholly new surroundings.

I am wondering, therefore, if you and I should not begin the consideration, *while the war is still on,* of discussing the whole subject with the Vatican and with the representatives of the Federal Council of Churches in America and some similar organizations in Europe.

The contact with the Jews has already been made through the Myron Taylor committee . . . which has concerned itself directly with the Jewish problem.

The contact with the Protestant churches can readily be made in this country and with the equivalent organizations abroad.

But a contact with the Catholic Church ought to be made directly with the Vatican itself, because this question is of infinitely more importance to European Catholics than to American Catholics.

It is my thought, therefore, that while there is no particular reason for haste, we might give consideration to sending at a later date a special Minister or Ambassador on *Special Mission to the Vatican,* in order that we could have a direct system of communication covering the subject of European Catholic refugees.

I am inclined to think that this is not only a practical idea but that it also puts the whole refugee problem on a broad religious basis, thereby making it possible to gain the kind of world-wide support that a mere Jewish relief set-up would not evoke.

You might think this over and talk with me about it at your convenience.[6]

On October 24 there was another luncheon at which the President discussed this new aspect of the refugees with Archbishop Spellman and said that a mission would be established soon after the adjournment of Congress. The next day a handwritten letter went from Madison Avenue to Pennsylvania Avenue saying:

I am very grateful to you for your kindness in having me with you yesterday. I did so enjoy the luncheon also. And I feel that as an American and as a Catholic I should thank you from my heart for what you desire to do, which I firmly believe will benefit humanity, our nation and every nation and benefit religion also.[7]

Between desire and execution, time still dragged on, and for Thanksgiving Day the Archbishop had a letter from the Apostolic Delegate saying that a cable from the Vatican had asked for a report on the most recent developments. Before sunset there was another handwritten letter dispatched to the White House:

> I hope you are well. As you so graciously permitted after our luncheon conversation I wrote to the Holy Father and if it is convenient for you to receive me any time any place, I would like to tell you what His Holiness said. He said of course that he thought it would be to the mutual benefit of nation and church and for the welfare of humanity. If you can spare a few minutes I would be grateful.[8]

This brought action and the final decision. A date was arranged for December 7, a day that was not yet associated with infamy. That morning the Archbishop went first to the Apostolic Delegation where he prepared a letter addressed to himself for the Delegate's signature, embodying assertions which the President had made to him on October 24. The text is important enough to quote:

> With a message dated yesterday the Cardinal Secretary of State has notified me that the Holy Father has received your letter of October 27th relative to the conversation which President Roosevelt had with Your Excellency on October 24th.
>
> The Holy Father received with great satisfaction the information that the President desires to appoint a mission to the Holy See to assist in the solution of the refugee problem and to treat other matters of mutual interest. The Holy Father was particularly pleased to know that the President has the intention of establishing this mission soon after the adjournment of Congress and before January 5, 1940.
>
> The Holy Father directs Your Excellency to convey to President Roosevelt an expression of deepest appreciation on his part and to say that he believes and prays that the resumption of relations between the United States and the Holy See will be most propitious, especially at the present time when both are making parallel endeavors for peace, the alleviation of sufferings, and other charitable and humanitarian purposes. You are further requested to represent to President Roosevelt that in the opinion of the Holy Father the proximate fulfillment of his gracious intention will be most conducive to the welfare of a world sadly torn by misunderstanding, malice and strife.
>
> After you have been accorded an audience with the President will you please communicate through the facilities of the Apostolic Delegation the approximate time that the President intends to make the announcement.
>
> I need only add to this message from the Cardinal Secretary of State that I am at the service of the President and Your Excellency.

That night he summed up his impressions in the diary.

> The President was wonderful to me. Luncheon lasted an hour and a

half and he agreed to recognize Vatican and send either Myron Taylor or Harry Woodring as Ambassador. Mr. Phillips was also considered. He agreed to make an announcement himself at Christmas as my letter from the Delegate which I left with the President was sufficient to give official assent of the Holy See. It was a wonderful day. Returned to New York with Frank Walker.

His bread-and-butter letter read:

Thank you so very much for yesterday. It was certainly an historic luncheon as well as an extremely pleasant one. I am grateful to you and I am grateful for you. I hope to hear that you will consider it timely to make the announcement for Christmas.[9]

Some uncertainty continued with regard to the actual date until Archbishop Spellman finally sent the following cable to Enrico Galeazzi: WORK WILL BE HAPPILY CONCLUDED AND ANNOUNCED DECEMBER TWENTY-FOURTH STOP TEXT OF LETTER (ADDRESSED TO HIS HOLINESS) WILL BE CABLED TOMORROW HAPPY CHRISTMAS

On December 23, a letter was given by the President to Archbishop Spellman, who in company with A. A. Berle, Assistant Secretary of State, transmitted it to the Holy Father through Archbishop Cicognani, the Apostolic Delegate. The same day a telegram was sent by the Department of State to the Embassy of the United States of America at Rome:

American Embassy
Rome (Italy)
164, twenty-third
The President is making public Sunday, December 24, the following Christmas letter to the Pope:

"Your Holiness:
Because, at this Christmas time, the world is in sorrow, it is especially fitting that I send you a message of greeting and of faith.
The world has created for itself a civilization capable of giving to mankind security and peace firmly set in the foundations of religious teachings. Yet, though it has conquered the earth, the sea, and even the air, civilization today passes through war and travail. . . .
I believe that while statesmen are considering a new order of things, the new order may well be at hand. I believe that it is even now being built, silently but inevitably, in the hearts of masses whose voices are not heard, but whose common faith will write the final history of our time. They know that unless there is belief in some guiding principle and some trust in a divine plan, nations are without light, and peoples perish. They know that the civilization handed down to us by our fathers was built by men and women who knew in their hearts that all were brothers because

they were children of God. They believe that by His will enmities can be healed; that in His mercy the weak can find deliverance, and the strong can find grace in helping the weak.

In the grief and terror of the hour, these quiet voices if they can be heard, may yet tell of the rebuilding of the world.

It is well that the world should think of this at Christmas.

Because the people of this nation have come to a realization that time and distance no longer exist in the older sense, they understand that that which harms one segment of humanity harms all the rest. They know that only by friendly association between the seekers of light and the seekers of peace everywhere can the forces of evil be overcome.

In these present moments, no spiritual leader, no civil leader can move forward on a specific plan to terminate destruction and build anew. Yet the time for that will surely come.

It is, therefore, my thought that though no given action or given time may now be prophesied, it is well that we encourage a closer association between those in every part of the world—those in religion and those in government—who have a common purpose.

I am, therefore, suggesting to Your Holiness that it would give me great satisfaction to send to you my personal representative in order that our parallel endeavors for peace and the alleviation of suffering may be assisted.

When the time shall come for the reestablishment of world peace on a surer foundation, it is of the utmost importance to humanity and to religion that common ideals shall have united expression.

Furthermore, when that happy day shall dawn, great problems of practical import will face us all. Millions of people of all races, all nationalities and all religions may seek new lives by migration to other lands or by reestablishment of old homes. Here, too, common ideals call for parallel action.

I trust, therefore, that all of the churches of the world which believe in a common God will throw the great weight of their influence into this great cause.

To you, whom I have the privilege of calling a good friend and an old friend, I send my respectful greetings at this Christmas Season.

Cordially yours,
FRANKLIN D. ROOSEVELT."

For your information similar letters were sent to the President of the Federal Council of the Churches of Christ in America [Dr. George A. Buttrick] and to Rabbi Cyrus Adler, as a recognized leader of the Jewish faith, except that instead of appointing a representative, these men were asked to confer from time to time with the President in Washington.

The President will likewise announce that he has appointed Mr. Myron

C. Taylor as his representative at the Vatican to take up questions arising out of the abnormal situation. The President contemplates that this representation will be for the duration of the war and to handle problems arising out of it. Mr. Taylor advises that because of his health, he will be unable to sail for some weeks, probably in February. It is planned that he will have merely the title of "Representative of the President," with the rank of Ambassador but without title. Unless problems require his continuous attendance in Rome, it is assumed that he will be able to spend most of his time at his villa in Florence, maintaining continuous office arrangements in Rome and coming there when needed.

HULL

The compliment to the Holy Father had thus been tempered by local politics and similar letters had been sent to a Protestant minister and a Jewish rabbi. Moreover, the mission as announced was temporary, though President Roosevelt had told Bishop Spellman that he intended it to be permanent, and Myron Taylor, instead of taking his place on an equal footing with the other diplomats in Vatican City, was merely the personal representative of the President. But the administration in Washington and the Holy See believed sincerely that when powerful ministerial associations realized how beneficial the arrangement was to the United States, they would permit the government to follow the lead of the civilized world. This proved in the end to be a forlorn hope.

The first reaction, however, was promising. Most of the editorial comment was favorable and the President's Secretary, Stephen T. Early, revealed that of more than four hundred telegrams received by Mr. Roosevelt over the Christmas weekend, only four "might be termed critical." Archbishop Spellman's statement, written in the White House on Christmas Day, summed up the attitude of the average Catholic:

As an American, living, working and willing to die for the welfare of my country and my countrymen, all of them, I am very happy that President Roosevelt has harmonized the voice of Pope Pius XII with his own clarion call for peace among nations and peoples.

It is opportune that, on the Vigil of the Anniversary of the Birth of the Prince of Peace, the President of the United States should take this action for peace. President Roosevelt is our leader, the leader of a free people, determined on peace for ourselves, desirous of peace for others.

We are a people who believe in, who practise and defend freedom of religion, freedom to disseminate truth, freedom of assembly, freedom of trade. It is timely that our President, intrepid enunciator of these principles and champion of them, should join with other forces for peace, with charitable and humanitarian influences.

Such an influence is the Catholic Church.

As an American I rejoice in this action of President Roosevelt.

It did not take a fortnight, however, for the four critical comments to become a roar of sectarian disapproval. Senator Josiah W. Bailey of North Carolina wrote almost immediately in the name of his constituents, protesting that the President's announcement had offended Protestant groups and did not describe Mr. Taylor's "messenger" duties. He received a characteristic reply:

DEAR JOSIAH:

I have yours of January tenth and I wish you could have been here the other day when I talked with some of the leading Baptists and Lutherans in regard to Mr. Taylor's going to the Vatican.

In the conduct of foreign relations, which is, of course, my responsibility, it is necessary for me to observe certain amenities of life. Whether we like it or not mere messenger boys, even when they are messenger boys sent by the President of the United States, eat in the servants' hall in foreign countries—and I could have hesitated to put Myron Taylor, who, after all, is a very great American, into such a position. If you were President you would not do it either.

Again, whether we like it or not there are certain titles which carry with them the right to sit at the supper table above the salt. Whether an American who is essentially acting as a messenger boy is called an Ambassador or by some other title ought to make very little practical difference in this country but makes a very great deal of difference in every other country, including, for example, Afghanistan, Tibet, London, Paris and Rome!

I am perhaps being a bit facetious but if some of my good Baptist brethren in Georgia had done a little more preaching from the pulpit against the K.K.K. in the '20s, I would have a little more genuine American respect for their Christianity!

The protest is due, of course, to a lack of appreciation of the difficulties and the niceties of conducting foreign affairs, and I am wholly charitable toward them—and, furthermore, I think the result of our conference was 100% good and that we shall hear little or nothing more of it.[10]

The President was as usual an optimist. The agitation against Mr. Taylor's appointment grew more intense with the passage of time. Adopting as their own the great principle of advertising that the public will believe anything if they hear it often enough, the hostile elements repeated again and again through every medium of communication that a mission to the Vatican violated the Constitution, implying as they said it did the union of church and state. The fact that the Constitution says nothing explicit about "the separation of church and state," and that even if it did, an exchange of diplomatic courtesies with the head of a foreign country would be quite irrelevant to the discussion of such a policy, was soon forgotten by millions of Americans.

On March 12, 1940, there was another solemn ceremony in St. Patrick's Cathedral when the pallium was conferred on Archbishop Spellman. This circular band of white wool received that day from the Holy Father was the symbol of the fullness of the episcopal power enjoyed by the Pope and shared in by archbishops, who might not exercise metropolitan jurisdiction without it. Once more there was a great gathering of prelates, priests, religious and laity as His Eminence, Dennis Cardinal Dougherty of Philadelphia, placed the pallium on the shoulders of New York's Archbishop. His Eminence of Boston was unable to attend. He had been invited to confer the pallium and had accepted, but at the last moment a letter had come from his secretary, Monsignor Minihan, saying:

I feel that if you knew the Cardinal's condition, you would want to release him from the obligation of coming to New York so early at what would seem to be great risk to his health. I know that H.E. is eager and anxious to be with you on that occasion because he was delighted to be asked and has mentioned it several times since. The doctor urged me to try to persuade H.E. to write to beg off. This I know he will not do but I am sure that if Your Excellency wrote and told him that in view of his condition, which has been brought to your attention, you wouldn't ask him to come, he would be greatly relieved in mind and deeply appreciative of your kindness.

In his solemn address delivered on the occasion, His Excellency, after making appropriate acknowledgments, devoted most of the text to the Taylor appointment.

I express gratification that President Roosevelt in his historic message of Christmas time sent his personal representative to the Holy See with the rank of an Ambassador in order that "parallel endeavors for peace and the alleviation of suffering would be assisted." . . . Full of faith and hope and warning are the words in the message of the President saying that "unless there is some trust in a divine plan, nations are without light and peoples perish." . . .

There are those who have not been in favor of this action of our President. . . . The only reason which the non-approvalists seem to have is the shibboleth of separation of church and state.

The Archbishop then briefly indicated the distinction between the ends of church and state, the historical background of American diplomatic relations with the Vatican, the temporal domain of Pius XII; and he referred to the fact that the United States maintained diplomatic relations with at least two countries, Great Britain and Japan, whose rulers were the religious leaders of their subjects.

The comments in the secular press were on the whole very complimentary, but the *Christian Century*, the *Christian Science Monitor*, the *Protestant* and others with a similar point of view on things Catholic, were severe in their criticism.[11] The *Jewish Advocate*, however, said editorially:

> The agitation in some Protestant circles to have Myron Taylor recalled from the Vatican is to be deplored. . . . We can't see any possible infringement on the constitutional guarantees for separation of church and state in this matter; to the contrary we regard it as a personal effort on the part of the President to keep informed on the European situation, to exchange opinions with others who seek peace, and to explore the roads ahead for restoration of a sane world.[12]

On April 17, 1940, the Archbishop wrote to President Roosevelt:

DEAR MR. PRESIDENT,—

I have just arrived back from another one of those memorable experiences of my life, another visit with you. I am deeply grateful. Though we were gloomier today than any day before, we must still continue praying, hoping and working. I thought all the way back to New York how well you articulate the thoughts and desires of all who still constitute the great majority of men and women of every country. Once more I thank you for the honor, the pleasure, the encouragement and inspiration you gave me and give me.

I enclose a press release from one Protestant group that seems to have a good word for us.

The press release referred to a leading editorial in the *Christian-Evangelist*, national weekly of the Disciples of Christ denomination. There it was stated that the *Christian Advocate*, the *Messenger*, the *Christian Leader*, and *Unity* had each approved the President's action.

Quoting the *United States Baptist*, which recently had predicted that the religious issue (the separation of church and state) would play a major part in the 1940 election, the editorial voiced regret that,

> . . . the opposition, unwillingly, we feel sure, is creating a vicious and un-American anti-Catholic prejudice. We fear that anti-Catholicism is still so deeply ingrained in many Protestant leaders in the United States that they are blinded with passionate prejudice and unable to see that Mr. Roosevelt has taken a tremendous forward step by mobilizing the strength of religious forces in this country in behalf of peace. The possibility of a just peace is the basic issue in this matter.[13]

After Pearl Harbor the agitation sank to a mutter, but as the end of the war drew near, there were reminders of the temporary nature of the appointment. The champions of the hostility of church and state remembered with some disquiet that Roosevelt's first letter to the Pope had said, "When the time shall come for the reestablishment of world peace on a surer foundation, it is of the utmost importance to humanity and to religion that common ideals shall have united expression," and they were convinced that even such an oblique reference to union of any kind was unconstitutional.

In January of 1945 a dying President went to Yalta. The dominance of Soviet Russia at that tragic meeting underlined for most observers the importance of uniting the moral forces of the West for the defense of what Roosevelt described in one of his happy phrases as "our way of life." It was, however, the occasion of 1600 Protestant ministers' following the lead of Kenneth Leslie, the editor of the *Protestant*, addressing a declaration to Roosevelt, Churchill, and Stalin, opposing "any attempt under whatever formula to involve the free democratic states [of which the Soviet was presumed to be one] in any deal with the Vatican state or its representatives."[14] Then, as usual, they mentioned something about "the representatives of any Protestant or Jewish establishment of religion," without indicating just which ones the world leaders would turn to for the solution of a crisis involving mankind. Archbishop Spellman made a few pointed remarks:

> It is difficult for me to believe there are 1600 ordained Ministers and religious leaders in our country who would put their names to a document offering insult to twenty-five million fellow Americans who are at least doing their share to win the war and serve and save our country; and whose religion teaches them to love their neighbor—every neighbor—even those who make it their business to sow cockle.

There were at once a dozen shouts like that of Gaetano Salvemini of the Harvard faculty:

> According to the Archbishop, there are two classes of American citizens—twenty-five million Catholics who have the right to command and one hundred million non-Catholics who have the duty to obey whenever the Pope is concerned.[15]

When on the death of Roosevelt, President Truman reappointed Myron Taylor there was a fresh outburst. "The shibboleth of church and state" had produced such mental confusion that one element called for the impeachment of our Chief Executive because he had written "Your Holiness, this is a Christian country." Deeply troubled, the Cardinal chose the Fordham commencement, June 12, 1946, as the setting for the following statement:

> From the earliest days of my priestly life, I have preached, prayed and labored to live as a true American and to live God's plan as a true Catholic, striving in charity to be all things to all men. I make no claim that anything I do or say represents the thought of twenty-five million Americans of Catholic Faith, or of more millions of Americans who are not of my faith, but I do believe that in fighting bigotry, untruth and dissension, I am a representative of the spirit of Freedom, Justice, Tolerance and Charity in which is grounded the life, the spirit and the hope

of the United States of America. I believe in and practice tolerance, for my religion teaches me to oppose even hatred with charity. But, when reunions of large groups of religious leaders, with the pretext of representing thirty or forty million Americans, sow seeds of dissension and disunion, I feel it my duty as an American and a Catholic to help defend our nation against such misrepresentations.

When President Roosevelt, an Episcopalian, reestablished for the eighth time in American history, the practice of sending a representative to the Vatican, he sought, by friendly association between the seekers of light and the seekers of peace, to overcome the man-made, war-mad forces of evil. He sought, by the cooperation of leaders in religion and leaders in government, to alleviate sufferings imposed upon peoples by godless men and nations and to help bring a lasting and just peace to mankind throughout the world. For one part of this mission he chose Myron Taylor, an Episcopalian of Quaker ancestry. And millions of Americans of all religious beliefs and their loved ones, members of the armed forces of our country, are everlastingly grateful for this mission. President Roosevelt himself repeatedly expressed his satisfaction and his gratification, and President Truman, a Baptist, on whom all this intolerant pressure is being centered, in asking Mr. Taylor to return to his post, said: "Mr. Taylor's mission was most helpful to the cause of peace and the alleviation of suffering brought about by the most awful conflict in the history of mankind and it will be, I am sure, equally useful in the future."

According to a quotation in last week's newspapers one representative of this ministerial group said: "We were given assurance that the appointment of Mr. Taylor was a temporary expedient to give the President the fullest opportunity to make his contribution to the peace. We were assured that Mr. Taylor's service as Ambassador to the Pope, might terminate at an early date, but would certainly terminate with the signing of the peace treaties." (June 6, 1946, A.P.—*World-Telegram*) . . .

Bigotry thrives on ignorance, and even intelligent people can be bigoted if they are not informed in fields of knowledge that have not come under their observation. I would like to believe that only ignorance is the reason for this illogical and harmful statement made by a man who claims representation of forty million American people. But a man of God, regardless of his sect, has a sacred duty to have knowledge of his subject before he speaks for others of his faith. However, bigots lay foundations of falsehood that have the appearance of truth, and thus they incite domestic strife, and sabotage the general welfare of our country. Surely these ministers of God know that even with the signing of peace treaties peace will be difficult to attain, yet they wish withdrawn from his mission a man who, by the statements of two Presidents, helped bring some measure of peace to this war-ridden world!

What reason then have these men of religion to make such demands

of the President of these United States? Is it the anti-Catholicism of
unhooded Klansmen sowing seeds of disunion within our treasured nation? I do not know what reply President Truman made to their impor-
tunities, but I wish to say I know some of the actions these men have
taken to promote and to provoke pressure upon the President. I know
that misrepresentative telegrams and letters have been sent to him and to
Senators and Congressmen. I know these men attempted to bolster their
intolerant attitude and acts by attempting, and in some cases succeeding,
in inciting others to join them. But I know, too, from the lips of *real*
and *great* Protestant and Jewish leaders, of their indignant refusals and
their honest abhorrence of such un-American tactics.

I know also that in addition to President Roosevelt's and President
Truman's conviction that the United States mission to the Vatican is
important to America, two men who have been candidates for the Presidency and two others who have held the high office of Secretary of State
have concurred that there is no issue of separation of church and state
involved in the accreditation of an Ambassador to the Holy See which,
according to the fears of this fearless group of defenders of America, is
"the chief objection to the appointment of Mr. Taylor." (June 6, 1946,
A.P.—*World-Telegram*) . . . .

At the present time there is need for the cooperation of all men of good
will to stave off the threatened ruin of civilization and to bring about the
reconstruction of the world on the basis of truth and justice. Pope Pius
XII not only has appealed for such cooperation but he has himself been
the outstanding example of the kind of good will towards all peoples that
is necessary if peace is to be restored among men. Our late President
Roosevelt and now President Truman have recognized this leadership of
the Holy Father and, being men of good will themselves, they have simply
sought to keep in touch with one who can help them immeasurably in
their work of peace and reconstruction. They have sent Mr. Taylor to the
Vatican as an Ambassador of good will. Only the absence of good will
can misrepresent his presence there or charge our last two Presidents with
violating the letter and the spirit of the American Constitution to keep
him there!

Meanwhile Mr. Taylor went quietly on, to the satisfaction of the White
House, accomplishing many of the varied tangibles and intangibles that
Roosevelt had had in mind, until January 18, 1950, when he offered his
resignation to President Truman in a long letter, which said in part:

When my service as Personal Representative of the President to the
Pope was undertaken at Christmas time in 1939, it was regarded by President Franklin D. Roosevelt and myself as a temporary mission, to be
terminated when circumstances permitted. At the end of hostilities, you
asked me to continue this service and I was happy to do so, again on a

temporary basis. To my great regret, personal considerations of a compelling nature make it necessary for me now to ask to be released from this service. Accordingly, I hereby tender my resignation as Personal Representative of the President of the United States of America to Pope Pius XII. . . .

In returning to private life, I wish to express my profound appreciation of the opportunity given me over the last ten years to serve under the wise leadership of two Presidents of the United States, in behalf of the cause of peace and humanity for which the free world fought the war and which it upholds today. I am also deeply gratified to have had the illuminating and inspiring experience of working for that noble cause in close cooperative association with Pope Pius XII, who exercises in Europe today, as He does in the whole world, a singularly significant and desperately needed moral leadership.[16]

His resignation was accepted with regret, and President Truman wrote to the Honorable Joseph P. Kennedy on February 3:

I have read with deep interest the thoughtful letter which you wrote on January thirty-first. It is indeed helpful to have all this background information concerning the origin of the Taylor mission from one who had so large and influential a part in the preliminary negotiations.

I am glad to tell you that His Holiness, the Pope, Mr. Taylor, the State Department and I are in complete accord as to the next step. The whole question is now under study at the State Department. Because of certain legislation which followed the discontinuance of our representation to the old Papal States, it may be necessary to seek authority from the Congress.

Meanwhile, everything is in abeyance until I have a report from the State Department. I appreciate very much your interest and may ask your counsel as things develop.

As it happened, nothing developed for eight months. By the following June, the Vatican had not yet been notified officially of the resignation and did not know whether this was an oversight or was intended to leave the impression that no change was contemplated. The Myron Taylor episode thus ended with an awkward pause.

In June, David Lawrence, the columnist, formulated the question in everyone's mind: "Could it be that President Truman is hesitating to make any decision until after the autumn Congressional elections?" It was the natural thing to suspect that he was, but around the first of September, Mr. Truman surprised the press by announcing at his news conference that he was considering the nomination of a regular diplomatic mission to the Vatican. This was taken up editorially by the Washington *Post*, which commented with approval, but added, "It is possible, perhaps even probable, that prejudice

may even at this stage of affairs be strong enough to block Senatorial confirmation of Mr. Truman's plan. . . . But this is the sort of prejudice that the
country can now ill afford."[17] It was, however, the sort that the country was
going to get. There was a warning rumble from the ministerial associations,
and the White House strategists decided on further study of the situation.

A year later, without previous notice, the President took a step which
should have flattered the proponents of Vatican recognition without unduly
frightening the adversaries. The situation was full of drama. On October 20,
a few hours before Congress was scheduled to adjourn, a member of the
White House press staff brought a four-line announcement to the press room
with the laconic remark, "This is hot." The announcement read: "Nomination sent to the Senate on October 20, 1951: General Mark W. Clark, Army
of the United States, to be Ambassador Extraordinary and Plenipotentiary of
the United States of America to the State of Vatican City." The Protestant
clergy, beginning with the President's own pastor, were enraged. Cardinal
Spellman issued the following statement:

> I am pleased at the action of President Truman in appointing an
> Ambassador to the Holy See. Certainly the United States and the Holy
> See have identical objectives of peace and it is most logical therefore
> that there should be a practical exchange of viewpoints in the search for
> this peace so devoutly desired by all peoples and especially "little
> peoples."
> I am also very pleased that President Truman has appointed to this
> post a distinguished, able and patriotic American as is General Mark
> Wayne Clark whose contributions to our country both as a military and
> civic leader have been outstanding.

Most congressmen refrained from immediate comment, and the press in
its editorials divided into three groups. The New York *Times* and a dozen
others were favorable to representation and the appointment of General
Clark. A second group agreed on the need for representation but criticized
the methods of the President. There were still others, including the influential Chicago *Tribune*, which were opposed for various reasons to sending
anybody to the Vatican. After sizing up all of them, the Brooklyn *Tablet*
remarked, "More than a few newspapers discerned the 'politics' in the situation and implied religion was being utilized to achieve a temporary, or
1952, political goal." The editorial said that the timing of the announcement
prevented "adequate consideration" and "the legality—from the point of
General Clark's availability—was rightly criticized as demonstrating a lack
of forethought." At first glance, General Clark looked like an excellent
choice. He was young, fifty-five, and like Myron Taylor an Episcopalian. He
had led the Allied forces in the capture of Rome and had remained there
to the satisfaction of the Italian people through most of the occupation.
Unfortunately, however, there was a law dating back to 1870 that prohibited

an Army officer from holding a civilian post in government, and Clark had
no intention of retiring from the Army. That precluded a recess appointment, so that before he could become ambassador, Congress would have
first to pass a bill of exemption and then a motion of approval. This would
take many months and give the opposition plenty of time to impress the
required number of congressmen.

Early in January, there was an announcement in Washington that the
White House had withdrawn General Clark's nomination at the general's
request, but Mr. Truman insisted that he still wanted an ambassador in the
Vatican. At the moment, there were five hundred ministers of the gospel at
his door protesting that "he had driven a sword deep into the heart of
Protestant America." Assembled in Constitution Hall by the American
Council of Christian Churches, they applauded the following pointed re-
marks:

> Communism is an enemy, we are all against it, but we have another
> enemy too, older, shrewder. It is Roman Catholicism and its bid for world
> power. In the United States it is Spellmanism.[18]

As the villain of the piece happened to be visiting in Rome, the international
press interviewed His Eminence at the American College on Humility
Street. One asked whether the President had consulted him on the Clark
appointment. The Cardinal answered that he had spoken only one sentence
to Mr. Truman on the subject, and that was when the President had said
that he would keep a representative at the Vatican "only until peace." His
Eminence had asked him then if he meant world peace, and when the answer was "yes," had announced that he was satisfied. An Italian correspondent requested a comment on the communist report that there was a direct
telephone line connecting Madison Avenue with the White House. The
Cardinal smiled and said that he had not talked to the President on the
phone in at least two years.

The day that His Eminence flew to Paris at the end of his visit in Rome,
January 17, L'Osservatore Romano carried an unsigned article on the front
page:

> The Vatican [it said] would like diplomatic ties with the United States,
> similar to those it has with other nations, in the interests of peace,
> but it has not and will not use pressure or "suggestions" of any sort to
> influence a decision by the United States. . . .
> The Holy See's wish in the case of diplomats accredited there is that
> they be "sent freely, according to normal criteria, according to the internal
> conditions of the country, and according to procedures established by
> law."
> "To speak therefore of Vatican 'pressures' or 'suggestions' or of other
> things of that kind is not only to invent out of whole cloth, but to invent

clumsily. We are also in a position to add that the so-called Clark case did not form the object of conversations between Pope Pius XII and Cardinal Spellman."

And there the matter has rested ever since. Mr. Truman's successor, with no pressure from Catholic America, seemed satisfied with sleeping dogs; a policy that is not likely to be changed by the present administration.

CHAPTER TWELVE

The Military Vicar

THE World Alliance for International Friendship through the Churches had sent out circulars announcing a very important meeting at Malines for August 10, 1914. The heroic Cardinal Mercier was to have presided, and hopes ran high that some way could be found at the last moment of slowing down the rumbling caissons of Europe. When the tenth of August arrived, all Belgium was in flames.

On September 3, 1939, the Pax Romana, with solemn pageantry, opened its annual congress for the first time in the western world. It had assembled in New York at the invitation of Fordham University, and its first official act was its presence at Pontifical Mass in St. Patrick's Cathedral. Archbishop Spellman was presiding. The Prince Regent of Luxembourg, with the Crown Prince Jean and the Auxiliary Bishop of Paris, was in the sanctuary. Student delegates had come from all parts of Europe to meet their fellows in a week of spiritual exercises and intellectual conferences, with the ultimate object, through international student co-operation, of international peace—the peace of Christ. Their great day came, but even on their knees before the altar in the cathedral they could hardly hear themselves pray above the rattle of sabers and the crash of guns. That very day Great Britain and France declared war on Nazi Germany.

The Archbishop on his throne listened intently to a sermon which tried to keep the viewpoint of the patient and eternal Christ. He knew that there were plenty of cynical moderns who saw a certain heartless humor in the situation of all these splendid young people who were praying and talking and playing together with the one object that their families might stop hating one another, and meanwhile were reading every day fresh evidence that European civilization was falling apart. He knew that men in the street were saying, "What good can they think they are doing? Why don't they give up and go back to whatever is left of home and get behind a machine gun like the rest? Physical strength is the only thing that matters anyway and all nations are equally immoral." He knew the cynics were wrong. He knew they were missing the point as usual; the Divine Point at which all creation comes to focus. He believed that Pax Romana made sense, and without knowing the magnitude of the part he was himself to play on a world-wide stage in the next six years, he took the simple resolution that in his work for peace he would never rest. There was no thought, of course, of static peace—the peace of the conquered and the dead. There was no dedication to the *status quo*. The peace he would seek was the peace of St. Thomas, who said, *"Pax effectus caritatis"*—"Peace is the effect of charity"; the peace of St. Augustine, who defined it as *"tranquilitas ordinis"*—"the tranquility of order"; the peace on the arms of his beloved Pius XII where he read *"Opus justitiae pax"*—"Peace is the work of justice." Again and again, in all parts of the world, before all sorts of audiences, he would return many times to his favorite theme: peace with charity, order, and justice.

The war had not come as a surprise to the Archbishop. It was more like the shock of a long-awaited death in the family. Versailles had made it possible. Hitler had made it inevitable. During the visit of Cardinal Pacelli three years before, someone at Mrs. Brady's dinner table had asked His Eminence in an offhand way about the situation in his beloved Germany. At the moment he was laughing heartily at an Americanism he had just learned, but when Germany was mentioned, a cloud passed over his face, he raised his slender expressive hands in a gesture of helplessness and answered, "Everything is lost!" By the fall of 1938 there could be no mistake. There was an influence at work in the Third Reich mightier and more sinister than greed for either place or gold. What Cardinal Faulhaber and Cardinal Innitzer were seeing through the broken windows of their palaces was the same influence that St. Jerome saw through his tears when they told him that Rome was burning, the same influence that was sweeping over North Africa when Augustine turned his face to the wall and died. For Alaric was back, and Genseric, and Attila the Hun—Attila who called himself the "scourge of God." The only difference was that the first Attila had never been a Christian, had never partaken of the sacraments. The early Huns had always been barbarians. The fact that the National Socialists were born in a civilized Fatherland, a glorious Germany rich in cultural traditions, dotted with churches whose lovely painted windows shone with German saints—this fact gave the 1938 campaign of frightfulness a very profound significance.

The next year, when Hitler on April 28 demanded the return of Danzig to Germany and a strip of land through the Polish Corridor, the new Archbishop-elect of New York was probably too busy answering letters of congratulation and winding up his affairs in Newton Center to give his full attention to the international crisis. By August 24, however, he was settled in New York and was deeply troubled to read of the Nazi nonaggression pact with Soviet Russia. Speaking the next day at the opening of the fifth national convention of the Society for the Propagation of the Faith, he recalled the heartaches of the First World War, when so many of his classmates in the Pontifical University had died in the service of their various countries. "I prayed then for deliverance," he continued, "as I pray this afternoon that God, the God of peace, will spare us, will spare us all, spare mankind, from the scourge of war and from the broken hearts of mothers, to which His Holiness Pope Pius XII referred so feelingly three days ago." Recalling the friendships among the Germans, French, Armenians, Bulgarians, Rumanians, Ruthenians, Irish, and others in his seminary class, friendships that were ended permanently through death in the war in some cases, he called on all at the meeting to unite in prayer "as the whole world totters on the brink of war, that God may spare us, that God may spare our fellowmen because, beneath the skin, the German heart, the Italian heart, the Russian heart, the French heart, the Irish heart, the Negro heart and the Oriental heart, beat as one. All of us have the same fundamental desires and rights for happiness if under God we strive for good."

A week passed. There was a wave of wishful thinking everywhere. The start of a universal war had been a matter of hours. Well, hours had passed, and now with the dreaded month of August drawing to a close, the poor common people of the world were looking up in bewilderment, afraid to smile as yet but actually hoping again for peace. They did not know that the panzer divisions were already rolling.

The war was just a month old when the Archbishop, picking up his private phone, heard a familiar voice say, "Hello. Spellman? This is Roosevelt. I have tragic news to give you. Cardinal Mundelein is dead." His Eminence had been for years a great source of strength to the President in the Middle West where social conservatism, isolationism, and hostility toward the pro-British policies of the Administration had been very troublesome. Now that he was gone, the question of his successor was of more than ecclesiastical interest. Everyone knew that the Cardinal was not alone in his enthusiasm for F.D.R. The Auxiliary Bishop of Chicago, the Most Reverend Bernard J. Sheil, was, if possible, more enthusiastic about the New Deal than his Ordinary. Here was a dynamic young man, fifty-one years of age, who had been the Cardinal's right hand as chancellor and vicar general before his consecration. He had distinguished himself as the founder of the Catholic Youth Organization and a patron of athletics, and almost equally as a champion of John L. Lewis and the CIO. In fact, it was acknowledged by friend and foe alike that he made no attempt to be neutral in labor questions, but was consistently opposed to management, particularly as it was represented by the National Association of Manufacturers. Sometimes it was intended as a compliment and sometimes not when he was identified as the only Catholic bishop in the country who talked like a labor leader. Roosevelt did not regard that reputation as a handicap; in fact he was surprised and distressed to learn that the promotion of the auxiliary bishop would not be automatic; that at the sole discretion of the Holy Father any priest in the country might be appointed to any vacant see. He was encouraged, however, by the assurance that recommendations could be made through the proper channels.

Thus it was that on one of Archbishop Spellman's many visits to the White House in connection with the possibility of diplomatic relations with the Vatican, the President managed to get around to the subject of Chicago. The liberal movement in the United States had suffered a great loss, had it not? He was convinced that there were few members of the Catholic hierarchy who fully shared Cardinal Mundelein's social views and were courageous enough to go all the way with an enlightened administration. In fact he could think of only one, Bishop Sheil. It was very important, therefore, if reaction was to be kept down, that this progressive be appointed as the next Archbishop of Chicago.

It was never easy to say "no" to Roosevelt, and particularly difficult now when his confidence had been built up by Harold L. Ickes and Frank Murphy, who assured him repeatedly that he was "on top of the world" and could go straight to the Vatican with any proposal.[1] The Archbishop, however, was silent for a moment and then tried to evade the issue, but pressed for an answer, said very slowly that he did not think it could be done. To the President's amazed question, "Why not?" he answered simply that Bishop Sheil was not considered by everyone to be the best administrator available. "What of that?" said Roosevelt. "Haven't you in every Catholic diocese a chancellor who can handle the routine of business?" The Archbishop agreed that there was such an official but added with a smile that only in New York was the chancellor able to handle the Ordinary! The President was rather hurt about the whole thing and told Harold Ickes afterward "that he could not depend upon Archbishop Spellman of New York to send any word to Rome because Spellman was too much concerned about his own red hat."[2]

When the announcement finally arrived that the Archbishop of Milwaukee, the Most Reverend Samuel A. Stritch, would be the successor of Cardinal Mundelein, Roosevelt commented to the Secretary of the Interior, who had been vigorously promoting the cause of Bishop Sheil, "Well, you and I have had a pretty severe blow today in Chicago."[3] Actually, the news was something of a relief to both of them. According to Ickes, they had feared the appointment of a bishop much less acceptable to the administration. Almost immediately, however, rumors began reaching the White House that the archbishop-elect was "out of sympathy with the program of our President and indeed on certain points in opposition to it." To silence this malicious gossip, Archbishop Stritch wrote to Archbishop Spellman, January 20, 1940: "It has not been hard to support the President for he has sought to protect the dignity of the individual and to emphasize the social nature of man. For my part I have been in full sympathy with his objectives and endorsed such of his proposals as came within the mandate of my office." The Archbishop of New York thanked him for his note, but pointed out that a troublesome clipping from the Milwaukee diocesan paper, *The Catholic Herald Citizen*, had been called to the attention of the President.

The Archbishop-elect of Chicago disclaimed responsibility for everything that appeared in the paper, saying, "The weekly is not censored before publication and from time to time carries statements which I do not approve." He then referred to all the favorable things which had previously been said about Roosevelt, and included an item published at his direction pointing out his own policy of abstaining from political action. The whole correspondence was then passed on to the White House by Archbishop Spellman, and it brought the following acknowledgment:

MY DEAR FRIEND:

Ever so many thanks for that nice letter of yours. I had hoped to get a chance to see you before leaving—but now I am off on Wednesday. I hope to see you soon after my return on March first.

I am delighted to see Archbishop Stritch's letter and I hope, too, that I can have the pleasure of seeing him in March. I am sure that he will prove a great success in the Chicago Diocese, not only along spiritual lines but also in pushing forward with the splendid social policies of the late Cardinal. Also, I hope that Bishop Sheil will receive recognition for the able assistance which he gave to my old friend.

Taking it all in all, I think things are going along all right and I have much to tell you when I see you next.

As ever, your old friend,
FRANKLIN D. ROOSEVELT

The outbreak of the war, which everyone knew would be world-wide, presented new and grave problems to Archbishop Spellman. It meant that the United States would have to call for volunteers to increase its armed forces. People even mentioned conscription. In any case, the number of Catholics in uniform would be impressive, as usual, and the Church would be called upon for a suitable staff of chaplains. In 1917, Auxiliary Bishop Patrick J. Hayes had been named Bishop Ordinary of the Army and Navy Chaplains and had remained in the post until his death. Although some suggested at the time that Washington would be a more appropriate headquarters for the military ordinariate, it was decided by the Holy Father to keep it identified with the See of New York. So on December 8, 1939, the day after the historic luncheon at the White House at which Roosevelt promised to send an ambassador to the Vatican, we find the Archbishop writing, with permission, to the President:

You will be pleased, I know, to hear that the Holy Father is going to announce in the Consistory of Monday that Father O'Hara of Notre Dame is going to be made a bishop and made a delegate to supervise the army and navy chaplains. I am to succeed Cardinal Hayes in the title of Military Vicar because it is deemed opportune for the present that the headquarters be kept in New York but Bishop O'Hara will have complete charge and authority as far as I am concerned and he will certainly have all my support. We hope to do a good job for the chaplains and with them for the welfare of the men in our country's service. . . .[4]

The preliminaries of this important development had begun in early November. It was clear that the religious problems of the Army and Navy could not be handled in any detail on the crowded desk of the Ordinary. He had to have a delegate of episcopal rank, and his choice for this important office was Father John F. O'Hara, C.S.C., since 1934 the dynamic president of Notre Dame University. Three factors had entered into the selection: Father O'Hara's personality and character—amiable, democratic, humble, energetic, brave, and spiritual; his record as prefect of religion for sixteen years, when he dealt with the souls of thousands of college men; his administrative skill and his instinct for public relations, displayed as president of a great educational institution. The only difficulty that presented itself was the fact that Father O'Hara did not want to be a bishop. He was looking forward to the end of his presidential term in 1940 and hoped to live out his active life as prefect of religion. On the morning of December 1, a letter from South Bend was on the Archbishop's desk, full of gratitude for the honor of the nomination, but firmly declining the appointment as Auxiliary Bishop of the Army and Navy. The same afternoon he stopped by Madison Avenue to say that the Apostolic Delegate had obliged him to accept. There is a brief entry in the diary: "I had a half-hour's talk with Father O'Hara before he left for the West. I am glad he accepted." One can almost see the smile of the experienced recorder.

The new auxiliary was named by Pope Pius XII Titular Bishop of Milasa and consecrated on January 15 in his beloved University Church. The consecrator was Archbishop Spellman, who lost no time in outlining the scope of his new assistant's responsibilities. At the luncheon following the ceremonies he announced:

> This is going to be one instance where the Ordinary of the Diocese will act as the Auxiliary Bishop because I enter upon my pastorate as Bishop of the Army and Navy Forces by delegating my powers to Bishop O'Hara. . . . I have complete confidence in Bishop O'Hara's carrying out everything that is expected of me.

Properly understood, the pledge was fulfilled. That he had no intention of being a figurehead, however, and of standing by idly while his assistants replaced him, was a foregone conclusion for everyone who knew the Military Vicar. Though giving his auxiliary all necessary latitude for a distinguished piece of work, he himself devoted to the armed forces a proportion of his attention that would have constituted a full-time effort for another man.

Thus began a period of anxiety for the new Military Vicar which was to last for two years and three months. Many of his fellow citizens were convinced that the United States could maintain a strict neutrality and let Europe disintegrate without risk to the New World, but no trace of this strange complacency is evident in any of the Archbishop's speeches delivered to various large and important groups at this critical period. His point of view was too close to the Holy Father's for any abstract speculation. The President was being bitterly criticized for his frank espousal of Great Britain's cause. People said we had made a mistake in saving the Empire in the First World War; that we should have listened to George Washington and avoided all foreign entanglements; that a negotiated peace with the Kaiser victorious would have been preferable anyway, avoiding, as it seemed, all the disastrous consequences of Versailles. But to the Archbishop the Second World War was not a war to save any particular country or class; it was a war to save human liberty, without which man could hardly achieve his end in life—the praise, reverence, and service of God. In the President he saw not "a scheming squire using the commonalty for his own purposes," but the Commander-in-Chief, with authority from God through the people, a knight in armor revolting eloquently against the vicious attacks of two pagan tyrants, and furthermore, a personal friend of unusual charm. It is true that, beginning in December 1940, an element of uncertainty crept into this estimate, when one of the pagan tyrants became a democrat and a bosom friend of the champion overnight, but till the end of the war the Archbishop's views of the cause and of the leader were to be substantially unchanged. Meanwhile, his interviews and his addresses continued to stress religious values rather than political.

In the beginning of this period his theme was peace, without specifying the aggressors, as when he addressed 2400 Cathedral High School girls in St. Patrick's Cathedral. "You represent," he said, "the 'White Host' that the Archdiocese of New York proudly and prayerfully elevates to the Throne of the Lord God of Hosts. Your voices are harmonized through faith and hope and love with the voices of youth all over the world praying that God in His mercy may calm this calamitous storm." Again, when prayers for world peace were offered in a meeting of 35,000 people at Fordham University, he insisted that they were praying for peace with justice for all. A little later, on a coast-to-coast hookup arranged by the Knights of Columbus, he was a little more explicit. "The peace of Christ," he said, "has never been the sepulchral silence that cries out over the ruins of the Temple of Justice. It has never been the Peace of Might over the Right. The Holy Father prays for peace and we pray with him, a peace wherein reason, justice and charity will prevail above madness, hatred and greed." At the training conference of the Chaplains Association of the Army of the United States, he referred to the Reds at home who were working in the interests of Soviet Russia when he said: "We should not be so democratic that we will allow others to come in and destroy our democracy. We must have freedom of speech, freedom of action, in fact, complete freedom, but we must draw the line when it comes to giving outsiders the freedom to destroy us." Communists and Bundists were alike condemned at Poughkeepsie, New York, where 20,000 members of the Holy Name Society heard him say: "When I went to school, freedom of speech consisted of speaking one's mind upon every subject that one wished but within laws of truth and also within the laws of justice. Now it seems to mean even permission and encouragement to those who would tear apart our country, tear down its flag, and destroy what is symbolized by that flag: our liberty and our opportunities to live lives as decent, peace-loving, law-abiding citizens." But at the Manhattan College commencement, Hitler was the target of his shaft. "We must face the inevitable conclusion that the present war is turning us back two thousand years to an era of barbarism caused by the selfishness of one individual."

As Military Vicar, the Archbishop was invited to open the National Convention of the American Legion, meeting at Boston in September 1940. The speech, which ranked with his best, reflected his attitude toward the most controversial issues of the moment. He began with an analysis of the veterans' motives when they sailed for France in the First World War, contrasting them with what were later called the real causes of the tragedy:

When the combatants put down their arms, historians took up the pen to expose the origins of the sanguinary struggle, and many causes of the war were listed in books that have been published in the last two decades. By these authors the World War was explained in its beginnings by the rivalry of nations for power and wealth, their quest for territorial expansion and imperial domination, their seeking of new markets and outlets for capital investment, their competition in exploiting backward people, motives, all of them, materialistic, sordid and ignoble.

If these were the underlying causes of the World War, you knew nothing of them. These were not the motives which stirred your minds and inspired you with the will for victory. Yours was an unselfish crusade. You fought for pure and high ideals.

The spark that flamed you into patriotic fervor was flashed by the President of the United States, and you judged it your task, whatever the sacrifice, to bring to accomplishment the ardent hopes that our Chief Executive had formulated in matchless sentences vindicating the inviolability of small nations, the security of democracy and the world rid of the threat and the actuality of war. Even though secretly mocked and later openly thwarted by foreign statesmen, these principles were sincerely proposed by President Wilson and by you as sincerely accepted.

We had learned bitter lessons from 1914 to 1919 without becoming cynics:

Despite the failure in the realization of our aims in the World War, we are still idealists. To be otherwise is impossible for Americans. But experience has taught us a measure of realism. We know now that we cannot draw the boundaries of States on the map of Europe so that race will never transgress upon race. We know now that we cannot bestow our democratic institutions on peoples opposed by natural feelings and traditions to our political system.

We know now that we cannot continue to remain unarmed when other countries have not imitated our peaceful example. We know now that it is our own pressing duty to defend ourselves, our lives, our liberties and our institutions. Interventionists, isolationists and those whose political thought lies between these two extremes all agree and must agree on the policy of national defense. . . .

It is better to have protection and not need it than to need protection and not have it. We Americans want peace and it is now evident that we must be prepared to demand it. For other peoples have wanted peace and the peace they received was the peace of death. Our good-will and the sincerity of our desire for peace have been demonstrated to the extent of sinking our own battleships. We can no longer afford to be moles who cannot see, or ostriches who will not see, for some solemn agreements are no longer sacred, and vices have become virtues and truth a synonym of falsehood. We Americans want peace and we shall prepare for peace, but not for a peace whose dilemmatic definition is slavery or death. . . .

I am a man of peace but gone is my hope of building a world safe for democracy on such foundations as the Treaty of Versailles. Vanished too is the mirage of many philanthropic optimists who cherished the vision of a world united in peace and fraternal charity beneath the aegis of science divorced from religion and around the altar of godless education. Blasted is the dream of a communistic universal brotherhood—blasted by the tell-tale rattle of machine guns and roar of cannon over Finland.

Science, knowledge, communism, these three great hopes of men, these three great deified abstractions, have wavered and failed beneath the pressure of human prejudice and selfishness and the spirit of wickedness and cruelty in high places. . . .

What is the answer? There is only one road to peace that I know of, the Highroad of Democracy, the road marked by the sign posts of the Ten Commandments, the road back to Christ and His teachings, in personal life, in national life, and in international life.

The speech was widely quoted and formed the subject of several editorials. Comment was for the most part enthusiastic, though isolationists, who were numerous and influential at the time, concluded with some apprehension that Roosevelt had found a new and powerful ally. Nor were they altogether mistaken. The strange fascination which the President seemed able to exercise almost at will had not spared the Archbishop of New York.

After one of Roosevelt's broadcasts, he learned of its effect at Madison Avenue from a handwritten note:

I sat alone and heard you tonight. All the while and for moments afterwards I sat enthralled and proud and grateful to you and for you. May God continue to bless America and our President.[5]

To this the President replied:

I need hardly tell you of my appreciation of that fine note which you wrote me on May twenty-sixth. It gives me strength and courage to have this assurance of such sympathetic understanding of my address to the nation, delivered in this time of grave anxiety.

For your expression of confidence I am more grateful than I can say and join my prayers with yours that God will continue to bless America.

Later the Archbishop forwarded some clippings to the White House, showing the Catholic response to the National Day of Prayer, and added: "I am still under the spell of my visit with you and I was pleased to read in Mrs. Roosevelt's column that my visit had a 'soothing' effect on you."[6] This is the earliest reference to the First Lady by His Excellency of New York in any of his papers.

As such communications were frequent, we are not surprised to find that the White House received a copy of the Boston speech before its delivery, with a card addressed to Miss LeHand, which read: "Dear Marguerite,— Hope the enclosed is along our President's line of thought."[7] She answered that it was. How closely it paralleled the administration's point of view appeared a month later, when Roosevelt was quoting from it very effectively. The occasion was the first drawing of numbers for Selective Service on October 29, to determine which 800,000 men would be drafted first, a delicate operation at best. Only the day before, the Commander-in-Chief had been at Fordham University in the company of the Archbishop and Governor Herbert Lehman for a formal review of the R.O.T.C., and, avoiding the emotional words "draft" and "conscription," had said to the boys on Edwards Parade: "You know that we are to take this muster—and I like to call it muster because that is an old word that goes back to Colonial days in America when every able-bodied man had an obligation to serve his community and his Country in case of attack."[8] This ingratiating term was so effective that he used it the next day on the radio, and further to ease a tense situation, read supporting messages from religious leaders of the so-called "Three Faiths." The Catholic message was considered particularly important because so many American Catholics of Irish and German ancestry were inclined to view the end of British dominance in world affairs with equanimity. For their benefit, excerpts were taken straight from the address to the American Legion convention, and in the opinion of Robert E. Sherwood the Archbishop's words were "stronger in justification of Roosevelt's position than any he himself uttered in his campaign."[9]

Two days later, a cordial letter of appreciation arrived at Madison Avenue:

MY DEAR ARCHBISHOP SPELLMAN:

Nothing could have been more heartening and reassuring, in my opinion, to the young men registered for possible service in the national defense, and to their families, than the message you gave to me to transmit to them on the occasion of the first drawing of numbers, Tuesday.

I don't have to tell you that I am deeply grateful to you, but I do want to express my belief that you must have made millions grateful—the young men themselves, their families and many, many others, not affected in the same personal way but deeply desirous in their hearts of confirmation of the sacredness of the cause in which we are all enlisted.

On the issue of conscription, there was an editorial in the *Christian Century* for November 1940 criticizing the government's policy and maintaining that Spellman gave wholehearted approval, while Buttrick and Israel, who had spoken for the Protestants and Jews respectively, indicated that theirs was a reluctant and conditional assent. The Archbishop sent the clipping to Roosevelt with a brief message: "Another characteristic editorial from the paper which was the worst against the Taylor appointment. I am glad that in their opinion I am always wrong."[10]

Meanwhile, Election Day was approaching, and strong emotions were in evidence on both sides. There were three main issues: private enterprise, intervention, and the indispensability of Roosevelt. While the Archbishop, of course, took no part in the campaign and issued no statements, his sympathies were known to be with the New Deal. He did not regard the Welfare State as "a threat to private enterprise." He did not believe that the President was "maneuvering us into an avoidable war with the object of intrenching himself in power." He had heard him promise the electorate "again and again" that their sons would not be sent into a foreign war, and he saw no reason for not believing him. But at the same time, he took the gravest possible view of the world situation. The erasing of Rotterdam, the defeat of France at Sedan, the miracle of Dunkirk, Italy's declaration of war, and the seemingly hopeless Battle of Britain demanded a type of leadership in Washington which, as far as he could see, only Roosevelt seemed to possess. In short, he was anxious to have a venerable tradition set aside and the President elected to a third term. So, as soon as the returns were in, a handwritten letter from Archbishop Spellman was dispatched to the White House, Wednesday, November 6, 1940, 1:00 A.M.:

Heartfelt congratulations and sincere prayerful good wishes and the assurances of continued faithful cooperation with you in every way possible for the welfare of our country.

My thoughts go back to four years ago today when you graciously included me in your luncheon to Cardinal Pacelli. I shall never forget that day and never cease to be grateful for that historic occasion.[11]

In acknowledgment the President wrote:

Ever so many thanks for that particularly nice letter, written after the election returns were in. I note you stayed up rather late that night!

I, too, remember very well your coming to Hyde Park with His Holiness. It was an occasion which I shall always remember.

I have just returned this morning from a week-end on the Potomac and feel considerably rested. I plan to go to Hyde Park for Thanksgiving and the week-end. I hope to have a quiet time.

On December 18, Hitler decided on the invasion of Russia and the communists in the United States had to do a *volte-face* overnight. Adjustments would be made eventually even in the highest levels of government, but not right away. The Archbishop's enthusiasm for his Commander-in-Chief continued and on December 31 there was another handwritten letter:

I wish you a most Happy New Year for our country and for yourself. I realize that real happiness is impossible in the present sad world situation; but the happiness that comes to each one who strives to do his utmost for his fellowman, as you have always done, must be your consolation.

I heard your radio address to all America and to all the world. In my opinion it was the truth; it was truly American, truly necessary and truly great. As always I remain faithful and loyal and desirous to serve and to help my Commander-in-Chief at all times and in every way.[12]

And after the inauguration he wrote again: "I have followed the ceremonies of the Inauguration over the radio and I have been thrilled by them. Your Inaugural message was superb."[13]

Thus began the fateful year of 1941. The Archbishop, who was occupied with the affairs of the archdiocese, war relief, and the military ordinariate now developing rapidly under Bishop O'Hara's direction, kept in touch with the President and grew more concerned every month with the lengthening shadows on the international front. Preaching on the second anniversary of the Holy Father's coronation, March 14, his words were grim:

Pius XII was destined by God to preside over the Church and guide the spiritual destinies of peoples at a time when all the evils condemned by preceding Pontiffs were to bring forth their most bitter fruits of cruel disastrous war, a war which is the culmination of the weakening of the foundation of the moral and religious ideas and ideals on which our civilization has been built. In the Sixteenth Century the Catholicity of Europe was shattered by the breaking up of Christian unity. The rejection of the supernatural and the inordinate glorification of human reason came in the Eighteenth and Nineteenth Centuries. And we of the Twentieth Century are witnessing the enslavement of man by the State, the cult of force, the deification of power, and the domination of right by might. Back once more the world has tumbled to the abyss of paganism and savagery. Christ and Christianity, humaneness and decency, truth and honesty have been swept aside.

A week later, five thousand friends attended a Solemn Pontifical Mass offered in St. Patrick's Cathedral for the conquered people of France. In a brief address the Archbishop recalled the many happy visits he had paid to that "fair and sweet" country, adding:

> I know the virtues of the French people and I know also they have some defects. But now we think only of their sorrows and sufferings, sorrows and sufferings undeserved. As a priest I preach love and as a priest I must be against the rulers of any land who preach hate. To preach hate is anti-religious and anti-God. In this sad, world-wide situation Catholics in every country and innocent non-Catholics, are suffering through no fault of their own. Our country is setting an example to the world in showing sympathy to all suffering peoples.

The Ambassador of France, Gaston Henry-Haye, who said that a similar Mass was being offered that day in Vichy, cabled to Marshal Petain "how magnificent and impressive the ceremony was."

Just before a state of "unlimited national emergency" was declared in Washington and the administration assumed the burden of helping Great Britain protect the convoys, the Archbishop celebrated the 150th anniversary of the Polish Constitution on May 3. Eighteen hundred Polish sympathizers who were in the cathedral were consoled to hear him say: "Humanly speaking, there seems to be no ray of hope on the blood-red horizon, but with eyes of faith we refuse to be discouraged and we look forward to the glorious day when peace and justice for all will prevail in this world. I shall never forget the anguish in the hearts of all of us when we began to realize for the first time what the future had in store for us."

The turn of the gallant British came on June 3 when, in the presence of Lord Halifax, Governor Lehman of New York, and other distinguished figures of public life, a Mass was offered for the subjects of King George VI. A cable arrived that day from Arthur Cardinal Hinsley, the Archbishop of Westminster: "In the name of all my fellow Bishops and the Catholics of Great Britain, on the occasion of the Solemn Pontifical Mass for the Suffering People of Great Britain at which Your Excellency is presiding, I express profound gratitude for the generous charity of America for war sufferers. God reward you all."

Meanwhile, the United States, like the protagonist in a Greek tragedy, was advancing step by step toward the dreaded abyss. Only a short year before, the Archbishop had been one of fourteen hundred guests to attend a dinner held on the eve of the Japan Day ceremonies at the New York World's Fair. Former Governor Alfred E. Smith, in a prophetic mood, had disclosed that the Japanese Building would not be torn down with the others at the close of the exposition, but would remain forever "an expression of good will and a symbol of lasting friendship." His Excellency Kensuke Horinouchi had assured those present, with all the sincerity of an ambassador, that Japan intended to stay out of the European War and "to keep the war out of Asia." Now, in July 1941, Japan was enraged by the passage of the Export Control Act and the freezing of her assets in this country. At the same time, Germany could watch with growing alarm the replacement of the British garrison in Iceland by Americans. Early in August, somewhere at sea, Roosevelt and Churchill, who could always swash a buckle with the best of them, met for a session that both must have relished keenly. These two masters of nineteenth-century rhetoric were to compose the Atlantic Charter in an atmosphere of high adventure and publish it on August 14. It throbbed on the airways and sparkled in the headlines for just a matter of months before taking its place beside the forgotten Fourteen Points of Woodrow Wilson. The meeting had not been wasted, however, for the Prime Minister could tell Parliament on his return that Roosevelt was ready to fight without being attacked. By October the President announced to the world: "We have cleared our decks and taken our battle stations!" but he should have added the words "rhetorically speaking," for on December 7 the American people discovered to their horror that we had in fact done neither.

Almost before the news of Pearl Harbor had reached the sidewalks, a businesslike statement was issued at Madison Avenue:

> As Archbishop of New York, I place all our resources, hospitals, institutions and personnel at the disposition of the Government. As Bishop in charge of the Catholic priests in the Army and Navy I can state that there are five hundred chaplains on duty at the present time. They have been an important factor in the building of the morale of our soldiers and sailors. They will be with them wherever they go and whatever they do. As an American and one of twenty-five million Catholic Americans I follow the identically glorious traditions of my country and my religion.

Soon after Christmas, His Excellency addressed the American people by radio, expressing a conviction that their cause was just and pointing out the role that religion should play in time of war.

> Americans, we have prayed for peace with justice. We shall continue to pray, but peace with justice can now come only through victory. Is that victory certain? No, it is not certain, but the sacrifice of 3000 American lives on December 7 has made victory more probable than it was before that infamous attack, for it has made America one.

The chief responsibility for victory is still on our soldiers, sailors, Marines and flying men, but essential responsibility is also on all the rest of us. Sleeping, wrangling America has awakened and is determined. Perhaps we are not yet fully awakened to the realization of the price we must pay in blood, tears and sweat, for in the words of Henry Luce, "The high resolve is yet to come to us that it would be better to leave America a heap of smoking stones than surrender it to the mechanized medievalism which is the Mikado or to the Anti-Christ which is Hitler."

We have been a generous people. We wanted peace, and we sank our battleships to prove it. We wanted friendship with the world and with Japan, and to prove it we made the armor plate for Japan's warships, furnished the oil to drive their engines and the gasoline to bring their planes to bomb us.

We shall not forget the blood that has been spilt, but we shall forget the irremediable past and the 15-month loss of our 24,000,000 man days of defense effort and the 10,000 unproduced planes. We shall forget everything but our honored dead and peace with justice after victory.

It is not alone our fighting men who must sacrifice. It is all of us together. All our man-power, military, industrial and agricultural, our resources and our resourcefulness fused together by our moral power, will not fail, cannot fail to bring us victory.

What will it profit us, however, to emerge victorious over attacks from abroad if at the same time we do not preserve the ideals of democracy at home and their indispensable supports of religion and morality? The answer is: It will profit us nothing, because democracy without the props of religion and morality collapses into anarchy and tyranny.

The happiness of the individual and the well-being of the nation may be destroyed not alone by foreign enemies but also by the lack of practical religious living and a fundamental morality based on the Ten Commandments. We have this faith in God expressed in the Magna Charta of our liberties and reaffirmed through our history.

"Religion," said our Commander-in-Chief, President Roosevelt, "is the source of democracy and of international good faith." The nation is composed of individuals, and the character of the national life of democracies, as long as they remain democracies, is determined by the common denominator of the moral and physical qualities of its citizens. Thus it is essential that men and women in the service of the country, not alone in the armed forces but in all branches of the Government, and men, women and children in civil life think of God and obey the laws of God.

The abandonment of Christ and His teachings, in personal life, in social life, in civic life and in international life, has brought us to the end of the world we have known. The way back to peace with justice through victory is in the identical order—personal righteousness, social decency, civic morality and international probity. . . .

Morale means courage, readiness to serve, high purpose. Morals is the sense of right and wrong, divinely taught, which makes a man strong in his duty to God, and morale makes him strong in his duty to country. Morals and morale blended together are the soul of our national life.

Religion and patriotism support and strengthen each other. Without religion and moral standards, patriotism is but a cloak. With religion and its moral standards, patriotism has a foundation, a strength and a permanence which comes from God. American morale draws its strength not alone from natural courage, but also from a just cause and a just God.

We know the facts. We face a situation forced on us. We wanted no land. We committed no economic wrong. We suppressed no civil liberties.

Our free press and free radio bring us the words of the leaders of the powers of darkness ranged against us, ofttimes false and sometimes ridiculous. The oppressed, suffering, deluded and eventually rebellious, defeated people of the nations ranged against us know nothing of the attitude of the United States except that they must know in their hearts that America is on the level and on the square. I do not think their leaders can squelch that thought, nor do I think that they can suppress the knowledge that America has been invariably victorious. And we shall be victorious again, cost what it may in blood, tears and sweat.

His views on America's purpose in entering the war were expressed on a coast-to-coast hookup March 23. The day before, he wrote to one of the President's secretaries, Grace Tully:

DEAR GRACE,—
Sorry not to have seen you last week. It was grand seeing the President. He may have a moment to glance over my radio talk tonight with my almost invariable reference to him in every talk that I give. This time I put him in company with a good Massachusetts Republican, President Coolidge.[14]

"Americans," he said, "are fighting for their God-given rights and every real American knows that he must fight, and, if necessary, die, for the principles that have had their noblest exemplification in history in the Government of the United States. I hold no enmity toward any people. Hatred has no place in my life. I love all men as brothers in Christ. But I am one of 130,000,000 Americans and millions and millions of other persons who are at war against any system of government which would destroy the things we cherish most. Franklin D. Roosevelt, more often than any other President, repeatedly has emphasized the truth that men who fulfill their duties to God are the pillars of a nation at war or in peace." The Archbishop warned that in the name of freedom we must not condone "false freedoms," the freedom to be cruel, the freedom to be obscene, the freedom to steal, and the freedom to spread disease, or America's liberty would succumb to tyranny. The war, he declared, was being fought for "our democratic way of life."

The following month he was still more specific in a sermon entitled "Two Victories," which was delivered in St. Patrick's Cathedral and on "The Church of the Air." It is full of the high idealism and simple faith in the rulers of the earth that mark the thinking of all patriots at the beginning of every war. There was no way in which he could have foreseen the appalling course of events that followed victory when he said:

> I do not think that I need to remind you that at present we are engaged in this war to maintain our existence. Nor do I need to remind you that charity tempered by justice and the merciful defense of the helpless millions of numerous enslaved nations constitute a Christian motivation for war. It is a motive that impels us to move onward to victory, and a victory, mark you well, that shall not have within itself the seeds of its own defeat. These seeds, hatred and revenge, bequeath to future generations only a heritage of all the evils that have followed in the wake of war: ill-will, distrust, ignorance, distortion of historical facts, selfishness, greed, cruelty and savagery. With such camp-followers of war, there can be no real victory, no real or final peace. . . .

> We of America fight today not only for human values, but also for those that are divine. It is true that our past has not been unsullied. In the pursuit of our inalienable rights to "life, liberty and the pursuit of happiness," we have certainly exaggerated the "pursuit of happiness" and distorted its meaning. Our lives at times have been selfish lives and some interpretations of liberty have unjustly encroached on the liberty of others. But despite our weaknesses and our mistakes, America's contemporary position for international rectitude, for international justice, for international generosity, is unparalleled in history. From her Founding Fathers, America received a human charter that has a divine sanction and implies a divine destiny. It is a consecrated America which we wish to preserve upon this earth, for which we fight and to which we give our consecrated service. We place our patriotism on the strong base of religion. For us the love of country is not a house built upon the shifting sands of revolutionary change, but a house built upon a rock which is God. . . .

> As an American I proclaim the common necessity of the defense of our beloved country. I shall never see her enslaved. I shall never see the sacred heritage of liberty torn from her, the democratic forms of government shorn from her. As a Catholic Priest, I point out the best way that I know to preserve our country strong and free, as the fundamental basis of all victory: the upbuilding of the citizen as an individual, a man who knows God and keeps God's Commandments. This is the best and essential contribution that each of us can make to the re-establishment of

peace and to the liberties of all peoples under all forms of government compatible with Christian life.

Summer in New York is a quiet time, when the Middle West moves in for excitement and the natives move out for the same purpose. After an amazing round of commencements, the Ordinary and his assistants can usually count on a little change of pace and even a brief vacation. So this year on July 30, Archbishop Spellman, by way of a rest, decided to visit all the chaplains in Alaska. A letter to the naval commandant at Seattle from Bishop O'Hara said that he expected to make the most of all the exigencies and obstacles of a fortified area "and will accept discomfort, broken schedules and war hazards as the order of the day. He also wishes to pay for his own transportation throughout."

Leaving Seattle then on August 2; traveling entirely by air; sleeping in cheap hotels, barracks, or a poor missionary's quarters; eating what, when, and where he could (at Galena his "supper consisted of a sandwich and a can of pineapple juice on top of a gasoline barrel"), he managed to visit in two weeks Prince George, Fort St. John, Whitehorse, Fairbanks, Galena, Nome, Anchorage, Kodiak, Cold Bay, Dutch Harbor, Unalaska, and Annette Island. Scattered over this vast area were fourteen Catholic chaplains. Most of them were completely surprised when he walked in on their loneliness and some asked, "Where did you come from, Father?" With some he could spend only a few hours, as all plans were subject to irregular and infrequent flights; with some he spent a day or two. Everywhere he was the seasoned tourist, writing letters full of scenery and statistics; everywhere the priest, observing the conditions of the little mission churches and the zeal and hardships of their pastors; but always and everywhere the Military Vicar, delighted with the efficiency, devotion, and success of the chaplains. One of the problems he met in the person of an unco-operative ranking chaplain was to arise so frequently in the next four years that it might be outlined here in some detail.

The post chaplain at Anchorage, Major Patrick J. Gleason, and the head chaplain, Colonel X, who is a Protestant, brought me to see General Buckner who is the Commander of all the Alaskan Defense Forces. General Buckner was very cordial and very kind. Colonel X started to do all the talking, and said that it would come up that I thought there were not enough Catholic chaplains in Alaska, and that of course there had to be Protestant chaplains in every place where the majority of men were Protestant, and if there were not more than 1200 men there could be only one chaplain, and, this one would, of course, have to be a Protestant. The second question that will come up, he said, was the term auxiliary chaplain to which he objected. At this point in the conversation I injected that I was able to bring up my own points, and I said that I did not admit that if the majority of a number of men were Protestant that, therefore, there should be no Catholic priest, because if that were the case, and the definition of a Protestant was a person who was not a Catholic, we would have very few Catholic chaplains. On the other hand, if the definition of a Protestant was one who attended Protestant services, and a definition of a Catholic was one who attended Catholic services, we would have few Protestant chaplains, and I did not think that would be fair.

In regard to the second point, I said that the term auxiliary chaplain was not intended to be a military designation in the strict sense, but an ecclesiastical title, because I said any Catholic priest cannot apply to become a chaplain in the Army without ecclesiastical sponsorship. In other words, a person desiring to be a chaplain needs, first the approval of his own Bishop, and then the application goes through the Military Ordinariate which endorses his application to the War Department. This was the reason, I added, why the character of the Catholic chaplains is of such an excellent type, because no one can apply for a chaplaincy with the endorsement of his Postmaster and a couple of citizens. I then explained that when there were not enough military chaplains to care for the Catholics in the Armed Services, that missionaries in those areas, such as Alaska, were called on to minister to the spiritual needs of these men. In these cases such missionaries enjoyed the designation of auxiliary chaplain. These explanations were perfectly clear to General Buckner to the chagrin of Colonel X.

The third thing that Colonel X wished to bring up was that I should be advised from going farther to the westward on this visitation. I explained to General Buckner that I would like to go to every post where the soldiers and chaplains were stationed, and for that reason I would like to visit the outposts on the Aleutian Islands, if it were agreeable to him. The General consented, and Colonel X was silenced.

Having set his heart on it, it was a foregone conclusion that Archbishop Spellman would get to every post where the soldiers and the chaplains had to go. Some of these places were apparently little sought after in the Army. There was, for example, an amusing publication in Kodiak, *What to Do in Case of Sunshine*, putting that commonest of blessings in a class with an air raid. From Dutch Harbor he wrote:

I dropped into the town of Unalaska, and went up the mountain to see some of the coast defenses, meeting two officers, Captain Martin and Captain Low from San Francisco, who were very easy to meet and to know. Wishing to say something pleasant and at the same time innocuous, I observed that this was wonderful air on top of the mountain. Captain Martin clutched his cigar from his mouth, turned around to face me squarely, and with an expression of earnestness far in excess of the requirements of the context said, "You can have it."

On his way back to Seattle, the trip to Annette Island from Sitka was, he wrote, "the worst trip I ever had by air and the most dangerous." It was in an Army transport plane for parachute troops, carrying a crew of three and nine pilots returning to the States. The Archbishop of New York was the only civilian.

It was a land plane flying over water between mountains, skimming the water sometimes no higher than fifty feet; skimming trees, barely avoiding mountains which loomed up suddenly through the stormy weather, and all the pilots in the plane were doing the equivalent of putting on the brakes in an automobile trying to help the pilot at the controls. So we were all happy when we landed at Annette Island.

And he was happy to be home in New York again, not only because of a safe return, but in the assurance that "his trip to Alaska had been the right thing." He remembered his parting with Father John McHugh in Nome:

When he bade goodbye at the airport he grasped my hand, thanked me for coming, and said, "I feel like a new man." I felt a little like an old man myself, and as a matter of fact, if I were much older I would not have been able to make the trip.

As it was, he was fresh enough to spend the next two weeks in an official visitation of Southwestern United States. This meant that from New York to New York he traveled 18,000 miles, interviewing 300 Catholic chaplains in 92 Army posts and Navy stations; an excellent dress rehearsal for the work that lay before him in other parts of the world.

His first day back on Madison Avenue offered an interesting study in delegation. On leaving for Alaska, he had instructed Auxiliary Bishop McIntyre to act in his absence with finality. "You can do everything," he told him, "but sell the Cathedral." Now on his return, His Excellency found that twelve priests of the diocese had been put on the chaplains list and that one of them, the Reverend John J. Flynn, was a pastor. That he did not approve of and explained with regret to Father Flynn that a mistake had been made. The pastor said Bishop McIntyre had approved his request. The Archbishop paused, and then said: "You're right. I gave him full authority. Go ahead and God bless you."

The presence of the Military Vicar had brought encouragement everywhere to men in the service who were just as disturbed as their families back home by a year of almost unbroken disaster. Events had been so difficult to understand. The Stars and Stripes were not supposed to retreat. The Armed Forces of the United States were more than a match for the rest of the world! Every good American knew that the Axis would collapse as soon as our boys entered the war. And yet from the beginning of January until Rommel finally lost the battle of supply, the Germans were calling the tune in North Africa, the Russians were retreating all along the line, and in the

Pacific area our own forces, the invincible Americans, were fighting with their backs to the wall. It was not possible that the great MacArthur had left Bataan, that Corregidor had surrendered, that Japan had driven us out of the Philippines. There had been, of course, a few rays of light in the gloom. Colonel James H. Doolittle had gotten through to Tokyo and Nagoya. The Coral Sea and Midway had spelled glory enough and to spare for the American Navy, but in the main the picture was one of defeat. While the Archbishop was spreading a spirit of hope in Alaska, news reached him of the tragic attempt of the Allies to land at Dieppe and of the savage resistance being offered by Japan at Guadalcanal. It was not until his return to New York that he read of the first real change in our fortunes. The Russians, aided as usual by General Winter, gained the initiative at Stalingrad in September, and about a month later, the Americans landed in French North Africa, and in the Pacific at Guadalcanal claimed a brilliant and decisive naval victory. He felt the end of the war could now be seen, but very far in the distance and not with absolute certainty.

As part of his long-range planning, the Archbishop on December 6 enlarged the National Catholic Community Center Building, which he had opened sixteen months before at 17 East Fifty-first Street, directly opposite the cathedral. A canteen which was added in the basement of the adjoining Cathedral College was destined to serve for the next three years some 630,-000 members of the armed forces. The Center itself was to continue after the closing of the canteen until the deactivation of the U.S.O. in 1947, offering its facilities in the intervening years to well over two million men.

Meanwhile the Military Vicar reported early in September to his Commander-in-Chief, who was delighted with the results of the tour in Alaska and the Aleutians. His visit to the White House coincided with the visit of the Prime Minister of Great Britain and Mrs. Churchill. Averell Harriman was the fourth guest at dinner.

The year 1943 opened auspiciously with the conference at Casablanca in French Morocco. Roosevelt and Churchill with their military staffs, together with General Henri Giraud and General Charles de Gaulle, met primarily to thrash out the difficult issue of French leadership. Almost incidentally, the invasion of Sicily was agreed upon and the postponement of the invasion of France, while the President's colorful pronouncement on unconditional surrender was not even on the agenda. Subsequent history, however, has altered the relative importance of these three items, writing many chapters on the dire results of Roosevelt's sudden inspiration. It came as a shock to the Archbishop, but he was able to write in 1945:

> We talked for an hour and during our conversation we discussed the phrase "unconditional surrender." The President said that its meaning had been misinterpreted and distorted and he told me the familiar story of the origin of the phrase. It was, President Roosevelt explained, the expres-

sion that General Grant had used when General Lee asked him for terms of surrender. When Grant gave his ultimatum to Lee, the armies of the South were short of provisions; but it was still possible for them to continue fighting, as General Lee could have retreated into Carolina and there joined the armies of General Johnston. When Lee heard the phrase "unconditional surrender," he is reported to have said: "But my men, what about them? What about their horses? They own their horses and they will need them for work on the farms." "We shall talk about that later," said General Grant, "but now, unconditional surrender." Lee capitulated, and Grant gave him more generous terms than he expected, and the Southerners were permitted to keep their horses and side arms and were given provisions.

However, "unconditional surrender," in its modern interpretation, means something very different, both here and abroad. One nation that America is fighting had for her objective the domination of the world and the enslavement of mankind, and in her dictionary "unconditional surrender" means "annihilation." Germany's desperate propagandists have planted and cultivated in the minds of her people the belief that the Allies intend a Carthaginian peace and that Germany, like Carthage, will be destroyed. Thus the fanatical German leaders incited their people to fight to the last man and woman; to fight to the last bullet, and every foot of the way. For people who have no hope of life prefer to die fighting and killing others instead of being merely killed themselves.

The President explained that we had no intention of destroying the German nation and of killing or enslaving eighty million German people, and he left no doubt in my mind that he realized America's responsibility, as a victor nation, for an enduring world peace. The end we seek and the terms on which we rightly insist, he said, are those which will eliminate the possibility of Germany ever again becoming an aggressor nation. The Germans designing total victory must now endure total defeat![15]

It was only when the Morgenthau plan for the annihilation of Germany started to take shape that doubts formed in the Archbishop's mind.

CHAPTER THIRTEEN

The Armed Forces

PREVIOUS to his own departure for Casablanca in January 1943, Roosevelt had suggested that the Archbishop, who was anxious to visit the overseas fronts, should plan to leave for Europe during the first week of February. On the President's return to the White House after the historic conference in North Africa, the following handwritten note from Madison Avenue was awaiting him:

> Welcome home! And thanks be to God for His protection of you, for His guidance to you! It was a wonderful thing in concept and in results. I am all ready to go myself as soon as you can conveniently have the time to receive me and give me a word or two of guidance.
>
> Judge Patterson has been kindness itself; I have my passport and all my inoculations![1]

The next day there was a telegram from Major General Edwin M. Watson, fixing February 4 at eleven-thirty for a farewell conference in Washington. The Archbishop wrote to some friends describing the occasion and the three or four hectic days that followed:

> The President looked well and was, as usual, extremely cordial and interesting. He told me some of the details of his trip, including his efforts to get General de Gaulle to come to Africa to meet General Giraud and of his repeated efforts to get them to act in friendly collaboration for the welfare of France. . . .
>
> The President made suggestions in regard to the people that I should visit and gave me letters to Generalissimo Chiang Kai-shek, Ambassador Phillips, General Eisenhower and the American Commanders in other war areas.
>
> Each time I see the President, I am more and more impressed with his stature as a great man, one of the great men of history and I hope and pray that he will lead this country on the road to victory, peace and prosperity. . . .
>
> I had luncheon with Colonel R. W. Ireland, who has arranged the air priorities for me. He had letters for me from General George, introducing me to all the Air Corps Commanders. The form was as follows:

"1. By personal direction of the President of the United States, Archbishop Francis J. Spellman, in his capacity as Military Vicar of the Armed Forces of the Army and Navy, is making a trip over the routes of the Air Transport Command.

"2. The President has requested that Priority Class I for air transportation be accorded to Archbishop Spellman and that his itinerary be arranged from point to point as he desires.

"3. All facilities of the Air Transport Command and courtesies of the Staff should be extended to Archbishop Spellman in order that his trip may be successful."

. . . With Colonel Ireland I went to call on the Under-Secretary of War, Judge Robert Patterson. I had already met him previously with Under-Secretary of the Navy, James Forrestal. They were personally directed by the President to make arrangements for my travel. Also on this occasion, I had the honor and pleasure of meeting, for the first time, Secretary of State Cordell Hull. . . .

Judge Patterson was most insistent on designating an American officer to accompany me at all times on my journey to make my path easy. I told him, however, that while deeply appreciating the courtesy, still I felt it was unnecessary since I had letters to various persons in the places which I intended to visit and also because I would feel embarrassed and disturbed if I had an officer solely at my service. . . . Judge Patterson saw my point of view and also agreed to permit me to buy my passage on the plane so that if anyone were asked about this aspect of the journey, the response could be made that I was paying my own expenses insofar as it was possible. Judge Patterson could not have been kinder and he had already prepared for me letters of introduction to Major General George Patton, Lieutenant General Dwight Eisenhower, Lieutenant General Frank M. Andrews, Major General Lewis H. Brereton, Lieutenant General Joseph W. Stilwell and Brigadier General John Bissell. . . .

I am certainly well fortified with letters!

I then went to the Apostolic Delegation and requested that a code telegram be sent to Rome informing His Holiness that I was leaving on Monday for Lisbon, Portugal, thence to visit the British Isles and Africa.

Then I returned to New York.

I have secured concentrated foods and vitamins so that I will not be any burden on any country I visit.

On Saturday morning, February 6th, I went to Boston and told Bishop Cushing of my intention. We had a fine talk and as usual, he approved of me and my acts.

I arranged for a family reunion, held at the Copley-Plaza, and I told my brothers and sisters of my plans. I told my father I was to be away but did not tell him my destination. It was a most happy occasion, after which I went with Bishop Cushing's chauffeur and my two sisters to Framingham to see my aunt in the Convent. On the way we stopped to see Miss Marguerite LeHand, President Roosevelt's secretary. . . . After a short but pleasant visit with Sister Philomena, we returned to Boston in time to meet Bishop Donahue, Bishop O'Hara, Bishop Cushing, Bishop McIntyre and Bishop McCarty who had come to attend the Chaplains' Dinner. . . . It was a most enjoyable evening.

Naturally, I said nothing of my immediate plans and intentions as I hope to be well on my way before it becomes publicly known. We all returned to New York on the midnight train.

I celebrated the nine o'clock Mass today in the cathedral for the members of the Newman Club Federation.

Shortly after Mass, I received a telephone call from the Apostolic Delegation saying that they were in receipt of a cablegram from the Holy See asking if it would be possible for me to prolong my visit so that I could visit Vatican City. I immediately contacted Grace Tully, who telephoned back a few hours later to say that the President was sending a memorandum to the Secretary of State to the effect that after my journey had been arranged, the Holy Father manifested a desire to see me. This memorandum also asked the Secretary of State to communicate with the Ambassador of the United States to Spain, Carlton J. H. Hayes, to make the arrangements, if the Italian Government permitted it, for me to go through belligerent territory to Vatican City. The President in his memorandum stated that Italy said after the last visit of Myron C. Taylor that it would not permit this to happen again, but the President thought that since my visit was purely on Church matters, the Italian Government might consent. I observed that I felt this was the responsibility of the Holy See and I contacted the Apostolic Delegation to tell them that they might inform the Vatican that from the part of the Government of the United States and from my own part there was no objection and if the Italian Government consented, the American Ambassador in Madrid might be notified.

. . . The Archdiocese of New York is in the charge of its vicar general, the Right Reverend Monsignor Joseph P. Donahue, P.A., who has in every way all the authority which I am empowered to give him. I have properly informed Bishop Donahue and Bishop McIntyre of this fact and of my prospective absence from the diocese. I have also informed Bishop O'Hara, Bishop McCarty and Monsignor Casey.

I am ready to go and I ask your prayers and assure you of a remembrance in mine. While I have had many great and wonderful journeys in the past, I realize that this is different in many ways and whatever the outcome, will be the outstanding experience of my life.

The night before his flight he penned a brief message to F.D.R.:

I am ready to go and this is my last letter before I leave. It is a letter of heartfelt thanks to you for *everything*; and the assurance on my journey of constant prayers for your welfare which is synonymous with the welfare of our country.[2]

On February 9 the Archbishop said good-by at the airport to Bishop O'Hara, Bishop McIntyre, and Monsignor Casey, his secretary. An air of uncertainty surrounded the whole adventure. He had no way of knowing that it would be twenty-four weeks before he would see New York again and that in the meantime he would travel 46,000 miles. He did not know even the extent of his itinerary, which would take him from New York to Portugal, Spain, Vatican City, Gibraltar, French Morocco, Algeria, England, Ireland, Scotland, Libya, Malta, Tunisia, Egypt, Palestine, Transjordan, Syria, Lebanon, Turkey, Iraq, Iran, Eritrea, Ethiopia, Anglo-Egyptian Sudan, Uganda, Kenya, Tanganyika, Madagascar, Mauritius, Mozambique, Union of South Africa, Belgian Congo, Rhodesia, French Equatorial Africa, Nigeria, Gold Coast, Ascension Island, Brazil, British Guiana, Puerto Rico, and back to New York.

It was not the air of uncertainty, however, that attracted the attention of the world press, but the air of mystery. It was the Germans who first broke the news of the trip while the traveler was flying from Lisbon to Madrid. What was he up to? It was unbelievable that the Military Vicar was going to perform the duties of a military vicar. Another possible motive was much more likely. It was understood on excellent authority that Roosevelt had entrusted him with power to open peace negotiations with the Axis, especially with Italy. He was going to Moscow to arrange a concordat between the Soviet and the Holy See. He was going to insure the victory of Russia by taking Finland out of the war. He was going to arrange matters with the allied governments so that the Holy Father would preside at the peace conference. Most picturesque of all, he was going to rescue the Pope and spirit him off to Brazil.

In Washington, President Roosevelt told a press conference the primary objective of Archbishop Spellman's trip to Europe was to visit military and naval units. Asked whether the Archbishop was on a mission for him or carrying any message to the Vatican, the President said he could not comment, but that he had seen the Archbishop before his departure. That was enough. The New York prelate was making ideological preparations for the third front. As he traveled, the rumors outran him. He had gone to Spain to persuade Franco on the subject of neutrality. He had unsuccessfully tried to have a meeting with Leon Bellard, French ambassador to the Vatican State. He had "maneuvered indirectly with the Rumanian, Hungarian and Finnish Ministers to the Vatican." He had unsuccessfully tried to have a talk with Bishop Mazzoli, papal envoy to Sofia, to sound out the antiwar spirit in Bulgaria. He had tried to improve Allied relations with Turkey. As the *Mainichi* observed in Tokyo with classic restraint: "It can be seen that Spellman was no longer a mere Catholic priest when he visited the Vatican, providing his purpose was anywhere near what has been conjectured."

If reliable reporters were a trifle excited, the professional anti-Catholics were hysterical. The *Nation* saw "a new axis being formed. It runs from Washington to Rome by way of Madrid. . . . The Vatican has become the rallying point of the reactionaries of the Continent, pro-Hitler and anti-Hitler alike."[3] The *New Republic* concluded: "Preserving from disruption under anti-Fascist disguise the clerical-Fascist regime in Italy if Mussolini has to decamp—this appears to be the plan of Vatican-British-American diplomacy."[4] The *Protestant* accused *Time* magazine of smoke-screening "the devious flittings of the dainty servant of Vatican intrigue" and asked two questions that were interesting in view of the fact that the Archbishop came in no contact with the enemy: "1) Under what democratic authority does a soldier-priest go to talk to the enemy, and 2) what does he say to the enemy and what does he hear from the enemy?"[5]

This anxiety found an echo in London, where on St. Patrick's Day, in the House of Lords, Josiah Wedgwood, of the pottery family, rose to speak on "The Present Situation of the War in North Africa" and spent the best part of an hour denouncing Archbishop Spellman and the Catholic Church. The most noble lords who were present listened in unaccustomed silence. There was not one "Hear! Hear!" until young Lord Cranborne, the Privy Seal, rose to say in a tired English voice that he congratulated Wedgwood on his success in offending such an extraordinary number of people by one speech.

Undismayed by the excitement he was causing, "the dainty servant of Vatican intrigue" was entering on six months of constant work and travel under the most trying conditions. "Always going places and always leaving them, always meeting people and always saying goodbye!" There were jeeps and planes, trains and boats, all kinds of weather, all kinds of food, and all kinds of human beings. His own reflections on the events and personalities around him were set down on his return in a book, *Action This Day*, which was serialized in *Collier's* before book publication and afterward syndicated by a newspaper chain. Resisting the temptation to quote generously from its pages, the story can perhaps be told from a different angle by placing together the impressions he made on others.

After a pleasant stopover in Portugal, where he met his old professor of North American College days, the Most Reverend Pietro Ciriaci, then Archbishop and nuncio at Lisbon and now Cardinal Prefect of the Congregation of the Council, the Military Vicar flew on to Madrid for his first important interview. Ambassador Carlton J. H. Hayes had been instructed by the State Department to show him every attention, in accordance with the following memorandum to Cordell Hull from the President:

Archbishop Spellman is about to leave by plane for Lisbon to inspect our troops in North Africa, and to go on to the Near East and India and China. He is, as you know, the Chaplain Bishop of the Army and Navy. He got word from the Vatican that the Pope hopes he will come to Rome from Lisbon and Madrid. I also hope he can do this if it can be arranged.

I suggest an immediate telegram to Hayes to see whether this can be worked out through the Papal Nuncio in Madrid. I take it it means crossing German-occupied France and also Italy. After Myron Taylor's visit it was intimated that the Italians would never allow it again but in view of the fact that this is wholly a church matter they might do so.

Will you wire Hayes to tell him that Spellman will see him very shortly in Madrid and to do what he can. Isn't this the best approach?[6]

The ambassador, who met the distinguished visitor at the airport in Madrid and had him as a house guest throughout his stay in Spain, wrote later:

He stood on no ceremony, and talked freely with many Spanish Catholics about the Church in America and its determined opposition to Nazism and support of our war effort. He was received, with special cordiality, by the Foreign Minister and by prominent ecclesiastics, including the Nuncio, the Spanish Primate (Archbishop of Toledo), the Bishops of Madrid and Barcelona, and Cardinal Segura of Sevilla, all of whom were naturally critical of Nazi doctrines and favorably disposed toward us. Finally, General Franco himself sent for Archbishop Spellman, and their conversation at the Pardo lasted two hours.

According to the report I had of this conversation, the Caudillo dwelt on much the same topics with the Archbishop in February, 1943, as he had with Mr. Myron Taylor in September, 1942: the menace of Communism, the necessity of suppressing it by force, the regrettable conflict between civilized Britain and Germany when they should be united against barbarous Russia, the theory of the two wars (the one in Europe and the other in the Pacific), the destructiveness of aerial warfare, the disastrous effects of a long war, the desirability of a negotiated peace. The Archbishop apparently argued the points, and drew from the Caudillo an admission that Germany couldn't possibly win the war, though he suspected no one would really win it except Russia.[7]

In the United States, where most of the non-Catholic public had followed the liberal press in backing the Leftists during the Spanish Civil War, the sentiment against Franco was very strong. The man in the street did not realize how much the Spaniard's friendly neutrality would mean to us in the North African campaign and was critical of the new attitude of toleration toward the Caudillo adopted by Churchill and Roosevelt. A good deal of unfavorable comment, therefore, followed the Archbishop's visit to the

Pardo, and when he described it later in *Collier's*, there were angry head-lines even in journals slightly to the right of *P. M.*

The trip to Vatican City by way of Barcelona and over the often traveled Mediterranean was full of nostalgia for one who had not seen the dome of St. Peter's for ten long years. Appropriately enough he was met by Enrico Galeazzi, and for ten days found himself the center of all eyes in Rome. "It is impossible," he said, "to mention the names of all those I saw and the great variety of things I was asked to do," so he kept them to himself for the rest of his life. All the resident Cardinals honored him with a visit and he spent many hours with the Holy Father.

The National Catholic Welfare Conference announced that the subjects of conversation had been exclusively ecclesiastical, but the principals made no announcement and even at this late date, we have only hints and specu-lations. They certainly discussed war prisoners and war relief, as well as the responsibilities of a military vicar, and everyone took it for granted that the interests of the Church in the impending invasion of Italy must also have been on the agenda.

The press continued to create the most sensational rumors on the role being played by the visiting prelate from New York even after his return to America.

On March 3, wearing the Holy Father's own chain and pectoral cross which he had received with tears at the last audience the previous day, when the Holy Father remarked that they might never meet again in this life, the Archbishop flew from the Guidonia Airport to Seville on the way to Gibraltar. The diary for March 4 notes that it was "in the Government paper that I arrived. Mr. [John N.] Hamlin says this is a first. He said that I had done more for good relations between Spain and U.S.A. in 24 hours than any other in a period of months." The British followed the Spanish lead, as indicated by the entry for March 6: "The Bishop of Gibraltar was very enthusiastic over my reception and the fact that for the first time since Queen Amalia of Portugal was here in 1911, Mass was said in the Govern-ment House."

It was fortunate that Spain and Rome had come between him and North Africa, his first objective. Otherwise the Military Vicar would have arrived at American headquarters in the midst of near-disaster. During his stay in Madrid, he received the news that Field Marshal Rommel had counterat-tacked General Eisenhower in central Tunisia and followed up his success with a thrust through Kasserine Pass. From February 17 to 27 the situation was critical. In the London clubs, visiting Americans had to hear plain lan-guage about "this fellow Eisenhower" from critics whose ideal was Field Marshal Montgomery. Even a naval aide on the spot wrote on February 23:

> The outstanding fact to me is that the proud and cocky Americans to-day stand humiliated by one of the greatest defeats in our history. This is

particularly embarrassing to us with the British, who are courteous and understanding. But there is a definite hangheadedness.[8]

By February 27, however, the Desert Fox had spent his force, and the situation steadily improved until by Monday, March 8, an air of confidence once more pervaded American headquarters:

> Archbishop Spellman of New York called on Ike today, bearing a letter of introduction from the President. It didn't seem to be necessary.
>
> At lunch today Ike said he had emphasized his own view to the Archbishop that all churches and other welfare agencies should extend help along humanitarian lines to any comers, regardless of nationality, race, creed or color. Ike had put this in his own vigorous language. The Archbishop had answered that the Pope had said the same thing, only "not quite in the same language." I asked Ike if he had been careful to avoid his usual adjectives and he said he had done his best. He was greatly impressed by the visitor.[9]

The next two weeks were filled with visits to camps and hospitals. One glimpse of the Military Vicar given by a correspondent could serve for almost any day. She described how he "said Mass today at a plain, hastily-built wooden altar in a small French cemetery over the grave of an American Chaplain. Afterwards the Archbishop shook hands with those present and told them that if they wished him to write to anyone back home when he returns to give him the addresses. He spent fifteen minutes taking down names."

This matter of writing home for the boys became in time one of the Vicar's greatest contributions to national morale during the war. It began with a suggestion from a wounded soldier who was unable to write himself and trusting enough to think that the Archbishop of New York, covering all fronts with a program that filled every waking hour, would have plenty of time to drop the folks a line and say that Joe was doing all right. By one of those extraordinary coincidences, the Archbishop of New York happened to be just that kind of man. It is estimated that in the course of his wartime journeying he took the names of tens of thousands of Joes and had friendly letters sent to their folks, exhibiting in this a rare blend of charity and efficiency.

On the seventeenth of March 1943, while he was being denounced in the House of Lords by Josiah Wedgwood for creating mischief in North Africa, his actions were recorded for the home front by an Irish Yankee in uniform:

> Bishop Spellman could have celebrated Mass in one of the large cities, but instead he journeyed to our location. We had little notice, but the word spread like wildfire of the Bishop's visit and officers and enlisted men alike rushed into town, availing themselves of any and all forms of

conveyance. All crowded into a small building ordinarily used for motion-picture shows, empty wooden bomb crates served as pews and a small altar was hastily erected on the stage.

And it was not Catholics alone who attended the St. Patrick's Day service for I noticed men of several other denominations among the over-flow throng. Bishop Spellman literally beamed as he entered the building, and his famous smile seemed to reach the farthest corner of the dimly lighted "cathedral." The service was scheduled for 6:30 p.m. and the Bishop arrived only a few minutes before. He walked to the stage, and here, in front of the altar and in front of the congregation, donned his vestments. . . . There was no room and no time for privacy. The beloved Bishop took the inconvenience in stride and the Mass started exactly on time. . . .

Before saying the last prayers, Bishop Spellman announced that al-though he didn't know how many of the men would have to return to their duties immediately, he would remain after Mass to greet all who desired. . . .

I think every Massachusetts man in the organization and in neighboring units attended the Mass and greeted the Bishop, and I feel sure that, as in my case, all will remember St. Patrick's Day 1943 for many, many years to come. Bishop Spellman's visit, his kind words, warm welcome, and friendly handshake seemed to bring all our loved ones closer. It was truly a great St. Patrick's Day for us all.[10]

On returning to General Doolittle's headquarters, news reached him of Cardinal Hinsley's death. This doughty Yorkshireman, Arthur Hinsley, Archbishop of Westminster, had been a symbol of religious co-operation in Britain through his "Sword of the Spirit," a movement which united for the first time Catholics, Anglicans, and Nonconformists in social and pa-triotic projects. Non-Catholics trusted him, and his heavy Yorkshire accent, frequently heard on B.B.C., had done much to remove the deep-rooted Eng-lish impression that Catholicism was a foreign thing. To the Prime Minister he was in many ways a tower of strength, so that Churchill was only half-joking when he said one night to Brendan Bracken, the Minister of Informa-tion, whom he had called in to help him select the next Archbishop of Canterbury, "I wish we could sell this to Hinsley."

The Cardinal's death, therefore, was a national loss, so Archbishop Spell-man, who had intended to visit the British Isles later on, changed his plans and took a plane at once for England. The only one available was a freighter, and his hazardous and uncomfortable trip, locked in the tail on top of the mailbags, without oxygen or sufficient covering, has been graphically de-scribed in *Action This Day*.

A New York priest who was in London at the time went down to Pad-dington Station with Archbishop William Godfrey, the Apostolic Delegate, as part of a welcoming group, and remembers vividly the appearance of the visitor when he left the train. He was not only very weary but showed the effects of too little oxygen over too long a time. He was highly nervous and irritable with the reporters—probably for the first time in his long career. This spirit of tension was communicated to his friends, especially to the Delegate's secretary who was driving the Delegate's car, and resulted in the loss of a fender and an exaggerated report to the States of a "smash up."

The next morning he looked as if he had just returned from a vacation when he stopped in at the Farm Street Church for a friendly call on the Jesuits and announced that he would attend the Lenten services at the cathedral that evening because an American was preaching the course. The report of his intention spread rapidly with the happy result that the sanctuary was full of purple and the pews bright with the familiar uniforms of our armed forces. At the funeral on Tuesday, the Archbishop of New York stood at the corner of the lofty catafalque and gave one of the benedictions. Meanwhile there was the usual round of hospitals, reception centers, and headquarters, the usual luncheons and teas and dinners. Now it was a group of his fellow countrymen gathered in the Sert Room of the Officers' Club on Park Lane, again it was a meeting of English prelates at the Delegate's table in Wimbledon. One afternoon he had just come from 10 Downing Street with an amusing story about the Prime Minister. Late in the evening of another day he was being called for in a London blackout at the darkened home of Anthony J. Drexel Biddle, then representative to the nations in exile, (and later United States Ambassador to Spain). The main object of his dinner with Ambassador Biddle was to discuss means of helping the displaced groups in London and we find a reference to the subject in the Archbishop's broadcast on the opening of the New York Catholic Charities drive on April 5: "I have promised $96,000 to help prisoners of war of all nationalities, to help suffering people in North Africa, to help St. Vincent de Paul Societies in every diocese in Ireland, British war orphans, Belgians, Greeks, Czechoslovaks, Dutch, Norwegians, Poles and Jugoslavs." Later he received the following letter from Biddle:

> I have pleasure in enclosing copies of various letters recently received expressing appreciation for the funds which you so generously made available for use by certain of the Allied Governments established here for welfare purposes connected with the war. I know how deeply touched all the recipients were by your generous gift.

Enclosed were letters from the Ministers of Foreign Affairs of Belgium, Czechoslovakia, Luxembourg, Greece, Norway, the Netherlands, and Yugoslavia.

Whenever one caught a glimpse of him during those days, he was smiling, taking messages, giving much-needed help to various institutions, and hurrying off to another appointment. Once he paused long enough to ask advice. He was going to Ireland, and he was uncertain about accepting an official invitation. Roosevelt had written to him in North Africa saying:

> Your trip has received universal acclaim and I know how useful it must have been across the waters. David Gray wants you to stay with him in Dublin but I told him I want you to use your discretion. Matthews in London will see you when you get there. My warm regards.

Unfortunately, David Gray was not popular as our minister in Ireland. He had had an explosive interview with Cardinal MacRory, and there was even talk of Dublin's asking for his recall. Both the Archbishop's friends who were consulted advised him to accept the hospitality of the Apostolic Delegate instead, but he decided to follow the President's implied preference and, risking the local criticism, stayed with Gray.

The soundness of his judgment appeared when on the first night of his visit, Prime Minister De Valera and Archbishop McQuaid of Dublin were both guests at the American Embassy, and later when Mr. Gray accompanied him to Armagh, where Cardinal MacRory had all the bishops of Northern Ireland for a luncheon in his honor. It was a difficult time for a close personal friend of the American President to visit Ireland. With the unassailable logic and devotion to principle that characterized Eire's war administration, De Valera had maintained its rights to neutrality in the face of veiled threats. Churchill and Roosevelt had not yet backed down from their blustering attitude and the Irish were a little grim about the whole thing, but where former emissaries of good will had only increased the tension, the Archbishop made new friends in what he described as a beautiful, beloved, but still "most distressful country."

After four crowded days he was back in London until April 5, when a few friends saw him off for Scotland on the *Edinburgh Express*. The blackout was almost total. There was some fog. He chatted with them about his plans for getting to India, China, and South Africa, said good-by with a big grin as if he were about to take a bus on Madison Avenue, and vanished into the darkness.

From Glasgow he flew back to North Africa and was soon immersed in visits to the chaplains and troops in Tripoli and Tunisia, with a fascinating two days on the gallant little island of Malta. Here, as Chaplain of the Sovereign Military Order of Malta in the United States of America, he left a gift of $5000 for the children.

Months later, a popular columnist mentioned the activities of the Military Vicar and received the following letter from a soldier recuperating behind one of the fronts:

> I'm sweating it out here in a hospital, after the Sicilian and African fighting, and I'm reading your column, and in it you mention Archbishop Spellman. If you used your whole column on him, Ed, you couldn't de-

scribe what his visit meant to all the boys over here. I had the honor and pleasure of shaking hands with him and talking to him, and his prayers have been with me through all of the fighting that our outfit has experienced. I've just learned from my mother that he sent her, and every other mother of every other boy he talked to, a swell letter and Ed, when a letter from the Archbishop arrives at 51st St. and 10th Ave., that is a red-letter day for the entire neighborhood.[11]

Planning to spend the Feast of the Resurrection in Jerusalem, the Archbishop flew to Cairo, where there was a situation that troubled the Holy Father. Though offered hospitality by ranking diplomats and generals, he chose this time to make his home at the Apostolic Delegation. It was a fortunate choice, for the Regent of the Delegation, London-born White Father, the Very Reverend Arthur W. Hughes, had been having a difficult time with certain British diplomatic and military authorities who wished to sweep the Middle East clear of Italian influence, not only political and military but religious and cultural as well. Missionary priests and brothers from Italy and Germany who had lived the best part of their lives working for the poor of Egypt without the slightest political interest in the Axis had been held in British concentration camps for three years while their churches and hospitals were being ruined with neglect. They were, it seemed, more harshly treated than the civilians, especially in case of illness. As a security measure, it was unwarranted and slightly ridiculous. Legally, it was unjustified in an Egypt that had refused to declare war on Italy though it was coerced into treating its Italian residents as enemy aliens. This was the sort of situation which the Archbishop could look into on his visitation of the camps without resorting to the cloak and dagger which so many thought he carried with him on his travels.

Father Hughes had been fighting a vigorous battle in defense of the Church's interests, but his protests and recommendations were, in the main, given the frustrating treatment of passive resistance. As the Archbishop relates in *Action This Day*, one of the first things he did in Egypt was to visit a group of interned Italian priests. His reaction was strong, motivated not only by sympathy but by a sense of justice. "In my opinion," he wrote, "they have been treated not only arbitrarily and unfairly but also with unnecessary harshness." When his book appeared in Cairo, the initiate, particularly the army officers in the higher echelons, were amused by the eloquence of His Excellency's silent treatment of the British ambassador, then Sir Miles Lampson, later to be elevated as Lord Killearn. Lampson had married the daughter of a Harley Street specialist named Castellani, who had later returned to Italy as Mussolini's surgeon-general in the Abyssinian campaign. Questions had been raised in Parliamentary circles about the fitness of having as His Majesty's ambassador in so strategic an area as Egypt a man whose wife was the daughter of "an infamous Fascist." This was generally thought to be the reason for the ambassador's brutality toward the unfortunate internees. Although the author of *Action This Day* was careful to include the name of every ranking civil and military personage with whom he had dealings along the way, Lampson was encased in a monumental silence, the deliberately forgotten man of the Middle East.

It was interesting [wrote the Reverend Francis W. Anderson, S.J., who was a guest in the Apostolic Delegation at the time] to observe the fascination that Archbishop Spellman's forthright manner and complete candor exercised on the professional diplomats. These qualities seemed to induce a strange hypnosis in these masters of evasion. They knew the Archbishop's visit to the Middle East was endorsed by President Roosevelt and Prime Minister Churchill, so the more he disclaimed the role of emissary on a secret mission, the more the diplomats were convinced that the case was otherwise. The more he insisted that his primary interest was the spiritual welfare of the military personnel subject to him as Military Vicar and shepherd of their souls, the more they invested him with an aura of mystery. All this, however, worked to the advantage of the Papal representative who was the Archbishop's gracious host, and Father Hughes' subsequent overtures, particularly to British officialdom, met with a far more cordial and sympathetic reception.[12]

The progress of negotiations is noted in the diary.

May 29:
    Had conference with Honorable Richard Casey, Minister of State, about treatment of Church, Delegate, internees, etc. He seemed agreeable.

May 31:
    Had another interview with the Honorable Richard Casey regarding improvement in Britain's treatment of Holy See, especially of Delegate.

June 8:
    I think Mr. Casey is showing great sympathy for the Church's viewpoint.

Not satisfied, however, to leave the solution entirely in British hands, he took the matter up with Roosevelt. To his surprise, however, the White House made no impression on London's confirmed policy of punishing Italians. Months passed. The following December nothing had been done. The President, after his return from Teheran, wrote from Washington in reply to a greeting:

MY DEAR ARCHBISHOP:
    It is mighty good of you to send me that nice note, and I send to you every possible good wish for 1944.

When I was in Cairo I had a very nice visit from the Very Reverend Arthur Hughes. We talked about the Italian priests and also the Italian nuns who were interned or detained in Egypt and in Ethiopia, and the day I left I called the whole matter to Churchill's attention and pleaded with him that these perfectly innocent people should be released, or at least allowed to do their work. I have not had any answer from the British as yet.

I ran across your trail on several occasions and all I can say is that everyone loved you everywhere you went. . . .

The principal reason for the popularity noticed by Roosevelt in Egypt was outlined later by Father Anderson:

One could not be close to the Archbishop, as was our privilege for the month of his sojourn at the Delegation, without being deeply impressed and edified by his utter selflessness. In spite of a crowded schedule, he was always accessible even to the lowliest and most anonymous of individuals. He would anticipate the embarrassment of the bashful and timid by taking the initiative with his warm and friendly approach. One little incident was typical. It was during a brief excursion to the Pyramids. Our guide was the brilliant Egyptologist, the Abbé Drioton, then Director of the Egyptian Department of Antiquities. While he was reading off and interpreting the hieroglyphics of one monument with the ease of a commuter scanning the morning's headlines, the Archbishop chanced to see two swarthy Ceylonese troopers of Britain's colonial army trying to screw up their courage to approach him. Leaving the Abbé and his Pharaohs of the XXIst Dynasty, the Archbishop walked over to the hesitant soldiers and struck up a conversation with them. They were Catholics. They would be more than honored to give the names and addresses of their parents to His Excellency so that he might write them of the meeting and assure them of their sons' well-being. As the Archbishop turned to rejoin his companions, he paused to offer his autograph in souvenir of their desert meeting across the world from their respective homelands. Eagerly the soldiers proffered the only paper they had in their possession, their well-thumbed British army paybooks. They were risking the displeasure of the army paymaster, but for them the signature of the Archbishop of New York was worth a dozen of his countersigns.[13]

From Cairo it was a two-hour flight to Tel Aviv, where he arrived on Spy Wednesday of Holy Week, going the same day by motor to Jerusalem. It was a great consolation in the midst of suffering and disaster to celebrate Holy Thursday in the Chapel of the Cenacle, Good Friday on the actual Via Crucis, and Easter Sunday at the Holy Sepulchre. Brother Anthony Bruya, O.F.M., who accompanied the Archbishop on his trip through Syria, Galilee, and Lebanon, wrote to Bishop O'Hara, "I might add that the mem-

ory of these days in the company of such a humble, devout and great man
will remain a cherished one with me."

Another crowded week in Cairo, and the Archbishop set out for Turkey
in spite of the fact that there had been some discussion with regard to the
timing of his visit, as appears in the following dispatch to Alexander Kirk,
the American minister to Egypt, from Laurence A. Steinhardt, our ambassador in Ankara:

> With reference to your telegram of March 29th to me, I should appre-
> ciate being advised as to whether the suggestion contained in your tele-
> gram has been sent to the State Department for its consideration. I ask
> this question because of the fact that the world press has generally con-
> strued Archbishop Spellman's trip abroad as having a political objective
> and because of the consequent conclusion in circles in Ankara that,
> following Mr. Churchill's visit, a visit by the Archbishop would be de-
> signed to accelerate the entry of Turkey into the war, to the embarrass-
> ment of the Turkish Government in its relations with the German
> Government.
>
> I should be grateful if you would inform Monsignor Spellman that, if
> the Department approves of the proposed visit, I should be glad immedi-
> ately to approach the Turkish Government on the matter; and, should it
> perceive no political objection to the visit, my wife and I would be glad
> to have him stay as our guest at the Embassy.

Having obtained the blessing of the State Department, the traveler continued on his way by plane to Aleppo and thence by the *Taurus Express*
to Scutari and across the Bosporus to Istanbul. It is worthy of note that
while he was on the train, Italy and Germany surrendered in North Africa,
and this was one more reason why his odyssey continued to be "a dopester's
goldmine yielding rumor at every seam." An A.P. dispatch reporting his
arrival added that "he will confer with a member of the Vatican Secretariat
of State, Emanuele Clarizio, who came from Rome especially for the
meeting." As usual, it took no time at all for the press to decide what the
principals must have talked about.

> The London *Evening Standard* said that "informed quarters" have ad-
> mitted existence of an "ultimate démarche" looking toward a compro-
> mise settlement in the Mediterranean. This proposal, according to the
> *Standard*, was believed elaborated in a special message from Pope Pius
> to Archbishop Francis J. Spellman of New York. The message was said
> to have been taken to Archbishop Spellman in Istanbul by a special Vati-
> can representative. According to the paper's entirely unconfirmed report,
> the proposal provides for immediate elimination of the Fascist Party and
> the introduction of a ten year period of "metamorphosis" during which

popular government would eventually be returned to Italy under guidance of an Allied Commission sitting in Rome.[14]

The U.P., however, quoted the Archbishop as saying that "the presence in Istanbul during his stay there of the Second Apostolic Delegate was a pure coincidence."

In the end it was the presence of the First Apostolic Delegate that made the occasion a matter of lasting interest, for this was Monsignor Angelo Roncalli, who would later become Nuncio in Paris, Cardinal Patriarch of Venice, and finally the Supreme Pontiff, John XXIII. He had met the American many years before through their mutual friend, Archbishop Borgongini-Duca, a classmate of Monsignor Roncalli, and seemed to enjoy being the perfect host. With the warmth and human charm now known to all the world the future Pope accompanied the Military Vicar on a round of official calls and invited all who might prove interesting to meet him at the Delegation. Among these was Chaim Barlas, head of the Jewish Agency in Jerusalem. At the moment the Hungarian Jews were in serious trouble and though His Eminence of New York tends today to make light of his part in the crisis, Barlas went on record in 1958 as saying that "the Cardinal's intervention was successful in averting their deportation."

On the departure of his visitor, Monsignor Roncalli presented him with a handsome silver plate, appropriately inscribed, whose sentimental value to the Archdiocese of New York has been greatly enhanced by subsequent events. It bears the Spellman coat of arms with four topazes, like the stones they would both receive one day from Pius XII.

In Germany for some months now, sentiment for a negotiated peace had been growing and parallel with it, an underground movement for the removal of Hitler. Franz von Papen, the German ambassador in Ankara, had been asked by the conspirators to sound out the Western Allies with regard to their future attitude, and described the incident nine years later in his *Memoirs*.

A member of the United States War Information Service stationed in Istanbul had already contacted me through Dr. Leverkuehn, a member of our Abwehr, with the information that Cardinal Spellman, The Archbishop of New York, intended to visit Turkey shortly. In fact, the Turkish Government had advised me as early as March that if the German Government would provide a representative with whom the Cardinal could exchange views, he would be prepared to include Turkey in the journey that he was making abroad. While in Berlin I had suggested to Ribbentrop that Dr. Leverkuehn would be a suitable representative. Ribbentrop had refused to entertain the idea, but now I raised the matter again. I was given to understand that the Cardinal had undertaken his journey at the request of President Roosevelt. However, the War Information Service representative advised me that Cardinal Spellman was not travelling in any official capacity and merely wished to obtain a picture of the situation in the Balkans and the Middle East. Ribbentrop had by now given a second flat refusal to any idea of such a contact and I was unable to arrange for any conversation with the Cardinal.[15]

Von Papen's attaché in Ankara also touched on this tale of a "might-have-been" in *Operation Cicero.*

Archbishop Spellman's visit to Ankara seemed to offer an excellent opportunity [to establish some sort of unofficial contact]. . . . Since the Ambassador would not compromise himself, even unofficially, in so delicate a matter, it fell to me to take the necessary steps to arrange a secret meeting between the Archbishop and this German. It might have been a chance for paving an earlier end to the war, thus saving mankind incalculable bloodshed and suffering. Nothing came of it. To put it briefly, Ribbentrop got wind of what was going on and put a stop to it just as ruthlessly as he knew how. No meeting ever took place.[16]

A third group interested in the Archbishop's trip to Ankara was the Dodecanesians. After centuries of subjugation by the Turks, they had passed to Italy in 1912; but now, with the surrender of Italy in Africa and her impending collapse all along the line, these hearty islanders saw a chance for reunion with Greece, their fatherland. The following letter acknowledges the help they received from His Excellency of New York:

RIGHT REVEREND ARCHBISHOP:
    The Dodecanesians "who have taken refuge" and reside here, wish to express their feelings of gratitude towards Your Grace for Your friendly efforts in respect to the liberation of the Dodecanese Islands (the Southern Sporades as they are also termed).
    We further wish to offer our heartfelt thanks, through Your Grace, to the Govt. of the United States which kindly be good enough to convey to the President in person, on Your Grace's return to Washington. The Govt. of the United States as is now well known had solicited Your Grace's good offices in furthering our cause for the freedom of the Dodecanese Islands which is one of the aims of the ASSOCIATED POWERS in their combined efforts to restore all "enslaved" and subjugated peoples.
    We trust that Your Grace on Your recent visit to Turkey will have testified to the goodwill of that Country (an Ally of Greece) to the liberation of the Greek Islanders and their union with their brethren of the Hellenic State. This after the Islands have been neutralized (as was the case when the Ionian Islands were handed over to Greece) and receive these safeguards which may be considered both adequate and REASONABLE.
    With the blessings of the Church and by a just international settlement, it is that we look toward Your Grace and the Govt. of the United States

as well [as] toward the British Empire for our freedom and Union with Hellas.

We have the honour once more to thank you, and soliciting Your blessing, to remain

Your Grace's Children in Christ,

| The Secretary | The Vice President | The President |
| Const. Cossyfakis | Michel Cladakis | Basile Agapitos |

It is pertinent to add parenthetically that their gratitude did not prevent their turning a deaf ear to the same Archbishop after the war when he pleaded with the Greeks not to confiscate the Roman Catholic cathedral on the Island of Rhodes. Ignoring their benefactor, they went ahead on the flimsy pretext that juridically it had been fascist property.

Finally, he continued without any atmosphere of mystery to co-operate with the Holy Father in his humanitarian efforts for the war prisoners of every nationality and wired from Istanbul to Robert D. Murphy, our Minister to North Africa and adviser to General Eisenhower on Political Affairs:

VATICAN INFORMS ME THAT DIFFICULTIES CONTINUE CONCERNING RECEPTION OF INFORMATION ABOUT PRISONERS OF WAR TAKEN IN ALGERIA AND TUNISIA. WOULD GENERAL EISENHOWER BE KIND ENOUGH SIMULTANEOUSLY TO FURNISH CARBON COPIES OF LISTS GIVEN TO RED CROSS TO REVEREND ARTHUR HUGHES APOSTOLIC DELEGATE CAIRO ASKING BRITISH AUTHORITIES TO FAVOR HIM USE OF TELEGRAPH FACILITIES TO VATICAN. STOP. VATICAN CONTINUES TO TELEGRAPH NAMES OF AMERICAN PRISONERS IN ITALY AND JAPAN. STOP. WHATEVER GENERAL EISENHOWER MR. MACMILLAN AND YOURSELF COULD DO WOULD BE DEEPLY APPRECIATED. WARM CONGRATULATIONS GENERAL EISENHOWER GENERAL SMITH. AFFECTIONATE REGARDS TO MESSMATES. NEXT STOPS ANKARA BAGHDAD TEHERAN CAIRO.

Mr. Murphy answered, "The question raised in your telegram May 15th is being referred to Washington for consideration." The consideration given was reflected in a letter from Under Secretary of State Sumner Welles to Archbishop Cicognani, the Apostolic Delegate, dated June 12, in which he explained that owing to the overburdened condition of the communication systems "the transmission by telegraph of the camp rosters [containing the names and addresses of prisoners] does not appear feasible." By September 29, however, there had been a change of heart, evident in a letter from Assistant Secretary of State Breckinridge Long:

The Service may now extend its activities to Italian prisoners of war in the hands of American authorities. General Eisenhower has been informed that he is authorized to furnish the Vatican Information Service with rosters of prisoners of war on a delayed basis, and to permit the transmission of welfare messages for Italian prisoners of war and persons of equivalent status in American custody.

The day that the Archbishop left Ankara for Aleppo on his way to Baghdad, Ambassador Steinhardt wrote to him:

An official communique was issued this morning by the Turkish Government to the effect that you and I had been received yesterday afternoon by President Ismet Inonu. In accordance with the customary practice, the communique did not disclose the subject matter of the conversation.

I have this morning sent a lengthy telegram to Washington describing the cordial reception accorded you by the President and giving a résumé of the conversation along the lines discussed between us yesterday.

Arriving unannounced in Baghdad, he was advised by the room clerk at the Tigris Palace Hotel to stay at Baghdad College which is conducted by the New England Jesuits. Eager as they were to entertain him, however, the Fathers explained that the American Minister, Mr. Thomas M. Wilson, was all prepared to receive him. One of the faculty members gives us a glimpse of his visit.

As soon as he arrived in the city, he telephoned the College. Weary as he must have been, and busy as he undeniably was, an invitation to visit him at the American Ministry, where arrangements were made for his brief stay, would have been an honor. But with the same thoughtfulness which will make his journey memorable to hundreds of thousands of soldiers, he offered to visit the College and say Mass there for the students.

The second group that will not forget his visit were 3,000 Polish soldiers at the R.A.F. air field some distance away. These were men who fought their way to freedom when their homes were blasted, their people crushed, and their military strength overwhelmed. Across the Balkans they trekked, across Asia Minor, until they were allowed to reorganize in Iraq. If ever men had a right to be homesick, these Polish soldiers, exiled in Iraq, had the right. That a man of the rank of Archbishop Spellman should seek them out to say a special Mass for them, did something for the spirit of those men that only the flaming soul of Polish fighting men can fully appreciate. For their Faith is something no tyranny in history has ever been able to crush, or exile to starve. This war has only made it stronger. Knowing that, and having met their fellow countrymen in England and in North Africa, Archbishop Spellman went considerably out of his way, early in the morning, fasting, to say a special Mass for them in their barracks at the air field. . . . From their soldier's pay they had saved enough money to commission a silversmith in Baghdad to make them a special chalice. Just as the Archbishop was about to begin Mass, they presented it to him, a token of gratitude that only Faith could have inspired. . . .[17]

The rector of the college, Father Francis B. Sargeant, S.J., described his coming as one of the "greatest things that ever happened to B.C. All were in admiration of his energy, for there was not a spare moment for himself during his stay here. They were more impressed with his simplicity and thoughtfulness and alertness; and all will long remember this stop on a journey which is doing so much good to so many." Coincidentally, the day before he visited the College, the New York *Times* said editorially that the Archbishop "seems instinctively to say and do the right thing. He is learned and accomplished but as humble as a fisherman-apostle. He is an American of whom all Americans can be proud."[18]

Before he left Baghdad for Basra, he was presented to the Prince Regent, Aboul Ilah, by the Premier, General Nuri Al Said, both one day to fall at the hands of assassins, and about the same time received a cordial invitation from Major General Donald H. Connolly, commander-in-chief of the United States forces in the Persian Gulf, to be his guest in Teheran:

> I take great pleasure in cordially inviting Your Excellency and your retinue to stay at my official residence as my guests during your stay in Teheran. . . . Subject to Your Excellency's approval, we have made the tentative plan to have Your Excellency celebrate Pontifical Field Mass for reception by this Command on Sunday morning Camp Amirabad. I look forward to meeting you at the airport.

The Minister in Baghdad, Mr. Wilson, replied:

> Archbishop Spellman received your message this morning and asks me to convey to you his deep appreciation of your invitation to stay with you. Archbishop Spellman is travelling unaccompanied. He departs for Basra this morning for a 24-hour visit and plans to proceed to Teheran sometime Saturday afternoon. He asks that his arrival be kept confidential to yourself and informal, and to avoid as far as possible any publicity. Archbishop Spellman will wire from Basra precise arrival time. Your plans for Mass on Sunday very acceptable. Both of us send our kind personal regards.

The account in his diary for May 29 of his audience with King Mohammed Riza Shah Pahlevi, who wanted "permission to enter the war on the side of the Allies," is not as interesting after the passage of years as his uneasy but still pertinent observations with regard to Soviet Russia. The influence of the White House appears in the passage from *Action This Day*:

> There is great admiration here [Iran] for the efficient manner in which the Russians are conducting the war. That admiration is expressed not only here but universally. The valiant defense of their country, the relentless pressing of the invaders from their soil, and the superb military, and national leadership the Russians have had in doing those things, merit

not only praise but gratitude. . . . England and America must ever ac-knowledge Russia's indispensable aid.[19]

Witnessing the transfer of our planes and tanks and trucks, and watching the white stars being painted over with red, gave him "a very definite sense of our cooperation."[20] He realized, however, from talking with Kaufman T. Keller, who had received orders to show the Reds everything that Chrys-ler was doing in the way of tanks and weapons, that the Soviet was not reciprocating. So he was worried about the ultimate consequences of the Russian victory, and wrote:

> There is a very strong impression throughout the Middle East that Russia has her own ideas about Peace and also about boundaries. More-over, Mr. Stalin is not obliged to ask anyone either inside or outside of Russia about putting his ideas into effect. . . . And my information is that two of the four freedoms as we understand them,—freedom of ex-pression and freedom of religion,—do not exist in Russia.[21]

Early in the spring, the Archbishop had received the following telegram from Alexander Kirk, the American minister in Cairo:

> Lieutenant General Theron asks me to transmit to you the following message which he has received from Field Marshal Smuts:
> "Please tell Archbishop Spellman that I have heard from Mr. Churchill and other sources of his intention to visit the Union and I am pleased at the news and look forward to meeting and exchanging views with him. Make any suitable arrangements for his transport."

Before starting for South Africa, however, there was an hour-long audience with Farouk I. This young king was only twenty-three years of age, and popular with devout Mohammedans for his religious observance and absti-nence from liquor and tobacco. The favorable impression made by His Majesty on His Excellency reminds us of the glowing tributes that were once written about Henry VIII of England, handsome and scholarly at twenty-three:

> Meeting King Farouk for the first time, the visitor is impressed by the strength of this youthful monarch and by the deep love which seems to surround him on all sides. One cannot but feel the most profound respect for the compactness of his thoughts, his sparkling wit and above all, his all-pervading patriotism and ardour.
> Of unpretentious design, King Farouk's desk is a perfect model of order. Towards the right of it is a single plate . . . with one single word which is the essence of all His Majesty's action: Patience.
> This is what I understood when I became aware of the peaceful atmos-phere created by the King which I am sure cannot escape the notice of the most casual observer. The general restiveness which meets the tourist

in any part of the country has been judiciously nutshelled in one phrase said to me by the King when speaking of Egypt's national aspirations: "The greatest force of the nation," he said, "is the people itself."

It is no wonder that this passage was quoted in the *Egypt Cultural Bulletin* seven years later, when at the age of thirty the name of Farouk was a byword in three continents.

With the Very Reverend Arthur Hughes as his companion, and travel orders reading "F. J. Spellman (Personal Representative of the President of the United States)," the Archbishop on June 11 took the weekly plane to Asmara on the way to Addis Ababa, where he met the grave little Emperor of Ethiopia. During an audience of one hour, Haile Selassie "said he would permit the immediate entrance of eight priests and eight Sisters and more later." The Military Vicar was now well out of the war zone, so until he left Africa for home, the entries in his diary concerned missionaries more than soldiers. There were stops in Khartoum and Mombasa. Passing through Tanganyika Territory, he stopped at Ndanda to await a plane. The following description of his visit by one of the Holy Ghost missionaries could be used, with a change of name, for most of his stops in Africa:

Before daylight broke over the horizon, in a strange country, the Africa of snakes, lions and cannibals, the Archbishop came walking alone to the Mission. He was not troubled although lions are sometimes roaming about these places.

There was a good number of Goans and natives that came to the Mass. His Grace, the Archbishop, was greatly pleased to see the Goan Community and spoke a few words to them. . . .

To our great joy the plane was delayed another day. We would have the pleasure of seeing the Archbishop again the next day. Again the natives came to assist at his Mass. After Mass he was pleased to talk to them. I was interpreter: "Dear friends," he said, "I come from very, very far. I am visiting the Christians of my own parish and of other American parishes. They are now spread throughout the world, sailing, flying, fighting. I was pleased to see that in all countries our soldiers have facilities to follow their religious duties; for us all, that is the most important matter. God above all. Never forget it. It is with great pleasure that I notice everywhere in Africa there are good Catholic communities, some with native priests, Brothers and Sisters. All of them performing their religious duties well. When I return home I will tell my people and know they will be very pleased to hear it."[22]

While visiting Madagascar, he was invited by the British Commander in East Africa on a rescue flight. All day they searched for the rafts with survivors of a ship torpedoed by a submarine in the shark-infested waters of the

Indian Ocean and came down at night on the distant island of Mauritius. There word reached them that the invasion of Sicily had begun.

When the Military Vicar arrived in the capital of Mozambique he found Archbishop Theodosia Gouveia finishing a new cathedral with the usual anxiety, and had the joy of donating an altar in the name of the New York Archdiocese. As a gesture of appreciation His Grace of Lourenço Marques presented the American visitor with a pair of ferocious lion skins which found their way eventually to Fordham.

Arriving in Pretoria from Lourenço Marques, the Archbishop was welcomed by the Prime Minister of the Union. In General Jan Smuts, then seventy-four years of age, he saw a real patriot who stood out as a great man in a generation of merely strong men, of blusterers, maneuverers, unscrupulous autocrats, and headline seekers. Their cordiality was mutual and immediate.

A Paulist priest in Johannesburg sent an unofficial report on the distinguished visitor to the folks at home:

> We invited the Archbishop to lunch for we were determined to get His Excellency alone, so that we could get some first-hand information about doings in America. . . . His Excellency's accent sure was music to our ears. The people were delighted with Archbishop Spellman, and the convents vied with one another in entertaining His Excellency. How the Archbishop bore up was a marvel to us. A little side remark—His Excellency is human just like we are. We saw him eagerly reading American papers on the library table that were several months old.[23]

It was still the traveler's intention to push on to India and China, but on his fifth day in Pretoria Bishop McIntyre cabled to say that both the Vatican and the White House were urging him to return to New York at once because of the military situation involving Rome:

> Received telegram that my trip was over. Mass at Sanatorium. Revised my schedule, cutting out Rhodesia, Kruger Park and other places. I am sorry I cannot continue the trip, but no one knows it yet but the Chinese Consul.

And on July 26 he noted:

> Mussolini resigns. Decided to go home. Cancelled engagements. Made me sad to do so. Goodbye to General Smuts. Placed plane at my disposal. Wired to President and Bishop McIntyre.

When it was known that he had left Pretoria two days after the resignation and imprisonment of Mussolini, "the dopesters" of the fourth estate went back to the "gold mine":

> The hand of Archbishop Francis J. Spellman of New York . . . was seen

in the downfall of Benito Mussolini. When the Duce was replaced as premier by Marshal Pietro Badoglio, it was recalled that Badoglio and the American churchman had conferred recently in Rome.[24]

Archbishop Spellman of New York, often mentioned as a possible middle man between Italy and the Allies, was hurrying north from South Africa.[25]

For his is the most potent, mysterious figure in the current world at war and the one best fitted to bring war-weary Italy to terms with the Allies. . . . The purpose for which Pope Pius XII called him from New York last February is revealed. For Archbishop Spellman is Rome-bound as fast as his chromium wings can fly to become apostolic intermediary in Italy's bid for peace.[26]

Archbishop Francis J. Spellman of New York, frequently mentioned as a possible go-between for peace negotiations between Italy and the Allies, canceled all remaining engagements in South Africa today and took off from Pretoria by plane for an undisclosed northern destination.[27]

The fact was he was headed at last, after six incredible months, for an overcrowded office on the second-floor front overlooking Fiftieth Street and Madison Avenue. The final stretch of 11,500 miles, up to the Gold Coast, across to Brazil, and on to Miami and New York, was covered in five days, with Holy Mass celebrated in a different country each morning.

On arrival, August 1, 1943, he held an overflow press conference in the old Victorian parlor of his episcopal residence, where he passed out an innocuous statement and declined to answer questions. One reporter began, "There have been some very persistent rumors—"

"There are also some very persistent reporters," retorted the Archbishop with a smile. So the distinguished gentlemen of the press filed out to write their stories under such headlines as this: SECRET OF LONG TOUR WELL KEPT.

CHAPTER FOURTEEN

President Roosevelt

THE President was in Canada for the first Quebec Conference, called to discuss plans for drawing Russia into full concert with the Western Allies, and word to this effect had been left in Miami by Stephen Early, his secretary:

> Kindly explain to the Archbishop in confidence that the President left Washington Friday for a week's rest in northwestern Canada PD Also in confidence explain that the President will not return to Washington until August ninth and that he left with knowledge of the Archbishop's return home PD Under these circumstances I have advised the State Department tonight of the Archbishop's expected arrival Sunday PD He will be met at the airport by a representative of the State Department who will endeavor to make any arrangements the Archbishop desires.

It was, therefore, September 2 before "his personal representative" visited Roosevelt at the White House for dinner with Winston Churchill, and talked with the President alone for an hour and a half on Friday morning, September 3. A two-page typewritten memorandum from the Archbishop's files, entitled "Here are a few outstanding points of the conversation," throws a rather interesting light on the thought processes of his host, the most influential man alive at the time:

Collaboration of the "Big Four":
It is planned to make an agreement among the Big Four. Accordingly the world will be divided into spheres of influence: China gets the Far East; the U.S. the Pacific; Britain and Russia, Europe and Africa. But as Britain has predominantly colonial interests it might be assumed that Russia will predominate in Europe. Although Chiang Kai-shek will be called in on the great decisions concerning Europe, it is understood that he will have no influence on them. The same thing might become true—although to a lesser degree—for the U.S. He hoped, "although it might be wishful thinking," that the Russian intervention in Europe would not be too harsh.

League of Nations:

The last one was no success, because the small states were allowed to intervene. The future League will consist only of the four big powers (U.S., Britain, Russia, China). The small states will have a consultative assembly, without right to decide or to vote. For example, at the armistice with Italy, the Greeks, Jugoslavs and French asked to be co-signers. "We simply turned them down." They have no right to sit in where the big ones are. Only the Russians were admitted, because they are big, strong and simply impose themselves.

Russia:

An interview with Stalin will be forced as soon as possible. He believes that he will be better fitted to come to an understanding with Stalin than Churchill. Churchill is too idealistic, he is a realist. So is Stalin. Therefore an understanding between them on a realistic basis is probable. The wish is, although it seems improbable, to get from Stalin a pledge not to extend Russian territory beyond a certain line. He would certainly receive: Finland, the Baltic States, the Eastern half of Poland, Bessarabia. There is no point to oppose these desires of Stalin, because he has the power to get them anyhow. So better give them gracefully.

Furthermore the population of Eastern Poland wants to become Russian. Still it is absolutely not sure whether Stalin will be satisfied with these boundaries. On the remark that Russia has appointed governments of communistic character for Germany, Austria and other countries which can make a communist regime there, so that the Russians might not even need to come, he agreed that this is to be expected. Asked further, whether the Allies would not do something from their side which might offset this move in giving encouragement to the better elements, just as Russia encourages the Communists, he declared that no such move was contemplated. It is therefore probable that Communist Regimes would expand, but what can we do about it. France might eventually escape, if it has a government à la Leon Blum. The Front Populaire would be so advanced, that eventually the Communists might accept it. On the direct question whether Austria, Hungary and Croatia would fall under some sort of Russian protectorate, the answer was clearly yes. But he added, we should not overlook the magnificent economic achievements of Russia. Their finances are sound. It is natural that the European countries will have to undergo tremendous changes in order to adapt to Russia, but he hopes that in ten or twenty years the European influences would bring the Russians to become less barbarian.

Be it as it may, he added, the U.S. and Britain cannot fight the Russians. The Russian production is so big that the American help, except for trucks, is negligible. He hopes that out of a forced friendship may soon come a real and lasting friendship. The European people will simply have to endure the Russian domination, in the hope that in ten or twenty years they will be able to live well with the Russians. Finally he hopes, the Russians will get 40% of the Capitalist regime, the capitalists will retain only 60% of their system, and so an understanding will be possible. This is the opinion of Litvinoff.

Hungary:

He likes the Hungarians. He wants them to come over. He would be ready to accept them on the Allied side as they are, if they come over.

Austria:

No plan for the Austrian Government in Exile is made or tolerated. There will be no opposition to a Russian dominated Communist Austrian Regime. The one thing that would save Austria from the Communists would be if Otto of Austria succeeded to gain that throne with the help of Hungary. But even then he would have to deal with the Russians.

Croatia:

He opposes the resurrection of Jugoslavia and favors an independent Croat and Slovene State. Churchill is for the *status quo ante.*

Germany:

Agreement has been reached between R[oosevelt] and Churchill, that Germany will be divided into several states. It will have no more central government, but will be under the domination of the Big Four, mostly Russia. There will be no peace treaty, but simply a decree of the Big Four. Before that hearings would be held, but these would have no influence. Germany would be divided into the following states: Bavaria, Rhineland, Saxony, Hesse, Prussia. Wurttemberg would become part of Bavaria, Saxony would take parts of Prussia. Hannover would become an independent state; Germany would be disarmed for forty years. No air force, no civilian aviation, no German would be authorized to learn flying.

Poland:

Poland, if re-established, would get Eastern Prussia.

Other Countries:

Plebiscites would be held in the following countries: France, Italy, Netherlands, Belgium, Norway, Greece. No plebiscite is to be expected in Czecho-Slovakia.

How far this type of "realism" reflected the thinking of Roosevelt's "favorite Bishop" can be gathered from the deep concern voiced at this time by the American hierarchy on the increasing influence of Soviet Russia in the distribution of the spoils of war. Its members agreed that secularism, exploitation, and totalitarianism whether Fascist, Nazi, or Communist, could never lead to a lasting peace, while Archbishop Spellman himself was urging everywhere that we keep the spirit of revenge out of our activities and "win the war without destroying our victory."

While the Archbishop was still a guest in the White House, word came that Montgomery had slipped two divisions across the Straits of Messina and the Allied invasion of the Continent was at last an accomplished fact. The joy of the news with its implication of approaching victory was tempered for many by the increased danger of the Holy Father's situation. The two-fold aspect of Rome as the capital of Italy and the center of the Catholic world was figuring prominently in most of the war plans on both sides. On the part of the Germans, its sacred character was regarded as an asset and although the city was not too important in a military sense, it figured in psychological warfare and lay on the line of railway communications. To the English, it was an unpopular symbol whose destruction would not be mourned. Back in the days of the blitz, Italian planes had appeared with the Nazis over London and the spirit of retaliation was strong. Antiquarian sentiment was rare in the rank and file and the fact that Rome was so closely identified with papal history struck no responsive chord in the hearts of English leaders. To the Americans, on the other hand, it was, as General H. H. Arnold himself described it, "a hot potato."[1] Catholics in the armed forces represented an impressive proportion of the nation's strength, while at home there were twenty-five million of their coreligionists who were for the most part loyal supporters of the President's policy.

Nearly a year before, on December 4, 1942, Archbishop Cicognani had left a memo with A. A. Berle of the State Department, asking that the Pope be assured at least informally and confidentially that Rome would not be bombed[2] and later in the same month there was a memo on the subject for Secretary Hull from the President's desk:

> In further reference to the desire of the Pope that Rome be not bombed, I really think that England and the United States could agree not to bomb Rome on condition that the City itself, outside of the Vatican, be not used in any shape, manner or form either by the Germans or the Italians for war purposes.
>
> I understand that today most of the Italian Departments have left Rome with their civil and military personnel, but that Germans, who are of course all military, are using Rome as their central headquarters.
>
> I should think that we might consider that it is up to the Vatican itself to propose that Rome be demilitarized. If that is accomplished there is no reason for us to bomb it.[3]

In May, His Holiness wrote to the President, expressing confidence that innocent people would "be spared as far as possible further pain and devastation, and their many treasured shrines . . . from irreparable ruin."[4] In his answer dated June 16, at the very time when the decision to bomb Rome was being made in Washington, Roosevelt wrote:

Attacks against Italy are limited, to the extent humanly possible, to military objectives. We have not and will not make warfare on civilians or against nonmilitary objectives. In the event it should be found necessary for Allied planes to operate over Rome our aviators are thoroughly informed as to the location of the Vatican and have been specifically instructed to prevent bombs from falling within the Vatican City.[5]

The meeting that sent the Prime Minister to the British War Cabinet and General Marshall to the American Chiefs of Staff for authorization to have Eisenhower carry out the bombing had been held at American headquarters in Algiers on June 2. Captain Harry C. Butcher noted the following day in his diary: "The Prime Minister had assured the President, after seeing Archbishop Spellman, that we would not bomb Rome for the present, but the Prime Minister now felt there was no tenable objection, as the marshaling yards are proper military objectives."[6]

"Marshaling yards" was the British term for freight yards, much affected by American officers. One of these yards was in the outskirts of Rome, but perilously close to the Papal Basilica of St. Lawrence-Outside-the-Walls, an ancient shrine dating back to Constantine the Great. Troop trains seldom formed there since Rome had no facilities for quartering large bodies of troops, but the bombing on July 19 seemed important enough to warrant the risk involved. A total of 521 planes participated, 272 heavies and 249 mediums.[7] There were many casualties, and San Lorenzo was badly damaged. Throughout the raid, a heartbroken Pope watched at the window of his study, and after the "all clear" went at once to comfort the wounded and the dying. His protest was addressed to the Vicar General of the district of Rome, not directly to the Allies, and expressed the anguished hope that Rome would not be bombed again. Here matters stood on August 1 when the Military Vicar finished his tour and arrived in New York.

Two days later, a second raid was called off at the last moment because of a report that the Italians were proposing to make Rome an "open city," but on August 14, an observer in Algiers wrote in his diary: "Yesterday we bombed Rome for the second time, and of course the BBC gave the operation liberal credit as American. What the repercussions will be from home we don't know." Three days later he noted: "Ike received orders from the Combined Chiefs to lay off bombing of Rome, pending settlement of the question of its becoming declared an 'open city.'"[8]

The Pope's reaction was described on August 25:

The Vatican complained bitterly over the second bombing of Rome, claiming another Church had been hit. Speaking repeatedly of the Eternal City, the secretary of the Vatican had reported to the American Diplomatic representative, Ambassador [sic] Harold S. Tittman, that the Holy See had prevailed on the Italians not to bomb Cairo or Athens, yet we had unhesitatingly socked Rome as well as other Italian cities where

Catholic churches were being demolished. Significantly, I thought, the Catholic hierarchy emphasized that Italian anger is being aroused by our bombings, particularly of Rome.[9]

The Archbishop of New York spent September 12 in Washington and noted in his diary:

> Talked all day with Enrico [Galeazzi]. Delegate and Monsignor Carroll had some news. I learned that I was appointed Apostolic Visitor to Sicily and Occupied Territories.

The official communication outlining the nature and scope of the mission was dated August 29 and signed by Cardinal Maglione, Secretary of State to His Holiness. In general, he was to render an account to the Pope of the religious situation in Sicily, noting the extent of the material damage done to religious institutions and suggesting plans for rehabilitation. Drawing on his wide pastoral experience, he was to advise the local hierarchy in their reorganization of parishes, their rebuilding the life of the seminaries, their revitalizing works of charity and Catholic Action. Finally, he was asked to devise some means of getting word through the Vatican to relatives on the mainland concerning their dear ones in Sicily. At the conclusion of the mission he was to report to the Holy Father in person. Before he could perform the duties of a delegate, however, the rapid advance of the Allies opened up communications between Rome and Sicily making it unnecessary for him to assume his new office.

Meanwhile, the situation in Washington, which His Excellency described as "awful," absorbed his attention. For the meeting with the President on September 15 at 3:30 P.M., it was decided that Archbishop Stritch of Chicago and Archbishop Mooney of Detroit should join Archbishop Spellman. That night the entry for the diary read:

> President suggested twenty-mile zone around Rome in which Germans would agree not to fight. It will be OK if he keeps his promise. I am glad the three of us went. The audience was one hour long. Returned to New York. Enrico [Galeazzi, who had arrived in New York from Rome on September 11th] wants to return at once. We got passage tomorrow.

Less than two months later, he wrote:

> November 6th:
> Vatican bombed.

> November 8th:
> Meeting at Delegation with Archbishops Stritch and Mooney. What to do for Holy See. . . .

Throughout the trying period of nearly a year, His Excellency of New York lost no opportunity to express the hope "that the leaders of our Allied armies will find it possible in their great military strategy to spare the Holy Father and the See city of the Catholic Church." Speaking to 75,000 Holy Name men at the Polo Grounds, he asked for prayers "that Rome, the city of the soul, eternal Rome, be spared destruction, and above all that Rome be not destroyed by us. . . ." This brought considerable newspaper comment, some of it emphasizing the slogan popular at the time to the effect that all the churches in Rome were not worth the life of one American soldier. This implied argument was referred to in an open letter His Excellency wrote to the editor of the New York *Journal-American*:

> Unless it could be irrefutably demonstrated that all the exigencies of military necessity had been explored, millions of hearts would be saddened if history were obliged to record that Rome was destroyed by Americans.
>
> Those who assert that the problem is a dilemma between saving lives and saving buildings appear to have oversimplified the situation; for according to authentic reports, the destruction of some buildings has provided the enemy with greater and stronger defenses.
>
> Military authorities have stated that Rome has little military value. If this be true, we pray that the "military necessity" involved in its occupation will not cost more precious soldier lives because of the "destruction of buildings."[10]

A special point had been given to the argument on military necessity by the recent tragic and senseless bombing of the Abbey of Monte Cassino on February 15, 1944, when the Americans at the insistence of General Bernard Freyburg, commander of the New Zealand Corps, dropped a total of some 576 tons of explosives on this beloved and historic spot, reducing it to rubble and killing the innocent peasants who had taken refuge there.[11] A heartbroken abbot told the Archbishop soon after, "I have no longer tears with which to cry." Of this ghastly blunder, General Mark W. Clark was to write eventually:

> I say that the bombing of the Abbey, which sat high on the hill southwest of Cassino, was a mistake—and I say it with full knowledge of the controversy that has raged around this episode. The official position was best summed up, I suppose, in a State Department communication to the Vatican's Undersecretary of State on October 13, 1945, saying that "there was unquestionable evidence in the possession of the Allied commanders in the field that the Abbey of Monte Cassino formed part of the German defensive system."
>
> I was one of the Allied commanders in the field and the one in command at Cassino, and I said then that there was no evidence the Germans were using the Abbey of Monte Cassino for military purposes. I say now that there is irrefutable evidence that no German soldier, except emis-

saries, was ever inside the Monastery for purposes other than to take care of the sick or to sightsee—and after the battle started, they didn't have a chance for any sightseeing. Not only was the bombing of the Abbey an unnecessary psychological mistake in the propaganda field, but it was a tactical military mistake of the first magnitude. It only made our job more difficult, more costly in terms of men, machines and time.[12]

At the moment, however, the press dispatches were conveying the impression that an important German observation post had to be wiped out even if it meant the destruction of a holy and historic landmark, so that too many protests were not thought to be in place; but because the Pope's villa in Castel Gandolfo had already received the same treatment,[13] there was a suspicion that the punitive attitude of England toward Italy was influencing American policy. The Archbishop wrote to Roosevelt on February 20, and the firmness of his tone marks an interesting development in their relations:

> I am greatly disturbed at the seeming helplessness of the Holy Father and the disregard of him and his pleadings. There are many other disturbed persons who have urged me to manifest publicly our feeling of sympathy with him. After my several talks with you and my repeated assurances to the Holy Father of our desire to show him every respect, I feel that I must do something to comfort him, and others who reverence him and are pained to see his home at Castel Gandolfo bombed by our airmen, the while the Vatican states that "no German soldier has been admitted within the borders of the neutral Pontifical Villa and that no German military whatsoever are within it at present." There are only helpless and homeless people refuged there. I have thought therefore that it would be opportune and necessary to make a statement on the occasion of the annual patriotic memorial Mass of the Knights of Columbus in St. Patrick's Cathedral on Washington's Birthday. I have just now prepared the draft of what I propose to say and in fact believe it necessary to state lest many people think me failing in my duty, and, what is even more important, think myself to fail.
>
> I realize, of course, that many will disagree with what I shall say, some indeed vehemently, but I believe the facts leave me no alternative. If, Mr. President, you see some different action that can be taken I shall be glad and grateful for your advice.[14]

The remarks to which he referred contained the following paragraphs:

> Thus hoping and praying, I must deplore the fact that the armed forces of our country have attacked the territory of a neutral state, thereby violating rights which are among those for which America is waging war. We have the word of the Pope, expressed by the Apostolic Delegate to the United States, that no Germans were there or had ever been allowed

there. In the winning of the war, let us keep not only the respect of others but also our own self-respect.

I also hope and pray that, as Britain once spared the Holy City of Mecca, military ingenuity will overcome "military necessity," which would destroy the Eternal City of Rome, the citadel of civilization.[15]

His Excellency returned to the subject March 12, the fifth anniversary of the Holy Father's coronation, and on April 1, at an Armenian liturgy in St. Patrick's Cathedral, he reminded 3500 people:

> It would be an ineradicable blot on this world of ours, this world that took its civilization from Rome, if all the exigencies of military necessity were not explored and found wanting before obliging history to record the fact that Rome had been destroyed by Americans!

Incidents continued to occur from time to time, like the Allied strafing of a fifty-two-unit Vatican motor and trailer convoy, plainly marked, near Chiusi; and although such minor outrages could be attributed to an irresponsible pilot who was not reflecting the policy of the administration in Washington, no one knew from day to day what that policy might become. It was, therefore, a great relief to Archbishop Spellman when Rome finally fell to the Allied forces on June 4, 1944, even though it meant a new set of problems to be discussed with the President. Roosevelt referred His Excellency's comments on the occupation to the Joint Chiefs of Staff and received the following memorandum:

> In connection with Archbishop Spellman's remarks on the use of Rome and its facilities by the Allied forces in Italy, the situation presently is as follows:
>
> General Wilson has laid down a policy that Allied troops stationed in Rome will be kept strictly to a minimum number although he does plan to set up rest camps near Rome and to use the facilities of the city for relaxation purposes. . . .
>
> So far as it is known here, the only important military installation which it is intended to establish in Rome is the administrative echelon of General Alexander's headquarters for the Allied Armies in Italy. . . .
>
> If you desire to comment on His Excellency's remarks, he might be assured that the Theatre Commander has stated his firm intention of holding Allied military installations in Rome to the minimum, consistent with expeditiously and efficiently getting on with the war and that Allied soldiers permitted to visit Rome are quartered outside the city in rest camps established for that purpose.

The previous month, the Military Vicar had proposed to his Commander-in-Chief that another visitation of the camps was in order, this time in the Pacific area. With his letter he had enclosed a copy of his newly published book, *The Risen Soldier,* a short, fervent meditation penned for the consolation of parents who had lost their sons in the war. The President replied:

DEAR FRIEND:

I am delighted to have that personally inscribed copy of your book, "The Risen Soldier." It is beautifully written and I feel it will be of great comfort to the mothers and fathers of our boys in the armed services. . . .

I would be perfectly delighted to have you make a trip to the South Pacific and Australia. However, the trip to China presents an interesting geographical problem. The hop from Australia to Ceylon and then through India to China is about 3,000 miles which I feel is taking too much of a risk. The hop can be made but I don't like risking it—especially for you.

When you decide you are ready to go, will you let us know and we will make the necessary arrangements with Secretary Forrestal and Patterson, as we did before. Also, of course I want to see you before you get off.

My best to you.

As events transpired, it was many months before the Military Vicar reached the Pacific Theater, but in the meantime, in addition to several important decisions with regard to diocesan administration, he turned his attention to the headquarters of the Military Vicariate, which in its development under Bishop O'Hara had kept pace with the complexity and expansion of the war.

The office of military chaplain was an ancient one in the Church, dating back to the Council of Ratisbon in 742, and even in the United States had its legal origin in a resolution of the Continental Congress, July 29, 1775, but until 1917 there was little organization among the scattered Catholic chaplains serving with the troops. Even as late as President Taft's administration, a Paulist Father, the Reverend Alexander P. Doyle, recommended chaplains to the government and remained their only ecclesiastical sponsor.[16] Their canonical faculties were granted by the Ordinary of the place where they happened to be stationed.

It was not until November 24, 1917, that Pope Benedict XV chose the Auxiliary Bishop of New York, the Most Reverend Patrick Joseph Hayes, D.D., as the first Bishop Ordinary of the Forces. He was given episcopal authority over all the Catholic Americans in the armed forces wherever they might be. The United States was divided into four regions or vicariates and over each was placed a vicar general. There was also a vicar general for Europe, assisted by two delegates. Compared with what had been done before, the organization was impressive when outlined by the Bishop in a letter to Cardinal De Lai a short time before the end of the First World War:

. . . However, all I have now at my disposition is 750 priests (of an estimated 1,000 required), of whom 600 have been commissioned by the Federal Government with my approval. I should like to add that at the present time there are in Europe 200 American priests and that by the first of January I hope to be able to have 1,000 priests serving in the Armed Forces. . . .[17]

Armistice Day came in a matter of two months. The armed forces melted away more rapidly than they had assembled, and most of the chaplains returned to their dioceses. Their records in the service had been notable. Cardinal De Lai, Secretary of the Consistorial Congregation in Rome, admitted that it was difficult to determine what should be the future attitude toward the spiritual care of the Army and Navy, but concluded that "for the protection of the discipline among the clergy and for the preservation of faith among the soldiers, it would seem to be useful to continue the Military Ordinariate and the Military Curia."[18] This meant in practice that the Vicar General, Monsignor George Waring, a veteran of the Chaplains Corps with a record of fourteen years of service in the Army, retained his rank and a secretary to keep in contact with the handful of chaplains still in uniform.[19]

Upon his appointment as the successor of Cardinal Hayes, the new Military Vicar made plans at once to meet the greatly expanded needs of the Second World War. His first step was the selection of Bishop O'Hara as his military delegate and the organization of adequate headquarters in the old Cathedral College on Madison Avenue. Accompanied by Father Robert E. McCormick, he called on Monsignor Waring, packed into one black bag all the correspondence of the Ordinariate and drove the whole organization home in a taxicab. The files recording baptisms and marriages followed. In January 1943 a second military delegate was appointed and consecrated in the person of the Redemptorist provincial, the Most Reverend William T. McCarty, C.SS.R., D.D. When Bishop O'Hara was promoted to the See of Buffalo, his place was taken by the Most Reverend William R. Arnold, D.D., a major general who had been Chief of Chaplains all through the war. On the promotion of Bishop McCarty to the See of Rapid City, South Dakota, the Military Vicar received an auxiliary vicar from the Diocese of Brooklyn, the Most Reverend James H. Griffiths, S.T.D., J.C.B. Six years later, Bishop Griffiths was named Auxiliary Bishop of New York, and one of the leading educators in the archdiocese, the Most Reverend Philip J. Furlong, D.D., Ph.D., succeeded him.

This succession of distinguished prelates was indicative of the Archbishop's determination to make the Military Ordinariate a solid and permanent source of authority and spiritual assistance in what has been called "the greatest mass missionary activity in the history of the Church in America and possibly in all the modern age." In the file of records kept at headquarters, there are nearly a million and a half cards listing besides first communions and confirmations, 468,494 baptisms and 294,411 marriages. In its permanent form, the organization was to consist of a military vicar, a military delegate, and an auxiliary to the vicar, assisted by an official ecclesiastical staff comprising a chancellor, vice-chancellor, two assistant chancellors and four other priests acting as secretaries, recorders, and archivists. In addition to this, there would be a lay staff of thirty-five. Fifteen years after the close of the shooting war, and seven years after Korea, the Ordinariate would still be supervising and directing the sacred apostolate of nearly 2410 priests in 35 countries.

During the hostilities, according to the records in the Washington offices of the Chief of Chaplains, there were 3270 Catholic chaplains commissioned in the service. Thirty-eight were killed in action, thirty-three were non-battle casualties, and ninety were wounded in action. Five hundred and seventy-eight in the Army and Air Corps received 827 decorations.[20] In addition, there were 2018 civilian priests who were designated as auxiliary chaplains to supplement the work of those who were commissioned. These cold statistics give, of course, only the vaguest impression of the impact made on our armed forces and through them on the United States by the priests and bishops who looked to the Military Vicar as their Ordinary.

Summer had come again and the Military Vicar was impatient to get back to his chaplains and the troops. On June 14 he visited the President and made preliminary arrangements for his trip. It was eight days after D day in Normandy, and the beachhead had just been secured. On July 6 he received the following letter from the Apostolic Delegate in Washington:

> I am receiving just now your note and I shall cable by code to the Vatican according your desire.
> This is the wording of the telegram which I received yesterday:
> "His Holiness wishes that the Archbishop of New York come to Rome for a short time, to treat several important questions."
> You will tell me if I have to give further information to the Cardinal Secretary of State.

Three days later Colonel Harold R. Maddux wrote to him:

> . . . . General Eisenhower and General Smith have been informed that you will proceed to Great Britain, departing from New York on 17 July 1944, and will visit the European Theater of Operations first. They have been further informed that upon completion of your visit, you will proceed to the North African Theater of Operations where you will visit Italy, and will then proceed to the Middle East, the Asiatic Theater, and the Southwest Pacific and Pacific Ocean Areas.

The Archbishop, however, wanted a little leeway in planning his itinerary, and was reassured by the following message:

In accordance with your wishes, a message is being dispatched informing the Commanding General, Allied Force Headquarters, Algiers, of the following:

"It is desired that no definite itinerary be planned for Archbishop Spellman until after his arrival in your theater. The Archbishop wishes first to proceed to Rome in order to carry out his mission and will then arrange his subsequent itinerary. Your proposal to have Chaplain, Major William J. Moran, meet the Archbishop at Casablanca is approved. . . ."

He was, as usual, well fortified with introductions, several from the President himself, couched in practically the same words as this one to Eisenhower:

My Dear Ike:

My old personal friend, Archbishop Spellman, needs no introduction to you, but I am hoping very much you will be able to see him while he is in your vicinity. He did a magnificent job on his last trip and I know you will do everything you can to be helpful.

His Excellency arrived in Rome on the morning of July 22, said Mass in St. Peter's, and the same day was received in audience by the Holy Father. Once more the rumors flew thick and fast. "Authoritative sources" dropped hints to newsmen that the Pope was trying to get a negotiated peace for Germany through the kind offices of President Roosevelt's old friend, the Archbishop of New York. The Archbishop denied it absolutely. "Vatican quarters also denied that a peace proposal was the subject of the Archbishop's conversations with the Pontiff or that the Pope was expected to come forward with any peace plan." Finally, "the State Department denied that it had any knowledge of peace proposals reported to be under consideration at the Vatican."[21] That quieted the rumors for a while.

Meanwhile the Archbishop had said Mass for a church full of American soldiers at the Gesù, with the usual greetings afterward and the collecting of addresses for letters to their families. A few days later, "wearing a garrison hat, a khaki suit, field boots and a green army muffler, he visited the American front lines at a point farther advanced than any ever reached by other notable visitors."[22] However, even at a distance which British officers thought safe for the King of England, there could always be a note of sudden tragedy:

Two German mines stepped on by an American soldier exploded with a terrific roar today within 300 yards of a table where King George VI of England, Lieutenant General Mark W. Clark, U.S. Fifth Army Commander, Archbishop Francis J. Spellman of New York, and General Sir Harold R. L. G. Alexander, Supreme Commander in Italy, were at lunch.

Although the concussion was felt at the luncheon table, none of the guests was hurt. The American soldier who inadvertently exploded the mines was killed.[23]

Back in Rome, the Vicar liked nothing better than helping the GI's feel at home in the Vatican, where, at his suggestion, military rank carried no precedence. In one boy's letter home we read:

> After the Pope left the hall, the crowd started to leave and down the aisle came Archbishop Spellman of New York. He walked down, shaking everybody's hand and asking them where they were from. When they told him, why he'd tell you more about people and places in your own home town than you had ever heard of before—not counting many people you know personally. Well, he sure has a wide scope of friends. He knows everyone. . . .
>
> I asked him if I could take his picture and he was so kind he took me over near a great big window and a guard came running over and pulled back the curtain to let the sunlight in. I was so excited I had him standing against the window instead of away from it, but he finally straightened me out and I snapped the picture. . . .[24]

Contact with the wonderful boys from home who streamed into the basilicas and crowded around the temporary altars at the front always brought deep consolation to their Military Vicar; but unfortunately, all the boys in uniform were not wonderful. One element constituted a grave problem in every country which was occupied by the American troops, and Italy was no exception. The people, prostrate and demoralized after their defeat, had looked forward to the coming of the Allies as their deliverers, only to find that they had exchanged a disciplined spoliation for an undisciplined. When the Germans had taken their chickens and cattle and cheese, they had done so under orders. Now the hapless Italians had to contend with private enterprisers in khaki who were "liberating" wrist watches and anything else that was loose. Moreover, the rich were poor and the poor were destitute. The Allied Military Government of Occupied Territory was described by Sumner Welles as disastrously inefficient, and the Allied Control Council (quoting from *Time*) was "a bumbling Anglo-American bureaucracy superimposed on the Italians; composed of one-fifth British brains and four-fifths American supplies—and neither adequate."

Here and there a few individuals among the Americans who held subordinate positions in the Allied Control Council vigorously protested against conditions which were not only causing unnecessary suffering to the Italian people but which threatened to do grave damage to Italian popular sentiment toward the United States. Their voices were invariably silenced in conformity with the order issued from Washington that all American officials, both military and civilian, were to "get along with the British." Before long this order was interpreted to mean that British policy directives were to be blindly obeyed whatever the effect on long-range American interests.[25]

The only figure in the prolonged crisis singled out for praise by Welles was Myron Taylor, but the Italians themselves added the name of Archbishop Spellman. In a letter addressed to him, the Under Secretary of State for Foreign Affairs wrote:

> In particular, the Italian Nation is grateful to Your Excellency for the recent action taken within the U.N.R.R.A. by the granting of help to Italy and expresses the hope that this will be the beginning of a true collaboration with the people. . . .

Relief and many other problems brought him into contact with all the important figures of the civil government—Prince Umberto, the Lieutenant General of the Realm, Premier Bonomi, and the aged Orlando, who at Versailles had been one of the Big Four.

For the Holy Father, his presence was doubly welcome at this juncture because of the death on August 22 of the Secretary of State, Luigi Cardinal Maglione. There were so many ways that a former member of the Secretariat could be helpful in a time of sudden confusion. This was the month, too, which saw Churchill, Admiral Standley, our Ambassador to Russia, Hugh Wilson, former Ambassador to Germany, Secretary of War Stimson, and many other distinguished English-speaking visitors paying their respects to Pope Pius XII. Under Secretary of War Robert P. Patterson related that he "called at the Vatican to see the Pope during my recent visit and was being led through a maze of corridors by Swiss guards when I saw Archbishop Spellman coming to meet me. You know the Archbishop is an old friend of mine and he got lost several times when he visited me in the Pentagon building. When he saw me there in the Vatican he smiled and greeted me with: 'Welcome to the Pentagon!' "[26]

During this month, at perhaps the lowest ebb of the fortunes of Italy, when most visitors and many Romans despaired of ever seeing a return of her self-respect, the Archbishop, out of the depths of his experience, analyzed the situation as follows:

> Italy cannot be amputated from the European economy; nor can she be sliced up as fair loot. Italy has a surplus of highly efficient technicians to help in her own reconstruction if she has the material and tools, and then she can take her place and pay her share among the nations of the world. Italy has the head, heart and hands to rebuild her economic structure if given a chance. She knows she must make her come-back the hard way, but in clearing away the wreckage strewn by Fascism and the war, the road back must not lead to economic and political ruin, making Italy a land of beggars, a land of slavery and a land of slaves.
>
> The uprising of the hungry and the unemployed would mean a sweep-

ing victory for Godless government, and the peace will be lost even as the war is won.[27]

On August 15, the American Seventh Army under Lieutenant General Alexander M. Patch landed on the French coast between Cannes and Toulon. The previous week, accompanied by General Thomas C. Darcy, the Archbishop had visited parachute troops and airborne soldiers in Corsica. Flying over from the Italian mainland in General Laurence C. Craigie's plane, he could see far below him in the water the transports filled with American boys on their way to the invasion of southern France. On the island he attended the briefings of some of the air missions and said Mass for the men who were to take part in the invasion. One sailor "asked me if I would write a postscript to a letter he had just written home. I wanted to, of course, but it was impossible to do so without the rain blotting out each word as I wrote it, so the lad suggested that we go under the tailboard of a truck. And we did."[28]

A few days after the landing, when Cannes was still occupied by the Germans, His Excellency flew to France with General Daniel Noce and Ambassador Robert Murphy, and "landed at San Tropez on the first airstrip that the Allies had bulldozed out of French soil in this invasion." For two weeks he remained with the Seventh Army in southern France as they advanced in three directions, east, west, and north, but never south because retreat was never to be considered. It was a time of horror, much too close to the realities of war, and relieved only by news of increasing victories which to a man with a heart brought only partial relief. "I have seen thousands of soldiers and have visited the wounded. I did not like to take names from the wounded because the matter is so delicate but when they asked especially, I did so. I am well, but rushed to the very limit."

Paris was liberated August 25 and the last day of the month, the Archbishop flew to England, where he landed at dawn just in time to see "a Flying Fortress, mortally wounded, come limping back from a mission. . . . Sprawling rag-doll figures of men parachuted from the plunging stricken plane as, fear-frozen, we awaited the inevitable plummet into the houses in its path. But just before the crash, almost like a human making a super-human effort, the plane heaved upwards, just missed the houses, and then crashed to earth in the open field! The superhuman effort had spared homes and lives, but had cost the life of the pilot."[29]

Again there were hours with diplomats, generals, prelates and chaplains, but days on end with the boys.

It was nearly dusk when I left the Embassy, but I wanted to try to get to the general hospital before nightfall. A general hospital may care for about two thousand patients, and while it takes a full day to go from bed to bed, as I always do, there was still time to go through many of the wards and say a word to each patient, and with one young pilot I spent nearly an hour. Each soldier has a story and each soldier is a story! When I talk man to man with individual soldiers, the dangers, horrors and consequences of war are most deeply impressed upon me. The airman longed to talk alone with some one, to open his mind and heart, and I was grateful to be that "some one." . . .

Just as I was leaving the hospital, I met a Chaplain I knew, and he invited me to stay the night with him. The day had been long and I was physically tired and emotionally tired. I gladly accepted his invitation, and went with him to his quarters in the hospital. Tired as I was, I did not go to bed, because the Chaplain wanted to talk to some one, and again I was grateful to be that "some one."[30]

An Oblate chaplain who acted as temporary aide to the Military Vicar recalled afterwards that:

His Excellency was tireless in his efforts to reach as many of the soldiers and WACs as possible.

When he heard there were three wounded priests in as many hospitals, he dropped all appointments to see each personally. Two of the priests had leg wounds from shrapnel, while the third had the thumb and first finger of the left hand blown off in the battle around the Falaise gap. The Archbishop said he would get a dispensation for this priest to say Mass.

And so it went, day after day, with the Archbishop saying Mass for thousands in air hangars, in hospitals and anywhere a crowd of GIs gathered. After each meeting he would speak to all present personally, taking their names and the names and addresses of the nearest of kin, with the promise to write back home that he had met them.[31]

The tide was turning rapidly now. News came from the Continent that the Allies were in the Pas-de-Calais and had occupied the bomb-launching area. The blackout was lifted and the lights went on in London after years of darkness, but when the Military Vicar flew again to France, this time to Normandy, and learned from General Eisenhower that preparations were being made for a winter campaign, his heart sank once more, realizing how many boys would ask him from their hospital cots if they were all going home for Christmas.

Arriving in Paris for the first time in twelve years, His Excellency went at once to pay his respects to the learned, heroic, and abused Cardinal Suhard. Throughout the occupation, the Nazis had made life difficult enough for him, and now the French Reds who had infiltrated the resistance movement were reportedly pressing for his resignation. To make matters worse, General de Gaulle who disagreed with the communists in everything else was unfriendly toward Cardinal Suhard. Thus a delicate situation was created when General de Gaulle asked the Archbishop of New York to celebrate a special

Mass for the GIs in Notre Dame without any reference to His Eminence of Paris. Cardinal Spellman told General de Gaulle that he needed permission from Cardinal Suhard, who welcomed his American visitor with quiet dignity and friendliness, making all the necessary arrangements for him at the cathedral. As a result of the occasion, the general's attitude changed to one of conciliation. During the services at Notre Dame, the Archbishop spoke to more than three thousand servicemen, warning them that:

> If there is only joy in victory then we have failed to win the war. Victory must carry the sober and somber realization that the cost of winning, which is so tremendous, must be paid for by our children and grandchildren. So the war must be won for a peace that will last. Our leaders must realize their responsibility in making a permanent peace and the people must do what is possible for a just peace. Soldiers must realize that a permanent peace is not only made by documents and the action of the state but also by the actions and the character of each soldier. And it is heartwarming to know that our soldiers are fulfilling their part.

A week later he was in Germany, where he joined General Courtney H. Hodges, commanding the First Army, just after the Siegfried line was breached.

> Archbishop Francis J. Spellman of New York celebrated Mass in the church of this German village [Kornelimünster] this morning for the American Army chaplains, German priests and a few of the inhabitants. [It was the first Mass for the Americans on German soil.] Those attending the service could hear the noise of the battle of Stolberg, a few miles away, where American and German soldiers were killing one another.
> Considerable significance may be attached to the fact that Archbishop Spellman chose a time when American armies have barely set foot on German soil, and when a battle still is raging nearby, to hold service in a German church. Many Germans have apparently taken seriously Adolf Hitler's warning that there is no difference between the Americans and "Bolshevik murderers," and that we mean to turn Germany over to the Communists.
> Archbishop Spellman's visit may be regarded as intended to dispel these fears or presumed fears.[32]

Of course he wanted to get closer to the front than the Church of St. Cornelius in Kornelimünster, and this time he had his way.

> Through days and nights [he wrote in *No Greater Love*] I heard the constant grumbling of artillery fire, the singing and crashing of German shells, and saw the flashing and splashing of our own. One night, under cover of darkness and fortified with a password, but feeling more fortified

by the company of two comforting MPs, I went to visit an outfit under the command of General Howell. The password was funny, but I knew it would not be funny if we forgot it! There was not even a ribbon of light. We groped through the darkness, hand in hand, and finally reached our destination, a dimly lighted cellar where we found the General. In the hubbub of noises, General Howell did not understand the officer who introduced us. He took one glance at me, turned to my companion and asked: "Does he speak English?"

I had never before, inside or outside, heard so much noise, nor seen so many people working in such a small space, yet everyone except myself knew exactly what he was doing and what was happening every minute. The General had his full quota of equipment, including the inevitable war maps, but this was the first headquarters I had visited where I was more interested in how I was going to get back than in the General's explanation of where his troops were and where they were going!

Early the next morning I said Mass for a group of our soldiers in the division of the First Army commanded by Major General Louis Alex Craig. . . . My vestments were camouflaged and a camouflaged net was stretched above the portable altar. All during Mass intermittent bursts from machine guns broke the continuous rumble of artillery fire, and the soldiers, who often use their helmets for seats, kept them on their heads except at the Consecration.

A sergeant who was part of his congregation during the battle for the Huertgen forest, outside of Aachen, wrote to his family:

This is a miserable day. I never saw one like it. It's cold, windy, rainy, and it even hailed a few minutes ago. We had the honor of having Archbishop Spellman visit us to offer Mass for the V Corps. We piled into open trucks and rode the few miles to the place where the service was being held. The rain and the wind were wicked, and I heard many remarks to the effect that a fellow had to be mighty religious to go out in this damn weather for service. But it was well worth it. We arrived at the place where the service was to be held and waited around for about half an hour. The Bishop was late because of the poor traveling conditions. But when he arrived he lost no time in starting Mass. The only protection he had was a sheet of canvas strung between four trees over the improvised altar in the woods.

The men, there must have been close to two thousand of them who had come to hear Mass, were gathered around the altar in all directions at least 150 feet deep. I never before saw such a large gathering of Catholic people who were facing such elements of nature as these, just to be able to be part of an expression of their faith. As the Bishop donned his vestments, everyone was silently waiting. . . .

The crowd just stood there during the Mass with their heads bowed and the rain beating down upon them. It was a humble gathering but it stirred the hearts and souls of all those present, I dare say. I received Communion from the Bishop as did about half of those present, and as usual, if not more so, I experienced that inner feeling which is quite inexplicable but known by those of us of our religion who believe in the miracle which our faith professes regarding the Sacrament. One could not help but admire Archbishop Spellman as he offered up Mass. He is a little man of considerable years, and the shelter afforded him little protection from the weather. When he gave Communion, he had to come out from under the shelter and I noticed that his vestments were drenched and just hung on his body and the water literally streamed down his bare head and over his face. Still he paid it not the slightest attention but went on with the service. After Mass he gave a short but inspiring sermon. He told us that this morning he saw what he had seen all over the world as he traveled to say Mass for the men on the front lines. He said that the gathering of us there as we stood in the cold wind and rain was indicative of what men all over the world were doing to be able to be closer to their religion. He illustrated that regardless of the environment, a man's soul and heart could find a home at the Mass no matter where it was held or the prevailing conditions. He said that this gathering was indicative of man's want for peace of mind, soul, and body, and that an expression such as this was, proved that we are a nation in whose hearts such things as war and destruction were alien and foreign and not a natural part.

His words were plain but they were inspiring and had I been in a massive Cathedral, I could not have been more deeply touched than I was as I stood there in the woods midst all the misery of the weather. I'll long remember this Mass and I'll long remember Archbishop Spellman. He certainly lifted the hearts of many men this morning.[33]

In spite of the incredible activity and distraction, His Excellency found time to jot down his experiences, with meticulous attention to detail, in letters to his father. That he was not, at this time, without certain scruples on the question of unfair competition with professional writers appears from the following lines written from Paris to his friends who were in charge at Madison Avenue:

Of course I have tried to be correct and I don't think really I have said anything new. Before any publication, however, I would certainly wish them to be read attentively by the American censor. The only one I had a doubt about, the one concerning General (Sir Frederick A.) Pile, I submitted to Brendan Bracken and it was censored and he wanted it *cabled* for publication somehow. I might leave the decision to Bishop O'Hara and Bishop McIntyre to decide but perhaps it is an unfair responsibility for them to assume. But if they and Grace Tully thought it okay, I would not oppose it. The returns would go to some charity like the Greater New

York Fund or the Foundling. If published, I think the order might have to be changed and they would certainly need better editing than I have been able to give them. I am writing as I am thinking and I remember Martin saying I might be depriving some professional writers of opportunities. I can't say "yes." So I leave it to you, for I am inclined to say "No" and I do say "No" if I must give a "yes" or "no" answer now after reading Miss Algase's letter, *not* because I do not believe that what I wrote might be interesting (she is kind enough to say that it is constructive), but because criticism of me might harm the Church. I remember Cardinal Gasparri's expression when he declined to write his memoirs: "What would be interesting I cannot write. What I can write would not be interesting." So therefore take all these considerations in mind and do what you think is best for the country and for the Church. That sounds awfully conceited as if I could do much for either. *Afterthought,* I think it will be difficult to overcome the hurdle that money is being paid for my articles and I have more, incredibly more, facilities than any correspondent, but again you think it over and decide *quite coldly.*

And "quite coldly" the decision was made by the Archbishop's associates, and the letters were published as *Action This Day,* first as a series in *Collier's* magazine and later between hard covers by Scribner's.

It was now less than three months since the Military Vicar had left home with the intention of circling the globe. While he was still in Paris, on September 11, he had received a mysterious message through SHSGS from Leo J. Crowley who was then the Foreign Economic Administrator: "Due to importance of matters arising here, where your assistance is most respectfully sought, advise your soonest return America, if you can reasonably do so. Please advise." The next day, a liaison officer in Rome had telegraphed: "In view of Mr. Crowley's message to you, please advise what disposition you wish made of items you left here. We all hope very much we will have an opportunity to see you before you return to U.S." At the same time, Myron Taylor wrote, saying: "We have a message from Mr. Leo Crowley through Secretary Hull, Washington, asking your earliest return to America due to the importance of matters requiring your assistance and requesting answer."

Not having any idea what "the matters arising" could be, His Excellency had cabled to Mr. Crowley: "Have only half completed trip which is regarded to be of importance. Cancellation will cause disappointment to many. Feel Archbishops Mooney, Stritch and Bishops McIntyre and O'Hara can speak for me." Under the same date, a message had gone to Bishop McIntyre in New York: "Leo Crowley requests my return for assistance in regard some unspecified matter. Advising him that Archbishop Mooney, Bishop O'Hara and yourself fully competent to act for me in every way. Feeling well and desire to continue unless you advise otherwise." Then two weeks had passed without any answer from Washington, and on September 26, Colonel Ray Ireland had written cryptically to the Archbishop in Germany: "Leo matter tabled satisfactorily."

With a sigh of relief His Excellency had begun to plan the rest of his trip when on October 5, during his second visit to Rome, a message reached him through the United States representative of the Advisory Council for Italy: "I wish to repeat that it is thought by some good friends of yours that you should return home soon. [signed] Hull." His answer this time was sent through Ambassador Kirk to Leo Crowley for Secretary Hull:

> Had understood from Bishop McIntyre that the matter which prompted your previous request for my return had been satisfactorily adjusted. Therefore I assume that some new reason prompts your present request. If it regards any situation in Italy I feel that Judge Marchisio who is returning to America in a few days can give a clear complete picture and I concur in his viewpoint. If however it regards the wish of the President to see me for whatsoever reason then I shall immediately and gladly return. Otherwise I would like to continue according to my itinerary. I shall not leave Rome until I have your reply.

At the bottom of the message there is a note in the handwriting of the Archbishop that the message was "answered through the Vatican and through Mr. Kirk that my presence is urgently requested and that my assumption that 'it is your friend who wishes you to return' is correct." As soon as he had confirmation that it was the President who wanted him home, he cabled at once to the Secretary of State: GLADLY CANCELLING PLANS AND LEAVING IMMEDIATELY ARRIVING NEW YORK SATURDAY NIGHT OR SUNDAY MORNING. PLEASE INFORM COLONEL IRELAND'S OFFICE ALSO CONFIDENTIALLY INFORM PORT AUTHORITIES AND HOUSEHOLD AND FAMILY.

It was only on his arrival home that he learned all the reasons for his mysterious recall. They concerned the tragic plight of the Italian people. A few days before the first message from Leo J. Crowley had warned him that his help was needed in Washington, a correspondent of the New York *Times* had described the situation in Rome as "alarming" and "terrifying." Infant mortality had risen in four years from 102.8 to 438 per 1000 for children in their first year. In June 1944 twice as many adults had died in Rome as in June 1943. Before the war a healthy Italian consumed about 3100 calories a day. Now under the Allied occupation, the basic ration was fixed at 664.7, roughly one-fifth of the pre-war average.[34] The people were starving in the streets and the blame was being laid on the severity of the Allied Control Commission which Anne O'Hare McCormick of the *Times* described as the *de facto* government of Italy, a body under the presidency and acting presidency of two British generals. Its lesser officers were about equally divided between the British and Americans, the former mostly older Army men and sometime colonial officials, the latter a heterogeneous lot just out

of the American Military Government schools. To forestall large-scale riot-
ing and social disintegration, Brigadier General William O'Dwyer was hastening home in September to plead with the President of the United States
for a more humane administration. This cruel and dangerous state of affairs
had been known the previous May to the War Relief Services of the National Catholic Welfare Conference whose members initiated negotiations
with Major General John H. Hilldring, director of the Civil Affairs Division
of the War Department, and Mr. Charles Taft of the State Department for
permission to send a group of six persons to Italy to do relief work.

A month later, Mr. Taft prepared a memorandum endorsing the request
of the War Relief Services and transmitted it to General Hilldring who reported after every possible delay had been created by the War Department
that he could not get permission through the Joint High Command. On
August 30, Mr. Leo Crowley telephoned to the general and was informed
that the difficulty was in the War Department itself. It was then that Mr.
Crowley talked with the President who sent a memorandum to the War
Department directing that four priests should be cleared at once for relief
work in Italy. At this juncture the first message went to Archbishop Spellman asking him to come home. Still nothing happened and Roosevelt was
annoyed to find at the end of September that his memorandum had been
effectively ignored. Another and stronger note went to the War Department;
the visas were finally issued, and the four priests left for Rome five months
late, about the time of His Excellency's arrival in New York.

The Archbishop landed at La Guardia Airport at 2:40 A.M. on October
16 and arrived unexpectedly at Madison Avenue about an hour later. As he
sat with Monsignor Casey briefly in the study exchanging bits of news before His Excellency could retire for a good, long, much needed rest, the
Monsignor remarked casually that Bishop Donahue intended to go down
that morning to St. Francis Xavier's, where Father Martin J. Scott was celebrating his diamond jubilee as a member of the Society of Jesus. The Archbishop, who could hardly keep his eyes open, said, "Tell him I'll go myself."
So, after sleeping an hour and a half and saying a seven o'clock Mass, he
was on the throne for the Jubilee Mass at eleven.

Two days later, the Military Vicar reported to his Commander-in-Chief.
That he fell under the spell all over again is evident from his letter to Roosevelt under date of October 23:

> My heartfelt thanks for the unforgettable experience of the luncheon
> on Wednesday. The occasions down through the last twelve years when
> I have had the privilege and the honor of being with you are indeed
> precious memories deepened and made more precious with time's pass-
> ing. I feel each time with greater force the strength of your being, as a
> man and as an American and *I do hope and pray with all my heart and*
> *soul that your desires* and efforts for the welfare of our country and for
> world peace will be realized; for, otherwise,—?

I was pleased to think that I could bring some little information which you deemed of value.[35]

By this time, however, the writer's sincere devotion to the President was already troubled by doubts. The more he thought about the policy of unconditional surrender and discussed it with military authorities of the highest rank, the more impossible it was for him to accept it. He could see that it not only stiffened German resistance and cost both sides innumerable casualties, but it made everything the Pope and he himself had been praying for seem so futile. The Holy Father's favorite phrase, repeated again and again, had been "Peace with Justice," but what armed forces had ever been just with an utterly prostrate foe? For the time being, the Military Vicar, like a good soldier, had worked hard to accept the explanation of his Commander-in-Chief that the phrase should be accepted as interpreted by General Grant. He tried to see the great American leader after the war, surrounded by a golden radiance, forgiving whole sections of the world and "giving them back their horses," but to complicate matters, the second Conference at Quebec had been held in September. There the plan of Secretary Morgenthau to annihilate the German people by dismembering their country and giving pieces of flesh to all the neighbors; by wrecking all the mines and factories and condemning seventy million human beings to live off a piece of land that would not feed half of them; a plan characterized by Secretary Hull as one of "blind vengeance," had been accepted by Churchill and Roosevelt almost without reservation. The President's comment afterward was a strange echo of the words falsely attributed to Marie Antoinette, "Let them eat cake." He wrote:

> I do not want them to starve to death but as an example, if they need food to keep body and soul together beyond what they have, they should be fed three times a day with soup from Army soup kitchens. That will keep them perfectly healthy and they will remember the experience all their lives. . . . The German people as a whole must have it driven home to them that the whole nation has been engaged in a lawless conspiracy against the decencies of modern civilization.[36]

The modest picture which had been in his mind of another Grant handing out horses had now advanced to the more impressive image of the Eternal Judge in the Valley of Josaphat.

On the same day that Hull had received the President's memo embracing the Morgenthau plan, he received another informing him that Morgenthau had presented at Quebec, in conjunction with the plan for Germany, a proposal of credits to Britain in the amount of six and a half billion dollars. The Secretary of State wrote later: "This might suggest to some the *quid pro quo* with which the Secretary of the Treasury was able to get Mr. Churchill's adherence to his cataclysmic plan for Germany. . . . This whole development at Quebec, I believe, angered me as much as anything that had happened during my career as Secretary of State."[37]

On Roosevelt's return to Washington, Hull found that "he did not seem to realize the devastating nature of the memorandum of September 15 to which he had put his 'O.K.—F.D.R.'" Later in the month, Secretary Stimson had a talk with the President from which he drew the same conclusion:

> He informed me [said Hull] that he had thereupon read to the President several sentences from the President's memorandum of September 15, concluding with the phrase "looking forward to converting Germany into a country primarily agricultural and pastoral in its character."
>
> Stimson informed me that the President was frankly staggered at hearing these sentences and said that he had no idea how he could have initialed the memorandum, and that he had evidently done so without much thought.

This ominous change that was coming over the President was not lost on the observant Archbishop. It brought back to his mind snatches of conversation that had disturbed him during the past year in many of their friendly visits together. He could recall the disarming smile with which Roosevelt would say, "The Pope is too worried about communism," and the rich tones of his voice as he expressed his sympathy with the great Soviet democracy. "Russia," he said one evening when they were sitting around after dinner in the White House, "has need of protection. She has been invaded twice, you know. That is why we shall give her part of Poland and recompense Poland with a part of Germany."

The Archbishop protested, "But your decision cannot cause a part of Poland to become Russia except by driving the population off their land. It is immoral to uproot people like that and take away their homes and their churches and even their cemeteries."

He remembered especially the interview the week before the President left for his conference with Stalin and Churchill at Teheran. It had shocked him profoundly that Roosevelt would go much more than halfway to meet the Red dictator in his own back yard, and he told him so. Nor was he reconciled when his "old friend" answered with a smile, "Don't worry. I know how to talk to Stalin. He is just another practical man who wants peace and prosperity."

The Archbishop answered, "He is not just another anything. He is different. You can't trust him. He'll never co-operate."

Worried as he often was, however, he would conclude that despite occasional signs of irresponsibility, coupled with loose social and political planning, F.D.R. was still a genius, a very charming genius, and able to end the horrors of a world war. It was not, therefore, a mark of blindness, inconsistency, or hypocrisy for the Archbishop to send the following letter when an ailing Roosevelt was elected to a fourth term:

Heartfelt congratulations on the verdict of your countrymen that at once gives approval to the way in which you have directed the Ship of State through twelve trying years and also is a vote of confidence in your guidance in the years that lie ahead. . . .

The President thanked his "old friend," sent his "affectionate regards," and invited him to the buffet luncheon after the inaugural on January 20.

The President's health was too precarious to risk a ride to the Capitol for the ceremony, and the oath was administered on the back porch of the White House. Robert Sherwood wrote later that "it was a short, simple ceremony, the brevity being due to the fact that the President was determined to stand up throughout it (I don't think that he ever wore his braces and stood up again)."[38] Frances Perkins and Mrs. Wallace were worried by his appearance. It seemed to Stettinius "that some kind of deterioration in the President's health had taken place between the middle of December and the inauguration of January 20th."[39] Yet almost immediately he set out on a long and difficult journey over a winter sea to determine personally the fate of half the world. When he reached Valetta, Malta, after a ten-day voyage on the heavy cruiser U.S.S. *Quincy*, Admiral King expressed alarm at his condition. Later, his one-time Special Assistant Secretary of the Navy and our former Ambassador to Soviet Russia, William C. Bullitt, was to write:

> At Yalta in the Crimea, on February 4, 1945, the Soviet Dictator welcomed the weary President. Roosevelt, indeed, was more than tired. He was ill. Little was left of the physical and mental vigor that had been his when he entered the White House in 1933. Frequently he had difficulty in formulating his thoughts, and greater difficulty in expressing them consecutively. But he still held to his determination to appease Stalin.[40]

The Archbishop in his office on Madison Avenue knew no more than the general public of what was going on behind closed doors somewhere in the Black Sea area, but when he found that his President had traveled 5700 miles, not to a neutral spot but to Russia because the Red dictator refused to leave home, he felt the humiliation as most Americans did. Fortunately for his peace of mind, he could not read the significant note slipped to the President by Harry Hopkins in the midst of a crucial discussion: "The Russians have given in so much at this Conference that I don't think we should let them down."[41] In any case, he was reassured when the New York *Times* said on February 13: "The alliance of the Big Three stands firm. Progress has been made. The hope of further gains is high. This conference marks a milestone on the road to victory and peace."[42] Wishful thinking was in the air.

When, therefore, the news came from Warm Springs, Georgia, a few weeks after Roosevelt's return, that the Commander-in-Chief was gone, the "old friend" in New York was sincere in his expressions of regret. His telegram to Mrs. Roosevelt came straight from the heart: NO WORDS CAN EXPRESS MY GRIEF AT THE DEATH OF THE PRESIDENT AND THE LOSS TO THE WORLD, THE NATION AND YOURSELF. I OFFER YOU MY PRAYERS.[43]

After a few months, however, as details of the things that were done at Yalta gradually seeped through to the American people, the Archbishop's old doubts and fears began to grow into genuine disillusionment. The climax came when His Excellency learned that his one-time ideal had handed over to Soviet Russia, not only southern Sakhalin but all the Kurile Islands too, for it stirred the memory of a certain evening at the White House just after his return from Alaska. It was a painfully vivid memory. Roosevelt had been summing up for his guest the events in the Pacific Theatre and pointing to a map on the wall that showed the Kurile Islands, said dramatically, "Those islands are a dagger aimed at the heart of America. They must never fall into the hands of an enemy." The Archbishop realized, with a sinking feeling, that the dagger was now in the hands of our most dangerous enemy and that a sick President had unwittingly put it there.

CHAPTER FIFTEEN

Temporalities

IT WAS now six years since the Auxiliary Bishop of Boston arrived on Madison Avenue for his installation in St. Patrick's Cathedral. The time had been so crowded with important matters extraneous to his episcopal duties that it comes as a surprise to find out how much had been accomplished during that period in the temporal administration of the archdiocese.

No distortion of values was involved when the new Ordinary turned his attention first to material things. It was common sense to find out what he had to work with before he started to work. He had known that there were financial problems which had not been solved since the dark days of 1929, but whether mercifully or not, no one had told him the whole truth. The first inkling he had of the real situation was from the tactless letter which lay among the welcoming flowers in his room when he retired for his first night's rest in New York. It was from his bankers, saying that the mortgages which they held on the property of the archdiocese aggregated "in the vicinity of $28,000,000" and suggesting that this sum could easily be increased. The letter ended with the words: "I am wondering whether you would be kind enough to see us for this purpose and if so, whether you would name a time at which we might call on you."

Two months later, there was an entry in the diary for July 19, 1939: "Saw Mr. X and Mr. Y of the Z National Bank and answered their letter which I received on the date of my installation saying that the archdiocese owed $28,000,000. The interview was very satisfactory to me, but not to them." In these two months, he had arranged savings in interest that already amounted to half a million dollars a year. It had not been easy. The bank which held the mortgages was charging six per cent and assured him that there could be no reduction. He inquired in other New York houses and found that with one exception the financial fraternity had such chivalrous ideals of professional courtesy that they would not enter into competition. The exception was the Bankers Trust Company, whose president, Seward Prosser, offered to lend the archdiocese $10,000,000 for ten years at two-and-a-half per cent. That made the rest easy. The Archbishop, being a "foreigner," knew that there were banks and trust companies outside of New York City, so on the next trip home he looked up some of his old friends in Boston and asked them if they were willing to take over part of his burden. They were more than willing. So on June 30 the diary reads: "Had Monsignor McIntyre come on from New York to talk to Frank Comerford. We also had a talk with Guy Cox of The John Hancock Life Insurance Company, and Serge Sermenenko of the First National Bank." The next day: "Returned to New York on the midnight train. Had interest on notes of Diocese reduced by one per cent and more, saving $100,000 in interest." By the end of July he wrote: "Still making progress in reducing interest. The Phoenix Life Insurance Company of Boston is now offering me money at three per cent for ten years and more."

On August 23 he could send to all the pastors and superiors in the archdiocese a letter which established him overnight in their loyal affection as the answer to a prayer:

One of the matters to which I have given attention since my installation has been the prospect of lightening the burden of debts which oppresses many of the parishes and the institutions of the archdiocese. I am pleased to report progress and to say that many banks have made substantial reductions in interest rates, for which we are most grateful. The parishes will be able to use these savings effected by lower interest charges to make substantial payments on the principal debts.

There are, however, some parishes which are weighed down with debts that they are absolutely unable to carry. These situations are due to unforeseen and unforeseeable circumstances, such as the depression and losses in the number of parishioners. . . .

It is clear that the accumulation of such situations has resulted in the creation of a diocesan problem, the solution of which requires the whole-hearted cooperation of all of us who are in a position to help. Each individual case must be considered as promptly as possible, and, if the welfare of souls, which must be the paramount determining factor in all of our actions, warrants the continuation of such parishes, then all of us should share in their maintenance and support. . . . I shall, therefore, welcome the practical cooperation of the pastors of any parishes who have balances of more than five thousand or ten thousand dollars. I invite the pastors of such parishes, who contemplate no immediate building or extensive repair programs, to come to my assistance in helping me to help others. At the present time I do not intend to make this a matter of obligation. . . .

I wish to avail myself of this occasion to make some general observations in regard to some parochial matters.

In the future no priest will be appointed pastor of a new parish until he has been provided with a tract of land free of debt and a certain amount of unencumbered money placed at his disposal so that he and his parishioners may reasonably hope to have a church and a rectory not only built but paid for within a maximum period of fifteen years.

Any parish priest who has a debt on his parish and at the same time has a credit balance greater than is prudently necessary for current or proximate expenses is expected to pay off as much of his debt as is possible and to pay it off at once to eliminate unnecessary interest charges.

Parish priests are reminded that they are not to make purchases of any securities or to sell any of their present holdings without consultation with and authorization from the Chancellor.

At this time I wish to give details concerning the very generous terms which the banks have offered to us to help us pay off our debts. . . .

The categories and the terms are as follows:

1. If a parish is in a position to pay off all of its debt in one year, that parish may borrow money at the rate of one and one-half per cent per year.

2. If a parish can pay off all of its indebtedness within five years, the money can be obtained at the rate of two per cent per year.

3. If a parish is able to pay off its entire debt in ten years, the rate will be two and one-half per cent per year.

4. If a parish is not able to pay off all its debt within a ten year period, but it can pay it off at the rate of three per cent per year, then the interest rate will be only an additional three per cent. In other words, a pastor who can pay six per cent a year on his total debt will have three per cent applied to principal payment and three per per cent to interest. If possible, it is, of course, highly desirable, and obviously so, to pay off more than six per cent per year, because all payments above three per cent of the interest will be applied to the reduction of the principal debt . . . This arrangement has been fixed for the next five years.

5. If a parish is able to pay off its debt at the rate of one and one-half per cent per year, which is a very slow rate of amortization, then the interest on such a debt will be at the rate of three and one-half per cent. In other words, with a five per cent annual payment, one and one-half per cent will be applied to the debt and three and one-half per cent to the interest. This concession has been obtained for a period of ten years, and, since the terms are very favorable for such a long term period, I recommend that parish priests take advantage of these terms and pay as much on the principal debts as is possible, since all payments in excess of three and one-half per cent will be used to reduce the principal debt.

We have these extremely low rates of interest for five and ten-year periods. We cannot hope to have them continued at these low rates after the expiration of these periods, so we must concentrate on debt reduction now.

There will be no necessity to change banks with which parish priests are now doing business, unless some bank does not desire to meet these conditions. There will be no expenses connected with the arrangements.

Praying for you and your devoted parishioners, and thanking you for your good will and cooperation, and assuring you of my own.

The "Reverend dear Father" to whom the letter was addressed soon received a new account book which would simplify and facilitate parish accounts, and an announcement that the Reverend Walter F. Kellenberg and the Reverend Edward J. Engels had been appointed "to supervise all transactions concerning insurance." The Archbishop advised consultation with these priests and strongly recommended public liability, workmen's compensation, and boiler insurance in addition to the fire insurance customarily carried. This was followed by a system of accident, health, and group life insurance for the members of the clergy and eventually for the brothers and sisters as well, which had the twofold effect of helping priests and religious meet their own hospital bills and at the same time lifting a financial burden from the sisters' hospitals. As a final touch of efficiency, the Archdiocesan Service Corporation was developed and expanded so that through it the agencies of the archdiocese could have surveys made of their insurance rates and coverage to determine whether or not savings could be effected.

In 1943 The Archdiocesan Reciprocal Loan Fund was set up. It is to all intents and purposes a real diocesan bank, so that since its foundation no parish or other institution under the jurisdiction of the Cardinal has arranged a loan or a mortgage elsewhere. It is a source of much consolation to a harassed pastor to know that no matter what his debt may be, his entire obligation is to his own diocese. It makes the question of foreclosure so academic.

Like carefully planned loans and insurance, the wise purchase and sale of real estate is an almost hidden factor in the over-all security of a diocese. Here again, New York has been farsighted. In his first twenty years, the Archbishop authorized 528 separate transactions, an average of about two a month, involving aggregate sums in excess of $132,000,000, an average of about $550,000 a month.

One almost incredible example must suffice. Cathedral College occupied the entire west side of Madison Avenue from 51st to 52nd Street, where the Look Building now stands, and the chancery was opposite on the corner of 51st. Together they comprised 37,500 square feet, and were sold in one year for $4,525,000. A new college was then bought on West End Avenue for $155,000. Soon after this, the Whitelaw Reid and Hubbard properties aggregating 32,600 square feet at Madison Avenue and 50th Street were acquired for $1,650,000. On the land there were buildings admirably adapted for chancery purposes which could not be duplicated for $2,500,000. Thus property was sold in one block for $125 a square foot and bought in the next block with suitable buildings already erected for $50 a square foot. In other words, overnight, the archdiocese had a new college and a new chancery and $2,720,000 for charitable and educational purposes.

On October 30, 1941, the first general membership meeting of the Institutional Commodity Services, a central purchasing agency, was held at the suggestion of Archbishop Spellman. Among other things, a plan to purchase milk in volume was discussed with all the procurators of institutions and administrators of hospitals present. Their participation was then, as it has been ever since then, entirely optional so that not all agreed to try it. But the shining fact remains that the creation of the Institutional Commodity Services just before the United States entered the war was an outstanding example of providential timing. The services rendered by the department went far beyond saving money in the purchase of food and other commodities. The problems of rationing, for example, were in many cases turned over to I.C.S. for advice and direction. At this time too, it was selected by the United States Department of Agriculture as an official agency for the distribution of surplus foods and in the years since then has channeled to eligible institutions nine million pounds valued at more than $2,500,000. These services would have justified its existence even if the total of goods purchased had not advanced steadily as the institutions of the archdiocese came to realize better the possibilities of I.C.S. The figure of $913,141 for the purchasing volume in 1942 was doubled by 1945 and for 1960 the total reached the impressive sum of $14,040,000. The savings were in proportion. During the war they were not great, $114,143 the first year, but I.C.S. did secure goods at the ceiling price and was able to insure the delivery of goods when they were difficult to obtain. In 1945, the minimum over-all savings were at least $250,000. In the report for 1960, when almost anything used in quantity could be ordered through I.C.S., the director announced with justifiable pride that he had saved $1,650,000 for the institutions and parishes wise enough to use the service.

Even more important in the over-all administration of temporalities was the establishment in 1939 of the Archdiocesan Building Commission. When Monsignor McIntyre was unable to suggest anyone in New York for the office of director, Mr. Fred Mack, who had been the architectural and structural adviser to the Sacred Heart Parish in Newton Center, was placed in charge. The general purpose of the new service and the success with which it was carried out are indicated in the remarks of a grateful pastor at the dedication of his new convent and chapel.

Under this arrangement, when a building is to be erected in the Archdiocese, the Building Commission helps the pastor or superior in the selecting of a reliable architect; once the general requirements of the building are known, the Commission supervises the plans and the drawing up of the specifications, asks for competitive bids and directs the actual construction. The pastor or superior has expert advice throughout all the building operations and I can tell you, from my own experiences, it is a blessing. While the building is going up, the Institution Commodity Services is on hand to help in the selection of the furnishings. Its representatives suggest the most reliable firms, check prices, see to the best discount and inspect the furnishings as they are delivered.[1]

Some idea of the rapid expansion of the program can be seen in the following breakdown of projected work issued by members of the commission on February 3, 1951, the year that saw the appointment of Monsignor Walter P. Kellenberg as director:

> Construction has begun or is about to begin on four new churches on Staten Island and in the Bronx under an estimated budget of $1,450,000. Six schools with auditoriums to serve temporarily as churches for the new parishes established by His Eminence in 1948, will be started in the next ten months at a cost of $3,150,000. Ten additional parochial schools and a dormitory at a Catholic girls' college are projected at a cost of $8,150,000. The sixteen schools will have a total capacity of 9,250 pupils.
>
> Three college projects consisting of Manhattan College's $2,000,000 Science Building and Engineering Building, ground for which was recently broken; relocation of Manhattanville College of the Sacred Heart on the former Ogden Reid Estate in Purchase, New York, the plans of which are in the early development stages at this time and assumed to approximate $7,000,000; Fordham's $2,000,000 building expansion program. These projects totaling $11,000,000 are in addition to those previously announced by Monsignor Kellenberg.
>
> A $2,000,000 wing will be erected for St. Vincent's Hospital. . . . The largest item in the hospital program is the $2,250,000 St. Francis Hospital in Poughkeepsie, now nearing completion. Two other up-state hospital additions, Our Lady of Victory in Kingston, and Good Samaritan Hospital in Suffern, and a nurses' home at St. Clare's Hospital bring the hospital program to $7,500,000.
>
> In the remainder of the program are three convents in Manhattan and the Bronx costing $1,950,000 and a $1,500,000 expansion planned for the children's homes at the Mission of the Immaculate Virgin on Staten Island.
>
> The present estimates for the entire program total $34,700,000.

These figures are a little confusing because of the listing of college projects conceived and carried out by groups that were in but not of the archdiocese and of projects which that year were only in the planning stage. As an over-all picture, they are important enough to record, but for a more accurate estimate of Archbishop Spellman's influence on the expansion of facilities we need to know what was finished in the course of a recent calendar year and how that compares with the achievements of a typical year before he arrived in New York.

The minutes of the diocesan consultors' meetings for 1936, when the depression was on the wane and the threat of war had not yet appeared, reveal the following program successfully completed: there were sixteen new buildings—two rectories, three churches, three schools and additions to eight institutions—erected at a cost of $1,883,000. There were, besides, substantial alterations to thirteen buildings at a cost of $345,000. The total expenditures for 1936 were $2,228,000.

The official report of the Archdiocesan Building Commission for 1958 lists the following diocesan projects as completed during that year: there were 61 new buildings—2 churches, 2 rectories, 26 schools, 14 convents, 6 institutions, 2 colleges and additions to 9 institutions—erected at a cost of $28,239,900. Still more impressive is the grand total of activity, reported by His Eminence during his last "Ad Limina" visit to the Holy Father. It covers the five years from 1955 through 1959. During that period, the building commission, now under the direction of the Right Reverend Monsignor Leonard J. Hunt, has supervised 1377 projects, costing $168,100,000. The breakdown is interesting:

Projects: 1955–1959

Churches	15	$ 11,625,000.
Schools	94	55,490,000.
Rectories	22	5,460,000.
Convents	60	24,440,000.
Institutions	30	42,685,000.
Total	221	$ 139,700,000.
Major additions, alterations and repairs on projects	1156	28,400,000.
Grand Total	1377	$ 168,100,000.

This underscores the fact that even though the scale of construction costs in 1959 was three times that of 1939, there was still in the intervening years an immense increase of building activity, and no one on the scene could doubt that the driving force behind most of it was the Ordinary of the diocese. Much of it originated with him and depended directly on him for funds. This was especially true of the great high schools, the major hospitals, and extraordinary parish churches. Everything was carefully studied and approved by him. The increase in the pressure of his work was reflected in the increase in the number and the added responsibilities of the archdiocesan consultors. Formerly they used to meet, all six of them, around a mahogany table in a small room next to the Archbishop's study. Now only the great hall in the chancery office is suitable. There, every month, thirty places are set and the Ordinary, surrounded by his vicars general, his auxiliary bishops, his chancellors, his deans and other officials, reviews every project in the archdiocese and many of the problems. The secretary of the meeting reads off the list: "Father Celestine of St. Bede's on Staten Island wants to build a new convent." There is a suppressed smile around the board as the Dean of Richmond rises to the occasion. Fifty such convents would be none too good for his district, and fifty more churches. The Archbishop agrees with him and after a little banter, appoints two consultors to visit the parish and make a report at the next meeting. His manner is informal, the tone of the group is relaxed and everyone speaks his mind, occasionally disagreeing with the expressed opinion of the Archbishop until a decision has been reached. Thereupon the ranks close and everyone co-operates for the success of the venture.

A brief outline of a few such ventures will have to substitute for a whole mass of important details since the laying of cornerstones, though one of a bishop's most significant functions, is very like the laying of other cornerstones by other bishops and the speeches delivered on such occasions are common to the Universal Church. Take the matter of Catholic hospitals in New York. Since 1939 construction projects completed have cost an impressive total of $48,209,905. Those now on the way reach $14,281,587. That would mean that in the course of 25 years the Ordinary will have had the quiet satisfaction of spending some $62,491,492 on hospitals alone. There are twenty of them, and most of them have seen the recent laying of a cornerstone or two, like Misericordia Hospital, dedicated in September 1958. This was one of the largest single building projects ever undertaken by the archdiocese and was erected on the Bronx River Parkway at a cost of $10,000,000, but St. Vincent's Hospital in the Village happens to be older and larger.

There are thirty-nine institutions for handicapped and neglected children, but the New York Foundling Hospital is one of the oldest and most picturesque. In addition to one university, which as the Archbishop's Alma Mater has had already more than its share of mention, there are eighteen colleges, three for men and fifteen for women, but Manhattanville was the first of the eighteen and has made the most spectacular move in recent years. Of high schools, private and diocesan, there are 99 at the moment. Cardinal Hayes High School was the first great educational venture on the part of the new Archbishop. So some detail with regard to these four institutions will be no slight to any of the others and will indicate a solicitude and helpfulness on the part of the Ordinary who has known no favorites.

St. Vincent's founded in 1849 was the first Catholic hospital on the East Coast where there are now 203. Progressing soon after to a red brick structure on Twelfth Street, it had expanded by 1939 around Seventh Avenue to Eleventh Street, occupying three buildings. Shortly after his arrival in New York, the Archbishop announced that an eight-story wing would be added on Eleventh Street, to be known at the urgent plea of Sister Loretto Bernard, as the Spellman Pavilion. The cornerstone was laid March

13, 1941, and the building dedicated in the early confusion of the war, January 4, 1942. The cost was $1,300,000. By the end of 1944, His Excellency was vaguely planning another building.

During his second visit to the front, when word had reached him in Rome that Al Smith was on his deathbed, he had cabled at once the last blessing of the Holy Father, following it with detailed instructions to Madison Avenue: "I think an exception should be made in his case and a eulogy preached —a formal eulogy from the pulpit. Will Monsignor Donahue preach it. He represents New York as well as the Archbishop of New York. Will Bishop McIntyre please pontificate." The former Governor of New York was to lie in state in St. Patrick's Cathedral, an honor only once before accorded a layman—Ignace Jan Paderewski—in the history of the archdiocese and meanwhile he would have a Memorial Mass in the American Church of Santa Susanna, with a choir from the Sistine Chapel.

Soon after returning to this country, the Archbishop said publicly: "His memory inspires and encourages me and that it may inspire and encourage others, I intend to erect a building that will perpetuate the name of Alfred E. Smith, a memorial that will render American, Catholic, friendly service to the people of his beloved City of New York." A few weeks later, the diary records: "Talked with Sister Loretto Bernard about an Alfred E. Smith Pavilion at St. Vincent's." The following May, 1945, the announcement was made that construction would begin as soon as possible on a sixteen-story, $3,000,000 addition to the hospital on Twelfth Street, to be known as the Alfred E. Smith Memorial.

During the summer, a campaign for funds was organized and in October it was formally inaugurated at a brilliant dinner. The national response was disappointing and building prices increased, so the time of the appeal was further extended. With the establishment the following year of the Alfred E. Smith Memorial Foundation, Inc., the dinner became an annual event of the first importance. On one such occasion, the Cardinal said:

> I give my heart's gratitude to Mr. Charles H. Silver, Vice President of the Foundation and Chairman of the Dinner Committee, who has tirelessly devoted himself to helping make this Annual Dinner so successful. Charles Silver is himself the President of a great hospital—the Beth Israel Hospital—and, in memory of Governor Smith, his friend and ours, I ask Mr. Silver to accept this gift of ten thousand dollars towards the needs of his own hospital. To the gracious, generous lady who once again has donated the entire costs of this dinner [later announced as an old friend of Roman days, Mrs. Evelyn Mendelssohn of Detroit], I offer tribute in my own name and in the name of all who will benefit from her munificent gift.
>
> Finally I express esteem for and gratitude to Gertrude Algase who originated this Annual Dinner to perpetuate the ideals and practices of

Governor Smith's devotion to the sick, the poor and the needy—an event that yearly contributes more than a quarter of a million dollars in supplemental funds toward the erection of the hospital that will bear the Governor's name, and who, with Monsignor John J. O'Donnell of the Archdiocese of New York, has again directed and brought to this happy conclusion another of these remarkable dinners.

The second year there was a $250-a-plate affair at which James A. Farley, the chairman, announced that the $3,000,000 goal had been reached. By the time the cornerstone was laid in May of 1949, the estimated cost had risen to $5,000,000, but the Foundation, with a regular source of income from the annual dinners which are usually addressed by international figures such as President Eisenhower, Prime Minister Churchill, Vice-President Barkley, and Secretary of State Acheson would be able to carry on for years without another organized drive. When Vice-President Nixon spoke at the Tenth Anniversary, the President expressed his satisfaction:

YOUR EMINENCE:
Recently Dick Nixon told me of the very cordial reception he had at the annual Alfred E. Smith Dinner. He spoke with particular gratification of your great courtesy to him.

I write this note, firstly, to thank you for the honor you did to a young man whom I consider to be a very splendid American. Secondly, I want to felicitate you on the great success of your Dinner, which seems each year to be a more notable event. Finally, it just seemed to me that it had been such a long time since I had communicated with you directly (I do hear of you often from Bernard Shanley) that I wanted to send along my very best wishes and warm greetings.

When I told Mamie of my intention to drop you a note this morning, she was insistent that I include her affectionate regard along with my own.
                                                    Sincerely,
                                        DWIGHT D. EISENHOWER

The next time Vice-President Nixon was invited he shared the program with dynamic young Senator Kennedy. Both guests were invited at the same time previous to their nomination as candidates for the Presidency. Reporters watched the smiling host for some slight indication of his preference but had to admit that his neutrality was perfect.

With the Dinner well established the Archbishop was soon ready for the next step, the replacement of the last remnant of the original hospital on the corner of Seventh Avenue and Twelfth Street. No name could have been more appropriate for the companion to the Smith Memorial than that of John J. Raskob. Devoted personal and political friends that they were, the two men had shared the triumphs and bitterness of 1928, and when Al bowed to the inevitable and retired to private life, it was as president of John's new building, the Empire State. Mr. Raskob had died on October 14, 1950, and the trustees of the John J. Raskob Foundation pledged an annual contribution of $150,000 that would in ten years cover one half the cost of the new twelve-story wing.

The present number of beds is 830 where there were in 1939 just 465, an increase of seventy-eight per cent. This was impressive enough, but does not represent the extent of the new obligations which have been assumed. The cost of operating a first-class hospital is soaring. It is interesting to note that in 1939, all the diocesan hospitals with a personnel of 3429, had operating expenses of $4,413,297. For 1960 with the personnel increased only two and a half times, the operating expenses were multiplied eight times to a total of $36,533,958. For St. Vincent's, the difference was proportionate. Its debt however, is lower today than it was in 1939 in spite of the fact that $15,000,000 have been spent in improvements and new construction.

Nothing daunted, then, the Archbishop turned his attention to the question of child care. It was always his policy to attack each problem as if he could depend on nothing but his ordinary resources and meanwhile to scan the horizon for a prospective benefactor. It had been so, for example, with a child caring project on the Pelham Parkway in the Bronx. He had bought the property with several buildings from the Gould Foundation for $925,000 and planned to spend $1,500,000 fixing it up. Only then did he look around. First there was an irresistible letter sent to a foundation offering a "bargain in philanthropy" which was courteously but firmly resisted. A few days later, driving back from a dedication, in the Bronx, an angel whispered in his ear the name of an old friend from Boston who had been doing rather well in real estate, Joseph P. Kennedy. So His Excellency promptly wrote him in a humorous vein, offering him the same tremendous bargain: a seven million dollar benefaction for only one and one half millions. The former ambassador, being a very shrewd investor, jumped at the opportunity and in due time, the Lieutenant Joseph P. Kennedy Home, named in memory of a heroic son who died in World War II, was opened for 280 homeless little boys and girls. So too with the next step at St. Vincent's. The need was pressing for the expansion of psychiatric care. Mental illness, if not actually on a sharp increase due to the strain and excesses of modern life, was more widely recognized than before and was overtaxing the facilities of the archdiocese. The crisis had to be met. The benefactor could be counted on to appear. So on August 14, 1953, plans were announced for a seven-story pavilion to be built for the care of mental patients at a cost of $2,500,000. By the time the cornerstone was laid, in April 1955, the Federal Government had reserved a grant in aid of $490,987, and Jacob L. Reiss had given $250,000 which at his death soon after became $500,000.

The story of St. Vincent's would be incomplete unless we mention other generous benefactors like Countess Mary Ann Robertson who provided the

Residence for Graduate Nurses; Countess Lillian Cronin who donated the Dr. Harold R. Cronin Research Building, and Mr. Leon Lowenstein who modernized the Clinic for Out-Patients which now bears his name. These are but a few among many contributors—all of whom have the everlasting gratitude of His Eminence—who, in fifteen years, have helped St. Vincent's become a great Catholic medical center, affiliated with the College of Medicine of New York University. On many occasions His Eminence has expressed regret at the closing in 1921 of the only Catholic medical school in the State of New York at Fordham.

The care of the sick has always been first on the list of the Archbishop's interests. His own bouts with ill health that have brought him three times to the threshold of death, his mother's invalidism of many years, and the fact that both his brothers, Martin and John, were doctors of medicine have made him acutely conscious of the problems, mental and emotional as well as physical, that can complicate the lives of the bedridden.

It was natural that his major effort would be in the development of Catholic hospitals, but his interest has extended beyond them. The Hospital Apostolate, organized in 1952 under the Right Reverend James G. Wilders, brings Mass on Sundays and Holy Days to fourteen of our large secular institutions, and bedside visits every day to their Catholic patients—416,000 visits in 1960. Finally, since Canon Law regards old age as a species of sickness, mention can be made here of the ten fine homes for the aged so very essential in these efficient times when science is reluctant to allow any of us to go to our reward, no matter how mature.

But high on the list of the Archbishop's interests, perhaps next to the sick, come the children, school children and orphans, disturbed children, but especially the wayward and abandoned.

His birthdays are always celebrated at Lincoln Hall, a protective institution that puts young delinquents back on the right track. On these annual occasions, the 292 boys, 33 brothers and a group of lay workers get all the birthday cake they can eat, while the Archbishop and the "born-in-May" group exchange a variety of presents. He gives them rosaries, prayer books, and a picnic, receiving in return a spiritual bouquet and a sacred vessel for the missions. But Christmas belongs to the abandoned babies who have been left on the straw, sometimes without swaddling clothes and no mother nearer than Mary. Beginning in 1946, His Excellency has had an old-fashioned party for them every year at the Waldorf with anywhere up to two thousand guests. There is always a wonderful tree with gifts for the children who are swarming all over the Archbishop and substantial checks for the unworldly Sisters of Charity. The first year brought in $35,000 for current expenses. By 1950 this total had been doubled. The entertainment world soon became interested and ran amateur shows and world premières for the foundlings, but the sinking fund begun by the Archbishop in 1944 and topping a quarter of a million dollars in ten years represents for the most part royalties from his articles and books. Of these, the most popular was *The Foundling*, a novel, his first and only novel, published in 1951. That a man with his routines, responsibilities, and distractions should attempt such a thing filled reviewers with amazement and the Literary Guild, which distributed the book as the June selection, persuaded him to answer for them in their review, *Wings*, the question that was in everyone's mind: "How did you come to do it?"

When I saw [he wrote] literally thousands of abandoned babies and children in the care of the Foundling Hospital—innocent victims of the economic, social and moral ills of mankind—my heart became even more heavily weighted with sadness, for all of these were, as now they still are, my sacred charges. And, the fact that my fatherhood is spiritual serves only to elevate and supernaturalize the outgoing of my heart to each and every one of them—from the tiniest babe in its crib, to the adolescent— all of whom are paying the price of poverty or injustice, or the penalty of another's sin and shame! . . .

It was from the spending of my own daily life in closeness and consciousness of this sacred responsibility that I conceived and wrote *The Foundling*. And, if through its message, even one little child shall find a mother's arms or a father's affection; if but one father and mother learn the lesson of love and strive harder to live better lives and keep together their God-given family; if men will learn to live peacefully in mutual respect for one another; then I have gained my goal, though it be reached at the cost of countless hours during five long, anxious years.

From out of the treasury of my precious experiences came *The Foundling*—its peoples and its places and, as I dreamed about the book, planning and organizing, I read volumes of letters from the library of the New York Foundling Hospital; and I read too every number of *The Homeless Child*, the magazine which tells the moving story of Mount Loretto which is the Mt. Mary of *The Foundling*.

And my characters? Peter and Paul are composite portraits of people I have known throughout my life's span. And, too, there are others who resemble the true person of friends and folks close to myself and my family; Sister Crescentia, a gifted musician of rare and beautiful character who actually died of tuberculosis; Mr. Mulrooney, the sacristan; the truly charitable, unforgetting Mr. Hecht; and Jim Randall, a man who worked on my father's farm, whose first name was really Jim, who taught me almost all I ever knew about the care of my father's and grandfather's horses. Another one of the characters that I remember from my earliest recollections is O. G. Healy, the weather-vane man atop the house where I spent my childhood and where my family lived for many years. Mr. Healy originally built the house for himself and designed a weather-vane to represent himself driving a lumber wagon with a colt and a little dog following behind it.

Why did I write *The Foundling?* I have tried to tell you, but the telling might be in one simple sentence. I wrote *The Foundling* because I had to write it, for it was conceived in the womb of my intellect and given birth by the love of my heart for little children and for all mankind!

The Foundling, with a sales record of half a million, including a paperback edition of 300,000, was ranked among the best selling novels of 1951, and the publisher was able to write to the author on May 23:

> Few books, over my more than forty years' association here, have received such uniformly enthusiastic reviews as your novel is getting. I think you will see now why I was able to reassure you, all along, when you had doubts about the book.

One of the "reviews" that pleased him most—it came closest to the spirit of the book—was from an old friend of his mother in Whitman:

> Among some magazines given me, I found your story, "The Foundling." I think it is such a sweet story. I liked Paul so much I hope he is a real person.
>
> I recalled an incident. I wonder if you remember it? You were an altar boy and Father Hamilton had a group of children from the Harrison Avenue Home in Boston to be placed in homes in Whitman. At the close, all were placed but one lone little boy. You asked your mother to take him in. She thought her own five "enough." You asked why and wanted more reasons—you would, you said, give him part of your food and part of everything you had. After you had exhausted all you knew, you accepted (as you always did when you were refused anything) very quietly and said no more. . . .

No one was surprised then to learn that the old Foundling on Lexington and Sixty-eighth Street was to be sold and a splendid new building was to rise on the east side of Third Avenue and Sixty-eighth Street.

When details were available, the news was even better. The old property had been sold for $48 a square foot and the new property on the opposite side of Third Avenue purchased twenty-four hours later for $22.50 a square foot, leaving approximately $3,000,000 to begin construction. This was completed at a cost of approximately $11,000,000 and on September 29, 1958, the babies were moved across Third Avenue with much fanfare into an air-conditioned eleven-story home big enough for 306 children, thirty sisters, thirty-four unmarried mothers, and a nursery school for 170.

Less sentimental but equally effective has been the handling of the educational problems that have confronted the Archbishop from time to time. On his arrival in New York, he found nothing for the boys that corresponded to Cathedral High School for Girls, and he realized that the city, in addition to parochial high schools, should have large central diocesan institutions as well. The first steps taken were characteristic. The educational details would be handled at the proper time. First he would have an adequate building. That involved an ecclesiastical financier, a real estate operator, and an architect. The diary for January 3, 1940, reads as follows: "Went with Monsignor McIntyre, John Reynolds and Dan Higgins to see property in the East Bronx. On way home John Reynolds passed down Concourse and indicated property at 153rd Street which he thought we might get for a high school. He and Dan Higgins got out of the car and looked it over. They thought it would be satisfactory. I said O.K. and we decided to buy it if the price was right." The price, $165,000 for thirty-eight lots, was apparently "right." No time was lost on plans and ground was broken for the new building on May 13. Taking advantage of this occasion, he said:

> I want to make an announcement this afternoon that I think will bring joy to you to hear, as it gives me great consolation to make, and that is that the name of this high school will be the Cardinal Hayes Memorial High School. I do this for many reasons. First of all because Cardinal Hayes, my predecessor, is also my inspiration and my ideal, and also because, beloved man as he was, he has also enshrined himself deeply and eternally in the heart of New York; and in dedicating this high school to Cardinal Hayes I really typify and symbolize what the high school stands for, those same two principles that I enunciated in the beginning, love of God and love of country.

The high school was to cost $3,000,000 and the money had to be raised. His Excellency admitted ". . . that in this enterprise I am departing from my hitherto invariable requirement, a requirement that I make also of parish priests, that they have the funds in advance, or at least half of them." He had "at least half of them" by the time of dedication, September 8, 1941, and had paid off the entire amount by March 1946, when he started planning for the Archbishop Stepinac High School in Westchester. By a quick, shrewd real estate decision, therefore, the first step was taken in giving the archdiocese its first great high school for boys, a splendid institution taught by diocesan priests and three congregations of brothers, which today, with four branches, has a total registration of 3311.

An equally wise decision on the part of the Archbishop, followed up by long and patient negotiations, gave Manhattanville College its new campus in Purchase. The Religious of the Sacred Heart had settled more than a century ago out in what was then the country—three miles to the north of New York City. In time they were engulfed by the creeping metropolis, and the neighborhood deteriorated so sharply that St. Nicholas Park and the surrounding streets were considered unsafe. Providentially enough, their neighbor to the north, the College of the City of New York, coveted the rolling acres of Manhattanville, but naturally enough, the nuns were senti-mentally attached to their old home and refused to sell. As the members of an exempt order, the Archbishop could only advise them in such matters, but his advice was extremely definite. On June 29, 1950, the director of the budget of the City of New York recommended a resolution for the acquisi-tion of Manhattanville College "by purchase, condemnation or otherwise" to be used as an addition to the College of the City of New York. "The total assessed valuation of Manhattanville is $2,852,000 of which $1,615,000 is on the land and $1,237,000 is on the improvements. No estimate is available of the cost under condemnation proceedings." The director of real estate and the director of the City Planning Commission both approved the resolu-tion in reports dated June 20, 1950.

For condemnation proceedings, a unanimous vote of the Board of Esti-mate is required, at times a difficult thing to obtain, but in the present instance its members realized that there would be no objection raised on Madison Avenue if the conditions were acceptable. By this time most of the lay trustees of the college had been brought around to the view of the Ordinary and asked his help in getting them a reasonable settlement. Mean-while an unusually attractive site had appeared on the market, the 250-acre estate which formerly belonged to Ogden Reid, located in Purchase, just west of the Hutchinson River Parkway. The asking price was $500,000 in cash. As the reluctant nuns were unwilling to borrow the amount, and the sale could not be delayed, the archdiocese bought the property and held it for a year, afterward presenting the college with a check that represented the accumulated interest. In the meantime the value of the land had risen from $2000 to more than $13,000 an acre. On October 27, 1950, the Man-hattanville campus was sold to the City of New York in record condemna-tion proceedings for $8,808,620, and the following May, ground was broken by the Religious of the Sacred Heart for a new college dormitory. This was the first step in a $14,000,000 building program that called for an academic building, two dormitories, dining hall, library, power plant, chapel, audito-rium, and gymnasium. By October 1952, the new Manhattanville was dedi-cated after an outlay of $9,000,000. It was another example of one man's foresight and courage.

By the fall of 1960, the archdiocese was ready for an appeal that made the anxious days of the Cardinal Hayes High School drive seem like an echo from another century. Back in 1940, the building of a $3,000,000 plant attracted national attention, but twenty years later, it was a backward university that could not boast that it needed ten times that amount for recreational purposes and research. With everyone thinking in terms of light years and billions of dollars, even the Catholic public had become difficult to shock and the needs of the Church in New York were very real. So a letter went out from the Cardinal's residence announcing the most ambitious project ever undertaken by the archdiocese. For the enlargement of seminary facilities and the building of new high schools, $25,000,000 would be needed. In 1940, $28,000,000 had been regarded as a crippling debt, even when shared by hundreds of churches and schools and hospitals. Now it was expected that that much could be raised in two months without any damage to the annual collections for Catholic Charities or to the individual building campaigns that were going forward in so many individual parishes. It would do for exhibit A in a study of contemporary American economy.

The first need was a new seminary. This was not to replace St. Joseph's at Dunwoodie which after sixty-four years was in excellent condition, but to help work out a new system that would make room for "the rich harvest of vocations which we prayerfully expect" and at the same time increase the efficiency of the training. For more than a century, the minor seminary had included four years of high school and two of college, while the major seminary offered two years of philosophy and four of theology. Henceforth, there would be three seminaries and the candidate for the priesthood would spend four years in each. The present Cathedral College would be reserved for high school, the present St. Joseph's for theology and the new St. Patrick's College with its chapel dedicated to the Curé of Ars would be built for the regular academic courses. Here the seminarians would spend four years as resident students, finish their philosophy and take their Bachelor's degree before going on to Dunwoodie. For this new institution, $5,000,000 would be required. The rest of the money collected would be used for the ever-expanding system of diocesan high schools.

The appeal was announced on September 7, 1960, and launched on October 7. The Victory Report was made on December 15. There was an amazing total of $35,438,619. By June 15 this had increased to $39,182,738.

Such an accomplishment seems all the more remarkable when we consider that New York is not an expanding diocese in the ordinary sense of the word. In 1900 there were already 1,000,000 Catholics here and in 1910 there were 1,219,920, with a large concentration in Manhattan Island. Following the First World War, however, a change occurred. Thousands of old parishioners moved into the Brooklyn and Newark Dioceses in the general trend toward the suburbs, and as most of the newcomers who took their places were Jewish or Negro, with very few Catholics in either group, it is not surprising that by 1948 the Catholic population had declined to 1,183,417, and that only in 1950, with the aid of the war babies and the Puerto Ricans, did it surpass the total of 1910. What does come as a surprise is that in such circumstances 32 new parishes were opened by the Archbishop in twenty years and 24 new churches besides, that replaced older and obsolete buildings.

Indispensable in solving social and religious problems of this kind is the great annual appeal for Catholic Charities. This was introduced in 1920 with a goal of $1,000,000. The World War just concluded had reduced the appeal for funds to a fine art, with committees, pledges, report luncheons, and thermometers, and Cardinal Hayes was one of the first members of the American hierarchy to profit by the technical experience gained. In organizing the Catholic Charities of the Archdiocese of New York which was incorporated in 1920 as a New York Membership Corporation, he unintentionally gave himself the title always associated with his name, the Cardinal of Charities. His successor, at his installation in St. Patrick's as Archbishop, emphasized his determination to continue the great work of his predecessor in the guidance of youth and the relief of suffering. The modest million of forty-two years ago has grown to $4,965,462.08 in 1960, but expenditures have increased to $4,921,579.13. This refers only to the expenditures of the Catholic Charities office. It does not take into account the many millions received and spent in the whole group of 192 health and welfare agencies.

The lion's share of more than three million has gone to Family Service and Child Care, with Health Services, Youth Activities, and Youth Counsel next in order. Half of the revenue comes directly from the parish collections, the other half from special gifts, legacies, funds and foundations. Over the years, a standing executive committee has been formed of dedicated laymen with John S. Burke as chairman and John A. Coleman as executive chairman who, working quietly for twelve months in every year, have the situation well in hand before the appeal opens in the archdiocese. The emphasis placed on the rare combination of efficiency and devotion strikes a responsive chord in every heart. As His Eminence expressed it, "What we as Catholics are unable to do, Catholic Charities sympathetically, understandingly, efficiently accomplishes for us. A fair and practical norm for giving is one day's income." The figure in the annual report for 1960 that gave His Eminence the greatest satisfaction was the item, "Appeal Expenses and Administrative Costs for the Year—$159,497.59," only five per cent of the total contributions. As the years go on, the sums collected may vary with the financial condition of the country, but the efficiency will continue to increase at headquarters and the appreciation of the good accomplished be ever more widely recognized. A major factor in this increased efficiency may be found in the new headquarters that were established at the extensive Russell Sage properties on Lexington Avenue when they were acquired in 1950 as the Catholic Charities Center.

Naturally enough, St. Patrick's Cathedral itself was not overlooked. First came the Lady Chapel, which is the subject of an entry in the diary, December 16, 1939: "Talked with Mr. Maginnis who was at luncheon and authorized him to approve design for altar in the Lady Chapel at approximate cost of $20,000 for which innumerable sketches have been made over a period of twenty years." The following April, the rectory was remodeled and modernized, though the Archbishop's house on the opposite corner was left unchanged. Driving along the East River, not long after, His Excellency told the president of Fordham that he was at long last going to replace the historic high altar of Cardinal McCloskey with one more splendid and liturgically more correct. The ingenuous Jesuit asked him, "What are you going to do with the old one?"

He turned impulsively and said, "Do you want it?"

The answer was yes. So all the precious inlaid marbles that had been given by the clergy of the diocese in 1878 were removed and rebuilt in the university church on the Bronx campus. As this venerable structure, however, had been before the Civil War the chapel for the diocesan seminary, the gift was generally considered sentimentally appropriate. The objection to the altar's remaining in St. Patrick's was mainly architectural. As originally designed, the cathedral had a flat east wall, and the old, high, carved stone reredos was appropriate enough. When the ambulatory and Lady Chapel were added, however, the unity of design was lost by the dividing effect of the straight line in the sanctuary, so that for many years there had been a standing offer from an anonymous benefactor to erect a severe marble altar without reredos or tabernacle, enclosed by a bronze baldachino, which would not cut off the view from west to east. The old rector of the cathedral, however, Monsignor Lavelle, would have none of it. He said that the new altar would go in over his dead body, and that is just what happened. For at his death, to acknowledge his distinguished services as rector of St. Patrick's for more than half a century, Monsignor Lavelle's body was placed in a crypt side by side with all the past Archbishops of New York, and just above him the beautiful new altar was built.

On July 12, 1945, a 125-pound block of masonry was dislodged above the Fifty-first Street entrance by the blasting in the neighborhood. Fortunately, the only damage that resulted was a dent in the pavement, but the realization of what could have happened started a chain of investigations that led to the exterior renovation of all three buildings, cathedral, archbishop's house, and rectory, at a total cost of over $3,000,000. This did not include the altar or the new bronze doors or the beautiful rose window over the main entrance or the glorious blue windows in the clerestory.

In meeting part of the great expense involved, His Excellency was fortunately able to draw on the princely bequest that was left to him about this time by Major Edward Bowes, who had made a fortune in radio. Of his $4,500,000 estate, he left $3,000,000 to the Major Bowes' Fund of St. Patrick's Cathedral, to be administered by his old friend, the Archbishop of New York. It all began with the major's aesthetic urge to plant trees around the cathedral. With this in mind he had asked to meet His Excellency and had come to the interview armed with a bundle of plans and renderings. His proposal was accepted at once with a "Yes. Thank you very much." When the chancellor suggested caution because Monsignor Lavelle was not partial to trees, His Excellency said with a grin, "If the Archbishop of New York can't plant trees around his own cathedral, I'm going back to Boston."

The acquaintance thus begun quickly ripened into friendship. Entries appear in the diary from time to time for the next three years, reporting visits back and forth, beginning with October 29, 1943: "Went to Rumson with Major Bowes. I shall accept his home for the Seminary," and ending with June 13, 1946: "Major Bowes died today." The last rites of the Church were administered by His Eminence, who offered a Solemn Pontifical Mass in the New York cathedral. The will directed that the Archbishop "shall in his sole discretion use and disperse the funds for the beautification of the interior and exterior of St. Patrick's Cathedral, or for the use of such charitable institutions as, in the sole discretion of His Excellency, Archbishop Spellman, shall accomplish the most good, His Excellency knowing my desire to help the poor, the sick, the widowed, the orphaned and the Sisters." Thus the fortune amassed through an amateur radio program became in the hands of a Most Reverend Almoner a source of help and comfort to suffering humanity in every part of the world.

An equally casual meeting resulted some years later in an even greater benefaction to the archdiocese, the most notable in its 150 years of history. Mrs. Mabel Gilman Corey, a stage celebrity at the turn of the century, and the widow of William E. Corey, one-time president of the U.S. Steel Corporation, called one day in 1956 to say that she would like to do something for the foundlings. Though not a Catholic, she proceeded to donate the Mabel Gilman Corey Auditorium for the new Foundling Hospital and began to take a deep interest in various forms of charitable work.

As His Eminence wrote in a letter to a friend just before Christmas in 1960: "I first met Mrs. Corey some dozen years ago when she was unable to dispose of her chateau in France and asked me if I could use it. I could not but consulted the Cardinal of Paris to see if it fitted in with any of his educational or charitable plans. In the end, nothing came of it, but Mrs. Corey realized that I had tried to help her and offered to put my name in her will. However, for many years I saw nothing of Mrs. Corey. When she became ill and asked my help, I requested the Trinitarian Sisters to receive her in the new home which I had purchased for them. It was then that the good lady proposed bequeathing something to the Archdiocese of New York. And so it was that three years ago, Mrs. Corey entrusted all her earthly possessions to the archdiocese and transferred the ownership to me as the Bishop."

The following letter, brief and colorless, disposed of approximately $5,000,000:

February 11, 1958

Chase Manhattan Bank
18 Pine Street
New York, N.Y.
GENTLEMEN:

I desire to transfer my bank balances and all securities and property belonging to me, of which you are custodian, to the Archdiocese of New

York. Will you please deliver to His Eminence, Francis Cardinal Spell-man, or his representative, a current statement of my assets and give your cooperation in promptly effecting the transfer of title.

Very truly yours,
MABEL GILMAN COREY

At the Cardinal's request, an officer representing the bank called on Mrs. Corey and said afterward that there was no question with regard to her desire, but added "Your Eminence must realize that the procedure is most unusual." "Unusual?" was the answer. "Unfortunately it is unique!"

We continue the Cardinal's narrative: "When I inquired about her religion and she had said that she had been to a Catholic school, I asked her if she would be interested in learning something about the Catholic Church. She said she would, so I instructed her in essential matters and baptized her. Until her death, she was a most fervent and devout Catholic." When the end came to the good lady at the age of eighty, in November 1960, His Eminence was presiding in Washington at the annual meeting of the American hierarchy. "Since she has done so much for the archdiocese" he wrote, "it was only proper for me to return at once to New York, offer her Funeral Mass and accompany her body to the Gate of Heaven Cemetery. Thus ended the unusual life of a wonderful lady."

Among the apostolic purposes to which the Corey fortune was devoted, we can mention the care of large and helpless groups of underprivileged Americans newly arrived in the city. Back in 1939 the Archbishop's first two Confirmation services had been in Harlem parishes, St. Aloysius and St. Charles Borromeo, and the "Negro problem" in New York was one of the first brought to his attention. As he saw it, the challenge in this under-privileged group, whose proven ability and patriotism immediately im-pressed him, was in their crowding, segregation, and lack of educational, social, and religious opportunities. The condition of the colored people in the South before the First World War had posed remote and almost academic questions to be solved by others a thousand miles away. But circumstances after the war, and the not entirely altruistic activities of local politicians, had increased the Negro population of New York with such amazing rapidity that during the twenty years before Archbishop Spellman came to the city, hundreds of thousands of Negroes had preceded him. As the swelling tide swept over Manhattan, north and south of 125th Street, one prosperous old Irish parish after another was submerged.

In 1943, on the occasion of the mass Baptism of sixty-one converts in St. Aloysius, the late Monsignor William R. McCann said, "Ten years ago the Catholic Church was not known in Harlem or was sneeringly referred to as the 'white man's Church.' Today it needs no advertisement, and is known as a potent instrument of good in our Negro community. . . . In those years over 5000 have received the light of Faith and Baptism, and we have created a record unequalled in the country."

Up to and including 1929, St. Mark's and St. Charles's were the only two parish schools in which colored children were enrolled. During the next ten years there was a marked improvement, but it was left to Archbishop Spellman to formulate the principle, even while opening new schools in Harlem that would be inevitably and exclusively colored: "There are no schools for Negroes. There are no schools for whites. There are only schools for all children." And again: "This is not a Negro school. This is a Catholic school which any Catholic child who is qualified may enter." When a socially prominent woman called on him to prevent Manhattanville College from accepting a colored girl as a student, he asked, "Is there anything wrong with her grades or her character? No? Then she has just as much right there as your daughter."

A step was taken beyond the ordinary church-school level when Monsignor Cornelius J. Drew, who had succeeded Monsignor McCann at St. Charles, set out to raise $1,000,000 for a community center for citizenship classes and adult education as well as for sports, dancing, and music. In presenting the first check for $10,000, Cardinal Spellman referred to newspaper reports that the national office of the Communist Party had been moved to Harlem:

> This was no surprise since we have been warned again and again that the Communist Party Line for 1952 would concentrate on the Negroes, and for years the Communists have been playing on their emotions in the hope of stirring up race hatred and mob violence. . . .
>
> Why will the Communists refuse to learn that the Negro is a peace-loving, God-loving, citizen, who, in spite of sins of segregation and discrimination, is aware of the advances of his race in our nation within these last years. Once he discovers that Communists are anti-religious and anti-American, the Negro wants no fellowship with Communism, and he resents the insinuation implied by the recent invasion into Harlem of the National Communist Party that Negroes will be easy prey for the propaganda, hatred and lies manufactured in Stalin's Moscow, smuggled into print by Soviet spies, and shouted by rabble-rousing Reds and Pinks. . . .
>
> To help promote a spirit of mutual understanding and forbearance among all fellow Americans and to contribute for youth and families of Harlem religious inspiration and training, we have authorized plans to be drawn for a new parochial school and community center in Harlem. This parochial school is a public school—with God added. And the community center will be a home for all the community. Confident that this new project will help to make Harlem healthier and happier and that the young and old will be benefited and assisted to be better citizens of our beloved country and of the Kingdom of God, gladly, proudly, do I give this check. . . .

There are now about 600,000 Negroes living in the archdiocese of whom perhaps 200,000 are Protestant and 50,000 Catholic. That leaves 350,000, a great city in itself, without any church affiliation of any kind. Zealous pastors in the old Irish parishes are bringing in converts at the rate of more than a thousand a year, but their Archbishop sees the fields still ripe for the harvest only a few blocks north of St. Patrick's Cathedral.

After the Second World War a new social and religious challenge was met successfully in New York. It was known as the Puerto Rican problem. Like the Germans and Irish of a hundred years ago, the Puerto Ricans have been facing a domestic crisis in recent years that has made emigration attractive if not imperative. With cheap air travel and a United States citizenship to level all quota barriers, they began to arrive at New York in great numbers, necessitating very serious civic and religious adjustments. These fellow citizens who could speak no English represented the poorest and most unfortunate classes in their beautiful homeland and were for the most part colored so that when they arrived by the thousand in cotton pants and straw hats, they gravitated to the outskirts of Harlem and other segregated districts of the city where they were welcomed by neither blacks nor whites. Little neighborhood boys swimming in the Harlem River would shout to each other: "The last one in is a Puerto Rican!"

Soon too many gangs were organized along language lines and New Yorkers who came into no contact with the newcomers blamed the increase in local crime entirely on the Puerto Ricans. The Cardinal Archbishop set about relieving conditions that must always arise in the little ghettos where new foreign language groups invariably gather. Churches were made available and school facilities enlarged for them, not in the spirit of enforced segregation, but because such groups instinctively preserve their identity for at least a generation. There are now more than 500,000 Puerto Ricans in the archdiocese and 150,000 Spanish-speaking Catholics from other parts of the world. To increase the number of Spanish-speaking priests who could minister to such a large group effectively, His Eminence established a special office in the chancery to co-ordinate Spanish Catholic Action, arranged for ten-week programs in Spanish for priests and religious, and established scholarships providing transportation and maintenance each year for ten seminarians from Dunwoodie who would spend their summer vacations serving as lay assistants to pastors in Puerto Rico.

Beginning in 1956 half the newly ordained priests have gone as well, so that by 1960 New York could point with pride to the impressive total of 200 priests in 104 parishes who have helped to solve the language difficulty. As a special mark of predilection, the Feast of St. John the Baptist was set aside for a Pontifical Mass to be celebrated for Spanish-speaking New Yorkers in St. Patrick's Cathedral. On the first occasion the Bishops of Ponce and San Juan made the journey from Puerto Rico to be present and thirty-seven hundred persons heard an eloquent sermon in Spanish delivered by the Most Reverend James H. Griffiths, D.D., Chancellor of the Military

Ordinariate. By 1956 the celebration had outgrown the cathedral and was moved to the campus of Fordham University where an estimated thirty-five thousand gathered for a Pontifical Mass and an all-day outing that included many picturesque and traditional features. The stadium on Randall's Island has since been selected as the official site for the annual observance.

As far as the Puerto Ricans are concerned, therefore, the pattern has been fixed and the future provided for, but the friendly interest of their Archbishop does not stop with local administration. He has made many trips to Puerto Rico where bands and enthusiastic choruses of children have greeted him with "The Sidewalks of New York," "When Irish Eyes Are Smiling," and "Hail, Hail, the Gang's All Here." One notable visit was in August 1958. Ponce and its Bishop, the Most Reverend James Edward McManus, C.SS.R., D.D., were celebrating with much solemnity the tenth anniversary of the Catholic University of Puerto Rico, and well they might. After so short a period they had every reason to be proud of five well-organized schools and 4908 carefully selected students. Among their several handsome buildings they could point to "The Cardinal Spellman Building" whose cornerstone had been laid by His Eminence—"The Godfather of the University"—ten years before.

Again in October of 1960 he flew down to consecrate the Most Reverend Luis Aponte Martinez, the new Auxiliary Bishop of Ponce and to enthrone as archbishop the Most Reverend James P. Davis who had been for many years Bishop of San Juan. It happened that the unfortunate controversy between the local bishops and the governor of the island was at its height and attracting more than ordinary attention in the United States because a Catholic was a candidate for the presidency. In consequence, the Cardinal was dogged by reporters at every step but shrugged them off good naturedly, protesting that he knew nothing whatever about politics. They all enjoyed that. At the formal dinner in the Governor's Residence he chatted amiably with the embattled Governor Munoz and the embattled Archbishop Davis and, by way of an after-dinner speech, reminisced on his more humorous experiences during the First World War!

CHAPTER SIXTEEN

Labor Relations

FROM a purely material point of view, the Ordinary of a great archdiocese finds himself in the role of a large-scale employer; from the spiritual point of view, he is the Father in Christ of most of the men who are employed on his projects. If his churches and hospitals and schools, convents, homes, and rectories represent an outlay of say $50,000,000 in a single year, it means that the archdiocese is paying $30,000,000 in wages to the building trades and has vast business relationships with labor unions. At the same time, as part of the Universal Church, sharing in her Magisterium, it has the obligation of teaching her doctrine, clarified by the last six Popes, on the moral aspects of these relationships.

Whenever appropriate, therefore, the Archbishop of New York has always presented the official attitude of the Church on the subject of social justice, particularly as it affects management and labor. Soon after his arrival he made it clear that all construction would be by union labor and from this policy he has allowed no deviation. In one crisis he found himself in open conflict with a union for two painful, much publicized months, but his views never changed. As they were explained on three notable occasions in New York and Buffalo, so they remained without disillusionment.

To the members of the New York Building Congress gathered at the Hotel Astor, May 27, 1947, he said: "It is a great and grave mistake to assume that any one class of Americans is naturally and inevitably hostile to any other class, that the wealthy and the workingman, employers and employees, are destined to live in mutual conflict." The Cardinal then quoted Abraham Lincoln and Theodore Roosevelt on the mutual rights of labor and capital, and endorsing their views, continued:

> Especially should these principles be practiced today when we are in a period where not only employer and employee alike, but our very country itself and every man in it, suffer from shortages and stoppages which threaten our economic strength and stability. Many people feel it imprudent to make commitments for capital expenditures because of rising costs of both labor and materials and as a result, a great number of projects, involving hundreds of millions of dollars, have been abandoned or postponed. I believe if this policy is continued and extended it can lead only

to the stalling of the wheels of our domestic economy, resulting in stagnation and depression. . . .

For myself, I am determined to go forward, although I have made it a rule—and steadfastly observed it throughout my life—personally never to spend $100 unless I had $100, and officially, as Archbishop of New York, never to undertake the construction of a building unless I had on hand half the amount of money necessary for its completion, . . . but I do now give you my promise to expend $25,000,000 for buildings to be constructed within the Archdiocese of New York. . . .

All this I promise to do because I have faith that the good-will and good works of Capital and Labor, of Employer and Employee, of all Americans, of every station in life, will be commensurate with my own, herein pledged and proven!

The Building and Construction Trades Council of Westchester County, New York, and also that of Greater New York, passed resolutions of appreciation, promising labor's full co-operation in the building program. The pledges given by the councils against work stoppage, which have never been revoked, were fulfilled, and Stepinac High School was finished in record time at a cost of $4,800,000.

The following September, at the Buffalo Centennial Eucharistic Congress, the Archbishop of New York drew a picture of carefully balanced responsibility without fear or favor:

Labor has the right and duty to expand its service and usefulness to the social body and to progress through orderly processes. Capital too has its right and duty to increase its usefulness to society through free enterprise, fair competition and reasonable profits. . . .

Christ, Who is God, sanctified Labor by toiling as a carpenter and it is Labor's duty to keep toil blessed, giving unbounded service for the happiness and prosperity of man as an avowal of his faith and trust in God. So, too, did Christ sanctify Capital, by calling laborers to work in His vineyard, paying to them their just hire. Shareholder with Labor, it is Capital's duty also to preserve itself blessed by fostering human happiness and prosperity, for no man should be slave nor master to another, but each should be servant to God and helpmate to his neighbor.

If Labor and Capital are to thrive and survive, they must serve as members of one social body, with singleness of purpose and diversity of functions united in the strong bond of service for the good of mankind, spirited by reverence and love of God, working together to do God's will on earth as it is done in Heaven. . . .

At the opening of the 85th annual convention of the New York State Federation of Labor in August 1948 the Archbishop returned to the subject of mutual responsibilities for preserving national security and freedom:

America's prosperity and happiness can be attained only through the full cooperation between Labor and Capital with full employment and fair wages. Yet millions of people are being taught—and tricked into believing that the benefits of security fall like manna from heaven. . . . A nation that gives to each of its citizens equal chances to earn his own and his family's keep has its right to receive from each of its citizens the highest service of which he is capable. And any man or any group of men who does not give full service for full pay contributes to the spiral of inflation, increases prices for his neighbor and himself, jeopardizes economic stability and invites Communistic disruption.

The right to regulate the use of wealth in the public interest is universally admitted. But in the essential interest of the common good for the common man we must also admit the right to regulate the terms and conditions of labor, and in the interest of the workingman himself we need set our faces like flint against mob-violence just as against corporate greed; against the lawlessness of workers, just as much as against the lawlessness of employers, remembering always that each must render justice to the other.

The following frank observations on the right to strike are interesting in the light of subsequent events:

Down through the years as Labor has struggled for its rights, an effective economic weapon has been evolved—the strike weapon—recognized in this and many other nations of free men, as lawful. However, this powerful, legal economic weapon should be used less frequently as Labor and Capital continue to work out their problems and differences in mutual respect and enlightened understanding following the principles of collective bargaining which jointly they have adopted for the well-being of all parties.

In fair collective bargaining rests America's greatest hope for future peaceful labor relations, but in its processes men must guard themselves against selfish, domineering minority groups opposed to our democratic form of government, groups that refuse to solve their problems through this just device and use strikes as smokescreens to wage political war against America. In no business, nor profession, nor craft, nor institution in America, is there any room for a man with a divided allegiance.

At the moment, the new Taft-Hartley Act was under bitter attack in all the unions of the country. At this same meeting, the Mayor of New York, William O'Dwyer, begged the convention "not to adjourn without passing resolutions calling on Congress to repeal the act" and George Meany the National Secretary-Treasurer of the AFL called it "the brain child of Big Business." But the Archbishop of New York, sacrificing a measure of applause, reminded the convention that the Taft-Hartley Act was the law of the land, and, like it or not, counseled the unions not to break it.[1] The New York *Sun* commented editorially:

> Considering the scene, the place, the time and the attendant circumstances, this was a courageous and forthright speech, courageously and forthrightly delivered.

Thus he always handled the theory of labor relations with the uncompromising confidence of one who knows the mind of the Church in such matters and is not afraid.

Where corruption was the issue he could be blunt and specific. He mounted his own pulpit, December 8, 1957, for an outspoken sermon on the labor crisis. In it he condemned the creation of dummy locals, the rigging of elections, extortion, acid throwing, graft, and the misuse of union funds, going straight to the heart of the matter when he said: "We must act and while there is still time, remove from power unscrupulous leaders and their underworld hirelings."

In individual cases, however, not only courage but good judgment comes into play. When a dispute among honest men breaks into print and each side asks the Archbishop of New York to make a statement in its favor, often enough it may be the prudent thing to make no statement at all. There was, for example, the controversial Wall Street strike during April 1948, in which the Association of Catholic Trade Unionists displayed placards on the picket line and sections of the Catholic press took sides with some emotion. Circumstances complicated the main issue, which was the right of a union shop agreement, and the conduct of sympathizers from the Seamen's International Union, who had joined the pickets, heightened the tension. There were, in consequence, critics on both sides when Madison Avenue remained neutral.

The following January, a celebrated case arose in which neutrality was impossible. It was the highly publicized cemetery strike. The Trustees of St. Patrick's Cathedral in the City of New York had been incorporated by special legislation in 1817. Their responsibilities included the care of diocesan cemeteries. There were no unions as we know them in existence at that early date, and even after a hundred years our gravediggers were continuing on their sad and solitary way. In December 1946, although by law non-profit religious corporations enjoy exemption, Cardinal Spellman encouraged the employees of Calvary and other Catholic cemeteries to organize, and accepted United Cemetery Workers Local 293 as their bargaining agent. In two years, the gravediggers' wages increased from $40.95 for a six-day, forty-five-hour week to $59.04 for a six-day, forty-eight-hour week; from $.91 an hour to $1.23. The average wage for manufacture in the United States, which included skilled labor, was at that time $54.77 for a forty-hour week.

Unfortunately, Local 293 was affiliated with the CIO Food, Tobacco, Agricultural and Allied Workers Union of America. The appropriateness of the affiliation is not at once apparent without a macabre imagination, and its desirability was questioned from the start. The trustees and their counsel, Godfrey P. Schmidt, were soon convinced that they had to deal with a communist-dominated union. One indication was that nothing was ever again quite satisfactory to the men. As a labor enthusiast described the situation:

> The last contract, which expired on December 31, 1948, was one of the best in the cemetery field, which is to the credit of both the union and management. Among other things, it provided for a health and welfare plan and pensions paid for by the employer. Nevertheless, by the admission of both parties, relations between the two were unsatisfactory. The last contract, for example, took ten months to negotiate. The union complains that there were frequent grievances in the day-to-day operations of the cemetery.[2]

On December 14, the union presented its conditions for the renewal of contract. There were minor improvements in the fringe benefits included, but the main point was forty-eight hours' pay for forty hours' work. In rejecting all the union's demands, Monsignor George C. Ehardt, director of cemeteries, wrote to the president of the union:

> It is the preachment of the Church to pay a living wage to a man for a decent day's work. These preachments the Trustees have always striven to put into practice and they are willing to do so now. Having the Bureau of Labor Statistics Index as a standard in the past, the Trustees are willing now again to consider an increase in salary based on this same Index. . . . If this Index furnished by the Department of Labor was fair in the past, it is fair now and to consider an increase in salary on this basis is the only just way, not only for the gravediggers who seem to be very solicitous about their own welfare, but for all our employees.
>
> These are the final deliberations of the Board of Trustees and I would ask you to bring this to the attention of the members of the Union and would also ask that the negotiations be resumed in the very near future with the idea of signing the contract under these terms and that the contract be signed by the end of the month, for we do not wish to have any retroactive salaries paid beyond this limit.[3]

The union had demanded an increase of 30 per cent, while the Monsignor's offer came to approximately 8 per cent. On receipt of the letter, the workers voted to strike within forty-eight hours, but in order to hold a meeting with management on January 10, took no action until January 13. On that day, some 240 employees of Calvary Cemetery staged a walkout, to be followed a month later by 47 men in the Gate of Heaven. In a letter sent to the individual workers and dated January 21, 1949, Monsignor Ehardt referred to the impossibility of having a forty-hour week in the cemetery since the dead had to be buried on Saturday and graves had to be opened for the Monday funerals:

> Because of poor and unprincipled leadership many of you have been led to believe that you have the right to commit such acts of cruelty to your fellow human beings. There have been brazen and grave infractions of rules and your Union leaders have always sustained the actions of the guilty employees even though they knew full well the dishonesty of their position. . . .
>
> We cannot but feel that your leaders did not fairly represent you, for many times they failed you when your best interests could have been better served by the proposals of the Trustees. When it came for you to decide upon a strike, you were not permitted the American way of freedom to express yourself by recourse to a secret ballot, even though it was a matter so serious that it might mean deprivation for your own children as well as making other people suffer.
>
> Despite the strike we are carrying on and will continue to do so. We hope that you, with all our loyal employees, will return to work as quickly as possible. However, we cannot let this matter rest on the basis of a mere invitation. The operation of the cemetery requires willing and able bodied workers. Therefore, we must inform you that unless you return by Monday, January 31st, 1949, at 7:30 A.M., we shall understand that you intend to sever your relationship with us.
>
> We are determined to continue the operation of our cemetery and have taken steps to insure the protection of our workers. Therefore let no one on the picket line or elsewhere intimidate you. We are convinced of the moral justice of our position and hope that you will understand your own obligations.[4]

The strike continued.

On February 10, Mr. Schmidt told the New York *Times* he favored submitting the dispute to an impartial board of three distinguished moral theologians outside the archdiocese. If the decision of the theologians favored the union, Mr. Schmidt said the cemetery's trustees would meet their demands. If the decision favored the trustees, then the union was to: (1) renounce affiliation with their communist-dominated international; (2) select a new negotiating committee; (3) continue their present contract with only the cost-of-living increase. The union agreed to this on condition that the management would be changed if the judgment of the theologians favored them. This killed the proposal.[5]

After six weeks, coffins containing hundreds of unburied dead were lying in open trenches, so the Cardinal dispatched telegrams to each of the strikers with the exception of the five members of the negotiating committee, inviting them to present their case to him personally. As he described the meeting:

Some 200 men attended including the members of the negotiating committee whom I permitted to attend the meeting in order to prevent further delay and added miseries. I stated my position in regard to Local 293, C.I.O. I invited the men as individuals to return to work immediately. Again I offered (though not bound by the Little Wagner Act) to permit them to form a new union provided that it was not in any way affiliated with a Communistic international union, to which each one of these men, I recently learned, contributed 70 cents every month. And in addition to all the fringe items which had been granted by the 1948 contract I promised the men a raise of 8% in wages (instead of the just 3% which had been previously offered according to the BLS Index)—a wage that is according to today's living standards and experts on economics more than a good and fundamentally fair wage.

A sub-committee of the workers' negotiating committee requested that the workers be given until 12 o'clock noon on March 1 to determine their action upon my proposal. To this request I acceded.

The offer was rejected 183–0. The Cardinal went a step further and agreed to deal with Local 293 if it disaffiliated from F.T.A.W., but insisted on a statement in writing that this would be done within forty-eight hours. He was told by the men that they were only a minority in the Local, which comprised 1000 members, but that they would urge disaffiliation at a Local meeting. Then they asked for further delay. Every twenty-four hours the unburied dead were increased by fifty or sixty and the total by now was well over a thousand, so the request for more time was refused. With this the bombshell exploded. In a statement to the press, the Cardinal said:

> Thus have the men and the union made their decision. And now I must make mine. This evening I shall go to Dunwoodie and suspend classes in the Seminary releasing all physically able seminarians to assist in the corporal work of mercy of burying the dead!

It was a dramatic and courageous step that was taken on March 3 when the Ordinary of the Archdiocese of New York led seminarians in sweat shirts and dungarees through the picket line at Calvary Cemetery. He knew he was courting criticism, but habitually careful as he was of public relations, he had reached the point where criticism was of minor importance to him. At a special meeting of the diocesan consultors called to discuss the crisis, some warned him that he was risking his popularity with the working classes and advised him to compromise. His answer was, "My popularity is not the point at issue. What is the right thing to do?"

Three weeks before, the brothers from Maryknoll had dug some graves at the Gate of Heaven in Westchester and had been accused by the Association of Catholic Trade Unionists of "strike-breaking and union busting."[6] Now the comments from some quarters became increasingly bitter.

The *Daily Worker* was, of course, delighted to headline an article, "Spellman to Lead in Cemetery Scabbing." The president of Local 293, CIO accused the trustees of "a vicious attempt to smash the union."[7] The chairman of the negotiating committee complained that "we support the seminaries and to allow the seminarians to take bread and butter away from the working people is wrong."[8] The Association of Catholic Trade Unionists backed up Local 293 and denied that its strike action was communist-inspired.[9] The Cardinal's answer to the outcry was to apply for an injunction against the strike and the pickets, on the ground that they were interrupting "an essential community service performed by a religious organization." The lawyer of the union insisted that it was "more important to recognize the right of workers to organize and bargain collectively in unions of their own choosing and to pay the living a just wage than to bury the dead."[10]

The smoke of battle increased. On March 4, the Cardinal led the seminarians back to Calvary through a battery of cameras. Long shovels in the hands of students who were used to nothing tougher than a baseball bat were clearing up a gruesome situation and making labor history. On the same day, the striking workers held a union meeting, which opened with the recitation of the Worker's Prayer. The men took an oath that they were opposed to communism and passed two resolutions. The first of these resolutions condemned "union-busting tactics in any employer, including the Catholic Church when it acts as an employer"; the second advocated disaffiliation from the allegedly communist International to which the Local belonged. The chairman of the negotiating committee, however, had said previously that "Communism is a false issue in this strike—and the Archbishop knows it."[11]

When the Cardinal was informed that the workers had disavowed communism, he expressed his approval, but added:

> It doesn't interest me too much just now because they have been promising that for two years. Each time I would ask them [the strikers' committee] to do this, they would promise, but they would come back to me and say something about having to report back to the union. They would ask for another 48-hour delay. Meanwhile, 50 more bodies would await burial and 50 more families would be bereaved. I cannot just say, "Pay the men more and pass the costs along to the people."

His Eminence said that he had received much mail praising his action and also "some criticism." "But none of the critics had any solution to my problem. I consider this an immoral and unjustifiable strike. I know of no other way to solve this problem that has confronted me for several weeks."

The chairman of the negotiating committee issued a statement for the press in which he asserted that the men held no animosity for the Archbishop, "but I believe from a labor relations point of view, that he has been ill advised. He should get a new secretary of labor."[12]

The Cardinal at the International Vatican Marian Year Stamp Exhibit in Philadelphia in 1954 looking at the only stamp which Pope Pius XII ever autographed. With him are Archbishop John F. O'Hara of Philadelphia and Sister Mary Fidelma of Regis College, Massachusetts, Curator of the Cardinal's Stamp Collection.

The Cardinal explaining the Index of Christian Art of Princeton University which he has just presented to the Vatican library.

Cardinal Spellman visits children in the New York Foundling Hospital, a charity close to his heart.

Cardinal Spellman visiting
His Holiness, Pope Pius XII,
at the time of the dedication
of the new American College
in Rome, October 14, 1953.

UPI

The heart-breaking sorrow of
losing a close friend and
companion in Christ is clearly
shown on the Cardinal's
face as he leaves Castel
Gandolfo after praying at the
bedside of the late Pope
Pius XII, October 9, 1958.

The Archbishop of New York greets a distinguished visitor, President Franklin Delano Roosevelt, on the latter's visit to New York City in 1940.

Cardinal Spellman welcomes Winston Churchill to New York City at St. Patrick's, March 20, 1946.

THE CARDINAL IN HIS ROLE AS MILITARY VICAR OF THE ARMED
FORCES OF THE UNITED STATES.

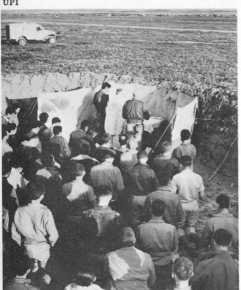

Saying Mass in the African Desert
for the men of the United States
9th Army Air Force, April 1943.

Archbishop Spellman celebrating
Mass for a group of patients
and personnel at an evacuation
hospital in Belgium during
World War II, September 27, 1944.

Major General W. G. Wyman of
the 9th Army Corps thanks
Cardinal Spellman for his visit to
his men in Korea in December, 1951.

Visiting troops of the 7th United
States Infantry Division at
Heartbreak Ridge, Korea, on
Christmas Day, 1951.

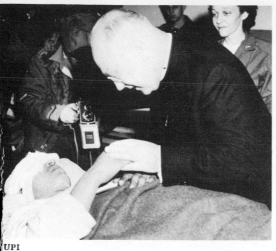

The Cardinal consoles a wounded
UN soldier at a front-line hospital
near Seoul, Korea, December 25, 1952.

The Cardinal in his uniform
as a Military Vicar.

Crossing Junk Bay on way to
visit Chinese refugee Camp in
Hong Kong, 1952.

At the United States Naval Station,
Argentia, Newfoundland,
January 1959.

Archbishop Spellman while visiting
the Italian front during World War II
meets King George VI of England
and General Mark Clark, 1943.

Cardinal Spellman with Generalissimo
Chiang Kai-shek, Formosa, January 1952.

Cardinal Spellman greeting President Eisenhower, guest of honor at the 50th
Anniversary Dinner of the National Conference of Catholic Charities in New
York City in 1960. With them are James Francis Cardinal McIntyre, Arch-
bishop of Los Angeles, Aloysius Cardinal Muench, of the Roman Curia, and
Richard Cardinal Cushing, Archbishop of Boston.

Francis Cardinal Spellman
pays homage to Pope John
XXIII at the Obeisance
Ceremony in the Sistine
Chapel, October 30, 1958,
symbolizing the Cardinals'
loyalty to their new
spiritual leader.

UPI

Archbishop Spellman as
Military Vicar visits the
Apostolic Delegate to
Turkey, Archbishop Roncalli,
now Pope John XXIII.
Istanbul, April 1944.

The newly-elected
Pope John XXIII receives
Francis Cardinal Spellman
in private audience.

UPI

General Douglas MacArthur leaves his car and embraces Cardinal Spellman as they meet on the steps of St. Patrick's Cathedral during the parade honoring the General on his return from the Far East, April 20, 1951.

Cardinal Spellman chats with President Truman at the Friendly Sons of St. Patrick Dinner, March 17, 1948.

Cardinal Spellman and President Eisenhower at the annual Alfred E. Smith Memorial Foundation Dinner, October 21, 1954.

Cardinal Spellman with presidential candidates, John F. Kennedy and Richard M. Nixon, at the Alfred E. Smith Memorial Foundation Dinner, October 19, 1960.

A fresh and painful phase of the situation was presented when seventy-five wives of the striking workers met on March 6 and adopted a resolution supporting their husbands' demands for a "decent wage for a five-day week." They criticized the "reckless and misguided charges of Communism" made against the men and insisted that their husbands had willingly gone on strike and had not been misled into it. A committee of five called on the Cardinal the following day, but left his residence saying they were "discouraged and disgusted." The leader of the committee said:

> The Archbishop promised us nothing. He wants the men to go back to work as individuals, not as union men, and he said he would not allow members of the strikers' committee to go back to work because they were ringleaders. . . . The Archbishop was adamant. He promised nothing except that the strikers could return with a small increase, but not as union men. He wants no part of the union. We got no place.[13]

Asked about the meeting, His Eminence told reporters: "I feel as badly for them as if it were my own mother in the same circumstances. They had nothing to offer me and I had nothing to offer them. I spoke to them for more than two hours." That day the number of seminarians working in the cemetery was increased to 200.

A rift in the clouds appeared on March 9, when 800 members of Local 293 voted to quit the F.T.A.W., CIO, and join the AFL Building Service Employees Union as Local 365. Two days later, the Cardinal and a spokesman for the new union announced that a settlement of the strike had been reached and the workers had returned to their jobs. The men received an increase of about 8⅓ per cent in their wages, bringing their pay up to $64.35 weekly. The current figure is $92.00 with fringe benefits. The dispute over hours was to be placed in the hands of a mediation board comprising a representative of management, one of the unions, and a neutral satisfactory to both parties. The union said that for the present the workers would continue the six-day week, and the question whether the adoption of a five-day week would affect the base weekly wage was left undecided.

David Sullivan, International Vice President of the Building Service Employees Union and President of its Local 32—B, publicly thanked the Cardinal for the settlement, and said that the strike would never have occurred if there had been "responsible union leadership." He assured the Cardinal of his support in carrying out the agreement that had been reached and promised that no such strike would occur under his leadership.[14]

His Eminence issued the following statement:

> Today my heart is lighter than it has been for many long weeks, for after awaiting a decision on the legality of the strike in Calvary and allied cemeteries, I have determined after the disaffiliation of the local union from the Communist-dominated parent union, to wait no longer to make

my own decision based upon the dictates of my conscience before the higher and only indisputable law—the law of God. True it is that there have been at stake economic principles, policies and practices. But, it is just as true there have been souls at stake—confused, misled souls—and I am a priest of God, striving to live in imitation of Him, the forgiving Good Shepherd of Souls.

Therefore, with thankfulness to Him, and to all who have given of their time, understanding and counsel, during the sad, troubled eight weeks past, and with a heart full of inexpressible admiration and gratitude for the seminarians who gave themselves in constant prayers and labors to help me keep faith with the living and the dead, I am happy to announce that the strike has been settled. . . .

Thus is brought to a close one of the most difficult, grievous, heart-breaking issues that has ever come within my time as Archbishop of New York, and it will be my daily prayer that if ever again the working men of this Archdiocese must make their choice between following their faith or faithless leadership they will, of their own free and immediate choice, choose—God.

As a token of his fatherly sympathy for the families that had gone through so much uncertainty and sacrifice, he sent a check to each of the strikers for sixty-five dollars. Monsignor Ehardt stated that the total of his gifts came to $17,870. A telegram signed by 275 employees of Calvary read as follows:

ON BEHALF OF ALL THE EMPLOYEES OF CALVARY CEMETERY, THE COM-MITTEE WANTS TO THANK YOU FOR YOUR GENEROSITY AND THOUGHTFUL-NESS FOR THE GIFT CHECKS YOU SENT US. PRAYING THAT THE FUTURE WILL BRING A HAPPIER RELATION BETWEEN US AND ASSURING YOU OF OUR CON-STANT PRAYERS IN YOUR BEHALF, WE REMAIN YOUR HUMBLE SERVANTS.

The attitude of the press was interesting. Most of the papers confined themselves to news service reports, but thirty-six wrote editorials supporting the position of the trustees. Most of them accepted the danger to the public health, the anguish added to bereaved families, and the link of Local 293 with a communist-dominated union as sufficient justification for the Cardinal's unusual action.

Thus the much publicized strike was settled. It was settled honorably, with no hard feelings left behind except in the ranks of the F.T.A.W., CIO. Ten years later, when labor staged its largest demonstration in the history of the United States and 115,000 men and women marched in the Labor Day parade, there in the reviewing stand waving and smiling back at their friends stood Governor Rockefeller, Mayor Wagner, David Dubinsky, and Cardinal Spellman.

CHAPTER SEVENTEEN

The Great Consistory

STRICTLY speaking, there are only six cardinalatial dioceses in the world, one for each of the six Cardinal Bishops. These are all situated in the neighborhood of Rome, and are for the most part sparsely inhabited districts that fifteen hundred years ago were populous and important. In a loose and popular sense, however, a diocese which has several times seen its Ordinary elevated to the purple, like Paris or Toledo, comes to be known as a cardinalatial diocese, and in this sense the term has been applied to New York. The first American to receive the red hat was Archbishop John McCloskey of New York, who was invested at old St. Patrick's on Mulberry Street in 1875, and since that time a similar honor has come to all his successors but one.

It was natural, therefore, that when the young Auxiliary Bishop of Boston was appointed to succeed Cardinal Hayes, it was rumored at once, even before his installation, that "Pope Piux XII would probably summon a consistory in November to fill some of the eleven vacancies in the College of Cardinals. . . . It was believed almost certain that one of the red hats would go to the Most Reverend Francis J. Spellman." As usual, the rumor was partly true. A secret consistory was held on December 11, 1939, but no cardinals were named, though a letter came the same month from Giuseppe Cardinal Pizzardo, saying:

DEAR EXCELLENCY,
    Little is wanting to call you Dear Eminence, and thus the beautiful dream of 1932 will be fulfilled.
    The Holy Father covers himself with glory. Everyone loves him for his angelic goodness and his constant work for peace.

The lull on the western front was not yet known as the "Phony Peace," and many even in Rome hoped that the World War could still be averted. By April of 1940, Italian circles were again predicting the appointment of new cardinals, and, as always, Archbishop Spellman was mentioned. The next year, however, November 25, the United Press quoted "authoritative Vatican circles" as saying that "Pope Pius XII has decided 'as a sign of mourning' not to name any cardinals until the war ends." For once the

"Vatican circles" seem to have been really "authoritative," for the often heralded consistory was not called until 1946.

In the meantime it was a little embarrassing for His Excellency of New York to parry the references and questions of tactless people on the subject of the red hat. Sometimes he would laugh and say he looked better in black. On the way to the front, he remarked that a khaki hat was safer. "Red is too good a target." To one old newspaper correspondent of Roman days he said, "You know, Tom, that on an average a man has to be seven years an Archbishop in New York before he gets to be a Cardinal."[1] Actually, McCloskey had waited eleven years, Farley nine, Hayes five; and Corrigan had been buried in the robes of an archbishop. There was not the slightest doubt in anyone's mind that if and when a consistory should be called, New York would be honored once more, but years were to pass with nothing on the subject recorded in the diary until September 30, 1945, when this brief entry was made: "Rome. His Holiness told me about Consistory plans." That was it.

Another three months passed. It was early in the morning of December 23 when Sergeant John D. Donaghue, on duty with the Army news service in New York, received the first flash from Rome that Archbishop Spellman was one of four American prelates nominated for the College of Cardinals. The others were Archbishop John J. Glennon of St. Louis, Archbishop Edward Mooney of Detroit, and Archbishop Samuel A. Stritch of Chicago. He telephoned at once to St. Patrick's Cathedral and gave the news to the pastor, Monsignor Joseph F. Flannelly, who informed the Archbishop and later made the first public announcement from the pulpit. The least excited man on Madison Avenue was the Cardinal-designate.

The news reached the family in Whitman when a neighbor who had been listening to an early broadcast telephoned to tell Mrs. Pegnam about her brother. It was almost as exciting as the day he was made a Very Reverend Monsignor, but when this American family got the new Prince of the Church on the phone, Pa just said, "Congratulations, Frank!" and the Prince answered, "I'll see you Tuesday afternoon, Pa!" That was the afternoon of Christmas, a feast he had spent in Whitman almost every year since ordination. When the town reporter asked him if this was not the happiest of all his homecomings, he shook his head. "The happiest," he said, "was the day I came home as a priest after five years away and said Mass for my father and mother."

The next day he was back in New York at a crowded desk, writing acknowledgments and trying to keep the news releases within reason. One of the first greetings to arrive came from an old and faithful friend who had guided him through the early mazes of his career in Rome, Archbishop Borgongini-Duca. By a quirk of fortune the apt pupil was receiving the purple six years before the old master. His Yankee school principal of former days, Archer M. Nickerson, wrote, "I have been happy in the thought that you were once a boy in my school and by your life you have honored that school as well as your parents, the Church and the town of your birth." The pastor of St. Thomas Episcopal Church, the Reverend Roelif H. Brooks, D.D., told his congregation:

> I am sure you will join with me in a message of congratulation to our neighbor the Archbishop, who has been raised to the rank of Cardinal. . . . And if you will pardon a personal reference may I tell you that at the time we lost our daughter, the Archbishop met me and said, "You know I try to get some exercise, and usually walk up Fifth Avenue, and since I heard of your sorrow, I never pass your Church without saying a prayer for you and your child."

The Association of Reform Rabbis wrote:

> It has been a source of encouragement to us . . . to note the many pronouncements you have made on the need for a greater brotherhood among men and your insistence that we in this country, in fact all the world, must give "to bigotry no sanction." We feel that you will carry this broad teaching, which is at once Christian and Jewish, into the larger sphere of your future ministry. . . .

But it took a virtually unknown soldier to hit the target with the following: "Whether you wear a red hat or otherwise you will always be G.I. Joe to me!"

Then there were the inevitable predictions of higher office and erroneous biographical details to be corrected. Rumors that he would become Papal Secretary of State were immediately revived, but three weeks later it became generally known that the Holy Father intended to keep the foreign office reins in his own hands with two pro-secretaries, Monsignor Giovanni Montini and Monsignor Domenico Tardini. On January 29, he read in the local press a UP dispatch from Nuremberg to the effect that:

> Archbishop Francis J. Spellman was identified today as the member of the Papal Secretariat of State's staff who smuggled the Pope's denunciation of Nazism into Germany in 1937.
>
> He flew from Rome to Paris, pretending he was on "normal business," it was learned, and then went on to Germany, where he got in touch with Catholic leaders.
>
> To the Catholics he handed a Papal Encyclical, which for the first time in hundreds of years was not in Latin but in German, for the German Church alone. The encyclical was duplicated and distributed to central points throughout Germany. On a given Sunday it was read simultaneously in all Catholic pulpits.

It was a picturesque but complete fabrication, inspired by his historic trip to Paris in 1931.

The women editors were interested in his new wardrobe. Would it really cost $10,000? No, it would not, even if it were all new. As a matter of fact, he was having Cardinal Hayes' robes cleaned and pressed. Had he decided on the list of those who would have the honor of being in his official party at the consistory? Now that was a sensible question, but the answer was not given until February 5, when the chancery released a list of forty-eight names.

The list was characteristic of the man who drew it up, partly official, partly personal, completely autobiographical except for the suites of Cardinal Glennon of St. Louis and Cardinal Tien of China whom he had invited to join him. There was his beloved family—sisters and brothers with their husbands and wives, and one niece, Mary Pegnam, in her naval uniform, to represent the second generation. Completing the representation from Whitman was the pastor of the Holy Ghost Church, Father John J. Starr. One old-timer who would have graced the occasion was not quite up to the journey and received the following letter:

DEAR MONSIGNOR OWENS:

I thank you very much for your note of January 20th. It brought me much joy to hear from you, and as you know without my telling you, if your health were better, you would be, with my father, among the first to come to Rome with me. I recall with affection and gratitude all your lifetime of interest in my welfare from the time that you and my mother conferred about giving me the name that I bear, through my boyhood, my college days, your visit to Rome for my Consecration and all the friendly contacts that we had during my years as a priest and a Bishop in Boston. I am grateful for your prayers and good wishes and also I thank you for your very generous gift. . . .

With affectionate regards, I am

Devotedly yours,
FRANK SPELLMAN
Archbishop of New York

To remind him of Fordham, His Eminence had asked three classmates and the president of the university. His North American College days were echoed by five of the dearest friends he had made in the seminary: his classmates, Bishop Bergan and Monsignors Quinn, McCarthy, and Killian, as well as an upperclassman, Bishop Louis F. Kelleher, who had meant so much to him in so many ways and who had prepared him for the historic repetition that attracted the first notice of Borgongini-Duca. Then there were friends of the intervening years and more recent friends made in New York. The Military Ordinariate was represented, the Society for the Propagation of the Faith, the Catholic Near East Welfare Association, the Catholic University, and the Knights of Columbus. The roster read like the table of contents for the story of his life. The remaining seats in the two chartered planes, *The Star of Rome,* a T.W.A. four-engine Constellation, and *The Colosseum,* a C-54 Douglas Skymaster, were assigned to twenty-five delighted newspapermen. Their stories would go to INS, UP, AP, *Life,* and a newsreel pool, as well as to specific newspapers in New York, Chicago, St. Louis, Boston, and Detroit. The resultant coverage of the Great Consistory for American readers was considered adequate.

On February 11, the first plane left La Guardia for Gander at eleven in the morning. The second plane, carrying the Cardinals-designate, left at one. Arriving at Shannon early the next day, the party was met by members of the Irish hierarchy and government officials who had arranged for Mass at St. John's Cathedral in nearby Limerick. In the course of his remarks to the people after Mass, the New York prelate said with feeling:

It is with a heart filled with gratitude that I come to Limerick on this occasion to offer Mass in this historic Cathedral. The thought uppermost in my mind this morning is that of my grandmother, my father's mother, Honora Hayes, who as a little girl left Limerick more than a century ago to come to the new world. She was one of the first Catholics to settle in my native town of Whitman. Her life was a life dedicated completely to the rearing of her children in the knowledge and worship of God, and inculcating in their hearts the love of their mother country, the United States of America. . . . I express also my veneration and appreciation of all that Ireland has given me, for my other three grandparents came from Ireland—one from Carlow, another from Tipperary, and a fourth from Cork.

The reporters looked at one another and murmured, "A perfect score!"

After breakfast, the Taoiseach himself, Eamon de Valera, accompanied the party to Killarney in an official train that had been stuffed with upholstery for one of Victoria's earlier visits to her so-called subjects. Like similar relics in England and on the Continent, it was in an excellent state of preservation and made record time from Limerick to the Lakes—the best time ever made on peat. There were more receptions, a tour to the Gap of Dunloe, and in the evening a state dinner at the best hotel. Mr. de Valera in greeting His Eminence admitted having been born in New York and was most gracious in his remarks about Americans in general. His Eminence in reply said that he had already delivered both his speeches and unfortunately had no more. Then he asked the Taoiseach if he knew what a "pinch hitter" might be, Mr. de Valera pleaded ignorance. So the Cardinal said, "I'll show you one," and thereupon called up one of the priests in the party to do the honors on the dais. It gave the evening an informality uncommon at state dinners, but not unexpected by those who knew His Eminence of New York. Cardinal Tien took the whole celebration in stride, relaxing a perfect composure only at the mention of the word "China," when he would smile and bow to the speaker as if he had not missed a thing.

In Paris, the American Ambassador, Jefferson Caffery, gave an afternoon reception at the Embassy that was a model of hospitality, but the post-war visit to the French capital by and large was anything but gay. For Mass in the great Cathedral of Notre Dame, each priest still was assigned one little piece of candle stuck in a bottle, which was carried from the sacristy by the server and carefully returned. Even when His Eminence gave Solemn Benediction at the main altar, there were only two candles burning. The streets were dark too, the streets of the City of Light, dark and dirty. The hotels were cold. The shops were shabby. Only the famous Flea Market, which seemed to be very much bigger than ever, was doing a thriving business. Everyone in the party had a feeling of relief when the two planes roared off the runway at Le Bourget and headed for Rome.

Instead of flying straight down the valley of the Rhone and over the island of Corsica, the inveterate tourist and perfect host, who continued to plan every step of the trip, had the pilots fly out of their course to circle Lake Geneva, Mont Blanc, and Monte Rosa, dear to the heart of the mountain-climbing Pope, Pius XI, then southward over the Ligurian Sea and Elba. When the dome of St. Peter's appeared, light gold in the late afternoon, all the old Roman students broke into a chant and everyone on both planes said prayers for the Holy Father. The runways at Ciampino were the temporary mattings of the battlefields, and everywhere along the road to the city were shell craters and overturned tanks in the ditches, but Rome itself, due solely to the presence of one man, had suffered less than any capital in the war zone. It was still occupied by the British and Americans, the people were demoralized, the swarms of unemployed were ominous, and the future was dark, but it was some consolation to realize that at least the city streets were unchanged and the churches, palaces, monuments and shrines were practically untouched.

That evening, on his arrival at the Grand Hotel, instead of gracefully retiring at once to his private apartments, the Cardinal-elect of New York stood in the lobby, list in hand, checking every member of the group and refusing to get ready for dinner until the humblest of them had been provided with a suitable room. In the days that followed, the Romans, who should have been used to everything, would stop in the street with an exclamation at the sight of a "neo-porporato," an eminent Cardinal-to-be, sitting up with a bus driver in the front seat and pointing out the sights to his fellow Americans! He managed to convey the impression, even in the midst of dazzling ceremonies, that somebody else was getting the red hat. As the editor of the Denver *Register* summed it up:

> I was happy to be able to be close to you in real life and to see what it was about you that has so captured the public fancy. I think that, in addition to the ecclesiastical qualifications that have made you an Archbishop and a Cardinal, it is your obvious enthusiasm, your painstaking

consideration for others, and, above all, the fact that, without ever losing dignity, you never parade pomp.

On Monday morning, February 18, the great five days began when the Holy Father, just before nine-thirty, opened the first secret consistory. Of the thirty-seven living members of the College of Cardinals, twenty-eight were present. Rapidly mounting the six steps to the throne, the Pope called attention to the "many and various difficulties" that had delayed his naming of the new cardinals. "Now at length with the conflict ended, although true peace does not yet shine upon anxious and troubled man, we are able to carry out the intentions which we have had in mind so long. . . . And since for the first time our worthy sons are selected from five parts of the world, . . . the well known Catholicity of the Church is placed in a new light." As the Pope read out the thirty-two names of the "neo-porporati," the cardinals present raised their zuchettos and bowed in assent.

At that moment, in ten different parts of Rome, groups were gathered about the Cardinals-designate to await the arrival of special messengers dispatched from the consistory with letters, or "biglietti," of notification. The four Americans had chosen the "Hall of the Hundred Days" in the Cancelleria, a splendid palace of the fifteenth century, which served incidentally as the model of the present chancery office in New York. Arrangements were to have been under the control of the Assistant Master of Ceremonies of St. Peter's Basilica, a large and impressive monsignore. Masters of ceremonies even in remote districts are always a little on the absolute side, used to clapping their hands and seeing the whole Church Militant genuflect, and here was the Assistant to the Master of Masters. So he clapped his hands and announced that only the immediate friends of Their Eminences would be admitted to the inner room. Everyone else would remain outside. Of course he had not counted on the American press, whose representatives, even before the arrival of the messenger, formed a flying wedge and made their grand entrance into the forbidden space, with most of Rome at their heels. The result was that when the Reverend Martin Gilligan, a member of the staff at the Secretariat of State, was formally announced at 10:05 A.M., Bishop O'Hara, the former president of Notre Dame, had to organize a powerful interference to get him through the line with his "biglietto." All the cardinals were to have made appropriate addresses, but when His Eminence of St. Louis, as the senior, had finished his brief and very touching remarks, with their prophetic reference to the late afternoon of his life, a photographer from Jersey City leaped over two lines of reporters in his way with the cry so beloved in Congressional circles, "Hold that, Cardinal!" and the notification ceremony was over.

The next day was devoted to the traditional exchange of visits among the old and new members of the Sacred College, known as the "ad calorem" visits—the warmth referred to being the warmth of charity. There was still time, however, for luncheon with Vittorio Orlando, now almost ninety years old, dinner with General Mark Clark, commander-in-chief of the American Occupation Forces in Austria, and an important broadcast to the United States from the chapel of the North American College in the old Via dell' Umiltà. The benches there were filled with friends, but memories that needed no space were crowding in everywhere. It did not seem to be thirty-five years since a young seminarian from Whitman had knelt in his "bags" and watched His Eminence of Boston pontificating at the altar. In his tribute to Pope Pius XII, who had raised him to the sacred purple, he said:

> Let truth outrun discretion. In the leadership of the world today he is the only certain embodiment of wisdom without wile, fortitude without brute force, vigor without violence. To him come the cries of men and of peoples. To him turn the eyes of the hungry, the naked, the oppressed. And from him come luminous counsel and boundless mercy. We of the Faith rejoice in his rule and guidance. . . .

Then he turned to the subject of his beloved archdiocese:

> Some will refer to the dignity of the Cardinalate as one that is unde-served. I say, however, that not inappropriately is it conferred on the church of New York of which I am not so much the head as a representa-tive. Permit me to pay tribute to that church, for I can do so freely because of its greatness, I am in no way the architect, in no way the builder. I guard the heritage that any man should guard without failure, so deeply rooted, so strongly reared are the walls of the city of God, that is the church of the City of New York.

Other days were even more crowded. In addition to attendance at the Vatican for three more consistories, an audience with the Pope to introduce two hundred American chaplains, two private audiences, and one for the members of his party who were received in the Holy Father's library, he carried out a schedule that prostrated every one of the friends who tried to keep up with him. Each morning he said Mass in one of the great basilicas or a favorite shrine, and once in Santa Maria in Via which had been the Titular Church of Cardinal Hayes. One afternoon it would be the dedica-tion of a building for an Italian Boys Town to house a hundred of the *"sciua-scia"* or shoeshine boys; another, a visit to the playgrounds of the Knights of Columbus where, as a former director, he felt peculiarly at home; or by way of contrast, a formal academy in the great hall of the Gregorian University with twenty-six other cardinals sitting in a great semicircle, ap-parently enjoying an hour of Latin verse and prose. They were afterward mobbed for autographs by unpredictable seminarians from every country in the world.

Cardinal Spellman's presence at a luncheon in his honor given by the United States Ambassador, Alexander C. Kirk, at the old Barberini Palace, passed unnoticed by the reporters, but a state dinner at the Spanish Embassy was described by the leftist press at home as the debut of the New York Cardinal "knee-deep in anti-democratic politics."[2] He was criticized too by the same element as the only American Prince of the Church to accept the invitation of Prince Umberto, the Lieutenant General of the Realm, for a reception to the Sacred College at the Quirinal Palace. Not to have accepted was to have missed one of the most picturesque and historic moments of the entire visit. It was the first reception held by the royal family since before the war, and the first reception held in the Quirinal for representatives of the Vatican since the Piedmontese seized this palace of Pope Pius IX in 1870. It was the first reception ever held by the House of Savoy for the College of Cardinals, and everyone present knew that it was the last. An era was ending in Italy, and though it ended with a touch of irony, it managed to end with splendor. The grand stairway was lined with thirty-five attendants holding candles, one to meet each of the expected cardinals at the carriage step and accompany him to the Throne Room. On the second floor, palace guards, each of them over six feet tall, with boots, cuirass and horsehair plume, presented arms for an hour without the flicker of an eyelash. After the formal reception, supper was served for royalty, the heads of government, and the members of the Sacred College, at tables set in the Hall of Mirrors, appropriately banked with blood-red roses. The other guests were in an adjoining room discussing quietly over their champagne the question in everyone's mind: How long? In two months' time, Umberto would be king, and in three months an exile. A less historic but more delightful evening was spent by Cardinal Spellman and his friends at the home of Count Enrico Galeazzi, where all joined with much enthusiasm in the singing of "The Fordham Ram."

However, nothing in this almost constant round of activity distracted in the least from the solemnity of the ceremonies at the Vatican. After the interval of one day for the "*ad calorem*" visits, a semipublic consistory was held in the Hall of Benedictions over the main entrance of St. Peter's. Special visitors arriving one hour early to secure their places on backless benches covered with green baize were entertained by the maneuvers of the seminarians, black and yellow and white and brown, who were lucky to have even standing room in the back of the Hall, but coveted the armchairs set aside for the bishops and diplomats. With a skill acquired over the centuries, they eluded the vigilance of the papal attendants, and when the Holy Father was borne in on the portable throne and nothing more could be done about it, fourteen innocent and dignified seminarians were in the bishops' chairs. Twenty-nine of the thirty-two cardinals created at the consistory were on hand. Accompanied each by three attendants, they knelt in quick succession before the Pontiff, who placed on their heads the biretta of red wool which was destined to be preserved for their remaining years under glass at the front door of their respective residences. When the youngest had made his obeisance and all had seated themselves in a semicircle about the throne, the dean of the group, Gregory Peter XV Cardinal Agagianian, once a fellow student of Cardinal Spellman at the University of the Propaganda and now Patriarch of the Armenians, expressed the gratitude of all to the Pope. Thereupon, in an unprecedented step, the Holy Father broadcast his reply to the world. Before him were some of the principal targets of totalitarianism, red and black—men like Sapieha, Frings, von Preysing, Mindszenty, von Galen—and when he spoke sternly of falsehood, imperialism, and the growth of a nation by the occupation of neighboring countries; of deportation, contempt for the individual, agnosticism, and a mechanistic view of society, as the major evils and errors of the modern world, he was looking into the upturned faces of confessors of the Faith—perhaps of future martyrs.

The next day, Thursday the twenty-first, the public consistory was held in St. Peter's. By sunrise, the city streets were full of American and British jeeps, command cars, and trucks. There were hundreds of chaplains who had thumbed their way from various parts of Europe and Africa, thousands of GIs and Tommies of all faiths and no faith, mingling with pilgrims from everywhere, and country people who had walked in from the Alban Hills. By eight o'clock the world's largest church was filled, except for the lucky box holders, who could afford a more leisurely breakfast.

Chatting amiably as Latins do in big churches, the crowds inspected the arrangements, many with a practiced eye—the two rows of facing seats for the cardinals and the throne of His Holiness erected above the tomb of St. Peter, the very spot where young Father Spellman had said his first Mass. It was approached by a dozen broad steps and was so proportioned as not to be dwarfed by Bernini's baldachino. Along the clerestory there was a novel touch—two rows of sun arcs that would make for better pictures. This last detail was to prove unpopular with the older members of the College, who frequently glanced up at the lights with scowls of disapproval, but the unwelcome glare made it possible for millions all over the world to join the lucky thousands in St. Peter's.

Soon after the royal family was seated (another first—the first time the House of Savoy had attended a consistory since 1870), the loud-speaker announced that the new cardinals were taking the oath to the Sacred College in the Chapel of the Blessed Sacrament, and presently the Supreme Pontiff made his traditional entrance on the *sedia gestatoria*. Non-Romans on such occasions begin by being a little shocked at all the hand clapping and the roar of "Long live the Pope!" but, with tears in their eyes, end up by joining in. The Pope looked radiant in a red cope and the tallest of gold miters, and ten years younger than he had in private audience. After all the old cardinals had made their obeisance individually at the throne, the consistorial advocates stepped forward to present for canonization Mother Frances Xavier Cabrini of New York, Mother Elizabeth Bichier des Anges, co-founder of the Daughters of the Cross, and two Jesuits, the Portuguese martyr John de Britto and the Italian apostle Bernadino Realino. Just before his final plea, the new cardinals filed in, each with his attendants, and were acknowledged by the crowd with a varying intensity of applause which could be measured. The favorite of the day was Clement August Cardinal von Galen, whose defiance of Hitler had impressed true lovers of liberty all over the world. Next came His Eminence of New York. He had received an excellent press on his arrival in Rome as an old and sincere friend of the people, and the *Capitale* had said editorially: "One day Italians will know how much he worked with the Pontiff and Myron C. Taylor to mitigate the armistice conditions." The same paper had suggested that he would soon be announced as the next Secretary of State. It was a great moment, then, for Romans as well as for New Yorkers and Whitmanites, when he mounted the twelve steps, his *cappa magna* fully extended, and knelt at the feet of his dearest friend, his father in Christ and his Most Holy Lord. As the attendant placed on his head first the hood of his *cappa magna* and then the great red hat with its shallow crown, wide brim, and trailing tassels—the hat used that day for all the investitures was the hat of the late Cardinal Merry del Val—the Pope said very distinctly in Latin:

For the praise of Almighty God and the honor of the Holy Apostolic See, receive the red hat, the special badge of a Cardinal's rank. By this you are to understand you must show yourself fearless, even to shedding your blood, in making our holy Faith respected, in securing peace for the Christian people and in promoting the welfare of the Roman Church in the name of the Father, the Son and the Holy Ghost. Amen.

The words were dramatic enough, and St. Peter's, the inner stage on which they were spoken, made them more dramatic still, but it was the outer stage, the ruins of the outer world, with Soviet Russia threatening every border, that made this one of the great scenes in the life of Pius XII. It was generally assumed at the time that when the American and British occupation came to an end, Tito would cross the Po and the communists would take charge of the ensuing chaos. No one was ready to say what would happen to the Holy Father and yet, as the 25,000 present that day looked at the slender old man on the throne, surrounded by fifty-seven other old men, few of them under sixty, the eldest in his nineties, they saw one force in the world that would certainly be flourishing after the red tide had ebbed. They remembered the tyrant's sneering question, "How many divisions has the Pope?"—and laughed at him for asking it.

As the last of the new cardinals returned to his place, the Pope stood for a moment, extended his arms full length in a great benediction, descended rapidly to the portable throne, and was carried around the altar and down the nave. The tremendous enthusiasm mounted to a pitch as he turned just before entering the Vatican, stood shoulder high among the people, and made again the Sign of the Cross with the words, "May the blessing of Almighty God, Father, Son and Holy Ghost, descend upon you and remain forever."

That afternoon His Eminence of New York, with a few chosen friends, drove to the old Casa San Giovanni on the Janiculum to await the formal delivery of his own ceremonial hat. As a mark of special predilection, and not of economy as Cardinal Glennon whimsically suggested, the Pope was sending him the very hat which he had himself received from Pope Pius XI just before Christmas in 1929. It looked enormous on the silver tray when presented with a bow by the Master of the Robes, and most prelates on such an occasion would have tried for just a moment to look like Richelieu. Cardinal Spellman grinned at the monsignor, who was as grave as a judge, and asked, "What shall I do now? Just take it?"

Later he was talking with Cardinal von Preysing about the custom always observed of never displaying the hat except when it is laid on the catafalque and then hung from the ceiling of the cathedral over a dead Cardinal's tomb until, like its owner, it disintegrates. He said that he had had a distraction at his meditation in St. Peter's when it occurred to him how much the scaffolding would cost when the time came to hang his hat from the ceiling of St. Patrick's. His Eminence of Berlin, who had lost his cathedral in an Allied air raid, remarked with a smile, "I have no trouble of that kind. I have no ceiling!"

One more consistory remained, and that a secret one. On the morning of the twenty-second, accompanied by one fortunate clerical attendant and a layman, the late William L. Galvin, treasurer of Catholic University, the new Cardinal presented himself with others of his rank in the Hall of Consistories for a ritual that brought back the days of Boniface VIII. The Pope first "closed their mouths," that is to say, forbade the newly created cardinals to exercise for the time being their advisory function, saying, "We close your mouth so that neither in consistory, nor in the congregations, nor in other functions as Cardinal can your advice be given." The purpose seems to have been to impress upon the novice cardinals the great gravity and responsibility of their advisory functions. Thereupon the Pope made an address, and after this brief interval—formerly it was several days—proceeded to "open their mouths," *aperitio oris*, saying, "I open your mouth so that in consistory, in congregations, and in other ecclesiastical functions your advice can be given."

Each cardinal then received the cardinal's ring set with a single topaz, a dark and reddish topaz, and each cardinal priest was assigned his titular church—his Roman parish. For this he accepts full responsibility, and it becomes the church in which he holds episcopal ceremonies on his visits to the Eternal City. Again, the Holy Father, mindful of the old days on Lake Constance, assigned to his former assistant one of the most ancient and most interesting in Rome, the titular church that had been his in the days of his cardinalate, the Church of Saints John and Paul. These martyrs, whose names occur in the Canon of the Mass, are known to have shed their blood in the fourth century, presumably under Julian the Apostate. Soon after, Byzantius, the Roman senator, converted his splendid home on the Caelian Hill into a Christian basilica, in which he placed their remains. Their tomb was known as a center of pilgrimage in the fifth century and still exists with its contemporary frescoes under the present structure, which dates from the twelfth century. Nine of the cardinals who preceded His Eminence of New York in this title were elevated afterward to the Papal Throne.

The Passionist Fathers, who are custodians of the church, met the Cardinal and his retinue with appropriate pomp when he came to take possession of his title and led him to the throne in the choir. His address, which was carried by radio and telephone to the New York crowds in St. Patrick's Cathedral, echoed the gravity of that moment in world affairs:

> Promotion of a spiritual rebirth is a mission of the Church—to bring light and law into life, to bring peace to mankind. It is her competency, her duty, to face a tidal wave of militant atheism, unbridled immorality, vile injustices, blinding hatreds and cruelties that in this atomic age of godless materialism threatens death to civilization, threatens the end of man's world. . . .

The only unpleasant incident to be recorded arose from a change in the plans for the return trip. It had been announced that a day and a half would be spent in Madrid to allow for a state dinner by General Franco in honor of Spain's new cardinals and the Spellman party, as well as for a visit to the Primatial See of Toledo as the guests of His Eminence Enrique Cardinal Pla y Deniel. The day after he took possession of his titular church, His Eminence of New York held a news conference whose tone was most unusual. As the newsmen themselves reported it:

> Francis Cardinal Spellman of New York [said the Philadelphia *Daily News*], obviously irritated by rumors and speculation over his projected visit to Spain, re-emphasized last night that the trip would be "wholly without political implication." He denied radio reports that he would carry a Papal letter to Generalissimo Francisco Franco. "I have no message to Franco and I will be carrying no message from anyone," he replied to a question at a press conference. . . .
>
> Persistent questions about a possible meeting with Franco caused Spellman to be sharper with newsmen than at any time since he began his trip to Rome. Asked if he thought his trip to Spain would not have political implications due to the controversial position of the Franco regime, he said: "There is no more political significance to that than to my stops in Ireland and France en route here. I have a right to go where I want to go."

Then turning to the *Herald Tribune* of New York—"Don't ask foolish questions," the usually affable Cardinal said rather tartly when asked whether he had a letter for Franco. "I am a guest of the Bishops of Spain. I'm going there and whatever they have planned, I'm going to do. I was told they are going to be given a reception by the Government. I was asked if I would attend and I said I would."

When the day came for the departure from Rome, the big TWA planes were still in France, delayed by bad weather, and it would be necessary to cancel the dinners that had been arranged in Madrid and Toledo if His Eminence was to reach New York in time for the public reception on Tuesday evening. Some reporters suspected that the storms had been contrived in order to relieve the Cardinal of unfavorable publicity in the anti-Franco American press, but he denied that there was any reason besides the weather for the change in plans and indicated that he would pay a courtesy call if time permitted.

"The stops going to and coming from Rome were taken in the interest of the great many members of my party who had never before been in those countries. It was to give them a break. Anything beyond the obvious is due to the genius of newspaper . . ." here he hesitated, evidently intending to say "reporters," but instead saying "readers."[3] The United Press reported that there was an uproar in Spanish circles over the change.

Arriving in Madrid, however, on March 3, His Eminence attended a reception at the United States Embassy, where he had a fifteen-minute visit with Foreign Minister Alberto Martín Artajo, and afterward paid courtesy calls on the Apostolic Nuncio and the Bishop of Madrid. That evening at seven-thirty, he was met at the airport in Lisbon by members of the Portuguese government.

After a brief stop at the palace of His Eminence Emmanuel Cardinal Gonçalves Cerejeira, the Patriarch of Lisbon, who had made the journey from Rome with the Americans, six of Cardinal Spellman's party accompanied him to the official residence of the Premier, Dr. Antonio de Oliveira Salazar, for dinner. The premier and the patriarch, who had been classmates in the seminary and who still make their annual retreat together, sat opposite each other at table, with Cardinal Spellman on the right of Dr. Salazar. The premier, a man at that time in his fifties, handsome and scholarly— like de Valera, much more professor than politician—proved himself a good conversationalist, that is, a good listener, was entertaining in French without being humorous, and seldom smiled.

The following morning, in a fleet of cars placed at their disposal and accompanied by officials of the government, the staff of the United States Embassy, and the premier himself, the Americans inspected the splendid system of roads fanning out in every direction from the capital. Their principal objective was the Jeronymos in Belem, the Westminster Abbey of Portugal, resplendent with the memory of Henry the Navigator, but on the way, the only Jesuit in the party pointed out the fortress of San Juliano, where hundreds of his brothers in Christ had been buried in the dungeons below sea level by the Marquis de Pombal, an eighteenth-century predecessor of the deeply religious Salazar.

After a luncheon as guests of the Portuguese government, the party resumed its journey, pausing only to refuel at the Azores and Gander. By 12:21 P.M. the next day, Tuesday, March 5, they were circling Whitman, Massachusetts, and at 1:30 P.M. arrived at La Guardia Airport. Ten thousand people were on hand, with the mayor, William O'Dwyer, many bishops, and members of the clergy, as well as state and city representatives, veterans' groups, and a police honor guard, to greet the Archbishop of New York, newly created and proclaimed Cardinal Priest of the title of Saints John and Paul. Aside from the insignia of his rank, he was easily recognized as the only traveler on either plane who looked as if he had had a vacation.

A fleet of twenty-five motorcycles, bearing the American, papal, and municipal flags, led the motorcade over the Triboro Bridge, pausing briefly at Cardinal Hayes High School. There he told the boys of the biggest thrill on the return journey:

> We flew three times around my home town of Whitman. We telegraphed ahead to my father that we were coming. I could see and recognize my own home and there on the lawn was my father waving to me. I couldn't see his face, of course, but I knew him.

When he reached his cathedral, the bells were pealing and the people in the streets were cheering him. At the door, he kissed the crucifix and sprinkled the congregation with holy water before proceeding to the high altar, where he read the Prayer of St. Patrick. Then, taking his place on the throne, in *cappa magna*, he presided during the Solemn Benediction of the Most Blessed Sacrament.

That evening there was a civic reception at the Metropolitan Opera House. Before an audience of more than 4500 people, including seventeen bishops, Governor Thomas E. Dewey of New York, Mayor O'Dwyer, and Postmaster General Robert E. Hannegan representing the President of the United States, His Eminence said:

> I would not even be remotely worthy of this honor were it not that I am aware that its greatest glory lies in its opportunity for service. This I have said before, and again I say, that in these days of chaos and crises while mankind is still engulfed in war-heated hatreds and bigotries, honors can be weighed, measured and considered only in terms of opportunity to serve. And service to the utmost and to the end I shall give. To serve my brother and share with him all honors bestowed upon me, all burdens imposed upon him, is the foundation of my faith and love for my fellowman. . . .

I pledge myself anew to love God and to serve Him only, striving ever to emulate Christ's Vicar on earth, unsparingly to spend myself for the spiritual and temporal welfare of you, my people.

And to you, my people, I make the plea for you too to adopt the motto: "Follow God."

The last episode in the journey to the Great Consistory took place in the St. Louis Cathedral on March 17 when Their Eminences of Chicago, Detroit, and New York met around the catafalque of John Cardinal Glennon. His great and kindly soul had returned to its Maker just twenty days after his elevation to the sacred purple "in the late afternoon of his life." There was to be no anticlimax for him, as there must inevitably be for any man who lives through such a month and then returns to the daily grind of administration. For the other American cardinals, the only higher climax conceivable would be their elevation to the Papacy and, in spite of repeated speculation in the press, no informed observers, least of all Their American Eminences, ever took that possibility very seriously.

CHAPTER EIGHTEEN

Educational Interests

IN THE misty pages of the Old Testament it was prophesied that the Messias would be a teacher as well as a priest and king. And so in the fullness of time He was. This office of teacher He handed on explicitly to His Apostles and their successors as a privilege and a responsibility that would last till the end of time. Hence every bishop is in virtue of his office an educator. In union with the Holy Father he represents the magisterium or teaching power of the Church. There have been periods in history when the atmosphere surrounding even secular affairs was such that his teaching could be confined to the pulpit and to pastoral letters—a confinement still pointedly recommended by the uninformed. In modern times, however, bishops have become, more than ever, conscious that their role of educator can no longer be fulfilled by a Sunday sermon. What they have to teach is a whole way of life. What they have to transmit to each generation is not only a deposit of revealed truth, but a set of values, an attitude toward every problem that can arise in human affairs. This task, in a society as naturalistic as ours, requires long and careful training of their flocks, in fact training from childhood to maturity, and makes the bishop not only a preacher but a schoolman involved with grammar schools, high schools, colleges, and universities.

In the case of Cardinal Spellman, his responsibilities were never accepted in a narrow sense and his many contributions to education at every level have been acknowledged by honorary degrees from forty-four institutions at home and abroad. Beginning with St. Joseph's Seminary at Dunwoodie, he found a handsome but venerable structure dating back to the early 1890's and eventually spent more than two and a half millions remodeling it. In addition to repairs and improvements he announced almost on his arrival in New York that he intended to build a well-planned modern library where a trained staff would be able to give professional service to modern students. The war intervened, however, and it was not until 1953 that the beautiful memorial library to Archbishop Corrigan was completed at a cost of approximately $1,000,000. Its first major project, suggested by the Catholic Theological Society of America and warmly endorsed by the Cardinal, who undertook the entire financial responsibility, was the compilation of the "International Union Catalog of Theological Source Materials." Its purpose is to locate all theological works published anywhere before 1800. During the first year, 510 titles were circulated among 107 libraries in the United States, Canada, and Europe with the result that nearly 8000 locations of the items and variations of them were reported. The gathering of the data and the editing of the catalog, which it is estimated will take twenty years to complete, is being carried on by the staff of the Corrigan Memorial Library at the seminary under the direction of the Very Reverend Monsignor John H. Harrington. When the time came for accreditation of the seminary by the Middle States Association the library was certainly an important factor, but only one, in the favorable impression made on the official examiners.

Earlier, the enthusiasm of the Cardinal was aroused by a work which had been inaugurated at Princeton in 1917 and was nearing a successful conclusion thirty years later. Professor Charles Rufus Morey had devoted his life and an endowment of three-quarters of a million dollars to the compiling of an index of 100,000 photographs and 500,000 cards listing all works of Christian art which can be dated prior to the year 1400. It was known as the Princeton Index of Christian Art.

Realizing that the art of the Church from the days of the catacombs to the Renaissance was not only the flower of Christian living but a key to its interpretation, His Eminence through the generosity of a friend secured a copy of the index for $50,000 and presented it to the Vatican Library. Complementing the gift, he set up a fund for administration, gave Father Harrington a year's leave of absence to superintend the arrangements, provided for a permanent staff, and initiated a program of bibliographical co-operation between the Vatican copy of the index and the great libraries of Europe. The pictures and cards now in the Vatican Library were housed for nine years on the first floor of the Pontifical Institute of Christian Archaeology, and there on June 6, 1952, the solemn dedication took place in the presence of several cardinals and many other distinguished guests. In two short years Professor Morey was quoted as saying that more scholars were using the index in Rome than in Princeton. His Eminence of New York had every reason to be gratified by the immediate results and wrote under date of July 27, 1954:

> I visit it each time I go to Rome and am greatly consoled to learn from the Curator, Dom Guy Ferrari, a learned and alert Benedictine, of the great number of years of drudgery and so-called research that this Index, the only one in Europe, has saved during the short time of its existence.[1]

A more positive achievement appeared in 1956 with the publication of the *Catalogo delle Publicazioni Periodici*, listing 8700 titles and locations of periodicals available in twenty-four libraries in Rome and two in Florence. The work was done in conjunction with the International Union of Historical Institutes and marks a new phase in the development of the Vatican

Library itself. This historic collection which was private until Leo XIII opened its resources to the learned world, now appears for the first time co-operating with scholars in the use of materials not on its own shelves.

It was not long before another index came to the Cardinal's attention. A young professor of philosophy at the seminary in Gallarate, near Milan, the Reverend Roberto Busa, S.J., conceived the idea of using the punch-card system of the International Business Machines for a verbal index of St. Thomas Aquinas, beginning with his *Contra Gentiles*. Samples of the cards were prepared and demonstrated in New York where everyone admitted that the method was bold, ingenious, and full of promise for reducing the endless mechanical labor of research. Then, as with so many useful and brilliant projects, there came a great calm. Nothing happened until His Eminence acted. He wrote to his old friend, the late Thomas J. Watson, chairman of the board of IBM, who responded enthusiastically. He wrote to the rector and the trustees of the North American College, proposing that space be allotted for the necessary machines in the graduate department on Via dell' Umiltà. In short, he did everything that Father Busa could not do for himself, realizing that in providing the instruments for important research, he was carrying out in a less obvious way the mandate given to the Apostles of teaching all nations.

It came as no surprise, therefore, that he has always given himself so unsparingly to the affairs of the Catholic University of America which is the special responsibility of the hierarchy in the United States. From the first board meeting he attended as Archbishop of New York, he has never been satisfied with generalities. He has always studied the agenda before-hand and has always been ready with the leading questions for which he is famous. In no time at all he discovered that the university was in serious financial difficulty and his diary records for April 3, 1940, a characteristic reaction: "I said I would refuse to approve the budget unless I could study it. For my pains I was 'rewarded' by being elected to the Executive Board." The outcome of his election can be inferred from a letter written in 1947 by the late William L. Galvin, then treasurer of the university, to the new chancellor, the Most Reverend Patrick A. O'Boyle, D.D., Arch-bishop of Washington:

As the new Chancellor of the University you are picking up the cleanest balance sheet the University has ever been able to exhibit from the day it was organized to date. . . .

Let there be no misgivings about where the credit for this condition belongs. It belongs entirely to Cardinal Spellman. As a member of the Executive Committee he took the work seriously and brought the ma-terial affairs of the University to their present sound stage. I think I am correct in stating that during his whole term on the Executive Committee he missed but one meeting.

This unusual blend of sound business and scholarly interest was to profit the university again in 1959. The need for a modern Catholic encyclopedia in English had been realized for many years. The original Catholic Encyclopedia had been published beginning in 1907 when its appearance was hailed as an important advance for the Church in the United States. Since then, efforts were made to keep it up to date by the publication of two supplements, but the passage of time made it quite obvious that these were not adequate substitutes for a complete revision or a new edition.

In 1958 the Catholic University opened discussions with the McGraw-Hill Book Company of New York with a view to producing an entirely new encyclopedia and, as chairman of the board of trustees, His Eminence guided the negotiations which resulted in a contract unusual in publishing practice. It was now possible for the university to make a major contribution to Catholic life through the preparation of the New Catholic Encyclopedia, and at the same time be assured of a large return from the sale of the proposed work without expense to the university.

The publication and distribution of the Catholic Encyclopedia and Supplement II had been carried on by the Gilmary Society, a membership corporation. In 1959 the board of directors of the society voted to transfer all the original rights and inventory of these publications to the Archbishopric of New York. To assist the university in its new and important project, His Eminence transferred these to Catholic University, as well as the rights to Supplement I, the Catholic Encyclopedia Dictionary, the Makers of the Catholic Encyclopedia, and all that had been published of the revision of the Catholic Encyclopedia.

On February 3, 1960, at the Teachers' Institute of the Archdiocese, the Cardinal announced his sponsorship of another encyclopedia, this one the Catholic Youth Encyclopedia in 10 volumes and 5,000,000 words to be developed in terms of the present and future needs of the secondary school curriculum. The rights and royalties to this series were assigned to St. Joseph's Seminary and the editorial staff organized with Monsignor John H. Harrington as editor-in-chief. As Archbishop of New York, His Eminence also signed a contract for the same staff to produce a multivolume history of the activity and influence of the Catholic Church in the United States. The pilot volume, on education, is scheduled to appear in 1963.

Our main interest, however, when we think of a bishop as an educator is in the way he provides for the schooling of his own flock. A brief summary of the responsibilities inherited was given in one of his addresses in 1941:

> Fordham, the largest Catholic University in our country, is the apex of the Catholic educational system in the Archdiocese of New York which comprises, in addition, nine colleges, eighty-seven high schools and academies and two hundred and seventy-five elementary schools.

Impressive as these figures were, the future was to see the building of eighty-one new elementary schools, the replacement of forty-six and additions made to still another eighty-seven with twenty-seven closed. For secondary education the figures would show an increase from eighty-seven to ninety-nine. In the single year 1955–56, His Eminence provided additional accommodations for 10,572 students from the first to the twelfth grades. Where in 1939–40 there were 119,429 pupils of all grades in the Catholic schools, in 1960–61 the number had risen to 216,013.

Meanwhile the teachers, who had increased from 3871 to 6176, were not neglected. Salaries were raised at every level, but still more significant of the Cardinal's personal interest were his plans for easing the financial burden involved in the degree preparation of his teaching religious. Higher education by 1952 had become a necessary step in the training of all parish school staffs, but an increasingly expensive one. Fordham University and other Catholic institutions had allowed substantial reductions to sisters and brothers ever since the First World War, but costs by now were getting beyond the reach of their still modest salaries. So in 1952, His Eminence instituted a subsidy program that would be responsible for sixty per cent of the tuition paid in the Fordham School of Education by religious teaching in parish and private elementary schools. Up to the summer of 1959, thirteen hundred religious had been assisted to the extent of $307,221.92.

Speaking at the celebration of the Fordham Centenary, just before the war reached the United States, the Archbishop of New York saw the success of his efforts and those of his predecessors in a kind of vision:

> Passing through this archdiocese and looking down upon it from the air church after church is seen and near the church, the school. Everywhere in teeming cities and country towns they dot the landscape. Erected with the voluntary contributions of the people, they are one glory of the Church. They represent faith, consecration, sacrifice and progress. Where, may I ask, will you find equal service to mankind, equal patriotic service to country?
>
> From many sources there comes the prediction that the future will be far different from the past. Any old order or any new order, if it is to endure, must not ignore the origin, the dignity, the rights, and the destiny of man. Those fundamentals are taught in every church and every school in the Archdiocese of New York. In all Catholic schools and colleges, 10,500 of them throughout our country, 94,000 teachers believe, teach and exemplify love of God, love of country, and love of fellowman, to 2,602,-000 students. These three loves are essentials of Catholic doctrine and we believe also that they are foundations of American democracy.

Many of his fellow countrymen were aware of the progress represented by the statistics he quoted, but found it deeply disturbing. Nor were they reassured by learning that "it would cost the City of New York more than twenty-seven million dollars annually to teach the children enrolled in Catholic elementary and high schools, to say nothing of the cost of providing sites and building schools, which at the present day's cost would represent a capital expenditure of approximately two hundred million dollars for the City of New York."

To many sincere, good people, as well as to the recognized purveyors of bigotry and hatred, the success of the Catholic schools was a threat to the country. They had been led to believe that the subjects of Rome would soon abandon their superstitions if exposed to the enlightenment of non-Catholic schools and colleges, and concluded that that was the real reason why the scheming hierarchy insisted on having every Catholic child in a Catholic school when the school and space were available. It was, as they saw it, one way to reinforce the political power of an alien Church. Moreover, the whole attitude of the bishops toward education was undemocratic. They were not acting as delegates of their flock. They seemed to think that their warrant was from the Shepherd instead of from the sheep.

To this traditional suspicion, new factors were now bringing new and different emphases. An older generation had disapproved the very existence of Catholic schools. Now there was some discussion of having them share in federal appropriations. As it appeared to one Methodist minister, there are "three reasons for the sudden sharpening of differences between Protestants and Catholics in America":

> The first is the new Catholic drive among the Negro and rural sections of the population, both of which are as traditionally Protestant as Latin America, say, is traditionally Catholic. . . .
>
> A second and widely argued source of cleavage is the Taylor appointment. . . .
>
> The most important issue between the faiths is in the field of education. . . . Catholics, in supporting legislation designed to make public funds available to parochial schools, object to having to support two sets of schools. Protestants, in opposing such legislation, point to the Canon Law of the Catholic Church as proof that Catholics are opposed to the whole concept of free, public education. Section 1217 of the Canon Law states that "Catholic children shall not attend non-Catholic, indifferent schools that are mixed, that is to say, schools open to Catholics and non-Catholics alike." According to Canon Law, such schools are to be tolerated only where there is no alternative.[2]

The broad issue of the place of religion in education found the non-Catholic world divided, a large part of it being entirely sympathetic with the Catholic point of view. In 1939, for example, the Chamber of Commerce of the State of New York (with a charter from George III) included in its annual report the following remarkable sentence:

> The United States cannot have or maintain a right system unless it is based on true religious principles and therefore, in spite of the fact that some hesitate to include religion in our educational program, we place it first.

This constituted an implied endorsement of the McLaughlin-Coudert Law, which had just been enacted by the state legislature, authorizing a released-time program for the teaching of religion to the children of the public schools. It provided that "absence from required attendance shall be permitted only for causes allowed by the general rules and practices of the public schools. Absence for religious observance and education shall be permitted under rules that the commissioner shall establish."

The State Council of Churches (Protestant) supported the law and was pledged to aid in making it effective. The president of the National Conference of Christians and Jews spoke in favor of the plan, but there were many critics in Jewish circles who feared that the practice of separating groups for religious study might tend to emphasize certain differences. Newbold Morris, president of the City Council and candidate for mayor of the City of New York, addressing the Jewish Teachers' Association on Lincoln's Birthday, 1941, characterized the law as "one of the saddest things that has ever happened."[3] His comment was promptly challenged. A year before, the Archbishop had said:

> We hope that those who are opposing the law will become more cooperative, if not for religious reasons then for patriotic reasons; if not for patriotic reasons, and if not for ethical reasons, then for economic reasons, because all they have to see is that religious education is valuable to youth today. The foundations of good citizenship are built on religious principles.[4]

Now, on Washington's Birthday, speaking at the Manhattan College alumni dinner, he referred to Newbold Morris' criticism without mentioning him by name:

> It is sad that such a man pledged and sworn to enforce and defend the laws of our state should try to sabotage those laws. I would like to know what is sad in seeing boys and girls learn about God, learn about their country, learn to love their country, learn to love their neighbors and learn to love decency.[5]

A month later, the president of the City Council, addressing a Protestant group, evidenced a change of heart:

> In fairness to the proponents of the released time law, [he announced] I should say that from what I have seen this system is operating smoothly and without evidence of ill feeling.
>
> There is a great need for bringing our people closer to God, for our children too often are being allowed to wander through a maze of doubt and cynicism without religious guidance.[6]

The fact was that Roman Catholic, Protestant, and Jewish agencies cooperated and after less than a year could report that in New York City

101,633 pupils were taking advantage of released time. The Public Education Association's report for the third year showed 28 per cent of the children in the city registered, 1 per cent Jewish, 4 per cent Protestant, and
23 per cent Catholic.[7] All over the country progress was made, but a hard
core of opposition from expected quarters was taking definite form. By 1945,
it had found a test case in Champaign, Illinois—the now celebrated Mc-
Collum v. Board of Education.

Mrs. Vashti McCollum, the wife of a professor at the University of Illinois
and the daughter of a militant freethinker, had a ten-year-old son attending
a tax-supported school where religious instruction was given as part of the
released-time program within the confines of the building. This last circumstance increased the possibility of success in ultimately challenging the whole
movement. The Board of Education pointed out to her that attendance
at the classes in religion was entirely voluntary, but she insisted that having
the other children take such instruction embarrassed her ten-year-old who
was a convinced rationalist, and that in any case it was a violation of the
First Amendment of the Constitution, made applicable to the States by
the Fourteenth.

The decision of the Circuit Court of Champaign County of Illinois, subsequently affirmed by a decision of the Supreme Court of Illinois, supported
the Champaign school board against Mrs. McCollum, insisting that the instruction was considered an "extracurricular activity," so that those who did
not attend had their regular subjects supervised by regular teachers during
the released time.

In her appeal to the United States Supreme Court, the plaintiff had the
support of the American Civil Liberties Union, the General Conference of
the Seventh Day Adventists, the Joint Baptist Conference on Public Relations, the Synagogue Council of America, and other religious groups who
filed briefs for an interesting variety of reasons that would form a long chapter in the history of American secularism. On March 8, 1948, the Court, in
an eight to one decision, ruled that the Champaign program was unconstitutional because, wrote Justice Hugo Black, the facts "showed the use of
tax-supported property for religious instruction and the close cooperation
between the school authorities and the religious council in promoting religious education. . . . And it falls squarely under the ban of the First
Amendment. . . . This is not separation of Church and State."[8] Justice
Robert H. Jackson, while concurring in the decision reached by the Court,
pointed out the irrational excess to which the rationalists were tending.

> While we may and should end such formal and explicit instruction as
> the Champaign plan and can at all times prohibit teaching of creed and
> catechism and ceremonial and can forbid forthright proselyting in the
> schools, I think it remains to be demonstrated whether it is possible,
> even if desirable, to comply with such demands as plaintiff's completely

to isolate and cast out of secular education all that some people may reasonably regard as religious instruction.[9]

Justice Stanley F. Reed filed a dissenting opinion, in which he directed attention to the many instances of the close association of church and state in American society, such as the required attendance of cadets at West Point and Annapolis at the academy chapel or elsewhere. He felt that the decision went beyond the separation which Jefferson and Madison contemplated, and beyond the constitutional prohibition of "an establishment of religion." Because of the importance attached in subsequent controversies to the fighting words "the separation of Church and State," Justice Reed may be quoted at some length:

The phrase "an establishment of religion" may have been intended by Congress to be aimed only at a state church. When the First Amendment was pending in Congress in substantially its present form, "Mr. Madison said, he apprehended the meaning of the words to be, that Congress should not establish a religion, and enforce the legal observation of it by law, nor compel men to worship God in any manner contrary to their conscience." . . .

The prohibition of enactments respecting the establishment of religion do not bar every friendly gesture between church and state. It is not an absolute prohibition against every conceivable situation where the two may work together any more than the other provisions of the First Amendment—free speech, free press—are absolutes. . . . This Court cannot be too cautious in upsetting practices embedded in our society by many years of experience. A state is entitled to have great leeway in its legislation when dealing with the important social problems of its population. A definite violation of legislative limits must be established. . . .

Devotion to the great principle of religious liberty should not lead us into a rigid interpretation of the constitutional guarantee that conflicts with the accepted habits of our people. This is an instance where, for me, the history of past practices is determinative of the meaning of the constitutional clause, not a decorous introduction to the study of its text. The judgment of the Circuit Court should be affirmed.[10]

Most conservative Protestants were as disappointed by the decision as the Catholics were, while "liberal" Protestants and most Jewish agencies regarded it as a victory. But meanwhile another issue was coming to a head in the field of education, which practically isolated American Catholics. This was the issue of federal aid, which, passing through several stages, reached its first climax as far as Cardinal Spellman was concerned in the defeat of the Barden Bill.

No great excitement had been aroused in 1930 when the Supreme Court upheld a decision of the Louisiana State Supreme Court permitting free nonreligious textbooks for pupils in private and parochial schools, on the ground that such assistance is given to pupils and not to institutions.[11] Little more attention was paid in 1946 to the National School Lunch Act, authorizing free lunches to children in private and parochial as well as in public schools. It was important that in those states which did not distribute lunches to any but public school children, the act provided that federal funds could be furnished directly and independently of the state school administration.

Where lunches, however, and textbooks failed to sound the tocsin, free bus rides were successful. The so-called New Jersey bus law, as passed by the state legislature in 1941, reads:

> Whenever in any district there are children living remote from any schoolhouse, the board of education for the district may make rules and contracts for the transportation of such children to and from school other than a public school, except such school as is operated for profit in whole or in part.[12]

The constitutionality of the law was contested before the New Jersey Supreme Court by a taxpayer named Everson and the Supreme Court held that the legislature had acted beyond its constitutional powers. The New Jersey Court of Errors and Appeals reversed this decision and the United States Supreme Court, on February 10, 1947, supported in a five-to-four decision the judgment of the Court of Errors and Appeals.

Justice Wiley B. Rutledge, in dissenting, struck the keynote of non-Catholic opposition.

> New Jersey's action therefore exactly fits the type of exaction and the kind of evil at which Madison and Jefferson struck. Under the test they framed it cannot be said that the cost of transportation is no part of the cost of education or of the religious instruction given. That it is a substantial and a necessary element is shown most plainly by the continuing and increasing demand for the state to assume it. . . .[13]

The Rutledge dissent was supported by the majority of law reviews and the entire Protestant press. Cardinal Spellman summed up the attitude of those who regarded the decision as a victory for Catholic taxpayers and for the cause of religious education in an address delivered at the Fordham University commencement the following June.

> A few months ago the Supreme Court of the United States rendered a decision which has attracted an unwarranted amount of sensational publicity, and which has stirred religious feeling to an alarming degree. . . .
>
> In high indignation some of our leading newspapers have denounced the decision as a dangerous departure from American principles, an egregious blunder which will lead to a union of Church and State, an attack upon our cherished free American public schools, the opening wedge in

breaking down the wall between Church and State. And with complete disregard for the absolutely clear language of the New Jersey law, which says that transportation service shall be provided for children attending both sectarian and non-sectarian private schools, several papers condemned the Court for showing favoritism to the Catholic Church. . . .

The editorials in the secular press, however, were mild in comparison with some others. . . . The headlines tell the story: "Methodist Bishops Attack Catholics," "Baptist Convention Told Wall Between Church and State Is Being Attacked," "Presbyterians Condemn Catholic Demands for School Aid." . . .

Once again a crusade is being preached against the Catholic Church in the United States. Once again the attack is directed not against Catholicism as such, not against Catholic dogmas or practices, not against the Catholic clergy, but against the Catholic Church as a social institution, as a cultural force in the United States. Once it was the tremendous influx of Catholic immigrants which stirred the attack on the Catholic Church; now it is the growth and expansion of Catholic education which is claimed to be a constant threat to the supremacy of public education in the United States.

Why is Catholic education thus attacked? Is it because in fact the public schools are Protestant schools, or at least schools which consciously or unconsciously are directed along Protestant lines?

For myself, I would never ask this question, but it has been asked and frankly answered by Mr. Justice Jackson. . . .

"Our public school, if not a product of Protestantism, at least is more consistent with it than with the Catholic culture and scheme of values. . . . It is organized on the premise that secular education can be isolated from all religious teaching so that the school can inculcate all needed temporal knowledge and also maintain a strict and lofty neutrality as to religion. The assumption is that after an individual has been instructed in worldly wisdom he will be better fitted to choose his religion."

This attitude is just one more example of the historical struggle to weave into the basic laws of the United States, elements of Protestant theology. It is assumed that the First Amendment's prohibition against "laws respecting an establishment of religion" lays down a rule of faith. It is assumed that all American people must agree to the dogma that in the sight of God all churches are of equal value. From this assumption it is concluded that any American who does not accept this brand of toleration is a heretic from the democratic faith. And the best that may be said for the dissenter is that he should not be persecuted, but definitely he is a sore-spot on the body politic—to be barely tolerated because the Constitution says he must.

Quite obviously, what is needed in the United States is a better understanding of the true relationship between Church and State in this country, and of just what is meant by their "separation." I doubt if some of those Protestant preachers realize that their incessant pleas for a *complete* separation of Church and State would strike a very discordant note in the ear of Thomas Jefferson. . . .

Our Founding Fathers certainly did not regard religious liberty as a concession of government. On the contrary, they demanded that our government acknowledge the citizens' right of conscience in religious matters as an inalienable right, always to be protected, never to be impeded either directly or indirectly. In their opinion and in the opinion of most Americans today, the right of religious freedom imposes a corresponding duty of religious toleration. It requires that all citizens respect the *civic* rights of each and every American, regardless of his religious affiliation. It means that as an American citizen and a Catholic, I may indeed not agree with the tenets of Protestantism, but I may not directly or indirectly deny to my Protestant friends any of their rights as American citizens. Is it not clear that when a Catholic school child is denied the use of a public school bus an injustice is done not to the *Catholic* child, but to an *American* child who happens to be a Catholic? What is really involved is a violation not of religious liberty but of civic equality. In this land of freedom, of inalienable rights, can there be any excuse, even one based on religious considerations, for treating any children as second-class citizens and denying them their right to civil equality? . . .

"Obviously, [wrote Justice Black] it is not the purpose of the First Amendment to cut off church schools from those services which are separate and indisputably marked off from religious functions. The state must be neutral in its relations with groups of religious believers and nonbelievers; it does not require the state to be their adversary. State power is no more to be used so as to handicap religions than it is to favor them."

Here is a sound working principle, one which does violence neither to taxpayers nor to the parents of parochial school children. It gives no preferment to any one religious denomination or to any one school system. It appeals to the fair-minded. It is subject to criticism mainly by the intolerant, who in their failure to win a victory in the court of law seek recourse in the shady corners of bigotry.

The reaction was immediate and violent. In a letter to the New York *Times*, the liberal point of view was expressed by three religious leaders:

What animates the anxiety of millions of American citizens with respect to the Roman Catholic Church is not to be found in the activities of the Catholic Church "as a social institution, as a cultural force," but rather in the political activities of members of the Roman Catholic hierarchy who, as representatives of a foreign power, have been carrying on unceasing propaganda and utilizing continuous and insistent pressure on press and radio and state and federal officials to break down our United States constitutional guarantee of separation of church and state.[14]

The *Christian Century* editorialized under the title "The Cardinal Looks for Trouble":

> There is no attack. There is, however, the beginning of a spirited defense against certain aggressive policies by which Roman Catholics are trying to get for their church certain special advantages from the government. . . . If Cardinal Spellman sees fit to consider that resistance to any program initiated by the hierarchy is equivalent to an attack upon the Roman Catholic Church, he is creating an anti-Catholic movement by definition, and he can easily bring on a real one.[15]

Criticism of the Supreme Court decision took concrete form in the organization of the "Protestants and Other Americans United for the Separation of Church and State"—familiarly known as the POAU. Who the "Others" might be was a matter of speculation, but the ringleaders were the usual Protestants who could always be depended upon to strike a gallant blow in defense of American liberties imperiled by Romish attacks. The central figure was G. Bromley Oxnam of the Methodist Church who appealed to a large group of admirers by combining extreme social liberalism with a religious conservatism that would have done credit to the sixteenth century. The POAU dedicated itself to the propagation of the idea that the First Amendment called for a wall to be erected between church and state and that the slightest assistance given to a child who attended any but a public school would break faith with the fathers of our country.

The Cardinal lost no time and minced no words in referring to this point of view.

> These bigots, who strangely squeal and identify themselves when one mentions unhooded Klansmen, have not yet insisted it is a violation of the American tradition of the separation of Church and State for members of a fire department to extinguish a blaze in a parochial school and to save children from burning to death and we do hope they will content themselves and satisfy their discriminatory thirsts at seeing little children left standing by the roadside in the snow as publicly-paid-for buses transport other American children to and from school.[16]

Thereafter suspicion increased on both sides as lines formed for a struggle. The so-called liberals, and as time went on, non-Catholics generally, saw in federal aid for auxiliary services the camel's nose under the tent. It was easy to convince them that all taxpayers of any and no religion would soon be helping to support parochial schools. To Catholics it seemed clear that the bitterness stemmed ultimately from the influence of secularism, that all-pervading philosophy which ignores the spiritual and the supernatural.

Those who follow this way of life, [wrote the Administrative Board of the National Catholic Welfare Conference] distort and blot out our religious traditions, and seek to remove all influence of religion from public life. Their main efforts are centered on the divorce of religion from education. Their strategy seems to be: first to secularize completely the public school and then to claim for it a total monopoly of education. . . .

Such was the setting for the Barden Bill (H.R. 4645) which was introduced in the House of Representatives on May 11, 1949. The bill was supported by the same group which backed Mrs. McCollum before the Supreme Court with the addition of the American Association for the Advancement of Atheism and the American Society of Freethinkers, who urged its passage as a victory over the Catholic Church. A superficial reading of the text was not too alarming. It aimed:

To provide for Federal financial assistance to the states in bearing certain costs of public elementary and secondary education. . . .
Section 2. . . . There is hereby to be appropriated
(1) $300,000,000 for the states . . .
Section 3. (a) To ascertain the amount payable to any state . . .
(1) multiply the number of children of school age in such state by $50; . . .
Section 5. Amounts paid to any state under this act shall be expended only for current expenditures for public elementary and secondary schools within such state. . . .
Section 7. For the purposes of this Act . . .
(2) The term "current expenditures" does not include expenditures for transportation or for interest, debt service, or capital outlay, and does not include expenditures for health services for the prevention, diagnosis or treatment of physical or mental defects or conditions.

The Barden Bill, in other words, would not allow a state to use federal funds for the transportation of parochial school children even if the state wanted so to use them.

One month later, His Eminence delivered an address at Fordham University entitled "Barden Bill—Brewer of Bigotry." He was in a fighting mood:

Congressman Barden, claiming to be a loyal American, holding a key position in our democratic government, is in truth violating, and inciting others to violate the very rights and freedoms upon which our democratic government was founded, [in proposing] a Bill that explicitly declares that all expenditures of Federal money for educational purposes shall be restricted to benefit only those children who attend public schools. While the Bill includes Catholic children for the purpose of receiving funds from the Federal Government it excludes these same children from the distribution and benefit of the funds allocated. . . .

I believe in Federal aid for needy States and needy children, but, unlike Congressman Barden, I believe in help for *all* needy children, including Catholic children whose parents prefer to give their children religious education. Catholics do not question the rightful place of the public tax-supported school in the American Democracy, but schools under religious control also exist by right and not by privilege or toleration. The Catholic school is an American school, equal in right with the public school because our theory of democratic government protects the inalienable rights of the human person to freedom of religion and freedom of education. . . .

Catholics, themselves taxpayers, save others of the nation's taxpayers half a billion dollars yearly through the voluntary support of parochial schools in addition to the capital expense of the buildings. We Americans must not stand idly by and watch our government spend three hundred million dollars according to legislation that would be unjust and discriminatory against millions of our nation's children. A vote for the Barden Bill is a vote against parental rights, against constitutional rights, against American education as a whole, against America herself! Fearlessly, forcefully, we must unite to demand equal rights for *all* America's children, and in justice we must oppose unequivocally any bill that fails to guarantee at least nonreligious textbooks, bus rides and health services for all the children of all Americans.

The address was widely quoted, bitterly assailed, and as bitterly defended. Bromley Oxnam, as the principal spokesman for the opposition, said:

Congressman Graham Barden of North Carolina deserves the commendation of the country rather than the condemnation of a Cardinal. As a loyal and wise legislator, Representative Barden insists upon the American principle that public funds shall be used solely for public education. The President's Commission on Higher Education made the same recommendation.

Cardinal Spellman has used the term "bigot" freely of late. Now we know what he means by it. Anyone who disagrees with the Cardinal, or who objects to the hierarchy putting its hand in the public treasury, is a bigot. . . .

Barden wants to preserve public education and to send federal aid to underprivileged areas for public schools. It is not "putting class against class" nor a "vote against constitutional rights." It is the preservation of American public education and its protection from a prelate with a prehensile hand.[17]

One of the most interesting comments on the other side came from the South:

Congressman Barden has never protested the use of public funds for religious purposes in his home state of North Carolina, James G. Mehegan, Kinston, N.C., Catholic layman, wrote in a letter to the Raleigh *News and Observer* which in an editorial comment admitted the soundness of Mr. Mehegan's objection.

"In today's *News and Observer*," Mr. Mehegan wrote, "I read Congressman Barden's lame defense of his iniquitous Federal aid to public schools bill and in the same issue I read 'Temple Baptist Church is holding services in Murphy School auditorium.'

"Will Mr. Barden make any protest about that? The Senate and House of our Congress is opened by prayer of Protestant Ministers. Has Mr. Barden ever made any protest? The State of North Carolina, for many years, has contributed vast sums of money to both white and Negro Protestant orphanages in Oxford. Mr. Barden has never protested. If the Catholic Church was the recipient of considerations as per above, the Bardens of the country would be very vociferous in crying 'Church and State.'"

The Raleigh *News and Observer* editorially expressed its conviction that "the old doctrine of separation of church and state is a sound American doctrine which should be everywhere observed," but said: "There is certainly much to be said for the statement of James G. Mehegan of Kinston that Southern Protestants have little right to talk of separation of church and state in Catholic areas so long as they approve the expenditure of State funds in North Carolina for Protestant Church schools."[18]

It was at this juncture that Mrs. Eleanor Roosevelt found the situation too delicate to let alone. In her column for June 23, 1949, titled "Mrs. Roosevelt Opposes Aid for Private Schools," she said the final word on every phase of a most complicated question:

The controversy brought about by the request made by Francis Cardinal Spellman that Catholic schools should share in Federal aid funds forces upon the citizens of the country the kind of decision that is going to be very difficult to make.

Those of us who believe in the right of any human being to belong to whatever church he sees fit, and to worship God in his own way, cannot be accused of prejudice when we do not want to see public education connected with religious control of the schools, which are paid for by taxpayers' money.

If we desire to see our children go to schools of any particular kind, . . . we are entirely free to set up those schools and to pay for them. . . .

It is quite possible that private schools, whether they are denominational schools—Catholic, Episcopalian, Presbyterian, Methodist, or whatever—or whether they are purely academic, may make a great contribution to the public school systems, both on the lower levels and on the higher levels. . . .

The separation of church and state is extremely important to any of us who hold to the original traditions of our nation. To change these traditions by changing our traditional attitude toward public education would be harmful, I think, to our whole attitude of tolerance in the religious area.

If we look at situations which have arisen in the past in Europe and other world areas, I think we shall see the reasons why it is wise to hold to our early traditions.

On July 8, she tried again:

I would like to make it clear once and for all that I believe in the right of any human being to worship God according to his conviction, and I would not want to see this right taken away from anyone.

Sometimes, however, I think church organizations are foolish because they do things that lead people to believe that they are not interested mainly in the spiritual side of the church, but that they have a decided interest also in temporal affairs. This may be harmful to the church's spiritual influence. . . .

Some people take me to task because they say our public schools are nonreligious. I would answer that I have no feeling against the use of a prayer which all children of all denominations could say in the public schools. In fact, I think there should be a great effort made to stress that education is not purely for material purposes, but is directed toward moral and spiritual aims and that religion plays a distinct part in achieving these ends.

But no school, private or public, can give any child a complete religious education. That must be done in the home, through the family and in the church. . . .

I do not want the public school system to be dominated by the Federal Government. That is why Federal aid should set only certain standards and not demand to control the schools of any state. But neither do I want church groups controlling the schools of our country. They must remain free.

On July 15, she was still at it:

I hate to continue an argument that many people think is based on prejudice, but something was written in a letter to me that seems worth mentioning. A gentleman writes that the Barden Bill was a discriminatory bill against the Negroes in the South. I have not read the bill carefully, and I have been rather careful not to say if I am for or against any particular bill or bills. . . .

There is no real reason why every school should not teach every child that one of the important aspects of our life is its spiritual side. It might be possible to devise a prayer that all the denominations could say, and it certainly ought to be possible to read certain verses from the Bible every day.

Referring to the place of religion in education, she showed the breadth of her point of view in these words: "It probably would do children no harm to learn to know some of the writings of other great religious leaders [none had been mentioned] who have led other great religious movements."

It was an unusually trying July that year, and Mrs. Roosevelt had keyed her mood to the month. It had always been her ambition to be stimulating, to strike sparks in the minds of all her readers. One who finally burst into flame was Cardinal Spellman:

July 21, 1949

Dear Mrs. Roosevelt:

When, on June 23rd in your column My Day, you aligned yourself with the author and other proponents of the Barden Bill and condemned me for defending Catholic children against those who would deny them their constitutional rights of equality with other American children, you could have acted only from misinformation, ignorance or prejudice, not from knowledge and understanding! It is apparent that you did not take the time to read my address delivered at Fordham University; and in your column of July 15th you admitted that you did not even carefully read and acquaint yourself with the facts of the Barden Bill—the now famous, infamous bill that would unjustly discriminate against minority groups of America's children. Unlike you, Mrs. Roosevelt, I did not make a public statement until I had studied every phrase of the Barden Bill; nor did I take issue with a man because his faith differed from mine. We differed, Congressman Barden and I, over the unimpeachable issue of equal benefits and equal rights for *all* America's children.

I had intended ignoring your personal attack, but as the days passed and in two subsequent columns you continued your anti-Catholic campaign, I became convinced that it was in the interests of all Americans and the cause of justice itself that your misstatements should be challenged in every quarter of our country where they have already spun and spread their web of prejudice. I have received hundreds of messages from persons of all faiths demanding that I answer you. I am, therefore, not free to ignore you.

You say you are against religious control of schools which are paid for by taxpayers' money. That is exactly what I, too, oppose. But I am also opposed to any bill that *includes* children who attend parochial schools for the purpose of receiving funds from the Federal Government while it *excludes* these same children from the distribution and benefits of the funds allocated. I believe that if the Federal Government provides a bottle of milk to each child in a public school it should provide milk for all school children. I believe that if Federal funds are used to transport children to public schools they should be used to transport parochial school children. I believe if through the use of Federal funds the children who attend public schools are immunized from contagious diseases that *all* children should be protected from these diseases.

"Taxation without representation is tyranny" was the cry that roused and rallied our pioneer Americans to fight for justice. *Taxation without participation* should rouse today's Americans to equal ardor to protest an injustice that would deprive millions of American children of health and safety benefits to which *all* our children are entitled. And the Supreme Court of the United States has declared that health and transportation services and the distribution of non-religious textbooks to pupils attending parochial schools do not violate our Constitution.

"The separation of church and state is extremely important to us who hold to the original traditions of our nation," you continue. But health and safety benefits and providing standard non-religious textbooks for all American children have nothing to do with the question of separation of Church and State!

I cannot presume upon the press to discuss, analyze or refute each inaccuracy in your columns—for they are manifold. Had you taken an objective, impersonal stand, I could then, in the same impersonal manner answer you. But you did not. Apparently your attitude of mind precluded you from comprehending issues which you either rigorously defended or flagrantly condemned while ignorant of the facts concerning both the Barden Bill and my own denunciation of it.

American freedom not only permits but encourages differences of opinion and I do not question your right to differ with me. But why I wonder do you repeatedly plead causes that are anti-Catholic? Even if you cannot find it within your heart to defend the rights of innocent little children and heroic, helpless men like Cardinal Martyr Mindszenty, can you not have the charity not to cast upon them still another stone?

America's Catholic youth fought a long and bitter fight to save all Americans from oppression and persecution. Their broken bodies on blood-soaked foreign fields were grim and tragic testimony to this fact. I saw them there—on every fighting front—as they equally shared with their fellow-fighters all the sacrifice, terror and gore of war—as alike they shared the little good and glory that sometimes comes to men as together they fight and win a brutal battle.

Would you deny equality to these Catholic boys who daily stood at the sad threshold of untimely death and suffered martyrdom that you and I and the world of men might live in liberty and peace? Would you deny their children equal rights and benefits with other sects—rights for which their fathers paid equal taxation with other fathers and fought two bitter wars that all children might forever be free from fear, oppression and religious persecution?

During the war years you visited the hospitals in many countries, as I did. You too saw America's sons—Catholic, Protestant and Jew alike—young, battered, scarred, torn and mutilated, dying in agony that we might learn to live in charity with one another. Then how was it that your own heart was not purged of all prejudices by what you saw these, our sons, suffer?

Now my case is closed. This letter will be released to the public tomorrow after it has been delivered to you by special delivery today. And even though you may again use your columns to attack me and again accuse me of starting a controversy, I shall not again publicly acknowledge you. For, whatever you may say in the future, your record of anti-Catholicism stands for all to see—a record which you yourself wrote on the pages of history which cannot be recalled—documents of discrimination unworthy of an American mother!

Mrs. Roosevelt, who said, "I am sure the Cardinal has written in what seems to him a Christian and kindly manner,"[19] answered with considerable zest on July 23:

YOUR EMINENCE:

Your letter of July 21st surprised me considerably.

I have never advocated the Barden Bill nor any other specific bill on education now before the Congress. I believe, however, in federal aid to education. . . .

It is fallacious, I think, to say that because children going to public schools are granted free textbooks in some states, free transportation or free school lunches, that these same things must be given to children going to private schools. Different states, of course, have done different things as they came under majority pressure from citizens who had certain desires, but basically by and large, throughout the country, I think there is still a feeling that the public school is the school which is open to all children, and which is supported by all the people of the country, and that anything that is done for the public schools should be done for them alone. I would feel that certain medical care should be available to all children, but that is a different thing and should be treated differently. . . .

Anyone who knows history, particularly the history of Europe, will, I think, recognize that the domination of education or of government by any one particular religious faith is never a happy arrangement for the people.

Spiritual leadership should remain spiritual leadership and the temporal power should not become too important in any church.

I have no bias against the Roman Catholic Church and I have supported Governor Smith as Governor and worked for him as a candidate for the office of President of the United States. I have supported for public office many other Roman Catholic candidates.

You speak of the Mindszenty case. I spoke out very clearly against any unfair type of trial and anything anywhere in any country which might seem like an attack on an individual because of his religious beliefs. I can not, however, say that in European countries the control by the Roman Catholic Church of great areas of land has always led to happiness for the people of those countries. . . .

I have no intention of attacking you personally, nor of attacking the Roman Catholic Church, but I shall, of course, continue to stand for the things in our government which I think are right. They may lead us to be in opposition to you and to other groups within our country, but I shall always act, as far as I am able, from real conviction and honest belief. . . .

I assure you I have no sense of being "an unworthy American mother." The final judgment, my dear Cardinal Spellman, of the unworthiness of all human beings is in the hands of God.

The exchange of letters created a sensation and both correspondents were criticized and commended. The nature of all the colorful organizations sponsored by Mrs. Roosevelt was examined by some commentators and a tabulation drawn up of the fifty-three references made to her in the report of the Dies Committee on Un-American Activities. She was hailed on the other hand as "one of the greatest women of American history" by those who condemned the Cardinal for his "craftiness and lack of candor." Bromley Oxnam told a radio audience:

It is not milk and medicine, books and buses! What he wants is the support of parochial schools by taxes levied on all the people. In a word, he seeks public funds for sectarian education. The Church not only wants public funds for private purposes, but must know that to drain off vast sums from public education is so to weaken it as eventually to destroy it.[20]

It was an anxious time for most of the prominent Democrats in New York. Bernard M. Baruch expressed admiration for both antagonists, and Mayor William O'Dwyer said, "I have great respect for the Cardinal, and equally great respect for Mrs. Roosevelt." But former Governor Herbert Lehman rushed loyally to Mrs. Roosevelt's side, while James A. Farley, who was cherishing a few Hyde Park memories of his own remarked dryly, "I am sure Cardinal Spellman gave considerable thought and great consideration to the contents of his letter to Mrs. Roosevelt before he wrote it."[21]

Bishops in various parts of the country, like Bishop Noll of Fort Wayne, Bishop Ready of Columbus, and Archbishop Rummel of New Orleans, added their voices to that of the Cardinal, while the Most Reverend Karl J. Alter, Bishop of Toledo, expressed in the following letter the general sentiment of the hierarchy:

The courage, determination and clarity with which you have stated the case of Catholic parents and their children for the right to participate in any federal benefits, has won the admiration of your confreres in the hierarchy.

It must have been with great anxiety that you debated in your own mind the particular procedure which you have followed; but it certainly was effective in lifting the entire issue from the back pages of our newspapers to headline news. It brought the whole controversy into focus.

I wish to assure you that your fellow Bishops in the hierarchy resent particularly any imputation that there is divided counsel among us and that we do not wholeheartedly support your position. That position is endorsed, I am sure, by each and every one of us.

On August 5, Mrs. Roosevelt told reporters she had no objection to meeting with the Cardinal. "I have never said that I had any objection to talking with Cardinal Spellman about our differences. But it seems to me that it is up to him to propose such a meeting."[22] The fact was, steps had already been taken in that direction the night before when His Eminence called her on the phone and asked her to go over a statement which he was about to release. She said afterward, "I have read it and think it is a clarifying and fair statement."

This historic clarification was published on August 5 and impressed the non-Catholic public as "showing a constructive and constitutional attitude toward the problems involved":

It is important that everyone should understand clearly what we are asking for under constitutional law, and, for what we are *not* asking. We are not asking for general public support of religious schools. In the State of New York, as in practically every other State, the State Constitution prohibits the use of public funds for the support of sectarian schools. The Supreme Court of the United States has interpreted the Federal Constitution in the same sense. Under the Constitution we do not ask nor can we expect public funds to pay for the construction or repair of parochial school buildings or for the support of teachers, or for other maintenance costs.

There are, however, other incidental expenses involved in education, expenses for such purposes as the transportation of children to and from school, the purchase of nonreligious textbooks, and the provision of health aids. These are called "auxiliary services." *The Federal-aid controversy revolves around these incidental benefits to school children and around them alone.*

Our New York State Constitution expressly allows the use of public funds for the transportation of children to *any* school, public or parochial. Fourteen other States follow the same non-discriminatory practice. Moreover, in some States public funds are used to provide nonreligious textbooks for the children in all schools, public and parochial. In all States many communities supply public health services to pupils in all schools. The Supreme Court of the United States has upheld these practices as constitutional.

What precisely are we asking for? We believe in Federal aid for needy States and needy children. We further believe that Congress should guarantee as it did in the School Lunch Act, that all children of whatever race, creed or color, no matter what schools they attend, will share alike in the "auxiliary services" for which these Federal funds are spent in the States. We do not think it should be left to each State to decide for itself whether or not to distribute Federal funds in a discriminatory way. And above all, we ask that Congress guarantee the use of Federal funds for health and transportation services to the two million eight hundred thousand of America's children attending parochial schools if they guarantee Federal funds for health and transportation services to other American children attending public schools.

We are asking Congress to do no more than to continue, in its first general aid-to-education measure, the non-discriminatory policy it has followed in the School Lunch Act and other Federal laws dealing with schools and schoolchildren. We do not want Congress, for the first time, to adopt a discriminatory policy in the field of education. This in no way undermines "the traditional American principle of separation of Church and State." We are asking only for what is constitutional and in accordance with America's previous policy and tradition.

The statement was in fact a clarification, but in outside circles generally, it was regarded as a strategic and prudent retreat. The Reverend Anson Phelps Stokes summed up this point of view.

Cardinal Spellman's statement was of epoch-making importance as far as church-state relations in the United States are concerned. It was the first time that the hierarchy, represented by one of its most prominent members, . . . recognized publicly that direct aid for the support of parochial schools was, under existing constitutions, laws and Supreme Court decisions, unconstitutional. Up to this time the Church had through many actions and through statements in authoritative utterances, and in books with the imprimatur of competent church authority, stated frankly its conviction that parochial schools, being practically free schools, should share with public schools in the distribution of federal funds for direct aid to education. . . .

This brought to a close a most interesting and illuminating public discussion, the general results of which should prove of benefit to the country, even though many non-Catholics may differ on the question of auxiliary aid, and many Catholics may regret that the Cardinal yielded on the matter of direct aid to parochial schools.[23]

Perhaps a fortnight after this, His Eminence called on Mrs. Roosevelt at Hyde Park. Her secretary explained that the visit had been unannounced and unplanned and added only that, accompanied by Monsignor Joseph A. Nelson, he had remained about three-quarters of an hour. In her column, Mrs. Roosevelt said: "The Cardinal had dropped in on his way to dedicate a Chapel in Peekskill. We had a pleasant chat and I hope the country proved as much of a tonic for him as it always is for me." The punch line was clever and the lady had the last word, but the Barden Bill was killed. The Cardinal had made his point and the matter rested for twelve years.

In 1960, Senator John F. Kennedy of Massachusetts was nominated for the presidency and waged a spectacularly successful campaign. In addition to the expected outbursts of Bible Belt bigotry, however, a great deal of sincere misgiving was evident among intelligent Protestants. They questioned the freedom from Church interference which a Catholic President might enjoy in the White House and were especially concerned with the possible benefits that might accrue to Catholic schools, in spite of what they interpreted as the obvious meaning of the Constitution. So whenever candidate Kennedy had a question period open to all, someone was sure to ask his views on federal aid to Church schools. His answer was always the same. He opposed such aid because he said, "it is unconstitutional under the First Amendment as interpreted by the Supreme Court." After his election but before assuming office, he appointed a "task force" of able men to advise him with regard to several pressing issues. One of these was education. Their proposals were published on January 6. Eleven days later, parish representatives of the Cardinal's campaign, meeting at Cardinal Hayes High School, heard an unusually spirited address from His Eminence on the subject of the "task force" proposals. The tone was sharp and the message directed to congressional opinion, which he was sure would not be in favor of making any American children second-class citizens. He said:

> In the lead editorial in the Chicago Catholic "New World" of January 14 it is stated: "One of President-elect Kennedy's 'task forces'—pointedly described by some as a 'tax force'—has proposed a nine billion, three hundred million dollar program of federal aid to education. Of the total amount, five billion, eight hundred million dollars would be allotted to public elementary and high schools."
>
> No Catholic schools or schools of other religious denominations are included in the Task Force proposal. For many millions of American parents, this means that they will be taxed more than ever before for the education of their children but that they cannot expect any return from their taxes, unless they are willing to transfer their children to a public grade or high school.
>
> The Task Force Committee which consists of six of our country's dis-

tinguished educators outlined a general program of financial assistance for all public schools as follows:

(1) "to provide $30 per annum a pupil, based on average attendance in public schools. The Boards of Education should be authorized to use the funds for construction, salaries or other purposes related to the improvement of education.

(2) "to provide $20 per child for states with personal income per student in average daily attendance in public schools that is below 70 per cent of the national average."

(3) "to provide an amount equivalent to $20 per child in average daily attendance in the public schools of the great cities (over 300,000 population) which are facing unique and grave educational problems."

I believe and I state that these recommendations are unfair to most parents of the nation's 6,800,000 parochial and private school children. Such legislation would discriminate against a multitude of America's children because their parents choose to exercise their constitutional right to educate them in accordance with their religious beliefs. Under these proposals parents would be compelled to surrender both freedom of mind and religion in the education of their children as a condition for sharing in federal education funds in direct violation of the liberties guaranteed by the first amendment to the United States Constitution.

In this day when according to the Communists' chief salesman Nikita Khrushchev, the Soviet Union is fighting to enslave the world by conquering men's minds, it is imperative that our nation provide every child with the teachings necessary to develop his moral and intellectual abilities to their highest potential. The requirements of the national defense as well as the general welfare of our country demand that, in educational opportunities, no child be treated as a second-class citizen. Hence, it is unthinkable that any American child be denied the federal funds allotted to other children which are necessary for his mental development because his parents choose for him a God-centered education.

To me it is also unthinkable that Congress would deny a child funds to study mathematics, science and languages simply because his parents supply additional funds for the study of religion. This would be penalizing both the child and his parents because of their religious beliefs.

As an American whose loyalties have been challenged only by Communists, I cannot believe that Congress would accept the proposals of the Task Force and use economic compulsion to force parents to relinquish their rights to have religion taught to their children. I cannot believe that Congress would discriminate against Lutheran, Baptist, Catholic or Jewish parents—Americans all—in the allocation of educational funds.

I cannot believe that Congress would enact a program of financial assistance to elementary and secondary education unless all children were granted equal educational privileges regardless of the school they attend. This procedure would insure the civil rights of independent school children and of their parents, and would then incorporate in the Task Force programs the first amendment principles of religious and academic freedom in the pursuit of truth.

Our Constitution not only demands that all children be treated alike regardless of their exercise of religion in the choice of school, but Congress has established many precedents of this equal treatment. To quote just a few:

In the Veterans' Readjustment Act of 1952 Congress provided for direct grants to veterans to enable them to pay tuition in the school of their choice. Many G.I.'s used these funds to pay tuition in the nation's 474 Protestant, 265 Catholic and 5 Jewish institutions of higher education.

In the War Orphans' Educational Assistance Act of 1956 Congress provided for direct grants to students whose fathers died as a result of the Second World War or the Korean Conflict. Many of America's orphaned students are using these grants to pay tuition in church-related colleges. And, in the National Defense Education Act of 1958 Congress provided for direct grants to graduate-fellows many of whom are pursuing their studies in universities under religious auspices.

A number of states have also adopted the method of direct grants to students in extensive scholarship programs which give the award winners freedom of choice in education.

It is a matter of record that programs of direct grants to students and children attending church-related schools do not breach the wall of separation of church and state. Discussing the G.I. bill, the President's Committee on Education beyond the High School observed that it "does not believe that this assistance to veterans was designed to help even indirectly, the institutions." This means that Congress can subsidize children and students without subsidizing the schools.

The Task Force Committee on Education calls for a flat grant of $30 annually for each public school child for all states. By denying this measure of equality to church-related school children and their parents, the Task Force proposals are blatantly discriminating against them, depriving them of freedom of mind and freedom of religion guaranteed by our country's Constitution whose first amendment was adopted to protect the individual person from government repression, the very danger implicit in the proposed program of the Task Force.

If Congress were to comply with the Task Force proposals as outlined by its committee, (and once again I express my faith that Congress would not do so), and compel a child to attend a state school as a condition for sharing in education funds, it would be engaging in thought control, which, as Justice Jackson remarked, "is a copyright of totalitarianism, and we have no claim to it."

Therefore, dear friends, in the hazardous present and the increasingly perilous future that we face, I beg your prayers that Americans may forever be free to worship God as conscience directs; prayers for our beloved country, her leaders and her people; prayers that, as we go forward to the great tasks ahead, we may rededicate ourselves to God with a single will for peace and righteousness for all!

Unfriendly sources called it "Spellman's blast at Kennedy" and were not slow to revive the old suspicion of "the camel's nose." Some said that they always knew that he was after government funds for his schools, even when he had protested that he wanted only fringe benefits, such as bus rides and lunch, ignoring the fact that scholarly reappraisal of the constitutional issues during the intervening years brought about a change in the Church's conception of the constitutional rights of parochial school children and their parents. They also failed to point out that the task force had not been satisfied to amend the old Barden Bill. It had essentially changed the situation by its proposed $9,300,000,000 grant for public schools, specifically excluding any help to children attending private and parochial schools.

The President-elect said nothing, took the oath of office on January 20 and a month later had a bill introduced into Congress which embodied the provisions suggested by the task force. The following week, the Administrative Board of the National Catholic Welfare Conference, composed of five cardinals and ten archbishops and bishops met in Washington, the very day that the President told a press conference with regard to federal aid to private schools, "There isn't any room for debate on that subject. It is prohibited by the Constitution and the Supreme Court has made that very clear. Therefore there would be no possibility of our recommending it."

After being pressed for details by reporters, the chairman of the Administrative Board, the Most Reverend Karl J. Alter, D.D., Archbishop of Cincinnati, on March 2 issued a statement to "summarize the discussion." The statement said that whether there ought to be federal aid depended on the objective economic facts, a point on which Catholic opinion was sharply divided, but that if there was federal aid, then in justice Catholic school children should be given the right to participate. The statement went on to suggest that there would be no violation of the Constitution if long-term, low-interest federal loans were made available to private as well as public schools. If children in private schools were excluded from a federal aid program, they would be the victims of discrimination and "there will be no alternative but to oppose such discrimination."

On March 13, Cardinal Spellman issued another statement, milder in tone than the first, but repeating its central theme: American children must not be penalized because their parents exercise a constitutional right to provide them with a religious education. He commended certain features of the President's program, paying tribute to the public schools of which he was himself a product, and offered, as an attainable objective, a program of federal aid that would accord equivalent benefits to children attending public and private schools without violating the Constitution. "The specifics," he said, "are matters for the discretion of Congress." Several possible programs were then suggested.

Most Catholics agreed with Bishop John J. Navagh of Ogdensburg who called this second statement "a magnificent plan of action, a bill of rights for Catholic children, a charter for complete equality," and several important Protestant and Jewish observers joined them. One of these was Charles H. Silver, the president of the Board of Education of New York and president of the powerful B'nai Jesurun, who endorsed the Cardinal's views at a hearing held by the House of Representatives Committee on Education and Labor. A little later, the lawyer for the Archdiocese of New York, Lawrence X. Cusack, in making a statement to the same committee, developed an entirely new angle. He gave warning that a program of discrimination might be in itself a violation of the Constitution. "The First Amendment," he said, "not only forbids a law 'respecting an establishment of religion,' it contains a second equally forceful prohibition, a clause directing that Congress shall make no law 'prohibiting the free exercise' of religion. Furthermore, the 'due process' clause of the Fifth Amendment prohibits the federal government from unreasonable discrimination in government programs."

It was not surprising then that when the subject of federal subsidy came up again at a White House press conference, the President was more guarded in his choice of words. This time he said that proposed forms of aid for private schools should be examined carefully by Congress; then the constitutional problems could be considered. Giving out constitutional opinion on each proposal as it comes up was obviously not one of his functions. The proposed bill should be passed first and then Congress could consider what to do in the other area. In any case, the administration would be delighted to co-operate. No wonder a New York newspaper editorialized at the time that "when Mr. Kennedy sent his Education Bill to Congress, he opened a king size can of worms." His political reasoning was considered sound. He had established his willingness to take a position contrary to an announced position of the Catholic hierarchy. And that was important to him for 1964. It was his constitutional reasoning that was weak. The decisions of the United States Supreme Court in the Everson, McCollum, and Zorach cases were not as cut and dried in their pertinency to the constitutional issue as the cases had once appeared and making school subsidies a constitutional issue brought a wave of opposition from expert opinion.

Moreover the advocates of help to parochial schools were not alone in their opposition to the administration's program of federal aid. Many who had no particular interest in Catholic education were not convinced with regard to the necessity and timeliness of such an outlay for any kind of schools. The governors and state legislatures were not asking for help. To the Society for Social Research, the classroom shortage seemed greatly exaggerated and local support adequate for the foreseeable future. It appeared that the National Educational Association and educators with various axes to grind, backed up by certain racial and sectarian groups, were doing most of the shouting. Some pointed out that, in the twenty-year period just elapsed, the national enrollment trend had been toward private and parochial schools by a ratio of three to one and in some quarters there were hopes of tipping the scales in the other direction with federal billions.

More organized opposition came from those who were uneasy about federal control of education. It was a foregone conclusion that conservative Republicans would be instinctively alarmed while Southern Democrats would see in this measure the end of local independence and, specifically, the end of segregation. Catholics were unjustly accused of placing special interests above the general good and as the struggle went on it was said that the public school aid bill was being held for ransom. The fact was that most Catholics, following the lead of Cardinal Spellman, were simply demanding justice. They began by rejecting the constitutional argument of the President because it seemed to them that federal aid to private schools would not tend to establish a State Church or prohibit the free exercise of religion and that, therefore, it did no violence to the First Amendment which was passed, after all, to preserve individual freedom, not to penalize it. On the positive side they saw in these lavish expenditures limited to public institutions the danger that the national interest would suffer through the resulting decline in private education and religious freedom. As one writer put it, "Free education must not be allowed to destroy freedom of education."[24]

Months passed, issues became more complicated and various compromises were suggested. Finally, the Senate passed two bills. The first and most important of these was the administration's original Aid to Education Act and the second was The National Defense Education Act Extension. In the House two similar bills and a third bill concerning federal loans and grants to promote higher education were reported on favorably by the House Committee on Education and Labor and reached the divided House Rules Committee. After considering and rejecting various amendments that were offered, the House Rules Committee voted 8 to 7, on July 19, to table all three. The President still hoped that the measures he favored could be brought to the floor of the House and adopted during the current session but all efforts to salvage them seemed to have collapsed by August 10 when the strategists of the administration agreed that it was useless "to put together some patchwork that would please nobody"[25] and further action should be postponed till the next session of Congress.

By August 14 it appeared that the notice of temporary surrender had been premature. Senator Wayne Morse of Oregon who had been entrusted by the President with the chief responsibility for his now famous Senate

Bill 1021, seeking general aid to public schools, spoke at the annual convention of the American Federation of Teachers, AFL-CIO, on the burning subject of federal aid for education. He became specific. "There are," he said, "those in this country who do not believe in our system of free secular education." He placed them in three categories, asserting of the third, "These people, and they include highly influential churchmen such as Cardinal Spellman, look upon the public schools as competitors . . . but I say in all sincerity that the adamant opposition of the higher Catholic clergy to an improvement to our public educational system, except upon their own terms, will lead to most unfortunate results . . . they are sowing a wind of discord which will result in a whirlwind of resentment when the people of this country learn the facts."

Having been mentioned by name, the Cardinal felt called upon to reply —the date was August 22: "We do not," he wrote in a press release, "as [Senator Morse] alleges, look upon [the public schools] as 'competitors' but as partners in the great work of educating America's children. . . . We do not believe that the best interests of this Nation can be served by making public school education a monopoly . . . It is our conviction that the Administration's proposal, put into legislative form by Senator Morse, is actually if not intentionally discriminatory, unwittingly anti-Catholic, and indirectly subversive of all private education. . . . One of the most unfair pressures was Senator Morse's ill-conceived and ill-timed warning that continued opposition will cause a flare-up of bigotry. Are Catholics no longer free, then, to speak their minds? . . . If Senator Morse feels that the economic needs of our schools call for a program of Federal Aid, let him propose legislation which will solve our educational problems in conformity with Constitutional principles and provide equal justice for all America's children. If, however, the Senator's convictions or sense of political expediency will not permit him to do this, then we beseech him at least to refrain from fanning the embers of religious discord. . . ."

This statement was released in the morning. The House met at noon and before dinnertime Senator Morse had delivered a reply which covers thirty-two pages of fine print in the Congressional Record. He wanted to make it clear that although he forgave the Cardinal's "unfortunate remarks" and had "the greatest respect for him," he felt that His Eminence's statement was "honeycombed with non sequiturs . . . had put words into his mouth and ignored what he had said." There was not the slightest bit of anti-Catholicism in him. On the contrary, he had been the stanchest supporter of federal loans for private schools—had proposed this solution as an amendment to a similar bill considered by the Senate during the Eisenhower administration and was still in favor of it, although out of loyalty to President Kennedy he now wanted it to be voted on as a separate bill instead of as an amendment. The Cardinal could not be more mistaken in his policy of "All or nothing"—and should be warned that he could not repeal the First Amendment by ignoring it. "If what the Cardinal is asking me to do, is to propose legislation which I am satisfied is unconstitutional, my answer to him is that I cannot oblige and accommodate. . . . It is not the Senator from Oregon who is fanning any embers of religious discord."

Senator Kenneth B. Keating of New York asked for the floor to say that he had made it a point to be present that day because of a rumor that a friend of his was about to be attacked. He congratulated Senator Morse on his restraint except for the reading of a few bitter editorials . . . "Cardinal Spellman is a man of deep personal conviction and unquestioned integrity. He is a great patriot who has demonstrated his love for his country and his great compassion for his fellowman in many ways . . . like every other American, he is entitled to make his position clear on any issue . . . I know from my mail . . . that the cardinal has wide support for his position . . . I am proud to speak as the cardinal's friend . . ."

Meanwhile the administration was in a determined mood and in spite of Speaker Sam Rayburn's warning that for this session, the issue of general federal aid to education was "dead as slavery" insisted on the passage of a compromise bill. The result was a much diluted measure, which no one was expected to find objectionable. Taking advantage of an old congressional custom known as Calendar Wednesday, the chairman of the House Committee on Education and Labor was able to bring the issue directly to the floor of the House on August 30, by-passing the Rules Committee altogether. The result was a stunning defeat for the administration. The compromise bill was smothered 242 to 169. In September, Congress passed a bill that merely extended for two years two expiring education programs, the National Defense Education Act, and a law providing grants to "Federally-impacted" school districts. It turned down a last minute plea by the President for a one-year stop-gap extension of both laws that would "provide the best assurance that reevaluation of legislation affecting education will take place early next year." One New York newspaper commented that it "would be naive not to admit that the chances for effective public school aid in 1962 have been painfully dimmed."[26] There was no comment from His Eminence.

CHAPTER NINETEEN

Postwar Problems

WHILE his elevation to the Sacred College was inevitably the climax of Cardinal Spellman's life, no one who knew him expected it to lessen either the pressure of his work or the importance of the decisions he would be called upon to make. The Great War had cooled off, it is true, and Roosevelt was dead. Then, too, the time had come in the administration of the arch-diocese when the innovations of a new regime had found their places in a pattern and even the most important accomplishments became repetitious. But new problems, postwar problems, were crying for solution on every side.

At home there was first of all the moral letdown always expected after the fighting ceases. As this had been the world's worst war, the letdown was worse than usual. Will Hays had sounded a warning in 1941 that evil forces in the motion picture industry here and abroad were preparing a flood of filth to be released on the return of peace, when they anticipated that sexual discipline would be relaxed. Similar forces were at work in theaters and publication offices. In fact, the downward trend was in evidence from the very beginning of hostilities.

Speaking on a national hookup under the auspices of the Knights of Columbus as early as 1942, the then Archbishop of New York summed up the position of the Church on the difference between self-defense and censorship:

> But nations may be destroyed not only by foreign enemies but also by internal decadence. Are our God-given rights also endangered by enemies within our borders? They most certainly are. Our freedoms are abused in the very name of freedom. . . . The fifth column of the saboteurs of our factories and public utilities has its counterpart in the filth of those who piously shout censorship if they are not permitted freely to exercise their venal, venemous, diabolical debauching of the mind and body of our boys and girls. I am against harmful censorship but that does not mean that I must condone those who wish to include among America's freedoms the freedom to kill the bodies and souls of their fellow Americans, the freedom to be cruel, the freedom to be obscene, the freedom to steal and the freedom to spread disease. If these false freedoms come, America's God-given rights will go; and America's liberty, the most pre-

cious of our possessions—dearer to us than life—will succumb to tyranny and America will die.

Later in the same year, speaking before the Anchor Club of the Police Department, he singled out the New York stage:

> Only this week I talked with a man renowned in the amusement business, a man who is not a Catholic, and he told me he has been obliged to get up and leave theaters in the city of New York in shame and horror at the utterances on the stage and the performances. . . . But what would happen if we tried to do something about it? We would be accused of "the crime of censorship"—accused by people hiding behind a smoke screen of their own depravity, their own lust, their own smugness, their own treason!

A similar address was delivered before five hundred judges and city and state officials at the annual conference of the New York State Association of Judges of Children's Courts.

In the course of time he singled out individual pictures condemned by the Legion of Decency and named names. The first of these was the *Two Faced Woman*, which unfortunately had been produced by one of the Cardinal's best friends, L. B. Mayer, as the following letter indicates:

DEAR L. B.,

First of all, I wish to say that for me personally the most painful duty that I have had to perform since I came to New York was in reference to the "Two Faced Woman." But I had, I felt and still feel, no alternative. I asked for time to refer the matter directly and personally and quietly to you. I was informed however that there was no time.

Father McClafferty had talked with a member of your organization in New York and had received no satisfaction. The company would refuse, as all companies were doing, to permit previews at any reasonable time before presentation in theaters. I was shown the advertising, the press reviews and was the told the picture was already being shown in several places and that the recommendations of the Legion of Decency, made immediately on seeing the film, were disregarded with just a tinge of indifference manifested. I was informed that absolutely no attention had been paid to the observations of the Legion of Decency in a general way and that it was a "now or never" situation.

I am not a member of the Bishops' Committee on Motion Pictures and I objected when some picture, I forget its name, was put on the "C" list just as it began to be shown in New York. This seemed to me to be unfair to the theater and to the company. It was explained to me at the time that no films had been available for a preview until just before the time it was to be exhibited in the theaters. Now I am as much in favor of the four freedoms as any American, but I did not feel that this was cricket; and furthermore I felt that you would not like it that no attention was paid to our representations; because I felt we saw eye to eye about as closely as was possible for any two men of good will to see; and besides that, I was, as you know, one of your greatest admirers and for you I had deep and genuine affection and *I still have*. . . .

I must say here that Mr. Rubin has been most considerate and I think he realizes that if the disposition shown now to effect a revision had been manifested sooner that the difficulty could and would have been avoided. . . .

Naturally I regret to have been the occasion of any financial loss to the company but on the first page of the "Catholic News" of this current week which I enclose there is an account of the evidence of good will on the part of the company in making every possible revision to meet the criticism. . . .

I shall send you some clippings and some letters taken at random, some favorable to me and some opposed to my position. But on the whole, I think they show that something had to be corrected. The thing I regret, however, and I repeat it in closing, is that this film produced by your company was the occasion of my action. . . .

Devotedly yours,
FRANCIS J. SPELLMAN

When His Eminence specified *Forever Amber* as one film that no Catholic could view "with a safe conscience," the producer said he would not "bowdlerize the film to placate the Roman Catholic Church,"[1] but later the president of the company reversed his earlier position and removed the objectionable material, saying that he wished "to correct an unfortunate impression created by statements made by us incident to the disapproval of the original version of *Forever Amber* by the Legion of Decency. These statements were interpreted as questioning the right of religious leaders to guide the adherents of their faith on moral questions. No such purpose was intended, neither was it our purpose to indicate any acceptance whatsoever of the theory that the popularity of a motion picture is a true criterion of its moral character."[2]

A still more serious challenge to public decency appeared soon after the war in a flood of foreign pictures, some of them superbly produced. One of these, called *The Miracle*, involved the Cardinal in a lawsuit that went to the United States Supreme Court and in a series of controversies that were frequently marked by bitterness. It is the story of an idiot girl. She is seduced by a stranger whom she believes to be St. Joseph and gives birth, miraculously as she thinks, in a church. The villagers then mock her by singing in her honor hymns to the Blessed Mother of God. When first seen by a member of the Legion of Decency in Venice in 1948, a vigorous protest was made, and previous to that it was condemned in Rome by the Pontifical Film Commission.

On December 12, 1950, it started its run in New York, branded by the National Legion of Decency as "a sacrilegious and blasphemous mockery of Christian religious truth." The showing was stopped on December 23 by the Commissioner of Licenses of the City of New York who found it "a blasphemous affront to a great many of our citizens."[3] The film distributor appealed and a judge of the Supreme Court of New York restrained the Commissioner from halting the picture on the grounds that the State Board of Regents, which had approved *The Miracle*, was supreme in the licensing of films. It developed that one person, not a member, had been allowed by custom to act in such matters for the board which in the present instance decided to review the decision of its representative. In the meantime, the protest had become identified with the Cardinal who had voiced his indignation publicly and was thought to be privately exercising an influence which had become legendary in non-Catholic circles. Picket lines appeared around the theater and the Fire Department moved in on the management because of overcrowding.

The producer cabled His Eminence from Italy, protesting that the theme of his play was deeply religious. The Protestants and Other Americans United for the Separation of Church and State sprang to the defense of the Constitution, declaring that Cardinal Spellman "had struck a blow against Democracy."[4] The *Daily Worker* agreed with POAU that His Eminence was trying to establish a "clerical political tyranny in violation of the United States Constitution." The American Civil Liberties Union and the Authors League of America sent a telegram to the Board of Regents protesting that "revoking licenses at the instance of private pressure groups would permit them to dictate what other Americans may or may not see,"[5] and the *Daily Compass*, radical successor to the unlamented *PM*, exploded through its editor: "My objection to this high-handed action is based on the Cardinal's command that the State forbid all citizens to exhibit or view the film, whether they be Roman Catholic or not; and the spineless subservience of the State to that order."[6]

Meanwhile an Albany Supreme Court Justice refused to restrain a three-man committee of the Board of Regents from holding a hearing on the picture and on February 16 the members "unanimously found that said motion picture *The Miracle* is sacrilegious and not entitled to be licensed under the provisions of Section 122 of the Education Law."[7]

Thereupon the American Jewish Congress urged the Court of Appeals to revoke the ban, contending that the "State has acted to prevent deviation from the religious views of a single group," and clamored again for the separation of church and state.[8] But the Court of Appeals sustained the verdict of the Board of Regents, finding that:

1. The film was "sacrilegious," since it "utterly destroys" the sacred concept of the relationship between Jesus and His parents.
2. The banning of the film did not constitute violation of the freedom

of the press, because pictures are "primarily a form of entertainment" and are not entitled to "absolute" freedom.

3. There was no interference with freedom of religion, since the government may regulate expression of religious views if the public welfare is at stake.

4. The Board had the power to revoke the license issued by their subordinate body, because the legislature intended they be given such power.

5. The word "sacrilegious" is a "sufficiently definite standard."

The United States Supreme Court, however, reversed the New York State Court of Appeals, with Justice Tom C. Clark delivering the opinion:

> The issue here is the constitutionality under the First and Fourteenth Amendments of a New York State statute which permits the banning of motion picture films on the ground that they are "sacrilegious." . . .
>
> It is urged that motion pictures do not fall within the First Amendment's aegis because their production, distribution and exhibition is a large-scale business conducted for private profit. We can not agree. . . .
>
> In seeking to apply the broad and all-inclusive definition of "sacrilegious" given by the New York courts, the censor is set adrift upon a boundless sea amid a myriad of conflicting currents of religious views, with no charts but those provided by the most vocal and powerful orthodoxies. New York cannot vest such unlimited restraining control over motion pictures in a censor. . . .
>
> It is not the business of government in our nation to suppress real or imagined attacks upon a particular religious doctrine, whether they appear in publications, speeches or motion pictures. . . .
>
> We hold only that under the First and Fourteenth Amendments a State may not ban a film on the basis of a censor's conclusion that it is "sacrilegious."[9]

By champions of the picture, this decision was considered "a humiliating defeat for Cardinal Spellman."[10] It was a humiliation, but only because it showed again how through technicalities our precious safeguards of liberty can be used to protect the very forces that are working against the best interests of the country. It was not a victory for the Cardinal, but neither was it a clear-cut defeat. When the next objectionable picture came along, called *The Moon Is Blue*, its producers were bold enough to go a step further and defy not only the National Legion of Decency but the Production Code Administration itself, which had been respected for twenty-three years. The Cardinal in his prompt and uncompromising denunciation showed no traces of any "humiliating defeat."

By 1956 even the Production Code Administration had compromised with the downward trend of public taste, to the point where a picture called

Baby Doll had received a certificate of approval under the so-called self-regulatory system of the Motion Picture Association of America. Condemned by the Legion of Decency as evil in concept and certain to exert a corrupting influence on those who saw it, its producers seemed to be using it as a trial balloon in their revolt against all restraint. Their actions had the appearance of a deliberate challenge which His Eminence did not care to ignore. Though in town for only a few days between his return from the Eucharistic Congress of Manila and his departure for Greenland, he mounted the pulpit in St. Patrick's, Sunday, December 16, to deliver a ringing condemnation:

> In the performance of my duty as Archbishop of New York, in solicitude for the welfare of souls entrusted to my care and the welfare of my country, I exhort Catholic people to refrain from patronizing this film under pain of sin.
>
> It has been suggested that this action on my part will induce many people to view this picture and thus make it a material success. If this be the case, it will be an indictment of those who defy God's laws and contribute to corruption in America.

There was the usual outcry. A much-publicized Protestant minister in the city hastened to patronize *Baby Doll*, and appeared in the next day's paper standing defiantly under a suggestive picture of the principal character. What he thought of the film was not clear from his statement, but no one could misinterpret his views of the Cardinal. Others made uncomplimentary remarks, and Catholics in foreign countries where juveniles are not allowed to see adult pictures were quoted against the Ordinary of New York as giving the banned film their limited approval. Instead of surrendering, however, to a disillusionment that would have been natural, His Eminence continued to strike out as vigorously as ever, realizing that in this kind of struggle often the only victory lies in unyielding resistance.

In much the same spirit of hope without delusion, he replied to an invitation which had come from Episcopal Bishop Horace W. B. Donegan to join a group of Protestants and Jews interested in civic reform:

> It is heartening to observe in the statements and actions of President Eisenhower, Bishop Donegan and other public-spirited citizens, a strong reaffirmation of the basic importance and essential needs of religion and editorial concurrence with these leaders that the remedies for the grave domestic problems confronting us are to be sought through the strengthening of the spiritual and moral forces which are basic to good citizenship. . . .
>
> Catholic Bishops of the United States have often expressed their concern about the dangers resulting from Secularism in our country. In September, 1947, they warned that "Secularism or the practical exclusion

of God from human thinking and living, is at the root of the world's travail today." In November, 1952, they stated that the real danger to our country comes "from the threatening disintegration of our social life, due to the weakening of religion as a constructive force." . . .

In the present acute concern with the social problems confronting our community, we are pleased to avail ourselves of the opportunity presented by the statement of Bishop Donegan to give renewed expression of our awareness on the part of Catholics of these problems as well as of our continued determination to contribute with all the spiritual resources at our disposal to their solution.

The realization, however, that "the threatening disintegration of our social life" was of prime importance to the United States only served to emphasize the importance of communism as an element of that disintegration.

The Cardinal had seen clearly for years that here was no mere wrong-headed economic theory or hotheaded form of politics. In the dialectic communism that had come to maturity in Russia, he saw from the very beginning what Germany's enemies had not allowed themselves to see: an implacable conqueror whose victory lay in spreading disorder and want. With a sense of dedication and a cunning that often seemed satanic in its origin, the agents of the Kremlin, here and abroad, were seeking to destroy the existing order by destroying all that supported it—religion, patriotism, and public decency. It alarmed him, therefore, that so many of his fellow Americans carried over into peacetime the double-talk and mental confusion which had been cultivated during the war for purposes of military strategy. Now that the shooting was over and the Axis was prostrate, now that a bitter year of disillusionment had passed since President Truman went to Potsdam and played Beethoven's *Minuet in G* for Stalin and Churchill, it was high time for a little plain speaking about the real objectives of the Soviet, and speak the new Cardinal did with tongue and pen.

The first fighting article after his return from the consistory appeared in the *American* magazine. It was titled "Communism Is Un-American," and well advertised ahead of time, created a considerable stir in newspaper circles.

It *can* happen here and everywhere that Communism, with its riot of rash promises, takes root. In America the seeds of confusion and disunion are spawning and spreading, and Communism is growing. In their efforts to wean Americans from Americanism, Communists unanimously revile and defile everyone whose opinions and convictions differ politically, socially or morally from their own. Their subtle, sinister schemings sway and mislead Americans who, in ignorance or weakness, yield to Communism their loyalty to God, to country and to their fellowman. . . .

Nor is it my duty to seek out those pseudo-Americans who would rob Americans of this heritage. That is the responsibility of informed and competent men in our government who are aware of un-American activities. But I feel that I would not be a true American if I did not express my conviction that no American can dare to compromise with the crooked courses of Communism, or surrender to it, without jeopardizing the security of our country. I feel that I would not be a true American if I entered into the conspiracy of silence and did not raise my voice above those who, privately and in whispers, talk about Communism, but neither act nor speak publicly against this insidious enemy of Americanism.

The *Daily Worker* was shocked that, surrounded as he was by all the dreadful suffering of the starving American wage earners, "Cardinal Spellman, in his first article since his appointment at Rome, finds nothing better to worry him than the old bugbear of 'communism.' In the magazine *American,* he uses all the familiar vocabulary, unbacked by a single fact that anyone can check on, to charge that communists are 'imposing a despotism' on this country. . . . By talking 'communism' he takes the heat off the employers."[11]

Two months later, Andrei Vishinsky and Ambassador Nicolai Novikof were among the representatives of the United Nations who attended Mass at St. Patrick's Cathedral, ostensibly to pray for peace. His Eminence happened to be in Boston at the time, addressing 15,000 members of the Confraternity of Christian Doctrine, and the visitors from the Kremlin shook hands before the camera with the Coadjutor Archbishop of New York, the Most Reverend J. Francis McIntyre. But even if the Cardinal had been on hand to exchange formalities with these human symbols of hate, he would not have changed a word in the article which appeared soon after in the *Cosmopolitan,* "Do We Want a Soviet Peace?" George Sokolsky called it "one of the sharpest statements I have read in recent months on the dangers of Russian conduct."

It is not [we read] in defense of my faith that I condemn atheistic Communism, but as an American in defense of my country, for while Communism is an enemy of Catholicism, it is also a challenge to *all* men who believe in America and in God. . . .

Two or three times in history there has been a peace that drenched the world in fear and held the fate of men relentless in its grip. And today like a chilling mist there hangs over the democratic nations the menace of a "Pax Sovietica" which . . . is being imposed upon Europe, with the goal of the dictators, One World—*Theirs!*

There was much favorable comment in the American press, and sharp criticism among the Reds, who saw him "attempting to carry out a Vatican plan" for world-wide reaction. The *Daily Worker* said his warning against a Soviet peace was a warning against any peace at all. There was a thinly veiled threat in the comment: "The Vatican might inform Cardinal Spellman that his preachments against the new democracies in Europe make it

more difficult for it to keep in step with its millions of communicants there."
Meanwhile the object of these attacks vowed publicly that:

> So long as my heart beats and breath lingers in my body, I shall never cease to pray and labor to protect America and warn and work against Communism and all the evils growing from out its rotted roots, for I believe that "Rebellion to tyrants is obedience to God."

Such was the message he repeated in many forms to many audiences in the years that followed—to mourners at Arlington National Cemetery on Decoration Day, to the FBI in Washington at their commencement, to the Veterans of Foreign Wars in their forty-seventh national encampment in Boston, and again in Milwaukee when he received the second Bernard Baruch Distinguished Service Award, to the thousands gathered for the World Peace Rally at the Polo Grounds, to audiences at innumerable dinners and graduations, to church congregations in all parts of the country.

This deep realization of what could happen in America came to the Cardinal not only by analyzing theories and reading recent history, but through his numerous contacts with communism's victims in other lands—Yugoslavia, Hungary, Czechoslovakia, and Poland. On October 6, 1946, at the World Peace Rally in New York, the heart of his address concerned the latest victim:

> I ask your prayers for Archbishop Aloysius Stepinac and his heroic priest-companions, whose only crime is fidelity to God and country, as steadfastly they refuse sinfully to save their lives at the price of losing their souls, yielding their loyalty to satanic Soviet sycophants. . . .
>
> "Dictatorship means unlimited power, resting on violence and not on law." This statement is not mine. It is the definition of Soviet Russia's own leader whose treacherous trademark of Communism is stamped upon his Yugoslav puppet who, following the perfidious pattern of communist godlessness, barbarism and enslavement, has already sealed the doom of this noble, humane priest as he is subjected to the agonies of a prolonged lynching!
>
> The confidence and conscience of the American people, already severely shaken by the unjustifiable, fiendish murder of our American aviators, and the execution of a brave soldier and patroit, General Draja Mihailovitch, have again been outraged by this latest infamy and affront to human dignity and decency. . . .
>
> But the spirit of Archbishop Stepinac will not die. . . . My fears are not for Archbishop Stepinac. . . . But the fear rests heavily upon me that we . . . may fail or refuse to realize that Communists, who have put to death thousands of innocent peoples across the seas, are today digging deep inroads into our own nation, and that here, too, they are tirelessly

trying to grind into dust the blessed freedoms for which our sons have fought, sacrificed and died. . . .

To commemorate the martyrdom of Archbishop Stepinac and the host of hard-dying men of God who in every country of the world laid down their lives in defense of these rights of man, it is my intention to honor his cherished memory by naming the next educational building to be erected in the Archdiocese of New York—The Archbishop Stepinac Memorial—thus ever to remind us of this great patriot of God and country, who found within himself, by Heaven's grace, a strength beyond the strength to live, a strength which is the strength, for what we love, to die.

This noble Archbishop for whom the prayers were offered did not die until 1960 but was sentenced to sixteen years in Lepoglava prison by Tito's communist courts. After five years, he was removed from the prison and confined within the limits of his native village of Krasic, where in 1953 he heard of his elevation by Pius XII to the Sacred College of Cardinals. During the first days of his imprisonment, Mrs. Franklin D. Roosevelt, who was honorary chairman of the American Committee for Yugoslav Relief, was asked by John F. Rapp of the New York State Board of the Ancient Order of Hibernians to aid "in our campaign to seek the release of Archbishop Aloysius Stepinac, Primate of the Roman Catholic Church in Yugoslavia, from his unjust sentence of sixteen years at hard labor." Mrs. Roosevelt's answer was brief but revealing.

Your letter addressed to me in care of The American Committee for Yugoslav Relief was forwarded to me. I am sorry but I fear that I cannot help you as you suggest. I understand the Archbishop took part in political affairs and the government now in power has jurisdiction in such matters.[12]

This was the troubled period when the Soviet and her slave states, with tacit sympathy from stranger quarters than Mrs. Roosevelt's, were advancing boldly against the Papacy. Taking a page from the England of the Tudors, they set about establishing national churches which were to be gloriously independent of everything but the local politicians. In Poland, Adam Cardinal Sapieha, the aged Archbishop of Cracow, successfully countered their moves at least until his lamented death in 1951. Czechoslovakia was less fortunate because less united than Poland. Archbishop Josef Beran of Prague found that the Church was being systematically confined within the walls of the sanctuary and its priesthood pressured into schism. In answer to a letter from Cardinal Spellman, Dean Acheson wrote under date of July 13, 1949:

MY DEAR CARDINAL SPELLMAN:

I appreciate very much your letter of June 29, 1949, concerning my statement to the press on June 23 with respect to the attack by the present regime in Czechoslovakia on the position of Archbishop Josef Beran and the suppression by the Communist authorities of religious rights and freedoms in that country. I assure you that this government continues to view such acts of persecution with concern and that the Department is giving close attention to developments affecting freedom of religion in Eastern Europe.

> Yours sincerely,
> DEAN ACHESON

Among the developments that were being given close attention was an inspired article in the communist organ *Rude Pravo* for August 3, which charged that the heads of an "organization X," including Allen Dulles and Francis Cardinal Spellman, had decided to make a martyr out of Archbishop Beran because they were displeased over the relaxing of East-West tension. The members of the organization, who were linked in some mysterious way with the Very Reverend John Baptist Janssens, General of the Society of Jesus, and Monsignor Montini of the Vatican Secretariat of State, were directing espionage, sabotage, and various other disturbances in countries that refused to submit to capitalism. The article characterized the Archbishop of New York as "the archenemy of everything that has the least connection with progress."[13] Soon, more than 150 Czech priests had been arrested for refusing to take the oath of loyalty to the government, and communist troops had occupied the archbishop's palace.

It was, however, in the tragic events of St. Stephen's Hungary that Cardinal Spellman was most involved. The Primate of Hungary, Josef Cardinal Mindszenty, Archbishop of Esztergom, had been elevated to the sacred purple at the same time as Cardinal Spellman. The acquaintance begun in the early spring of 1946 at the consistory ripened into friendship the following year when His Eminence of Esztergom, who was returning after the Marian Congress in Ottawa, was for several days a house guest of His Eminence of New York. The sky above him was already red. In his first pastoral letter, October 18, 1946, the new primate had sized up the situation in Budapest:

> It is with great pain that we must agree with the words of the English Foreign Minister when he said that it would appear in Hungary that one totalitarian dictatorship was being relieved by another.[14]

That was the background for a remark he made at a Hungarian-American reception in New York:

> I am pleased to look about and see smiling Hungarians for the first time in years. Although there are smiles where I come from, the two are not the same because of the ordeals our people in Hungary are suffering. Yet there is a spiritual bond which holds Hungarians together regardless of where they are and what is happening to them.

General elections will be held in Hungary on August 31st but observers believe that, as in Poland, the Red Forces now in control of the government will be able to perpetuate that control.[15]

Later, recalling the primate's visit to the United States, Cardinal Spellman said that the Hungarian prelate had foreseen "the role he was destined to play in the present enslavement of his nation. Only a year ago when I had the honor to have the Cardinal as a guest in my home, he was asked by someone if he did not fear to return to Hungary. Calmly, simply, he answered: 'Why should I fear to return? That is where my flock is. Ultimately all that my enemies can take from me is my life.'" At the end of the visit, there was a brief entry in the Spellman diary for July 7: "Cardinal Mindszenty left. I had the impression I was saying goodbye to a martyr. He asked me smilingly if I would name a school after him if he were imprisoned."

On the prelate's return to Hungary, the situation continued to deteriorate until on June 18, 1948, the Hungarian Parliament, by an overwhelming majority, passed the bill nationalizing the nation's 4813 Catholic schools. That day, at the instruction of His Eminence, all the church bells of Hungary rang for a quarter of an hour.

His last pastoral letter was dated November 18, 1948:

> For many weeks, attempts have been made to stage "resolutions" directed against me in all the townships and village communities of Hungary. I am blamed for counter-revolutionary plots and activities hostile to the people, because of the Marian celebrations in 1947–1948. . . .
>
> I look on calmly at this artificial whipping up of the waves. In the place where I stand, not by the grace of any party, but by the grace and confidence of the Holy See, seething waters are not an extraordinary phenomenon. History lives in change.
>
> Of my predecessors, two were killed in action, two were robbed of all their possessions, one was taken prisoner and deported, one was assassinated, our greatest one was exiled. . . .
>
> Of all my predecessors, however, not one stood so bare of all means as I do. Such a systematic and purposeful net of propaganda lies—a hundred times disproved and yet a hundred times spread anew—has never been organized against the seventy-eight predecessors in my office. I stand for God, for the Church and for Hungary. This responsibility has been imposed upon me by the fate of my nation which stands alone, an orphan in the whole world. Compared with the sufferings of my people, my own fate is of no importance.[16]

Half an hour before his arrest, the cardinal managed to put down on an old envelope the following statement and pass it on:

> I have partaken in no conspiracy whatsoever. I shall not resign my

episcopal see. I shall not make any confession. If, however, despite this you should read that I confessed or that I resigned, and even see it authenticated by my signature thereto, regard that as merely the consequence of human frailty; and in advance I declare such acts null and void.[17]

After being duly processed by the ministers of justice, however, the same cardinal on the second day of his trial called this very statement "null and void."[18]

The trial, which began on February 3 and ended with a sentence of life imprisonment on February 8, was described by one reporter as "a well rehearsed but poorly produced play." Mayor O'Dwyer called it "a lynching party," Governor Dewey "a mock formality, an insult to religion and a cruel parody of justice," Dean Acheson "wanton persecution," and President Truman "the infamous proceedings of a kangaroo court."[19]

Most of the evidence was based on a collection of documents found at the cardinal's residence and acknowledged by him in an abject confession. László Sulner and his wife, Hannah Fischer, the handwriting experts who testified that the papers were not forgeries and that the defendant's "confession" was not written under duress, reversed themselves a few days later when they reached the safety of the American Zone, saying that they themselves had testified under duress and that the cardinal's "confession" seemed to have been obtained with the use of drugs.[20]

Three of the points raised by "the documents" afterward published by the Hungarian Government involved Cardinal Spellman. They were supposed to have established that there was a plot to restore the monarchy: that Mindszenty had met Archduke Otto, heir to the throne of Hungary, in Chicago before coming East to consult with His Eminence of New York, who had been a go-between entertaining both the primate and the archduke, and had not only given large sums of money to advance the royal cause, but had used his influence to keep the United States from restoring the Holy Crown to the sovereign people of Hungary. There was, of course, some truth in all of it, with a great deal of deliberate distortion.

It was no secret that Cardinal Mindszenty, like the vast majority of his countrymen, regarded the Russian conquest of Hungary as a national tragedy. For him and millions of others, the Hapsburgs were symbols of legitimacy, order, and Christianity, and the personable Otto a worthy representative of his family. Regarding the supposed meeting at a monastery near Chicago, the archduke stated that "the first I heard of it was in the newspapers. As to the supposed representation of all Hungarian Catholics, which a Hungarian communiqué said had been conferred on me by the Cardinal, it is hard to imagine that a Primate should delegate such representation upon a man who, so to say, has been principally a political character."[21] But of the discussion in New York, we read in Mindszenty's "confession": "Spellman then said he thought it necessary that I should give a letter of commission to Otto which would enable him abroad to represent Hungarian Catholics. . . . After writing the letter, I gave it to Cardinal Spellman."[22] The archduke, asked by the press to confirm the report, said it was true, but that Cardinal Spellman would be in a better position to comment on it.[23] Father Zakar, the Primate's unfortunate secretary, who went to pieces during the trial, described in detail alleged relations between Cardinal Mindszenty and Cardinal Spellman, Archduke Otto, and the American Minister to Hungary, Selden Chapin:

> Father Zakar said that he had attended one New York meeting between the two Cardinals but had waited in an anteroom while the Primate conferred with Archduke Otto and, on another occasion, with the Archduke's mother, Empress Zita. Father Zakar also testified that Cardinal Spellman had told Cardinal Mindszenty that the Hungarian royalists should hold themselves ready in case of an opportunity to take power. Cardinal Spellman also was alleged to have spoken of a post-World War III Central European bloc under American auspices.[24]

His Eminence of New York had already denied (December 29) that Cardinal Mindszenty had informed him of any royalist plot to put Archduke Otto on the Hungarian throne, and even the unhappy Primate, reduced to a moral shadow of himself, while he "confessed" to the court that he had "committed the majority of those deeds" with which he was charged, denied leading a movement "to destroy the democratic system of the State." The charge of a plot, however, was resurrected on October 10 and brought before the fifty-nine-nation special political committee of the United Nations General Assembly by Dmitri Manuilsky, Foreign Minister of the Soviet Ukraine. He accused Cardinal Spellman of giving Cardinal Mindszenty $30,000 in 1947 to finance a plan to undermine the Republic and restore Otto to the throne. Answering the charge, His Eminence said:

> If for $30,000 democracy, with its freedoms, could be secured in any of the countries under Soviet domination, all our soldiers and their relatives would know that it was the greatest bargain since Manhattan was bought from the Indians.
>
> The Catholic people of the United States and all other humanitarian Americans have been contributing not only through the Government but through private agencies to help the poor of the war stricken areas of the world. All our money goes for three purposes, food, clothing and medicine, and our task would be less formidable if these people were not still terrorized and tyrannized. We gave much more than $30,000. Through our war relief services we gave millions of dollars, food and medicine.[25]

To the accusation, however, concerning the Holy Crown of Hungary, there was more substance and shortly before the trial began, Cardinal Spellman issued the following statement through the chancery office:

Newspaper reports from Hungary have referred to communications between Cardinal Mindszenty and myself concerning the Crown of St. Stephen. When the Cardinal was in America he expressed the desire that this Crown be kept from the Communist leaders because he regarded it as a religious relic since it was a gift of Pope Sylvester to St. Stephen and for a thousand years has been held in the highest reverence by the people of Hungary. At the Cardinal's request I wrote to Secretary Patterson and received a reply from Secretary Royall who has given me permission to release this exchange of letters:

"July 28, 1947

"DEAR JUDGE PATTERSON:

Cardinal Mindszenty, Primate of Hungary, has asked me if I would intercede with you to have every possible care taken of the Sacred Crown of Hungary which is both a relic of the first King of Hungary, St. Stephen, given to him by Pope Sylvester in the year 1000, and also a juridical emblem of the apostolic Kingdom of Hungary. The Crown was carried away by Hungarian refugees into American territory in 1944 and is now in the possession of the Supreme American Military Command. The Crown is an object of great veneration among the Hungarian people and Cardinal Mindszenty asks that the Supreme American Military Command if possible safeguard it in this country or entrust it to the care of His Holiness, Pope Pius XII.

With kind regards and best wishes, I remain

Your sincere friend,
FRANCIS CARDINAL SPELLMAN
Archbishop of New York

HON. ROBERT PATTERSON
War Department
Washington, D.C."

"11 August 1947

"YOUR EMINENCE:

Your letter dated 26 [*sic*] July 1947, addressed to Judge Patterson interceding on behalf of Cardinal Mindszenty, Primate of Hungary, with respect to the Sacred Crown of Hungary, now in the custody of the military authorities in Austria, was duly received.

Since the restitution of sacred relics other than to the government of origin is not properly within the discretion of the Military Government authorities, I have taken the liberty of forwarding a copy of your letter to the Department of State requesting its careful consideration of your request.

Sincerely yours,
KENNETH C. ROYALL
Secretary of War"

From the Department of State to which Secretary Royall referred my communication, I received no reply. But, during the ensuing months I continued to receive requests from Europe concerning the safeguarding of Hungary's sacred relic. The following letter is my answer to one of these whose identity, for his security, I do not reveal. The answer to all other inquirers was similar.

". . . I have submitted the matter for the consideration of those who are regarded as well versed in International Law. It is their viewpoint that while we might regret the necessity of giving the Crown of St. Stephen into the hands of those who have so little regard for this great spiritual leader and patron of Hungary, I am informed nevertheless that the Crown is considered to be the property of the Hungarian people. This Crown was spirited away from Hungary by the retreating Nazi forces when the Soviets advanced on Budapest—at least this is the way I am informed by reliable Hungarian authorities in this country. The Crown was captured in Austria by the advancing American armies. Thus, it came into the possession of the Americans.

"Since the ratification of the peace treaty with Hungary, the United States Government acknowledges the Government of Hungary as presently existing, as a de jure Government. Consequently, if the Government of Hungary requests the American authorities to hand over the Crown of St. Stephen as 'loot' which was captured from the retreating Nazis, it is the opinion of those I have consulted that the United States Government may be obliged by International Law to accede to the request.

"On the other hand, it would be impossible for the United States Government to send the Crown of St. Stephen to the Holy See because in so doing, it would be conveying to the Holy See that which is, according to the principles of International Law, 'loot' which the Nazis took from Hungary. Consequently, it might be a cause of greater embarrassment to the Holy See if the Communists of Europe were to publicize throughout Europe the fact that the Holy See had thus innocently become the possessor of so-called 'stolen goods.' As a matter of fact, the Hungarian Government might request the Holy See to transmit the Crown immediately to Hungary under the threat of penalizing the Church in Hungary.

"All things being considered, I fear that there may be no legal way in which the United States authorities may retain the Crown of St. Stephen and certainly there is no way which is adequate under the prescriptions of International Law whereby the Crown might be entrusted to the Holy See. This is, of course, only my opinion, but it is the answer I am giving to all who have consulted me about this matter, and you will well understand that any measures taken must be within the framework of International Law.

Very sincerely yours
FRANCIS CARDINAL SPELLMAN"

Three days after the appearance of the statement, on January 11, the State Department announced that present circumstances were inopportune for returning the Crown of St. Stephen to the Hungarian Government.[26]

The pattern had now been established, and almost every important trial staged in the slave states thereafter dragged in the name of Cardinal Spellman. After the imprisonment of Cardinal Mindszenty, many of his responsibilities were assumed by Archbishop Josef Groesz of Kalocsa, whose duty it was to keep in contact with the Holy See and resist all pressure for the establishment of a national church. He was arrested therefore in May of 1951 and brought in for sentence the following month. With the same mystifying calm that had shocked the Western World in Cardinal Mindszenty, he confessed to everything required of him. Robert Vogeler of the International Telegraph and Telephone Company, who was released from a Hungarian jail about that time, suggested what might have happened to the prelate. He described his own confession as "rubbish." He said that he was slapped, questioned for hours without rest, food, or sleep, and was subjected to such physical, moral, and mental pressure that his will to resist was gradually worn away.[27] In any case, Archbishop Groesz involved Pope Pius XII, Cardinal Spellman, and Monsignor Montini of the Vatican Secretariat of State in a fantastic plot to make himself the head of the state with the title of *Homo Regius*.[28] His sentence was fifteen years in prison but in May 1956 he was released and restored to his diocese where he was part of a very puzzling picture until his death in 1961.

In 1953 it was Poland's turn, and Bishop Czeslaw Kaczmarek of Kielce was placed on trial for his life. On September 18, the communist Warsaw radio announced that a former Polish government official, whom it identified as "Ghromecki, the Bishop's former political adviser," had testified that the Archbishop of New York tried during World War II to bring the United States into the war on Hitler's side. He told the judge that "Spellman enjoyed extraterritorial rights and made trips to the Vatican in order to facilitate the conclusion of a compromise peace and the launching of a joint attack against the East by Nazi Germany, Great Britain and above all, the United States—with the Vatican's blessing."[29]

His Eminence gave the following statement to the press:

> It is a long time since I have replied to false accusations against me by the God-hating, freedom-hating Communist puppets now terrorizing, brutalizing and tyrannizing half the world and openly ambitioning, with the help of traitors, many even within our own country, to enslave the rest of the world.
>
> I feel, however, that I must protest against the vicious crime of the sentencing of Bishop Czeslaw Kaczmarek of Kielce, Poland, to prison for twelve years because he "confessed" that he transmitted secret information through me to officials of the United States Government.
>
> I declare that never in my life have I known this man nor had I even

heard his name before his "trial" began. Therefore I denounce the "trial" as a fraud and a mockery. I pronounce the verdict absurd and cruel and characterize the officials of the court and their instigators as cowardly criminals who in the Communist world of contradictions, will probably have meted out to them punishment befitting their evil, barbaric crimes.

What has been said about me has been published in American papers. I hope that my reply will be printed in the papers of Moscow, Warsaw, Belgrade, Budapest and Bucharest, and broadcast by the Voice of Siberia.

Demoralized as they were by their defeat, the Italians were regarded as another easy prey for communism. Most observers on the spot predicted that the withdrawal of American and British forces of occupation would signal the end of orderly government. The Holy Father, however, rallied the men and women of Italy to use their ballots, and at the critical juncture from out of nowhere came a man named De Gasperi. Highly recommended to President Truman by Myron Taylor, he visited America for help in 1947, minimizing as far as he could the alarmist stories about the political situation that had preceded him. Letters reaching the Cardinal, however, minimized nothing. Said one, just before Christmas: "We are so heavily pressed, and our present situation is so grave and exceptional, that these considerations do not restrain me from addressing you this appeal. Your Eminence will forgive our insistence; for you are best qualified to realize its urgency and warmth."

His Eminence was urged to do what he could, not officially but through friends, for Mario Di Stefano, assistant to the Italian ambassador in Washington, who had been entrusted by his government with the important mission of arousing Italians to a realization of the communist danger through the letters of their friends and relatives in the United States. By January 27, 1948, Di Stefano could report grounds for positive hope, and on March 17, in the presence of President Truman, the Cardinal said:

And one month from tomorrow as Italy must make her choice of government, I cannot believe that the Italian people, whom I learned to know and to love as I spent with them thirteen of the most precious years of my life, will yield their Faith and America's friendship to Soviet Russia's Communist pressure and propaganda. I cannot believe that the Italian people will choose Stalinism against God, Soviet Russia against America —America who has done so much and stands ready and willing to do so much more, if Italy remains a free, friendly, unfettered nation.

There is a memorandum in the Cardinal's files reading: "On this date, April 20th, the news came that the party of Christian Democracy had been successful over the Communists."

By May of 1953 another crisis had arisen in Italy, and the people of the Archdiocese of New York received a pastoral letter from their Archbishop:

Impressed with the seriousness of the present election issues and encouraged by the success of the letter writing campaign of 1948, I ask that you urge your good people to write *immediately* to relatives, friends and acquaintances in Italy. Ask them to point out the benefits that are and will be theirs under a free government as contrasted with the slavery imposed by the Communists wherever they have seized power. Ask them to warn that the choice is between Christianity and Atheism, Godliness and Godlessness.

At home, meanwhile, the American people were undertaking a serious reappraisal of the lenient attitude toward communism which had been quietly building up during the excitement of war. This was reflected in Congress by a number of special investigating committees in both Houses. Senator William E. Jenner, as chairman of the Senate Internal Security Subcommittee, was examining the power of the left wing in education and in government. Representative Harold H. Velde, as chairman of the House Committee on Un-American Activities, drew attention to Red influences at work among entertainers and the ministers of the various churches. But it was Wisconsin's junior Senator, the late Joseph R. McCarthy, who became a symbol of the whole movement. As chairman of the Senate Permanent Subcommittee on Investigations, he ranged over a wide and interesting field: the Voice of America, our overseas libraries, ships in trade with Red China, and even sensitive areas in the armed forces. It was soon evident that many groups in our complex citizenry, not all of them Red by any means, were in violent opposition to his general purposes or at least to his methods of procedure. Some of his colleagues, notably Senator Jenner and Representative Velde, shared his point of view and adopted his general manner of approach, but they were fortunate in not having a vulnerable Irish name.

Such was the background of a press conference that was held in Milwaukee, August 3, 1953:

Questions on Senator McCarthy at the press conference were handled slowly and gingerly by the 64-year-old Cardinal, who measured each word as he spoke.

"I have never met Senator McCarthy," he began. "I have never had any telephone conversations with him or received a letter from him. I have never seen him on television. All I know about him is what I read in newspapers. There are three things I will say about Senator McCarthy. He was a Marine, and having been with the Marines myself, the fact that a man was a Marine places him very high in my book as regards patriotism. He is against Communism and he has done and is doing something about it. He is making America aware of the danger of Communism. He has been elected Senator from his native State, and no one is known better than by his neighbors. I am willing to accept the verdict of the citizens of Wisconsin concerning Senator McCarthy."[30]

By the following fall, Western Europe, where resentment toward the United States increased with every billion dollars contributed, had joined the hue and cry against what the communists were the first to call "Mc-Carthyism." The Cardinal regarded this as part of an over-all misunderstanding, and took the occasion of an important address in Brussels to place his country in the proper light. On October 23, he was the guest of the *Grandes Conférences Catholiques* in the Palace of Fine Arts. For an audience of 4000 which included the entire Belgian cabinet, he chose for his topic, "America, Grateful Child of Mother Europe." After a gracious introduction, His Eminence came to the point with characteristic honesty:

It seems, in these latter days, that certain critics in Europe have not honored the canons of constructive criticism in their judgments of America. They see us only in our worst light. Their purpose in criticizing seems designed to hurt, not to help. The litany of tired, jaded charges against us is run through with little or no attempt made to understand our true nature as a people. Thus to such critics we are a grossly materialistic nation. We are vulgar, preoccupied with trivia, possessing neither culture nor soul. We are the New Carthage, all wealth and no spirit. We have no God but money and we have no concern for anyone but ourselves. Such, then, is the picture painted of us by these critics and the conclusion they draw is that since there is little to choose between Russia and America, a plague is pronounced on both their houses.

Is America then so scabrous? Has she so quickly forfeited her fair name? . . .

I do not think so and I will tell you why. Within the last decade I have visited every part of the globe and have thrice circled the earth! I trudged with soldiers over the battlefields of Europe, Africa, the Middle East and the Far East. I entered Belgium with the troops of liberation and my heart beat faster at the sincerity and warmth of the welcome which the Belgian people gave to us. . . .

That America responded as she did is not due to any desire on her part to satisfy imperialistic ambitions, nor is it inspired by a homely desire to export what is called "The American Way of Life." America's generosity, her desire to share her substance with those less fortunate springs from a deep evangelical motive. . . .

From her rich bounty, America has given unstintingly and for this she expects no praise but she does hope she will be spared the carping criticism that she is all wealth and no spirit. America seeks not to buy the friendship of any other nation. She knows there is no price for true friendship. If her present role in world history is proof of materialism and lack of spiritual insight, then America's patronizing critics have much to learn from her! . . .

Another matter which has subjected America to widespread criticism in Europe has been the Congressional inquiries into the infiltration of Government by Communists. Judging from the hysterical tone of the criticism, one would imagine that it is no longer possible in America to keep one's good name. Nothing could be further from the truth. We are still a free people who cherish freedom. No American uncontaminated by Communism has lost his good name because of Congressional hearings on un-American activities.

However, there are many individuals who have seriously compromised themselves by a flat refusal to state whether they are now or have been Communists. It is impossible for me to understand why any American should refuse to declare himself free of Communist affiliation *unless he has something to hide*. In that event he deserves to be held in suspicion because he constitutes a threat to our country's freedom which has been won at too great a cost to be lightly lost. There is no reason to doubt the aim of the Communists. The history of Communist treachery all over the world is tragic and the subjugation by them of one country after another makes grim reading.

Our American Government would be utterly naive if it did not take all the necessary steps to preserve its own existence. It has the right to know the kind of men it employs. It has the right to expect that its citizens will not have a divided loyalty. The Communist has such a divided loyalty and has given abundant proof of the treachery such a division spawns. We have seen how he bides his time, using all the words and forms of free men only to mask his evil intent until such occasion is given him for betrayal. *We do not intend in America to give him that occasion if we can prevent it.*

Congressional inquiries into Communist activities in the United States are not the result of any mad legislative whim. There are strong reasons for these inquiries and we thank God we have begun while there is still time to do something about it. In too many instances the awareness of Communist intrigue has come when it is too late. The anguished cries and protests against "McCarthyism" are not going to dissuade Americans from their desire to see Communists exposed and removed from positions where they can carry out their nefarious plans. If American prestige is going to suffer in Europe because of this understandable desire we have to keep our free society immune from Communist subversion, then it seems more a reflection upon European standards of honor and patriotism than on ours. . . .

Having said this, and I say it in no spirit of harshness but rather with a plea for better understanding, it remains for me now to tell you how deep is the debt that America owes to Europe. . . .

The enumeration of all that Europe and especially Belgium has done for the material, cultural, moral, and religious progress of the United States was followed by a return to the main theme:

But it is my heart's firm belief, as I feel it must be yours too, that the ideal attitude for the present day sons of Belgium and her sister-countries should be one not of resentment of a new world's seeming prosperity but rather one of justifiable pride, gratification and affection. For America, the daughter of Europe, is a grateful child who aids her mother in her hour of need, not in a spirit of arrogance, but with a profound satisfaction that America is able to repay, in some small measure, her tremendous debt.

Postwar disillusionments had clarified the Cardinal's conviction that the influence of Moscow was lethal. There was no point in trying to meet it halfway. Moscow had already clarified its conviction with regard to the Cardinal. By 1960 the exchange of compliments was picturesque.

For his Christmas Tour in 1959, the Military Vicar had visited the troops in Germany, Turkey, Libya, Morocco, and Spain. According to Red reports: in Germany, he had "spied" on the Soviet defenses along the communist border; in Turkey, he had a friendly conference with Archbishop Athenagoras in Istanbul, where these two enemies of human freedom had discussed the possibility of reunion, while in Adana he must have given directions to Francis Gary Powers who was planning at the time to fly his deadly U-2 over a peace-loving country. To crown it all, in Spain he was shameless enough to go on pilgrimage to the Valley of the Fallen with its enormous basilica. He knew that this had been erected by the villainous Franco in memory of the fascist rebels who had ended the glorious Red rule in the peninsula. He had even called it publicly "a symbol in the world's fight against Communism." So in March, when the mild and gallant Maryknoll Bishop James A. Walsh, already sixty-eight, was sentenced by the Chinese communists to twenty years in prison, Radio Moscow announced that "he had been sent to China by the Vatican with Cardinal Spellman to set up anti-revolutionary organizations."

Summer came and with it another International Eucharistic Congress, this time in Munich where twenty-one cardinals, one hundred bishops, one thousand priests, and 1,200,000 pilgrims had gathered from all parts of the world. It was not reprehensible in Soviet eyes to visit Dachau and dedicate a chapel on the site of Nazi paganism, but the New York Cardinal had visited the Czech border again and worse still had preached an inflammatory sermon in the Munich Cathedral. He had likened communism to "a wild beast of the forest—making this the most dangerous summer since 1939." Soviet Russia he called "once a fanatic, now a realistic threat." Was it any wonder that Moscow dubbed him "The Archangel of Atomic War"?

In September, Nikita Khrushchev made a historic tour of the United States at the invitation of President Eisenhower. Some Americans in high place still harbored the delusion that the bear who walked like a man was a man, and that if Ivan only knew how much we loved peace, the war clouds would vanish. His Eminence was more realistic. He did not blame President Eisenhower for hopefully turning every stone, and he told him on the telephone that he would pray for a successful outcome, but when he summoned the whole archdiocese to attend Holy Hour services in every church on the eve of Khrushchev's arrival, he solemnly warned of "disasters that may yet come. Within this very hour on the wings of silence, death could ride forth from out a far off land." No wonder the cathedral was packed to the doors on September 14 and the air tense, as he prayed with a devout flock, for his country and his President.

On his Christmas visitation to Alaska, along the DEW Line, (Distant Early Warning Line), through northern Canada, Baffin Land, Labrador, Newfoundland, and Greenland, His Eminence told the men and their families, "I realize the degree of your personal sacrifice and dedication, and cannot express my gratitude enough. For without you, not only America would be lost but the world would be in chaos." Such sentiments showed plainly enough that "he had sold himself, body and soul to the Pentagon." But, worst of all, before leaving New York, he had written out a Christmas message that was read at Midnight Mass in St. Patrick's Cathedral and carried by television and radio throughout the entire country. In it he spoke of sharing the feast of the Prince of Peace with the servicemen "as they keep their lonely watch in the Northlands" and was reminded of a "fearless, lawless, Godless enemy" who had advanced "a blueprint of disarmament that would mean the murder of the whole free world." This time Radio Moscow became hysterical. It described how just when the simple worshipers in the cathedral were praying for "Peace on Earth," a rasping voice was heard shouting "Down with Peace! We do not need disarmament. Arm! Arm! Arm!" The faithful had thought at first that they heard the voice of the devil —but it was Spellman's. By the time the program was relayed through Budapest, the rasping voice had increased to a "tremendous howling that came down from the cupola!" This was an obvious fabrication. St. Patrick's has no cupola.

Meanwhile, Soviet tanks were beginning to roll in Cuba and by Christmas of 1960, there were 38,000 refugees in the United States. Most of them were responsible businessmen and their families who had been allowed to leave their country with no more than five dollars apiece and were now destitute in Florida, so the Cardinal before starting for the Arctic had sent President Eisenhower $10,000 to be used for their relief. Fidel Castro was quick to inform the world that Spellman and the millionaire Kennedy had an imperialistic pact! Of course he could not have been more mistaken. So at the first news conference, after the return of His Eminence from Greenland, when asked to comment on the dictator's remark, he said with a chuckle, "I want to be fair. I'll make another contribution, so that Mr. Castro can get hospital treatment. I think he needs it." This was widely quoted and when he followed it up later with a letter, asking homes and jobs for refugees who had now reached 60,000 in the Miami area, Moscow warned that "Spellman is trying to arm the criminals who fled from Cuba."

Throughout these postwar years, years of growing tension and misunderstanding of disillusionment and fear, the Cardinal remained reasonably optimistic. He told the National Convention on Housing in Chicago, "I am not a pessimist by race, temperament, or grace. I believe in America and her high destiny." He also believed in the United Nations as part of America's destiny and looked to it for many valuable solutions, but this belief did not preclude an occasional doubt and several words of honest criticism.

When the Security Charter was framed at Dumbarton Oaks in 1944, the N.C.W.C. Administrative Board, of which His Eminence was a member, advanced a few suggestions which, unfortunately for the world at large, were not accepted by the framers. For example: ideologies which violate the rights of man should be uprooted by a universal and democratic institution before which every nation could stand on its rights and not on its power. There should be a world court whose authority would be not merely advisory but strictly judicial, a court in which no nation should sit in judgment on its own case. Here assistance should be found for prostrate nations, and the means for revising treaties. The moral and philosophical principles which were implicit in these suggestions were not peculiar to the Catholic hierarchy. They represented the hopes of men of good will all over the world, hopes that were not to be fulfilled in San Francisco. So when the bishops saw that the United Nations Charter was merely the best compromise that could be arranged with Soviet Russia, they prophesied:

> A nation which refuses to accord to its own people the full enjoyment of innate human rights cannot be relied upon to cooperate in the international community for the maintenance of a peace which is based on the recognition of national freedom. Such a nation will pursue its own selfish international policy while paying lip service to international cooperation.[31]

Nevertheless, they came to the conclusion a year later that, in spite of its inequities and its betrayals, "our country acted wisely in deciding to participate in this world organization."[32] It was better than nothing.

So it was with Cardinal Spellman. Time and again, he deplored the indifference of the United Nations to Divine Guidance, their exclusion of Ireland and Spain and every civilized country that might prove embarrassing to the Kremlin, and above all, their cynical attitude toward the liquidation of Poland, Estonia, Latvia, Lithuania, and the Atlantic Charter. But it was better than nothing and when New York City formally turned over several tracts of land on the East River to the United Nations, His Eminence pronounced the invocation. Similarly, on his return from England on October 6, 1950, he told reporters he had written a prayer for the United

Nations at the request of John Golden, chairman of the United Nations Day Committee, because he firmly believed in it. The statement was particularly significant because at the time the Israelis were challenging the authority of the world body on the internationalizing of Jerusalem.

Palestine had been a sore spot in international relations ever since the Balfour Declaration of 1917 which proposed that this Arab territory should be returned to the foreign descendants of a people who had ruled it from time to time thousands of years before. When Franklin Roosevelt was on his way home from the fateful conference at Yalta in 1945, he conferred with King Ibn Saud aboard the U.S.S. *Quincy* at Bitter Lake, Egypt, and Fleet Admiral William D. Leahy, who was present, made note of the most important part of the interview:

> The King, with great dignity and courtesy, and with a smile, said that if Jews from outside Palestine continued to be imported with their foreign financial backing and their higher standards of living, they would make trouble for the Arab inhabitants. When this happened, as a good Arab and as a true believer, he would have to take the Arab side against the Jews and he intended to do so.[33]

According to Sumner Welles, the dying President favored the establishment of an independent Commonwealth of Palestine as a national Jewish homeland, but did not believe that Arabs or Christians should be deprived of their equal political and religious rights.[34] With the latter sentiment, the Archbishop of New York was in complete agreement. Attacks on the Christians were already an old story in September 1948, when the N.C.W.C. in Washington made public a detailed report on lootings and profanations in Catholic institutions, including the theft by Israeli soldiers of a ciborium containing consecrated hosts. His Eminence was deeply concerned and had been for a long time. On January 3, 1947, we read in his diary: "Long talk with Ambassador George Wadsworth of Iraq about Holy Places enclave in case of partition of Palestine"; and four months later: "Authorized Monsignor McMahon to present Christian interests in Palestine before United Nations."

This was the late Right Reverend Monsignor Thomas J. McMahon, who had been since 1943 national secretary of the Near East Welfare Association, of which the Cardinal was president. The association is directly under the Sacred Oriental Congregation, of which His Eminence was named a member in 1946. This new Congregation was separated in 1917 by Benedict XV from the four-centuries-old Sacred Congregation of the Propagation of the Faith. In 1938 its competence was enlarged and it became the direct mission aid of the Holy Father for Near and Middle Eastern lands. It was, therefore, Cardinal Spellman who, when tragedy shrouded the Holy Land, seconded the wishes of Pope Pius XII in founding the Pontifical Mission for Palestine and has been responsible ever since for raising the funds necessary for its support. On June 7, 1947, Monsignor McMahon filed a plea with the United Nations Assistant Secretary General in charge of trusteeship affairs for the right to be heard by the Assembly Political Committee on creation of the projected Palestine Inquiry Commission. In the brief, prepared with His Eminence, it was stated:

> It is manifestly false to assert that "Christianity is not an indigenous force in Palestine." It is also false to charge that "as an organized religion, Christianity is the creation of Rome and always represented in the East the introduction of a foreign civilization." . . .
>
> Christian apprehension is not purely academic. There is now living in Palestine a sizable minority of 51,000 indigenous Roman Catholics.[35]

The application for a hearing was rejected.

In November, the General Assembly voted to partition Palestine into two independent states and an international enclave of Jerusalem comprising the municipality and some surrounding villages, to be placed under an International Trusteeship System. The Israelis accepted the arrangement. The United States and Russia stood shoulder to shoulder in supporting this partition. The following spring Britain ceased to govern Palestine on May 14, 1948. Israel proclaimed her independence and was attacked by five neighboring Arab nations. At this time, on the eve of his departure for Australia, Cardinal Spellman sounded a note of concern:

> As the Holy Land's fateful hour impends and as I depart on a trip that will take me half way around the world to celebrate the Centenary of the Catholic Church in Melbourne, I repeat my plea and my prayer made over a year ago that not only the Holy City, but all sanctuaries precious to Christians as well as to Jews and Moslems, be spared from chaos, bloodshed and destruction.
>
> War must not bloody the soil nor desecrate the scene of the sacrifice of the Prince of Peace. For if men and nations who profess to believe in God defy God and defy His Holy Homeland, how can they condemn Godless barbarism in others?
>
> My plea on behalf of the sanctuaries and minorities of Palestine is not new, for mine was almost the lone Christian voice in America when I filed a brief with the United Nations pleading, in God's name, for protection of the Holy Places.
>
> May God grant wisdom and charity to all factions that in their hour of decision they may spare the centuries-old symbols of our only hope for a better and more peaceful world.

Despite this and many similar appeals from other world leaders, a bloody war had broken out between Arabs and Israelis. After two ineffectual truces a final cease-fire took place on January 9, 1949, with Jerusalem occupied by both parties and with other boundary lines vastly different from those envisaged by the General Assembly in 1947.

Following all the bloodshed and the flight of refugees, on Good Friday, April 15, 1949, Pope Pius XII called for the internationalization of Jerusalem and unhampered access for the faithful to the Holy Places there and elsewhere in Palestine. Dr. Chaim Weizmann, the Israeli President, pledged his nation to safeguard the Holy Places and said that Israel would support and encourage international controls for their immunity and protection. He insisted, however, that the Israeli Government would retain control over the Jewish section of Jerusalem. In the meantime, Monsignor McMahon was making a four months' inspection tour of the troubled Middle East where he witnessed indescribable suffering and on his return conferred with the Cardinal concerning additional relief measures for the 800,000 starving Palestinian Arabs who had been driven from their homes during the fighting. At the recommendation of His Eminence, the Holy Father in June appointed the Right Reverend Monsignor head of a world-wide organization for relief in Palestine.

On the occasion of his visit to this country, President Weizmann was invited to dinner at Madison Avenue with Aubrey S. Eban, now known as Abba Eban, Israeli representative with the United Nations. No statements on the nature or result of their talk were issued, but it was an open secret that the subject was free access to the Holy Places. In an interview aboard the *Queen Mary* before he sailed for Europe, President Weizmann said that his talks with President Truman and Cardinal Spellman had been "very useful. They cleared up several important misunderstandings in connection with Jerusalem. The interview with Cardinal Spellman was arranged through the good offices of the President of the United States." When asked whether his talks with the Cardinal had settled the Jerusalem problem, Dr. Weizmann replied, "It was not settled, but the talks cleared the way for a settlement. I hope to see a settlement soon."[36] The same day, Monsignor Francis J. Murphy issued the following statement for His Eminence:

> In reply to the requests of the press for comment on the statement made by President Chaim Weizmann of Israel that at a meeting with Cardinal Spellman "several important misunderstandings on the Palestine matter were cleared up" it seems necessary to state first of all that on the occasion of the meeting the Cardinal made it clear that he had no authority to make any agreements on any matters concerning the position of the Catholic Church in Palestine.
>
> The Cardinal stated he was one of the Bishops who, at the annual meeting in Washington, signed a statement asking that the internationalization of Jerusalem, as agreed on by the United Nations on Nov. 29, 1947, and then accepted by the Zionists, be implemented.
>
> Dr. Weizmann stated that "our aims in the Jerusalem question though

not identical are nevertheless reconcilable." This is confirmation by Dr. Weizmann himself that there is still existing divergency of views. Unfortunately, this divergence reaches matters fundamental, namely, whether internationalization, as agreed upon among the United Nations, will be effected or evaded.

The rest of the story is one of humiliation for the United Nations. In September 1949, the Reverend Raphael Quinn, secretary to the Roman Catholic Custodian of Holy Places, charged elements of the Israelis with the responsibility for the ruin of a number of shrines. The following March, the United Nations was expressing regret for the negative attitude shown by the representatives of Israel and Jordan and reminded them sternly that the boundaries set in the Assembly resolutions must be respected, but by June 1950, the Trusteeship Council had handed the ticklish issue back to the United Nations Assembly. In January 1953, Cardinal Spellman, interviewed in Beirut, said, "The United Nations had previously decided the internationalization of the Holy City and I believe this decision must be carried out," and on the same subject, eight months later, Charles Malik, the delegate from Lebanon, quoted him at some length in the Assembly:

Recalling the Assembly's resolutions demanding the internationalization of Jerusalem, the Cardinal declared that he wished "to point out and condemn the effrontery of a member of the United Nations, the State of Israel, which has, without right and in defiance of these resolutions and votes, tried to make the 'new city' of Jerusalem its capital."

The Cardinal said that "on two prior occasions this association has found it necessary to present to the United Nations protests against the overextension of Israel." He requested that the U.N. "proceed to the implementation of its decisions" to make Jerusalem international.

Meanwhile, the Secretary-General, Dag Hammarskjold, received a letter from Monsignor McMahon on behalf of the Near East Welfare Association complaining against Israel's transfer of her foreign ministry from Tel Aviv to Jerusalem and protesting that the shift violated past Assembly recommendations. The letter also opposed countersuggestions by Israel for "functional" internationalization of the Holy Places, saying: "The Catholic body throughout the world, as is evidenced by the repeated statements of their leader, Pope Pius XII, will not be contented with a mere internationalization of the Holy Places." And so it went with some monotony in 1954, in 1955, and in 1956, and yet His Eminence continued to defend the United Nations.

When Hungary and Egypt were invaded in the fall of 1956, he signed the statement issued by the hierarchy of the United States at the close of their annual meeting in Washington.

It has been the hope of humankind [they wrote] that a means adequate to the necessity might be found in the concert of the United Nations. This is neither the time nor the place to review its history or to pass judgment on its achievement. If there have been mistakes in its decisions and faltering in its procedures, that is no more than a commentary on our human condition. The fact remains that it offers the only present promise we have for sustained peace in our time, peace with any approximation of justice.

In February 1955 Secretary-General Dag Hammarskjold invited the Holy See to participate in the International Conference on the Peaceful Use of Atomic Energy. This was to convene in Geneva the following August. To the disappointment of the committee in charge, Monsignor Domenico Tardini sent regrets explaining that the Vatican had neither the technicians nor the services necessary to be helpful. At that point, Dr. Ralph Bunche, United Nations Undersecretary for Special Political Affairs, called at Madison Avenue to urge reconsideration because of "the psychological significance involved," and to explain that the delegates were not expected to be profoundly versed in nuclear science.

Cardinal Spellman was sympathetic to the appeal of Dr. Bunche that the Vatican reconsider its decision. As a direct result of his intervention on the matter, the Vatican decided to send two representatives, Professor Henri Medi and Father Henri de Riedmatten, who played an important part at the conference in bringing delegates together and in drawing attention to the larger aspects of the problem. This precedent was followed at the Second International Conference on the Peaceful Uses of Atomic Energy in 1958, when Mr. Frank Folsom, Father Theodore M. Hesburgh, and Father de Riedmatten represented the Holy See. Incidentally, Mr. Folsom and Father Hesburgh saw service again during the formative stages of the International Atomic Energy Agency in Vienna in 1957.

Meanwhile conditions were far from ideal in the great glass house of many flags. There were alarming straws in the wind: shifting majorities, newly elected member nations pathetically unprepared for their responsibilities, and all too soon, an ugly spirit of rule or ruin that would lead to scenes of boorishness and violence; but His Eminence clung to the point of view of the American hierarchy that the United Nations, weak and divided under attack, was still a great deal better than nothing.

CHAPTER TWENTY

Across the Pacific

THE Archbishop had already set his heart on a trip to the Orient when
he visited Europe and Africa in 1943. Leaving London, he had announced
at Paddington Station that he was on his way to India and China, but circumstances had forced a postponement for two crowded years. By the summer of 1945, the European phase of the war was over and it was apparent
that Japan could not hold out much longer. If the Military Vicar was to see
his boys and their chaplains in action, he would have to go at once to the
Pacific area.

An invitation to make the inspection tour arrived on July 8, couched in
the stiff and formal language of the Armed Services. It was signed by the
Chief of Chaplains, U.S.N., and the Acting Chief of Chaplains, U.S.A.:

The Secretary of War and the Secretary of the Navy invite you, or a
representative designated by you, to visit each of the theaters of operation
or the composite areas designated below. [These included the Pacific
Ocean area and the Southwest Pacific area, India-Burma and China
areas.]

The Secretary of War and the Secretary of the Navy have been impressed and much gratified by the beneficial effects upon the morale of
the personnel of the armed forces, resulting from your previous visitations. They believe that further visitations, as indicated above, would be
most helpful in maintaining the morale of the personnel mentioned and
of their relatives and friends in the churches at home and thereby be a
vital contribution toward the successful termination of the war effort.

Nothing more was necessary. The Military Vicar accepted at once.

For August 4, the diary reads: "Bob Hannegan came to luncheon. He will
issue stamp for Al Smith. Wishes me to see President Truman before I go
to the Pacific." By this time world events were really galloping. On August
7, we read: "First atomic bomb fell on Hiroshima. Got inoculations and
wrote for passport." On August 8, there was an entry: "Russia declares war
on Japan. Harry Luce and Joe Kennedy came to see me to ask if I would
ask President Truman for five or six days' truce to give Japan a chance to
surrender." Even those who six months before had been eager for the sup-

port of Soviet arms in Manchuria realized now what a postwar problem was being created. For August 10, we read: "Japs offer to surrender under terms of Potsdam. Worked frantically all day and took train to Washington." The next day:

John L. Sullivan accompanied me to President Truman. It was a historic meeting. Secretary of State Byrnes came in with document to be sent to Japan accepting provision to retain Emperor. President read it to me. Saw Secretary Forrestal and Bob Hannegan and James Byrnes. Very nice to me too, and Leo Crowley. Flew back to New York and prepared broadcast for V-J Day.

A letter written shortly after outlines his impressions of Mr. Truman:

Everything about him confirmed the opinion one has from reading about him, reading what he says, hearing him speak over the radio. He seems to be Mr. Average American endowed with supreme good will and a desire to do what is the right thing. I was greatly impressed by his humility, his sincerity, his frankness and his general attitude toward every problem, relying on God's help and on man's help to assist him in the performance of his varied, difficult and weighty tasks. . . .

During our conversation the President said, "I didn't want this responsibility, never expected to have it but now that I do have it, I am going to do my level best. I realize the problems of peace are tremendously difficult, but, at any rate, they are the problems of peace and not war. We hope to have the answer from the Japanese in a few hours." He impresses me as a man who is not going to be evasive. He is going to give you an answer whenever it is possible and he is going to try to give the right answer.

The President was kind enough to give me letters of introduction to General MacArthur and Admiral Nimitz and he told me that when victory came he would ask the people to go to their churches to thank God for it. He was very natural when I expressed appreciation for the reference he had made to the deity and the support that he had given to religion and he said, "Why shouldn't I? Where would I be without the blessing of God?" The President is a man who is full of life and certainly very healthy. I pray that he will continue to have strength and health to face the grave tasks ahead, the gravity of which he fully realizes. He said, "I will do the best I can from day to day and rely on God's help and the best advice I can get to assist me."

On the President's desk were two stacks of telegrams, the vast majority urging him to refuse the Japanese offer of surrender. Only a few favored acceptance. The Archbishop pointed to the few and said, "Mr. President, these are from people whose sons are in the service!"

Back to New York for twenty-four hours and on August 12 the Archbishop cleared his desk and drove to La Guardia. The next evening, he had dinner with forty-five chaplains of the San Francisco District and left the Oakland airport at 9:30. When he awakened it was 11:48 Greenwich Central Time and the first pilot, Lieutenant Paul Wessner, told him and his traveling companion, Admiral James L. Kaufman, that President Truman had just announced the war was over.

I went [he writes] forward and sat in the pilot's seat, looked at the star-studded heavens and said a prayer of thanksgiving. Deep darkness was below us but the altimeter told me that we were two miles above the Pacific Ocean. I asked the navigator our position and he gave it to me. (29-40 N Lat.; 142-50 W Long.)

The plane flew into Honolulu along the same route the Japanese had taken on the fatal day of Pearl Harbor and as it passed over Diamond Head, a huge arched rainbow followed it like an omen of peace. For two days there was the usual round of field Masses, visitations, and presentations. Six thousand attended his jubilant Mass of Thanksgiving in the Bloch Arena at Pearl Harbor, and another 3000 in the Schofield Barracks where he shook hands with an estimated 1200. At a reception on the battleship *New York*, the Ordinary of New York was given the battle flag that had flown on the ship at Iwo Jima and Okinawa. (Today this hallowed flag in its bronze standard is at the main entrance to St. Patrick's Cathedral.) At ten o'clock on the night of the fifteenth, the Archbishop left for Kwajalein and Eniwetok.

On arriving at Guam, the Archbishop presented the letter of introduction which President Truman had written to Admiral Nimitz, and was received with great cordiality. "This," said the admiral as he showed him to the room which was known as that of the Secretary of the Navy, "is your home." And home it was for a week, while side trips were made to Saipan, Tinian, and finally to Iwo Jima. On this now famous island, he celebrated Mass for the Army in the evening and the Navy the following morning, noting in his diary: "It was a thrill to be on Mount Suribachi!" One unpleasant duty marred the visit to Guam. He had to tell poor Bishop Olano, a Spaniard, that his nationality was against him in these critical times, and that the government had insisted that he be replaced by an American. The bishop answered philosophically, but with a touch of bitterness, "This is just what the Japanese said and did." And so it was that the Most Reverend Miguel Angel Olano, O.F.M. Cap., D.D., was made Assistant at the Pontifical Throne on August 20, 1945, and transferred to the Philippine Islands.

One of the lighter moments occurred when the Military Vicar was visiting a wing of the 20th Air Force. The Chief Intelligence Officer, Harry W. Besse, described afterward how the Archbishop of New York,

came into my office with several generals and colonels and I was asked to show him on the maps and with photographs what we had been doing. . . . Just as I was about to start the briefing, the squawk box we used for interoffice communication opened up. A friend of mine said, "Besse, there's a little fellow in a clergyman's collar coming over to see you with some generals. Give him the $2 show." I tried to shut him up, but he went on until he had finished and I told him abruptly that they were in my office. I went through the whole thing and was pretty embarrassed by the situation. When I was finished, Cardinal Spellman thanked me and said quietly, "That show, Colonel, was worth at least $3."[1]

Meanwhile, the following telegram had arrived from General Douglas MacArthur in Manila: MY HEARTIEST WELCOME TO YOU. I AM LEAVING FOR THE NORTH AT DAYBREAK MONDAY, AUGUST 27TH. I HOPE YOU MAY BE ABLE TO ARRIVE BEFORE THAT TIME AS I ANTICIPATE WITH PLEASURE PERSONALLY GREETING YOU. So on Sunday the twenty-sixth, at 1:00 A.M., the Military Vicar left Guam for the Philippines.

His first Mass was celebrated at Cebu in driving rain and the rubble of war. The cathedral had three walls standing, and on one of them was a tablet in memory of Bishop Thomas Augustine Hendrick, whom he had once seen back in the Fordham days. Arriving at Manila, he found a tragic ruin, more battered proportionately than any capital in Europe, but hospitality was universal. From President Osmeña, the Apostolic Delegate, and the American generals and admirals, down to the humblest native soldier, everyone had a smile for Archbishop Spellman. In a crowded week that took him as far as Cebu in the south and San Fernando in the north, to hospitals, churches, mess halls, and schools, and even included the official Mass of Thanksgiving for victory and liberation in Rizal Stadium, nothing impressed him more deeply than his meeting with General Douglas MacArthur:

> The breadth and depth of the General's conversation amazed me [he wrote afterward in a letter home] and I really contributed nothing to it, as I was spellbound listening to him and admiring his philosophy which is based on Lincoln's statement: "I do the best I know how, the very best I can and I mean to keep doing so until the end." . . .

> He has been able not only to get along with his armies, but he is received by the Filipinos and Australians as he is esteemed by his own countrymen. Archbishop Duhig, of Brisbane, Australia, said that the Australians admired MacArthur as much as do the Americans and the Filipinos believe in and trust him as much as, even more than any single one of their leaders. . . .

> Concerning only one matter did General MacArthur show resentment and that was the criticism by an American journalist of General MacArthur when he said, "By the grace of Almighty God our forces stand again on Philippine soil consecrated in the blood of two peoples." The

journalist said that the credit of the return should be given to the soldier and not to God and General MacArthur said, "That remark hurt me because it showed to what baseness some men had fallen."

It is certainly inspiring to see generals who give more than lip service to religion. There seem to be three classes of C.O.s in the service. Some are antagonistic. They make the job of the chaplain more difficult. Others are indifferent. These speak well of the chaplains and look on religion as something that other people need. And then there are the men who hear the Word of God and follow it.

Admiral Barbey invited the Vicar to be his guest aboard the *Catochtin*, the flagship of the Seventh Amphibious Force Fleet, as he convoyed the 24th Infantry Division from the Philippines to Korea for V-J Day, but because of the Mass in Rizal Stadium His Eminence had to fly to Okinawa and meet him there. Unfortunately, a serious typhoon which did great damage to the shipping in Buckner Bay delayed them in Okinawa the better part of a week.

During the time I spent on the island [he wrote later] I was the guest of General James H. Doolittle and visited many of our units. I saw the caves and the trenches that were used by the Japanese in the stubborn defense of their last bastion. We can never thank God enough that the Emperor surrendered because of the terrific casualties that would have followed an assault on Japan. Some hotheads wanted Japan to be assaulted anyway and the Emperor to be tried as a war criminal. If that insane policy had been followed, I do not know when the war would have ended. But the MacArthur formula was very sound: that the eighty million Japanese people would obey the Emperor and the Emperor would obey him. That is why when we went to Korea, we saw the Japanese soldiers, fully armed, regiment after regiment of them, march up, stack their guns, and walk away prisoners of war. I was in the jeep with Admiral Barbey as we rode from Inchon to Seoul for the surrender, and while General Hodge was accepting the surrender by the Japanese generals, I was offering Mass in the Cathedral in Seoul.

Arriving in Japan two days later, he found himself in the confusion of a great Empire lying in ruins:

The day that I met General Robert L. Eichelberger, Commander of the 8th Army, was the day that Tojo attempted suicide. . . . Now it is the practice of the newspapermen to ask as a sort of routine question, "Do you contemplate hara-kiri?" While I was at supper with General Eichelberger I got the news of the suicide of Field Marshal Hajime Sugiyama, Commander of the First Japanese General Army, who had been chief of staff during most of the war and twice Minister of War. Yesterday

General Homma who ordered the death march on Bataan was surrendered by the Japanese themselves.

But order was already beginning to appear, partly as a result of MacArthur's enlightened policies and partly as a result of the Japanese temperament. People of every class had been bowing from the hips to the man on the red carpet for 2000 years, and now that an American general was on the red carpet, they kept on bowing.

A special feature of the visit is described by an American navigator writing to his wife:

DEAREST MARY,

Today we had the honor of flying Archbishop Francis J. Spellman to Hiroshima. . . . Leveridge offered Archbishop Spellman the co-pilot's seat, where he sat and enjoyed most of the flight.

Upon landing we unloaded the jeep and trailer. The Archbishop and party were unable to get all the way into Hiroshima because of landslides along the road. When we took off again we flew over the city at 500 feet and circled it many times. The Archbishop saw the remains of the city from the co-pilot's seat.

From here we headed for Osaka. His Excellency was asked if he would like to fly the airplane. He said he would like to try. He received about ten minutes stick-time and did surprisingly well. When the Archbishop wasn't engaged in conversation or taking in the sights he read his prayer book. . . .

The next day the Archbishop was off for China, in response to an invitation from General Chiang Kai-shek, stopping once more at Okinawa on the way. Landing in Liuchow, the ceiling closed in, and he spent his first night in a tent pitched on a mud flat.

The starvation [he wrote his father] and the squalor, and the misery that I saw there were equal to any similar sight I have ever seen anywhere. Some French missionary gave me a portion of his matting placed on the ground to sleep on, and this was part of a shack where he and other emaciated people who were still able to walk, would pick up the dying people in the streets and bring them into this wall-less structure so that the rain would not fall directly on them, and as soon as one died, the body was taken out and a new body, still living, given the vacated place.

There was excitement in Kunming when the following message was received at Chihkiang:

C-46 Pilot Sandegs #7938, departed Yontan Strip, Okinawa for Foochow, ETA 220348 Zebra. This plane feared lost. Archbishop Spellman aboard. Pass to Theater Hqs. Military Attaché, Army and Navy Commanders. Urgent. 28 September.

The missing C-46 referred to had wandered some 200 miles off its course in Central China for two and one-half hours with the gas supply running dangerously low, but was located subsequently and shepherded back to safety at Liuchow. Here His Excellency was the house guest of Lieutenant General Albert C. Wedemeyer and was entertained by Archbishop Yu Pin of Nanking, who introduced him to all the bishops of Free China gathered there to greet him. Chiang Kai-shek showed him every courtesy during his stay of two days and promised to rehabilitate the German missionaries.

Kunming was the only stop on the way to Calcutta, which was reached on September 26. The plan of the Military Vicar was to remain only a few hours and proceed by the same plane, but Chaplain Patrick E. Nolan of St. Augustine, Florida, had plans of his own. Said he, "We have waited three years for Your Excellency and have scheduled two and a half days of hospitality. You can't disappoint the men." With incredible courtesy, the passengers on the plane agreed to wait over in Calcutta, so the Vicar bowed gracefully to the obvious will of God and Chaplain Nolan. In one hospital there was a touching picture he never forgot. Two victims of polio were in adjoining rooms. One was a non-Catholic aviator who had volunteered to bring back a Catholic boy stricken in the jungle with the dread disease. Now the rescued soldier was on the road to recovery and the Good Samaritan was breathing his last.

The Archbishop's staccato account in the diary of his usual breathless round of duties is less revealing than the following letter from a staff sergeant to his parents:

I never saw a man with more junk than Archbishop Spellman had with him. He had two suitcases full of files, papers, pictures, speeches and stories. And truthfully, I don't think he knew where a single thing was, or where he could lay his hands on anything he wanted. He didn't even want to attempt to clean it up either. One of the suitcases couldn't be opened because he had lost the key to the lock. We called up the Base Utilities and one of the guys came over and fixed it for him. All this pleased the Archbishop very much. After a while we started to work.

He asked me to mail back to St. Patrick's Cathedral in New York a lot of the souvenirs and gifts he had picked up all along the route from the Philippines up to Japan and down to China and at last to Calcutta. Included was a present from General Chiang Kai-shek. . . . The Archbishop is giving the dedication speech at the opening of the Al Smith Memorial in New York on October 4th, and we worked up his speech for that occasion yesterday morning. He wouldn't have had time to work it up if he had waited until he arrived home back in the States.

It was well past noon when we finished, and he said if I wasn't doing anything later he would like me to come back in the evening to take care of some more of his unfinished work. . . .

I came back last night after knocking the speech for the dedication out on the typewriter all afternoon. Before we started to work the Archbishop suggested that we raid the refrigerator downstairs. (Only the generals have them.) . . . So after bringing back some ice in a bowl plus some charged water and coke, we set to work. That continued until close to midnight, after which we called it a day. I said goodnight to him, and he told me that he was going to read for several more hours before hitting the sack. After the strenuous day he had had, I couldn't imagine why he wanted to stay up another minute.[2]

By way of relaxation, he flew all the next night to Karachi, said Mass for the troops, saw the chaplains, flew all day to Cairo, and the next night on to Rome. The diary records laconically enough: "His Holiness told me about Consistory plans and we discussed other matters." Twenty-four hours in Paris was time enough to call on Cardinal Suhard and the Apostolic Nuncio, bless some trucks leaving for Germany, confer at length with General Larkin and Father Edward Swanstrom about war relief services, and give a dinner for all the chaplains in the metropolitan area. At the Azores, the Archbishop discovered that he was more expendable than a general when he was allowed to proceed in weather that was not considered safe for a distinguished military figure, and the diary records for October 3: "Arrived in New York at 3:00 A.M. Did not go to bed but worked on speech for Al Smith banquet."

Thus his first trip around the world, like his travels in the Near East and Africa, had been in the role of Military Vicar chiefly concerned with the welfare of his chaplains and the religious progress of Catholics in the service. But his interest in the missionaries who were constantly crossing his path, while secondary, became deeper with each contact. His Excellency wrote that his visits to the missions were "an absorbing interlude in the course of my visits to the soldiers. These missionaries are soldiers also, soldiers whose term of enlistment never ends. They are never mustered out of service because of age, sickness or injury; their battles are continuous on all fronts, in all parts of the world." He was impressed by the men themselves, by the work that they were doing for God, and by the effect they had on the military personnel. The boys in uniform were often inclined to self-pity on finding themselves "stuck in this hole for six months," until they met a man who had stuck himself in the same hole for life and was happy in his vocation. It was, however, on the Vicar's next trip to the Pacific which he took in the role of Cardinal Archbishop that the latent missionary in him fully emerged.

An invitation had come from the venerable Archbishop of Melbourne, the Most Reverend Daniel Mannix, to help him celebrate the centenary of his archdiocese and of the establishment of the hierarchy in Australia. This was the patriot whose heroism in the cause of Irish freedom had been front-page news in the early twenties, but regard for a great prelate was only one motive which moved the Cardinal to accept. He was like an explorer who had scaled all but one peak. He had never been to Tasmania, and the sands of life were running out. So he assembled a retinue of associates and friends whose stamina might stand up under the test and left for "down under" on April 23, 1948. The fifteen members of the party represented ten dioceses and included Archbishop Gerald T. Bergan of Omaha, Bishop Michael Browne of Galway, Ireland, and Bishop James A. Walsh of Maryknoll, who was to remain in China, eventually as a prisoner of the communists.

They were welcomed in Sydney by the charming and democratic Norman Cardinal Gilroy, Archbishop Giovanni Panico, the Apostolic Delegate, and by Premier James McGirr. Thus began a round of Pontifical Masses, concerts, cornerstones, teas and sermons and speeches that took them to Canberra, Melbourne, Hobart, and Brisbane as the guests of prelates, prime ministers, governors, and lord mayors. There was also a brief but most successful trip to Auckland and Wellington which publicized the Church's anti-communism and increased its prestige in predominantly Protestant New Zealand.

May 18 might have been the end of the trip and of several interesting careers. Flying from Brisbane to Darwin, they arrived at Camooweal in the sheep country. As they tried for a landing, the brakes failed them, and before the plane could be halted it had demolished a frame building and sliced an automobile in two. Once more His Eminence had brushed the fringes of eternity. In arranging for space on a replacement plane, a question of surplus weight arose, and Monsignor Quinn suggested that they jettison the bag that contained the speeches since that was their heaviest possession.

Someone with a passion for statistics counted in just seven days out of the month-long visit, thirty-two addresses for His Eminence and fifty for Monsignor Fulton J. Sheen, a professor at Catholic University, who was being groomed by the Cardinal for higher things. In a letter home, His Eminence wrote:

> The speeches here are outnumbered only by the number of times a person is expected to eat. There is breakfast—there is morning tea—there is lunch—there is afternoon tea and then there is just tea, at six o'clock and then before one goes to bed, one has supper, which consists only of cold meat, salads, desserts, cheese, crackers and an assortment of beverages, including tea. . . .
>
> I have been obliged to write a number of new speeches because, unfortunately, all those that I have given have been published in their entirety in all the papers in Australia as well as broadcast every time. Even Monsignor Sheen has been obliged to recite Mary Dixon Thayer's poem to Our Lady twice, and it was mentioned in the paper for that reason that

it must be "clearly a favourite of Monsignor Sheen for he recited it in his speech at the laity reception at Xavier College on Sunday, May 2, and again at the end of his Holy Hour sermon at St. Francis' Church on Thursday, May 6." So I have to be extremely careful what I say in this part of "a sin-shackled God-hating world." And all Australia seems now to be very conscious "that discord, disunity and disloyalty breed war." Certainly they are all aware that I am against Communism and they are also aware that "Archbishop Mannix has led a life full of mercy deeds." Despite my valiseful of speeches and sermons, I have been so hard-pressed that I spent many hours that I should have spent in sleep writing some verses for the close of the Centenary. On Saturday night Msgr. Quinn read it and thought it was too long, and I agreed with him. . . . Msgr. Quinn and Father Killian have told me that on two occasions I spoke too long, and Msgr. Quinn even emphasized it by saying I was all right for the first hour—as if I ever spoke that long!

It is significant that Cardinal Spellman, who was always so aware that glamour was not one of his many gifts, never hesitated to risk comparison with the most popular ecclesiastical orator of the day and could report with a smile:

> The only uneven bias manifested thus far was that Monsignor Sheen had three fat wreaths hung around his neck in Honolulu while mine was adorned with only one delicate one. But I am still ahead of him in Indian tribal headdresses and I think, too, in moccasins.

No personal humility, however, prevented him from demanding the honor due to his rank as a Prince of the Church, and when a public official committed a *faux pas*, it was not to be overlooked.

> I had been invited [he wrote home] to call on the Governor of Tasmania and would have been glad to do so, as I did in Melbourne, but since the Governor of Victoria put in the paper that he had sent his Aide-de-camp, Major Campbell, to return the call I made on him, I decided I would not call on any more Governors unless they returned my call, so with that proviso I went to call on Admiral Binnie, the Governor of Tasmania.

The original plan for the group had been to finish with the formalities in Australia and lapse into the role of tourists for a little visit to the missions of China before slipping quietly home again, but on returning to Sydney they found telegrams inviting them to be the guests of the various governors from Batavia and Singapore to Nanking. There was still another from Admiral Badger asking them to include in their itinerary Tsingtao, the headquarters of the Pacific Fleet, and floods of invitations from the Philippines. They were clearly in for another speech or two.

In Batavia and Singapore, their brief stays were spent for the most part with the local gold braid and in Bangkok, the Prime Minister of Siam, Philbun Songkhram, who cabled later to say, "The spiritual comfort derived from conversation with Your Eminence is still vivid in my mind," not only attended the dinner given by the French ambassador in honor of the distinguished visitors, but sent gifts by the Air Marshal of Siam to the plane at 4:30 the next morning. With all their social obligations, however, they had taken time out to make a two-day tour of the main Catholic institutions of Bangkok where they "found that the Faith was prospering in a free atmosphere." Describing a very pleasant dinner he had with the missionaries in the city to celebrate the ninth anniversary of his transfer to New York, the Cardinal wrote home to Whitman:

I cannot refrain from expressing once more my admiration for these men and women and in a special way for the men and women of Maryknoll. I referred to them as the greatest American Mission Order only to have Monsignor Sheen, who followed me on the speaking program, say that he would go farther than that and say that they were the greatest missionary order in the Church. Not wishing to engage in any debates with the redoubtable Monsignor, I decided not to continue the discussion, but the conclusion is that we all think that we shall be fortunate indeed if when the Lord calls us to render an accounting of our stewardship, we may go to the same place as the missionaries.

Flying to Saigon over the famous ruins of Angkor Wat in Cambodia, His Eminence said on his arrival, "We have flown out of our way to come here because of our great admiration for these missionaries, especially in these days when eight priests, three of them French, five Annamites, have been massacred." Later, he wrote to his father: "What feelings come over one meeting these missionaries and realizing that one is associating with men who may be martyrs tomorrow!"

From Saigon it was a five-hour flight to Canton. Here they were entertained with lavish Chinese hospitality, but His Eminence could not get the missionaries out of his mind.

All China [he wrote] has suffered from the war, and the missionaries —men and women—despite their stout hearts and extraordinary graces, their indefatigable zeal and unquenchable ardor for souls, nevertheless show signs of malnutrition and other sufferings. And incidentally I am going home broke but nevertheless happy because at least for a few days I have been able to do some little favors for the men and women who are in the front trenches of Christ's Army.

In Hong Kong, next on the schedule, the party was entertained by the Governor, Sir Alexander Grantham, and Lady Grantham. There were "the usual visits to the institutions, including the Salesian Fathers who in every place we visit are doing remarkable work with boys. . . . I have helped them a little in every city I visited and, in fact, every community I visited I have helped a little and when you think that on an average I visit ten different institutions a day and make an average of six or seven talks a day, you can see that I am busy." A flying boat took him off for a day's excursion to Macao where the Portuguese governor and the bishop wanted him to see every church in the city. He begged off, however, pleading that he had not seen all the churches in New York after nine years there and did not think it was necessary in nine hours to see everything in Macao.

From Hong Kong, the party flew to Manila where, after two receptions, they were just in time for a state dinner of fifty-eight covers given by President Quirino in the Malacañang Palace. The president had just moved in himself after the ravages of war had been repaired and the Cardinal, who was his first guest, sized him up as "a genial character despite the excruciating humiliations and sufferings that he has endured through the years of occupation and I think that he is a very spiritual man and also of sufficient strength of character to be a leader if he can conserve his health."

The next morning, after Mass at the Convent of the Good Shepherd, His Eminence found that he was expected to visit the Hospital of the Philippine Veterans and be at the American Embassy by 10:30. He compromised by spending three and a half hours with 1360 soldiers and remarked that "the poor fellows seemed to appreciate it." One, a Mohammedan Moro, kissed his ring and later explained to his surprised companions in the ward, "That is all right. He is a man of God. He belongs to us too." Meanwhile, His Eminence had called at the Embassy, had met the mayor at City Hall, and had gone to lunch with the chaplains in the Army Headquarters at the Philippine University Area. His fourth speech of the day was made at the Tala Leprosarium where, as he said, he was "privileged" to give Benediction for the ambulatory lepers. Among them was Mrs. Josefina Guerrero who had performed valued intelligence service for the United States Army with great danger to herself. Already dear to her own countrymen, she was decorated that very day by the United States government. On the way back to Manila, he stopped at Novaliches to see the Jesuit novices, sixty-eight young Filipinos, made another address at Army headquarters to the personnel of the station and wound up in the evening with a dinner for the Philippine bishops at Archbishop O'Doherty's palace.

So it went for two more feverish days and on the thirty-first, the Cardinal and his drooping companions were welcomed in Shanghai by representatives of the government, Archbishop Yu Pin and American consular officials.

The first entire morning was spent in Zi Ka Wei which is under the Jesuits and the Helpers of the Holy Souls. St. Ignatius, the Cathedral, was thronged with people and after Mass, I visited the old folks and the young folks, those who went to school, the deaf and dumb, and all the many different groups cared for by the charity of the priests and the Sisters.

Unusual, too, was a visit to the schools for Russian emigrés, the boys in the charge of the English Jesuits, the girls in the charge of the Irish Sisters of St. Columban. Both priests and sisters had changed from the Latin to the Oriental rite. But the feature of these days in Shanghai which lingered longest in the Cardinal's memory was the invitation to ordain thirteen young Chinese, seven of them Jesuits and six, diocesan seminarians. His Eminence answered that "it would be a great privilege. Native vocations are the barometer whereby we realize the good will of those who hear the Gospel." The ordination was held very early in the morning, with ceremonies beautifully carried out, and pervaded by the haunting consciousness that if China should go communist, these zealous young priests might well be called upon to shed their blood for the Faith.

By nine o'clock, the Americans were on a chartered plane of China National Airways headed for Nanking. At teatime, they went to the house of the premier, a geologist turned statesman, where they got the distinct impression that it is easier to make a politician out of a scholar than a scholar out of a politician. In the evening there was a dinner given by Generalissimo Chiang Kai-shek.

Many thought [wrote the Cardinal] that this was the high point of the trip and it certainly was one of the most extraordinary honors given to us. He was most friendly to me and most frank in discussing China's present problems and China's plight. I had conferred with the American Ambassador and I followed the Ambassador's suggestion in my conversation with President Chiang Kai-shek. The dinner was extraordinarily cordial and both the President and I made speeches.

At a dinner given the next night by the American ambassador, there was another private conversation about conditions in China. They were, apparently, most ominous and all agreed that only through proper and adequate American aid, promptly supplied and efficiently distributed, could there be any hope of avoiding the horrors of Red domination.

The beloved missionaries, however, were not neglected. There was Mass for the California Jesuits who had a college in Nanking and a note that "American organization and American spirit, as well as American money, seemed to have produced an excellent and greatly appreciated institution." Then after breakfast a change of plans and a four-hundred-mile detour took them to Hankow in response to an invitation of a graying, weather-beaten bishop. This was the Most Reverend Edward J. Galvin of Hanyang, founder of St. Columban's Society, who had suggested that seeing the Cardinal would give courage to the poor Catholics who were so close to the enemy. His Eminence wrote afterward:

This city is practically surrounded with Communists and Bishop Galvin had seen his life work impaired and his property destroyed on at least two occasions and yet again he calmly faces the future. We had special permission to land on this field in Hankow which was a military field and from which planes were taking off every few minutes to bring supplies to the beleaguered armies of the Generalissimo. We had Benediction of the Blessed Sacrament and two speeches in the church. The whole town had turned out for the occasion with bands and firecrackers and parades. But we managed to do everything necessary with the help of the American Consul in a little more than one hour. . . .

We left Hankow to fly directly to Peiping where we were met by Cardinal Tien and, I think, the largest crowd to greet us on arrival at any city on our journey. There were bands and people and more parades. Cardinal Tien brought us to his home where we had an opportunity of meeting many good Chinese Bishops, priests and people. There were sixteen Bishops in all. . . .

I think I reached my low point in resistance in Peiping because at the dinner of the Catholic University after seven successive Chinese meals, after excessive heat and excessively little sleep, I was really tired. So the Cardinal and the Mayor were nice enough to let me speak before the end of the dinner so that I could have a little time to myself to prepare the Catholic Family Hour broadcast scheduled for the evening.

Before dawn, the party took off for Tsingtao where Admiral Oscar C. Badger, Commander of the Naval Forces in the Western Pacific, was their host. Again there was but one absorbing topic of conversation.

Admiral Badger spoke for nearly two hours about the situation in China and how vital it is for American interests that Northern China be kept from the Communists. The good in all this ominous portent is that two American military officials, General Barr and Admiral Badger, agree with Ambassador Stewart as to what should be done and Generalissimo Chiang Kai-shek, they believe, agrees with them. I do hope that they can persuade the American people to continue Chinese aid for if they do so, it will be well also for American interests. The Chinese Communists, however, appear most optimistic that they will dominate China within five years.

But meanwhile the visit had not been fruitless.

"He's China's number-one missionary today," said a priest in Peiping about Cardinal Spellman.

"The Cardinal's coming was providential," said another observer. "He personifies qualities that have gained increased prestige for the Church out here during the past decade. His arrival gave an occasion for this favorable sentiment to crystallize and to be expressed in manifestations that have drawn still more attention to the Faith. Where Christians are undergoing persecution by Communists, their morale has been uplifted by the Cardinal's visit."

"People everywhere liked the way the Cardinal and his party came. It was benign. It was modern. He met everybody with a smile. Everywhere he proved his own interest, and stimulated local interest, in the missions and works of charity."

On June 7, arriving in Japan from Tsingtao, His Eminence was greeted by the Apostolic Delegate, the Archbishop of Tokyo and a representative of General MacArthur who told him that the members of his party were all the general's guests during their stay in the city. The favorable impression made on the Cardinal by his host in 1945 was deepened.

The General [he reported later] looked about the same as he did at our last meeting. He has a very efficient organization and all his men seem very devoted to him. He is a great man, a great soldier and a great statesman.

In the forty-eight hours at their disposal, there was time for only two dinners. The MacArthurs gave one and for the other, Major General Charles A. Willoughby was host at the Imperial Hotel. All the highest ranking officers of the American and other armies, together with the members of the Diplomatic Corps, were present with the exception of the Russians. The Russians had accepted General Willoughby's invitation and sent caviar, but changed their minds just a few hours before the dinner. Fortunately, they did not ask to have the caviar returned and the Cardinal rather enjoyed getting so much out of the Soviet Union.

The next morning, June 9, His Eminence had a thirty-minute audience with Emperor Hirohito which started groundless rumors that his object was to discuss the possible conversion of His Imperial Majesty to Catholicism. The fact was, he found the Emperor "very nervous and timid, but things went along pleasantly enough and we talked on subjects of general interest."

I did most of the talking at the interview, which was attended only by Archbishop Marella, Archbishop Bergan, Bishop Walsh and myself. After about twenty minutes I got up to go and thanked the Emperor only to have the interpreter say the Emperor wanted to keep on talking. He talked to Archbishop Bergan and then told Bishop Walsh of the efforts which the Maryknoll Fathers made to stop the war in the very beginning, when the Maryknoll Fathers were the media of communications between the Emperor and President Roosevelt.

A few hours later, the Cardinal and his party were on the plane speeding home to the United States after a fifty-two-day journey that covered 43,000 miles and proved to be a marathon of eloquence. His Eminence wrote to his father: "Two or three of the men have suffered a bit, but I think a week or two at home will put them on their feet again." He admitted that he had been tired out before he left New York, but went on to say that the excitement of the trip had been so relaxing that he was now completely rested. His over-all impressions were summed up at a press conference in Los Angeles.

This trip has made me prouder than ever I have been, (if that be possible) of being an American:

Proud to be a fellow citizen of our military leaders who brought to Japan the most peaceful and orderly occupation the world has ever known, exchanging peace for war, understanding for hate, reconstruction for destruction;

Proud to be brother to our missionaries who left their beloved homeland, America, to bring the message of the gentle Christ to a pagan world, saintly men and women whose lives of sacrifice and hardship can be endured and understood only in the shining light of God's grace;

Proud too of my countrymen for helping to feed the sick and starving, for never in the annals of history has any nation so generously, so selflessly served the suffering as America is doing, as daily she pours out the Gospel measure, full and overflowing, to the misery-ridden peoples of the world.

First in his love among these "misery-ridden peoples" came the heroic men and women he had known in the Philippine Islands. That outpost of Western civilization, Catholic for four long centuries, had suffered greatly from two campaigns, one of conquest and one of liberation. In bloodshed, hunger, and humiliation, the cost had been beyond computing and even the material damage was staggering. In their study of the Church's reconstruction problem, the bishops and religious superiors estimated that it would take forty million dollars to re-establish normal activities on a minimum basis, while the War Damage Corporation admitted that Catholic churches and Church-connected property had suffered to the extent of $125,000,000. About half the churches in the Islands had been destroyed or were in need of major repairs. To meet this crisis, the Philippine hierarchy took immediate action. The Catholic Welfare Organization was established in early 1945 by the then Apostolic Delegate to the Philippines, Archbishop William Piani, and turned over to the bishops in the Islands who elected Archbishop Gabriel M. Reyes of Cebu as chairman of the Administrative Board, with Bishop Constancio Jurgens of Tuguegarao and Bishop Mariano Madriaga of Lingayen as its members. The first executive secretary was the Reverend John F. Hurley, S.J., who had been throughout the war the Jesuit superior of the Philippine Missions.

As far back as his first visit to Manila in 1945, Archbishop Spellman had dedicated himself to this particular cause and on his return home had brought the situation to the attention of the Administrative Board of the hierarchy of the United States and its chairman, the Dominican Archbishop McNicholas of Cincinnati. The board then arranged for the approval by Rome of direct liaison between the two hierarchies of the United States and the Philippines and their two administrative organizations, the National Catholic Welfare Conference and the Catholic Welfare Organization. Thus the Philippine hierarchy would be represented before the United States Government in the matter of their war claims. The Archbishop of New York maintained throughout a close and detailed interest in the deliberations of Congress which culminated in the Philippine Rehabilitation Act of 1946 with its appropriation of $400,000,000. There was special provision in the Act for the war damages sustained by churches of every denomination, but as the total amount represented only a fraction of what the people as a whole had lost, the $400,000,000 had to be prorated. The amount assigned to the churches was further reduced by the decision of the U.S. Philippine War Damage Commission to deduct for depreciation. This meant that ecclesiastical buildings, being in the main much older though not less substantial than commercial buildings, would be credited with less than ten per cent of their replacement value. It was Archbishop Spellman who pointed out to Congress the inequity of the situation and the importance of rebuilding Church property as a step in the control of communism. As a result, in early 1952 another bill was passed, Public Law 303, which was an amendment to the War Claims Act of 1948 and which allowed full replacement costs to compensate for the loss of nonprofit schools, hospitals, and other welfare institutions. The money was to be paid through the liquidation of enemy assets then being held by the American government in lieu of reparations. His Eminence had previously enlisted the help of many prominent citizens requesting Congress to pass the War Claims Act of 1948 which was principally for the benefit of civilian internees and prisoners of war, including all the American priests, brothers and sisters held by the Japanese. In addition, Public Law 303 now provided supplementary benefits for all former American prisoners of war in the Philippines and elsewhere, including Filipinos who had served as part of the armed forces of the United States. In the preparation of the original property claims filed under the Philippine Rehabilitation Act of 1946, the Archbishop of Chicago, His Eminence Samuel Cardinal Stritch, arranged for the American Board of Catholic Missions, of which he was chairman, to contribute a subvention of $50,000 for the services of a competent attorney.

As a result of the fair and objective presentation of the vast damages suffered and of the simple honesty and legitimacy of the petition made by the combined hierarchies of the United States and the Philippines, the Reverend John F. Hurley, S.J., could report to His Eminence that, as of the closing date, March 28, 1955, the Catholic churches, schools, hospitals, and other welfare institutions in the Philippines, as well as certain of their personnel, had received the aggregate sum of $22,966,574 in payment of their several categories of war claims. Father Hurley, in a letter to his Jesuit superiors, wrote in 1953:

> No report, no matter how brief, could omit the absolutely essential part played by Cardinal Spellman. In fact, take the Cardinal out of the picture and the picture disappears. In other words, the Cardinal was a condition *sine qua non* and without his continuous and effective aid, the Church in the Philippines would not have collected a single dollar of the above.

That took care, however, only of those Philippine institutions that were affiliated with corresponding institutions in the United States. To save the others, a new claims bill was introduced into Congress which passed both Houses before the end of July 1956. That His Eminence was not a disinterested spectator seems clear from the following excerpt of a letter dated August 3 and signed by the Most Reverend Egidio Vagnozzi, Titular Archbishop of Myra and Apostolic Nuncio in Manila:

> Without the personal interest and intervention of Your Eminence we could never have hoped to have the Bill introduced and approved. To Your Eminence, to Congressman McCormick, to the N.C.W.C. and all those who contributed in any measure to the passage of the Bill, I wish to convey the undying gratitude of the Philippine Hierarchy, the Filipino people and myself.

Back in New York after his illuminating tour of the East, the Cardinal was proud, as he told the press in Los Angeles, of his country's role in the postwar rehabilitation but admitted to his friends that he was uneasy about the future. Having followed events so closely during the years that began with Pearl Harbor, he did not toward the end expect too much from victory. His speeches during the war reflect a decline from confidence that the outcome would be an enduring peace with justice to the realization that leftists would get in at the end and ensure another war by building up the power of the Soviet. From 1946, then, to 1950 was a period of prayer and watchful waiting.

One pleasant interlude in the growing uncertainty was the inauguration of the Korean Government on August 15, 1948. His Eminence sent a note of congratulation to Syngman Rhee which read: "I was very glad to hear of your election as President of Korea and I wish to offer you my heartiest congratulations. I wish you every success in your new position and promise a prayerful remembrance of you in your work and also for the welfare of the Korean people." And the new President replied: "I have taken great pleasure in appointing Mr. John Myun Chang, one of our eminent Catholic leaders, to head the delegations to the United Nations conferences to be held in Paris in September. I have instructed him to arrange for a visit to the Vatican as my special envoy to His Holiness the Pope. Monsignor Byrne has informed the Vatican and asked for the opening of the way for this good-will mission. I hope this will bring the Korean nation and the Catholic Church even closer in understanding and cooperation."

In the two short years that followed, the United States withdrew its troops from Korea and, to the amazement of the well informed, intimated its indifference to the fate of that critical area so that General Douglas Mac-Arthur could write to the Cardinal: "I am most grateful for the kindly renewal of your invitation to attend this year's Memorial Dinner for that great American, Alfred E. Smith, but the existing tensions in the international sphere foretell to a certainty that next October will see me still at my post of duty here." Ten days after the letter was sent, Korea was invaded by the communists and on June 27, 1950, His Eminence called upon the Catholics of the archdiocese to offer special prayers "on behalf of the unfortunate populace of Korea, which has been so brutally assaulted. In this moment which is one of tragic importance for us and for the whole world, we Americans who believe and trust in God will not lose heart, neither will we be unmindful of the supreme power of prayer." The next month, the Military Vicar was looking for more chaplains:

The Navy [he wrote] was seeking fifty chaplains; the Army, forty; and two hundred new chaplains were needed for all the United States.

From all these facts you can readily understand that we have to face not only an emergency, but a crisis. The Church of New York must gird itself immediately to meet the challenge. No indictment of "Too little and too late!" must be leveled against us, the spiritual shepherds of souls.

After a desperate year of successes and reverses, with communist China definitely in the war, and the papers full of Heartbreak Ridge and the Punch Bowl, a letter came to Madison Avenue from General James A. Van Fleet, dated October 22, 1951. It read:

On behalf of the soldiers of the Eighth Army, now fighting the cause of freedom in Korea, I sincerely extend a cordial invitation to you to come to Korea for a visit.

We are mindful of the fact that the present duties of your office give little or no time for extended activities outside of your diocese. Nevertheless, we know from past experience during the last war, that your interest in the American Forces and those of our Allies, fighting all over the world, were indicative of your great love for them. Your visits on the several battle fronts helped to promote the morale and spiritual life of the soldiers. We know that the families of our soldiers also were especially happy that you were with their loved ones on the battle fronts all over the world. Your warm understanding and fatherly solicitude for the soldiers of all Faiths welded a bond of friendship among the different creeds in our Nation and preached to the whole world a lesson of peace and good will. . . .

General Collins and General Ridgeway will be in Korea on 27 October and I am going to take the liberty of mentioning to them the great good which your visit will accomplish.

The Cardinal's answer was characteristic.

I have your letter of October 22nd and I thank you very much for your invitation to visit the soldiers of the Eighth Army. I consider this invitation a command and I shall be happy to leave New York by Pan American Airlines for Tokyo on December 19th or 20th at the latest in order that I may be in the three most difficult places and as near to the front as possible on Christmas Day. I would much prefer bringing Christmas to our boys in Korea than being in St. Patrick's Cathedral on that day. I shall remain as long as is necessary to visit every combat unit.

I would like to keep this information confidential until the 19th of December if this is possible.

The general's final comment was: "I know of no greater good that can come to the Eighth Army."

During a stop at San Francisco, the Cardinal said to reporters: "I am going out as a priest to see the boys. I am going there to offer Mass, to visit as many troops as possible, to visit as many hospitals as possible. I was there on September 8, 1945. I entered Korea with our troops. Everybody was happy. We thought we had not only victory but peace. Now"—and he paused with a weary half smile—"it's different."

The Cardinal said his first Christmas Mass in the chapel of the I Corps. The second Mass was offered at the Division Headquarters of the First Marine Division. Some three thousand marines, many of them just off the battle lines, attended the Mass and four hundred and fifty of them received Holy Communion. It was nearly noon when he reached the site of his third Mass after a trip by helicopter. Let Father Patrick O'Connor of the Columban Fathers take up the story:

Three thousand men formed an open-air congregation. Many came straight down from the mountainside bunkers and foxholes that form the front line. . . . The setting for this Mass was one of the most impressive that even this war-shadowed land of jagged skylines and poignant memories can offer. The front line was only three thousand yards ahead. The dull roar of artillery sounded intermittently. Behind the altar, covered and shielded by tenting, a gaunt gray ridge towered over the improvised sanctuary. It was Heartbreak Ridge. Today it became Heart-Lift Ridge. This Christmas Mass, the Sacraments, the Cardinal's coming and his words would lift up hearts of men who by late afternoon would be back on the mountain line.

When it became clear that the chaplains would not have time to hear the confessions of all who wished to receive, His Eminence gave general absolution and nearly one thousand men went to Holy Communion. After the Mass, Cardinal Spellman, with General Van Fleet, attended a Christmas dinner with one hundred and sixty-eight enlisted men, men representing all the platoons of one regiment. They were of all denominations and were selected for merit. That afternoon, bad weather forced the Cardinal's party to abandon their copters and take to the jeeps instead. At one point, deep snow and ice made it necessary for His Eminence and General Van Fleet to get out with the rest and push the cars back on the road. By nightfall, conditions made it impossible to continue and the group spent the evening with the Mobile Surgical Hospital of the 7th Division.

On December 28, the Military Vicar went aboard two hospital ships, the *Jutlandia* and the *Repose*, visiting every single wounded boy on board. The next day, the commanding officer of the *Repose* wrote to His Eminence:

> I have had ample opportunity to observe the patients as they lay in their bunks in the hospital, and I say to you in all sincerity; that never have I seen such an "uplift" given any group of men such as you gave them, as you passed through the various wards and had a cheerful word of greeting for every man. . . . You brought Faith, Hope and Love into the hearts of us all.

It was the second rigorous winter our troops had known in Korea. There were no major offensives in progress, just seesaw actions fought for observation with exploratory attacks mostly at night, but the hardship everywhere was great. If morale was low, however, it was not because of the suffering. It was because the international statesmen had their hearts set on a draw, it was because there was a tendency at home to belittle the whole thing as a "police action," and because the boys still found it difficult to understand why they had to suffer to take another ugly brown patch of a country they had never heard of before. It was no mere courtesy, therefore, when General Van Fleet described the visit as "a blessing and an inspiration to all of us in Korea—the soldiers will never forget your visits on the battle fronts that so greatly raised their morale and spiritual welfare." And Major General Lyman L. Lemnitzer wrote: "Your Eminence's presence on our own front lines has brought the hope and renewed confidence that we in Korea enjoy the spiritual backing of our people at home, a thing so essential to every fighting man."

In addition, there were stacks of letters from chaplains, Chinese prisoners of war, privates and American mothers with the usual forwarded "Gee Ma, guess what happened to me" accounts of the Cardinal's visit. The following is typical.

> There was an enormous crowd but I got in a position where I could both see and hear him when he gave his sermon. (It reminded me of the Sermon on the Mount.) Everyone appreciated his giving up Christmas at

home in order to be here. It was bitter cold and I thought his hands must have got awfully cold during the Mass. . . .

He had about ten other priests with him and they were hearing confessions in bushes, trucks and every conceivable object they could find. At the sermon he said that although he had his helpers he wanted to try to give everyone personal Communion, even though it would take considerable time—and it did—but it was an honor I wouldn't have missed for the world. We were all packed in like sardines and slowly in a line edged forward to where he was standing and then knelt down on the ground to receive from him. . . .

I was thankful for the opportunity of seeing him. Sort of sets you at peace.[3]

No priest could read such letters and convince himself that it would be just as apostolic to stay at home for Christmas.

Returning briefly to Japan after an exhausting week in Korea, the Military Vicar made a round of the hospitals and flew to Okinawa and Formosa, arriving on January 5. His time on the island was spent in official calls, ecclesiastical and civil, with dinner the second evening at the home of Chiang Kai-shek. That the time was not wasted appears from the following letters. The superior general of the completely Chinese "Congregation of the Disciples of the Lord" wrote later: "Your visit will give us a new courage, a new comfort, a new hope, a new consciousness that we are not alone, isolated on this island of Taiwan, but that millions of Catholics of America are with us, with their prayers and their help."[4] How consoled the good Father would have been had he known by a revelation that in 1960 there would be 182,-450 Catholics on Taiwan, plus 45,643 under instruction, with 648 priests, 490 sisters and 1029 catechists. The First Lady of Nationalist China was also deeply impressed by the Cardinal's visit:

After your departure from my home this evening [she wrote] I fell to musing over our conversation, mainly on the unprecedented historic role the Mother Church is playing in taking the lead against tyranny and oppression of our God-given freedom and human dignity, and the sensitive heed of the Holy Father in responding to the cries and heartbreaks of his children on China Mainland as well as elsewhere behind the Iron Curtain.

Almost without conscious volition, my hand sought the paint brush. The result is depicted on this small piece of paper, my memory of Ali-Shan, the highest mountain range on Formosa. . . .

Would you be so kind as to deliver it to the Holy Father for me? I should like to have him receive it from you, Cardinal, who have been with us. Will you please tell him that Ali-Shan represents the Mother Church, and the almost invisible houses under the trees, the suffering people of the world who look up to Ali-Shan with hope and faith? . . .

Need I tell you what an immense inspiration your presence is to our people, not only those in Free China, but also those on China Mainland who live in misery and terror under the grounding hoofs of Satan? Your visit brings to us a much-needed assurance that we in our struggle against tremendous odds, both physical and military, are not forgotten and that man lives not by bread alone, not even if augmented by guns when spiritual strength is absent!

Yours cordially,
MAYLING SOONG CHIANG

In Manila, His Eminence conferred with President Quirino, the Apostolic Nuncio, and the Philippine hierarchy, addressed the students at the new Ateneo out in Quezon City and visited the veterans hospitals. January 9 found him in Hong Kong where he had "the privilege" of greeting nine expelled American missionaries as they stumbled across the border from Red China at the Lo Wu railroad station. When the Cardinal offered to arrange for their passports and take them home with him to America, they answered quietly that they had come to the missions for life and if Red China would not take them back, they hoped to serve in some other field afar.

On a previous visit he had been able through the generosity of friends to provide six new centers of missionary activity in the city, consisting each of a chapel, hall, convent, and rectory. This time he had the consolation of baptizing one hundred converts in one center.

After a stop in Calcutta, the Cardinal went on to Delhi and got in a hurried look at the unhurrying Taj Mahal. Later in the day he talked with Prime Minister Nehru for nearly an hour. Questioned by reporters afterward as to what role Christianity would play in the East, he answered: "East or West the role of Christianity is the same—that of promoting the service of God, the love of humanity and the cause of peace." Two days in Rome and on to Rocquencourt in France, the Supreme Headquarters of the Allied Powers in Europe, where he met his old friend, General Eisenhower, for a two-hour conference. The only thing that was not mentioned was politics! Photographers asked him to pose before a militay map in the offices of Brigadier General Anthony J. Drexel Biddle, Deputy Chief of Staff for National Affairs, but the Cardinal declined. "No," he said, "I am interested only in the spiritual aspects of SHAPE, not the military." As he walked over and stood before a large American flag, he added: "Now here is a perfect background." On January 20, the Military Vicar landed at Logan Airport, Boston, concluding a thirty-two-day trip that had covered 28,000 miles. He was just in time to assist Archbishop Cushing in the dedication of Our Lady of the Airways Chapel before leaving for Whitman to visit his father.

Knowing the situation as he did, His Eminence spent the next year trying to awaken the American people to the futility of the peace talks as they were being conducted in Panmunjom. He stressed the inhumanity of returning the prisoners of war to North Korea and death, the stupidity of making further concessions and permitting the communists to build airfields from which to strike, the folly of admitting Russia as a neutral "when her planes and guns are killing our boys." The Red press in the United States commented on his views coldly and scornfully. Moscow, referring to the Christmas visit, said he "blessed with holy water the U.S. flags covered in shame and U.S. arms stained with innocent blood." The communist newspaper *Trybuna* in Warsaw wrote that the Cardinal, while in Korea, "encouraged the American aggressors to continue their bloody exploits," and added: "Shortly after his visit they began to employ bacteriological warfare."

In April his friend General Douglas MacArthur returned from Japan under a White House cloud. The Cardinal, regarding him as the greatest American living, was embarrassed by an unfortunate column which appeared in *Osservatore Romano* taking sides and sharply criticizing the dismissed general. It had to be pointed out that Count Bernucci was only a columnist and spoke for no one but himself, least of all for His Holiness the Pope. When the parade of welcome passed St. Patrick's Cathedral, the General left his car and greeted His Eminence on the steps, a gesture that irritated the representatives of the leftist press, and later when the Veterans of Foreign Wars invited Cardinal Spellman to ride with General MacArthur at the head of the Loyalty Day Parade, there was a Protestant outburst demanding that the Right Reverend Horace W. B. Donegan, Episcopal Bishop of New York, should also have a place in the car. It ended by the Cardinal suggesting that the two churchmen march on foot with a Negro clergyman between them.

To the surprise of no one who knew the Military Vicar, the New York chancery office issued the following statement on December 5, 1952:

> As last year, I am going to Korea to celebrate Mass in three different sectors of the front on Christmas Day and in other sectors during the rest of the eight days which I shall spend in Korea.
>
> While I will be leaving my own New York during this holy season, I am sure that all will understand that the very spirit of Christmas demands that I bring solace and spiritual comfort to America's brave, beloved soldiers on far-flung battle fields.

Messages poured in from the top ranks of the military that echoed the wire of President Syngman Rhee: "We assure you that the entire nation heartily welcomes your visit."

His Eminence began the trip to Korea on December 18.

> I am going to Korea bearing messages of love from hundreds of American families. I am bringing with us manifestations of the love of the people of America for their loved ones in the form of 100,000,000 cigarettes, 50,000 religious medals and 15,000 holy cards. These are symbols of the unity of the folks back home. I am going to Korea even though

it is a sad place. Nevertheless, I shall be happy there because I shall be with our American soldiers. I hope you in America have a happier Christmas knowing that I shall be with your sons.

For the Midnight Mass on Christmas, the Military Vicar was at Headquarters, I Corps, with artillery fire rumbling in the distance. His second Mass was with the First Marine Division at an altar erected in the open air. Of the 2500 marines who attended the Mass, 750 received Communion. His third Mass, said in the afternoon, was for 800 men of the Second Division. When he sat down to Christmas dinner afterward, it was the first time he had eaten since the previous evening. During the eight days of his Korean visit, the Cardinal addressed an estimated 30,000 men; shook hands with 22,000; gave thirty talks, mostly in the open; visited every United States division, two Korean divisions and eight hospitals. He spent a day with the Navy and Air Force and met chaplains of all branches of the service, Korean bishops, priests, foreign missionaries, sisters, orphans, and prisoners of war. During his stay in the combat zone, His Eminence celebrated Mass twelve times for servicemen and took the names of seven thousand to whose relatives he wrote. The mail bags flying home were full of letters like this from the Air Force Base in Taegu.

> The day before a U.S.O. show had been here in the same place. Rory Calhoun, Debbie Reynolds, etc., but this little man with nothing but a wrinkled paper in his pocket made far more impression on the boys than anyone else. I was so proud he had come, and prouder still I had met him.[5]

On the way home, His Eminence stopped at rain-sodden Beirut on January 11. As he trudged through the mud to visit hut after hut of Arab DPs, he declared that he had never seen such misery, even in China. Leaving the Lebanese capital at four-thirty in the morning, he traveled by the *Comet*, a jet airliner, and reached Rome just in time for the consistory at which his former chancellor, James Francis Cardinal McIntyre, was raised to the Sacred Purple. Questioned by reporters upon his return to New York, the Cardinal told them: "My final reaction to the world picture is one of bafflement because I can see no end to the present situation."

Hence it was a source of special consolation to read in the report of the Military Ordinariate for 1952 that 1030 commissioned chaplains had administered 23,000 baptisms in one year. This compared with 19,795 baptisms administered by the 3085 chaplains of 1945. The small corps had also performed 8000 marriages and assisted 800 ex-servicemen to enter a seminary or novitiate.[6]

Before the next Christmas came around, the fighting had ceased, but the problem of morale had become more acute with time hanging heavy on the soldiers' hands, no visitors and no shows of the U.S.O., so the Cardinal announced that he was going to Korea again. Everything now was better organized, quarters were more comfortable, traveling safer than in the bitter winter of '52, but the novelty was gone forever and for ordinary men, constant repetition creates a chore. Still His Eminence went to Korea year after year, and he was not getting any younger though his secretaries preferred to have one of his doctor-brothers tell him that. When they did, he listened to them both very dutifully and decided by way of compromise that before the journey of '55, he would make a two-week visit to the Northeast Air Command in Greenland as a kind of trial run to see if he was in condition. Flying 7000 miles in five days with Lieutenant General Glenn O. Barcus of the Northeast Command, he was within 800 miles of the North Pole. The temperature was averaging thirty degrees below zero and the traveler learned that in a thirty-mile gale human flesh freezes in thirty seconds. But he saw all his chaplains and blessed all his boys and was back in New York on December 10 with six days to prepare for the Far East.

The following Friday, His Eminence was off again to Alaska leaving many head-shakers behind him. From Anchorage he wrote triumphantly:

> I wish that some of those who were opposed to my Christmas trip to the Far East could have stood by my side as I greeted the people, and at least one in every ten persons said, "Thank you very much for coming." I do not know how many in New York, as I greeted them after Midnight Mass at Christmas, would have commented, "Thank you very much for staying at home."

In Japan he dedicated the first parish church in the country under the patronage of St. Patrick as he had done the previous year in Seoul and flew around Fujiyama in an Air Force jet. He was delighted with everything and wrote to his secretary, Monsignor John M. Fleming:

> I had to put on just as much apparatus as I wore at the time I was catapulted from the deck of the *Wisconsin* with the exception of the survivor suit. . . . Lieutenant Colonel Allen McDonald let me fly the ship for about ten minutes and its flight is so smooth and its response so easy that even a bird could not enjoy flying as much as we did. We had a large crowd of people at the take-off and on our welcome back to the field.

Describing the Christmas Masses, he said: "As usual, I was supremely happy offering the Holy Sacrifice of the Mass with these defenders of our country and for our country's life and world peace. . . . This day in my life was as hard and as compact and as fatiguing as any day that I can recall." And then after describing twelve hours of activity without a break, he concluded: "It is amazing how well acquainted one can be in such short time with people. Just so far on this trip I have met at least forty people whose association and companionship I enjoyed immensely."

This was nothing, however, compared with the thousands who felt they had met him and had "enjoyed the experience immensely." In a letter from Saigon, dated January 16, 1956, Monsignor Joseph J. Harnett wrote to Monsignor, later Bishop, Edward E. Swanstrom, director of the War Relief Services:

The Cardinal arrived as scheduled on the afternoon of January 5th, and was received at the airport by a formal reception committee and by practically every important personality in the city; but most important of all were the 10,000 refugees who came to the airport to greet him. The Cardinal won all their hearts immediately by walking around among them, giving them his blessing and smiling very benevolently on them. On the way in from the airport, the streets were lined with people who had come out to see the Cardinal with welcome banners. The crowds along the way were increased many times when the Cardinal got out of the car to walk in front of it in order that the people might have a chance to see him and that he might have a chance to give them his blessing. I'm sure he walked at least a mile and perhaps a mile and a half to the Cathedral of Saigon where he was welcomed by the Bishop and by another crowd that overflowed the Square in front of the Cathedral. After the prayers before the high altar, another reception ceremony was held in the Square itself with the usual speeches of welcome, et cetera. The Cardinal once more walked all around among the people, giving them his blessing and giving them a chance to see him closeup. It was a wonderful reception ceremony and the people were entirely thrilled by the whole thing.

. . . Everywhere the Cardinal went, he won everyone and I am sure that in the 2-½ days that he was here, he saw and was seen by at least two hundred thousand people. Within two hours after his arrival, probably 20,000 people saw him, although the newspapers estimate the number at 50,000.

At the Mass that was celebrated for the refugees the next evening at the "Enwah", there were at least 30,000 and possibly 40,000 people present for it. During the visit of the Cardinal to the Shrine of the Blessed Mother at La-Vang, and to Hué, many many more thousands of people saw him and received his blessing.

. . . The people here, Catholics, Buddhists and those who practice no religion at all, have become very devoted to him and certainly regard him as one of Vietnam's most important and most devoted friends. . . .

It was extraordinary that so many far off lands had come to realize that this prelate from America who could not speak their language and saw them so briefly on his world-round flights was really very close to them.

The previous October, for example, the Korean Government had honored the Cardinal by erecting a stone monument with a long and complimentary inscription in front of the new rehabilitation center for blind Korean veterans. "They gave me a gift," he wrote later, referring to a visit with the Syngman Rhees at Pusan, "and I gave them $10,000 for the institute they established last year in my name for blind soldiers. They wanted me to visit it but that was impossible so I said I would do it next year—if next year comes."

It came and there is every reason to believe that many more years will follow it. In any one of them, Francis Cardinal Spellman as Military Vicar will be aptly described as he was at the Pentagon on June 30, 1947, when Secretary of War Robert P. Patterson presented him with the Medal of Merit "in accordance with the order issued by General George Washington at his headquarters in Newburgh, New York, on August 7, 1782, and pursuant to an Act of Congress, . . . for extraordinary fidelity and exceptionally meritorious conduct." The citation read in part:

> His services have been characterized at all times by his magnanimous spirit, his eminent wisdom, his ecclesiastical statesmanship, diplomacy, and high patriotism. As a representative of American Catholicism, Cardinal Spellman brought encouragement and high inspiration, first to the chaplains, then to all military personnel, including the high command, wherever he went.

CHAPTER TWENTY-ONE

Because He Wanted To

W E HAVE seen Cardinal Spellman on his rounds of duty in the arch-diocese. We have seen him in all parts of the world dutifully raising the morale of the boys in the armed forces. Is his life just one duty after another? Doesn't he do anything merely because he wants to? A man who thinks nothing of working eighteen hours a day; who says with a grin, "I don't get to bed very early so instead of saying night prayers I say my morning prayers twice!" ought to be able to fit in a few private activities here and there. What does he do with his free time? For one thing, he writes.

In high school he won prizes for his essays. In college he was on the staff of the Fordham *Monthly*. As a young priest he wrote for the *Pilot*, the diocesan paper of Boston, and translated two of Borgongini-Duca's popular spiritual books. *The Word of God*, published in 1921, had an introduction by the Apostolic Delegate, the Most Reverend John Bonzano, who praised "the literary craftsmanship of Father Spellman." This was the beginning of an important friendship. Thirty-five years later, a new illustrated edition was announced. In 1924, *In the Footsteps of the Master* appeared and this time Cardinal O'Connell wrote an introductory letter in which he wished the volume "every success and a large circle of readers." The work was well received and ran into two editions.

During his seven years in Rome, there was little opportunity for anything but diaries, letters, and an occasional sermon, but even after the return to Boston brought a little more leisure, the Muse was still silent. In 1937, Macmillan tried to interest him in doing the life of Pope Pius XI, but no one knew better than he the difficulties involved in writing the biography of a distinguished living prelate and nothing came of it.

It was not, in fact, until 1942, three years after his elevation to the See of New York, that Archbishop Spellman compiled his first original book. At that time he would have been busy enough without a war on his hands. The tangible mechanics of his great archdiocese were more than an ordinary person could handle with efficiency and there were many intangible elements in the picture that eluded even the *Catholic Directory*. For example, the fact that New York is the leading metropolis of the New World, that its streets are better known on the fringes of civilization than the names of most other American cities, and that every distinguished visitor to the Western Hemisphere winds up sooner or later at Rockefeller Center, has created a special burden for the Archbishop which is none the lighter for being unofficial. So that even if all the world were at peace, no one would have been surprised if he had confined himself to interviews, extemporaneous talks, and an occasional sermon or address. Now, however, the war had come to complicate still further his life and his work. A tremendous Army and Navy had been recruited, a consoling proportion of the fighting forces was Catholic, as usual, and the grave responsibility of caring for their spiritual needs had fallen on the Archbishop of New York. His pace was incredible, using up aides and hosts, generals, monsignori and auxiliary bishops as the riders of the Pony Express used to use up relays of fast horses. No one just then could have thought of a more humorous remark than to say that the Archbishop was writing a book. But he was. He was creating time at the end of crowded and tired days to write patriotic addresses and sermons as well as long, interesting letters home to his father, which were soon destined to become the chapters of a gripping narrative. In fact, during three years of wartime activity, he wrote three books.

The first, *The Road to Victory*, was an interpretation of the war in terms of our Catholic Faith. The tone was the tone of the pulpit, the matter, eternal truths applied to temporary disorder and presented with reverence and dignity. The nucleus of the volume was a baccalaureate address which the Archbishop had delivered at West Point, May 27, 1942, on the two victories to be won in "the battle of life and the battle for your country's life." It appeared afterward in the *Congressional Record* and one of the ten thousand reprints came to the desk of Gertrude Algase, the successful literary agent of Monsignor Fulton J. Sheen. It was she who persuaded His Excellency to expand these ideas of victory into a book with the addition of other addresses and sermons. Thus began the Archbishop's second creative period. It was to bear fruit in a shelf of slender volumes, and a shower of royalties poured into the coffers of various charitable and educational organizations over a million dollars.

The second book of this period, *Action This Day*, was an immensely interesting piece of reporting, written exactly as the Archbishop talks. God had given him an extraordinarily observant eye and a prodigious memory, both of which were conspicuous in this series of intimate and natural letters. Of course, the account is not complete to the last detail and several fascinating books could be written on the material which was not emphasized. Thus, of his talk with Generalissimo Franco he says only, "We covered a great deal of territory"; of his two talks with De Gaulle, "We discussed the tragedy of France"; of his historic meeting with Pope Pius XII, "I was with His Holiness about two hours." Still the book is filled with incidents of great historic importance, related with the simplicity and objectivity of one who has been watching history in the making for many years and has taken a hand in it himself more than once.

The third book published in rapid succession, *The Risen Soldier,* was entirely different from the other two. If the first was a sermon, and the second good conversation, the third was a lyric. The Archbishop did not rise to conscious verse until the end, but the mood throughout was one of highly personalized emotion springing from an experience referred to in *Action This Day.* It happened that one evening, His Excellency, somewhere in England, blessed a group of American boys who were setting out on a bombing mission and then waited "on the windswept airstrip" for their return. Some were missing when the count was made and, meditating on their sacrifice, the author was reminded of another Warrior's eternal and triumphant sacrifice. Such is the tone of the prose that one hardly adverts to the change when blank verse at the end leads up to this:

> *And if it be*
> *My blood should mingle reverently with Christ's,*
> *His Son's, in this my final missioning,*
> *Shall I not whisper with my dying breath—*
> *"Lord, it is sweet to die—as it were good*
> *To live, to strive—for these United States, . . .*

These three little volumes, signed "Francis J. Spellman," did much at this critical time not only to inform and console our own people, but to strengthen the confidence of the whole country, for thousands of readers who never met him formed of the author the same impression that the author formed of Winston Churchill, "He follows Socrates' 'Know Thyself.' He also knows the world. He has 'gone places.'"

A few cold statistics are significant enough to be included in the record. Published in October by Scribner's, 19,000 copies of *The Road to Victory* were sold the first month and by February, the number had risen to more than a quarter of a million. This total included a paper-back edition of fifty thousand, sponsored by Major Edward Bowes, who sent them to editors, clergymen, public libraries, and educational institutions, and also a special military edition distributed among the armed forces by the National Headquarters of the Holy Name Society. Three thousand copies were sent to His Eminence, Arthur Cardinal Hinsley, Archbishop of Westminster, to be sold in the interests of British War Charities. *Action This Day* was first sold to *Collier's* magazine and nine months later published by Scribner's. When *The Risen Soldier* was ready, *Collier's* again asked for the pre-publication rights and Scribner's first printing was forty thousand copies. It was received by reviewers with unusual enthusiasm and the file of letters from tail gunners and chaplains and mothers whose boys never came back was ample reward to an Archbishop who stole time out of the middle of the night to write it. As a film possibility, it was brought to the attention of Louis B. Mayer of

Metro-Goldwyn-Mayer in Hollywood and the diary for May 9, 1944 records: "Gave Mr. Mayer through Miss Algase and Mr. McGuinness 60-day option on film rights of *Risen Soldier*." This option they exercised, paying $50,000, the only time this high price was ever paid for a story in verse of about ten thousand words. The script was to be prepared by Cyril Hume who wrote on November 2:

> Naturally I am more than happy that you like so well the shape that *The Risen Soldier* has taken. However you need not fear that you have unduly puffed up my vanity. The splendid power of your basic conception, together with the beauty of the New Testament narratives made it inevitable, in the hands of any competent writer, that something exceptionally fine would result.

Two months later, James K. McGuinness advised him:

> We have forwarded to you by air mail today two copies of the script of "The Risen Soldier" for you to read at your convenience. . . . Enthusiasm for the script is extraordinarily high among those who have read it here, two of the most enthusiastic here being Leo McCarey and John Ford, who are two of the finest directors in motion pictures.

About the same time, Mr. Mayer expressed his own high hopes:

> Since reading your comment on the treatment and development of "The Risen Soldier," as explained by Mr. Reid, I am more hopeful and confident than ever that we can give to the world an unparalleled story of hope, love of country and faith in God. Such a story could only come from one inspired and with an intellect capable of analyzing the deepest of human emotions, and a heart that beat in perfect sympathy for the distressed soul.

The following September, however, the *Catholic Register* of Denver charged that the Hollywood producers were scrapping a number of films with a religious background, convinced that the public was in a mood to appreciate nothing but "escape" and "light" themes. It was reported that in consequence the filming of *The Risen Soldier* had been "retarded." This proved to be an understatement. "When the devil was sick, the devil a monk would be," but now the war was practically over. The film rights and the finished script were returned to the author. The picture was never made.

Meanwhile, a fourth volume had appeared in July 1945. Like *Action This Day*, it was a collection of letters describing, this time, his second visit to the armed forces, entitled *No Greater Love—The Story of Our Soldiers*. Once again the author had his reward in the unsolicited letters that poured in from consoled and reassured Americans. A popular weekly with an acknowledged talent for earthy news remarked about this time: "A prolific writer of prose and verse, Archbishop Spellman is also one of the world's highest paid (he gives the money to charities); he has made $250,000 from his writing in the last three years. Last year *Good Housekeeping* paid him the highest price ever paid for a single poem." The reference was to "Our Sleeping Soldiers," seventy-two lines of blank verse, ending on the author's favorite note:

> *They ask for men the just peace they have fought for*
> *The better world that they have died to build.*

On October 5, 1945, the Archbishop noted in his diary: "Dick Berlin decided to buy 'Our Sleeping Soldiers' for $5000. Then he decided to give $10,000. I guess it is the largest sum ever paid for such a work." The following April, Time Incorporated followed suit and gave the Foundling Hospital $2000 for a similar poem, *Resurrection,* published in *Life.* This was also included in a volume of thirty-six pages which appeared at the time of the Great Consistory called *Prayers and Poems,* his fifth publication in as many years. Meanwhile, with the author's elevation to the College of Cardinals, the demand increased and the articles, poems, prayers, introductions, and addresses that flowed from his tireless pen were eagerly sought after. Two prayer books, *Heavenly Father of Children* and *Cardinal Spellman's Prayer Book,* as well as a collection of prayers and poems entitled *What America Means to Me* sold 186,000 copies. These, however, were overshadowed by his first and only novel, *The Foundling.* This has already been described at some length in an earlier chapter.

Thus the ten years that placed him under the greatest strain, spiritually and physically, stimulated his desire and power of expression to an extraordinary degree. Many would have been content to write what he wrote in wartime without doing what he did. In all probability, the inspiration and the unusual response will not be repeated, but writing will certainly be a part of the Cardinal's day.

A more relaxing pastime is the pursuit of a hobby which dates back to his days in the North American College—stamp collecting. As a seminarian, he recognized its historical and cultural value and years later stated in an address to the National Federation of Stamp Clubs in Washington, D.C., that,

> Stamps are miniature documents of human history. They are means by which a country gives sensible expression to its hopes and needs; its beliefs and ideals. They mirror the past and presage the future. They delineate cultural attainments, industrial works, domestic, civil and social life. In a word, these vignettes give a vivid picture of the world, its occupants and their multifarious endeavors.

His collection is well known in the world of philately and has been seen in whole or in part at more than one hundred major exhibits throughout the United States and in seventeen foreign countries as well. Many of the volumes were presented to him by heads of governments on the occasion of significant visits during the war. They are grouped under topics as well as places of origin, like the volumes on "Churches and Cathedrals," and "Saints" and "The Madonna." One series of particular interest was issued by Nicaragua in September 1959. Six stamps bearing the arms or the portrait of the Cardinal commemorate his visit to the country as Papal Legate at the Eucharistic Congress. Another item sent to him by a refugee from Hitler's Germany is one of two which were saved when the Nazis destroyed the edition because of its religious nature. Thus, by means of stamps, His Eminence has integrated history, geography, art, and literature with religion as the central theme. His collection may be classed briefly as a general one with specialized areas in the United States, Vatican City, Monaco, Jahore, Poland, and the Universal Postal Zone. Speaking at the dinner marking one hundred years of American philately in 1947, he said:

> Stamp collectors are an international fraternity whose enthusiasm lags neither in war nor in peace. In their common association many differences are submerged and many potential disagreements held in abeyance while they are made one by their common avocation. Multiplied sufficiently, such pleasurably peaceful human contacts are the ingredients for a leaven of universal accord. And religion, essentially an individual and collective tranquility, is deeply concerned with culture and is profoundly interested in the dissemination of exact historical knowledge. The Irish say, "There is history on our stamps," thinking perhaps of Mulready, a Clare man, the designer of the first postal cover in history. Precisely at this point, philately, which demands concentrated study and presumes a proper knowledge of many fundamentals, does its greatest service as the handmaid of culture. Philately makes us think.

Soon after young Bishop Spellman was appointed pastor of Sacred Heart in Newton Center, he found a studious and interested nun on the faculty of the high school, Sister M. Fidelma, to whom he entrusted the care of his collection. On his appointment to the Archdiocese of New York, he arranged that she should continue to care for his stamps in Regis College, near Boston. Fifteen years later, His Eminence wrote to Mother Euphrasia of Mount St. Joseph Academy:

> I desire to give my stamp collection to the Sisters of St. Joseph in tribute to my aunt, Sister Mary Philomena, for fifty-four years a member of your congregation.
> I further desire to give to the Sisters of St. Joseph the sum of five thousand dollars to establish a fund, the principal and interest of which may be used for the additional purchase of stamps at the discretion of the Rev. Laurence B. Killian, at present Parish Priest of Sacred Heart Church, East Boston. . . .

At this time I wish to express deepest gratitude to Sister Fidelma to whom I entrusted this collection fifteen years ago. Her interest and indefatigable intelligent labors have contributed to make this collection one of the most important private collections in the world.

To the dismay of Sister Fidelma and of all good philatelists, some experienced thieves broke into Regis College in the spring of 1959 and made off with substantial portions of the collection. The stamps were stolen with evident discrimination and their value was estimated at nearly $100,000. No trace has yet been found of thieves or loot. The only consolation that has come to the good nuns has been the news that they are soon to have a new building, the gift of Mabel Gilman Corey, to be known as the Cardinal Spellman Philatelic Museum. This will house also the former treasures of the National Philatelic Museum in Philadelphia as well as several private collections of great value, including the famous Baron Wrangle Collection, unique in the world of stamps, a gift of Monsignor Charles H. Doyle of Ladycliff College, Highland Falls, New York; the Thomas V. Ferrari general collection; and the Edward Nowak Collection of twenty volumes of the world's Polish stamps.

A second interest which his friends profess to find more appropriate in a great administrator is the interest the Cardinal has always had in coins. He has a complete set of every gold dollar ever minted in the United States. It is thought that there are only two such sets in existence. One gem of the collection is a twenty-dollar piece of 1907, a rare type, with high relief wire edge and a sandblast proof. There is only one other known copy and none is found in the Smithsonian Institution.

Such pursuits as these do well enough for that solitary winter evening when the blizzard has canceled an important engagement, but never take the place of travel as the Cardinal's most congenial occupation. From the day he left Whitman to see the sights in the national capital until he arrived back in New York after his latest trip around the world, His Eminence has always been stimulated by faces and places and events, if not by sheer activity and speed. Since 1941, he has had the further satisfaction of spiritual and patriotic accomplishment. The prestige that his office brings to any national or international event and the lubricating influence of his personality have advanced the cause of peace and the salvation of souls, adding meanwhile to the fullness of his life and the zest he finds in living it.

While most seasoned travelers shrink from the regimentation of a pilgrimage, His Eminence has led as many as four of them in five successive years, meeting everybody and going every place as if he were on his first trip abroad. At his table on shipboard, he entertains a dozen different pilgrims at every meal and the sharpest eye has yet to discover a trace of boredom. Every time he appears on deck he is surrounded by autograph-seekers and patiently has his picture taken with every one of them. Whenever the buses leave the hotel to visit "the famous ruins," His Eminence is in the front seat, pointing out all the sights with anecdotes, and this after almost forty years of constant travel.

There was, for example, the Holy Year Pilgrimage of five hundred New Yorkers, the first to leave the United States in 1950. At Fatima, in the pouring rain, the Cardinal read a special poem he had composed for the event. In Malta, this old friend of war days and chaplain of the Knights of Malta in America was given a wild ovation by more than a hundred thousand people when he appeared on a balcony of the governor's palace. In Rome, he celebrated Mass at the high altar in St. Peter's on the seventy-fourth birthday of the Holy Father. There were civic celebrations in Nice and Cannes and the Cardinal's departure from Barcelona was delayed four hours as a crowd of 15,000 with two bands jammed the pier to wish him "Bon Voyage."

The following year, he led three hundred pilgrims to the Canadian shrine of Ste. Anne de Beaupré to offer prayers for peace and in 1952 six hundred from thirty different States to Barcelona for the Eucharistic Congress. There were eighty members of the clergy accompanying him to Spain, including seven archbishops and bishops. At Lisbon, a very characteristic incident occurred. His Eminence was informed on May 23 that his aunt had died, Sister Mary Philomena of the Sisters of St. Joseph. She was the former Katherine Conway, his mother's sister and eighty-five years of age. To the surprise of those who did not know him, he left the pilgrimage at once and took the first available plane for Boston, arriving at five the next morning. After celebrating the Requiem Mass, he went on to New York, rejoining the pilgrims in Spain on May 26. There was no indication that he thought the 7000-mile trip at all unusual.

For the arrival in Barcelona of the Papal Legate, Frederico Cardinal Tedeschini, His Eminence of New York took his place with hundreds of other Americans on some improvised bleachers along the curbstone of the wide and shady Rambla. When the cavalcade of official cars swept by, nearly two hours late, the expression on the faces of the very distinguished occupants as they recognized a Prince of the Church sitting patiently by the wayside, was one of the few amusing incidents of the congress. In the course of the week, Cardinal Spellman gave an address at the university on "The Eucharist and Personal and Family Peace." He was a little nonplussed on arriving at the auditorium to find that two members of the Sacred College had been invited to give the same address at the same hour in the same place. With the wisdom of Solomon, however, the audience was divided and each of the eminent speakers occupied a separate hall. Later in the afternoon, His Eminence presided at a great outdoor rally of employees and employers, offering prayers with them for social peace throughout the world. He was deeply moved one morning, as were 80,000 other pilgrims, by the ordination to the priesthood of 813 deacons from ten nations. Four archbishops and seventeen bishops took their places at twenty-one altars arranged in a circle around the Barcelona Sports Stadium with about forty deacons prostrate before each altar and for more than two hours the silence was broken only by the words of the liturgy. After a state dinner given by Generalissimo Franco and a trip to Majorca for the dedication of a church and a new college, nothing remained but participation in the stupendous last procession and the Benediction which closed the congress.

Three years later, there was a striking example of the good that can be accomplished by an official visit when the Cardinal's party, after the Eucharistic Congress in Rio de Janeiro, stopped over in Uruguay. They had intended to include Argentina in their itinerary, but just at that time, President Peron's attacks on the Church were reaching a climax, so it was decided that Montevideo, in spite of its historic anticlericalism, should be substituted for Buenos Aires. What happened to the anticlericalism in the presence of a tactful Cardinal, who had the twofold handicap of being not only a cleric but a Yankee as well, appears from the following letters:

> Here, he was Official Guest of the country, and was given such a reception as was not accorded to either the then Prince of Wales in 1922, or to Prince Humbert in 1923 when they came here as "Huespedes Oficiales." The *Prince* of the U.S. Catholic Church was received in a princely fashion. . . . The U.S. Ambassador, Mr. McIntosh, outdid himself. He gave at the Embassy one of the greatest receptions I have seen. Present were not only the President and his Council, but also every English-speaking Catholic in Montevideo.[1]

> From every point of view your visit to Montevideo was very successful. Your fame and reputation as an outstanding American and as a great religious leader in the United States had preceded you and had aroused great interest in your visit. It is unnecessary for me to say that you made a wonderful impression upon everyone who had the privilege of coming in contact with you, and this includes people from every station in life. Your visit, I feel, represented a very substantial contribution to the further development of cordial relations and better understanding between the peoples of Uruguay and of the United States.[2]

> The balance of your visit has been of great importance in the public relations of the Church and our leading political forces which, as you know, had kept a very "liberal" attitude towards Catholicism in the last 50 years.
> The magnetic influence of your presence and the extraordinary sympathy aroused by you in all your various actions while in Montevideo, were responsible for many unprecedented changes that took place, including the Presidential luncheon (never before had a Church dignitary been given one) and also the "new look" on the editorials of the leading paper

"El Dia" that used to call the Holy Father, Mr. Pacelli . . . and never wrote God with a capital "G"! . . .

The farewell statements were a true success and everybody was moved. The President and the Archbishop later published your telegrams in their own newspapers.[3]

Like widening circles in a pool, the effects of the visit to Montevideo became more gratifying with time. The following December, President Battle Berres was passing through New York. Although His Eminence was preparing to leave for his Christmas visit to Korea, he was glad to share his few precious moments with him because as he explained, "He had been so generous with the gift of his time to me when I visited Uruguay." That meant two dinners and a luncheon in various places besides the reception at St. Patrick's and dinner in the residence afterward.

In April 1959 a devastating flood left 50,000 people homeless in Uruguay. This brought an urgent cable to the Cardinal from Miguel Páez Vilaro of "Caritas," the Catholic Relief Agency in Montevideo: IF MONSIGNOR SWANSTROM AGREES COULD OFFER DONATION BEHALF CATHOLIC WELFARE DIRECTLY TO PRESIDENT.

This appeal had a history as long as the history of the Catholic Relief Services, N.C.W.C. Under various titles and in various circumstances, this committee, representing the American hierarchy, has been alleviating misery far and near for forty years. The Most Reverend Edward E. Swanstrom, Auxiliary Bishop of New York, is the present Executive Secretary and Cardinal Spellman, though never Episcopal Chairman, has made it one of his favorite extracurricular activities. Thus when the United States began to distribute its surplus foods to needy parts of the world, the government offered to pay the freight charges only to areas on its official list. His Eminence, noting that many destitute missions had been overlooked, authorized a gift to C.R.S. from the Archdiocese of New York of $250,000 to take care of exceptions. The following year, less than half the fund defrayed the ocean freight costs of five and a half million pounds of supplies going to ten countries and led the government to include on its list almost all the mission territories. So that when "Caritas" in Montevideo cabled to Madison Avenue for relief, the Cardinal had only to call on Bishop Swanstrom and assistance was on its way. To the surprise and delight of local Catholics, His Excellency President Martin R. Echegoyen not only accepted the gift (it was the first time in fifty years that the government of Uruguay had acknowledged any help from Catholic sources), but expressed his warm gratitude through press, radio and television. The official communiqué ended with the words: "The President was extremely moved by the generous offer of the Catholic Relief Services. He will cable Cardinal Spellman to express the deep thanks of government and people for his noble attitude."

Early the following year the Consejo Nacional de Gobierno authorized the president to confer the Medalla de la Filanthropia on His Eminence. It was the first time a foreigner had ever been so honored and Señor Páez Vilaro was ecstatic. The presence of President Eisenhower in Montevideo added to the solemnity of the ceremony when the Cardinal's medal was delivered to the Uruguayan ambassador to take with him to Washington and Señor Vilaro wrote:

> Your Eminence can very well imagine how much I was moved by such events in this country of mine, where for 50 years no important official has stepped into a church.

In December 1960 the new president, Benito Nardone, was received in audience by Pope John XXIII, the first Uruguayan chief of state ever to visit the Vatican, and was awarded the Grand Cross of Pius IX. President-elect Haedo who was in the party (they change office every year in Uruguay) called on Antonio Cardinal Barbieri to ask if it would be possible to have a Eucharistic Congress in Montevideo during his term with Cardinal Spellman as the Papal Legate. Uruguay had come a long way in five short years.

On the Feast of All Saints, 1956, the Holy Father wrote to His Eminence: "As Our personal representative you may in Our name and with Our authority preside over the National Eucharistic Congress in the Philippine Islands to be held in Manila." Accompanied therefore by three monsignors and a papal marquis, all New Yorkers, the Cardinal, acting for the first time as a Papal Legate, arrived on the scene November 28 at 6:40 in the morning to be greeted by the Apostolic Nuncio, the Archbishop of Manila, the Most Reverend Chairman of the Congress, a representative of the chief executive, an impressive array of the military, two bands, garlands of flowers, and a nineteen-gun salute. After the usual formalities and speeches, a motorcade proceeded to the Malacañang Palace where he was to be the guest of the late President Ramon Magsaysay for the six short days of his visit. These days were crowded with the impressive religious events that have become traditional on such occasions, interspersed with civic ceremonies, dinners, dedications and receptions. Old-timers smiled with satisfaction when the Papal Legate laid a wreath at the monument of Dr. José P. Rizal. This national hero had been in his day a notorious anticlerical, but before his execution by the Spaniards as a revolutionist he had made his peace with the Church.

Only one thing marred the success of the Congress and that was the tail end of a typhoon. There were lashing winds and torrential rains that almost broke up the first night's meeting in confusion and would have ruined the women's day and even the solemn closing when more than a million Filipinos were present had not the people pulled themselves together after the first panic and bravely faced the elements. The last Pontifical Mass, celebrated at the Luneta, the great park that looks over at Corregidor across the bay, was the occasion of a national event of great importance. President

Magsaysay knelt bareheaded in the pouring rain to read a solemn dedication of the Philippines to the Sacred Heart of Jesus. It was at this Mass too
that the Papal Legate made his principal address. He referred to the terrifying events in Hungary as "the results of apathy and appeasement, procrasti-
nation and compromise, broken promises and unfulfilled pledges," and after
a stinging attack on the Soviet communists as "God-hating, lustful beasts
masquerading as men," besought the people of the Philippines: "Hold fast
to your Faith, for Faith is the one force that communism cannot conquer,
God's miracle which alone can save civilization."

Consoled as he was, however, and thrilled by the warm Faith of the
Philippines, the American in Cardinal Spellman was deeply disturbed by the
bitter criticism of his country that filled the Manila press and found himself
once more acting as a go-between. In a letter to a friend dated December
6, 1956 we read:

> On Monday evening I had a long talk with Mr. Horace Smith at the
> American Embassy. He told me of Mr. Bendetson's intention to return
> to the United States on Thursday, a decision which I thought was a cor-
> rect one as it appeared to me impossible for any just decisions to be made
> in an atmosphere where the papers were continually criticizing the United
> States and Mr. Bendetson.
>
> The climax of all that I read came with a statement by a Philippine
> Congressman named Roces who stated that technicians should be brought
> to the Philippines from European countries because unlike the United
> States the European countries would have no ulterior motive in assisting
> the Philippines. I agreed to talk to President Magsaysay about the situa-
> tion and after a quiet dinner with him, I explained the seriousness of the
> situation and told him that he could have complete confidence in the sin-
> cerity and the ability of Mr. Smith and that after the bitterness of the
> panel discussion had subsided, discussion on a diplomatic level might be
> initiated to solve remaining difficulties. The President seemed impressed
> and agreed to send for Mr. Smith and talk to him personally and pri-
> vately. It would certainly be catastrophic if the Philippines which we have
> twice helped to liberate and for which we have done so much econom-
> ically and in other ways would obligate us to withdraw from the bases
> which we have built at such great cost.

The Papal Legate, after sixteen hours of speeches, receptions, decorations,
ceremonies and processions, caught up with his mail: he was sorry to learn
of the death of Monsignor Barry and Father Reilly; he was pleased that
Mrs. *Blank* was well adjusted to her new life in the Mary Manning Walsh
Home, concerned about Chaplain James J. Killeen who had been injured
in a helicopter accident and would visit him when the party touched at
Honolulu, delighted that Monsignor *Blank's* operation was successful and

thankful to Almighty God that the McCarthy boy was expected to recover from his injuries.

The next day, as Military Vicar, he visited the armed forces in Okinawa, saying Mass for 2500 marines in the open air and making the usual round of the hospitals before flying on to Tokyo in a commercial plane. His first day in Japan, where he was the house guest of General and Mrs. Lyman L. Lemnitzer, he spent with the Air Force, his second with the Navy and his last with the Army. Somehow he found time to baptize the week-old baby of a sailor in Yokosuka before hastening home to gather the babies of the Foundling Hospital around him for their annual party. Christmas he shared with the North East Command. For Midnight Mass he was in Greenland at Thule, "the jumping off place," and afterward flew ten hours to celebrate the afternoon Mass at Goose Bay Air Base in Labrador.

Three years later he was appointed by the newly elected Pope John XXIII to represent His Holiness in Guatemala as Papal Legate to the first Central American Eucharistic Congress. The local situation was delicate and his success was a tribute in about equal measure to his personality and long experience. More illuminating than the notes jotted down by the Legate himself or even his official report to the Holy See is a memorandum written by the United States Ambassador, Lester Mallory, to the State Department in Washington, March 5, 1959. The ambassador is not a Catholic.

> The visit of His Eminence Francis Cardinal Spellman, Archbishop of New York, to Guatemala from February 11 to 15 as Papal Legate to the First Central American Eucharistic Congress probably exerted greater pro-American influence here than any event in recent years. . . .
>
> On his arrival the morning of February 11, the Cardinal was received with pomp and ceremony beyond the normal calls of protocol and courtesy. . . . No personal warmth or sympathy for the Cardinal was involved. On the contrary, many religious persons deplored the Pope's choice of an American as his personal representative, while appreciating his uncommon gesture in sending a Legate to a regional Congress. Highly placed officials admitted to some predisposition against the Cardinal, rooted partly in anti-clericalism, and a mixture of coolness and veiled hostility was palpable when the visit began. It was quickly dissipated. A staunch anti-clerical has stated with feeling that the Cardinal's "humility, goodness and lack of ostentation" won everyone, reflecting credit on the Church and on the United States. . . . It seems apparent that he succeeded at least in prying open some minds long closed to things and persons American. . . .
>
> The reception at the Embassy residence on the night of February 11 led off the social events connected with the Congress. . . . Most of the high visiting church dignitaries attended and the observation has been heard that no better way could have been found to demonstrate the cordial religious coexistence in the United States and the respect accorded Roman

Catholicism there. A local anti-clerical who has attended the Embassy functions for thirty years described the reception as the "best premeditated" and most successful in his experience. He echoed the deep impression made on the Guatemalan guests by the Cardinal's act in leaving the reception line with the Ambassador to go to the kitchen to meet the servants. . . .

At Chichicastenango, Cardinal Spellman descended from his automobile several hundred yards before reaching the church and walked the rest of the distance, preceded by native drums and standard bearers and surrounded by thronging Indians. He blessed them and received their homage with visible emotion. The incense-spewing altars on the church steps; the candles, rose petals and offerings to the dead that fill the central aisle of the church itself; the Indian costumes on processional images of Saints; all the things which so offend the sense of propriety of the local Spanish priest elicited no sign that the Cardinal found them strange or out of place. As he walked to the high altar, as he was invested with ceremonial robes in sight of the congregation, and as he performed the Mass, an emotion was generated that no one present, Catholic or Protestant, was able to choke back. . . .

The Embassy believes that Cardinal Spellman's visit to Guatemala deserves careful study by those concerned specifically with the problem of relations with Latin America. . . . It cannot be too highly recommended that the fullest advantage compatible with dignity be taken of the non-official activities abroad of such figures as Cardinal Spellman who, by force of their personalities and strong convictions as Americans in the service of humanity, contribute greatly to the prestige of the United States and to understanding of its aims and character.

In addition to its effect on local anticlericalism, anti-Americanism, and the little frictions that sometimes exist between Catholic missionaries of various backgrounds and temperaments, between Spaniards, for example, who see paganism in certain Indian customs and Americans who do not, the visit of the Papal Legate was to be a step in the direction of peace between Mexico and Guatemala. In a letter to friends at home His Eminence wrote:

I had two long talks with the President and told him of the desire of the President of Mexico to have peace between the two countries, and I found that President Ydigoras was even more desirous, and anxious to let the past be forgotten. I asked the Papal Nuncio to send a telegram making an appointment for me to see the President of Mexico on the evening of February 20th so that I could convey this message and ask the two parties to come to some new agreement.

So after five days of honors, ceremonies, sunburn, fatigue and immense consolation in Guatemala, His Eminence enjoyed five days of elaborate hospitality in Nicaragua, Honduras, Costa Rica, and El Salvador. At each airport, there was a twenty-one gun salute and distinguished members of the president's party greeted the arriving plane. Formalities completed, a motorcade was formed which proceeded through the principal streets so that thousands of people, freed from business because of a declared holiday, could acclaim His Eminence.

Arrived at the cathedral, he was always greeted warmly by the archbishop and the papal nuncio, before the Te Deum was chanted. A reception followed in the archbishop's residence for the ecclesiastical dignitaries and priests, and afterward there was a second reception at the president's palace, for government officials and prominent citizens. It was usually during the state dinner that His Eminence was presented with the highest decoration of the country. The following morning, he celebrated Mass at the local cathedral, and after breakfast, visited the various Catholic institutions where he often presented generous checks to continue the charitable work. Luncheon was usually held at the home of some prominent Catholic before driving to the airport where the heads of state, other civic officials, and the hierarchy bade a ceremonious but cordial farewell.

In Mexico City His Eminence stopped at the presidential palace to report the peaceful aspirations of President Ydigoras. His host directed that the plane be held during their conference. Everything was very pleasant and augured well for the future, but President López Mateos made no commitment as he said it would be necessary to consult the cabinet.

In addition to Eucharistic Congresses there were so many important and sometimes historic journeys that to preserve proportion only a few words can be given to each. There was the meeting in London in 1950 attended by seven cardinals, twelve archbishops, and forty-six bishops commemorating the restoration of the Catholic hierarchy in England and Wales. His Eminence of New York preached to over 2,250 sisters at a Solemn Pontifical Mass in Westminster Cathedral.

Today, after centuries of brave living, England's little flock of faithful have grown into a multitude, with its Hierarchy re-established and its temples spread over the land. Come again Tyburn or Tower Hill, there shall always be Fishers and Mores, multitudes of them, to bear witness to Christ and His Church.

. . . For myself I will not shirk my bounden duty, nor shall I shield myself with the shield of the cross which I wear upon my breast. And if it comes that I, like Cardinal Mindszenty and the hosts of other dauntless priests, and nuns and people, be crucified for fearlessly practicing my Faith, then with God's grace I am ready—for naught but death can silence me. . . .

Then there was the special journey to Brazil in 1951 to assist at the nation's first celebration of Thanksgiving Day. Surrounded by the pomp of an official welcome in Rio, he recalled his visit of 1938 when, as "Father" Spellman, a young Auxiliary Bishop rode the streetcars and sightseeing buses unrecognized. This time there was a Pan American "Te Deum" in the cathedral, sermons, addresses, luncheons and dinners, decorations and honorary degrees, but in between he managed to do some sightseeing and visit the factories and slums. The same program was repeated in Saõ Paulo. At the moment the communists were working hard for a foothold in Brazil and most of the Cardinal's remarks had some reference to this danger.

The human person [he said at the Governor's Palace in Saõ Paulo] is more than a thing or an animal. He is an individual subject to a moral law that gives direction and purpose to his life—a life which is free, happy and stabilized only when he remains true to his human nature by preserving obedience to this moral law. But a crass and cruel materialism has separated our culture from its religious and moral relationship and robbed us of the creative and life-giving spirit, divorcing the Divine from the human, religion from life and morality from the ways of men and the procedures of government. Disunity and war are the monstrous offspring of this death-dealing dualism and the result is a refined barbarism that eventually drops its mask and we behold the terrors and the tragedies of totalitarian tyranny.

After a week in Brazil, he paid visits of state to Peru, Bolivia, Ecuador, Colombia, and Venezuela. Everywhere the hospitality was lavish. All the United States ambassadors foresaw an improvement of international relations from the impression he made on those in control. The various governments considered it an honor to entertain him. The devout welcomed him as a Prince of the Church, the undevout as a great American. The missionaries were happy that he was both. As one Maryknoller expressed it:

The full results of your visits to these Latin American countries will never fully be known, but you can be sure they brought tremendous benefits—and gave a truly great impetus to the prestige of the Church. Your presence, and the publicity it received, was of special help to all Religious Communities who have come down from the United States. It is surprising how many people in Latin America still think of the U.S. as a pagan and Protestant land where Catholicism is unheard of. This idea is on the wane—and I am sure your visit will have helped to dispel it even more.

The same results followed a visit to Mexico City in 1956 for the funeral of the late Archbishop Luis María Martínez. They were described by Auxiliary Bishop Loras T. Lane of Dubuque in a letter dated March 17:

In conjunction with my attendance at the consecration of Bishop John L. Morkovsky, Auxiliary Bishop of Amarillo, I spent a few days in

Mexico City. It was just after the funeral of the late Archbishop Martínez which Your Eminence had attended. As it is my good fortune to know Spanish, I read the accounts of the funeral in the Mexican papers and talked with many of the people. On all sides there was profound gratitude and appreciation for your kindness and charity in honoring them and their beloved Archbishop by presiding at the funeral rites. Your visit was one of the finest things that has happened in many years for the good of the Church and State in Mexico. It seems that the Church there has taken on new strength as a result. The editorials in the secular papers went to great length in extolling the benefits and recognition conferred upon the Mexican people because of your kindness and consideration.

In February 1956, Ciudad Trujillo was the scene of an International Catholic Cultural Congress for World Peace and Cardinal Spellman was a guest of honor. In response to a complimentary address made by the "Benefactor," General Rafael L. Trujillo, he said: "The Dominican Republic has been among the first to recognize the need for the solidarity of the Americas: the threat to the Americas of World Communism. Perhaps long after your physical achievements have disappeared, you will be remembered for your courage and wisdom in this regard." The following October, when the International Fair of Peace and Friendship was held in San Domingo, the main thoroughfare was named for the Cardinal Archbishop of New York.

All the visits of His Eminence to the Vatican accompanied by two or three ecclesiastics or sometimes alone have been too numerous to be included, but some were too notable not to be. In 1950, for instance, following the dedication of the Lieutenant Joseph P. Kennedy Home for Children, he flew to Rome, arriving unfortunately after the Holy Father had obtained the unanimous approval of thirty-five cardinals and four hundred and ninety patriarchs, archbishops, and bishops to the proclamation of the Assumption of the Blessed Virgin Mary as an Article of Faith. He was present, however, the next day in the great Piazza of St. Peter's when the proclamation was read to seven hundred thousand people.

More important was the part he played in the dedication of the new North American College on the Janiculum Hill. During the crowded days of the Great Consistory in 1946, His Eminence attended the meeting of trustees that started wheels turning and over the next three years set the pace for the alumni in their campaign to raise $350,000 for the chapel. His own gift was the main altar with the inscription, *"To the Mothers of the Sons of Alma Mater,"* and the mosaic behind the altar representing the Assumption of Our Blessed Lady in memory of Francesco Cardinal Borgongini-Duca. In addition he donated several altars in honor of his parents, his predecessors in the Archdiocese of New York, Cardinal O'Connell, Bishop Kelleher, Countess Mary Young Moore, and Enrico Galeazzi.

Most impressive of all, he was able to effect certain economies that netted trustees $936,878, about one-quarter of the cost of the North American College. He had learned that certain American motion picture companies were anxious to dispose of four million dollars in blocked lire which they could not use outside of Italy. In his capacity as Treasurer of the North American College, the Cardinal convinced Minister Giulio Andreotti of the Italian Treasury that it would be in the interests of Italy to release the lire for the building of the American College and thus be an immediate help to Italian industry as well as continuous assistance to the Italian economy. The transaction was completed, and four million dollars in Italian lire were purchased for three million dollars in the United States. This augmented the contributions of the hierarchy, clergy, and laity of the United States, so that the entire cost of the college was on hand. Such was his interest in the project that when the time came for the dedication in the fall of 1953, the fact that he had been very ill, too ill to consecrate Bishop Dargin and Bishop Kellenberg, was not taken into consideration. He appeared at the Polo Grounds three days after the consecration for the annual Holy Name Rally, took a helicopter to Idlewild and flew to Rome. There he had the official honor and deep personal satisfaction of greeting the Supreme Pontiff who officiated personally at the ceremonies and of proposing in Latin the traditional toast "To His Holiness" at the luncheon which followed.

From Rome, the Cardinal flew to Munich and two days later, his friends in New York were alarmed to read that he had suffered a heart attack in Vienna and was seriously ill. His own version, given to reporters on his return to Idlewild made light of the whole episode: "I was not ill, I was exhausted. The diagnosis was made by a reporter in Paris with a pencil rather than by a doctor in Vienna with a stethoscope." He said he went through a "terrific ordeal" in Munich. He went from bed to bed, from person to person, visiting refugees. "I felt that whatever the cost to me I should visit these people who are without homes or hope, to give them what help I could." He had broadcast nine times to nine Iron Curtain countries. "That took a lot out of me," he said. "When I arrived in Vienna I had no commitments so I took a day off and disappointed no one except the reporters."

On the way home, he had addressed the *Grandes Conférences Catholiques* in Brussels, been received in audience by His Majesty King Baudouin, and started a building fund at a Paris Communion breakfast to erect a Catholic Church for United States citizens living in the French capital. This gift, like the others, was disbursed by His Eminence as trustee of contributions entrusted to him by friends and benefactors for religious, charitable and educational purposes. That same afternoon, His Eminence, as Archbishop of New York, spoke at Ste. Croix Cathedral in Orléans, presenting a million francs for its restoration, and after a conference the next day at the Supreme Headquarters of the Allied Powers in Europe with his old friend, General Alfred M. Gruenther, was ready to proceed to Ireland. All in all, it was just another quiet little trip.

The following autumn, 1954, there was a flying visit to Rome still more characteristic. Word had come that Cardinal Spellman's old teacher, patron, and friend who thirty years before had opened the most important doors in the Vatican to an inexperienced young American, Francesco Cardinal Borgongini-Duca, was dead. All engagements were canceled on Madison Avenue, reservations secured on the first available plane and when the Princes of the Church took their places at the obsequies, some with short memories were impressed to see the Cardinal Archbishop of New York among them. The spiritual testament of the deceased appended to his will was worthy of a great and humble man. In it he asked forgiveness for his sins and thanked all those, beginning with the Blessed Mother and his own dear earthly mother, who had helped him serve God and save his soul. There was an echo of the past in the words: "I wish to thank all my benefactors, my associates, my co-workers, my assistants, and among them certainly the first place must go to His Eminence Francis Cardinal Spellman, for their charity toward me and their solicitude for me."

Here in the United States he is always available whenever a brother bishop says that his presence can help the cause of the Church, so that no month goes by without two or three plane trips that have nothing to do with his own responsibilities: a fiesta in Santa Fe, jubilees in Omaha and Rochester, consecrations, centenaries, and funerals everywhere, as well as great events like the dedication of the National Shrine of the Immaculate Conception in Washington when he celebrated its first Pontifical Mass in the presence of other Princes of the Church.

His last two visits to Chicago were made just to express his sympathy. Samuel Cardinal Stritch had been a close friend for years. They had been elevated on the same day to the College of Cardinals and when the Holy Father announced that the venerable Archbishop of Chicago was to be Pro-Prefect of the Sacred Congregation for the Propagation of the Faith with residence in Rome, the heart of Cardinal Spellman was full of sympathy and understanding as he wired his "enthusiastic support for the first American Cardinal designated a Cardinal of the Roman Curia." On the eve of the new Pro-Prefect's departure he was honored in New York by a reception and dinner, with four cardinals, the Apostolic Delegate, and eighty-one archbishops and bishops in attendance. His illness on arrival in Rome and his death soon after touched the heart of the nation and the Cardinal Archbishop of New York went to the obsequies not only for the sake of protocol but "because he wanted to." That was also the reason that brought him back in January for the funeral of all the little children who perished in the tragic fire at Our Lady of the Angels School. As one priest put the sentiments of Chicago into words: "Compassion is much better expressed by symbol and gesture. Your thoughtfulness in undertaking a journey through the bitter cold to be with us on that darkest of all Fridays was a symbol that gave more comfort than human eloquence ever could."

Duty or pleasure may take His Eminence every place else in the world, but with Boston it is habit. After twenty-two years in New York his accent still betrays his heart and no one is ever surprised to hear that he is up in Massachusetts again. One recent visit, however, deserves a special place in the chronicle. The beloved Richard Cardinal Cushing announced in the spring of 1958 that the new $3,000,000 school under construction in Brockton, another and larger shoe center close to Whitman, would be called the Cardinal Spellman Central High School. It was dedicated in the fall as part of the sesquicentennial celebration of the Boston Archdiocese and His Eminence of New York, recalling that in boyhood days he used to sell the Brockton *Enterprise*, expressed his gratitude and donated $100,000 to be used on the auditorium. He asked that this be known as the Cardinal Cushing Auditorium so that "thus we shall be closely associated in memory as we have been in life for nearly four decades of priesthood."

The donation of $100,000 was part of a purse that had been presented to His Eminence as Archbishop of New York on the occasion of his silver jubilee as a bishop. To include the elaborate observance of this event in his own diocese among the things he did "because he wanted to" is slightly whimsical because as it happened the program was just what he did not want. He did not want a big ceremony in New York and he did not want a purse. His plan called for a quiet celebration of his twenty-fifth anniversary in Rome, but prelates of his own household by way of a pleasant surprise sent out invitations and accepted gifts before he was aware of their loyal intentions, so that he "found himself involved in the public ceremony of September 7 at the Yankee Stadium." It was quite a ceremony. A great platform and attractive altar had been arranged on the diamond and everyone in the American hierarchy who could make the trip was there, including all the cardinals and the Apostolic Delegate. Francis Cardinal McIntyre, Archbishop of Los Angeles, so long identified with the New York chancery, preached a warm and appropriate sermon. In reply the jubilarian said in part:

What can a full heart say to those embraced within it, in devoted love and gratitude! What is the yardstick to measure the heart's deep affection and appreciation? No greater gift can any man offer than his life to share, work, suffer and if need be to die in dedicated service as priest and friend. This gift I offered to you, dearly beloved, when first I came among you, a stranger to most of you, eighteen years ago. This I have striven to give these many years, wanting to be one with you, living and working in harmony and friendship. This gift has been yours all the days and years I have been with you, no matter how far away from you I have flown— South America, Europe, Asia, Africa, Australia. I have circled the earth many times to be with your dear ones as their Chaplain, father and friend, but each visit with them was also offered for you, because it was in your name that I went forth across land and sea and through the air to be with your sons and daughters bravely serving in the Armed Forces of our country. My whole life and soul and all my priestly works have belonged to you since that other wondrous and awesome day when I was installed as Archbishop of New York. Whatever I have been privileged to do, with God's grace, we have done together, even as this day too is yours as well as mine. . . .

One treasured experience I recalled was the day forty-one years ago, just before my ordination to the priesthood, when I attended Mass and received Holy Communion on Holy Thursday 1916 from the hands of His Holiness, Pope St. Pius X. Solemnly, I reflected, I am about to receive Holy Communion from the blessed hands of the Holy Father and, soon I too, shall be a priest, with the sacred privilege of offering the Sacrifice of the Mass, the greatest power possessed even by our beloved Vicar of Christ. . . .

God has been generous and merciful in all the sixty-eight years of my life, and on this day so sacred to me, I fervently pray that many others of His sons and daughters will answer Christ's call to the priesthood and religious life so that they too may know the happiness of which there is no greater in this earthly life!

Many have been the blessings of my own priesthood, but I have none more precious than the privilege that has been mine as Christ's missionary, to help lessen, even a little, the pain and loneliness of our soldier sons who lived, suffered and died in the far places of the earth, in the wars of our times. It was just twelve years ago tomorrow, September 8, 1945, that I entered Korea with the American occupational forces and witnessed the soldiers of Japan file by and lay down their arms in surrender. V.E. Day and V.J. Day were past and millions of hearts were joyful at the prospect of peace. Millions of hearts were too sorrowful because of the loss of their loved ones, but consoled by the thought that their anguished sacrifices had been offered in the cause of peace. They knew not then that the peace with justice for all peoples which their sons, husbands and fathers, sweethearts and brothers had courageously sacrificed to gain, would not come to pass, even unto this very day.

Dear friends, in loving tribute to these our sons who gave their lives that we might live in peace, let us together re-avow our loyalty and love for our great and noble nation, and pledge our determination to cherish and keep inviolate the priceless blessings which we enjoy as free Americans, as daily we unite in prayers for peace—that just and enduring peace which God alone can bring to men, for truly there is no human hope for peace!

On the practical side, unknown to His Eminence, his vicar general, Monsignor John J. Maguire, had given all the clergy and parishes of the archdiocese the opportunity to celebrate the jubilee with contributions toward a surprise testimonial. It was characteristic of the jubilarian that he promptly decided to use the gift of $3,179,589.00 to assist in the construction of a new high school. The consultors then prevailed upon His Eminence to permit the new school to be called the Cardinal Spellman High School of New York.

But brilliant as was the New York observance, the Cardinal carried out his original plan of having the real celebration in Rome. In his first letter home he wrote:

> The Editor of *Look* Magazine was anxious to get some pictures from which to make a selection illustrating articles which *Look* Magazine intends to publish. The Editor wished to send a photographer in the plane with me and while it seemed strange to me to send someone such a long distance to take pictures, I said I would have no objection and I gave them the number of the flight indicating that it was a tourist flight. The Editor answered that it would be the first time any of his men would travel other than first class. I said I knew no easier way to save three hundred dollars on a round trip ticket from New York to Rome than traveling tourist. . . .
>
> The Holy Father has sent me a picture which he had framed in a silver frame for me and the inscription reads: "To our beloved son Francis Joseph Cardinal Spellman, Archbishop of New York, on the occasion of the Silver Jubilee of his episcopal consecration received from our hands on September 8th, 1932, gratefully recalling his unfailing filial devotion, generous charity and zealous activity, we impart from our heart as a mark of particular favour our loving Apostolic Benediction. Vatican City—September 8th, 1957. Pius p.p. XII."

"The greatest friend he ever had" received him in audience soon after his arrival and the following account occurs in a letter written the next day:

> His Holiness was all smiles and looked very well. In fact just the same as I have remembered him during the past thirty years with the minimum of the effects that three decades must make in the life of a person. I tried to follow the protocol of genuflections as I approached His Holiness, but I was unable to complete them until His Holiness embraced me and told me of his joy at seeing me again. It seemed to me that His Holiness bears the terrific burdens of His office with greater tranquility than the last time I was privileged to be in His presence in January of 1956. His Holiness discussed some of these burdens with me and He is fully aware of the earnest desire of the bishops, priests and laity of the United States to cooperate with him in every possible way. He said that America was the source of some of His greatest consolations. I told His Holiness of the spiritual life of the Archdiocese giving special mention to our efforts to

care for the Spanish-speaking people of New York and told His Holiness that one of every three Catholics in the Archdiocese was Spanish-speaking. I told His Holiness of the great school expansion in the United States giving details of the progress in the four dioceses with which I was most familiar, Boston, Philadelphia, Los Angeles, and New York. His Holiness is aware of the great sacrifice of the Catholics to provide school accommodation and smilingly His Holiness recalled the controversy in which I became involved concerning the Barden Bill. Our conversation was very intimate and chronology seemed to melt away and I felt that our relations were almost the same as they were during the weeks I was privileged to be His Holiness' companion on the shores of Lake Constance. His Holiness noticed the cross and chain which I was wearing and which was the one His Holiness wore during His years as Archbishop, as Cardinal, as Secretary of State and as Holy Father until the day in 1943 when I visited Rome during the German occupation and His Holiness took from His shoulders this cross and chain and gave them to me. His Holiness asked me twice if there was some request I had to make of Him and I replied that I had none. My desire was only to serve Him in any way possible to the best of my ability. . . .

Two days later was the actual anniversary of the day when he became Bishop Spellman and the following account, brief as it is, gives just a glimpse of the glorious solemnity that is Rome for most of us:

Leaving the American College I went outside of Rome to a retreat where I spent Thursday and Friday in preparation for my Mass at the altar of the Chair in the apse of St. Peter's Basilica. I had expected a very simple ceremony and of course the Mass itself was very simple, but there were five Cardinals, many Archbishops and Bishops, Generals of different religious orders, members of the diplomatic corps, students of the North American College and two hundred and fifty American pilgrims of the Young Christian Workers. Students of the North American College served my Mass and the choir of St. Peter's sang a number of motets before and during the Mass. Cardinal Pizzardo, Cardinal Ottaviani, Cardinal Micara, Cardinal Ciriaci and Cardinal Arriba y Castro were the Cardinals present and the Generals of the Society of Jesus, the Dominicans, the Passionists and several other communities. . . .

There was a luncheon afterward given by Bishop Martin J. O'Connor, the rector of the American College, in the great hall of the Palace of the Knights of the Holy Sepulchre and later in the afternoon, he completed his formal calls on the cardinals who were in the city at the time. On his return to New York at the end of "a wonderful week", he received the following message from Pope Pius XII:

Since We follow always and with particular affection your daily and arduous work, We know with what zeal you give yourself to the spiritual welfare of that chosen part of the Catholic flock which, mindful of your outstanding virtues, We entrusted to your wise care. Whence it is that you, too, Venerable Brother, in the remembrance of your Episcopal consecration, can justly repeat with St. Paul: "His grace in me hath not been void." Continue, therefore, your precious apostolate with the same fervor and serenity of spirit, assured that nothing consoles and cheers Our heart more than the zealous fruitful apostolate of the Shepherd of Souls.

CHAPTER TWENTY-TWO

The Closing of a Volume

IT STARTED out like any other pilgrimage. The world was celebrating the centenary of Our Lady's apparition at Lourdes in 1858 and Cardinal Spellman was taking six hundred Americans on the Greek ship *TSS Olympia* to pray at the Shrine in the Pyrenees, visit the Pope, and tour the Mediterranean. They sailed in gay spirits from New York on September 8 with a send-off arranged by Monsignor John J. O'Donnell, who had erected a long streamer on the pier reading on one side *BON VOYAGE* and the other *WELCOME HOME CARDINAL SPELLMAN*. No one was supposed to see the reverse until October 13. When that date arrived, however, the streamer was forgotten. The pilgrims were back, but the Cardinal was not with them. He was in Rome assisting at the funeral of Pius XII.

A smooth passage of seven days in what is called "a happy ship" and everyone was in the mood for southern France. Passing through Bordeaux was the occasion of placing flowers on the tomb of the first Bishop of Boston, Cardinal Cheverus, who died as Archbishop of Bordeaux, but Lourdes was the first objective. Though the weather was weepy and uncertain the air of Faith was compensation enough for the thousands of pilgrims who crowded the little town. There was Mass one day in the Grotto, the next in the Basilica of Pius X. His Eminence of New York spoke in Rosary Hall on "Mary," together with Cardinals Ottaviani and Tappouni. The Apostolic Legate, Eugene Cardinal Tisserant, gave a dinner for all the members of the Sacred College present for the centenary and nearly two hundred archbishops and bishops attended.

Overland to Bilbao on the Bay of Biscay took the party through a corner of Spain and the American Ambassador, John Davis Lodge, met His Eminence at the border. There was a brilliant dinner in his honor at the home of the Spanish Foreign Minister, Alberto Martín Artajo, before his return to the *TSS Olympia*. From the port of Vigo a pilgrimage was made to Santiago de Compostela where the traditional tomb of St. James the Greater has been venerated for more than a thousand years. As a devout pilgrim His Eminence knelt before Fernando Cardinal Quiroga y Palacios and was invested as "an Elder Brother of the Archbrotherhood of the Glorious Apostle Saint James."

In the new basilica at Fatima whose atmosphere does so little to foster devotion the Cardinal spoke in Portuguese and English, helping his pious group to relive the events of 1917. At the station on their return to Lisbon the official car was waiting to take His Eminence to the old fortress in Estoril where Prime Minister Antonio Oliveira Salazar was spending the summer months. The hospitality was quiet but most cordial. Stopping briefly at Gibraltar, Malaga, and Palermo, the Greek ship headed joyously for ancient Crete and Athens. Here the leading newspaper *Kathimerini* struck an ominous note: "There are many who believe that the tremendous education, vast knowledge of languages and administrative capabilities of Cardinal Spellman may force the Conclave of Cardinals to break a tradition of four centuries by not electing an Italian as the next Pope."

The last thing His Eminence had in mind was a conclave and his own election was not there at all. He saw as many Catholic institutions as he could reach, met Prime Minister Karamanlis and Archbishop Makarios, the patriot of Cyprus (he had been presented to the King and Queen of Greece on a previous visit), and hastened to rejoin his pilgrims. Their arrival in Malta was the occasion of a public holiday and as they entered the Port of Valletta thousands of cheering people lined the shores. The papers ran editorials and everyone from the archbishop, the governor general, and the prime minister down made this third visit of Cardinal Spellman a sort of home coming.

Landing at Naples they were soon in Rome, the second principal objective of the pilgrimage. In a letter to friends, His Eminence wrote:

> October 3rd was the day scheduled for our audience with the Holy Father. On that day I said Mass in the Church of Santa Susanna, which is the Church of Cardinal Mooney and the American Church in Rome. The pilgrims, with religious articles on their arms, in satchels and in boxes, arrived at Castel Gandolfo at nine o'clock so that leisurely we could proceed to the Papal Palace for our audience, which was scheduled for nine-thirty. The previous day we had heard that the Holy Father was not as well as usual, in fact that he had had recurrent hiccups. I knew that His Holiness had promised to see our group in special audience and that we were to have the privilege, unusual at the present time, of being greeted by His Holiness individually. Along with that procedure arrangements had been made for benches on which we could sit while His Holiness spoke to us. We were all grouped in the courtyard and I thought it was about time to proceed upstairs, when Monsignor Nasalli Rocca came to me all aflutter and said that His Holiness was having violent hiccups and he did not think it well for His Holiness to meet each pilgrim as I had expected. I was relieved that it was possible for His Holiness to see us and speak to us.
>
> Promptly at nine-thirty the doors on the little balcony opened and our Holy Father appeared to be greeted affectionately by our pilgrimage

group. They were singing the Lourdes hymn as His Holiness appeared and listened approvingly until the hymn was over.

There was a moment of silence and then the Holy Father spoke to them about the angels:

> Dearly beloved pilgrims; receiving you at the beginning of this month of October, We could not refrain from leaving with you a brief word of paternal exhortation to awaken and sharpen your realization of the invisible world about you—"for the things that are seen last for a moment, the things that are not seen are eternal" (2 Cor. 4, 18)—and to foster a certain familiar acquaintance with the Angels, who are so constant in their solicitude for your salvation and holiness. You will spend, God grant it, an eternity of joy with them; begin to know them now.

As the pilgrims prepared to leave the courtyard,

> suddenly the Holy Father appeared again at another window, waved to us and blessed us once more, and smiling, extended his hands in a most affectionate manner.
>
> When I was ushered upstairs to be received in private audience, I could see that His Holiness was not at all well and three times I tried to leave and he bade me remain, thanking me for the help that I had given him in many ways. Of course, I replied that it was a joy to be able to do anything I could to lighten his tremendous burden. We talked about our early years together and especially of the weeks I had been permitted to be with him in Switzerland. During the few minutes I was with him, His Holiness had the hiccups and it was most disturbing to me to see him thus afflicted. Several times he asked if there was anything I wanted to ask of him and I said there was nothing, that I was very grateful to him for receiving the pilgrims, especially when he was not feeling well. He offered me rosaries, as many as I wished, and I took a half-dozen. His Holiness then gave me medals to distribute to all the pilgrims. Once more we embraced and said farewell.

While the party went on to Genoa and the Riviera, the Cardinal flew to Vicenza to say Mass for the American troops located there. His reception was enthusiastic. After dedicating a school in nearby Verona and visiting more of his boys in the armed forces, he rejoined the pilgrimage in Nice and stopped long enough for a call at the Palace of Monaco.

Homeward bound, the TSS *Olympia* was approaching Gibraltar on October 6. At 2:00 P.M. Monsignor Terence J. Cooke, Vice Chancellor of the Archdiocese of New York, was called to the ship's phone by the New York *Journal-American* to learn that the Holy Father had suffered a stroke and had received the last rites. His diary picks up the narration:

> Immediately I went to the dining room where His Eminence, according

to his custom, was having luncheon with his pilgrims. His Eminence received the message with his usual calm and self-composure but with deep sorrow. That afternoon several phone calls were received from the press in Lisbon, Paris, Rome and New York. Since our ship-radio was occupied with ship-to-shore messages, we used a portable Zenith Transistor Radio to follow the news broadcasts.

In addition to the regular devotions, which included meditation and Mass each morning and pilgrimage devotions consisting of rosary, sermon and benediction, a vigil of prayer before the Blessed Sacrament for the intention of the Holy Father was organized with His Eminence's approval by pilgrims under the leadership of the Knights of Malta and the Knights and Ladies of the Holy Sepulchre. Their spirit was marvelous! Their fervor reminded me of my days at Dunwoodie as a seminarian during the Forty Hours Devotion. The "Olympia" had become a cathedral at sea.

The next day we were happy to hear that the Holy Father's condition had improved and that he was able to speak a few words. Earlier His Eminence had sent the following cable:

TUESDAY OCT. 7TH
EXCELLENCY DELLACQUA—VATICAN CITY
PILGRIMS SORROWSTRICKEN HOLY FATHERS ILLNESS OFFERING MASSES AND HOLY COMMUNIONS FOR HIS HOLINESS MAINTAINING TWENTY FOUR HOUR VIGIL OF PRAYERS BEFORE THE BLESSED SACRAMENT.

CARDINAL SPELLMAN

In the morning His Eminence received an answer from the Pope:

WEDNESDAY OCT. 8TH
HIS EMINENCE FRANCIS CARDINAL SPELLMAN
ARCHBISHOP OF NEW YORK S.S. OLYMPIA IAR
WE FEEL CONSOLED AND COMFORTED IN OUR ILLNESS BY THE PRAYERFUL MESSAGE WHICH YOU HAVE SENT TO US AND WITH THE ASSURANCE OF OUR SINCERE GRATITUDE WE IMPART TO YOU AND YOUR PILGRIMS OUR PATERNAL APOSTOLIC BLESSING.

POPE PIUS XII

This was probably the last message sent by Pius XII.

Together we all offered prayers of joy and gratitude. But the cable was quickly followed by the sad news that His Holiness had suffered a second stroke and once more we were besieged by calls from the various news agencies. Everyone wanted to know His Eminence's plans. We would not give any information, but His Eminence had told me and Captain Sigalas that if the Pope lived beyond nine-thirty on Thursday morning, when we would be passing the Island of Terceira in the Azores, he would continue on ship to New York, but if his death came before that hour he would leave the ship and return to Rome.

At 4:45 A.M. on October 9 I was called to the telephone to answer a dozen calls. The first was from the Associated Press. The Holy Father had died and a statement was requested from His Eminence. It was five o'clock in the morning when I knocked on His Eminence's door and told him the sad news. He seemed to know it already but the grief in his heart was clearly discernible on his weary countenance. His first inclination was to go immediately and offer Mass but he decided to wait a short time so that the pilgrims could be with him. I went to the Captain's cabin and arranged for telegrams to be sent ahead to Terceira which we would reach at 9:00 A.M. When I returned to His Eminence he had a statement prepared which was given to the press by telephone. It read as follows:

THE DEATH OF HIS HOLINESS POPE PIUS XII MEANS THE DEPARTURE FROM AMONG US OF THE MOST IMPARTIAL, MOST DEVOTED PEACEMAKER IN OUR WEARY, WARRING WORLD. DURING HIS LONG, LABORIOUS LIFE OF PRAYER, SACRIFICE AND ACTION, PIUS XII DEDICATED HIMSELF TOTALLY TO THE SERVICE OF GOD, AND TO THE WELFARE OF ALL THE CHILDREN OF GOD. IN HIS GREAT PATERNAL, PASTORAL HEART, HE EMBRACED EACH INDIVIDUAL MAN, WOMAN AND CHILD OF EVERY RACE, COLOR, CULTURE AND CREED. POPE PIUS XII, LIKE HIS DIVINE MASTER, WAS FRIEND TO EVERY MAN, AND I AM SURE THAT ALL PERSONS OF GOOD WILL JOIN THE CATHOLIC WORLD IN MOURNING THE LOSS OF A LOVING AND BELOVED HOLY FATHER. OF MY PERSONAL LOSS I SHALL SAY ONLY THAT HIS HOLINESS WAS THE GREATEST FRIEND I EVER HAD AND I UNITE MY PRAYERS WITH MULTITUDES BESEECHING ALMIGHTY GOD FOR THE BLESSINGS I KNOW HE HAS ALREADY GRANTED, AN ETERNAL REWARD TO ONE OF HIS SAINTS.

FRANCIS CARDINAL SPELLMAN

Meanwhile all the pilgrims were called and prayed the Rosary in the chapel. His Eminence then offered a Requiem Mass for Pope Pius XII and under the expert direction of Father Curtin, all the priests formed the choir. The Cardinal's Mass was followed by thirty-one Masses for the Holy Father. After Mass His Eminence said that he wished to bid farewell to all the pilgrims before leaving the ship. His intention was to disembark as soon as possible and he instructed us to proceed immediately to New York "so that we would not be late getting home." Even at this time of great personal sorrow his only thought was for the welfare of everyone else but himself. After His Eminence spoke to the pilgrims, he shook hands with each one. A short time later a launch with American officers and Portuguese authorities came out to our ship, their flag at half-mast, and took His Eminence aboard. From the launch he kept waving his hand and smiling until he was out of sight. The pilgrims tried to sing the Lourdes hymn but their voices were hoarse and choked. As the "TSS

Olympia" steamed homeward, a plane circled the ship three times. It was the Cardinal. He waved goodbye and we did too.

The rest of the account can be pieced together from subsequent letters written by the Cardinal to his friends:

By good fortune I knew the Commanding General at the American Air Force Base on Terceira, Brig. General George B. Dany, as he had been most helpful to me in planning my trip to Thule in Greenland a few years ago at Christmas time. I had met his wife at that time and both the General and his wife were on the dock when I landed.

General Dany had already made reservations for me to fly by a Venezuelan plane departing around noon for Lisbon. A Brazilian plane then took me from Lisbon on a non-stop flight to Rome. The plane was delayed three hours and I thought the passengers would be displeased, but instead they were most charitable and cordial.

I arrived in Rome at midnight on the day the Pope died. Bishop O'Connor and Count Galeazzi and others met me at the plane and brought me immediately to Castel Gandolfo. Only five days had elapsed since I had my audience with our Holy Father and it was a shock to see his remains. Many thoughts swirled through my brain—memories of the past and bewilderment about the future. Count Galeazzi and I remained about fifteen minutes and then we returned to Rome about one o'clock in the morning.

The body of the Holy Father was carried in solemn procession from Castel Gandolfo to St. Peter's with all Rome lining the road for miles. Affection and sorrow seemed to be universal and some of the old people along the way must have been struck by the contrast between the events of 1958 and those of 1878 when Pope Pius IX was buried. On that sad occasion, which incidentally fell within the lifetime of Eugenio Pacelli, an anticlerical mob had attacked the funeral cortege as it crossed the bridge of Sant'Angelo at midnight, with the intention of throwing the Pope's body into the Tiber. Only the courage and energy of the faithful had prevented this outrage and the press everywhere showed a minimum of sympathy. Eighty years later it seemed as though the Papacy did not have an enemy in the free world. In every country outside the Iron and Bamboo Curtains the last illness, death, and burial of Pius XII were reported in detail with a degree of respect and esteem beyond all precedent. Obscure priests in various parts of America had telephone calls and letters of condolence from non-Catholic strangers on the loss of the Holy Father, recalling to mind what a tower of strength he had been to Protestants and Jews through all the darkness of World War II.

The next morning His Eminence had a visit from Mother Pasqualina who was distraught with grief. This venerable nun from the community at

Menzingen in Switzerland had watched over the late Pontiff for a quarter of a century, supervising all the details of his domestic arrangements. Now, with tears she had brought a number of mementoes to an old friend who years before as a young American monsignor had been so close to Cardinal Pacelli. Among them were the last cassock he wore, the very one he used at Castel Gandolfo that day when he spoke to the pilgrims about the angels, and the last zucchetto which she had placed on his head after death.

When the fully vested body of the Pope had been three days on a great catafalque, surrounded by a forest of tall candles, there were three funeral Masses in the crowded basilica attended by nearly all the cardinals and the representatives of nearly all the civilized nations, including the United States. After the last Mass, five absolutions were given, one by his most devoted disciple, and the entombment took place in the crypt close to St. Pius X. With the forthrightness of Latins who are not unusually sensitive about the facts of death, the nails were hammered into the box with such vigor that the silent mourners down by the jubilee door could follow the ceremony.

The Pope was dead and buried, but the business of the Church had to go on, so the next morning:

> There was an assembly of the Cardinals at ten-thirty o'clock and I was the first present at this meeting and at all subsequent meetings which were held daily in the Consistorial room, presided over by Cardinal Tisserant, the Cardinal Dean and Cardinal Aloisi Masella who was selected as Camerlengo. At other times I kept by myself at our beautiful North American College. Time has gone by rather quickly even though I continue to be somewhat depressed by it all. I say Mass in the chapel adjoining my room and have my meals with the faculty, except the evening meal when I go to Count Galeazzi's home.

Nearly two weeks passed and His Eminence again wrote to his friends:

> Tomorrow we enter the Conclave and if the election is over in two days, the probability is that the coronation will take place on November 9th. I decided to ask Monsignor Francis F. Reh, the Rector of the Seminary, and Monsignor Edwin B. Broderick, my secretary, to come to Rome to be with me for the Conclave. Monsignor Reh is a Prelate and, therefore, cannot go into the Conclave, but he is very helpful to me with his knowledge of Rome and of people. Monsignor Broderick never had an opportunity to see Rome and Monsignor Reh has been very kind to act as his guide. I did ask Count Galeazzi to go with me into the Conclave since each Cardinal can bring two persons with him, but the Count decided for very good reasons that it would be better for him to remain on duty instead of being isolated. So I invited the Very Reverend Monsignor George A. Schlicte, Vice Rector of the American College, to be my com-

panion. Monsignor Schlicte is from Boston, a graduate of Annapolis who was a Commander in the Navy during the war, and who then studied for the priesthood here in Rome.

As they were preparing to leave the North American College to go into residence at the Vatican, His Eminence was saddened by the sudden death of the beloved Cardinal Archbishop of Detroit:

Cardinal Mooney had arrived three days before the Conclave. He had attended one meeting of the Cardinals and was present at the Mass on Saturday morning. We arrived back at the North American College in time for luncheon. He looked well and was in good spirits during the meal. As we left the dining room together, he said he was tired and asked how long he would have to rest. We were supposed to be in the Vatican at three-thirty and it was then two o'clock so I replied that he would have at least half an hour. I packed my suitcase and was ready to leave when Monsignor Broderick came into my room and said, "I hate to tell you but I think Cardinal Mooney is dead." In a few minutes I went up to his room and found Cardinal McIntyre saying the prayers for the dying. The Cardinal had already been anointed and Doctor Rocchi was ministering to him. After a few minutes the doctor stood up and without saying a word, stretched out his hands with an expression of futility which clearly told us that a dear friend was dead. It is true that for four or five years Cardinal Mooney had known that this was the way in which God would call him, and he had told me a number of times that I would read some morning in the paper that he was dead and always asked me to pray for him.

Despite the fact that he expected a sudden death, however, it was a great shock to all of us who had been with him only an hour before, and also a subject for deep meditation. I expressed my condolences to Monsignor Breitenbeck who had been for many years his devoted and efficient secretary and intimate friend. It was decided then that the body would be returned to the States the next day, and from the Vatican I believe we saw the Constellation flying home with his remains, because it flew very close to the Vatican area and all planes had been requested to detour during the Conclave. All during the Conclave the empty chair and desk that he was to have occupied bore his name.

There are several of the Cardinals who are very old and very feeble. From day to day one wonders if they will survive. However, after Cardinal Mooney's sudden death one is jostled into the consideration that perhaps one who is younger and does not anticipate proximate death may go before the others whose appearance makes death seem more proximate.

Even without this grim reminder of their own mortality, the ceremonies and the strange surroundings in which the cardinals and their attendants found themselves created an atmosphere of austerity and recollection. It was not, of course, as grim as Gregory X intended it to be when he established the Law of the Conclave in 1271. His own election had taken two years and nine months and to prevent the recurrence of such an abuse he prescribed that all the electors with one servant each were to be locked in one large room without curtains. After three days each meal would be reduced to one dish and after five more days to bread and water—with wine of course. The next Pope was elected in one day.

Times have changed and now each cardinal has two attendants and sometimes a suite of rooms, often with a kitchenette where a smart secretary can boil an egg. So it was in Monsignor Bocci's comfortable six-room apartment which had been divided and assigned to Cardinal Spellman, his old friend, Cardinal Pizzardo, and their four secretaries. That helped. Moreover, Monsignor Schlicte happened to be the experienced buyer for the North American College and so, with a few creature comforts that had not been expected, life went on. The fourth day His Eminence wrote:

> Attendance at the Conclave has been awesome for me as I think of the great responsibility of each Cardinal and of the tremendous burden that will be imposed upon the Cardinal who will succeed Pope Pius XII. As you know, there are four votes each day, and one indeed has to take a solemn oath that he will vote for one who, before God, he thinks worthy to be the successor of St. Peter. I am about the half way mark in the matter of seniority and, therefore, my place is down near the entrance.
>
> Naturally living in the Vatican brings back hosts of memories, and last evening walking by myself in the Cortile of Saint Damasus, with a full moon, which I saw last in Athens on our pilgrimage towards Rome, thoughts of the first time I saw Pope Pius X in that Cortile and of all the associations and experiences I have had in Rome during the past forty-seven years gave me plenty of opportunity for reflection.

That letter was finished at noon. Before he retired for the night His Eminence had written another:

> This is the evening of October 28th. On the eleventh ballot, the first balloting of this afternoon, we elected a wonderful Holy Father, Cardinal Roncalli, who will be known as Pope John XXIII.
>
> This afternoon and early evening were packed with drama. It was surprising that as His Eminence received the necessary number of votes, two-thirds plus one, there was no demonstration of any kind. The total was read, the ballots were collected, and we all gathered around the throne of Cardinal Roncalli as he accepted the burden laid down by Pope Pius XII. The new Holy Father then went into the sacristy to vest and reappeared before us in white cassock and white zucchetto. When he returned to the Sistine Chapel, he read the oath of office and then seated himself on the throne, and each one of us in order went up to offer him our congratulations and render homage and our pledge of obedience.

The Holy Father is a very genial person and was very cordial to all of us. He embraced each one of us, and a particularly moving moment occurred when he left the throne and walked down to greet Cardinal Tien who was on a stretcher. Another emotional moment came when the Holy Father was accepting the burden of Papacy. He removed his red skull cap and placed it on the head of Monsignor Di Jorio, the Secretary of the Conclave, thus making him the first Cardinal in this Pontificate. This was a custom which had been interrupted after the death of Pope Leo XIII, when Cardinal Sarto, also Patriarch of Venice like Cardinal Roncalli, removed his skull cap and placed it in his pocket and not on the head of Monsignor Merry del Val. It was a month before the Monsignor was made Cardinal Secretary of State and the custom lapsed for fifty-six years.

We all thought that we could go home then, but we were told we must remain in the Vatican overnight for the second obeisance to the new Holy Father at nine o'clock tomorrow morning. Immediately after the election of the Holy Father, the Papal Master of Ceremonies, Monsignore Enrico Dante lighted the fire that would consume the ballots and give off a puff of white smoke—the signal to the outside world that a new Pope had been elected, while the Sistine Choir for the first time acclaimed Pope John XXIII as Peter. "Thou art Peter and upon this rock I shall build my Church." Never before had it been so full of significance for me. I thought of all the Pontiffs I had known in my lifetime—Pius X, Benedict XV, Pius XI, Pius XII and now—. My memory went reaching back through the centuries—back to St. Peter and Our Lord Himself.

(The next year in welcoming the New Apostolic Delegate to the United States—the Most Reverend Egidio Vagnozzi—Cardinal Spellman would say, "We shall find Pope John in Your Excellency as we find Peter in John and Christ in Peter!")

After the Cardinals had sung the Te Deum, at least those Cardinals who could sing, the Holy Father went to the loggia to bless the throng assembled in St. Peter's Square. The Cardinals were grouped on other loggias and were deeply moved to see the throngs wildly cheering at the blessing of the city and of the world. The band played the pontifical hymn and searchlights played on the balcony of the Holy Father and on the great crowd in the piazza. Walking back to my room after the ceremony of the benediction one Cardinal very friendly with the new Pope overtook me and placing his hand on my shoulder said, "Now we shall liberate you from New York." I explained, however, that I did not wish to be liberated and that I looked forward to returning to my duties there sometime in mid-November.

As we left the Piazza of St. Peter a full moon was rising and the Noble Guards, the Palatine Guards and other military units started to march away. The day was over. Another day was beginning.

Later in the week he had more news for those at home:

> Today, All Saints Day, I had my first formal audience. It lasted three-quarters of an hour and the Pope was calm, unhurried and most cordial. His Holiness came to the door to greet me and said that Cardinal Tardini, whose audience had just finished, had told him it was against protocol for him to stand up to receive visitors, and he had replied that he would stand up to receive me.
>
> He is very much at home in the role of Holy Father and at the same time most humble. He asked me for any suggestions I might have to make and said that I could always communicate directly with him if I had any ideas of what should be done or should not be done. I recommended the Cause of Mother Seton to His Holiness and he made immediate note of it and I am sure that we shall get prompt action.
>
> There is, of course, a tremendous contrast between Pope Pius XII and Pope John XXIII. The latter will not make as many speeches as his predecessor and is handicapped by being unable to speak English, but he certainly has remarkable energy and a great capacity for work, so I think that there will be more Consistories during his Pontificate and fewer vacancies in the Sacred College.
>
> After the audience I went to call on Cardinal Tardini and we had a chat for about ten minutes. He is now in charge of the entire Secretariat of State and most influential.

The elaborate preparations for the crowning of the new Pope were hurried at his own request because the Holy Father realized from experience what it would mean to all the cardinals and bishops not resident in Rome. Most of them had been away from their dioceses for nearly a month and some like His Eminence of New York for nearly two. So the date was moved up to November 4, establishing something of a record at the Vatican. The crowd that gathered that morning was enormous; the ancient five-hour ritual was gorgeous and meticulously correct but familiar to only a few. With all his years in Rome, it was new even to Cardinal Spellman.

He had been a boy in first-year high when Pius X was crowned. He might have seen the coronation of Benedict XV because it happened during his time at the North American College, but on September 3, 1914, he was looking at "the white ceiling of a little room in the Yolanda Hospital of Milan." When the turn came for Pius XI, Father Spellman was too busy in Boston selling the *Pilot* and when the new Pope was Pius XII, Cardinal O'Connell saw no reason why his Auxiliary Bishop should go to Rome so he had stayed at home reading all the accounts in a state of suppressed excitement. This then was the first time that he was part of the pageantry and yet when the Dean of the Sacred College placed the triregnum on the brow of John XXIII with the traditional reminder that he was the father of princes and kings, Cardinal Spellman was not immune from distraction. The novelty of the scene could not crowd out a flood of memories.

When a man has lived a full and colorful life, has seen the world, has been too close to war, and has met all kinds of people, nothing can seem completely new to him. Every crisis is just a turn in the road he has taken before. Every citation read at him sounds strangely familiar, and every joy the echo of an earlier joy. Toward sunset, the jubilees and anniversaries and galloping birthdays begin to coalesce in one great golden glow. Thus it was with the Cardinal. One morning he found himself at three score and ten. Messages poured in from the Pope, the President, a radio operator in Alaska, a fireman in the Bronx and hundreds of well wishers all over the world. It was close to his twentieth anniversary as Archbishop of New York and his forty-third as a priest, so his old friends the reporters made the most of it. How did he feel? Twenty years older than when he started the job. Was he going to retire? No. He enjoyed his work and nobody could make him retire. He would rather burn out than rust out.

On his seventy-first birthday he had the spiritual joy of ordaining his nephew, Marian's boy, the Reverend John W. Pegnam. On his seventy-second, in 1961, he went as usual to Whitman for a visit to the old church where he learned to serve Mass, to the Dyer School where he learned to read and write, and to the family graves in the little cemetery where he learned what is meant by the Communion of Saints, but this time there were clouds in the sky. Something was wrong with those glasses. On his return to the city, the doctor broke the bad news that the trouble was not with the glasses but with a retina which had become detached. He was shaken as anyone would be. He knew that it meant weeks in a hospital with eyes bandaged for days, and then convalescence in the seminary; complete rest for a man who had forgotten a long time ago how to rest. But on the way to the operating room on May 9, he told the doctor that he would like to go to the Fordham commencement on June 14, and receive his Insignis Medal in person on the fiftieth anniversary of his graduation day.

When the day arrived, to no one's surprise, he came out of seclusion, got caught with the rest in the downpour of rain on the campus, received the Insignis Medal, done in gold for the first and only time, and presided with appropriate informality at a dinner on Madison Avenue for his five surviving classmates. That evening, the past came strangely alive. The same Jack Coffey was there who had ended young Spellman's dreams of baseball glory by being too good at shortstop, and together they analyzed everything from batting averages to the teaching methods of their old professors. The Cardinal's Boswell, sitting between them, heard for the first time that his subject had once been a boxing champion in the featherweight class, and wondered what other important details had escaped his years of research.

In the course of conversation, Vincent Harcourt Isaacs was mentioned, but it was at the Fordham alumni dinner held in honor of His Eminence that this boy from the British West Indies became the central figure of the evening. To the Cardinal he was a symbol of everything that was best in youth, and while the thousand diners waited for humorous anecdotes and comments on the international situation, fifty years melted away and Frank Spellman from Whitman who lived on the second corridor in First Division talked about Vincent Isaacs from Kingston, Jamaica, "actor, debater, and scholar," as well as his own young ideal of an intellectual man. He had kept for more than forty years a copy of the last letter written by Vincent to his mother before he left for the front, and quoted the words that appealed to him most:

> To you, I owe through God, all that I am . . . That may not be much from the worldly point of view, Mother, but let me tell you some little secrets. You gave me the instincts of a gentleman at birth; you gave me the education that counts more than all the book-learning in the world— it was you who taught me to love and to fear God, and it is to you, Mother, that I owe that something which makes me as much at home in the presence of a king as I am in that of a chimney-sweep. Whatever there is of good in me, I owe to you, and the bad I owe to myself for not having followed you.

Those who were closest to His Eminence looked up as he was reading. Was this particular paragraph in quotation marks? Was it Vincent talking about a little mother in Kingston, or Frank talking about a little mother in Whitman?

On the program for that evening, a warm tribute worthy to be the last page in a long biography was written by the Most Reverend James E. Kearney, D.D., the Bishop of Rochester:

> When Ellen Spellman looked at her baby in a little New England town some seventy-two years ago, she probably did not consider it a very momentous decision when she said, "I'll call him Francis." Just which of the famous saints who bore the name was in her mind, we do not know. What we do know is that the choice seems to have been inspired, for in the apostolate of that son there have been combined all the special virtues that marked the three outstanding saints that bore the name: the little Man of Assisi, the great de Sales of Geneva and the patron of missionary zeal, Francis Xavier. Combining the Christian simplicity of purpose, devotion to the poor, the sick and the orphaned that marked the life of the Saint of Assisi, with the culture and pastoral zeal of the great Francis de Sales, he has still found time for a challenging and often dangerous apostolate as the Shepherd in Christ of our Armed Forces, just like the adventurous apostolate of the greatest of the missionaries, Saint Francis Xavier. So let us say that the little mother in Whitman years ago probably never realized that she was a prophetess too when she said, "I'll call him Francis."

Notes

SOURCE

CHAPTER II
1. Roger Butterfield, "Cardinal-Designate Spellman," *Life*, XX, Jan. 21, 1946, 104.
2. Dedham *Transcript*, Apr. 28, 1939.
3. Francis J. Spellman, *Action This Day*, New York: Charles Scribner's Sons, 1943, pp. 105–6.
4. *Ibid.*, p. 140.
5. Letter from Monsignor Gill to author, Sept. 26, 1953.
6. *Ibid.*

CHAPTER III
1. Quoted in Rev. Henry A. Brann, D.D., "The American College in Rome," The Catholic Encyclopedia (ed. C. G. Hebermann *et al.*), New York: Appleton, 1907, I, 424.
2. Boston *Globe*, May 13, 1916.

CHAPTER IV
1. Letter from Monsignor Haberlin to author, Sept. 21, 1953.

CHAPTER V
1. Boston *Post*, Nov. 2, 1925.
2. Carlo Prati, *Popes and Cardinals in Modern Rome* (trans. E. I. Watkin), New York: Lincoln MacVeagh, The Dial Press, 1927, pp. 129–30.
3. Thomas B. Morgan, *Speaking of Cardinals*, New York: G. P. Putnam's Sons, 1946, p. 125.
4. "The Oratory of St. Peter in Audience with the Pope," translated from the *Corriere d'Italia*, Dec. 10, 1925.

CHAPTER VI
1. Quoted in Most Reverend Jan Olav Smit, *Angelic Shepherd, The Life of Pope Pius XII* (adapted into English by Rev. James H. Vanderveldt, O.F.M.), New York: Dodd, Mead & Co., 1950, pp. 56–57.
2. Thomas B. Morgan, A *Reporter at the Papal Court*, New York, Longman's, Green & Co., 1937, p. 217.
3. Boston *Pilot*, Feb. 16, 1931.
4. Thomas B. Morgan, *The Listening Post*, New York: G. P. Putnam's Sons, 1944, pp. 185–86.

5. Address to the Friendly Sons of St. Patrick, Jan. 8, 1940 in *Proceedings of the Quarterly Meeting of the Society*, January 1940, pp. 135–36.
6. Wilfred O'Malley, "The Story of the Eucharistic Congress," *The Far East*, XV, July 1932, 10.

CHAPTER VII

1. New York *Journal-American*, Apr. 29, 1939.
2. Letter from Sister M. Reginald, C.S.J., to author, Aug. 3, 1953.

CHAPTER VIII

1. New York *Times*, July 17, 24, 1936.
2. *Ibid.*, Sept. 17, 20, 26, 1936.
3. Quoted in *ibid.*, Sept. 3, 1936.
4. *Ibid.*, July 26, Aug. 5, 6, Sept. 4, 1936.
5. *Ibid.*, Sept. 26, 1936.
6. Letter from Reverend Charles E. Coughlin to author, May 5, 1954.
7. New York *Times*, Nov. 5, 1936.
8. *Ibid.*, Nov. 8, 1936.
9. Memorandum from Roberta Barrows to Henry M. Kannee, October 28, 1936. Roosevelt Library, President's Personal File, 4404 (Francis J. Spellman), 1935–45. Hereafter cited as R.L., P.P.F.

CHAPTER X

1. Morgan, *Speaking of Cardinals*, pp. 134–35.
2. New York *Sun*, Mar. 3, 1939.
3. Boston *Herald*, Apr. 25, 1939.
4. Boston *Globe*, May 23, 1939.

CHAPTER XI

1. New York *Herald Tribune*, Oct. 3, 1939.
2. In October 1933, before Roosevelt's meeting with Litvinoff to discuss the recognition of Soviet Russia by the United States, the Vatican requested Cardinal Hayes to raise the question of religious persecution in that unhappy country. His Eminence appointed the Very Reverend Robert F. Keegan to represent him at the White House. Monsignor Keegan was received November 1, 1933 and presented a memorandum covering the following points:
(A) Freedom of conscience for Russians and foreigners,
(B) Freedom of worship, public and private,
(C) Liberation of those imprisoned for their Faith,
(D) Cessation of propaganda against God.
Cardinal Hayes, in a note marked "confidential," wrote on November 2: "The President conferred with the Monsignor for more than one hour in his private study, receiving him most cordially and substantially accepting the points of the memorandum." Cardinal Spellman Papers.
3. New York *Times*, Mar. 3, 1939.
4. Letter from Archbishop Spellman to President Roosevelt, May 27, 1939. R.L., P.P.F.
5. *The Memoirs of Cordell Hull*, New York: Macmillan, 1948, I, 713.
6. *F.D.R., His Personal Letters, 1928–1945*, (ed. Elliott Roosevelt), New York: Duell, Sloan and Pearce, 1950, II, 930–32.
7. Letter from Archbishop Spellman to President Roosevelt, Oct. 25, 1939. R.L., P.P.F.

8. Letter from Archbishop Spellman to President Roosevelt, Nov. 30, 1939. R.L., P.P.F.
9. Letter from Archbishop Spellman to President Roosevelt, Dec. 8, 1939. R.L., P.P.F.
10. *F.D.R., His Personal Letters, 1928–1945,* II, 988–89.
11. *Christian Century,* LVII, March 25, 1940, 405; *Christian Science Monitor,* September 3, 1940; *Protestant Digest,* III, February 1940, 1–9.
12. *Jewish Advocate,* Apr. 26, 1940.
13. Quoted in Religious News Service, press release, Mar. 30, 1940.
14. New York *Herald Tribune,* February 12, 1945.
15. *Nation,* CLX, April 21, 1945, 471.
16. *Exchange of Letters Between His Excellency, Harry S. Truman, President of the United States, and the Honorable Myron C. Taylor, on his Retirement as the Personal Representative of the President of the United States to His Holiness, Pope Pius XII,* January 18, 1950, n.p., pp. 7, 11.
17. Editorial in the Washington *Post,* Sept. 6, 1950.
18. Reverend Carl McIntire, President of the International Council of Christian Churches, quoted in New York *Times,* Jan. 25, 1952.

CHAPTER XII
1. *The Secret Diary of Harold L. Ickes,* New York: Simon and Schuster, 1953–54, III, 56.
2. *Ibid.,* III, 65.
3. *Ibid.,* III, 110.
4. Letter from Archbishop Spellman to President Roosevelt, Dec. 8, 1939. R.L., P.P.F.
5. Letter from Archbishop Spellman to President Roosevelt, May 26, 1940. R.L., P.P.F.
6. Letter from Archbishop Spellman to President Roosevelt, Sept. 5, 1940. R.L., P.P.F.
7. Card from Archbishop Spellman to Miss LeHand, Sept. 20, 1940. R.L., P.P.F.
8. *Fordham Alumni Magazine,* VIII, January 1941, 15.
9. Robert E. Sherwood, *Roosevelt and Hopkins, An Intimate History* (revised edition), New York: Harper and Brothers, 1950, p. 190.
10. Note from Archbishop Spellman to President Roosevelt, Nov. 19, 1940. R.L., P.P.F.
11. Letter from Archbishop Spellman to President Roosevelt, Nov. 7, 1940. R.L., P.P.F.
12. Letter from Archbishop Spellman to President Roosevelt, Dec. 31, 1940. R.L., P.P.F.
13. Letter from Archbishop Spellman to President Roosevelt, Jan. 20, 1941. R.L., P.P.F.
14. Card from Archbishop Spellman to Miss Tully, Mar. 22, 1942. R.L., P.P.F.
15. Francis J. Spellman, *No Greater Love,* New York: Charles Scribner's Sons, 1945, pp. 2–3. With reference to the President's explanation of the term "unconditional surrender," Cordell Hull noted: "The President had a comprehensive knowledge of American history, which he had studied thoroughly and intensively. It was not at Appomattox, however, that Grant demanded unconditional surrender, but at Fort Donelson

in 1862, when he received the surrender of General S. B. Buckner."
The Memoirs of Cordell Hull, II, 1574.

CHAPTER XIII

1. Letter from Archbishop Spellman to President Roosevelt, Feb. 1, 1943. R.L., P.P.F.
2. Letter from Archbishop Spellman to President Roosevelt, Feb. 8, 1943. R.L., P.P.F.
3. Freda Kirchwey, "The New Axis," *Nation*, CLVI, March 6, 1943, 330.
4. Gaetano Salvemini, "Pius XII and Fascism," *New Republic*, CVIII, March 8, 1943, 309.
5. Kenneth Leslie, "What About Spellman?" *Protestant Digest*, IV, February-March 1943, 1–2.
6. Roosevelt to Hull, Feb. 7, 1943, *F.D.R., His Personal Letters, 1928–1945*, II, 1399–1400.
7. Carlton J. H. Hayes, *Wartime Mission in Spain, 1942–1945*, New York: Macmillan, 1945, p. 98.
8. Harry C. Butcher, *My Three Years With Eisenhower*, New York: Simon and Schuster, 1946, p. 268.
9. *Ibid.*, p. 275.
10. Letter from PFC Carl Ryan to Honorable Thomas Dorgan, Mar. 26, 1943, quoted in extension of remarks of Honorable Thomas J. Lane, April 22, 1943, *Congressional Record*, Appendix, 78 Cong., 1 sess., A2035–36.
11. Letter from Staff Sergeant Edward Flynn, n.d., quoted in Ed Sullivan's column, New York *Daily News*, Oct. 24, 1943.
12. Letter from the Reverend Francis W. Anderson, S.J. to author, Feb. 4, 1955.
13. *Ibid.*
14. New York *Journal-American*, May 19, 1943.
15. Franz von Papen, *Memoirs* (trans. Brian Connell), London: Andre Deutsch, Ltd., 1952, pp. 499–500.
16. L. C. Moyzisch, *Operation Cicero* (trans. C. Fitzgibbon and H. Fraenkel), New York: Coward McCann, Inc., 1950, p. 93.
17. Reverend Clement J. Armitage, S.J., "Archbishop Spellman Visits Baghdad," *Jesuit Missions*, XVII, September 1943, 212.
18. New York *Times*, May 20, 1943.
19. Spellman, *Action This Day*, p. 145.
20. *Ibid.*
21. *Ibid.*, p. 146.
22. Copy of letter from the Reverend E. Gattang, C.S.Sp., Nov. 9, 1943. Cardinal Spellman Papers.
23. Copy of letter from the Reverend Claude J. Collins, C.S.P. and the Reverend Henry P. Fisher, C.S.P., Jan. 18, 1944. Cardinal Spellman Papers.
24. Boston *American*, July 26, 1943.
25. New York *World-Telegram*, July 28, 1943.
26. Boston *American*, July 28, 1943.
27. Boston *Globe*, July 28, 1943.

CHAPTER XIV

1. Henry H. Arnold, *Global Mission*, New York: Harper and Brothers, 1949, p. 513.

2. *Memoirs of Cordell Hull*, II, 1560.
3. Roosevelt to Hull, Dec. 18, 1942, *F.D.R., His Personal Letters, 1928–1945*, II, 1382.
4. Letter from Pope Pius XII to President Roosevelt, May 19, 1943, *Wartime Correspondence Between President Roosevelt and Pope Pius XII* (Introduction and Explanatory Notes by Myron C. Taylor), New York: Macmillan, 1947, p. 90.
5. *Ibid.*, pp. 91–92.
6. Butcher, *op. cit.*, p. 323.
7. Lewis H. Brereton, *The Brereton Diaries, 3 October 1941–8 May 1945*, New York: William Morrow & Co., 1946, p. 195.
8. Butcher, *op. cit.*, pp. 378–79, 389–90.
9. *Ibid.*, p. 398.
10. Open letter from Archbishop Spellman to William A. Curley, reprinted in Baltimore *American*, Apr. 2, 1944.
11. Mark W. Clark, *Calculated Risk*, New York: Harper and Brothers, 1950, pp. 314–18.
12. *Ibid.*, p. 312.
13. Twelve years later, the Congress of the United States voted $964,199.35 in damages to pay the Holy See. *Time*, LXVIII, July 9, 1956, 39.
14. Letter from Archbishop Spellman to President Roosevelt, Feb. 20, 1944. R.L., P.P.F.
15. *Ibid.*
16. Letter from President William H. Taft to Reverend John J. Burke, editor of the *Catholic World*, August 10, 1912. Quoted in letter from Miss Alice G. Walsh to the Rt. Rev. Msgr. James H. Griffiths, October 10, 1945, Office of the Military Ordinariate, Miscellaneous, Historical File. Hereafter cited as O.M.O.
17. Letter from Bishop Hayes to Cajetan Cardinal De Lai, August 29, 1918. Quoted in "Memorandum for Dr. Theodore Maynard," O.M.O.
18. Letter from Cardinal De Lai to Bishop Hayes, May 18, 1921. Quoted in *ibid.*, O.M.O.
19. At the time of the death of Cardinal Hayes, there was a total of 31 commissioned chaplains in the Army, 19 in the Navy, and 67 in Veterans' Hospitals.
20. Letter from Reverend Patrick J. Ryan to Monsignor Griffiths, Nov. 8, 1946; and from Reverend George A. Rosso to Monsignor Griffiths, November 5, 1946, O.M.O. The Navy did not list the decorations received by chaplains according to the religious denomination of the officers.
21. New York *Herald Tribune*, July 25, 1944.
22. New York *Journal-American*, July 27, 1944.
23. Philadelphia *Inquirer*, July 30, 1944.
24. Letter from Staff Sergeant Fred Lawrence to family, n.d. Quoted in Chelsea *Record*, Aug. 23, 1944.
25. Sumner Welles, *Where Are We Heading?*, New York: Harper and Brothers, 1946, pp. 131, 137, 141–42.
26. Washington *Times-Herald*, Aug. 31, 1944.
27. Spellman, *No Greater Love*, pp. 24–25.
28. *Ibid.*, pp. 39–41.
29. *Ibid.*, p.54.
30. *Ibid.*, pp. 56, 61.

31. Reverend John T. Tracy, O.M.I., "Ye Merrie Olde England," *The Oblate World*, VII, February 1945, 5.
32. New York *Herald Tribune*, Sept. 23, 1944.
33. Copy of letter from Sergeant John C. Bass to family, Sept. 24, 1944. Cardinal Spellman Papers.
34. New York *Times*, Sept. 5, 1944.
35. Letter from Archbishop Spellman to President Roosevelt, Oct. 23, 1944. R.L., Tully, Spellman Folder, Box 144.
36. *The Memoirs of Cordell Hull*, II, 1602–03, 1606.
37. *Ibid.*, II, 1613–14, 1618, 1621.
38. Sherwood, *op. cit.*, p. 846.
39. Edward R. Stettinius, Jr., *Roosevelt and the Russians* (ed. Walter Johnson), New York: Doubleday & Co., 1949, p. 73.
40. Quoted in *ibid.*, pp. 5–6.
41. Sherwood, *op. cit.*, p. 860.
42. Quoted in Stettinius, *op. cit.*, p. 4.
43. Copy of telegram from Archbishop Spellman to Mrs. Eleanor Roosevelt, April 12, 1945. Cardinal Spellman Papers.

CHAPTER XV
1. Reverend Henry P. Fisher, C.S.P., quoted in *Catholic News*, Nov. 1, 1952.

CHAPTER XVI
1. New York *Sun*, Aug. 2, 1948.
2. John C. Cort, "The Labor Movement—The Cemetery Strike, I," *Commonweal*, XLIX, February 18, 1949, 471.
3. Letter from Monsignor Ehardt to Joseph Manning, Jan. 4, 1949, quoted in *ibid.*
4. Quoted in *ibid.*, pp. 471–72.
5. Cort, "The Labor Movement—The Cemetery Strike, II," *Commonweal*, XLIX, March 18, 1949, 563–65.
6. Roger K. Larkin quoted in New York *Times*, Feb. 19, 1949.
7. Joseph Manning quoted in Boston *Globe*, Mar. 3, 1949.
8. Edward Ruggieri quoted in New York *Post and Home News*, Mar. 3, 1949.
9. *Labor Leader*, Mar. 14, 1949.
10. John Sheehan quoted in Brooklyn *Eagle*, Mar. 4, 1949.
11. New York *World-Telegram*, Mar. 7, 1949.
12. *Ibid.*
13. *Ibid.*
14. New York *Sun*, Mar. 11, 1949.

CHAPTER XVII
1. Morgan, *Speaking of Cardinals*, p. 142.
2. "The Shape of Things," *Nation*, CLXII, March 2, 1946, 245.
3. New York *Journal-American*, Mar. 2, 1946.

CHAPTER XVIII
1. Letter from Cardinal Spellman to author, July 27, 1954.
2. Reverend Alson J. Smith, "The Catholic-Protestant Feud," *American Mercury*, LXV, November, 1947, 536–42.
3. New York *Daily News*, Feb. 23, 1941.

4. Bronx *Home News*, Oct. 25, 1940.
5. New York *Daily News*, Feb. 23, 1941.
6. *Catholic News*, Mar. 22, 1941.
7. Anson Phelps Stokes, *Church and State in the United States*, New York: Harper and Brothers, 1950, II, 543.
8. *McCollum v. Board of Education* 333 U.S. 209–10, 212 (1948)
9. *Ibid.*, p. 235.
10. *Ibid.*, pp. 244, 255–56.
11. *Cochran v. Louisiana State Board of Education* 281 U.S. 370 (1930).
12. *Everson v. Board of Education of the Township of Ewing* 330 U.S. 3, note 1 (1947).
13. *Ibid.*, p. 46.
14. Letter from Stanley I. Stuber, National Director of Public Relations, Northern Baptist Convention; Clyde R. Miller, Associate Professor of Education, Teachers College, Columbia University; Guy Emory Shipler, editor, *The Churchman*, to New York *Times*, June 14, 1947.
15. Quoted in New York *Sun*, June 20, 1947.
16. Syracuse *Post-Standard*, Oct. 24, 1947.
17. *Christian Science Monitor*, June 21, 1949.
18. *Catholic News*, Aug. 6, 1949.
19. New York *World-Telegram*, July 26, 1949.
20. New York *Herald Tribune*, Aug 8, 1949.
21. Baruch quoted in New York *Sun*, July 26, 1949; O'Dwyer in New York *Journal-American*, Aug. 3, 1949; Lehman in New York *Daily News*, July 24, 1949; Farley in *Catholic News*, July 30, 1949.
22. New York *Herald Tribune*, Aug. 5, 1949.
23. Stokes, *op. cit.*, II, 755, 758.
24. Charles W. Whelan, "Public Aid Not Public Schools" *America*, CV, July 15, 1961, 528–29.
25. New York *Times*, August 11, 1961.
26. New York *Times*, September 13, 1961.

CHAPTER XIX
1. Reported in indirect discourse, New York *Times*, Oct. 24, 1947.
2. New York *Times*, Dec. 5, 1947.
3. Quoted by Cardinal Spellman in statement issued Jan. 7, 1951, reprinted in New York *Herald Tribune*, Jan. 8, 1951.
4. New York *World-Telegram & Sun*, Jan. 10, 1951.
5. New York *Post*, Jan. 18, 1951.
6. New York *Daily Compass*, Feb. 18, 1951.
7. New York *Times*, Feb. 17, 1951.
8. New York *World-Telegram & Sun*, June 23, 1951.
9. *Joseph Burstyn, Inc.* v. *Wilson, Commissioner of Education of New York, et al.* 343 U.S. 497, 501, 504–6 (1952).
10. New York *Daily Compass*, May 28, 1952.
11. New York *Daily Worker*, June 6, 1946.
12. Letter from Mr. Rapp to Mrs. Roosevelt, April 14, 1947; from Mrs. Roosevelt to Mr. Rapp, April 29, 1947, quoted in "Mrs. Roosevelt's Views," *Catholic News*, May 10, 1947.
13. New York *Times*, Aug. 3, 1949.
14. *Cardinal Mindszenty Speaks*, New York: Longmans, Green & Co., 1949, p. 62.
15. *Faith*, August 1948, 5.

16. *Cardinal Mindszenty Speaks*, pp. 209–12.
17. *Ibid.*, p. 216.
18. New York *Sun*, Feb. 4, 1949.
19. Gabriel Pressman quoted in *Catholic News*, Feb. 19, 1949; O'Dwyer in New York *Journal-American*, Feb. 7, 1949; Dewey in New York *Times*, Feb. 3, 1949; Acheson in New York *Journal-American*, Feb. 9, 1949; Truman in New York *Post and Home News*, Feb. 10, 1949.
20. New York *Times*, Feb. 10, 1949.
21. New York *Journal-American*, Jan. 6, 1949.
22. Copy of "Documents on the Cardinal Mindszenty Case," published by the Government of Hungary. Cardinal Spellman Papers.
23. North Tonawanda *News*, Jan. 5, 1949.
24. New York *Times*, Feb. 4, 1949.
25. New York *Times*, Oct. 13, 1949.
26. New York *Herald Tribune*, Jan. 11, 1949. On August 27, 1956, it was being "held in trust and safekeeping by the United States as property of a special status." Letter from Deputy Under Secretary of State Robert Murphy to Cardinal Spellman, Aug. 27, 1956. Cardinal Spellman Papers.
27. Boston *Herald*, June 23, 1951.
28. Brooklyn *Eagle*, June 22, 1951.
29. New York *Post*, Sept. 18, 1953.
30. Milwaukee *Journal*, Aug. 4, 1953.
31. New York *Times*, Nov. 19, 1944.
32. New York *Herald Tribune*, Nov. 18, 1945.
33. William D. Leahy, *I Was There*, New York: Whittlesey, 1950, pp. 326–27.
34. Welles, *op. cit.*, pp. 264–65.
35. Los Angeles *Tidings*, May 14, 1948.
36. New York *Herald Tribune*, May 6, 1949.

CHAPTER XX
1. Boston *Post*, Feb. 20, 1947.
2. Letter from Staff Sergeant Raymond J. Boylon to Mrs. Bridget Boylon, Sept. 27, 1945, quoted in Pittsburgh *Catholic*, Nov. 1, 1945.
3. Michael Kenealey, U.S.M.C., quoted in letter from Mrs. Alis M. Kenealey to Cardinal Spellman, Jan. 15, 1952. Cardinal Spellman Papers.
4. Letter from Reverend Joseph Yang, C.D.D., to Cardinal Spellman, Jan. 7, 1952. Cardinal Spellman Papers.
5. Letter from Mrs. Paul T. Eagen to Cardinal Spellman, Jan. 14, 1953, quoting her son. Cardinal Spellman Papers.
6. *Catholic News*, Feb. 7, 1953.

CHAPTER XXI
1. Reverend William Grant, quoted in letter from Archbishop O'Hara to Cardinal Spellman, Aug. 22, 1955. Cardinal Spellman Papers.
2. Letter from Ambassador Dempster McIntosh to Cardinal Spellman, Aug. 3, 1955. Cardinal Spellman Papers.
3. Letter from Miguel Páez Vilaro to Cardinal Spellman, Aug. 9, 1955. Cardinal Spellman Papers.

Index